Patterns for College Writing

A Rhetorical Reader and Guide

Fourth Edition

Patterns For College Writing

A Rhetorical Reader and Guide

Fourth Edition

LAURIE G. KIRSZNER
Philadelphia College of Pharmacy and Science

STEPHEN R. MANDELL
Drexel University

St. Martin's Press   New York

Senior Editor: Nancy Perry
Development Editor: Michael Weber
Project Management: EDP, Inc.
Cover Design: Darby Downey
Cover Art: Esther Frederiksen

Library of Congress Catalog Card Number: 88-60556
Copyright © 1989 by St. Martin's Press, Inc.

Manufactured in the United States of America.
21
hijkl
For information, write
St. Martin's Press, Inc.
175 Fifth Avenue
New York, NY 10010
ISBN: 0-312-01231-4

Acknowledgments

NARRATION

Maya Angelou, "Finishing School." From *I Know Why the Caged Bird Sings* by Maya Angelou. Copyright © 1969 by Maya Angelou. Reprinted by permission of Random House, Inc.

Donna Smith-Yackel, "My Mother Never Worked." Copyright 1975 by *Women: A Journal of Liberation*, 3028 Greenmount Avenue, Baltimore, Maryland, 21218.

Martin Gansberg, "38 Who Saw Murder Didn't Call the Police." Copyright © 1964 by The New York Times Company. Reprinted by permission.

Lou Ann Walker, "Outsider in a Silent World." From *A Loss For Words* by Lou Ann Walker. Copyright © 1986 by Lou Ann Walker. Reprinted by permission of Harper & Row, Publishers, Inc.

George Orwell, "Shooting an Elephant." From *Shooting an Elephant and Other Essays* by George Orwell, copyright 1950 by Sonia Brownell Orwell, renewed 1978 by Sonia Pitt-Rivers. Reprinted by permission of Harcourt Brace Jovanovich, Inc., the Estate of the late Sonia Brownell Orwell, and Martin Secker & Warburg Ltd.

DESCRIPTION

Andrea Lee, "The Beriozka." From *Russian Journal* by Andrea Lee. Copyright © 1979, 1980, 1981 by Andrea Lee. Reprinted by permission of Random House, Inc.

Maxine Hong Kingston, "Photographs of My Parents." From *The Woman Warrior: Memoirs of a Girlhood among Ghosts* by Maxine Hong Kingston. Copyright © 1975, 1976 by Maxine Hong Kingston. Reprinted by permission of Alfred A. Knopf, Inc.

Joan Didion, "Salvador." From *Salvador* by Joan Didion. Copyright © 1983 by Joan Didion. Reprinted by permission of Simon & Schuster, Inc.

N. Scott Momaday, "The Way to Rainy Mountain." First published in *The Reporter*, January 26, 1967. Reprinted from *The Way to Rainy Mountain*, copyright © 1969, The University of New Mexico Press.

E. B. White, "Once More to the Lake." From *Essays of E. B. White.* Copyright © 1941 by E. B. White. Reprinted by permission of Harper & Row, Publishers, Inc.

EXEMPLIFICATION

Laurence J. Peter and Raymond Hull, "The Peter Principle." Chapter 1 from *The Peter Principle*

Acknowledgments and copyrights are continued at the back of the book on pages 600–601, which constitute an extension of the copyright page.

PREFACE

In preparing the fourth edition of *Patterns for College Writing,* we have made many changes large and small, but our original purpose and approach remain the same. As before, our main concern is practical: to help students prepare for writing assignments not only in the English classroom but in their other college courses. Our approach combines precept and example: discussions of writing procedure and rhetorical pattern are immediately illustrated by one or more annotated student papers and then followed by a series of professionally written pieces for analysis and discussion in the classroom.

Many instructors have found that in a single volume *Patterns* answers their needs both for a writing textbook and for an anthology—with the extra benefit that the two are coordinated. We are confident that these instructors will find the fourth edition significantly improved in both aspects—its discussions fuller and clearer, its readings more varied and more interesting. The many other instructors who have used *Patterns* mainly as an anthology will find the fourth edition still very manageable for that purpose and considerably strengthened by the new selections.

As before, the book begins with a comprehensive introductory chapter devoted to the writing process. We have carefully revised this chapter in response to suggestions from users of the third edition, adding new material on purpose and audience, thesis statements, formal and informal outlines, and writing on a computer. In Chapter 1 we explain to students how they can move confidently through the process of invention by understanding their assignment; recognizing the limits set by a paper's length, purpose, audience, and occasion, as well as by their own knowledge; narrowing a subject to a workable topic; generating ideas through various invention techniques; and formulating a thesis. The chapter goes on to discuss arrangement, analyzing the parts of the essay in some detail. Finally, we consider drafting and revising, illustrating our discussion with a preliminary draft of a student essay followed by its two successive revisions, all accompanied by analysis.

The introductory chapter of *Patterns for College Writing* is followed by nine additional chapters, each discussing and illustrating a pattern of development that students will use in their college writing assignments: narration, description, exemplification, process, cause and effect, comparison and contrast, classification and division, definition, and argumentation. Each chapter begins with a comprehensive introduction that first defines and illustrates the rhetorical pattern and then provides a thorough analysis of one or more annotated student papers to show how the chapter's concepts can be applied to particular college writing situations. Each of these introductions has been rewritten in the interests of greater completeness and clarity, and each now begins with a paragraph-length illustration of the pattern to be discussed. Those who know the third edition will find the greatest changes in the treatments of cause and effect, classification and division, and argumentation—patterns which are especially difficult to teach but which are among the most important for academic work.

Each chapter then goes on to illustrate the pattern with a number of reading selections, diverse in subject and style, by professional writers. Like the student examples in the introductions, these essays are not intended to be imitated (though they may serve as stimuli for student writing). Rather, in the possibilities they offer for arranging material and developing ideas, they are meant to be analyzed and understood. In this edition we have retained the essays that our colleagues felt were most useful to their students and that our own students enjoyed the most. We have replaced other, less favored readings with fresh, timely selections that will interest students (for example, William Zinsser's "College Pressures," Joseph Lelyveld's "Rule of Law," and, in the argumentation chapter, two sets of paired essays taking opposing points of view on controversial issues—bilingual education and animal experimentation). Both student and professional essays now encompass an even greater variety of styles and cultural perspectives than before, while offering a more evenly balanced representation of subject matter from different fields of study.

As before, each reading selection is followed by four types of questions designed to help students measure their comprehension of the essay's content, their understanding of the author's purpose and audience, their recognition of the stylistic and structural techniques used to shape the essay, and their sensitivity to the nuances of word choice and figurative language. As in previous editions, with every selection we include a "Writing Workshop" of suggestions for student writing. Many of these ask students to respond to a specific situation and to consider a specific audience and purpose, thus making their assignments not only more concrete but also more interesting. New to the fourth edition is the "Thematic Connections" feature, which suggests other essays in the text that are thematically related to each selection. At the end of each chapter is a comprehensive list of writing topics, many of which ask students to make connections among several essays in the chapter.

The book's final section, "Essays for Further Reading," offers five classic, challenging essays that do not conform to any single pattern of development. New to this edition is a helpful glossary of terms.

In this fourth edition, we have continued to adhere to our original approach, as defined in the book's first three editions. We hope that by offering interesting and accessible reading selections, by fully analyzing student writing that represents many academic disciplines, by stressing the importance of purpose and audience in our questions and assignments, and by presenting writing as a flexible, individualized process, we may encourage students to approach college writing not as a chore but as a challenge. We continue to be guided by what our own students have taught us: When writing is presented as a skill that can be learned and applied to projects in many fields, students will work to master that skill.

Friends, colleagues, students, and family all helped this project along. Of particular value were the responses to a questionnaire sent to users of the third edition, and we thank each of the instructors who responded so frankly and helpfully: Thomas Allen, Riverside Community College; Ronnie Susan Apter, Central Michigan University; Diana Azbell, Orange Coast College; David W. Baker, Frederick Community College; Greg Barnes, Drexel University; Margie N. Barre, Tulsa Junior College; Brenda Black, Mesa College; Martin L. Bond, Delta State University; Mary Kate Brennan, SUNY College at Buffalo; Edward F. Burgess, Sacramento City College; Judith A. Burnham, Tulsa Junior College; Donna M. Campbell, SUNY College at Buffalo; David Cole, Quinnipiac College; Debra Conner, Parkersburg Community College; Barbara G. Cooper, University of Maryland—Baltimore City; Joseph Cosenza, St. John's University; Charles Cudney, Walla Walla Community College; Darlene Davis, Franklin and Marshall College; James Dean, University of Wisconsin—Parkside; Eden Allen Delcher, Towson State University; Yolanda T. DeMola, Fordham University; J. K. Van Dover, Lincoln University; H. Yvonne Elliott, Virginia Western Community College; Margaret Endress, Angelo State University; James P. Erickson, Wichita State University; Mary Francis Everhart, City College of San Francisco; Louise Excell, Dixie College; Joan Ferrell, Southeastern Illinois College; Joyce Flamm, Eastern Arizona College; Rose Ann Fleming, Xavier University; Francine Foltz, City College of San Francisco; David D. Fong, Bellevue Community College; Jeanne Froeb, Tulsa Junior College; Margaret Geiger, John Carroll University; Jean George, University of North Carolina—Chapel Hill; A. J. Glazier, California State College—San Bernadino; Steven C. Glogger, Community College of Philadelphia; Rosaire Hall, Minneapolis Community College and Metro State University; Phyllis R. Hamilton, Frederick Community College; William Harrell, University of Maryland; Betty Hart, Fairmont State College; Mechthild Hesse, Lane Community College; Charles Hill, Gadsden State Community College; Sharon Hockensmith, University of Texas at San Antonio; Craig Hoffman, Cañada College; Barbara Hunter, Wilbur Wright College; Terry F. Itnyre, Cypress College; Eugene W. James, Highline Community College; Faye Kachur, Indiana University—Northwest Campus; Kenneth Kaleta, Glassboro State College; Diane B. Kamali, Portland Community College; Judith C. Kuhns, Drexel University; Richard Larschan, Southeastern Massachusetts University; Stanley A. Larson, University of Wisconsin—Oshkosh; David Louie, Knox College; D'Ann Madewell, North Lake College; Alicya Malik, Cochise College; Joseph Maltby, University of Hawaii—Manoa; Glenn Man, University of Hawaii; Nedra Martz, University of Wisconsin—Oshkosh; Linda Mason, Western Michigan University; Howard A. Mayer, University of Hartford; Sara McKinnon, University of Southern Colorado; Elizabeth Mills, Georgia Southern College; Harriot Murton, Imperial Valley College; Thomas O'Brien, Prairie State College; Paul O'Dea, Parkland College; Linda L. O'Rourke, Monroe Community College; Dianne Peich, Delaware County Community College; Willene Perkins, Gadsden State Community College; Skaidrite Picciotto, Borough of Manhattan Community College; Francis Polek, Gonzaga University; Carole Quine, Catonsville Community College, University of Maryland—Baltimore City; Alfred L. Recoulley, Southern College of Technology; Patrick Ruffin, Drexel University; Edward Sams, Cabrillo College; Joyce Schenk, El Camino College; Gerald J. Schiffhorst, University of Central Florida; Susan Schiller, Sacramento City College; Winfield P. Scott, Richland Community College; Lucy R. Shaver, Cochise College; Anne Slater, Frederick Community College; Gregg A. Smith, Shoreline Community College; Fiona Sohns, West Valley College; Anne E. Spicer, Wayne Community College; Theodore L. Steinberg, SUNY College at Fredonia; Joan Stelmack, Community College of Allegheny County—South Campus; David Stooke, Marshall University; David Tammer, Eastern Arizona College; Phyllis M. Taufen, Gonzaga University; Miriam M. Taylor, Southern College of Technology; Raymond Terhorst, University of Maryland—Baltimore City; David J. Thomas, West Liberty State College; Mary Tookey, Eureka College; John S. Tumlin, Southern College of Technology; J. Kenneth Van Dover, Lincoln University; Robin Visconti, Grossmont College; Robert C. Wess, Southern College of Technology; Michael A. Williams, Spring Hill College; Darvin V. Wilson, Chabot College; and Paula Yaeger, Portland Community College.

We are also grateful to the following colleagues, who provided useful commentary on various drafts of this new edition: Doris Adler, Howard University; Cher Brock, North Harris County College; Joyce Flamm, Eastern Arizona College; Ann Higgins, Gulf Coast Community College; Susan Norton, Trident Technical College; Fay Rouseff-Baker, Parkland College; Phil Sipiora, University of South Florida; Barbara Sloan, Santa Fe Community College; and Gene Wright, North Texas State University.

Special thanks go to Joyce Flamm of Eastern Arizona College for revising the Instructor's Manual for this edition and to Anne Vandenberg, who prepared the draft of the glossary.

We have benefited as well from the encouragement, cooperation, and editorial care of the staff at St. Martin's Press, especially Michael Weber and Nancy Perry. Above all, on the home front we thank Mark, Adam, and Rebecca Kirszner and Demi, David, and Sarah Mandell.

Laurie G. Kirszner
Stephen R. Mandell

Contents

are created equal, that they are endowed by their
Creator with certain unalienable rights, that among
these are life, liberty, and the pursuit of happiness.''

ESSAYS FOR FURTHER READING   535

"Behold! human beings living in an underground den,
which has a mouth open toward the light and reaching
all along the den; here they have been from their childhood, and have their legs and necks chained so that they
cannot move, and can only see before them, being
prevented by the chains from turning round their heads."
"I think it is agreed by all parties that this prodigious
number of children in the arms, or on the backs, or at
the heels of their mothers, and frequently of their
fathers, is in the present deplorable state of the
kingdom a very great additional grievance; and,
therefore whoever could find out a fair, cheap, and easy
method of making these children sound, useful members
of the commonwealth, would deserve so well of the public
as to have his statue set up for a preserver of the nation."
"Why has every man a conscience, then? I think that
we should be men first, and subjects afterwards. It is
not desirable to cultivate a respect for the law, so much
as for the right. The only obligation which I have a
right to assume is to do at any time what I think
right."
". . . It seemed to me, reviewing the story of
Shakespeare's sister as I had made it, that any woman
born with a great gift in the sixteenth century would
certainly have gone crazed, shot herself, or ended her
days in some lonely cottage outside the village, half
witch, half wizard, feared and mocked at."
"In our time, political speech and writing are largely
the defence of the indefensible. . . . Thus political
language has to consist largely of euphemism, question-
begging and sheer cloudy vagueness."

Thematic Guide
to the Contents
Arranged by Subject

SPORTS AND RECREATION

HISTORY AND POLITICS

SCIENCE AND TECHNOLOGY

LANGUAGE AND LITERATURE

ETHICS, JUSTICS, AND RELIGION

SOCIETY AND CULTURE

Patterns for College Writing

A Rhetorical Reader and Guide

Fourth Edition

1

The Writing Process

Every essay in this book is the result of a struggle between a writer and his or her material. If the writer's struggle is successful, the finished essay is welded together without a seam, and the reader has no sense of the frustration the writer experienced while hunting for the right word or rearranging ideas. Writing is no easy business, and even a professional writer can have a very difficult time. Still, although no simple formula for good writing exists, some approaches to writing are easier and more productive than others.

At this point you may be asking yourself, "So what? What has this got to do with me? I'm not a professional writer." True enough, but during the next few years you will be doing a good deal of writing. Throughout your college career, you will need to write midterms, final exams, quizzes, lab reports, and short essays. In your professional life you may have to write progress reports, proposals, business correspondence, memos, and résumés. As diverse as these assignments seem, they have something in common: They can be made easier if you are familiar with the writing process—the way in which effective writers begin with a subject, decide on a thesis, and eventually put together an essay.

In general, the writing process has three stages. During *invention*, sometimes called *prewriting*, you decide exactly what you will write about. Then you gather ideas and information to support or explain what you want to say. During the next stage, *arrangement*, you decide how you are going to organize your ideas. And finally, during *drafting* and *revision*, you write your essay, progressing through several drafts as you reconsider ideas and refine style and structure.

But although these neatly defined stages make discussing the writing process easier, they do not represent the way people actually write. As any writer knows, ideas do not always flow easily from the pen or computer keys, and the central point you may set

out to develop is not always reflected in the essay that you ultimately write. Often writing progresses in fits and starts, with ideas
occurring unexpectedly or not at all. In fact, much good writing
evolves out of a writer's getting stuck or being confused and continuing to work until ideas begin to take shape on the page or on the
screen.

The writing process that we discuss throughout this book reflects
the concerns and choices that writers have at various stages of composition. Because writing can be such an erratic process, the writing
process does not move in a linear fashion, with one stage ending
before another begins. In fact, the three stages overlap. Most
writers engage in invention, arrangement, and drafting and revision
simultaneously—finding ideas, considering possible methods of organization, and looking for the right words all at the same time.

In addition, no two writers approach the writing process in exactly the same way. Some people outline; others do not. Some take
elaborate notes during the prewriting stage; others keep track of
everything in their heads. But regardless of these differences, one
thing is certain: The more you write, the better acquainted you will
become with your personal writing process—the one that works for
you—and with ways to modify it to suit various writing tasks. The
rest of this chapter will help you to define your needs as a writer
and to understand the options available as you face the diverse writing assignments you will encounter both in and out of college.

STAGE ONE: INVENTION

Invention, or prewriting, is an important part of the writing process. Oddly enough, many people totally ignore this stage, either because they underestimate the importance of preparation or because
they simply do not know how to plan to write. In college and afterward, you will often be given an assignment, at least a general one,
and you may be tempted to plunge into a first draft immediately.
Before writing, however, you should take the time to probe your
subject and decide what you wish to say about it.

Your first step should be to make sure you understand the assignment. Next, limit your subject by considering your essay's length,
purpose, audience, and occasion, as well as what you know about
the subject. Using techniques like freewriting, questions for probing, and brainstorming, you then can move from your subject—

which may be very broad—to a manageably narrow topic. These techniques will also prepare you to gather and organize ideas and facts until, finally, you are able to formulate a *thesis*—the main idea of your essay, the point you want to make.

Understanding the Assignment

Almost everything you write in college will begin as an assignment. Some assignments will be direct and easy to understand:

Write about an experience that changed your life.
Discuss the procedure you used in this experiment.

But others will be difficult and complex:

According to Wayne Booth, point of view is central to the understanding of modern fiction. In a short essay discuss how Henry James uses point of view in his *Turn of the Screw*.

Therefore, before beginning to write, you need to understand what you are being asked to do. If the assignment is a written question, read it carefully several times and underline its key ideas. If the assignment is read aloud by your instructor, be sure to copy it accurately because a missed word can make quite a difference. Whatever the case, do not be afraid to ask your instructor for clarification if you are confused. Remember that an essay, no matter how well written, will be unacceptable if it does not fulfill the assignment.

Setting Limits

Once you are certain you understand the assignment, you should consider its length, purpose, audience, and occasion, as well as your own knowledge of the subject. Each of these considerations limits what you will say about your subject and simplifies your writing task.

Length. Often your instructor will specify an approximate length for a paper, or your writing situation will determine how much you can write. Your word or page limit has a direct bearing on your paper's focus. For example, you would need a narrower topic for a two- or three-page essay than for a ten-page paper. Similarly, during an hour exam you could not discuss a question as thoroughly as you might in a paper prepared over several days.

If your instructor sets no length, consider how other aspects of the assignment might indirectly determine length. A summary of a chapter or an article, for instance, should be much shorter than the original, whereas an analysis of a poem usually will be longer than the poem itself. If you are uncertain about the appropriate length of your paper, discuss ideas for the paper with your instructor.

Purpose.   Your purpose sets another limit to what you say and how you say it. For example, if you were to write to a prospective employer about a summer job, you would emphasize different aspects of college life from those you would stress in a letter to a friend. In the first case, you would want to persuade the reader to hire you. To do so you might include your grade-point average or a list of the relevant courses you took. In the second case, you would want to inform and perhaps entertain. You might share anecdotes about dorm life or describe one of your favorite instructors. In both cases, your purpose would help determine what information you need to evoke a particular response in your audience.

In general, you can classify your purpose for writing according to your relationship to the audience. Your purpose in a piece of writing can be to express feelings or impressions to your readers. *Expressive* writing includes diaries, personal letters, and journals. Quite often you write narratives and descriptions that fall into this category (although they could fall into other categories as well). Your purpose can also be to inform readers about something. *Informative* writing includes much of the writing that you do in college. Essay examinations, lab reports, book reports, expository essays, and some research papers are primarily informative. Finally, your purpose can be to persuade readers to think or act in a certain way. *Persuasive* writing includes editorials, argumentative essays, and many other essays and research papers. When you seek to persuade, your emphasis is on how best to convince your audience to accept your assertions.

In addition to these general purposes, you can have a number of more specific purposes. For example, in addition to informing, you may also want to analyze, entertain, hypothesize, assess, summarize, question, report, recommend, suggest, evaluate, describe, recount, request, or instruct. Suppose that you wrote a report on the incidence of AIDS in your community. Your general purpose might be to *inform* readers of the situation, but you might also want to *assess* the progression of the disease and to *instruct* readers how to avoid contracting the virus that causes it.

In college, regardless of the specific purpose or purposes you wish to achieve in a particular writing assignment, you always write to demonstrate your mastery of the subject matter, your reasoning ability, and your competence as a writer. When assigning a college paper, your instructor may provide some guidelines about purpose. In many cases an assignment (such as a discussion of the economic causes of the Spanish-American War) may seem to require only an informative paper. But a successful paper will usually do more than provide information. It will convince readers that you know what you are talking about and that your point deserves their thoughtful attention.

Audience.   To be effective, your essay should be written with a particular audience in mind. Audiences, however, can be extremely varied. An audience can be an *individual*—your instructor, for example—or it can be a *group*, like your classmates or coworkers. Your essay could address a *specialized* audience, like a group of medical doctors or economists, or a *general* or *universal* audience whose members share no particular expertise, like the readers of a newspaper or news magazine.

When you write most college essays, the audience is your instructor, and the purpose is to convince him or her that your facts are valid and your conclusions are reasonable and intelligent. Other audiences may include classmates, professional colleagues, and members of a community. Considering the age and sex of your audience, its political and religious values, its social and educational level, and its interest in your subject may help you to define it. For example, if you were selling life insurance, the sales letters you prepared for people with young children would probably differ from those you prepared for single people. Likewise, you might promote a local park from one angle for retired people and from another for working couples.

Often you may find that your audience is just too diverse to be categorized. In such cases, many writers imagine a universal audience and write for it, making points that they think will appeal to many different readers. Sometimes, writers try to think of one typical individual in the audience—perhaps a person they know—so that they can write to someone specific. At other times, writers solve this problem by finding a common denominator, a role that interests or involves all those in the audience. For example, when a report on toy safety asserts, "Now is the time for concerned consumers to demand that dangerous toys be removed from the market," it automatically casts its audience in the role of "concerned consumers."

Once you have defined your audience, you have to determine how much or how little its members know about your subject. In addition, you should decide how much background information your readers need before they will be able to understand the discussion. Are they highly informed or relatively uninformed? In the first case, assuming a detailed knowledge of your subject, you would make your points directly. In the latter case, you would have to include definitions of key terms, background information, and summaries of basic research. Keep in mind that even an expert in one field will need background information in an area with which he or she is unfamiliar. If, for example, you were writing an essay analyzing the characters in Joseph Conrad's *Heart of Darkness*, you could assume that the literature instructor who assigned the novel was familiar with it and would not need a plot summary. Still, that same instructor might not know a great deal about African political history and might appreciate some background information. However, an essay for your history instructor that used *Heart of Darkness* to illustrate the evils of European colonialism in nineteenth-century Africa would need some plot summary. Just because your history instructor knows a lot about African colonialism does not mean that she is familiar with Conrad's novel.

Occasion.   In academic writing, the occasion is most often a classroom writing exercise or an at-home assignment. Although these situations may seem artificial, they serve as valuable practice for writing you do outside the classroom—for example, writing a memo or a report for your job, writing a letter to your representative in Congress, or preparing a flyer for an organization. Each of these occasions, in or out of college, requires a special approach to your writing. A memo to your co-workers, for instance, might be informal and more limited in scope than a report to your company's president. A notice about a meeting, sent to your fellow beer-can collectors, might be strictly informational, whereas a letter to your senator about preserving a local historical landmark would be persuasive as well as informational. Similarly, when you are preparing a classroom exercise, remember that college writing is somewhat formal and should contain precise diction and correct grammar and spelling. Keep in mind, however, that there are different kinds of classes, each with different occasions for writing. A response suitable for a psychology class or a history class might not be acceptable for an English class, just as a good answer on a quiz might be insufficient on a midterm.

Knowledge.   Obviously, what you know (and do not know) about a subject limits what you can say about it. Before writing about any subject, you should ask yourself the following questions:

What do I know about the subject?
What do I need to find out?
What do I think about the subject?

Different assignments or writing situations require different kinds of knowledge. A personal essay may draw on your own experiences and observations; a term paper will require you to gain new knowledge through research. Although your experience riding city buses might be sufficient for an impromptu essay in composition class, you will need to research the subject of rapid transit for an urban sociology paper. Sometimes you will be able to increase your knowledge about a particular topic easily because of your strong background in the general subject. At other times, when a general subject is new to you, you will need to select a specific topic particularly carefully so that you do not get out of your depth. In many cases, the time allowed to do the assignment and its page limit will guide you as you consider what you already know and what you need to learn before you can write knowledgeably.

EXERCISES

1. Decide if the following topics are appropriate for the stated limits. Write a few sentences for each topic to justify your conclusions.
    a. A *five-hundred-word paper*: A history of the Louisiana American Civil Liberties Union
    b. A *two-hour final exam*: The role of France and Germany in the American Revolutionary War
    c. A *one-hour in-class essay*: An interpretation of Andy Warhol's painting of Campbell's Soup cans
    d. A *letter to your college paper*: A discussion of your school's investment practices

2. Make a list of the different audiences to whom you speak or write in your daily life. (Consider all the different types of people you see regularly, such as your family, your roommate, your instructor, your boss, your friends, and so on.)

    a. Do you speak or write to each in the same way and about the same things? If not, how do your approaches to these people differ?
    b. Name some subjects that would interest some of these people but not others. How do you account for these differences?
    c. Choose a subject, such as your English class or local politics, and describe how you would speak or write to each audience about it.

Moving from Subject to Topic

Once you have considered the limits of your assignment, you need to narrow your subject to a workable topic within those limits. Many writing assignments begin as broad areas of interest or concern. These *general subjects* always need to be narrowed or limited to specific *topics* that can be reasonably discussed. For example, a subject like DNA recombinant research is certainly interesting. But it is too vast to write about except in a vague and generalized way. You need to narrow such a subject into a topic that can be covered within the time and space available.

Subject	*Topic*
DNA recombinant research	One use of DNA recombinant research
Herman Melville's *Billy Budd*	Billy Budd as a Christ figure
Constitutional law	One result of the Miranda ruling
Microcomputers	A comparison of the Apple Macintosh SE and the IBM PC 50 computers

As these examples illustrate, a topic does more than a narrow general subject. A topic also defines the manner in which you will treat a subject.

To narrow a general subject, you need to explore the topics it contains that fall within your limits and to consider what you have to say about each topic. Do not make the mistake of skipping this stage of the writing process, hoping that a topic will suddenly come to you. Not only will you waste time with this haphazard approach, but you also may fail to realize the potential of your subject. Instead, you can use three of the most productive techniques—freewriting, questions for probing, and brainstorming—to help you narrow your subject and generate ideas. Like most other writers, you will probably discover by trial and error which of these methods of invention work best for you.

Getting Started: Freewriting

You can use freewriting at any stage of the writing process—to narrow your subject, to generate information, or to find a thesis— but it is particularly useful as a way to get started. *Freewriting* is just what the term implies. Begin writing for a fixed period, usually five or ten minutes, and write down everything that comes to mind. Do not worry if your ideas do not seem to relate to your subject. The object of freewriting is to let your ideas flow. Often your best ideas will come to you as a result of unexpected connections that you make as you freewrite. When you freewrite, you should not pay attention to spelling, grammar, or punctuation. Your goal is to get your ideas down on paper so you can react to them. If you find that you have nothing to say, write down anything until ideas begin to emerge—and in time they will. The secret is to *keep writing.*

After completing your freewriting, read it and look for ideas that you can use in your essay. Some writers underline ideas they think they might explore in their essays. These ideas may become supporting information for the writing topic, or they could become subjects for other freewriting exercises. For example, if after reading your freewriting you find a promising idea, you can free-write again, using your new idea as your focus. This technique— called *looping*—can yield a great deal of useful information and can help you arrive at a workable topic. In fact, many writers do a free-writing draft of an essay *before* they do a more structured version. In this way, they concentrate on ideas and do not become bogged down in the more formal aspects of writing.

If you do your freewriting on a computer, you may find that star-ing at your own words can cause you to freeze. Or you may find that you are paying so much attention to what you are writing that your ideas just do not flow. A possible solution to these problems is to turn down the brightness until the screen becomes dark and then freewrite. This technique allows you to block out distracting ele-ments and to focus on your ideas. Once you finish freewriting, turn up the brightness and see what you have. If you have expressed an interesting idea, you can move it onto a new page and freewrite again.

Here is a ten-minute freewriting assignment that a student, Laura Gastin, did on the subject "An event that had an impact on my life."

> Write for ten minutes—ten minutes—at 9 o'clock in the morning, She must be kidding—Just what I want to do—Don't stop—Don't stop—Hungry—I didn't even have breakfast. Great. Just spilled coffee on my paper. Remember the time Dad spilled a whole pot and burned his hand. Mom wasn't home and I bandaged it. I was eight or nine I guess. The doctor at the emergency ward asked who did the professional job of bandaging. He told me that I should think about becoming a doctor. Maybe he was kidding or maybe he was just humoring a kid. Who knows? That was the first time I ever thought about it. Before that—nurse or teacher. I remember the whole thing clearly. Probably could write about it—Before etc. My teachers—my parents. Why not?

After some initial floundering, Laura arrived at an idea that could be the basis for her essay. Although the incident that Laura describes must be expanded, her freewriting has helped her arrive at a possible topic for her essay.

EXERCISES

1. Assume that you were asked to write a short in-class essay for your composition class. Do a ten-minute freewriting exercise on one of the following subjects. Do not stop; keep writing until you focus on a narrowed topic.
   a. Running
   b. Movies
   c. Baseball
   d. Music
   e. Books
   f. Vacations

2. Read what you have just written, and write a one-sentence summary of the topic you have arrived at. Freewrite about this topic for another ten minutes to generate ideas that you could use in your essay. Underline the ideas that seem most useful.

Focusing on a Topic: Questions For Probing

When you probe your subject, you ask a series of questions about it. These questions are useful because they reflect ways in which your mind operates: finding similarities and differences, for instance, or dividing a whole into its parts. By running through the list of questions, you can probe your subject systematically. Of course, not all questions will work for every subject. Still, any question may lead to many different answers, and each answer is a possible topic for your essay.

What happened?
When did it happen?
Where did it happen?
What does it look like?
What are its characteristics?
What are some typical cases or examples of it?
How did it happen?
What makes it work?
How is it made?
Why did it happen?
What caused it?
What does it cause?
What are its effects?
How is it related to something else?
How is it like other things?
How is it different from other things?
What are its parts or types?
How can its parts or types be separated or grouped?
Do its parts or types fit into a logical order?
Into what categories can its parts or types be arranged?
On what basis can it be categorized?
How can it be defined?
How does it resemble other members of its class?
How does it differ from other members of its class?
What are its limits?

When applied to a particular subject, even a few of these questions can yield many workable topics—some you might never have considered had you not asked the questions. By applying this approach to a general subject, such as "the Brooklyn Bridge," you can generate more ideas and topics than you need:

What happened? A short history of the Brooklyn Bridge
What does it look like? A description of the Brooklyn Bridge
How is it made? The construction of the Brooklyn Bridge

What are its effects? The effect of the Brooklyn Bridge on American writers

How does it differ from other members of its class? Innovations in the design of the Brooklyn Bridge

At this point in the writing process, you mainly want to explore possible topics, and the more ideas you have, the wider your choice. So write down all the topics you think of. You can even repeat the process of probing several times to uncover topics that are still more limited. For instance, you might begin probing the subject of television programs and decide you are interested in writing about game shows. But that topic is still very broad, so you might probe again, arriving at a narrower topic: types of game-show contestants. Once you have generated many topics, eliminate those that do not interest you or that go too far beyond your knowledge or are too complex or too simple to fit the limits of the assignment. When you have discarded these weaker ideas, you will still have several left, and you can select from these possible topics the one that best suits your paper's length, purpose, audience, and occasion, as well as your knowledge of the subject.

If you are writing on a computer, you can store your questions in a file that you can return to every time you have a new topic to probe. Having easy access to the questions makes it more efficient to use them. In addition, you can keep copies of your responses for each essay. Not only will you be able to keep a complete record of your prewriting activities, but you can easily determine what invention techniques work best for you.

EXERCISES

1. Indicate whether the following are general subjects or topics for a short essay. Be prepared to explain your decisions.
   a. An argument for gun control
   b. A comparison of metal and fiberglass skis
   c. Macroeconomics
   d. Two creation stories in the Book of Genesis
   e. Waterfowl and fresh-water plants
   f. The Haber process for the fixation of atmospheric nitrogen
   g. Michelangelo's Sistine Chapel paintings
   h. The advantages of term over whole life insurance
   i. Skiing
   j. An analysis of the McDonald's television marketing strategy
   k. The Book of Genesis

2. Choose two of the following subjects, and generate topics from each by using as many of the questions for probing as you can. (Assume that the essay you are preparing is due in three days for your English class and that it should be about one thousand words long.)
   a. Television programs
   b. Computers
   c. Pocket calculators
   d. Print advertisements
   e. Teachers
   f. Video games
   g. Styles of clothing
   h. Doctors
   i. Motorcycles
   j. Radio stations
   k. Diets
   l. Fatherhood or motherhood
   m. Grading
   n. Social problems
   o. Politics

Finding Something to Say: Brainstorming

After you have decided on a topic, you still have to find something to say about it. Brainstorming is a method of invention that can help you to do this. Like freewriting, brainstorming is a method of free association for generating ideas. By the time you brainstorm, however, you usually have a topic in mind, so brainstorming is often more focused.

You can brainstorm in a group, exchanging ideas with several students in your composition class and writing down the useful ideas that come up. Or, you can brainstorm individually, quickly writing down every fact, idea, or association you can think of that relates to your topic. Your list might include words, phrases, statements, or questions. Jot them down in whatever order you think of them, allowing your thoughts to wander freely. Some of the items may be inspired by your class notes; others may be ideas you got from reading or from talking with friends. Still other items may be ideas you have begun to wonder about, points you thought of while working toward your topic, or thoughts that spontaneously occur to you as you brainstorm.

An engineering student planning to write a ten-page research paper for his composition class on the advantages and disadvantages of alternate energy sources made this brainstorming list:

Alternate Energy Sources

Solar
Fusion
Wind
Tidal
Nuclear
Nuclear technology already exists and is widely used
Nuclear plants can leak radioactivity (Chernobyl)
Synthetic fuels
Steam power plants
Free fuel source for solar
Solar technology exists but is not widely used
Inefficiency of solar collectors
Efficiency of fusion reaction
Difficulty of containing fusion reaction
Solar collectors safe
Disposal of nuclear wastes—dangerous
Proliferation of plutonium
Breeder reactors
Sophisticated technology still not developed for fusion
Fusion relatively clean—little radioactive waste
Unlimited fuel source for fusion—H_2O
Limited uranium resources
Solar—no waste—no pollution
Oil could run out by 2020
Limited energy resources
Gas crisis of 1970s
Congress and president worried?
Development money
Certain alternate sources still too expensive
Coal gasification
Shale oil
Decontrol
Raising prices
Rationing
Heating
Cars and transportation
Electricity

The student who wrote this brainstorming list was obviously at no loss for ideas. After reading his list over several times, he decided that he would concentrate on the advantages and disadvantages of the three alternate energy sources with which he was most familiar:

nuclear, solar, and fusion. He knew he could research these three sources of energy in his college library, and he felt confident that they could be clearly explained in nontechnical language for his composition instructor and classmates.

Making an Informal Outline

The next step in the writing process is to organize your ideas by grouping the items from your brainstorming list under a few broad headings, thereby creating an *informal outline*. An informal outline can take many forms and can be prepared at various stages of the writing process. Quite often an informal outline is just a list of your major points, perhaps presented in some tentative order; sometimes, however, it will include some supporting details or suggest a pattern of development. Informal outlines do not detail the major divisions and subdivisions of your paper or the relative importance of your ideas; they simply suggest the shape of your emerging essay.

Here is how the engineering student grouped his ideas about the advantages and disadvantages of nuclear, solar, and fusion power.

Nuclear Power
Nuclear technology already exists and is widely used
Nuclear plants can leak radioactivity (Chernobyl)
Limited uranium resources
Disposal of nuclear wastes—dangerous

Solar Power
Solar technology exists but is not widely used
Inefficiency of solar collectors
Solar collectors safe
Free fuel source
No waste—no pollution

Fusion Power
Sophisticated technology still not developed
Difficulty of containing fusion reaction
Unlimited fuel source—H_2O
Relatively clean—little radioactive waste

The informal outline above represents only a rough sketch of one possible way to arrange material. At this point in the writing process, neither the order of points nor the writer's emphasis is fixed.

Neither are the supporting details nor the pattern of development. In the course of his work, the student will experiment with different ways of arranging his ideas until eventually he is able to sum up in one sentence a possible main idea for his essay: "Although nuclear, solar, and fusion power are promising energy sources, each also has disadvantages."

EXERCISE

Suppose that your English composition instructor has given you the following list of subjects and told you to select one for a five-hundred-word essay, due in two days. Prepare three of these subjects following the procedures for invention just discussed. First, do five minutes of free-writing on the three subjects that are most appealing. Next, apply the questions for probing. Then, pick the best topic developed from each subject and brainstorm about it. Finally, select the ideas about each topic that you would use if you were actually writing the paper, and group them into an informal outline.

a. Grandparents
b. Science-fiction movies
c. Gay rights
d. Divorce
e. The draft
f. Fast-food restaurants
g. Music
h. The motion picture rating system
i. The death penalty
j. Cats
k. Television comedy

Formulating a Thesis

Once you have decided what your essay is going to discuss, your next job is to formulate a thesis. Your *thesis* is the main idea of your essay; it is the central point that your essay supports.

The word *thesis* at one time denoted an argumentative statement, one that took a firm stand on an issue. But the definition of *thesis* has broadened considerably over the years. Now, the term is commonly used to identify the main idea of an essay whether or not it is argumentative. In this sense, every essay has a thesis.

An effective thesis statement clearly expresses your essay's main idea. What this means is that a thesis does more than just present your essay's topic; it indicates what you will say about your topic, and it signals what your approach toward your material will be.

The following thesis, from the essay "Grant and Lee: A Study in Contrasts" by Bruce Catton (chapter 7), clearly communicates the main idea the writer will support.

> They [Grant and Lee] were two strong men, these oddly different generals, and they represented the strengths of two conflicting currents that, through them, had come into final collision.

This thesis indicates that the essay will compare and contrast Grant and Lee; more specifically, it reveals that Catton's approach to his material will be to present the two Civil War generals as symbols of two historical currents that were also in opposition. If Catton's thesis had been less fully developed—if, for example, he had said, "Grant and Lee were quite different from each other"—it would have communicated no more than the essay's title, and it would have failed to signal the essay's purpose or approach—or its real subject—to his readers.

Your thesis evolves from your purpose, and it is an expression of that purpose. Whether your purpose for writing is to evaluate or analyze or simply to describe or recount, your thesis communicates that purpose to your readers. In general terms, your purpose may be to express your feelings, to present information in a straightforward manner, or to persuade. Accordingly, your thesis can be *expressive*, conveying a mood or impression; it can be *informative*, perhaps listing the major points you will discuss or presenting an objective overview of the essay to follow; or it can be *persuasive*, taking a strong stand or outlining the position you will argue.

The three thesis statements below express different purposes.

> The city's homeless families live in heartbreaking surroundings. (Purpose—to express feelings)

> The plight of the homeless has become so serious that it is a major priority for many city governments. (Purpose—to inform)

> The only responsible reaction to the crisis at hand is to renovate abandoned city housing to provide suitable shelter for homeless families. (Purpose—to persuade)

Whether your thesis is expressive, informative, or argumentative, it is always more than a title, an announcement of your subject, or a simple statement of fact. A descriptive title is useful because it orients your reader, but it is seldom detailed enough to reveal much about your essay's purpose or direction. An announcement of your subject can reveal more, but it is stylistically intrusive. Finally, a statement of fact—for instance, a historical or scientific fact or a statistic—is typically a dead end and therefore not worth developing in an essay. A statement like "Alaska became a state in 1959" or "Tuberculosis is highly contagious" or "The population of Greece is about 10 million" provides your essay with no direction. However, a judgment or opinion in response to a fact *can* be an effective thesis—for instance, "The continuing threat of tuberculosis, particularly in the inner cities, may make it necessary to conduct more frequent diagnostic tests among high-risk populations."

To gain an appreciation of the differences among titles, announcements, statements of fact, and thesis statements, compare the statements in each of the following groups.

Title:	The 55-Mile-Per-Hour Speed Limit: Pro and Con
Announcement:	In the following pages, I will examine the pros and cons of doing away with the 55-mile-per-hour speed limit on most state highways.
Statement of Fact:	Ohio has increased the speed limit from 55 to 65 miles per hour.
Thesis:	The federal government should withhold highway funds from any state that decides to increase the speed limit on state highways from 55 to 65 miles per hour.

Title:	Orwell's "A Hanging"
Announcement:	This paper will discuss George Orwell's attitude toward the death penalty in his essay "A Hanging."
Statement of Fact:	In his essay Orwell describes a hanging that he witnessed in Burma.
Thesis:	In "A Hanging" George Orwell shows that capital punishment is not only unpleasant but immoral.

Title:	Alternate Energy Sources
Announcement:	This essay will explore some alternatives to oil, gas, and electricity.
Statement of Fact:	Nuclear, solar, and fusion are three alternate energy sources.
Thesis:	Although nuclear, solar, and fusion power are promising energy sources, each has drawbacks that would keep it from replacing traditional energy sources.

To communicate your essay's main idea, an effective thesis should be clearly and specifically worded. Often, it is expressed in one com-

THE WRITING PROCESS 19

plete sentence. Also, it should speak for itself (it is not necessary to say, "My thesis is that . . . " or "The thesis of this paper is . . . "). The thesis statement should be pertinent to the rest of the essay, giving a fair indication of what follows and not misleading readers about the essay's direction, emphasis, content, or point of view. Vague language, confusing abstractions, irrelevant details, or overly complex terminology have no place in a thesis statement.

Naturally your thesis cannot include every point you will discuss in your paper. Still, it should be specific enough to indicate to your readers the direction in which your essay is going. The statement "The new immigration law has failed to stem the tide of illegal immigrants" does not give your essay much focus. Which law will you be examining? Which illegal immigrants? Of course your thesis cannot mention every idea you will explore, but it should define the scope of your discussion. Keep in mind, too, that your thesis should not make promises that your essay is not going to keep. If you are going to discuss just the effects of the new immigration law, do not emphasize in your thesis the sequence of events that led to the law's passage.

The following thesis statement fulfills the requirements for an effective thesis. It clearly indicates what the writer is going to discuss, and it establishes a specific direction and purpose for the essay.

> Because it fails to take into account the economic causes of illegal immigration, the 1986 immigration law is an inadequate solution to the problem of illegal immigration from Mexico into the United States.

With this thesis, the writer is committed to a position and can easily move ahead and present the facts and reasoning that will support it. Furthermore, readers have been shown where the essay is headed and so will not have to puzzle out just what the writer means to say.

Implying a Thesis. Although every essay should have a clear sense of purpose, not every kind of writing requires an explicitly stated thesis. Sometimes a thesis may only be *implied*. Like an explicitly stated thesis, an implied thesis conveys your essay's purpose, but the purpose is not directly stated in a single sentence. Instead, it is suggested by the selection and arrangement of the essay's points. Although using an implied thesis requires that a writer plan and organize especially carefully, many professional writers whose essays are included in this book prefer this option because it is more subtle than a stated thesis. The advantages of an implied thesis are especially apparent in narratives, descriptions, and some arguments where the writer wants readers to feel that they have reached their own conclusions. In most college writing, however, you should state your thesis explicitly to avoid any risk of being misunderstood.

Arriving at a Thesis.   No fixed rules determine when you formulate your thesis; the decision depends on such variables as the scope and difficulty of your assignment, your knowledge of the subject, and your own method of writing. Sometimes, when you know a lot about the subject, you may formulate a thesis before brainstorming or even before probing your subject. At other times you may wait until you have a chance to review all your material and draw it together into a single statement that indicates your position on the topic. Occasionally, your assignment may specify a thesis statement by telling you to take this or that position on a given topic. Whatever the case, you should arrive at your thesis before you begin to write the first draft.

Keep in mind that the thesis you develop at this point is a *working* or *tentative* thesis. As you write, you will continue to discover new ideas and will probably move in directions that you did not anticipate when you formulated the working thesis. Still, because your working thesis gives you guidance and purpose, it is essential at the initial stages of writing. As you draft your essay, make certain that you review the points that you make and revise your thesis accordingly.

EXERCISES

1. Assess the strengths and weaknesses of the following as thesis statements. Note which ones would most effectively establish the direction of an essay.
   a. Myths and society.
   b. Myths serve an important function in society.
   c. Contrary to popular assumptions, myths are more than fairy stories; they are tales that express the underlying attitudes a society has toward important issues.
   d. Today, almost two marriages in four will end in divorce.
   e. Skiing, a popular sport for millions, is a major cause of winter injuries.
   f. If certain reforms are not instituted immediately, our company will be bankrupt within two years.
   g. Early childhood is an important period.

h. By using the proper techniques, parents can significantly improve the learning capabilities of their preschool children.

i. Fiction can be used to criticize society.

j. Fiction, in the hands of an able writer, can be a powerful tool for social reform.

2. Rewrite the following factual statements to make them effective thesis statements. Make sure that each thesis is clearly and specifically worded.

   a. A number of hospitals have refused to admit patients on public assistance because they feel that such patients do not have the resources to pay their bills.

   b. Several recent Supreme Court decisions say that art that contains a sexual theme is not pornographic.

   c. Many women earn less money than men because they drop out of the workplace during their child-rearing years.

   d. People who watch television more than five hours a day tend to think the world is more violent than people who watch less than two hours of television daily.

   e. In recent years the rate of suicide among teenagers—especially middle- and upper-middle-class teenagers—has risen dramatically.

3. Read the following sentences adapted from *Broca's Brain* by Carl Sagan. Then, formulate a one-sentence thesis statement that draws together the points that Sagan makes about robots.

   a. Robots, especially robots in space, have received derogatory notices in the press.

   b. Each human being is a superbly constructed, astonishingly compact, self-ambulatory computer—capable on occasion of independent decision making and real control of his or her environment.

   c. If we do send human beings to exotic environments, we must also send along food, air, water, waste recycling, amenities for entertainment, and companions.

   d. By comparison, machines require no elaborate life-support systems, no entertainment, no companionship, and we do not feel any strong ethical prohibitions against sending machines on one-way, or suicide, missions.

   e. Even exceptionally simple computers—those that can be wired by a bright ten-year-old—can be wired to play perfect tic-tac-toe.

   f. With this . . . set of examples of the state of development of machine intelligence, I think it is clear that a major effort over the next decade could produce much more sophisticated examples.

   g. We appear to be on the verge of developing a wide variety of intelligent machines capable of performing tasks too dangerous, too expensive, too onerous or too boring for human beings.

   h. The main obstacle seems to be a very human problem, the quiet feeling that there is something threatening or "inhuman" about machines. . . .

   i. But in many respects our survival as a species depends on our transcending such primitive chauvinisms.

   j. There is nothing inhuman about an intelligent machine; it is indeed an expression of all those superb intellectual capabilities that only human beings . . . now possess.

4. For three of the following general subjects and topics, go through as many steps as you need to formulate effective thesis statements.
   a. The importance of your family
   b. Writing
   c. AIDS
   d. The difficulty of adjusting to college
   e. One thing you would change about your life
   f. Air pollution
   g. Space exploration
   h. Humor in television commercials
   i. The objectivity of newspaper reporting
   j. Television evangelism

STAGE TWO: ARRANGEMENT

Each of the steps discussed so far represents a series of choices you have to make about your topic and your material. Now, before actually beginning to write, you have another choice to make: how to arrange your material into an essay. This extremely important choice determines how clear your essay will be and how your audience will react to it.

Sometimes deciding how to arrange your ideas will be easy because the assignment specifies a particular pattern of development. This may often be the case in a composition class where the instructor may assign, say, a descriptive or a narrative essay. Also, certain assignments or examination questions suggest how your material should be structured. Probably no one except an English composition instructor will say to you, "Write a narrative," but you will have assignments in other courses that begin, "Give an account of. . . . " Likewise, few teachers will explicitly assign a process essay, but they will do so indirectly when they ask you to explain how something works. Similarly, an examination question might ask you to trace the events leading up to an event. If you are perceptive, you will realize that this question calls for either a narrative or a cause-and-effect answer. The important thing is to recognize the clues that such assignments give, or those you find in your topic or thesis, and to structure your essay accordingly.

One clue to the emerging structure of your essay may be found in the questions that proved most helpful when you probed your subject. For example, if questions like "What happened?" and "When did it happen?" suggested the most useful material, you might consider structuring your paper as a narrative. The chart that follows links various questions to the patterns of development they suggest:

Questions	Pattern
What happened? When did it happen? Where did it happen?	Narration
What does it look like? What are its characteristics?	Description
What are some typical cases or examples of it?	Exemplification
How did it happen? What makes it work? How is it made?	Process
Why did it happen? What caused it? What does it cause? What are its effects? How is it related to something else?	Cause and Effect
How is it like other things? How is it different from other things?	Comparison and Contrast
What are its parts or types? How can its parts or types be separated or grouped? Do its parts or types fit into a logical order? Into what categories can its parts or types be arranged? On what basis can it be categorized?	Classification and Division

What is it?
How does it resemble other
members of its class?   } Definition
How does it differ from other
members of its class?
What are its limits?

Notice that the terms in the right-hand column—narration, description, and so on—identify some useful patterns of development that
can help order your ideas. The rest of this book explains and illustrates these patterns.

Formal Outlines

Once you have arranged your ideas into an informal outline, formulated a thesis, and identified an emerging pattern of development,
you may want to construct a *formal outline* for your essay. Whereas
informal outlines are preliminary lists that simply remind the writer
what points to make in which order, formal outlines are multilevel,
detailed constructions. The complexity of your assignment will determine how detailed an outline you need. For most short papers,
informal outlines like the ones included in chapters 2–10 will usually
be sufficient. For a longer, more complex essay, however, a formal
outline may be needed.

Your outline should follow certain conventions of numbering, in-
dentation, and punctuation to map out the shape of your paper's
body. Group main headings under Roman numerals (I, II, III, IV,
etc.) flush with the left-hand margin. Indent subheadings under the
first word of the heading above. Use capital letters for major points
and numbers for subtopics, and capitalize the first letter of the first
word of both topics and subtopics. Make your outline as simple as
possible, avoiding overly complex divisions of ideas. Many of the
outlines you do will probably not have to go beyond a third-level
heading (1, 2, 3, etc.).

Thesis: _____
_____

    I. _____
        A. _____
            1. _____
            2. _____

      a. _____

      b. _____

  B. _____

II. _____

The headings in your outline can be presented either as topics or as complete sentences ("Advantages and disadvantages" or "Solar energy has advantages and disadvantages"). In either case, all headings and subheadings at the same level should be stated in parallel terms. If Roman numeral I is stated as a noun, II, III, and IV should also be. In addition, each heading must contain at least two subdivisions. You cannot have a *1* without a *2* or an *a* without a *b*.

To construct an outline, review your thesis and all the points compiled during prewriting. As you examine the list, you will see that certain subheadings emerge and that some points seem more important than others. Write down the points from your informal outline, grouping them under the appropriate subheadings. When you revise, make sure that each point supports your thesis. Points that do not should be rewritten or discarded entirely. In addition, make certain that your outline follows the proper format. If you use a computer to outline, you can easily add or rearrange the ideas with which you are working. Do not delete points, however, until you are sure that you do not need them.

The following topic outline follows the format that we have just discussed. Notice that the outline focuses on the body of the paper and does not include the introduction or conclusion—these are usually written after you have drafted the body. (Compare this formal outline with the informal outline on p. 15 in which the writer simply grouped his notes under three general headings.)

Alternate Energy Sources

Thesis: Although three energy sources are being proposed as alternatives to fossil fuels, their disadvantages outweigh their advantages.

  I. Nuclear energy
    A. Advantages
      1. Existing technology
      2. Widely used technology
    B. Disadvantages
      1. Limited uranium resources
      2. Dangerous nuclear wastes
      3. Radioactive leaks from plants

        a. Three Mile Island
        b. Chernobyl
     4. High cost of plants
  II. Solar energy
     A. Advantages
        1. Safe energy generation
        2. Free fuel
        3. Low waste—no pollution
     B. Disadvantages
        1. Inefficient technology
        2. Expensive energy
        3. Exotic equipment
        4. Geographic limitations
  III. Fusion energy
     A. Advantages
        1. Unlimited fuel source—H_2O
        2. Little radioactive waste
        3. High energy production
     B. Disadvantages
        1. Undeveloped technology
        2. High costs
           a. Research
           b. Development
           c. Construction

This outline enables the writer to order his points so that they support the thesis. It serves as a useful guide that reminds the writer to arrange and support his points so that the advantages and disadvantages for each of the three energy sources are clear.

Parts of the Essay

No matter what pattern of development you use, an essay should have a beginning, a middle, and an end—that is, an *introduction*, a *body*, and a *conclusion*.

The Introduction.   The opening of your essay, usually one paragraph and rarely more than two, introduces your subject, engages your reader's interest, and often states your thesis. But in so short a space, there is obviously no room for an in-depth discussion or even a summary of your topic.

You can introduce an essay and engage your readers' interest in a number of ways. Here are several you can employ:

1. You can give some background information and then move directly to your *thesis*. This approach works well when you know that the audience is already interested in your topic and that there is no reason not to come directly to the point. It is especially useful for exams, where there is no need or time for subtlety.

> With inflation taking its toll, many companies have understandably been forced to raise prices, and the oil industry should be no exception. But well-intentioned individuals begin wondering whether high prices are justified when increases occur as frequently as they do. It is at this point that we should start examining the pricing policies of the major American oil companies.
>
> (economics take-home exam)

2. You can introduce an essay with a *definition* of a relevant term or concept. (Keep in mind, however, that the "According to *Webster's Dictionary* . . . " formula is overused and trite.) This technique is especially useful for research papers or examinations where the meaning of a specific term is crucial.

> Democracy is a form of government in which the ultimate authority is vested in and exercised by the people. This may be so in theory, but recent elections in our city have caused much concern for the future of democracy here. Extensive voting-machine irregularities and ghost voting have seriously jeopardized the people's faith in the democratic process.
>
> (political science paper)

3. You can begin your essay with an *ancedote* or *story* that leads into or prepares for your thesis.

> Upon meeting the famous author James Joyce, a young student stammered, "May I kiss the hand that wrote *Ulysses*?" "No!" said Joyce. "It did a lot of other things, too." As this exchange shows, Joyce was an individual who valued humor. This tendency is also present in his final work, *Finnegans Wake*, where comedy is used to comment on the human condition.
>
> (English literature paper)

4. You can begin with a *question*.

> What was it like to live through the holocaust? Elie Wiesel, in *One Generation After*, answers this question by presenting a series of accounts about individuals who found themselves thrust into Nazi

death camps. As he does so, he challenges some of the assumptions
we hold in our somewhat smug and highly materialistic society.

(sociology book report)

5. You can also begin with a *quotation*. If it is well chosen, it can
interest your audience in reading further.

"The rich are different," said F. Scott Fitzgerald more than fifty
years ago. Apparently, they remain so today. As any examination of
the tax laws shows, the wealthy receive many more benefits than do
the middle class or the poor.

(business law essay)

No matter which method you select, your introduction should be
consistent in tone and approach with the rest of your essay. If it is
not, it can misrepresent your intentions to your reader and even destroy your credibility. (For this reason, the introduction is often the
last part of a rough draft to be written.) A technical report, for instance, should have an introduction that reflects the formality and
seriousness of the occasion. The introduction to an autobiographical
essay or a personal letter, on the other hand, should have an informal and relaxed tone.

The Body Paragraphs.   The middle section, or body, of your essay supports and expands your thesis. The body paragraphs present
the detail, such as examples, descriptions, and facts, that will convince your audience that your thesis is reasonable. To do their job,
body paragraphs should be unified, coherent, and well developed.

Body paragraphs should be unified. A paragraph has unity when
every sentence directly relates to the main idea of the paragraph.
Sometimes the main idea of a paragraph is stated in a *topic sentence*. Like a thesis, a topic sentence acts as a guidepost and makes
it easier for readers to follow your discussion. Although where you
place a topic sentence depends on your purpose and your subject,
beginning writers often make it the first sentence of their paragraph.

At other times, the main idea of a paragraph is *implied* by the
sentences in the paragraph. Professional writers frequently use this
technique because they believe that in some situations—especially
narratives and descriptions—a topic sentence can seem forced or
awkward. As beginning writers, it is easier for you to use topic sentences. Not only will topic sentences emphasize the ideas that you

are discussing in each paragraph, but they will also keep you on track by reflecting the major divisions of your outline.

Whatever strategy you use, remember that each sentence in a paragraph should reflect your purpose and should develop the main idea of the paragraph. If the sentences in a paragraph do not do this, the paragraph is said to lack unity. In the following excerpt from a student essay, notice how the topic sentence unifies the paragraph by summarizing its main idea.

> Built on the Acropolis overlooking the city of Athens in the fifth century B.C., the Parthenon is an excellent example of Greek architecture. It was a temple of the gods and was very important to the people. Although at first glance its structure seems to be perfect, on closer examination it becomes clear that it is a static, two-dimensional object. As long as you stand in the center of any of its four sides to look at it, its form will appear to be perfect. The strong Doric columns seem to be equally spaced, one next to another, along all four of its sides. But if you take a step to the right or left, the Parthenon's symmetry is destroyed.

This paragraph identifies the Parthenon as an excellent example of Greek architecture. The explicit topic sentence, located at the beginning of the paragraph, enables readers to grasp the writer's point immediately. The examples that follow all relate to that point. The whole paragraph is therefore focused and unified.

Body paragraphs should be coherent. A paragraph is coherent if it is composed of sentences that smoothly and logically connect to one another. Coherence can be achieved through three devices. First, you can repeat key words to carry concepts from one sentence to another and to echo important terms. Second, you can use pronouns to refer back to key nouns in previous sentences. Finally, you can use transitional expressions to show chronological sequence (*then, next, after that*); cause and effect (*as a result, therefore*); addition (*first, second, and, furthermore*); comparison (*similarly*); and contrast (*but, however, still, nevertheless*). These strategies for connecting sentences can spell out for your readers the exact relationships among your ideas. The following paragraph, from George Orwell's "Shooting an Elephant," uses all three techniques to achieve coherence.

> I got up. The Burmans were already racing past me across the mud. It was obvious that the elephant would never rise again, but he was not dead. He was breathing very rhythmically with long rattling gasps, his great mound of a side painfully rising and falling. His

mouth was wide open—I could see far down into the caverns of pale pink throat. I waited a long time for him to die, but his breathing did not weaken. Finally I fired my two remaining shots into the spot where I thought his heart must be. The thick blood welled out of him like red velvet, but still he did not die. His body did not even jerk when the shots hit him, the tortured breathing continued without a pause. He was dying, very slowly and in great agony, but in some world remote from me where not even a bullet could damage him further. I felt that I had got to put an end to that dreadful noise. It seemed dreadful to see the great beast lying there, powerless to move and yet powerless to die, and not even be able to finish him. I sent back for my small rifle and poured shot after shot into his heart and down his throat. They seemed to make no impression. The tortured gasps continued as steadily as the ticking of a clock.

In this paragraph Orwell keeps his narrative coherent by using transitional expressions (*already, finally, when the shots hit him*) to signal the passing of time. He uses pronouns (*he, his*) in nearly every sentence to refer back to the elephant, the topic of his paragraph. Finally, repetition of key words like *shot* and *die* (and its variants *dead* and *dying*) also link the paragraph's sentences together. The result is a coherent, cohesive whole.

Body paragraphs should be well developed. A paragraph is well developed if it contains the examples, facts, and discussions readers need to understand the main idea. If a paragraph is not adequately developed, your readers will feel that they have been given only a partial picture of your subject. Just how much information you need depends on your audience, your purpose, and the claims you make in your topic sentence.

Should you find that you need more information in a paragraph, you can consult the brainstorming list created during your prewriting. If the list does not provide enough material to develop your main idea sufficiently, you can freewrite or brainstorm again, review your notes, talk with friends and instructors, read more about your topic, or go to the library and do some research. Your assignment and your topic will determine the kind and amount of information you need. The following paragraph by a student writer marshals a good deal of concrete information to support the assertion made in the topic sentence.

Just look at how our society teaches males that extravagance is a positive characteristic. Scrooge, the main character of Dickens's *A Christmas Carol*, is portrayed as an evil man until he is rehabilitated—meaning that he gives up his miserly ways and freely distributes gifts and money on Christmas day. This behavior, of course, is re-warded when people change their opinions about him and decide that perhaps he isn't such a bad person after all. Diamond Jim Brady is another interesting example. This individual was a financier who was known for his extravagant taste in women and food. In any given night, he would consume enough food to feed at least ten of the many poor who roamed the streets of late nineteenth-century New York. Yet, despite his selfishness and infantile self-gratification, Diamond Jim Brady's name has become a synonym for the good life.

This student writer provides two examples to support her assertion that society teaches males that extravagance is a positive attribute. Her literary and historical examples are not only complete but also carefully chosen and effectively presented.

In addition to making sure that your body paragraphs are unified, coherent, and well developed, you need to arrange your material according to the pattern of development you have chosen. For instance, an essay in which you discuss the causes of Hitler's defeat in Russia could be organized following a *cause-and-effect* pattern:

Introduction: Thesis
Body
    Cause 1:   The Russian winter
    Cause 2:   The opening of a second front
    Cause 3:   The problem of logistics
    Cause 4:   Hitler's refusal to take advice
Conclusion

A lab report on the synthesis of aspirin could be organized like this, following a *process* pattern of development:

Introduction: Thesis
Body
    Step 1:   Mix 5 g. of salicylic acid, 10 ml. of acetic anhydride, and 1–2 ml. of sulphuric acid.
    Step 2:   Wait for the mixture to cool.
    Step 3:   Add 50 ml. of water and collect on a Büchner filter.
    Step 4:   Dry the residue.
    Step 5:   Recrystallize the aspirin from benzene.
Conclusion

These patterns, and others, will be outlined and analyzed in detail throughout the rest of this book.

The Conclusion. Readers remember best what they read last, and so your conclusion is extremely important. Always end your essay in a way that reinforces your thesis and your purpose.

Like your introduction, your conclusion should be brief. In a short essay, it can be as brief as one sentence and most often is no longer than a paragraph. Regardless of its length, however, your conclusion should be consistent with the content of your essay. Therefore, it should not introduce new points or material that you have not discussed earlier. Frequently, a conclusion will end an essay by restating the thesis. Like thesis statements, effective conclusions need no announcement, and you should avoid beginning your conclusion with the artificial phrase *In conclusion.*

Conclusions can be as challenging to construct as introductions. Here are several ways to conclude as essay:

1. You can conclude your essay by simply reviewing your main points and *restating your thesis.*

> Rotation of crops provided several benefits. It enriched soil by giving it a rest; it enabled farmers to vary their production; and it ended the cycle of "boom or bust" that had characterized the prewar South's economy when cotton was the primary crop. Of course, this innovation did not solve all the economic problems of the postwar South, but it did lay the groundwork for the healthy economy this region enjoys today.
>
> (history exam)

2. You can end a discussion of a problem by *recommending a course of action.*

> While there is still time, American engineering has to reassess its priorities. We no longer have the luxury of exotic and wasteful experiments such as automobile airbags. Instead, we need technology grounded in common sense and economic feasibility. That Volkswagen, rather than an American company, developed an outstanding and inexpensive passive restraint system illustrates how far we have strayed from old-fashioned Yankee ingenuity.
>
> (engineering ethics report)

3. You can conclude with a *prediction.* Be careful, however, that your prediction is supported by the points you have made in the essay. The conclusion is not the place to make new points or change direction.

> It is too late to save parts of the great swamps in northern Florida, but it is not too late to preserve the Everglades in the southern part

of the state. With intelligent planning and an end of the dam building program by the Army Corps of Engineers, we will be able to halt the destruction of what the Indians called the "Timeless Swamp."

(environmental science essay)

4. You can also end with a *quotation*. If selected carefully, it can add weight to an already strong essay.

In *Walden*, Henry David Thoreau said, "The mass of men lead lives of quiet desperation." This sentiment is reinforced when you drive through the Hill District of our city. Perhaps the work of the men and women who run the health clinic on Jefferson Street cannot totally change this situation, but it can give us hope to know that some people, at least, are working for the betterment of us all.

(public health essay)

STAGE THREE: DRAFTING AND REVISION

After you generate material and decide on a tentative arrangement for your ideas, your next step is to draft and revise your essay. Keep in mind that.even as you carry out these activities, you may have to do more brainstorming and further refine your tentative thesis.

Writing Your First Draft

The purpose of your first draft is to get your ideas down on paper so you can react to them. While writing your draft, you may discover new directions for your essay. If a new idea occurs to you, follow it through. Some of your best writing will come from unexpected turns or accidents. You should think of the first draft as a releasing of the ideas that you have been gathering about your topic. For this reason, don't let worries about correctness or word choice interfere with the flow of your ideas. All you want to do is keep your momentum until you finish the first draft. Later, when you write the second or third draft, you can polish your writing, and then you can go on to edit for grammar, punctuation, and mechanics.

Revising Your Essay

Remember that revision is not something to do after your paper is finished. It is a continuing process during which you consider the logic and clarity of your ideas as well as their effective and correct expression. Thus, revision is not simply a matter of proofreading or editing, crossing out one word and substituting another; it means reexamining and rethinking what you have done (re-vision) and may involve extensive addition, deletion, and reordering of whole sentences or paragraphs as you reconsider what you want to communicate to your audience.

After you have written your first draft, you should put it aside for several hours or even a day or two if you have the time. This "cooling-off" period enables you to distance yourself from your essay so that you can go back to it and read it more objectively. When you read it again, you can begin to revise.

If you have time, you can start your revising by setting up a revision and editing checklist (see pp. 45-46) and applying it to your essay. As you move systematically from the whole essay to the individual paragraphs to the sentences and words, you can assess your paper's effectiveness. First, check your thesis statement to see if it is still accurate. Is it clear and specific? Is it consistent with the body of your essay? If you departed from your original goal while you were writing, you will need either to revise the thesis so that it accurately sums up the ideas and information contained in your essay or to remove any unrelated sections—or to revise them so that they are relevant to your thesis.

Next, look at your body paragraphs to see if they need strengthening. Are they unified? Coherent? Well developed? Do the points you make support your topic sentences and your thesis? Are the points themselves convincingly supported? You might have to add more facts or examples to one paragraph to make it as strong as the others.

Consider your introductory and concluding strategies. Are they appropriate for your material, your audience, and your purpose? Do they reinforce your thesis?

Now look over your sentences. Are they correct? Effective? Interesting? Are there any sentences that might be added or deleted or relocated?

Consider the words you use. Are there any additions or substitutions you feel you should make?

Finally, give careful attention to your title. Creating the first impression your reader will have of your essay, your title should arouse interest in what you will be saying. Usually, single word titles ("Love") and cute ones ("The Cheery Cheerleader") do little to draw a reader into your essay. To be effective, a title should reflect your purpose and your tone. The essays in this book illustrate a number of types of titles that you can use.

Type	*Model*
Unusual topic	"The Beriozka"
Question	"Who Killed Benny Paret?"
Topic + question	"The Civil Rights Movement: What Good Was It?"
Controversy	"Animal Rights vs. Human Health"
Topic + controversy	"Television: The Plug-In Drug"

Only now, after doing all your revision, should you go back and edit your essay. Polish sentence structure, check spelling, and make sure punctuation and grammar are correct. Revision and editing can take a lot of time, so do not be discouraged if you have to go through three or four drafts of your essay before you think it is ready to hand in.

Even if you do not have time to reconsider your written work this thoroughly, you might want to check the logic of your essay's structure by making a review outline. Such an outline of what you have actually written can be useful as a revision tool. Either an informal outline or a formal one can show you whether any important points have been omitted or misplaced. An outline can also show you whether your essay follows the pattern of development you have chosen. Finally, an outline can clarify for you the relationship between your thesis and your support paragraphs.

Another revision strategy you might find helpful is seeking peer criticism—in other words, asking a friend to read your essay and comment on it. Sometimes peer criticism can be quite formal. An instructor may require students to exchange papers and evaluate their classmates' work according to certain standards, perhaps by completing a formal checklist. Often, however, peer criticism is informal. Even if your friend is unfamiliar with your material, he or she can still tell you honestly whether you are getting your point across—and maybe even advise you on how to communicate more effectively. (Of course, your critic should only be your reader, not your ghost writer.)

How you revise—what specific strategies you decide to use—depends on your own preference, your instructor's directions, and the time available. Like the rest of the writing process, revision varies from student to student and from assignment to assignment.

If you revise on a computer, you can add, delete, and move information quickly and effortlessly. Still, some writers have difficulty revising on a computer screen. One reason is that most screens show only a portion of a page and it is difficult to revise if you cannot see an entire page. Because pages cannot be compared side by side, the connection between ideas becomes unclear. Therefore, many writers find that they have an easier time revising if they print a hard copy of their essay and make their changes on paper. After they complete their changes, they enter them into the computer.

By using the global *find* and *replace* commands, you can change overused words and check punctuation. Spelling checkers will locate misspelled words in your paper, and text analysis programs can scan for grammatical errors, sexist language, jargon, and wordy or vague expressions. (Naturally, you should ask your instructor's permission before you use such programs.) Remember, however, that even though your computer can help you find these errors, it cannot do your revising for you. The decision about whether to move a paragraph, to change a thesis, or to add or delete information is yours and yours alone.

The following three drafts of an essay were written by a student, Kevin Ingram, for his composition class. His assignment was to choose an issue important to students at his college. Kevin's choice of topic was easy because he was the freshman representative to a faculty committee charged with investigating whether entering students should be required to purchase microcomputers. His work on the committee had led him to believe that the advantage of such a requirement outweighed any disadvantages, so his thesis was clear from the beginning. As part of his process of invention, Kevin prepared this informal outline before he began writing his essay:

Introduction: Thesis—The advantages of having a computer outweigh the disadvantages.
Advantage 1: Word processing
Advantage 2: Spreadsheets
Advantage 3: Science software
  Conclusion: Restatement of thesis

Here is the handwritten rough draft of Kevin's essay:

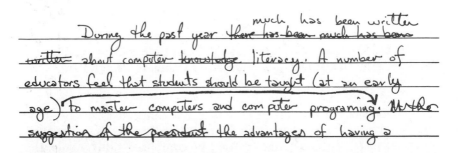

computer outweigh ~~this minor The it~~ the disadvantages ~~of the.~~

The computer's ability to do word processing makes it a useful ~~thing~~ tool for students. If students were required to use a word processor ~~for the~~ in one's composition courses. They would gain skills ~~and would use them~~ that would help ~~them~~ throughout their four years of college ~~the university now has~~ tentative plans to install printing stations on ~~campu Students would use these printers in the way they use duplicating machines.~~

Business ~~students~~ majors ~~would also gain a lot from their computers~~ Most computers have spread sheet programs that ~~are perfect for anyone who works with numbers.~~ enable students to carry out calculations. Accounting majors could do financial analysis, budget modeling, and inventory control. ~~Management majors could do far more than just spread sheet analysis. In~~ enable students to restructure a work sheet by adding and ~~addition~~ spread sheets ~~programs enable you to work on~~ deleting information. ~~numbers~~ Some programs, ~~would~~ even enable students to ~~the~~ make high quality graphics. ~~They can transfer information from one format to another and~~

~~Science majors~~ students ~~would~~ also benefit ~~from computers. The computer would also be help science majors.~~ For example, ~~As the preliminary report to the faculty published in the school paper pointed out.~~ Chemistry majors could simulate chemical reactions. Students could ~~try to~~ simulate chemical reactions, and bond atoms together. Biology majors could use computers to ~~carry out test~~ ~~the reaction of certain substances on plants or animals~~

visualize the DNA molecule. Students could simulate gene splicing:

~~Computers could add~~ Computers would add ~~a lot~~ much to our curriculum. For this reason ~~I feel~~ ~~I believe~~ computers should be required of all entering freshmen.

Revising the Rough Draft

After writing this rough draft, Kevin put it aside for a few hours and then reread it. As a result, he was able to see a number of areas that needed revision

The Introduction.   First, Kevin realized that he would have to present more detail in his introduction, which was too abrupt and did not lead up to his thesis gradually. He decided to add more background information concerning the debate about computers at his college and to acknowledge in his thesis statement that tuition would increase if computers were required of all entering freshmen. By doing so, he hoped to soften his stance and present a more reasonable image of himself to his audience. At this point, Kevin also added a working title that described the subject of his essay.

The Body Paragraphs.   Kevin knew that to make his case he would have to give several good examples of the uses students could make of computers. After reading his draft carefully, he decided to develop the discussion in each of his three body paragraphs further. For his first body paragraph, he thought of an example to prove how word processing skills could benefit students. He then did some brainstorming to expand his discussion in the second body paragraph about spreadsheet programs. Finally, after reviewing his third body paragraph, he concluded that he needed more material about gene splicing and simulating chemical reactions.

To make certain that his sentences led smoothly into one another, Kevin added transitional words and phrases whenever he could and rewrote entire sentences when necessary. He also found places where he could signal the progression of his thoughts by adding words and phrases like *therefore, for this reason, naturally, for example*, and *as a result*. In addition, Kevin tried to repeat key words from sentence to sentence so that important concepts would be reinforced.

The Conclusion. Kevin's biggest concern was that his readers would accept the points of his argument but still not accept his conclusion. He knew that the major argument against his position was that the benefits of the computer did not justify its cost. Although he had mentioned this point in his introduction, Kevin realized that a discussion of this issue in his conclusion—where it would remain fresh in his readers' minds—would be most effective. He decided to add such a section to his last paragraph and make sure that it led smoothly and logically to his last sentence. By rewriting his conclusion, Kevin reinforced his thesis and provided closure to his essay.

The following typed draft incorporates Kevin's revisions as well as some preliminary editing for spelling, punctuation, and grammar.

COMPUTERS

During the past year, much has been written about computer   1
literacy. A number of educators feel that students should be
taught at an early age to master the intricacies of computers
and computer programming. Now that a special faculty committee
has been appointed to investigate the possibility of requiring
all freshmen to purchase microcomputers, the issue gains added
importance. Although the cost of buying a computer would
slightly increase the cost of attending college, the advantages
of having a computer would more than make up for this.

The computer's ability to change words and sentences makes   2
it a good tool for college students. If students were required
to use a word processing program, they would gain skills that would
help them through four years of college. The university now has
tentative plans to install printing stations at key points
throughout campus. Students would be able to use these stations
much the way they now use duplicating machines. They would write
their papers at home on their computers and have their papers
typed on high-speed printers.

Most computers have spreadsheet programs that enable   3

students to work with numbers. Accounting majors could do financial analysis, budget modeling, and cash flow analysis. Some programs even enable students to convert numbers to graphs.

Chemistry majors could simulate chemical reactions on the computer. With the proper software, students could bond atoms together to form compounds. If a student attempted to combine two incompatible atoms, the computer would tell the student why the bonding would not take place. Biology majors could work with the structure of the complex molecule DNA. In short, the computer would make it possible for science majors to examine things that it would be impossible for them to see otherwise.   4

The price of the microcomputer would present problems to some students. The $1600 cost of the computer, however, would be spread over a four-year period adding only $400 a year to each student's tuition. University officials have assured both students and faculty that sufficient scholarship money will be available so that no student will suffer a financial hardship. This fact, plus the benefits of the computer, make me believe that computers should be required of all entering freshmen.   5

Revising the Second Draft

Kevin could see that this second draft was quite a bit better than the first. He had expanded the body paragraphs and sharpened his focus. But after thorough rereading and analysis, he discovered a number of ways in which his essay could still be improved.

The Title.   Kevin's original title was only a working title, and now he wanted something more descriptive. A humorous title was inappropriate, so after some experimentation he decided on the title "Computers Go to College." Not only was this title catchy, it was also descriptive: it prepared readers for what was to follow in the essay.

The Introduction.   Although Kevin was now more satisfied with the tone of his introduction, he identified two problems. Because the term *computer literacy* in his first sentence might not be familiar to his audience—freshman composition students—Kevin decided to define this term. Next, in reviewing his thesis, he found that by eliminating wordiness he could make it more effective.

The Body Paragraphs. After reading his first body paragraph, Kevin thought that he should sharpen his diction. In sentence one, for example, he decided to substitute *manipulate* for *change* and *useful* for *good.* He also recognized that the entire discussion concerning printing stations was irrelevant and that what he needed was a specific example to show how students could make use of word processing skills.

In his second body paragraph, Kevin had identified a specific use that accounting majors could make of the computer, but he found he had not explained spreadsheet programs in enough detail or shown how other business students could make use of them. Therefore, he decided to expand this discussion. Because the last sentence of the paragraph seemed to be an afterthought, he decided to delete it.

Kevin thought that the third body paragraph was his best, but even so, he knew his discussion of simulating chemical reactions could be smoother. He also realized that he would have to expand his discussion of the manipulation of the DNA molecule for readers not familiar with this subject.

In going over his body paragraphs to check for unity, Kevin discovered that none had an explicit topic sentence. To make sure that his readers could follow his reasoning, he added a strong topic sentence for each of the body paragraphs:

The most obvious application of computers is word processing.
Computers have a number of applications that business majors would find useful.
Science majors would also find the computer useful.

The Conclusion. Although Kevin knew he had to deal with the problem of a computer's cost, in rereading he decided that beginning his conclusion with this drawback was not very effective. Instead, he decided to discuss this disadvantage in a separate body paragraph and to use his conclusion to remind his readers of the advantages he had already discussed. He could then end his essay by restating the thesis.

Based on this analysis, Kevin revised and edited his draft, producing this final version of his essay.

COMPUTERS GO TO COLLEGE

Introduction (giving background)   During the past year, much has been written   1
about computer literacy--the ability of an individual
to use a computer. A number of educators think that
students should be taught to master the intricacies
of computers at an early age. Now that a special
faculty committee has been appointed to study the
possibility of requiring all freshmen to purchase
microcomputers, the issue gains added importance.

Thesis   Although the cost of buying a computer would increase
tuition, the advantages of having a computer outweigh
the disadvantages.

Advantage 1   The most obvious application of computers is   2
word processing. The computer's ability to change
words and manipulate sentences and paragraphs makes
it a useful tool for college students. If students
were required to use a word processing program in
their first-year composition courses, they would gain
skills that would help them with all their college
writing assignments. Revising an essay, for example,
would become an easy task. Students would no longer
have to sort through pages of scribbles and crossed-
out passages to create a clean draft. With the
computer, students could print out a clean copy of an
essay in progress, make changes, and then easily
insert the changes into the computer. Within minutes,
students would have a completed essay ready to hand
in to their instructors.

Advantage 2   Computers have a number of applications that   3
business majors would find useful. Most computers
have spreadsheet programs that enable students to
develop worksheets and carry out calculations. With
spreadsheets, students could easily restructure a
worksheet by adding and deleting information. Some

programs enable students to convert numbers to charts, files, or words. Accounting majors, for instance, could do financial analysis, budget modeling, and cash-flow analysis. Management majors could do forecasting, inventory control, and ''what if'' analysis. Most important, spreadsheets would enable students to concentrate on the significance of numbers rather than on calculating and arranging them.

Advantage 3   Science majors would also find the computer   4
useful. For example, chemistry majors could study chemical reactions with the computer. With the proper software, students could simulate the process of combining atoms to form molecules. If a student attempted to combine two incompatible atoms, the computer would tell the student why the reaction could not take place. Biology majors could use the computer to visualize the complex molecule DNA. By changing the amino acid groups on the DNA chain, students could simulate gene splicing and gain insight into genetics and microbiology. In short, the computer would make it possible for science majors to examine phenomena that they could not see under normal laboratory conditions.

Discussion of   Naturally, requiring computers is not without   5
major   its drawbacks. For example, the price of a
drawback   microcomputer would present problems to some
students. The $1600 cost of hardware, however, would be spread over four years, adding only $400 a year to each student's tuition. University officials have assured both students and faculty that sufficient scholarship money will be made available so that no student will suffer financial hardship.

Conclusion: summary of major points	Clearly, however, requiring students to purchase microcomputers has a number of advantages. Students would learn to use a valuable tool, and they would gain an understanding of processes that would be impossible to experience by traditional means. These
Restatement of thesis	advantages make it clear that the university should move ahead with its plans to integrate computers into the freshman curriculum.

6

7

Reviewing the Final Draft

The Introduction.   By first defining the term *computer literacy* and then putting into perspective the question of requiring students to purchase computers, Kevin's introduction supplies the background that readers need to understand the essay's thesis. To demonstrate to his audience that he is looking at the issue reasonably, Kevin goes on to concede that buying a computer will increase tuition. Even so, his thesis clearly maintains that the advantages—the subject of the paper—outweigh the disadvantages.

The Body Paragraphs.   Kevin supports his thesis by presenting examples of the educational advantages students would gain by owning a computer. He discusses each advantage in a separate paragraph and introduces each paragraph with a clearly stated topic sentence. Following each topic sentence are the facts that support it. Perhaps the major weakness of Kevin's paper is that he could have used still more specific information. In his first body paragraph, for example, he says that computers would help students learn certain writing skills, but he never demonstrates that these skills would be useful in courses other than freshman composition. In his second and third body paragraphs, Kevin says that students could carry out certain operations with the computer. He does not, however, mention specific business or science courses or explain whether students would be required to buy the software he describes. Although he makes good points, Kevin could strengthen his essay by presenting more detailed information to support his thesis.

In his fourth body paragraph, Kevin admits the potential problem of the computer's price, a point he mentioned in passing in his introduction. Although these costs are real, he says, they will not represent a substantial increase in tuition. This fact, plus the school's guarantee of financial aid, will make computers a welcome addition to the academic program. Kevin's decision to place this paragraph before his conclusion makes good sense. By refuting the major objection to his thesis, he prepares the way for the restatement of his thesis in the conclusion.

The Conclusion. Kevin begins his conclusion by summarizing the major points of his essay. He wants to make sure that his audience does not forget the implications of the material he has presented. Kevin ends his conclusion with a restatement of his thesis. This tactic provides closure to his essay and ensures that his major point will stay with his audience after they have finished reading.

REVISION CHECKLIST

You can use the following checklist to help you revise your essays. After you have applied the questions to the introduction, body, and conclusion of a paper, you can go on to revise sentence style and word choice and edit for grammar, punctuation, and mechanics. As you become a more confident writer, you will develop your own approaches to the writing process.

I. Introduction/Thesis
   A. Is the topic sufficiently narrowed?
   B. Is the thesis accurate, clear, and specific?
   C. Does the thesis indicate the direction your essay will take?
   D. Is your introduction appropriate for your material, audience, and purpose?
II. Body
   A. Is the topic sufficiently developed? Do any points need strengthening?
   B. Do the points you make support your topic sentences and your thesis?
   C. Does the essay have a clear pattern of development?
   D. Are the paragraphs well developed?
   E. Are the paragraphs unified?
   F. Are the paragraphs coherent?
III. Conclusion
   A. Is your conclusion interesting?
   B. Does the ending follow from your strongest points?

Each of the essays in the chapters that follow is organized around one dominant pattern of development. It is not at all unusual, however, to find more than one pattern used in a single essay. For example, a narrative essay might contain an introduction that is descriptive. As you can see, these patterns are not to be followed blindly but should be adapted to your subject, your audience, and your writing occasion.

2

Narration

WHAT IS NARRATION?

A narrative tells a story by presenting events in an orderly, logical sequence. In the following paragraph from *The Glory and the Dream*, William Manchester summarizes the sequence of events that led to the Montgomery, Alabama, bus boycott, an action that many believe began the civil rights struggle in the 1950s.

> Her name was Rosa Parks, she was forty-two years old, and on Thursday, December 1, 1955, she was very tired. She found a seat on a Montgomery bus, but when the bus filled up the driver told her to stand so a white man could sit there. It was an old southern custom for Negroes to surrender their seats to whites. It was also against the law for anyone to disobey a bus driver's instructions. Mrs. Parks thought about it for a moment and then said she wouldn't move. At that moment, Eldridge Cleaver later wrote, "somewhere in the universe a gear in the machinery had shifted."

Narration can be the dominant pattern in many types of writing—formal, such as history, biography, autobiography, and journalism, as well as less formal, such as personal letters and entries in diaries and journals. Narration is also an essential part of casual conversation, and it underlies tall tales, speeches, and news and feature stories presented on television or radio. In short, any time you "tell what happened," you are using narration.

Although a narrative may be written simply to recount events or to create a particular mood or impression, in much college writing narration presents a sequence of events in order to prove a point. For instance, in a narrative essay about your first date, your purpose may be to show your readers that dating is a bizarre and often unpleasant ritual. Accordingly, you do not simply "tell the story" of your date. Rather, you select and arrange details of the evening that show your readers why dating is bizarre and unpleasant. As in any other kind of essay, you may state your thesis explicitly ("My experiences with dating have convinced me that this ritual should be abandoned entirely"), or you may imply your thesis through the selection and arrangement of events.

Narrative writing may be part of an essay that is not primarily a narrative. In an argumentative essay in support of stricter gun-control legislation, for example, you may devote one or two paragraphs to a story of a child killed by a handgun. These narrative paragraphs, though only a small portion of the essay, still have a definite purpose. They support your point that stricter gun-control laws are needed.

In this chapter, however, we focus on narration as the dominant pattern in a piece of writing. During your college career, you will have many assignments that call for such writing. In an English composition class, for instance, you may be asked to write about an experience that was important to your development as an adult; in European history, you may need to relate the events that led to Napoleon's defeat at the Battle of Waterloo; in a technical writing class, you may be asked to write a letter of complaint reviewing in detail a company's negligent actions. In each of these situations (as well as in case studies for business management classes, reports for criminal justice classes, and many additional assignments), the piece of writing has a structure that is primarily narrative, and the narrative is presented to make a point.

The skills you develop in narrative writing will also be helpful to you in other kinds of writing. A process essay, such as an account of a laboratory experiment, is like a narrative in that it outlines a series of steps in chronological order; a cause-and-effect essay, such as your answer on an economics midterm that directs you to analyze the events that led to the Great Depression, also resembles narrative in that it traces a sequence of events. A process essay, however, presents events to explain how to do something, and a cause-and-effect essay presents them to explain how they are related. (Process essays and cause-and-effect essays are dealt with in chapters 5 and 6, respectively.) Still, writing both process and cause-and-effect essays will be easier if you master narration.

Narrative Detail

Narratives, like other types of writing, need rich, specific detail if they are to be convincing. Each detail should help form a picture for the reader; even exact times, dates, and geographical locations can be helpful. Look, for example, at the following excerpt from the essay "My Mother Never Worked," which appears in its complete form later in this chapter.

> In the winter she sewed night after night, endlessly, begging cast-off clothing from relatives, ripping apart coats, dresses, blouses, and trousers to remake them to fit her four daughters and son. Every morning and every evening she milked cows, fed pigs and calves, cared for chickens, picked eggs, cooked meals, washed dishes, scrubbed floors, and tended and loved her children. In the spring she planted a garden once more, dragging pails of water to nourish and sustain the vegetables for the family. In 1936 she lost a baby in her sixth month.

In this excerpt, the list of details makes the narrative genuine and convincing. The central figure in the narrative is a busy, productive woman, and the readers know this because they are presented with a specific list of her actions.

Narrative Variety

Because narratives are often told from one person's perspective, and because they usually present a series of events in chronological order, a constant danger is that all the sentences will begin to sound alike: "She sewed dresses. . . . She milked cows. . . . She fed pigs. . . . She fed calves. . . . She cared for chickens. . . . " A narrative without sentence variety may affect your readers like a ride down a monotonous stretch of highway. You can avoid this monotony by varying your sentence structure—for instance, by alternating sentence openings, inverting subject-verb order, or combining simple sentences: "In the winter she sewed night after night, endlessly. . . . Every morning and every evening she milked cows, fed pigs and calves, cared for chickens. . . . "

Narrative Order

Many narratives present events in exactly the order in which they occurred, moving from beginning to end, from first event to last. Whether or not you follow a strict chronological order, though, depends on the purpose of your narrative. If you are writing a straightforward account of a historical event or presenting a series of poor management practices, you will probably want to move efficiently from beginning to end. In writing personal experience essays or fictional narratives, however, you may choose to engage your reader's interest by beginning with a key event from the middle of your story, or even from the end, and then presenting the events that led up to it. You may also begin in the present and then use a series of flashbacks, shifts into the past, to tell your story. Whatever ordering scheme you use, it should shape and direct your narrative.

Verb tense is an extremely important clue in writing that recounts events in a fixed order because tenses show the temporal relationships of actions—earlier, simultaneous, later. When you write a narrative, you must be especially careful to keep verb tense consistent and accurate so your readers can easily understand the time sequence. Naturally, there are times when you must shift tense to reflect an actual time shift in your narrative. For instance, convention requires that you use present tense when discussing works of literature ("When Hamlet's mother *marries* his uncle . . . "), but a flashback to an earlier point in the story calls for a shift from present to past tense ("Before their marriage, Hamlet *was* . . . "). Nevertheless, it is important to avoid unnecessary shifts in verb tense because such unwarranted shifts will make your narrative confusing.

Together with verb tenses, *transitions*—connecting words or phrases—are the most precise indicators of the relationships among events in time. Transitions can indicate to readers the order in which events in a narrative occur, and they also signal shifts in time. Transitions commonly used for these purposes in narrative writing include *first, second, next, then, later, at the same time, meanwhile, immediately, soon, before, earlier, after, afterwards, now,* and *finally.* In addition to these transitions, specific time markers—such as *three years later, in 1927, after two hours,* and *on January 3*—indicate how much time has passed between events. Without these guides narratives would lack coherence, and readers would be unsure of the correct sequence of events.

STRUCTURING A NARRATIVE ESSAY

Like other essays, narratives usually have an introduction, a body, and a conclusion. If it is explicitly stated, your essay's thesis will, in most cases, appear in the *introduction.* Once the thesis is established, the *body* of your essay will recount the series of events that makes up your narrative, following a clear and orderly plan. Finally, the *conclusion* will give your reader the sense that your story is complete, perhaps by restating your thesis.

Suppose you are assigned a short history paper about the Battle of Waterloo. You plan to support the thesis that if Napoleon had kept more troops in reserve, he might have defeated the British troops under Wellington. Based on this thesis, you decide that the best way to organize your paper is to present the five major phases of the battle in strict chronological sequence. An informal outline of your essay might look like this:

Introduction:	Thesis—Had Napoleon kept more troops in reserve, he might have broken Wellington's line with another infantry attack and thus reversed the outcome of the battle of Waterloo.
Phase one of the battle:	Napoleon attacks the Château of Hougoumont.
Phase two of the battle:	The French infantry attacks the British lines.
Phase three of the battle:	The French cavalry stages a series of charges against the British lines that had not been attacked before. Napoleon commits his reserves.
Phase four of the battle:	The French capture La Haye Sainte, their first success of the day but an advantage which Napoleon, having committed troops elsewhere, cannot maintain without reserves.
Phase five of the battle:	The French infantry is decisively defeated by the combined thrust of the British infantry and the remaining British cavalry.
Conclusion:	Restatement of thesis—Had Napoleon had reinforcements ready to capitalize on his capture of La Haye Sainte, he could have broken through the British lines with another infantry attack.

By discussing the five phases of the battle in chronological order, you clearly demonstrate the validity of your thesis. In turning your informal outline into a historical narrative, you realize that exact details, dates, times, and geographical locations will be extremely important. Without them, your mere assertions will be open to question. In addition, to keep your readers aware of the order in which the events of the battle took place, you plan to select appropriate transitional words and phrases carefully and to pay special attention to verb tenses.

The following essay is typical of the informal narrative writing many freshmen are asked to do in English composition classes. It was written by Anne Chan Mandel, a student who grew up in Shanghai, in response to the assignment, "Write an essay about an episode from your childhood."

MY BROTHER AND GENERAL CRAB

Introduction   I often think of my brother. I just received a   1
letter from him recently. It says:

Dear "little" sister,   2

Forgive me for calling you "little" sister
because I still can't get used to saying your
name even though you are grown up now. When I
saw your picture which you took on the beach of
Okracoke Island in North Carolina, it reminded
me of my little sister with bare feet running
along the bank of the river. Your smile is still
as joyous as before and your posture still like
a little girl's. I guess you don't know how much
happiness this picture gives to me and how much
I miss the times when we were together. Do you
remember in Shanghai, that night when we were
catching General Crabs? . . .

Flashback: Of course I remember! At that time I was eight   3
Narrative   years old and my brother was nine. Because our ages
begins   were close to each other, I was his little tail,
following him everywhere. I remember he wasn't happy
with this at first and often complained to my mother.

Dialogue   "Mom, I'm going out to play Big Soldier Will   4
Catch the Japanese Ghost, but Mei Mei (younger
sister) wants to go with me. She is too little for
the game."

"I want to go, I want to go!" I said loudly. I   5
ignored his complaining.

"Well, you are the older brother," my mom said   6
to him. "You should share your fun with Mei Mei,
shouldn't you?"

It was true that I liked to play with boys. They   7

were brave, did not get angry at each other that easily, and had lots of ideas for fun. Especially my brother: he knew much more than I did, and he always seemed like an expert to me. He knew how to make kites and moon festival lanterns and even how to catch fish. Following him, being his "little tail," was my way to have fun. Finally he had to accept the fact that losing a little bit of freedom by bringing mei mei with him was better than staying home.

One evening, we were going to Huong Po River with our   8 cousins and friends. I saw my brother taking a bamboo basket, flashlight, and chopsticks from home.

"What are we going to do?"   9

"We are going to catch General Crab," he   10 replied secretively.

"Oh, yeah!" I was jumping in the air, very   11 excited by this idea.

When we arrived on the bank of Huong Po   12 River, the moon hid in the clouds. A few little stars were blinking their eyes at us. The river was dark and quiet; only on the surface was there some reflection of lights from several boats which were moored near where the ferry was waving on the water.

We started to search for holes which had been   13 made by crabs. My brother seemed more professional than the other kids. He could judge correctly which one had a crab in it and which one didn't. The mud was very soft under our feet. The pressure of our footsteps easily changed the shape of the hole.

"It fools you if you don't watch carefully,"   14 my brother explained to me. "See this one, it looks like a comfortable home for a crab, but actually it's a snake hole." I looked at it anxiously. "This one over here," he continued on like an expert while I was holding the flashlight for him, "seems like

nothing special, but can you see? They deposited dirt
out to both sides of the hole and the front and back
are clear. This is their habit when they build their
house." He started to use the chopstick, probing
into the hole. "Now we have to get General Crab
angry," he explained to me. "They will use their
claws to fight with my chopstick. Then, finally. . . . "

Climax of narrative

He pulled the chopstick out of the hole.
"Look how tight they pinch on the chopstick!"

Really, that was very exciting for both of us. I   15
looked at the crab; it was bigger than my palm, grey
and bony. Eight legs were moving in the air, and it
didn't give up pinching the chopstick. I imitated the
movement of the crab like a dancer, using my arms and
legs. The sound of our laughter went through the dark
sky all the way to the moon behind the clouds. That
night we caught at least 15 crabs. Poor guys, they had
to stay in the bamboo basket until we got home. Then,
the next day. . . .

Conclusion: Aftermath of episode

"Why do you call the crabs 'General'?" I asked   16
my brother one day.

"Because they have strong shells and claws. And   17
they are good fighters."

Last sentence reinforces thesis

Again, he seemed like an expert.   18

Points for Special Attention

Introduction.   Anne's introduction uses a very effective strategy
to arouse reader interest. She begins with a simple statement—"I
often think of my brother"—that her entire essay will develop. She
then quotes a portion of a letter from her brother in which he expresses his affection for her and asks whether she remembers a particular incident from their childhood. Her answer to this question—
"Of course I remember!"—moves readers smoothly into the body of
the essay.

Thesis. Anne's assignment was to recreate an episode from her childhood, and her narrative is an affectionate memoir. The essay's thesis—the point of the narrative—is stated in paragraph 7, and all the details in the narrative contribute to this thesis. The first sentence establishes her brother's central position in her life, and later Anne twice refers to herself as his "little tail" and three times refers to her brother as the "expert" to whom she deferred. Throughout, the essay communicates a strong sense of how Anne looked up to her brother, and the last sentence reinforces this impression.

Structure. The body of Anne's essay consists of a flashback to her childhood. She begins by explaining and illustrating the relationship between her brother and herself. Once she has established her respect for him ("he always seemed like an expert to me"), she introduces the key episode on which her essay focuses: the hunt for General Crab. The balance of the essay proceeds in chronological order, working up to the climax or high point of the story: the capture of the first crab. The essay has no formal concluding paragraph, but the last sentence is isolated in a separate paragraph for emphasis.

Detail. Personal narratives like Anne's are especially dependent on detail because the authors want readers to see and hear and feel what they did. To present an accurate picture of the events she describes, Anne supplies all the significant details she can remember: the names of the games the children played, specific place names, the way the stars and the river looked, the feel of the mud, and the way the crab struggled when Anne's brother caught it. She could have presented even more detail—descriptions of her mother, or of her brother's friends, for instance—but she chose not to because she wanted to keep her account focused on her brother.

Dialogue. Anne characterizes her brother, her mother, and herself—and their relationship with one another—by means of dialogue. As a result, her narrative is more interesting and more immediate than it would be if she had simply described events. (Notice that, as convention requires, Anne begins a new paragraph each time a different person speaks.)

Sentence Variety. Anne's sentences are, for the most part, sufficiently varied to sustain reader interest. She avoids monotonous strings of choppy sentences and varies sentence openings. In paragraph 13, however, all of her sentences begin with the subject:

> We started to search for holes which had been made by crabs. My brother seemed more professional than the other kids. He could judge correctly which one had a crab in it and which one didn't. The mud was very soft under our feet. The pressure of our footsteps easily changed the shape of the hole.

If Anne had combined some sentences and varied her openings, this paragraph could have been clearer as well as less monotonous.

> As we started to search for holes which had been made by crabs, I could see that my brother seemed more professional than the other kids. He could judge correctly which one had a crab in it and which one didn't. Because the mud was very soft under our feet, the pressure of our footsteps easily changed the shape of the hole.

With these revisions, the exact sequential and logical relationships between ideas are clearer and the paragraph is more coherent.

Verb Tense.   Maintaining clear chronological order is very important in narrative writing, where unwarranted shifts in tense can confuse readers. Knowing this, Anne is careful to avoid unnecessary shifts in tense. She does shift from past tense to present, but this shift is necessary to distinguish events that happened at different times. Although the first sentence of Anne's essay uses present tense to indicate a habitual action ("I often think . . . "), with paragraph 3 her narrative switches to past tense to indicate that the events described took place before the essay was written.

Transitions.   In "My Brother and General Crab" Anne effectively uses transitional words like *finally* and *when* as well as more specific time markers like *One evening, at that time, that night,* and *one day*. Most often, though, she relies on the dialogue to advance the action and to carry her readers along through the story's action.

The selections that follow illustrate some of the many possibilities open to writers of narrative essays.

FINISHING SCHOOL

Maya Angelou

Maya Angelou (originally Marguerita Johnson) was born in 1928 in St. Louis and grew up in Stamps, Arkansas, with her brother Bailey and her grandmother ("Momma"), who owned a general store. Later Angelou studied dance and toured Europe and Africa performing in Porgy *and* Bess. *She also starred in the off-Broadway play* The Blacks, *was Northern Coordinator for the Southern Christian Leadership Conference, worked as a newspaper reporter in Egypt and Ghana, and wrote four autobiographical volumes and several books of poetry. "Finishing School" is a chapter from* I Know Why the Caged Bird Sings *(1969), Angelou's vividly evocative memoir of her childhood. In this selection she explores a theme she returns to often: her inability to understand the ways of the town's whites and their inability to understand her.*

Recently a white woman from Texas, who would quickly describe herself as a liberal, asked me about my hometown. When I told her that in Stamps my grandmother had owned the only Negro general merchandise store since the turn of the century, she exclaimed, "Why, you were a debutante." Ridiculous and even ludicrous. But Negro girls in small Southern towns, whether poverty-stricken or just munching along on a few of life's necessities, were given as extensive and irrelevant preparations for adulthood as rich white girls shown in magazines. Admittedly the training was not the same. While white girls learned to waltz and sit gracefully with a tea cup balanced on their knees, we were lagging behind, learning the mid-Victorian values with very little money to indulge them. . . .

We were required to embroider and I had trunkfuls of colorful dishtowels, pillowcases, runners and handkerchiefs to my credit. I mastered the art of crocheting and tatting, and there was a life-time's supply of dainty doilies that would never be used in sacheted dresser drawers. It went without saying that all girls could iron and wash, but the finer touches around the home, like setting a table with real silver, baking roasts and cooking vegetables without meat, had to be learned elsewhere. Usually at the source of those habits. During my tenth year, a white woman's kitchen became my finishing school.

Mrs. Viola Cullinan was a plump woman who lived in a three-bedroom house somewhere behind the post office. She was singularly unattractive until she smiled, and then the lines around her eyes and mouth which made her look perpetually dirty disappeared, and her face looked like the mask of an impish elf. She usually rested her smile until late afternoon when her women friends dropped in and Miss Glory, the cook, served them cold drinks on the closed-in porch.

The exactness of her house was inhuman. This glass went here   4
and only here. That cup had its place and it was an act of impudent rebellion to place it anywhere else. At twelve o'clock the table was set. At 12:15 Mrs. Cullinan sat down to dinner (whether her husband had arrived or not). At 12:16 Miss Glory brought out the food.

It took me a week to learn the difference between a salad plate, a   5
bread plate and a dessert plate.

Mrs. Cullinan kept up the tradition of her wealthy parents. She   6
was from Virginia. Miss Glory, who was a descendant of slaves that had worked for the Cullinans, told me her history. She had married beneath her (according to Miss Glory). Her husband's family hadn't had their money very long and what they had "didn't 'mount to much."

As ugly as she was, I thought privately, she was lucky to get a   7
husband above or beneath her station. But Miss Glory wouldn't let me say a thing against her mistress. She was very patient with me, however, over the housework. She explained the dishware, silverware and servants' bells. The large round bowl in which soup was served wasn't a soup bowl, it was a tureen. There were goblets, sherbet glasses, ice-cream glasses, wine glasses, green glass coffee cups with matching saucers, and water glasses. I had a glass to drink from, and it sat with Miss Glory's on a separate shelf from the others. Soup spoons, gravy boat, butter knives, salad forks and carving platter were additions to my vocabulary and in fact almost represented a new language. I was fascinated with the novelty, with the fluttering Mrs. Cullinan and her Alice-in-Wonderland house.

Her husband remains, in my memory, undefined. I lumped him   8
with all the other white men that I had ever seen and tried not to see.

On our way home one evening, Miss Glory told me that Mrs. Cullinan couldn't have children. She said that she was too delicate-boned.   9
It was hard to imagine bones at all under those layers of fat. Miss Glory went on to say that the doctor had taken out all her lady organs. I reasoned that a pig's organs included the lungs, heart and liver, so if Mrs. Cullinan was walking around without those essen-

tials, it explained why she drank alcohol out of unmarked bottles. She was keeping herself embalmed.

When I spoke to Bailey about it, he agreed that I was right, but he also informed me that Mr. Cullinan had two daughters by a colored lady and that I knew them very well. He added that the girls were the spitting image of their father. I was unable to remember what he looked like, although I had just left him a few hours before, but I thought of the Coleman girls. They were very light-skinned and certainly didn't look very much like their mother (no one ever mentioned Mr. Coleman). 10

My pity for Mrs. Cullinan preceded me the next morning like the Cheshire cat's smile. Those girls, who could have been her daughters, were beautiful. They didn't have to straighten their hair. Even when they were caught in the rain, their braids still hung down straight like tamed snakes. Their mouths were pouty little cupid's bows. Mrs. Cullinan didn't know what she missed. Or maybe she did. Poor Mrs. Cullinan. 11

For weeks after, I arrived early, left late and tried very hard to make up for her barrenness. If she had her own children, she wouldn't have had to ask me to run a thousand errands from her back door to the back door of her friends. Poor old Mrs. Cullinan. 12

Then one evening Miss Glory told me to serve the ladies on the porch. After I set the tray down and turned toward the kitchen, one of the women asked, "What's your name, girl?" It was the speckled-faced one. Mrs. Cullinan said, "She doesn't talk much. Her name's Margaret." 13

"Is she dumb?" 14

"No. As I understand it, she can talk when she wants to but she's usually quiet as a little mouse. Aren't you, Margaret?" 15

I smiled at her. Poor thing. No organs and couldn't even pronounce my name correctly. 16

"She's a sweet little thing, though." 17

"Well, that may be, but the name's too long. I'd never bother myself. I'd call her Mary if I was you." 18

I fumed into the kitchen. That horrible woman would never have the chance to call me Mary because if I was starving I'd never work for her. . . . 19

That evening I decided to write a poem on being white, fat, old and without children. It was going to be a tragic ballad. I would have to watch her carefully to capture the essence of her loneliness and pain. 20

The very next day, she called me by the wrong name. Miss Glory 21 and I were washing up the lunch dishes when Mrs. Cullinan came to the doorway. "Mary?"

Miss Glory asked, "Who?"   22

Mrs. Cullinan, sagging a little, knew and I knew. "I want Mary to   23
go down to Mrs. Randall's and take her some soup. She's not been feeling well for a few days."

Miss Glory's face was a wonder to see. "You mean Margaret,   24
ma'am. Her name's Margaret."

"That's too long. She's Mary from now on. Heat that soup from   25
last night and put it in the china tureen and, Mary, I want you to carry it carefully."

Every person I knew had a hellish horror of being "called out of   26
his name." It was a dangerous practice to call a Negro anything that could be loosely construed as insulting because of the centuries of their having been called niggers, jigs, dinges, blackbirds, crows, boots and spooks.

Miss Glory had a fleeting second of feeling sorry for me. Then as   27
she handed me the hot tureen she said, "Don't mind, don't pay that no mind. Sticks and stones may break your bones, but words . . . You know, I been working for her for twenty years."

She held the back door open for me. "Twenty years. I wasn't much   28
older than you. My name used to be Hallelujah. That's what Ma named me, but my mistress give me 'Glory,' and it stuck. I likes it better too."

I was in the little path that ran behind the houses when Miss   29
Glory shouted, "It's shorter too."

For a few seconds it was a tossup over whether I would laugh   30
(imagine being named Hallelujah) or cry (imagine letting some white woman rename you for her convenience). My anger saved me from either outburst. I had to quit the job, but the problem was going to be how to do it. Momma wouldn't allow me to quit for just any reason.

"She's a peach. That woman is a real peach." Mrs. Randall's maid   31
was talking as she took the soup from me, and I wondered what her name used to be and what she answered to now.

For a week I looked into Mrs. Cullinan's face as she called me   32
Mary. She ignored my coming late and leaving early. Miss Glory was a little annoyed because I had begun to leave egg yolk on the dishes and wasn't putting much heart in polishing the silver. I hoped that she would complain to our boss, but she didn't.

Then Bailey solved my dilemma. He had me describe the contents   33
of the cupboard and the particular plates she liked best. Her favorite

piece was a casserole shaped like a fish and the green glass coffee cups. I kept his instructions in mind, so on the next day when Miss Glory was hanging out clothes and I had again been told to serve the old biddies on the porch, I dropped the empty serving tray. When I heard Mrs. Cullinan scream, "Mary!" I picked up the casserole and two of the green glass cups in readiness. As she rounded the kitchen door I let them fall on the tiled floor.

I could never absolutely describe to Bailey what happened next, 34 because each time I got to the part where she fell on the floor and screwed up her ugly face to cry, we burst out laughing. She actually wobbled around on the floor and picked up shards of the cups and cried, "Oh, Momma. Oh, dear Gawd. It's Mamma's china from Virginia. Oh, Momma, I sorry."

Miss Glory came running in from the yard and the women from 35 the porch crowded around. Miss Glory was almost as broken up as her mistress. "You mean to say she broke our Virginia dishes? What we gone do?"

Mrs. Cullinan cried louder, "That clumsy nigger. Clumsy little 36 black nigger."

Old speckled-face leaned down and asked, "Who did it, Viola? 37 Was it Mary? Who did it?"

Everything was happening so fast I can't remember whether her 38 action preceded her words, but I know that Mrs. Cullinan said, "Her name's Margaret, goddamn it, her name's Margaret." And she threw a wedge of broken plate at me. It could have been the hysteria which put her aim off, but the flying crockery caught Miss Glory right over her ear and she started screaming.

I left the front door wide open so all the neighbors could hear. 39

Mrs. Cullinan was right about one thing. My name wasn't Mary. 40

COMPREHENSION

1. What is Angelou required to do in the white woman's kitchen? What things does she find unfamiliar in the household?

2. Why does Angelou feel sorry for Mrs. Cullinan at first? When does her attitude change?

3. Why does Mrs. Cullinan's friend recommend that Angelou be called "Mary"? Why does this upset Angelou so deeply?

4. When Angelou decides she wants to quit, but realizes she cannot quit "for just any reason," how does Bailey help her resolve her dilemma?

5. What does Angelou actually learn through her experience? In what sense, then, does the kitchen really serve as a finishing school?

PURPOSE AND AUDIENCE

1. Is Angelou writing for Southerners, blacks, whites, or a general audience? Point to the specific details to support your answer.

2. Angelou begins her narrative by summarizing a discussion between herself and a white woman. What is her purpose in doing this?

3. What is Angelou's thesis?

STYLE AND STRUCTURE

1. What image does the phrase *finishing school* usually suggest? How is the use of this phrase ironic in view of its meaning in this selection?

2. How does Angelou signal the passage of time in this narrative? Identify some transitional phrases that show the passage of time.

3. How does the use of dialogue highlight the contrast between the black and the white characters? In what way does this strengthen the narrative?

4. What details does Angelou use to describe Mrs. Cullinan and her home to the reader? How does this detailed description help advance the narrative?

5. What is Angelou's tone? Is she angry, amused, or matter-of-fact? Quote specific words and passages that illustrate the tone.

VOCABULARY PROJECTS

1. Define each of the following words as it is used in this selection.

   tatting (2)   barrenness (12)
   sacheted (2)   ballad (20)
   impudent (4)   construed (26)
   embalmed (9)   dilemma (33)
   pouty (11)   shards (34)

2. According to your dictionary, what is the difference in meaning between *ridiculous* and *ludicrous* (1)? Between *soup bowl* and *tureen* (7)? What is the effect of Angelou's distinctions?

3. Try substituting an equivalent word for each of the following, but pay careful attention to the context of each in the narrative.

perpetually (3)   peach (31)
exactness (4)   biddies (33)
station (7)

Does the writer's original choice seem best in all cases? Why, or why not?

WRITING WORKSHOP

1. Think about a time in your life when an adult in a position of authority treated you unjustly. How did you react? Write a narrative essay in which you recount the situation and your responses. Would you act differently today? Explain.

2. What institution served as your "finishing school?" Tell how you learned the skills you needed there.

3. Write a narrative essay in which you retell an incident from a work of fiction—specifically, an incident that serves as a character's initiation into adulthood. In your essay, explain how the experience helped the character to grow up.

THEMATIC CONNECTIONS

- "The Civil Rights Movement: What Good Was It?" (p. 283)
- "Three Kinds of Discipline" (p. 391)

MY MOTHER NEVER WORKED

Donna Smith-Yackel

*Although this essay draws on personal experience, it makes a gen-
eral point about what society thinks of "women's work." According to federal law, a woman who is a homemaker is entitled to Social Security benefits only through the earnings of her husband.
Thus, a homemaker who becomes disabled receives no disability
benefits, and her husband and children are allowed no survivors'
benefits if she should die. Although this law has been challenged in
the courts, a woman who does not work for wages outside the home
is still not entitled to Social Security benefits in her own right.
Without explicitly stating her thesis, Donna Smith-Yakel comments on this situation in her narrative.*

"Social Security Office." (The voice answering the telephone 1
sounds very self-assured.)

"I'm calling about ... I ... my mother just died ... I was told to 2
call you and see about a ... death-benefit check, I think they call
it ... "

"I see. Was your mother on Social Security? How old was she?" 3

"Yes ... she was seventy-eight. ... " 4

"Do you know her number?" 5

"No ... I, ah ... don't you have a record?" 6

"Certainly. I'll look it up. Her name?" 7

"Smith. Martha Smith. Or maybe she used Martha Ruth 8
Smith? ... Sometimes she used her maiden name ... Martha Jera-
bek Smith."

"If you'd care to hold on, I'll check our records—it'll be a few mi- 9
nutes."

"Yes. ... " 10

Her love letters—to and from Daddy—were in an old box, tied 11
with ribbons and stiff, rigid-with-age leather thongs: 1918 through
1920; hers written on stationery from the general store she had
worked in full-time and managed, single-handed, after her gradua-
tion from high school in 1913; and his, at first, on YMCA or Soldiers
and Sailors Club stationery dispensed to the fighting men of World

War I. He wooed her thoroughly and persistently by mail, and though she reciprocated all his feelings for her, she dreaded marriage. . . .

"It's so hard for me to decide when to have my wedding day— that's all I've thought about these last two days. I have told you dozens of times that I won't be afraid of married life, but when it comes down to setting the date and then picturing myself a married woman with half a dozen or more kids to look after, it just makes me sick. . . . I am weeping right now—I hope that some day I can look back and say how foolish I was to dread it all." 12

They married in February, 1921, and began farming. Their first baby, a daughter, was born in January, 1922, when my mother was 26 years old. The second baby, a son, was born in March, 1923. They were renting farms; my father, besides working his own fields, also was a hired man for two other farmers. They had no capital initially, and had to gain it slowly, working from dawn until midnight every day. My town-bred mother learned to set hens and raise chickens, feed pigs, milk cows, plant and harvest a garden, and can every fruit and vegetable she could scrounge. She carried water nearly a quarter of a mile from the well to fill her wash boilers in order to do her laundry on a scrub board. She learned to shuck grain, feed threshers, shock and husk corn, feed corn pickers. In September, 1925, the third baby came, and in June, 1927, the fourth child—both daughters. In 1930, my parents had enough money to buy their own farm, and that March they moved all their livestock and belongings themselves, 55 miles over rutted, muddy roads. 13

In the summer of 1930 my mother and her two eldest children reclaimed a 40-acre field from Canadian thistles, by chopping them all out with a hoe. In the other fields, when the oats and flax began to head out, the green and blue of the crops were hidden by the bright yellow of wild mustard. My mother walked the fields day after day, pulling each mustard plant. She raised a new flock of baby chicks—500—and she spaded up, planted, hoed, and harvested a half-acre garden. 14

During the next spring their hogs caught cholera and died. No cash that fall. 15

And in the next year the drought hit. My mother and father trudged from the well to the chickens, the well to the calf pasture, the well to the barn, and from the well to the garden. The sun came out hot and bright, endlessly, day after day. The crops shriveled and died. They harvested half the corn, and ground the other half, stalks and all, and fed it to the cattle as fodder. With the price at four cents 16 a bushel for the harvested crop, they couldn't afford to haul it into town. They burned it in the furnace for fuel that winter.

In 1934, in February, when the dust was still so thick in the Minnesota air that my parents couldn't always see from the house to the barn, their fifth child—a fourth daughter—was born. My father hunted rabbits daily, and my mother stewed them, fried them, canned them, and wished out loud that she could taste hamburger once more. In the fall the shotgun brought prairie chickens, ducks, pheasant, and grouse. My mother plucked each bird, carefully reserving the breast feathers for pillows.   17

In the winter she sewed night after night, endlessly, begging cast-off clothing from relatives, ripping apart coats, dresses, blouses, and trousers to remake them to fit her four daughters and son. Every morning and every evening she milked cows, fed pigs, and calves, cared for chickens, picked eggs, cooked meals, washed dishes, scrubbed floors, and tended and loved her children. In the spring she planted a garden once more, dragging pails of water to nourish and sustain the vegetables for the family. In 1936 she lost a baby in her sixth month.   18

In 1937 her fifth daughter was born. She was 42 years old. In 1939 a second son, and in 1941 her eighth child—and third son.   19

But the war had come, and prosperity of a sort. The herd of cattle had grown to 30 head; she still milked morning and evening. Her garden was more than a half acre—the rains had come, and by now the Rural Electricity Administration and indoor plumbing. Still she sewed—dresses and jackets for the children, housedresses and aprons for herself, weekly patching of jeans, overalls, and denim shirts. She still made pillows, using feathers she had plucked, and quilts every year—intricate patterns as well as patchwork, stitched as well as tied—all necessary bedding for her family. Every scrap of cloth too small to be used in quilts was carefully saved and painstakingly sewed together in strips to make rugs. She still went out in the fields to help with the haying whenever there was a threat of rain.   20

In 1959 my mother's last child graduated from high school. A year later the cows were sold. She still raised chickens and ducks, plucked feathers, made pillows, baked her own bread, and every year made a new quilt—now for a married child or for a grandchild. And her garden, that huge, undying symbol of sustenance, was as large and cared for as in all the years before. The canning, and now freezing, continued.   21

In 1969, on a June afternoon, mother and father started out for town so that she could buy sugar to make rhubarb jam for a daugh-   22 ter who lived in Texas. The car crashed into a ditch. She was paralyzed from the waist down.

In 1970 her husband, my father, died. My mother struggled to re-   23
gain some competence and dignity and order in her life. At the reha-
bilitation institute, where they gave her physical therapy and
trained her to live usefully in a wheelchair, the therapist told me:
"She did fifteen pushups today—fifteen! She's almost seventy-five
years old! I've never known a woman so strong!"

From her wheelchair she canned pickles, baked bread, ironed   24
clothes, wrote dozens of letters weekly to her friends and her "half
dozen or more kids," and made three patchwork housecoats and one
quilt. She made balls and balls of carpet rags—enough for five rugs.
And kept all her love letters.

"I think I've found your mother's records—Martha Ruth Smith;   25
married to Ben F. Smith?

"Yes, that's right."   26
"Well, I see that she was getting a widow's pension. . . . "   27
"Yes, that's right."   28
"Well, your mother isn't entitled to our $255 death benefit."   29
"Not entitled! But why?"   30
The voice on the telephone explains patiently: 31
"Well, you see—your mother never worked."   32

COMPREHENSION

1. Why wasn't Martha Smith eligible for a death benefit?

2. What kind of work did Martha Smith do while her children were growing up? List some of the chores she performed.

3. How does the government define *work?*

PURPOSE AND AUDIENCE

1. What is the essay's thesis? Why is it never explicitly stated?

2. This essay appeared in *Ms.* magazine and other journals whose audiences are sympathetic to feminist ideals. Could it just as easily have appeared in a magazine whose audience was not? Why, or why not?

3. How can you tell that this essay's purpose is persuasive?

4. The author mentions relatively little about her father in this essay. How can you account for this?

STYLE AND STRUCTURE

1. Is the title effective? Why, or why not?

2. What constitutes the essay's introduction? Its conclusion? How are the introduction and conclusion set off from the body of the essay?

3. The author could have outlined her mother's life without framing it with the telephone conversation. Why does she include this frame?

4. What strategies does the author use to indicate the passing of time in her narrative?

5. This narrative piles details one on top of another almost like a list. For instance, paragraph 13 includes this sentence: "My town-bred mother learned to set hens and raise chickens, feed pigs, milk cows, plant and harvest a garden, and can every fruit and vegetable she could scrounge." Why does the author list so many details?

6. In paragraphs 20 and 21, what is accomplished by the repetition of the word *still*?

7. Would the point of the narrative have been made as effectively if it had been written as a straightforward essay on injustice toward women who work at home? Explain.

VOCABULARY PROJECTS

1. Define each of the following words as it is used in this selection.

   scrounge (13)   reclaimed (14)
   shuck (13)   flax (14)
   shock (13)   fodder (16)
   husk (13)   intricate (20)
   rutted (13)   sustenance (21)

2. Try substituting equivalent words for those italicized in this sentence. Be prepared to discuss how your substitutions change the sentence's meaning.

   He *wooed* her *thoroughly* and *persistently* by mail, and though she *reciprocated* all his feeling for her, she *dreaded* marriage. . . . (11)

3. Reread paragraph 16. Which words convey a sense of hopelessness? What details reinforce this feeling?

4. Throughout the narrative, the author uses very concrete, specific verbs. Review her choice of verbs, particularly in paragraphs 13–24, and comment on how such verbs serve the essay's purpose.

WRITING WORKSHOP

1. If you can, interview one of your parents or grandparents (or another person you know who might remind you of Donna Smith-Yakel's mother) about his or her work, and write a chronological narrative based on what you learn. Include a thesis that your narrative can support.

2. Write Martha Smith's obituary as it might have appeared in her hometown newspaper. If you are not familiar with the form of an obituary, read a few in your local paper.

3. Write a narrative account of the worst job you ever had. Include a thesis that expresses your negative feelings.

THEMATIC CONNECTIONS

- "Photographs of My Parents" (p. 117)
- "The Company Man" (p. 440)

38 WHO SAW MURDER DIDN'T CALL THE POLICE

Martin Gansberg

*Martin Gansberg, a native of Brooklyn, New York, was born in
1920 and was on the staff of the* New York Times *for some forty
years. He has also taught at Fairleigh Dickinson University and
written for popular magazines. The essay reprinted below was
written for the* New York Times *two weeks after the murder it recounts. The entire country was shocked by this incident, which has
been the subject of countless articles and editorials, as well as a
television movie. Indeed, the murder of Kitty Genovese is still
cited today as an example of public indifference. Gansberg's article
is frequently anthologized; its thesis, though not explicitly stated,
retains its power.*

For more than half an hour 38 respectable, law-abiding citizens in   1
Queens watched a killer stalk and stab a woman in three separate
attacks in Kew Gardens.

Twice their chatter and the sudden glow of their bedroom lights   2
interrupted him and frightened him off. Each time he returned,
sought her out, and stabbed her again. Not one person telephoned
the police during the assault; one witness called after the woman
was dead.

That was two weeks ago today.   3

Still shocked is Assistant Chief Inspector Frederick M. Lussen, in   4
charge of the borough's detectives and a veteran of 25 years of homicide investigations. He can give a matter-of-fact recitation on many
murders. But the Kew Gardens slaying baffles him—not because it
is a murder, but because the "good people" failed to call the police.

"As we have reconstructed the crime," he said, "the assailant had   5
three chances to kill this woman during a 35-minute period. He returned twice to complete the job. If we had been called when he first
attacked, the woman might not be dead now."

This is what the police say happened beginning at 3:20 A.M. in the   6
staid, middle-class, tree-lined Austin Street area:

Twenty-eight-year-old Catherine Genovese, who was called Kitty   7 by almost everyone in the neighborhood, was returning home from her job as manager of a bar in Hollis. She parked her red Fiat in a lot adjacent to the Kew Gardens Long Island Rail Road Station, facing Mowbray Place. Like many residents of the neighborhood, she had parked there day after day since her arrival from Connecticut a year ago, although the railroad frowns on the practice.

She turned off the lights of her car, locked the door, and started   8
to walk the 100 feet to the entrance of her apartment at 82-70 Austin Street, which is in a Tudor building, with stores in the first floor and apartments on the second.

The entrance to the apartment is in the rear of the building be-   9
cause the front is rented to retail stores. At night the quiet neighborhood is shrouded in the slumbering darkness that marks most residential areas.

Miss Genovese noticed a man at the far end of the lot, near a   10
seven-story apartment house at 82-40 Austin Street. She halted. Then, nervously, she headed up Austin Street toward Lefferts Boulevard, where there is a call box to the 102nd Police Precinct in nearby Richmond Hill.

She got as far as a street light in front of a bookstore before the   11
man grabbed her. She screamed. Lights went on in the 10-story apartment house at 82-67 Austin Street, which faces the bookstore. Windows slid open and voices punctuated the early-morning stillness.

Miss Genovese screamed: "Oh, my God, he stabbed me! Please   12
help me! Please help me!"

From one of the upper windows in the apartment house, a man   13
called down: "Let that girl alone!"

The assailant looked up at him, shrugged, and walked down Aus-   14
tin Street toward a white sedan parked a short distance away. Miss Genovese struggled to her feet.

Lights went out. The killer returned to Miss Genovese, now trying   15
to make her way around the side of the building by the parking lot to get to her apartment. The assailant stabbed her again.

"I'm dying!" she shrieked. "I'm dying!"   16

Windows were opened again, and lights went on in many apart-   17
ments. The assailant got into his car and drove away. Miss Genovese staggered to her feet. A city bus, O-10, the Lefferts Boulevard line to Kennedy International Airport, passed. It was 3:35 A.M.

The assailant returned. By then, Miss Genovese had crawled to   18
the back of the building, where the freshly painted brown doors to the apartment house held out hope for safety. The killer tried the first door; she wasn't there. At the second door, 82-62 Austin

Street, he saw her slumped on the floor at the foot of the stairs. He stabbed her a third time—fatally.

It was 3:50 by the time the police received their first call, from a man who was a neighbor of Miss Genovese. In two minutes they were at the scene. The neighbor, a 70-year-old woman, and another woman were the only persons on the street. Nobody else came forward. 19

The man explained that he had called the police after much deliberation. He had phoned a friend in Nassau County for advice and then he had crossed the roof of the building to the apartment of the elderly woman to get her to make the call. 20

"I didn't want to get involved," he sheepishly told police. 21

Six days later, the police arrested Winston Moseley, a 29-year-old business machine operator, and charged him with homicide. Moseley had no previous record. He is married, has two children and owns a home at 133–19 Sutter Avenue, South Ozone Park, Queens. On Wednesday, a court committed him to Kings County Hospital for psychiatric observation. 22

When questioned by the police, Moseley also said that he had slain Mrs. Annie May Johnson, 24, of 146–12 133d Avenue, Jamaica, on Feb. 29 and Barbara Kralik, 15, of 174–17 140th Avenue, Springfield Gardens, last July. In the Kralik case, the police are holding Alvin L. Mitchell, who is said to have confessed that slaying. 23

The police stressed how simple it would have been to have gotten in touch with them. "A phone call," said one of the detectives, "would have done it." The police may be reached by dialing "O" for operator or SPring 7–3100. 24

Today witnesses from the neighborhood, which is made up of one-family homes in the $35,000 to $60,000 range with the exception of the two apartment houses near the railroad station, find it difficult to explain why they didn't call the police. 25

A housewife, knowingly if quite casually, said, "We thought it was a lovers' quarrel." A husband and wife both said, "Frankly, we were afraid." They seemed aware of the fact that events might have been different. A distraught woman, wiping her hands in her apron, said, "I didn't want my husband to get involved." 26

One couple, now willing to talk about that night, said they heard the first screams. The husband looked thoughtfully at the bookstore where the killer first grabbed Miss Genovese. 27

"We went to the window to see what was happening," he said, "but the light from our bedroom made it difficult to see the street." The wife, still apprehensive, added: "I put out the light and we were able to see better." 28

Asked why they hadn't called the police, she shrugged and replied: 29
"I don't know."

A man peeked out from a slight opening in the doorway to his 30
apartment and rattled off an account of the killer's second attack.
Why hadn't he called the police at the time? "I was tired," he said
without emotion. "I went back to bed."

It was 4:25 A.M. when the ambulance arrived to take the body of 31
Miss Genovese. It drove off. "Then," a solemn police detective said,
"the people came out."

COMPREHENSION

1. How much time elapsed between when Kitty Genovese was first
   stabbed and when the people finally came out?

2. What excuses did the neighbors make for not having come to Kitty
   Genovese's aid?

PURPOSE AND AUDIENCE

1. This article appeared in 1964. What effect was it intended to have on
   its audience? Do you think it has the same impact today, or has its
   impact diminished?

2. The author of this article tells his readers very little about Kitty Genovese. Why, for instance, doesn't he tell us what she looked like? How
   might additional details have changed the impact of the essay?

3. What is the article's main idea? Why does Gansberg imply his thesis
   rather than stating it explicitly?

4. What is Gansberg's purpose in describing the Austin Street area as
   "staid, middle-class, tree-lined"?

5. Why does Gansberg provide the police department phone number in
   his article?

STYLE AND STRUCTURE

1. The author is very precise in this article, especially in his references
   to time, addresses, and ages. Why?

2. The objective newspaper style is dominant in this article, and yet the
   author's anger shows through. Point to words and phrases that reveal his attitude toward his material.

3. Identify the transitions in the article. Characterize the kinds of expressions that are used.

4. Because this article was originally set in the narrow columns of a newspaper, there are many short paragraphs. Would it be more effective if some of these brief paragraphs were combined? If so, why? If not, why not? Give examples to support your answer.

5. Examine the dialogue. Does it strengthen the author's presentation? Would the article be more compelling without dialogue? Why, or why not?

6. This article does not have a formal conclusion; nevertheless, the last paragraph sums up the author's attitude. How?

VOCABULARY PROJECTS

1. Define each of the following words as it is used in this selection.

   stalk (1)   punctuated (11)
   baffles (4)   sheepishly (21)
   staid (6)   distraught (26)
   adjacent (7)   apprehensive (28)

2. Try substituting an equivalent word for each of the words above, being sure the context supports each word you have chosen. Discuss the differences your changes make.

3. The word "assailant" appears frequently in this article. Why is it used so often? What impact is this repetition likely to have on the reader?

WRITING WORKSHOP

1. In your own words, write a ten-sentence summary of the article. Try to reflect the author's order and emphasis as well as his ideas.

2. Rewrite the article as if it were a diary entry of one of the thirty-eight people who watched the murder. Outline what you saw, and explain why you decided not to call for help.

3. If you have ever been involved in or witnessed a situation where someone was in trouble, write a narrative essay about the incident. If people failed to help the person in trouble, note why you think no one acted. Or, if people did act, tell how.

4. Write an essay narrating an incident in which you should have acted differently but for some reason did not.

THEMATIC CONNECTIONS

- "Salvador" (p. 123)
- "Violence in the Morning" (p. 156)

OUTSIDER IN A SILENT WORLD

Lou Ann Walker

Born in 1952, Lou Ann Walker was educated at Ball State University and at Harvard, where she studied comparative literature. Walker has been a staff writer for New York, Esquire, Cosmopolitan, *and other magazines, and she has published articles in many national publications, including the* New York Times *and* People *(for which she wrote about a deaf street gang). In addition, Walker received a Rockefeller Foundation Humanities grant to do research about hearing children of deaf parents. In her 1986 book,* A Loss for Words: The Story of Deafness in a Family, *from which this selection was adapted, Walker describes her own experiences as a hearing child of a mother and father deaf from infancy. In particular, she recounts the difficulties she faced when, as a young child, she had to take on the responsibility of serving as her parents' interpreter. Throughout the book, and in this excerpt as well, Walker explains how she came to realize that her parents' world was one in which she would always be an outsider.*

When I was born, the obstetrician looked at my mother and traced the hour-glass figure of a woman. It was his way of telling her she had had a baby girl. The doctor then walked over and clapped his hands near my head to see if I would respond. He went back to my mother and, smiling, pointed to his ears and nodded. Everyone in the delivery room was relieved I was a "normal" baby.   1

Dad passed out cigars to the men at work and cradled his arms to let them know his wife had given birth. He pulled out the small white notepad he always carried and wrote "girl."   2

I was their first child. It was 1952, in Blackford County, Ind.   3

Before I was born, Mom and Dad paid $65—more than a week's salary—for a baby cry box, designed to alert deaf parents when their children cry. They placed the dark-brown plastic box, shaped like a radio, next to my crib and wired it to a lamp by their bed. As I cried, the box transmitted an impulse to the bulb, which flashed on until I paused for breath.

My parents worried about how I would learn spoken language. So when I was barely 2 years old, they bought a television set (one of   5 the first in Montpelier): a hulking affair with a tiny screen. Sitting in my small green rocking chair, I would watch that screen for hours on end, developing what was, for Indiana, a strange, accentless speech. Now and then, I would rush off to sign to Mom or Dad what I had heard about the outside world, about the outbreak of polio, or who had won the baseball game.

I acted as interpreter and guide for my patents the entire time I   6
was growing up. I was an adult before I was a child. I was painfully shy for myself, squirming away when the attention was focused on me, but when I was acting for my mother and father I was fine. I made their doctors' appointments. I interpreted when my mother went to the doctor and told him where it hurt and when he told her what medicine to take. I told the shoe repairman what was wrong with a shoe. When we received a call, I was usually the one to relay to Mom and Dad that a friend had died. This was my life. I didn't know any other.

It has taken me most of my adult life to figure out my own place   7
in the world. We were outsiders, my two younger sisters, my parents and I. It was as if we were clinging together for safety. But while there were unbreakable bonds between us, there was also an unbridgeable chasm. For despite my parents' spirit and their ability to get along, their world is the deaf—it is something separate, something I am intimate with yet can never really know.

In a family in which there is deafness, guilt is a constant undercur   8
rent. Thousands of times during my mother's life when she misinterpreted what someone said, she watched the other person, particularly my father, grow impatient or become angry because she seemed so slow. She had learned early on that it was easier, not only for herself but for everyone else as well, if she simply smiled and nodded. My own grandparents—none of whom had a hearing impairment—constantly exhorted me to "be good"; they themselves felt guilty for not doing more for their children and hoped somehow I would make up for things. But that phrase—I heard it a thousand times as I was growing up: Be good. Be good. Even now I hear it rasping through my head like a handsaw, pushing and pulling, through a plank. How could I ever be good enough?

*   *   *

Children of deaf parents rarely run away from home. Instead, they   9
hide. It's one of those odd phenomena. You don't have to go out the door, because your parents can't hear you rustling or giggling.

Besides, you feel too strong a sense of responsibility to leave. Something might happen. You might be needed. Still, for a few minutes you have to get away from that awesome adult role. My sister Jan found a nook under my parents' bed. I curled up in the spot behind the back seat of our red Volkswagen Beetle.

I'm not sure when I decided Mom and Dad were spies. At one point or another, most children think they are adopted. I never saw it that way. At about the age of 8 I was convinced Mom and Dad had been sent to check up on me. They were pretending not to hear so that they would know everything I was saying and denounce me for it.

The tests I devised were simple but fairly ingenious. One of my ploys was to go into another room and scream "Mom! Help!" Nothing. Then I would drop a book on the floor and hold my breath. Still nothing. I would throw myself with a thud on the carpet. Nobody came to check.

Other times I would sit on the floor in the living room and watch them while they read the paper. I wanted to see if they would make a mistake. I would sit for long periods watching the back of my mother's newspaper. When she brought the two sides together to turn the page, she would catch me staring at her.

"What's the matter?" she signed, her forehead wrinkled.

"Nothing."

"Why are you looking at me?"

(The one thing that completely unhinged her was someone staring at her—at home, in a restaurant, anywhere.)

"Oh, sorry, Mom. I was just thinking," I signed, index finger circling my brow.

She would go back to her newspaper and peer around the corner a couple of times, not able to figure out what I was up to.

One night before I went to bed, I fixed the phone cord just so. The next morning it was in exactly the place I had left it. And the next. And the next.

A few years later, while vacationing in New York, Mom and Dad and I were at the beach. The sun was setting and the sky was a fiery red purple. Mom and I stood, arms linked, watching the waves.

"What does it sound like?" Mom signed.

I wrinkled my forehead and held out my hand palm up, hand searching, to show I was thinking of an answer. Then I made a little gurgling sound with my lips. Mom looked at my lips thoughtfully, then turned back to watch the waves hitting the rocks and made her own lips gurgle.

A minute later, Dad came over. He had been watching some fish-   23
ermen.

"What does it sound like?" he signed, pointing to the ocean.   24

Mom grinned and signed that she had just asked me the same   25
question. Then she made the little lip movement for him. The three
of us stood and watched the waves and the sunset. I tried to imagine
the scene without the sound and, suddenly, everything before my
eyes turned black and white, like a silent movie.

A little while later we got on a ferryboat. As we leaned over the   26
rails watching the cars being loaded and the dock hands at work,
Mom grabbed my arm excitedly.

"Music!" she signed, and she moved to the beat.   27

"No, Mom! It's the engine." and I slapped a fist into my palm in   28
time with the pistons.

"I think music," and she did a little dance.   29

Mom and Dad drove me out to Harvard the fall I transferred   30
there. I had just spent two years at Ball State University, in Mun-
cie, Ind., with some vague idea that I wanted to be a teacher of the
deaf. When the program turned out to be less than I expected, and
when I didn't feel I was getting enough challenge in my other
classes, I applied to four Eastern colleges and was accepted.

As I looked up at the backs of my parents' heads, I sank down   31
low in the car's rear seat. Filling out the application, I had made
prominent mention of the fact that my parents were deaf. The entrance essay, which was supposed to be about me, was actually
about them. Many applicants use a father's or grandfather's degree
to get into the family alma mater, but neither of my parents had set
foot in a college. The irony that I was shamelessly using my deaf
parents to get into Harvard was not lost on me. I knew that though
I would willingly and openly tell people my parents were deaf and
would briefly answer questions, I would refuse to elaborate further.
It was all too complicated.

Through most of the 16-hour trip to Cambridge, I brooded over a   32
freshman reading list—the kind given to high-school seniors that
includes all the books they should have read by the time they ma-
triculate. I had read very little of what was on that list.

I sat in the back seat, worrying that I would have nothing to dis-   33
cuss in the dining hall. And every once in a while I would look up to
watch my parents' conversations.

When the highway was deserted, Dad could shift his eyes from   34
the road to Mom's hands. When traffic got heavy, he had to watch
the road, and then his glances were shorter. If he wanted to pass a

car he would hold up an index finger at Mom, signaling her to suspend the conversation for a moment. It was always easier for the driver to do the talking, although that meant his signs were shortened and somewhat less graceful. He would use the steering wheel as a base, the way he normally used his left hand; his right hand did all the moving.

Curled up in the seat, I noticed there was a lull in the conversation. 35
Dad was a confident driver, but Mom was smoking more than usual.

"Something happened? That gas station?" Mom signed to me. 36
"No, nothing," I lied. 37
"Are you sure?" 38
"Yes, everything is fine." 39

Dad and I had gone in to pay and get directions. The man behind 40
the counter had looked up, seen me signing and muttered, "Huh, I didn't think mutes were allowed to have driver's licenses." Long ago I had gotten used to hearing comments like this, but I never could get used to the way they made me churn inside.

Mom was studying me. Having relied on her visual powers all her 41
life, she knew when I was hiding something. "Are you afraid of going so far away from home? Why don't you stay in Indiana?"

"Mom, no! Cut it out." 42

She turned and faced front again. Dad hadn't seen what either of 43
us said, but he had caught the speed and force of my signs from the rear-view mirror, and he could feel the tension coming from behind him. Mom had struck several nerves in me. Not only was I stepping into foreign territory (I hadn't been able to afford to visit any of the schools to which I had applied), but, back home in Indiana, none of my relatives or friends had been enthusiastic about my going East. To Hoosiers, Harvard meant highbrow and snooty.

When she saw the first sign for Boston on the turnpike, Mom 44
tapped Dad's arm rapidly. Soon we were crossing a bridge over the Charles River. Another sign said "Cambridge."

Dad pointed to the sign and turned to look at me. In the corner of 45
his eye was the beginning of a tear.

"I never thought my daughter would go to Harvard," he signed. 46
"I'm so proud." To sign "proud," he started with his thumbs at waist level and drew them up his chest, sitting a little straighter as his chest welled up. Dad would have been content no matter what college or job I chose, but this was a dream he—a linotype operator at a newspaper—never had. Mom, who was then a film librarian, felt the same way; no one in her family had ever gone to college.

The strain of all those miles was suddenly washed away. I smiled 47
and leaned over to kiss his cheek. Mom patted my hand and then

my face. She was unaware of the long low hum of affection coming from her throat.

The dormitory to which I was assigned was pathetic—a cinder-block room with upended tables and chairs. There was litter in the hallway, the bathrooms were filthy and the kitchen had an unidentifiable smell. My dreams of wood-paneled, leather-armchair splendor were not coming true.   48

"Your room at Ball State was cleaner," Mom said, the sign for "clean" being one palm drawn neatly over the other. I glared at her.   49

It seemed that only the overstudious "nerds"—whom Harvard termed "wonks"—had also arrived this early. All the glamour that might still be attached to Harvard disappeared when a peculiar-looking character with mechanical pencils in his pocket, frizzy hair and enormous, twitchy eyes, came into my room. He jumped as I began translating what he was saying into sign for Mom. I felt several worlds collide.   50

As soon as the last box was moved into the room, I told Mom and Dad they could go to their hotel. I said I needed to plunge into Harvard life. But if I had been honest with myself, I would have known that I was as embarrassed at having them meet the wonk as I was at having the wonk and the rest of Harvard meet my deaf parents.   51

A couple of hours later, my parents and I had an early dinner together and then we said our goodbyes. They were leaving early the next morning for the drive back to Indianapolis. Standing on the sidewalk outside the restaurant, I was in a hurry to get on with things. We hugged and kissed. Mom reached over to smooth the hair from my face.   52

"Promise you'll write often," she signed.   53

"I always do, Mom."   54

Back in the dorm, I unpacked. My roommate had also arrived. Laura was the first person I had ever met from California. A junior with long, wavy dark hair, she was beautiful, long-legged and sinewy. She didn't look at all like my image of the studious 'Cliffie.   55

We talked for a couple of minutes and, except for throwing a sheet over the top of her bed, she didn't bother to arrange any of her things. Instead, she went off to talk to the guy with the pencils.   56

Laura came back. "Howard told me your parents are deaf and dumb. He said he saw you using sign language. That's pretty neat."   57

I cringed. I didn't want to sound priggish, correcting her for saying "dumb." "Um, well, I don't know if I would exactly call it that."   58

At 9:15, Laura announced she was going to bed and took off all her clothes. Throwing them across the room onto a dusty chair she   59 had carried up from the basement, she dived under the sheet to rest on top of the bare mattress.

I had never seen anyone sleep nude in my life. There was some- 60 thing in the nimbleness of her movement after she had taken her clothes off that told me there were a number of things I was going to learn at Harvard that I hadn't foreseen.

I put on my nightgown, dressing with my back to Laura, carefully 61 pulling the gown to my ankles before reaching under to remove my skirt. I crawled into my crisp bed—made by my mother—and we talked for a few minutes more. Suddenly, Laura directed a foot at the light switch.

In the dark, I felt more forlorn than ever. I waited until I thought 62 she was asleep, got up, put my clothes back on and walked outside. I didn't know where I was going. I headed toward what looked to be the busiest street and discovered Massachusetts Avenue. Mom and Dad had told me that was where the Holiday Inn was situated. I wandered up and down the sidewalk and found myself in front of their hotel.

I made my way to their room on the third floor and, as I raised 63 my knuckles, it dawned on me that knocking would do no good. I knew they were awake; I could hear the television. I took a notebook paper out of my purse and bent down to shove it underneath the door, working it in and out. There was no response. I tried crumpling up a small piece of paper to throw into the room, but I couldn't get it between the jamb and the door. I pounded on the gray metal, thinking they might feel the vibration. I must have stood there for 20 minutes, hoping Dad might come out to get ice from down the hall or perhaps go to the car to retrieve a bag. But he didn't.

COMPREHENSION

1. According to Walker, hearing children of deaf parents are forced to take on responsibilities which their counterparts with hearing parents do not face. List some of these responsibilities.

2. What are some of the mechanical aids that helped the Walker family compensate for the parents' deafness?

3. What does Walker mean in paragraph 6 when she says, "I was an adult before I was a child"?

4. Why did Walker feel a constant need to "be good"?

5. Why, according to Walker, do children of deaf parents rarely run away from home?

6. Why does Walker think that using her parents' deafness to gain acceptance to Harvard is ironic?

PURPOSE AND AUDIENCE

1. What is the essay's thesis? Where is it stated?

2. This essay addresses a general audience, one made up largely of hearing people. How might Walker have changed her essay's content and emphasis if she were addressing an audience of psychological counselors who work with deaf parents and their children? An audience of hearing children of deaf parents?

3. Is Walker's purpose in this essay to gain sympathy for her situation, to criticize her parents, or to win greater acceptance for or understanding of deaf people? Does she have a combination of these purposes, or a purpose or purposes not listed here? Explain.

4. How does the incident described in the essay's two final paragraphs support Walker's thesis?

STYLE AND STRUCTURE

1. The essay begins with a brief anecdote. How does this strategy add to the effectiveness of the narrative?

2. Why is the information in paragraph 3 isolated in a brief paragraph? What function does this paragraph serve in the essay?

3. In addition to reproducing conventional dialogue, Walker also occasionally describes the signs she or her parents make to indicate speech. Where does she do this? How does this technique enhance the essay?

4. In the early paragraphs of her essay, Walker moves in time from the day of her birth, to her parents' lives before she was born, to her childhood years. How does she signal these time shifts to her readers?

5. In general, Walker's tone in this essay is involved and subjective. Does she ever seem to abandon this tone in favor of a more impersonal tone and style? If so, where and why?

6. What does the incident recounted in paragraphs 20–29 add to the essay? Would the essay be stronger without it? Explain.

7. Beginning with paragraph 48, Walker describes the physical surroundings of Harvard and some of the people she encounters there. What function do these descriptions serve?

VOCABULARY PROJECTS

1. Define each of the following words as it is used in this selection.

   chasm (7)   sinewy (55)
   exhorted (8)   dumb (57)
   phenomena (9)   priggish (58)
   Hoosiers (43)

2. Walker calls her essay "Outsider in a Silent World." Review the selection and list all the words Walker uses to suggest her "outsider" status (for example, *"normal"* in paragraph 1 and *strange* in paragraph 5).

WRITING WORKSHOP

1. Consider how someone you know copes with a physical, emotional, or cultural handicap. Write a balanced, objective narrative essay in which you explain what this person has had to overcome to accomplish specific educational, social, or personal goals.

2. Using details from Walker's life, write a narrative essay in which you support the following thesis: "Lou Ann Walker's parents were in many important ways isolated from society, and yet they managed to function well in it." Make sure that your focus is on the parents, not on Walker herself.

3. During Walker's first day at Harvard, she feels the gap between her old life and her new life quite acutely. Write a narrative of your first day at college, exploring the distance between the world you were entering and the one you were leaving.

THEMATIC CONNECTIONS

- "Aria: A Memoir of a Bilingual Childhood " (p. 348)
- "Dyslexia" (p. 448)

SHOOTING AN ELEPHANT

George Orwell

Born Eric Blair in 1903 in Bengal, India, George Orwell was brought up in England and was only nineteen when he joined the British police force in Burma. Unhappy in his role as a defender of British colonialism, a system he despised, and wanting to be a writer, Orwell left Burma after five years to live and write in London and Paris; later he fought in the Spanish Civil War. As a reporter and a socialist, Orwell wrote about the living conditions of English miners and factory workers; he sought to expose the dangers of totalitarianism in his widely read novels Animal Farm *(1945) and* 1984 *(1949). He died in 1950. "Shooting an Elephant," set in Burma, relates an incident that clarified for Orwell the nature of British rule. Notice that Orwell uses an extended narrative to support his thesis and includes much specific detail to increase its impact.*

In Moulmein, in Lower Burma, I was hated by large numbers of people—the only time in my life that I have been important enough for this to happen to me. I was sub-divisional police officer of the town, and in an aimless, petty kind of way anti-European feeling was very bitter. No one had the guts to raise a riot, but if a European woman went through the bazaars alone somebody would probably spit betel juice over her dress. As a police officer I was an obvious target and was baited whenever it seemed safe to do so. When a nimble Burman tripped me up on the football field and the referee (another Burman) looked the other way, the crowd yelled with hideous laughter. This happened more than once. In the end the sneering yellow faces of young men that met me everywhere, the insults hooted after me when I was at a safe distance, got badly on my nerves. The young Buddhist priests were the worst of all. There were several thousands of them in the town and none of them seemed to have anything to do except stand on street corners and jeer at Europeans.

All this was perplexing and upsetting. For at that time I had already made up my mind that imperialism was an evil thing and the sooner I chucked up my job and got out of it the better. Theoretically—and secretly, of course—I was all for the Burmese and all against their oppressors, the British. As for the job I was doing, I hated it more bitterly than I can perhaps make clear. In a job like that you see the dirty work of Empire at close quarters. The wretched prisoners huddling in the stinking cages of the lockups, the grey, cowed faces of the long-term convicts, the scarred buttocks of the men who had been flogged with bamboos—all these oppressed me with an intolerable sense of guilt. But I could get nothing into perspective. I was young and ill-educated and I had had to think out my problems in the utter silence that is imposed on every English-man in the East. I did not even know that the British Empire is dying, still less did I know that it is a great deal better than the younger empires that are going to supplant it.* All I knew was that I was stuck between my hatred of the empire I served and my rage against the evil-spirited little beasts who tried to make my job im-possible. With one part of my mind I thought of the British Raj as an unbreakable tyranny, as something clamped down, in *saecula saeculorum*,** upon the will of prostrate peoples; with another part I thought that the greatest joy in the world would be to drive a bayonet into a Buddists priest's guts. Feelings like these are the normal byproducts of imperialism; ask any Anglo-Indian official, if you can catch him off duty.

One day something happened which in a roundabout way was en-lightening. It was a tiny incident in itself, but it gave me a better glimpse than I had had before of the real nature of imperialism—the real motives for which despotic governments act. Early one morning the sub-inspector at a police station the other end of the town rang me up on the phone and said that an elephant was ravaging the bazaar. Would I please come and do something about it? I did not know what I could do, but I wanted to see what was happening and I got on to a pony and started out. I took my rifle, an old .44 Win-chester and much too small to kill an elephant, but I thought the noise might be useful *in terrorem*. Various Burmans stopped me on the way and told me about the elephant's doings. It was not, of course, a wild elephant, but a tame one which had gone "must."*** It had been chained up, as tame elephants always are when their attack of "must" is due, but on the previous night it had broken its chain and escaped. Its mahout, the only person who could manage it when it was in that state, had set out in pursuit, but had taken the wrong direction and was now twelve hours' journey away, and

3

---

*EDS. NOTE—Orwell was writing in 1936, when Hitler and Stalin were in power and World War II was only three years away.

**EDS. NOTE—From time immemorial. *Raj*: sovereignty.

***EDS. NOTE—That is, gone into an uncontrollable frenzy.

in the morning the elephant had suddenly reappeared in the town. The Burmese population had no weapons and were quite helpless against it. It had already destroyed somebody's bamboo hut, killed a cow and raided some fruit-stalls and devoured the stock; also it had met the municipal rubbish van and, when the driver jumped out and took to his heels, had turned the van over and inflicted violences upon it.

The Burmese sub-inspector and some Indian constables were waiting for me in the quarter where the elephant had been seen. It was a very poor quarter, a labyrinth of squalid bamboo huts, thatched with palm-leaf, winding all over a steep hillside. I remember that it was a cloudy, stuffy morning at the beginning of the rains. We began questioning people as to where the elephant had gone, and, as usual, failed to get any definite information. That is invariably the case in the East; a story always sounds clear enough at a distance, but the nearer you get to the scene of events the vaguer it becomes. Some of the people said that the elephant had gone in one direction, some said that he had gone in another, some professed not even to have heard of an elephant. I had almost made up my mind that the whole story was a pack of lies, when we heard yells a little distance away. There was a loud, scandalized cry of "Go away, child! Go away this instant!" and an old woman with a switch in her hand came round the corner of a hut, violently shooing away a crowd of naked children. Some more women followed, clicking their tongues and exclaiming; evidently there was something that the children ought not to have seen. I rounded the hut and saw a man's dead body sprawling in the mud. He was an Indian, a black Dravidian coolie, almost naked, and he could not have been dead many minutes. The people said that the elephant had come suddenly upon him round the corner of the hut, caught him with its trunk, put its foot on his back and ground him into the earth. This was the rainy season and the ground was soft, and his face had scored a trench a foot deep and a couple of yards long. He was lying on his belly with arms crucified and head sharply twisted to one side. His face was coated with mud, the eyes wide open, the teeth bared and grinning with an expression of unendurable agony. (Never tell me, by the way, that the dead look peaceful. Most of the corpses I have seen looked devilish.) The friction of the great beast's foot had stripped the skin from his back as neatly as one skins a rabbit. As soon as I saw the dead man I sent an orderly to a friend's house nearby to borrow an elephant rifle. I had already sent back the pony, not wanting it to go mad with fright and throw me if it smelled the elephant.

The orderly came back in a few minutes with a rifle and five cartridges, and meanwhile some Burmans had arrived and told us that the elephant was in the paddy fields below, only a few hundred yards away. As I started forward practically the whole population of the quarter flocked out of the houses and followed me. They had seen the rifle and were all shouting excitedly that I was going to shoot the elephant. They had not shown much interest in the elephant when he was merely ravaging their homes, but it was different now that he was going to be shot. It was a bit of fun to them, as it would be to an English crowd; besides they wanted the meat. It made me vaguely uneasy. I had no intention of shooting the elephant—I had merely sent for the rifle to defend myself if necessary—and it is always unnerving to have a crowd following you. I marched down the hill, looking and feeling a fool, with the rifle over my shoulder and an ever-growing army of people jostling at my heels. At the bottom, when you got away from the huts, there was a metalled road and beyond that a miry waste of paddy fields a thousand yards across, not yet ploughed but soggy from the first rains and dotted with coarse grass. The elephant was standing eight yards from the road, his left side towards us. He took not the slightest notice of the crowd's approach. He was tearing up bunches of grass, beating them against his knees to clean them and stuffing them into his mouth.

I had halted on the road. As soon as I saw the elephant I knew   6
with perfect certainty that I ought not to shoot him. It is a serious matter to shoot a working elephant—it is comparable to destroying a huge and costly piece of machinery—and obviously one ought not to do it if it can possibly be avoided. And at that distance, peacefully eating, the elephant looked no more dangerous than a cow. I thought then and I think now that his attack of "must" was already passing off; in which case he would merely wander harmlessly about until the mahout came back and caught him. Moreover, I did not in the least want to shoot him. I decided that I would watch him for a little while to make sure that he did not turn savage again, and then go home.

But at that moment I glanced round at the crowd that had fol-   7
lowed me. It was an immense crowd, two thousand at the least and growing every minute. It blocked the road for a long distance on either side. I looked at the sea of yellow faces above the garish clothes—faces all happy and excited over this bit of fun, all certain that the elephant was going to be shot. They were watching me as they would watch a conjurer about to perform a trick. They did not like me, but with the magical rifle in my hands I was momentarily worth watching. And suddenly I realized that I should have to shoot

the elephant after all. The people expected it of me and I had got to do it; I could feel their two thousand wills pressing me forward, irresistibly. And it was at this moment, as I stood there with the rifle in my hands, that I first grasped the hollowness, the futility of the white man's dominion in the East. Here was I, the white man with his gun, standing in front of the unarmed native crowd—seemingly the leading actor of the piece; but in reality I was only an absurd puppet pushed to and fro by the will of those yellow faces behind. I perceived in this moment that when the white man turns tyrant it is his own freedom that he destroys. He becomes a sort of hollow, posing dummy, the conventionalized figure of a sahib. For it is the condition of his rule that he shall spend his life in trying to impress the "natives," and so in every crisis he has got to do what the "natives" expect of him. He wears a mask, and his face grows to fit it. I had got to shoot the elephant. I had committed myself to doing it when I sent for the rifle. A sahib has got to act like a sahib; he has got to appear resolute, to know his own mind and do definite things. To come all that way, rifle in hand, with two thousand people marching at my heels, and then to trail feebly away, having done nothing—no, that was impossible. The crowd would laugh at me. And my whole life, every white man's life in the East, was one long struggle not to be laughed at.

But I did not want to shoot the elephant. I watched him beating   8 his bunch of grass against his knees, with the preoccupied grandmotherly air that elephants have. It seemed to me that it would be murder to shoot him. At that age I was not squeamish about killing animals, but I had never shot an elephant and never wanted to. (Somehow it always seems worse to kill a *large* animal.) Besides, there was the beast's owner to be considered. Alive, the elephant was worth at least a hundred pounds; dead, he would only be worth the value of his tusks, five pounds, possibly. But I had got to act quickly. I turned to some experienced-looking Burmans who had been there when we arrived, and asked them how the elephant had been behaving. They all said the same thing: he took no notice of you if you left him alone, but he might charge if you went too close to him.

It was perfectly clear to me what I ought to do. I ought to walk   9 up to within, say, twenty-five yards of the elephant and test his behavior. If he charged I could shoot, if he took no notice of me it would be safe to leave him until the mahout came back. But also I knew that I was going to do no such thing. I was a poor shot with a rifle and the ground was soft mud into which one would sink at every step. If the elephant charged and I missed him, I should have about as much chance as a toad under a steam-roller. But even then I was not thinking particularly of my own skin, only of the watchful yellow faces behind. For at that moment, with the crowd watching me, I was not afraid in the ordinary sense, as I would have been if I had been alone. A white man mustn't be frightened in front of "natives"; and so, in general, he isn't frightened. The sole thought in my mind was that if anything went wrong those two thousand Burmans would see me pursued, caught, trampled on and reduced to a grinning corpse like that Indian up the hill. And if that happened it was quite probable that some of them would laugh. That would never do. There was only one alternative. I shoved the cartridges into the magazine and lay down on the road to get a better aim.

The crowd grew very still, and a deep, low, happy sigh, as of people   10
who see the theatre curtain go up at last, breathed from innumerable throats. They were going to have their bit of fun after all. The rifle was a beautiful German thing with cross-hair sights. I did not then know that in shooting an elephant one would shoot to cut an imaginary bar running from ear-hole to ear-hole. I ought, therefore, as the elephant was sideways on, to have aimed straight at his ear-hole; actually I aimed several inches in front of this, thinking the brain would be further forward.

When I pulled the trigger I did not hear the bang or feel the kick—   11
one never does when a shot goes home—but I heard the devilish roar of glee that went up from the crowd. In that instant, in too short a time, one would have thought, even for the bullet to get there, a mysterious, terrible change had come over the elephant. He neither stirred nor fell, but every line on his body had altered. He looked suddenly stricken, shrunken, immensely old, as though the frightful impact of the bullet had paralyzed him without knocking him down. At last, after what seemed a long time—it might have been five seconds, I dare say—he sagged flabbily to his knees. His mouth slobbered. An enormous senility seemed to have settled upon him. One could have imagined him thousands of years old. I fired again into the same spot. At the second shot he did not collapse but climbed with desperate slowness to his feet and stood weakly upright, with legs sagging and head drooping. I fired a third time. That was the shot that did for him. You could see the agony of it jolt his whole body and knock the last remnant of strength from his legs. But in falling he seemed for a moment to rise, for as his hind legs collapsed beneath him he seemed to tower upwards like a huge rock toppling, his trunk reaching skywards like a tree. He trumpeted, for the first and only time. And then down he came, his belly towards me, with a crash that seemed to shake the ground even where I lay.

I got up. The Burmans were already racing past me across the   12
mud. It was obvious that the elephant would never rise again, but
he was not dead. He was breathing very rhythmically with long rat-
tling gasps, his great mound of a side painfully rising and falling.
His mouth was wide open—I could see far down into the caverns of
pale pink throat. I waited a long time for him to die, but his breathing did not weaken. Finally I fired my two remaining shots into the
spot where I thought his heart must be. The thick blood welled out
of him like red velvet, but still he did not die. His body did not even
jerk when the shots hit him, the tortured breathing continued without a pause. He was dying, very slowly and in great agony, but in
some world remote from me where not even a bullet could damage
him further. I felt that I had got to put an end to that dreadful noise.
It seemed dreadful to see the great beast lying there, powerless to
move and yet powerless to die, and not even to be able to finish him.
I sent back for my small rifle and poured shot after shot into his
heart and down his throat. They seemed to make no impression. The
tortured gasps continued as steadily as the ticking of a clock.

In the end I could not stand it any longer and went away. I heard   13
later that it took him half an hour to die. Burmans were bringing
dahs* and baskets even before I left, and I was told they had
stripped his body almost to the bones by the afternoon.

Afterwards, of course, there were endless discussions about the   14
shooting of the elephant. The owner was furious, but he was only an
Indian and could do nothing. Besides, legally I had done the right
thing, for a mad elephant has to be killed, like a mad dog, if its owner
fails to control it. Among the Europeans opinion was divided. The
older men said I was right, the younger men said it was a damn
shame to shoot an elephant for killing a coolie, because an elephant
was worth more than any damn Coringhee coolie. And afterwards I
was very glad that the coolie had been killed; it put me legally in the
right and it gave me a sufficient pretext for shooting the elephant. I
often wondered whether any of the others grasped that I had done
it solely to avoid looking a fool.

COMPREHENSION

1. Why was Orwell "hated by large numbers of people" in Burma?

2. Orwell had mixed feelings toward the Burmese people. Explain why.

3. Why did the local officials want something done about the elephant?

*EDS. NOTE—Heavy knives.

4. Why did the crowd want Orwell to shoot the elephant?

5. Why did Orwell finally decide to kill the elephant? What made him hesitate at first?

6. Why does Orwell say at the end that he was glad the coolie had been killed?

PURPOSE AND AUDIENCE

1. One of Orwell's purposes in telling his story is to show how it gave him a glimpse of "the real nature of imperialism." How does the story illustrate this?

2. Do you think Orwell wrote this essay to inform or to persuade his audience? How did Orwell expect his audience to react to his ideas? How can you tell?

3. What is the essay's thesis?

STYLE AND STRUCTURE

1. What is the function of Orwell's first paragraph? Where does the introduction end and the narrative itself begin?

2. Orwell uses a good deal of descriptive detail in this essay. Locate some details that you think are particularly vivid or strong. Why is detail so important?

3. Point out some of the transitional words and phrases Orwell uses to indicate the passing of time. Why are they so important in this essay?

4. The essay includes almost no dialogue. Why do you think Orwell's voice as narrator is the only one the reader hears? Is this a strength or a weakness? Explain.

5. Why does Orwell devote so much attention to the elephant's misery (paragraphs 11 and 12)?

6. Orwell's essay includes a number of editorial comments inserted into his text between parentheses or pairs of dashes. What kind of comments are these? Why are they set off from the text?

7. Compare the following passages: "Some of the people said that the elephant had gone in one direction, some said that he had gone in another . . . " (paragraph 4); "Among the Europeans opinion was divided. The older men said I was right, the younger men said it was a damn shame to shoot an elephant . . . " (paragraph 14). How do these passages reinforce the theme expressed in paragraph 2 ("All I knew

was that I was stuck between my hatred of the empire I served and my rage against the evil-spirited little beasts . . . ")? Can you find other examples that reinforce this theme?

VOCABULARY PROJECTS

1. Define each of the following words as it is used in this selection.

   baited (1)   ravaging (5)
   perplexing (2)   miry (5)
   oppressors (2)   garish (7)
   lockups (2)   conjurer (7)
   flogged (2)   dominion (7)
   supplant (2)   magazine (9)
   prostrate (2)   cross-hair (10)
   despotic (3)   remnant (11)
   labyrinth (4)   trumpeted (11)
   squalid (4)   pretext (14)
   professed (4)

2. Use your dictionary to help you determine the origins as well as the definitions of these words:

   coolie (4)   mahout (6)
   paddy (5)   sahib (7)

3. Because Orwell is British, he frequently uses words or expressions that an American writer would not be likely to use. Substitute an idiomatic American word or phrase for each of the following, making sure it is appropriate in Orwell's context.

   raise a riot (1)   inflicted violences (3)
   rang me up (3)   a bit of fun (5)
   rubbish van (3)   I dare say (11)

WRITING WORKSHOP

1. Orwell says that even though he hated British imperialism and sympathized with the Burmese people, he found himself a puppet of the system. Write a narrative essay about a time when you had to do something that went against your beliefs or convictions.

2. Orwell's experience taught him something not only about himself but also about something beyond himself—the way imperialism worked. Write a narrative essay that reveals how an incident in your life taught you something about yourself and about some larger social or political force.

3. Write an objective, factual newspaper article recounting the events Orwell describes.

THEMATIC CONNECTIONS

WRITING ASSIGNMENTS FOR NARRATION

1. Trace the path you expect to follow to establish yourself in your chosen profession, considering possible obstacles you may face and how you expect to deal with them. Include a thesis that conveys the importance of your goals.

2. Write a personal narrative in which you look back from some point in the far future on your own life as you hope it will be seen by others. Use third person if you like, and write your own obituary; or, assess your life in the form of a letter to your great-grandchildren.

3. Write a travel narrative. In an essay about a trip you took, include a thesis to convince your audience to take a similar trip. Be sure to pay careful attention to detail in describing the physical setting, activities, and people central to your narrative.

4. Write a historical narrative tracing the roots of your family or your hometown or community.

5. Write an account of one of these "firsts": Your first date; your first serious argument with your parents; your first experience with physical violence or danger; your first extended stay away from home; your first encounter with someone whose culture was very different from your own. Make sure your essay includes a thesis that your narrative can support.

6. George Orwell and Martin Gansberg both deal with the consequences of failing to act. Write an essay, story, or news article in which you recount what would have happened if Orwell had *not* shot the elephant or if one of the eyewitnesses *had* called the police right away.

7. Maya Angelou's "finishing school" was Mrs Cullinan's kitchen. What would Lou Ann Walker have considered her finishing school? Write a narrative from her point of view, including a thesis statement that makes her reasons clear.

8. Write a short narrative summarizing a class, a short story, a television show, a conversation, a fable or fairy tale, or a narrative poem. Include as many details as you can.

9. Write a narrative about a time when you were an outsider, isolated because of social, intellectual, or ethnic differences between you and others. Did you resolve the problems your isolation created? Explain. (If you like, you may refer to the Angelou, Walker, or Orwell essays.)

10. Imagine a meeting between any two characters in this chapter's essays. Using dialogue as well as narrative, write an account of this meeting.

3

Description

WHAT IS DESCRIPTION?

Description tells what something or someone looks like. In the following paragraph from *Teaching a Stone to Talk*, Annie Dillard relies on sense impressions and figurative language to paint a word picture of the jungle in Ecuador.

> When you are inside the jungle, away from the river, the trees vault out of sight. It is hard to remember to look up the long trunks and see the fans, strips, fronds, and sprays of glossy leaves. Inside the jungle you are more likely to notice the snarl of climbers and creepers round the trees' boles, the flowering bromeliads and epiphytes in every bough's crook, and the fantastic silk-cotton tree trunks thirty or forty feet across, trunks buttressed in flanges of wood whose curves can make three high walls of a room—a shady loamy-aired room where you would gladly live, or die. Butterflies, iridescent blue, striped, or clear-winged, thread the jungle paths at eye level. And at your feet is a swath of ants bearing triangular bits of green leaf. The ants with their leaves look like a wide fleet of sailing dinghies—but they don't quit. In either direction they wobble over the jungle floor as far as the eye can see. I followed them off the path as far as I dared, and never now an end to ants or to those luffing chips of green they bore

Before we make judgments about the world, before we compare or contrast or classify our experiences, we describe what we observe. Scientists observe and describe whenever they conduct experiments, and you do the same thing whenever you write a paper. In a comparison-and-contrast essay, for example, you may describe the performance of two cars to show that one is superior to the other. In an argumentative essay, you may describe a fish kill in a local river to show that factory pollution is a problem. Through description, you introduce your view of the world to your readers. If your readers come to understand or share your view, they are more likely to accept your conclusions and judgments as well. Therefore, in almost every essay you write, knowing how to write effective description is important. In this chapter, we focus on descriptive writing as a strategy for a whole essay.

A narrative essay presents a series of events; it tells a story. A descriptive essay, on the other hand, tells what something looks like or what it feels like, sounds like, smells like, or tastes like. Description can also go beyond personal sense impressions. Novelists can create imaginary landscapes, historians can paint word pictures of historical figures, and scientists can describe physical phenomena that they have never seen. When you write description, you use language to create a vivid impression for your reader. As we mentioned in Chapter 2, a good narrative may depend heavily on descriptive details. It is important, however, not to confuse these two types of writing. A narrative always presents events in time, in some sort of chronological order, whereas a description presents things in spatial rather than temporal order.

You can use description to support an implied or explicit thesis. Writers often use an implied thesis when they describe a person, place, or thing. This technique allows them to convey the narrative's *dominant impression*—the mood or quality that is emphasized in the piece of writing—subtly through the selection and arrangement of details. When they use description to support an idea or assertion, however, many writers prefer to use an explicitly stated thesis. This strategy eliminates ambiguity by letting readers see immediately what point the writer is making—for example, "The sculptures that adorn Philadelphia's City Hall form a catalog of nineteenth-century artistic styles." Whether you state or imply your thesis, the details of your narrative essay must work together to create a single dominant impression. In many cases your thesis may simply be the statement of the dominant impression; sometimes, however, your thesis may go further and make a point about the dominant impression.

Objective and Subjective Descriptions

There are two basic approaches to description: objective and subjective. In an *objective* description, you focus on the object rather than on your personal reactions to it. Your purpose is to convey a literal picture of your subject. Many writing situations require precise descriptions of apparatus or conditions, and in these cases your goal is to construct as accurate a picture as possible for your audience. A biologist describing what he sees through a microscope and a historian describing a Civil War battlefield would both write objectively. The biologist would not, for instance, say how exciting his observations were, nor would the historian say how surprising she thought the outcome of the battle was. Newspaper reporters also try to achieve this cameralike objectivity, and so do writers of technical reports, scientific papers, and certain types of business correspondence. Of course, objectivity is an ideal for which writers strive but never achieve. Any time writers select some details and eliminate others, they are not being completely objective.

In the following descriptive passage, Thomas Marc Parrott aims for objectivity by giving his readers all the factual information they need to visualize Shakespeare's theater.

> When James Burbage built the Theatre in 1576 he naturally designed it along the lines of inn-yards in which he had been accustomed to play. The building had two entrances—one in front for the audience; one in the rear for actors, musicians, and the personnel of the theatre. Inside the building a rectangular platform projected far out into what was called "the yard"—we know the stage of the Fortune ran halfway across the "yard," some twenty-seven and a half feet.

Note that Parrott is not interested in responding to or evaluating the environment he describes. Instead, he chooses impersonal words that are calculated to convey sizes, shapes, and distances. His use of adjectives such as *two* and *rectangular* reflects this intent. Only one word in the paragraph—*naturally*—suggests that the author is expressing an opinion.

In contrast to objective description is *subjective* or *impressionistic* description, which discloses your personal vision or your emotional responses to what you see and tries to get your readers to share them. These responses are not necessarily expressed directly, through a straightforward statement of your opinion or perspective. Often they are revealed indirectly, through your choice of words and phrasing. If an assignment in freshman English required that you describe a place of special meaning to you, you could convey your subjective reaction to your topic by selecting and emphasizing details that showed your feelings about the place. For example, you could write a subjective description of your room by focusing on several objects—your desk, your window, and your bookshelves—and conveying all the impressions these things bring back to you.

Your desk could be a "warm brown rectangle of wood whose top contains the scratches of a thousand school assignments."

A subjective or impressionistic description should convey not just a factual record of sights and sounds but also their meaning or significance. For example, if you objectively described a fire, you might include its temperature, its duration, and its dimensions. In addition to these quantifiable details you might describe, as accurately as possible, the fire's color, its movement, and its intensity. If you subjectively described the fire, however, you would include more than these unbiased observations about it. Through your choice of language and your phrasing, you would try to re-create for your audience a sense of how the fire made you feel: your reactions to the crackling noise, to the dense smoke, to the sudden destruction.

In the following passage, Mark Twain subjectively describes the Mississippi River.

> I still kept in mind a certain wonderful sunset which I witnessed when steamboating was new to me. A broad expanse of the river was turned to blood; in the middle distance the red hue brightened into gold, through which a solitary log came floating, black and conspicuous; in one place a long, slanting mark lay sparkling upon the water; in another the surface was broken by boiling, tumbling rings, that were as many-tinted as an opal.

In this passage, Twain uses language that has emotional connotations—*wonderful*—and comparisons that suggest great value—*gold, opal*—to convey his feelings to the reader. By noting the red color, the solitary log "black and conspicuous," and the "boiling, tumbling rings," he shares with his readers his vivid perception of sunset on the river.

Neither of the two approaches to description exists independently. Objective description almost always contains some subjective elements, and subjective description needs some objective elements to convey a sense of reality. The skillful writer adjusts the balance between objectivity and subjectivity to suit the topic, thesis, audience, purpose, and occasion of an essay.

Objective and Subjective Language

As the passages by Parrott and Twain illustrate, both objective and subjective descriptions depend on specific and concrete words to convey, as precisely as possible, a picture of the person, place, or thing that the observer is describing. But objective and subjective descriptions use different kinds of language. Objective descriptions rely on precise, factual language that details your observations without including your attitude toward the subject. They describe things with words and phrases so unambiguous that many observers could agree that the descriptions were appropriate and exact. Subjective descriptions, however, generally rely on richer and more suggestive language than objective descriptions. Subjective descriptions are more likely to rely on the *connotations* of words, their emotional associations, than on their *denotations,* or dictionary definitions. They may deliberately provoke the individual reader's imagination with striking phrases or vivid comparisons. For example, a subjective description might compare the behavior of an exotic peacock spreading its feathers to that of a pet Siamese cat posturing and posing, thus evoking a lively image in the reader's mind.

Although both kinds of description may use comparisons to evoke a subject, subjective descriptions rely more on elaborate or imaginative comparisons. When you write subjective descriptions, you can compare two similar things, using the familiar parakeet to describe the unfamiliar peacock. Or, instead of comparing two things that are alike, you can find similarities between things that are unlike, such as the peacock and the cat, and provide a fresh view of both. Such special comparisons are known as *figures of speech.* Three of the most common are simile, metaphor, and personification.

A *simile* compares two things that are unlike, using *like* or *as.* These comparisons occur frequently in everyday speech, for example, when someone claims to be "happy as a clam," "free as a bird," or "hungry as a bear." As a rule, however, you should avoid these clichés in your writing. Effective writers constantly strive to use original similes. In his short story "A & P," John Updike uses a striking simile when he likens people going through the checkout aisle of a supermarket to balls dropping down a slot in a pinball machine.

A *metaphor* identifies two unlike things without using *like* or *as.* Instead of saying that something is like something else, a metaphor says that it *is* something else. Twain uses a metaphor when he says that "a broad expanse of the river was turned to blood."

Personification endows animals or objects with the qualities of human beings. If you say that the wind whispered or that the engine died, you are using personification.

Your purpose and audience determine whether you should use predominantly objective or subjective description. Legal, medical, technical, business, and scientific writing assignments frequently require objective descriptions, but even in these areas you may be encouraged to tailor your descriptions so that they develop your own interpretations and arguments. Still, in all these instances, your purpose is primarily to give your audience factual information about your subject. In contrast, an assignment that specifically asks for your reactions demands a subjective or impressionistic description.

Sometimes inexperienced writers load their subjective descriptions with empty words like *beautiful, tasty, disgusting*, or *scary*. They may confuse their own reactions to an object with the qualities of the object itself. To produce an effective description, however, you must do more than just *say* something is wonderful—you must *picture* it as wonderful to the reader, as Twain does with the sunset. Twain does in fact use the word *wonderful* at the beginning of his description, but he then goes on to give many concrete details that make the experience vivid and specific for his readers.

Selection of Detail

All good descriptive writing, whether objective or subjective, relies heavily on specific details that enable readers to visualize what you are describing. Your aim is not simply to *tell* your readers what something looks like but to *show* them. Every person, place, or thing has its special characteristics, and you must use your powers of observation to detect them. You then must select the concrete words that will convey your dominant impression, that will enable your readers to see, hear, taste, touch, or smell what you describe. Do not be satisfied with "he looked angry" when you can say, "His face flushed, and one corner of his mouth twitched as he tried to control his anger." What is the difference? In the first case, you simply identify the man's emotional state. In the second, you describe his appearance by providing enough detail so that readers can tell not only that he was angry but also how he revealed the intensity of his anger. Of course, you could have provided even more detail by noting the man's beard or his wrinkles or any number of other features. In a given description, however, not all details are equally useful or desirable. Only those that contribute to the dominant impression you wish to create should be included. In describing a man's face to show how angry he was, you would probably not describe the shape of his nose or the color of his hair. (After all, the color of somebody's hair does not change when he or she gets angry.) The number of details you use is less important than their quality and appropriateness. To avoid a seemingly endless list of details that blur the focus of your essay, you must select and use only those details relevant to your purpose.

The level and knowledge of your audience also influence the kind of detail that you include. For example, a description of a DNA molecule written for first-year college students would contain more basic details than a description written for junior biology majors. In addition, the more advanced description would contain details—a series of amino acid groups, for instance—that would be inappropriate for freshmen.

STRUCTURING A DESCRIPTIVE ESSAY

When you write a descriptive essay, you begin with a brainstorming list of unorganized details, which you proceed to arrange in a way that supports your thesis and communicates your dominant impression. For example, you can move from a specific description of an object to a general description of other things around it. Or you can reverse this order, beginning with the general and proceeding to the specific. You can progress from the least important feature to a more important feature until you finally focus on the most important one. You can also move from the smallest to the largest item or from the least unusual to the most unusual detail. You can present the details of your description in a straightforward spatial order, moving from left to right or right to left, from top to bottom or bottom to top. Finally, you can also combine organizing schemes, using different schemes in different parts of the essay. The particular strategy you choose depends on the dominant impression you want to convey, your thesis, and your purpose and audience.

Suppose your English composition instructor has assigned a short essay describing a person, place, or thing. After thinking about the subject for a day or two, you decide to write an objective description of the Air and Space Museum in Washington, D.C. because you have visited it and many details are fresh in your mind. The museum is large and has many different exhibits, so you realize at once that you will not be able to describe them all. Therefore, you decide to concentrate on one, the heavier-than-air flight exhibit, and you choose as the topic for your essay the particular display that you remember most vividly: Charles Lindbergh's airplane, *The Spirit of St. Louis*. You brainstorm to recollect all the details you can, and when you read over your list, you immediately see that the organizing scheme of your essay could be based on your actual experience in the museum. You decide to present the details of the airplane in the order in which the eye takes them in, from front to rear. The dominant impression you wish to create is how small and fragile *The*

Spirit of St. Louis appears. Your thesis is your statement presenting this impression. An informal outline for your essay might look like this:

Introduction: Thesis—It is startling that a plane as small as *The Spirit of St. Louis* was able to fly across the Atlantic.
Front of plane: Single engine, tiny cockpit
Middle of plane: Wing span, extra gas tanks
Rear of plane: Limited cargo space filled with more gas tanks
Conclusion: Restatement of thesis

The following student essays both illustrate the principles of effective description. The first one, by Joseph Tessari, is an objective description of the light microscope. The second, by Mary Lim, is a subjective description of an area in Burma.

THE LIGHT MICROSCOPE

Introduction   The simple light microscope is widely used in   1
the scientific community. The basic function of the
microscope is to view in great detail objects or
biological specimens that would otherwise be
invisible to the naked eye. Light microscopes come in
a variety of shapes and sizes, all having different
degrees of magnification and complexity. Most
microscopes, however, are made of metal or plastic
(primarily metal) and stand approximately ten to
Thesis   thirteen inches tall. A description of the
microscope's design illustrates its function.

Description of   A simple light microscope consists of several   2
stand   integrated parts. The largest piece is the stand. The
stand (black in this example) is a single metal
structure that has vertical and horizontal sections.
The horizontal piece rests on the tabletop and is
wishbone-shaped. The vertical section stands
approximately nine inches tall and is shaped like a

question mark. These two sections join at the base of the wishbone.

Description of optic tube

Attached at the top of the vertical piece of the stand is a black metal tube approximately three to four inches long. One entire side of this optic tube is attached to the end of the vertical stand and, therefore, sits in front of the stand when viewed from the side. 3

Description of eyepiece

Sitting directly on top of this tube is a silver cylinder called the eyepiece. The eyepiece, slightly smaller in diameter than the optic tube, is approximately two inches long. The top of the eyepiece is covered with a clear glass lens called the fixed lens. The lens and the cylinder together make up the entire eyepiece. 4

Description of coarse adjustment knobs

On the stand, adjacent to the point where it meets the optic tube, are two silver knobs--one on each side of the microscope. When rotated, these coarse adjustment knobs raise and lower the optic tube. This raising and lowering of the tube focuses the object being viewed. 5

Description of objective lens

Attached to the bottom of the optic tube is a movable disk which, when viewed from the side, makes a forty-five degree angle with the front of the optic tube. The side of the disk in the front of the microscope is higher than the back of the disk. Two small silver cylinders are attached, one hundred eighty degrees apart, to the bottom of this movable disk. These cylinders have small glass lenses covering the unattached ends. Each cylinder lens has a different magnification power. This entire piece (disk and lenses) is called the objective lens. When the objective lens is in place, the eyepiece, optic tube, and objective lens fall in a vertical line. 6

Description of viewing stage
Directly below the objective lens, attached to the bend in the question mark of the vertical stand, is a horizontal metal plate called the viewing stage. It is square with a small hole cut out in the center. This circular hole is approximately the same diameter as the objective lens and is also along the same vertical line. On either side of the hole, attached to the back of the stage, are metal clips that hold the specimen in place.

7

Description of diaphragm
Connected to the underside of the stage is a flat circular diaphragm that can be rotated to vary the amount of light passing through the hole in the stage.

8

Description of mirror
A few inches below the stage, sitting in the opening of the wishbone base, is a small circular mirror. It is centered along the vertical line of the eyepiece, optic tube, objective lens, and stage opening. The mirror can pivot around a horizontal axis and is attached to the stand by a Y-shaped structure. (The mirror sits in the opening of the Y.) When the mirror is moved, light from some source is reflected up into the viewing apparatus (objective lens, optic tube, and eyepiece).

9

Conclusion
The simple light microscope has been an extremely useful biological tool for many years. It has been responsible for a significant number of important scientific advancements, such as pasteurization, immunization, sterilization, cures for diseases, and better understanding of human anatomy and physiology. With modern technology newer and more complex instruments, such as the electron microscope, are being developed. Still, the light microscope remains an important tool that aids members of the scientific community in their research.

10

Points for Special Attention

Objective Description. Joseph Tessari, a toxicology major, wrote this paper as an exercise for a class in scientific writing. Ilis assignment was to write a detailed, factual description of an instrument, mechanism, or piece of apparatus or equipment used in his study of his major field. Because he was to write an objective description, he does not react subjectively to the microscope, tell how it works, or stress its advantages and disadvantages. Instead, he simply details the microscope's physical features. Joseph's thesis emphasizes his purpose and conveys his straightforward intention to his readers.

Objective Language. Because his essay is written for a class in scientific writing, Joseph keeps his objective description technical. His factual, concrete language concentrates on the size, shape, and composition of each part and on each part's physical relationship to the other parts and to the whole. He does not use subjective language or elaborate figures of speech.

Structure. Joseph chose to describe the microscope piece by piece. He starts at the bottom of the microscope with its largest part—the stand. He next directs the reader's attention upward from the optic tube to the eyepiece and then downward past the coarse adjustment knobs to the bottom of the optic tube (where the objective lens is located), down to the viewing stage, the diaphragm, the mirror, and the light source. In his introduction, Joseph comments on the microscope's purpose and general appearance; in his conclusion, he summarizes the microscope's historical significance and briefly considers its future.

Selection of Detail. Joseph Tessari's assignment identified his audience as a group of well-educated nonscientists. He was told he could assume that his readers would generally know what a microscope looked like but that he would have to describe the individual components in detail.

Unlike "The Light Microscope," Mary Lim's essay uses subjective description so that readers can share, as well as understand, her experience.

THE VALLEY OF WINDMILLS

Introduction   In my native country of Burma, strange   1
happenings and strange scenery are not unusual. For
it is a strange land that in some areas seems to have
been ignored by time. Mountains stand jutting their
rocky peaks into the clouds as they have for
thousands of years. Jungles are so dense with exotic
vegetation that human beings or large animals cannot
even enter. But one of the strangest areas in Burma

Description   is the Valley of Windmills, nesting between the tall
(identifying
the scene)   mountains near the fertile and beautiful city of
Taungaleik. In this valley there is beautiful and
breathtaking scenery, but there are also old,
massive, and gloomy structures that can disturb a
person deeply.

Description   The road to Taungaleik twists out of the coastal   2
(moving toward
the valley)   flatlands into those heaps of slag, shale, and
limestone that are the Tennesserim Mountains in the
southern part of Burma. The air grows rarer and
cooler, the stones become grayer, the highway a
little more precarious at its edges until ahead,

Description   standing in ghostly sentinel across the lip of a
(immediate
view)   pass, is a line of squat forms. They straddle the
road and stand at intervals up hillsides on either
side. Are they boulders? Are they fortifications? Are
they broken wooden crosses on graves in an abandoned
cemetery?

These dark figures are windmills standing in the   3
misty atmosphere. They are immensely old and
distinctly evil, some merely turrets, some with
remnants of arms hanging derelict from their snouts,
and most of them covered with dark green moss. Their
decayed but still massive forms seem to turn and

Description   sneer at visitors. Down the pass on the other side is
(more distant
view)   a circular green plateau that lies like an arena

below, where there are still more windmills. Massed
in the plain behind them, as far as the eye can see,
in every field, above every hut, stand ten thousand
iron windmills, silent and sailless. They seem to
await only a call from a watchman to clank, whirr,
flap, and groan into action. Visitors suddenly feel
cold. Perhaps it is a sense of loneliness, the cool
air, the desolation, or the weirdness of the arcane
windmills--but something chills them.

**Description
(immediate
view contrasted
with city)**

As you stand at the lip of the valley, contrasts   4
rush as if to overwhelm you. Beyond, glittering on
the mountainside like a solitary jewel, is Taungaleik
in the territory once occupied by the Portuguese.
Below, on rolling hillsides, are the dark windmills,

**Conclusion
(thesis)**

still enveloped in morning mist. These ancient
windmills can remind you of the impermanence of life
and the mystery that still surrounds these hills. In
an odd way, the scene in the valley can disturb you,
but it also can give you an insight into the contrasts
that seem to define our lives here in Burma.

Points for Special Attention

Subjective Description. One of the first things you notice when
you read Mary's essay is her use of vivid details. The road to Taungaleik is described in specific terms: it twists "out of the coastal
flatlands" into the mountains which are "heaps of slag, shale, and
limestone." The iron windmills are decayed and stand "silent and
sailless" on a green plateau that "lies like an arena." Using language
in this way, Mary creates her dominant impression of the Valley of
Windmills as dark, mysterious, and disquieting. Her language
is no less specific than Joseph Tessari's, but she uses it to create a
different kind of dominant impression. The point of her essay—the
thesis—stated in the last paragraph, is that the Valley of Windmills
embodies the contrasts that characterize life in Burma.

Subjective Language and Figures of Speech. Mary conveys the
sense of foreboding she felt by describing the windmills in several

different ways. Upon first introducing them, she questions whether these "squat forms" are "boulders," "fortifications," or "broken wooden crosses," each of which has a menacing connotation. After telling the reader what they are, she personifies the windmills by describing them as dark, evil, sneering figures with "arms hanging derelict." She sees them as ghostly sentinels awaiting a call from a watchman to spring into action. Through this figure of speech, Mary masterfully re-creates the unearthly quality of the scene she witnessed in Burma.

Structure.   Mary's purpose in writing this paper was to give her readers the sensation of actually being in the Valley of Windmills in Burma. She uses an organizing scheme that takes readers along the road to Taungaleik, up into the Tennesserim Mountains, and finally to the pass where the windmills wait. From the perspective of the lip of the valley, she describes the details closest to her and then those farther away, as if following the movement of her eyes. She ends by bringing her readers back to the lip of the valley and contrasts Taungaleik "glittering on the mountainside" with the windmills "enveloped in morning mist." Through her description, she builds up to her thesis, about the nature of life in Burma. She withholds the explicit statement of her main point until her last paragraph, when readers have been fully prepared for it.

The following essays illustrate different types and uses of description, sometimes more than one in the same essay. Pay particular attention to the difference between objective and subjective description.

THE BERIOZKA

Andrea Lee

Andrea Lee was born in Philadelphia and received a Bachelor and a Master of Arts degree in English from Harvard University. Her most recent work is Sarah Phillips, *a semiautobiographical novel about the coming of age of a young black woman. In 1978, she and her husband, a doctoral candidate in Russian history, went to live for one year in Moscow and Leningrad. Because they were young, spoke Russian, and lived in a dormitory at Moscow State University, they saw more of the real Russian life than many American diplomats or journalists who tend to live among foreigners. They also became friendly with their fellow students who were curious about American life. The following selection is from Lee's book* Russian Journal *(1981), which is based on the journal entries she kept during her year in the Soviet Union.*

The diplomatic food store on Vasilevsky Island is located on an exceedingly drab industrial street where there are several factories, and a steady stream of poorly dressed men and women going by with hugh bundles of food and necessities in bulging plastic suitcases or net bags. Many of these people slow down to stare as they pass the diplomatic store, which has the veiled, suggestive appearance of all Soviet *beriozki.* On this muddy street, filled with pits and rubble and lined with shabby buildings, the unmarked store window, with its snowy pleated draperies over a tasteful arrangement of pebbles that look almost Japanese, is a mysterious and angelic presence, a visitation of luxury to a world that lives without it. Outside the store are often parked a few shiny foreign automobiles with diplomatic or business-community license plates—or equally shiny Soviet cars, usually the discreet black Volga. These are minutely examined by the heavily laden passers-by. Occasionally a workman with a gnarled frostbitten face will eye the cars and spit scornfully, muttering, "Foreigners!"

Inside, the shop consists of two rooms, and to enter them from the street is like passing into another dimension; the carefully decorated interior, in fact, has a suggestion of the feeling of intimacy and luxury found in an expensive Western boutique. The larger room holds every expensive brand of European and American beer, wine, liquor, cigarette, and candy, all artistically set out on mirrored shelves that reflect the soft lighting and the red carpet on the floor. There is a section devoted to Soviet beverages—Armenian and Georgian wines and brandies, flavored vodkas, the rare "balsam" liqueur from the Baltic region—many of which are unobtainable on the open market. In front of the shelves are a couple of comfortable armchairs, and near these is an attractive laminated wooden desk where normally sit two pretty English-speaking Soviet girls in stylish Western outfits. These girls greet customers, sizing them up with the expertise of snobbish salespeople around the world; sometimes, depending on the apparant rank of the customer, they actually fill and push the little shopping carts. (We students are definitely not important enough to have our carts pushed. Living among Russians and arriving on foot as we do, we form the lowest of the castes allowed in the store, slightly below, say, the African diplomats, who receive only the most perfunctory smiles from the young women.)

The second, smaller room is filled with canned goods—usually   3 German, Russian, or Bulgarian—and an array of marvelous fresh meats, dairy products, and produce, all of which are Russian, and most of which are superior to anything one can buy on the open market or at the *rynok*. The beef is all prime, the hamburger particularly, so lean that fat must be added to it. There is liver, which Russians love, and which is almost impossible to buy for rubles, since it is reserved for restaurants serving foreigners and stores like this one. In the produce section are big bags of hothouse cucumbers and tomatoes, the same vegetables that have been selling for ten to fifteen rubles a kilo in the peasant markets this winter. In general, the prices at the diplomatic stores are very low. The payment procedure is this: the foreigner pays his own currency for a booklet of ruble coupons redeemable for goods only in these special stores. Right now, a diplomatic ruble costs about a dollar forty. Even with the disadvantageous exchange rate, the store is full of bargains: a bottle of Cointreau costs about three rubles; a sack of precious tomatoes, about two rubles; a bottle of Starorusskaya (considered one of the best Russian vodkas), a ruble fifty.

Last week when I was at the store, a middle-aged foreign woman   4 from the Brahmin caste that receives obsequious service from the salesgirls was doing some shopping. She had a finely made-up, rather imperious face, and was swathed in handsome sheared beaver, the kind of coat Russians rarely see, because the best Russian furs are exported. One of the salesgirls, a curly-headed blonde in a denim jumper, was pushing her cart and urging her to buy some lettuce. "It's just in today, madame," she said in her birdlike English. "Greenhouse lettuce! Our first this winter!"

"I don't know," said the woman, also in English but with an ambiguous European accent. "So far I've not been very impressed with your Soviet vegetables. But send some to me tomorrow." She raised a thin hand to her lips, and I saw her fingers glittering with diamonds. At the desk, the other salesgirl, a redhead, gently packed the woman's few purchases into a plastic bag, totted up the bill in graceful flourishes on a piece of paper, and reverently received the coupons. As the woman went out, the blond salesgirl sighed, and then said to her companion in rapid Russian, "That coat—oh, my goodness! And the boots, did you see the boots? All the women are wearing that style now. What a life!"

I had been pushing my own cart around. When I came up to the desk, they treated me with absent-minded civility, and I felt very annoyed. I was annoyed partly because I, too, longed for a fur coat and diamonds, but mostly because I knew that these young women shared with me a knowledge of the contrast between the two worlds of the Soviet Union: the hidden world where luxury and snobbery reign for privileged Russians—and especially for foreigners—and the harsh life of the working class on the outside, where even the plastic shopping bags from the *beriozki* are coveted luxuries. The workers on the street can't see inside the diplomatic store, and the foreigners, climbing into their cars and driving back to their segregated luxury apartments, can't possibly know what life is like for the average Russian. But I, trudging through the streets, speaking Russian and visiting Russian friends, know what both sides are like, and so do these young women, far better that I. So how, I wondered, could they sit there, so prettily painted and manicured, ready to shepherd rich women around this mirrored, carpeted room, without any trace of ugly cynicism crossing their faces? I told myself it was the universal Soviet pragmatism I've seen so clearly in Valerii and my other friends: the philosophy is to find your niche, make your adjustments, and then live without considering it. Like Intourist guides, and other Russians whose jobs involve close contact with foreigners, the salesgirls probably have KGB affiliations and probably, also, the privilege of shopping in the special "closed" stores for upper-level Russians. They are young, pretty girls, and the diplomatic-store job is clearly quite a pleasant one.

Just as I was leaving the store last week, something happened 7
that occasionally occurs in these special stores. Normally, the door-
man, a short, fat man with bulging eyes and a grotesquely upturned
nose, is on guard to keep ordinary Russians from entering, but at
that moment he was pausing to smoke a foreign cigarette and to
lean over the desk to say something confidential to the two girls;
the door, moreover, was open to allow some of the fresh balmy afternoon into the store. An old woman dressed in a worn black wool
coat, a gray wool scarf, and a pair of rubbershod *valenki*—unmistakably a woman from that stream of populace passing in the grimy
street outside—appeared suddenly in the doorway. *"Ostorozhno!*
[Watch out!]" hissed one of the salesgirls, and the guard leaped over
to the door and began to back the old woman out, speaking in a firm,
officious voice as if to a child. "Now, grandmother, this isn't for you.
This is a special store, for foreigners . . . " The *babushka* pretended
to be deaf and slow-witted, but it was clear that she knew what she
was doing, and had been drawn there out of curiosity. As the guard
backed her out, her head swiveled around and she took in the whole
glittering two rooms. It was amazing to watch her wrinkled red face,
on which there struggled a remarkable mixture of astonishment and
avidity, as if she'd just discovered, and longed to plunder, an entirely new world.

COMPREHENSION

1. What is a beriozka? Who is allowed to shop in it?

2. What does the beriozka on Vasilevsky Island look like? How does it
   contrast with its surroundings?

3. What things are sold in the beriozka?

4. What is Lee doing in the Soviet Union? Why is she allowed to shop
   at the beriozka?

5. According to Lee, what two worlds exist in the Soviet Union? What
   does Lee mean when she says that the old woman discovered a new
   world that she "longed to plunder"?

PURPOSE AND AUDIENCE

1. Is Lee's general purpose in writing this essay to express her feelings,
   to present information, or to persuade her readers? How can you tell?

2. What is Lee's thesis? Is it implied or explicit?

3. What evidence does Lee give to support her thesis?

4. What knowledge does Lee assume her audience has about her subject? What does this tell you about the audience she has in mind?

STYLE AND STRUCTURE

1. Locate the images that Lee uses in her essay to contrast "the two worlds of the Soviet Union." How do these images help convey her meaning?

2. Underline the adjectives that Lee uses to describe the ordinary Russians. How do these words help her make her point?

3. Is the essay an objective or subjective description? What leads you to your conclusion?

4. What is the organizing scheme of Lee's description? What other scheme might she have used? Is hers the best scheme for the topic? Explain.

5. Why does Lee end her essay the way she does? How effective is this concluding strategy? Can you think of a strategy that would be more effective?

VOCABULARY PROJECTS

1. Define each of the following words as it is used in this selection.

visitation (1)	obsequious (4)
minutely (1)	imperious (4)
gnarled (1)	ambiguous (5)
laminated (2)	pragmatism (6)
perfunctory (2)	balmy (7)
disadvantageous (3)	officious (7)
Brahmin (4)	avidity (7)

2. Using a dictionary, write down at least one synonym for each of the vocabulary words above. Then, locating each word in the essay, determine how closely the synonym approximates the author's original word choice. Finally, write a paragraph in which you summarize your findings concerning synonyms.

3. Make a list of the words that Lee uses to characterize the salesgirls in paragraphs 6 and 7. Why does Lee choose the words she does? What is the dominant impression that Lee tries to convey?

WRITING WORKSHOP

1. Choose a place you are familiar with and write an objective description of it. Then, write a subjective description of the same place.

2. Examine your surroundings and select a person or thing that contrasts sharply with them. Write an essay in which you, like Andrea Lee, describe this person or thing so that you convey the sense of contrast to your readers.

3. Visit a store that you have never been to before and, like Andrea Lee, describe it in detail. Include the physical details of the store and of the people who shop there.

THEMATIC CONNECTIONS

- "The Arab World" (p. 337)
- "Rule of Law" (p. 397)

PHOTOGRAPHS
OF MY PARENTS

Maxine Hong Kingston

Maxine Hong Kingston was born in Stockton, California, in 1940. She graduated from the University of California at Berkeley and taught high school English and mathematics in California and Hawaii, where she now teaches creative writing at the University of Honolulu. Her first book, The Woman Warrior: Memories of a Girlhood Among Ghosts *(1975), won the National Book Critics Circle Award. Her second book,* China Men *(1980), also received critical praise. In "Photographs of My Parents," an excerpt from* The Woman Warrior, *Kingston describes some old photographs of her mother and father. By doing so she conveys their strength and dignity as well as the cultural differences that separate China from America.*

Once in a long while, four times so far for me, my mother brings   1
out the metal tube that holds her medical diploma. On the tube are gold circles crossed with seven red lines each—"joy" ideographs in abstract.* There are also little flowers that look like gears for a gold machine. According to the scraps of labels with Chinese and American addresses, stamps, and postmarks, the family airmailed the can from Hong Kong in 1950. It got crushed in the middle, and whoever tried to peel the labels off stopped because the red and gold paint came off too, leaving silver scratches that rust. Somebody tried to pry the end off before discovering that the tube pulls apart. When I open it, the smell of China flies out, a thousand-year-old bat flying heavy-headed out of the Chinese caverns where bats are as white as dust, a smell that comes from long ago, far back in the brain. Crates from Canton, Hong Kong, Singapore, and Taiwan have that smell too, only stronger because they are more recently come from the Chinese.

Inside the can are three scrolls, one inside another. The largest   2
says that in the twenty-third year of the National Republic, the To

---

**EDS. NOTE—That is, stylized Chinese characters for the word *joy*.

Keung School of Midwifery, where she has had two years of instruction and Hospital Practice, awards its Diploma to my mother, who
has shown through oral and written examination her Proficiency in
Midwifery, Pediatrics, Gynecology, "Medecine," "Surgary," Therapeutics, Ophthalmology, Bacteriology, Dermatology, Nursing and
Bandage. This document has eight stamps on it: one, the school's
English and Chinese names embossed together in a circle; one, as
the Chinese enumerate, a stork and a big baby in lavender ink;
one, the school's Chinese seal; one, an orangish paper stamp pasted
in the border design; one, the red seal of Dr. Wu Pak-liang, M.D.,
Lyon, Berlin, president and "Ex-assistant étranger à la clinique chir-
ugicale et d'accouchement de l'université de Lyon";* one, the red
seal of Dean Woo Yin-kam, M.D.; one, my mother's seal, her chop
mark** larger that the president's and the dean's; and one, the number 1279 on the back. Dean Woo's signature is followed by "(Hackett)." I read in a history book that Hackett Medical College for
Women at Canton was founded in the nineteenth century by European women doctors.

The school seal has been pressed over a photograph of my mother   3
at the age of thirty-seven. The diploma gives her age as twenty-
seven. She looks younger than I do, her eyebrows are thicker, her
lips fuller. Her naturally curly hair is parted on the left, one wavy
wisp tendrilling off to the right. She wears a scholar's white gown,
and she is not thinking about her appearance. She stares straight
ahead as if she could see me and past me to her grandchildren and
grandchildren's grandchildren. She has spacy eyes, as all people recently from Asia have. Her eyes do not focus on the camera. My
mother is not smiling; Chinese do not smile for photographs. Their
faces command relatives in foreign lands—"Send money"—and posterity forever—"Put food in front of this picture." My mother does
not understand Chinese-American snapshots. "What are you laughing at?" she asks.

The second scroll is a long narrow photograph of the graduating   4
class with the school officials seated in front. I picked out my
mother immediately. Her face is exactly her own, though forty years
younger. She is so familiar, I can only tell whether or not she is
pretty or happy or smart by comparing her to the other women. For
this formal group picture she straightened her hair with oil to make
a chinlength bob like the others'. On the other women, strangers, I

---

*EDS. NOTE—Foreign ex-assistant (teacher) at the surgical and maternity clinic of
the University of Lyons (France).
**EDS. NOTE—Chinese seal.

can recognize a curled lip, a sidelong glance, pinched shoulders. My mother is not soft; the girl with the small nose and dimpled underlip is soft. My mother is not humorous, not like the girl at the end who lifts her mocking chin to pose like Girl Graduate. My mother does not have smiling eyes; the old woman teacher (Dean Woo?) in front crinkles happily, and the one faculty member in the western suit smiles westernly. Most of the graduates are girls whose faces have not yet formed; my mother's face will not change anymore, except to age. She is intelligent, alert, pretty. I can't tell if she's happy.

The graduates seem to have been looking elsewhere when they 5
pinned the rose, zinnia, or chrysanthemum on their precise black dresses. One thin girl wears hers in the middle of her chest. A few have a flower over a left or right nipple. My mother put hers, a chrysanthemum, below her left breast. Chinese dresses at that time were dartless, cut as if women did not have breasts; these young doctors, unaccustomed to decorations, may have seen their chests as black expanses with no reference points for flowers. Perhaps they couldn't shorten that far gaze that lasts only a few years after a Chinese emigrates. In this picture too my mother's eyes are big with what they held—reaches of oceans beyond China, land beyond oceans. Most emigrants learn the barbarians' directness—how to gather themselves and stare rudely into talking faces as if trying to catch lies. In America my mother has eyes as strong as boulders, never once skittering off a face, but she has not learned to place decorations and phonograph needles, nor has she stopped seeing land on the other side of the oceans. Now her eyes include the relatives in China, as they once included my father smiling and smiling in his many western outfits, a different one for each photograph that he sent from America.

He and his friends took pictures of one another in bathing suits 6
at Coney Island beach, the salt wind from the Atlantic blowing their hair. He's the one in the middle with his arms about the necks of his buddies. They pose in the cockpit of a biplane, on a motorcycle, and on a lawn beside the "Keep Off the Grass" sign. They are always laughing. My father, white shirt sleeves rolled up, smiles in front of a wall of clean laundry. In the spring he wears a new straw hat, cocked at a Fred Astaire angle. He steps out, dancing down the stairs, one foot forward, one back, a hand in his pocket. He wrote to her about the American custom of stomping on straw hats come fall. "If you want to save your hat for next year," he said, "you have to put it away early, or else when you're riding the subway or walking along Fifth Avenue, any stranger can snatch it off your head and put his foot through it. That's the way they celebrate the change of

seasons here." In the winter he wears a gray felt hat with his gray overcoat. He is sitting on a rock in Central Park. In one snapshot he is not smiling; someone took it when he was studying, blurred in the glare of the desk lamp.

There are no snapshots of my mother. In two small portraits, however, there is a black thumbprint on her forehead, as if someone had inked in bangs, as if someone had marked her. 7

"Mother, did bangs come into fashion after you had the picture taken?" One time she said yes. Another time when I asked, "Why do you have fingerprints on your forehead?" she said, "Your First Uncle did that." I disliked the unsureness in her voice. 8

The last scroll has columns of Chinese words. The only English is "Department of Health, Canton," imprinted on my mother's face, the same photograph as on the diploma. I keep looking to see whether she was afraid. Year after year my father did not come home or send for her. Their two children had been dead for ten years. If he did not return soon, there would be no more children. ("They were three and two years old, a boy and a girl. They could talk already.") My father did send money regularly, though, and she had nobody to spend it on but herself. She bought good clothes and shoes. Then she decided to use the money for becoming a doctor. She did not leave for Canton immediately after the children died. In China there was time to complete feelings. As my father had done, my mother left the village by ship. There was a sea bird painted on the ship to protect it against shipwreck and winds. She was in luck. The following ship was boarded by river pirates, who kidnapped every passenger, even old ladies. "Sixty dollars for an old lady" was what the bandits used to say. "I sailed alone," she says, "to the capital of the entire province." She took a brown leather suitcase and a seabag stuffed with two quilts. 9

COMPREHENSION

1. What did Kingston's mother study in China?

2. Kingston says that in a photograph her mother has "spacy eyes." What does she mean? Why don't Chinese smile for photographs?

3. What is the "barbarians' directness" that Kingston mentions? What does her use of this term show?

4. How do the photographs of Kingston's father show him to be different from his wife?

5. What qualities of Kingston's mother and father do the photographs reveal? What do they conceal?

PURPOSE AND AUDIENCE

1. What preconceptions does Kingston believe her readers have about Chinese men and women?

2. Does Kingston identify with her audience or her parents? Explain.

3. In general terms, what is Kingston's purpose in writing this essay? More specifically, what points does she wish to convey to her readers?

4. In your own words, state the thesis of this essay.

STYLE AND STRUCTURE

1. What is the organizing scheme for this description?

2. Where is the transition from the description of the mother to the description of the father? Is it effective? Why or why not?

3. What effect does Kingston achieve by describing the single and group portraits one after the other?

4. What does Kingston mean when she calls the smell of China "a thousand-year-old bat"? What type of figurative language is she using?

5. How does Kingston use the photographs to fill in bits of her parents' history?

6. What is the dominant impression that Kingston wants to create with her description?

VOCABULARY PROJECTS

1. Define each of the following words as it is used in this selection.
   proficiency (2)   therapeutics (2)
   ophthalmology (2)   enumerate (2)
   pediatrics (2)   tendrilling (3)
   gynecology (2)   bob (4)
   dermatology (2)   emigrates (5)

2. Look up the suffix -ology and determine its meaning. List ten other words that also contain this suffix.

3. Why does Kingston use the word scroll to refer to her mother's certificates?

WRITING WORKSHOP

1. Select several pictures from a family album, and describe them. Try to organize your writing in a way that links your pictures together.

2. Find a picture of a famous person in a book or magazine. Describe the picture, inferring as many character traits as you can from the expression or attitude of the subject.

3. Based on what you can gather from the descriptions of the photographs, describe the personalities of the two people mentioned in the essay.

THEMATIC CONNECTIONS

- "Aria: A Memoir of a Bilingual Childhood" (p. 348)
- "Historical Fiction, Fictitious History, and Chesapeake Bay Blue Crabs, or, About Aboutness" (p. 406)

SALVADOR

Joan Didion

Joan Didion was born in 1934 in Sacramento, California. After graduating from the University of California at Berkeley in 1956, she worked as an editor for Vogue *and then for the* Saturday Evening Post, National Review, *and* Esquire. *Her essays have been collected in* Slouching Towards Bethlehem *(1968),* The White Album *(1979), and* Essays and Conversations *(1984). In addition, she has authored four novels,* Run River *(1963),* Play It as It Lays *(1970),* A Book of Common Prayer *(1977), and* Democracy *(1980). Her latest book is* Miami *(1988). In 1982 Didion traveled to El Salvador, a Central American country that was being torn apart by civil war. The result of her visit was the book* Salvador *(1983), which paints a portrait of a country engulfed by fear and political violence. The following selection, from the very beginning of the book, presents her initial impressions of El Salvador and focuses on the "mechanism of terror" that she sees operating everywhere in El Salvador's capital city of San Salvador.*

The three-year-old El Salvador International Airport is glassy and 1
white splendidly isolated, conceived during the waning of the Molina "National Transformation" as convenient less to the capital (San Salvador is forty miles away, until recently a drive of several hours) than to a central hallucination of the Molina and Romero regimes, the projected beach resorts, the Hyatt, the Pacific Paradise, tennis, golf, water-skiing, condos, *Costa del Sol*; the visionary invention of a tourist industry in yet another republic where the leading natural cause of death is gastrointestinal infection. In the general absence of tourists these hotels have since been abandoned, ghost resorts on the empty Pacific beaches, and to land at this airport built to service them is to plunge directly into a state in which no ground is solid, no depth of field reliable, no perception so definite that it might not dissolve into its reverse.

The only logic is that of acquiescence. Immigration is negotiated 2
in a thicket of automatic weapons, but by whose authority the weapons are brandished (Army or National Guard or National Police or Customs Police or Treasury Police or one of a continuing proliferation of other shadowy and overlapping forces) is a blurred

point. Eye contact is avoided. Documents are scrutinized upside down. Once clear of the airport, on the new highway that slices through green hills rendered phosphorescent by the cloud cover of the tropical rainy season, one sees mainly underfed cattle and mongrel dogs and armored vehicles, vans and trucks and Cherokee Chiefs fitted with reinforced steel and bulletproof Plexiglas an inch thick. Such vehicles are a fixed feature of local life, and are popularly associated with disappearance and death. There was the Cherokee Chief seen following the Dutch television crew killed in Chalatenango province in March of 1982. There was the red Toyota three-quarter-ton pickup sighted near the van driven by the four American Catholic workers on the night they were killed in 1980. There were, in the late spring and summer of 1982, the three Toyota panel trucks, one yellow, one blue, and one green, none bearing plates, reported present at each of the mass detentions (a "dentention" is another fixed feature of local life, and often precedes a "disappearance") in the Amatepec district of San Salvador. These are the details—the models and colors of armored vehicles, the makes and calibers of weapons, the particular methods of dismemberment and decapitation used in particular instances—on which the visitor to Salvador learns immediately to concentrate, to the exclusion of past or future concerns, as in a prolonged amnesiac fugue.

Terror is the given of the place. Black-and-white police cars cruise 3 in pairs, each with the barrel of a rifle extruding from an open window. Roadblocks materialize at random, soldiers fanning out from trucks and taking positions, fingers always on triggers, safeties clicking on and off. Aim is taken as if to pass the time. Every morning *El Diario de Hoy* and *La Prensa Gráfica* carry cautionary stories. "*Una madre y sus dos hijos fueron asesinados con arma cortante (corvo) por ocho sujetos desconocidos el lunes en la noche*": A mother and her two sons hacked to death in their beds by eight *desconocidos*, unknown men. The same morning's paper: the unidentified body of a young man, strangled, found on the shoulder of a road. Same morning, different story: the unidentified bodies of three young men, found on another road, their faces partially destroyed by bayonets, one face carved to represent a cross.

It is largely from these reports in the newspapers that the United 4 States embassy compiles its body counts, which are transmitted to Washington in a weekly dispatch referred to by embassy people as "the grimgram." These counts are presented in a kind of tortured code that fails to obscure what is taken for granted in El Salvador, that government forces do most of the killing. In a January 15 1982 memo to Washington, for example, the embassy issued a "guarded" breakdown on its count of 6,909 "reported" political murders between September 16 1980 and September 15 1981. Of these 6,909, according to the memo, 922 were "believed committed by security forces," 952 "believed committed by leftist terrorists," 136 "believed committed by rightist terrorists," and 4,889 "committed by unknown assailants," the famous *desconocidos* favored by those San Salvador newspapers still publishing. (The figures actually add up not to 6,909 but to 6,899, leaving ten in a kind of official limbo.) The memo continued:

> "The uncertainty involved here can be seen in the fact that responsibility cannot be fixed in the majority of cases. We note, however, that it is generally believed in El Salvador that a large number of unexplained killings are carried out by the security forces, officially or unofficially. The Embassy is aware of dramatic claims that have been made by one interest group or another in which the security forces figure as the primary agents of murder here. El Salvador's tangled web of attack and vengeance, traditional criminal violence and political mayhem make this an impossible charge to sustain. In saying this, however, we make no attempt to lighten the responsibility for the deaths of many hundreds, and perhaps thousands, which can be attributed to the security forces. . . . "

The body count kept by what is generally referred to in San Salvador as "the Human Rights Commission" is higher than the embassy's, and documented periodically by a photographer who goes out looking for bodies. These bodies he photographs are often broken into unnatural positions, and the faces to which the bodies are attached (when they are attached) are equally unnatural, sometimes unrecognizable as human faces, obliterated by acid or beaten to a mash of misplaced ears and teeth or slashed ear to ear and invaded by insects. *"Encontrado en Antiguo Cuscatlán el día 25 de Marzo 1982: camison de dormir celeste,"* the typed caption reads on one photograph: found in Antiguo Cuscatlán March 25 1982 wearing a sky-blue nightshirt. The captions are laconic. Found in Soyapango May 21 1982. Found in Mejicanos June 11 1982. Found at El Playón May 30 1982, white shirt, purple pants, black shoes.

The photograph accompanying that last caption shows a body with no eyes, because the vultures got to it before the photographer did. There is a special kind of practical information that the visitor to El Salvador acquires immediately, the way visitors to other places acquire information about the currency rates, the hours for the museums. In El Salvador one learns that vultures go first for the soft tissue, for the eyes, the exposed genitalia, the open mouth. One learns that an open mouth can be used to make a specific point, can be stuffed with something emblematic; stuffed, say, with a penis, or, if the point has to do with land title, stuffed with some of the dirt in question. One learns that hair deteriorates less rapidly than flesh, and that a skull surrounded by a perfect corona of hair is a not uncommon sight in the body dumps.

All forensic photographs induce in the viewer a certain protective numbness, but dissociation is more difficult here. In the first place these are not, technically, "forensic" photographs, since the evidence they document will never be presented in a court of law. In the second place the disfigurement is too routine. The locations are too near, the dates too recent. There is the presence of the relatives of the disappeared: the women who sit every day in this cramped office on the grounds of the archdiocese, waiting to look at the spiral-bound photo albums in which the photographs are kept. These albums have plastic covers bearing soft-focus color photographs of young Americans in dating situations (strolling through autumn foliage on one album, recumbent in a field of daisies on another), and the women, looking for the bodies of their husbands and brothers and sisters and children, pass them from hand to hand without comment or expression.

> "One of the more shadowy elements of the violent scene here [is] the death squad. Existence of these groups has long been disputed, but not by many Salvadorans. . . . Who constitutes the death squads is yet another difficult question. We do not believe that these squads exist as permanent formations but rather as ad hoc vigilante groups that coalesce according to perceived need. Membership is also uncertain, but in addition to civilians we believe that both on- and off-duty members of the security forces are participants. This was unofficially confirmed by right-wing spokesman Maj. Roberto D'Aubuisson who stated in an interview in early 1981 that security force members utilize the guise of the death squad when a potentially embarrassing or odious task needs to be performed."
>
> *From the confidential but later declassified January 15, 1982 memo previously cited, drafted for the State Department by the political section at the embassy in San Salvador.*

The dead and pieces of the dead turn up in El Salvador everywhere, every day, as taken for granted as in a nightmare, or a horror movie. Vultures of course suggest the presence of a body. A knot of children on the street suggests the presence of a body. Bodies turn up in the brush of vacant lots, in the garbage thrown down ravines in the richest districts, in public rest rooms, in bus stations. Some are dropped in Lake Ilopango, a few miles east of the city, and wash up near the lakeside cottages and clubs frequented by what remains in San Salvador of the sporting bourgeoisie. Some still turn up at El Playón, the lunar lava field of rotting human flesh visible at one time or another on every television screen in America but characterized in June of 1982 in the *El Salvador News Gazette*, an English-language weekly edited by an American named Mario Rosenthal, as an "uncorroborated story . . . dredged up from the files of leftist propaganda." Others turn up at Puerta del Diablo, above Parque Balboa, a national *Turicentro* described as recently as the April–July 1982 issue of *Aboard TACA*, the magazine provided passengers on the national airline of El Salvador, as "offering excellent subjects for color photography."

I drove up to Puerta del Diablo one morning in June of 1982, past   9
the Casa Presidencial and the camouflaged watch towers and heavy concentrations of troops and arms south of town, on up a narrow road narrowed further by landslides and deep crevices in the road bed, a drive so insistently premonitory that after a while I began to hope that I would pass Puerta del Diablo without knowing it, just miss it, write it off, turn around and go back. There was however no way of missing it. Puerta del Diablo is a "view site" in an older and distinctly literary tradition, nature as lesson, an immense cleft rock through which half of El Salvador seems framed, a site so romantic and "mystical," so theatrically sacrificial in aspect, that it might be a cosmic parody of nineteenth-century landscape painting. The place presents itself as pathetic fallacy: the sky "broods," the stones "weep," a constant seepage of water weighting the ferns and moss. The foliage is thick and slick with moisture. The only sound is a steady buzz, I believe of cicadas.

Body dumps are seen in El Salvador as a kind of visitors' must-   10
do, difficult but worth the detour. "Of course you have seen El Playón," an aide to President Alvaro Magaña said to me one day, and proceeded to discuss the site geologically, as evidence of the country's geothermal resources. He made no mention of the bodies. I was unsure if he was sounding me out or simply found the geothermal aspect of overriding interest. One difference between El Playón and Puerta del Diablo is that most bodies at El Playón appear to have been killed somewhere else, and then dumped; at Puerta del Diablo the executions are believed to occur in place, at the top, and the

bodies thrown over. Sometimes reporters will speak of wanting to spend the night at Puerta del Diablo, in order to document the actual execution, but at the time I was in Salvador no one had.

The aftermath, the daylight aspect, is well documented. "Nothing   11
fresh today, I hear," an embassy officer said when I mentioned that I had visited Puerta del Diablo. "Were there any on top?" someone else asked. "There were supposed to have been three on top yesterday." The point about whether or not there had been any on top was that usually it was necessary to go down to see bodies. The way down is hard. Slabs of stone, slippery with moss, are set into the vertiginous cliff, and it is down this cliff that one begins the descent to the bodies, or what is left of the bodies, pecked and maggoty masses of flesh, bone, hair. On some days there have been helicopters circling, tracking those making the descent. Other days there have been militia at the top, in the clearing where the road seems to run out, but on the morning I was there the only people on top were a man and a woman and three small children, who played in the wet grass while the woman started and stopped a Toyota pickup. She appeared to be learning how to drive. She drove forward and then back toward the edge, apparently following the man's signals, over and over again.

We did not speak, and it was only later, down the mountain and   12
back in the land of the provisionally living, that it occurred to me that there was a definite question about why a man and a woman might choose a well-known body dump for a driving lesson. This was one of a number of occasions, during the two weeks my husband and I spent in El Salvador, on which I came to understand, in a way I had not understood before, the exact mechanism of terror.

COMPREHENSION

1. What does Didion mean in paragraph 2 when she says that the only logic in El Salvador is "that of acquiescence"?

2. Why is terror the "given" of El Salvador?

3. According to Didion, who does most of the killing in El Salvador? What evidence does she present to support this assertion?

4. What special kind of practical information do visitors to El Salvador acquire immediately?

5. What is a body dump?

6. What is the "exact mechanism of terror" that Didion mentions in her conclusion?

PURPOSE AND AUDIENCE

1. What is the dominant impression that Didion creates with her description of El Salvador?

2. What does Didion hope to achieve by including graphic descriptions of atrocities?

3. In paragraph 7 Didion includes the text of a memo drafted by the American embassy in San Salvador. What is her motivation for doing so?

4. How can you tell that Didion's purpose in this selection is persuasive as well as informative?

5. Does Didion state her thesis explicitly, or does she imply it? Explain why she chose the strategy she did.

6. Is Didion addressing an audience that she believes knows a lot or a little about conditions in El Salvador? Explain your answer.

STYLE AND STRUCTURE

1. Why does Didion begin her book with a description of the El Salvador International Airport? Explain her reference to "National Transformation."

2. Paragraphs 1 and 2 act as an introduction to the selection. In what way do these paragraphs set the stage for the rest of the selection?

3. Explain Didion's use of imagery at the end of paragraph 2 when she says that a visitor immediately learns to concentrate on certain brutal details "to the exclusion of past or future concerns, *as in a prolonged amnesiac fugue.*"

4. Throughout this selection, Didion alternates objective commentary supported by evidence with subjective description. What does she achieve by this strategy?

5. Explain Didion's use of the language of a travel guide in paragraph 10, when she describes the body dump as "a kind of visitors' must-do, difficult but worth the detour."

6. In her conclusion, does Didion simply summarize the ideas that she presents in her conclusion, or does she expand on those ideas? Explain.

VOCABULARY PROJECTS

1. Define each of the following words as it is used in this selection.

   acquiescence (2)   obliterated (5)
   brandished (2)   laconic (5)
   dismemberment (2)   vigilante (7)
   decapitation (2)   bourgeoisie (8)
   amnesiac (2)   uncorroborated (8)
   fugue (2)   vertiginous (11)

2. Throughout this selection, Didion uses Spanish words and phrases. After identifying these words and phrases, determine why Didion includes them and how she conveys their meaning to her readers.

WRITING WORKSHOP

1. Write an essay in which you describe a place or experience that was frightening to you. As Didion does, vary your subjective account with objective description.

2. Assume that you are a Salvadoran, and write a letter to a relative who lives in the United States describing conditions in your country. Use information from Didion's essay and from an article that you find in the library that describes conditions in El Salvador in 1982. Include a thesis.

3. Go to your college library and consult *The New York Times Index, The Readers' Guide to Periodical Literature, The Humanities Index* or *The Social Sciences Index* to find articles that describe conditions in El Salvador today and write a description like Didion's.

THEMATIC CONNECTIONS

- "Rule of Law" (p. 397)
- The Declaration of Independence (p. 484)

THE WAY TO RAINY MOUNTAIN

N. Scott Momaday

N. Scott Momaday was born in Oklahoma in 1934. He graduated from the University of New Mexico in 1958 and was awarded a Ph.D. from Stanford University in 1963. He received a Guggenheim Fellowship in 1966 and taught English at the University of California–Santa Barbara, at Berkeley, and at Stanford. In 1969 he won a Pulitzer Prize for his first novel, House Made of Dawn. *His second book,* The Way to Rainy Mountain *(1969), is a collection of Kiowa legends and folk tales. The following essay is excerpted from the autobiographical introduction to* The Way to Rainy Mountain *in which Momaday traces the migration of the Kiowas to Oklahoma. By focusing on his grandmother, he effectively evokes the passing of the old ways that his grandmother embodies.*

A single knoll rises out of the plain in Oklahoma, north and west   1
of the Wichita Range. For my people, the Kiowas, it is an old landmark, and they gave it the name Rainy Mountain. The hardest weather in the world is there. Winter brings blizzards, hot tornadic winds arise in the spring, and in summer the prairie is an anvil's edge. The grass turns brittle and brown, and it cracks beneath your feet. There are green belts along the rivers and creeks, linear groves of hickory and pecan, willow and witch hazel. At a distance in July or August the steaming foliage seems almost to writhe in fire. Great green-and-yellow grasshoppers are everywhere in the tall grass, popping up like corn to sting the flesh, and tortoises crawl about on the red earth, going nowhere in the plenty of time. Loneliness is an aspect of the land. All things in the plain are isolate; there is no confusion of objects in the eye, but *one* hill or *one* tree or *one* man. To look upon that landscape in the early morning, with the sun at your back, is to lose the sense of proportion. Your imagination comes to life, and this, you think, is where Creation was begun.

I returned to Rainy Mountain in July. My grandmother had died   2
in the spring, and I wanted to be at her grave. She had lived to be very old and at last infirm. Her only living daughter was with her when she died, and I was told that in death her face was that of a child.

I like to think of her as a child. When she was born, the Kiowas   3

131

were living that last great moment of their history. For more than a hundred years they had controlled the open range from the Smoky Hill River to the Red, from the headwaters of the Canadian to the fork of the Arkansas and Cimarron. In alliance with the Comanches, they had ruled the whole of the southern Plains. War was their sacred business, and they were among the finest horsemen the world has ever known. But warfare for the Kiowas was preeminently a matter of disposition rather than of survival, and they never understood the grim, unrelenting advance of the U.S. Cavalry. When at last, divided and ill-provisioned, they were driven onto the Staked Plains in the cold rains of autumn, they fell into panic. In Palo Duro Canyon they abandoned their crucial stores to pillage and had nothing then but their lives. In order to save themselves, they surrendered to the soldiers at Fort Sill and were imprisoned in the old stone corral that now stands as a military museum. My grandmother was spared the humiliation of those high gray walls by eight or ten years, but she must have known from birth the affliction of defeat, the dark brooding of old warriors.

Her name was Aho, and she belonged to the last culture to evolve   4
in North America. Her forebears came down from the high country in western Montana nearly three centuries ago. They were a mountain people, a mysterious tribe of hunters whose language has never been positively classified in any major group. In the late seventeenth century they began a long migration to the south and east. It was a long journey toward the dawn, and it led to a golden age. Along the way the Kiowas were befriended by the Crows, who gave them the culture and religion of the Plains. They acquired horses, and their ancient nomadic spirit was suddenly free of the ground. They acquired Tai-me, the sacred Sun Dance doll, from that moment the object and symbol of their worship, and so shared in the divinity of the sun. Not least, they acquired the sense of destiny, therefore courage and pride. When they entered upon the southern Plains, they had been transformed. No longer were they slaves to the simple necessity of survival; they were a lordly and dangerous society of fighters and thieves, hunters and priests of the sun. According to their origin myth, they entered the world through a hollow log. From one point of view, their migration was the fruit of an old prophecy, for indeed they emerged from a sunless world.

Although my grandmother lived out her long life in the shadow of   5
Rainy Mountain, the immense landscape of the continental interior lay like memory in her blood. She could tell of the Crows, whom she had never seen, and of the Black Hills, where she had never been. I wanted to see in reality what she had seen more perfectly in the

mind's eye, and traveled fifteen hundred miles to begin my pilgrimage.

Yellowstone, it seemed to me, was the top of the world, a region 6 of deep lakes and dark timber, canyons and waterfalls. But, beautiful as it is, one might have the sense of confinement there. The skyline in all directions is close at hand, the high wall of the woods and deep cleavages of shade. There is a perfect freedom in the mountains, but it belongs to the eagle and the elk, the badger and the bear. The Kiowas reckoned their stature by the distance they could see, and they were bent and blind in the wilderness.

Descending eastward, the highland meadows are a stairway to 7 the plain. In July the inland slope of the Rockies is luxuriant with flax and buckwheat, stonecrop and larkspur. The earth unfolds and the limit of the land recedes. Clusters of trees and animals grazing far in the distance cause the vision to reach away and wonder to build upon the mind. The sun follows a longer course in the day, and the sky is immense beyond all comparison. The great billowing clouds that sail upon it are shadows that move upon the grain like water, dividing light. Farther down, in the land of the Crows and Blackfeet, the plain is yellow. Sweet clover takes hold of the hills and bends upon itself to cover and seal the soil. There the Kiowas paused on their way; they had come to the place where they must change their lives. The sun is at home in the plains. Precisely there does it have the certain character of a god. When the Kiowas came to the land of the Crows, they could see the dark lees of the hills at dawn across the Bighorn River, the profusion of light on the grain shelves, the oldest deity ranging after the solstices. Not yet would they veer southward to the caldron of the land that lay below; they must wean their blood from the northern winter and hold the mountains a while longer in their view. They bore Tai-me in procession to the east.

A dark mist lay over the Black Hills, and the land was like iron. 8 At the top of a ridge I caught sight of Devil's Tower upthrust against the gray sky as if in the birth of time the core of the earth had broken through its crust and the motion of the world was begun. There are things in nature that engender an awful quiet in the heart of man; Devil's Tower is one of them. Two centuries ago, because they could not do otherwise, the Kiowas made a legend at the base of the rock. My grandmother said:

"Eight children were there at play, seven sisters and their brother. Suddenly the boy was struck dumb; he trembled and began to run upon his hands and feet. His fingers became claws, and his body was covered with fur. Directly there was a bear where the boy had been. The sisters were terrified; they ran, and the bear after them. They came to the stump of a great tree, and the tree spoke to them. It bade them climb upon it, and as they did so, it began to rise into the air. The bear came to kill them, but they were just beyond its reach. It reared against the tree and scored the bark all around with its claws. The seven sisters were borne into the sky, and they became the stars of the Big Dipper."

From that moment, and so long as the legend lives, the Kiowas have kinsmen in the night sky. Whatever they were in the mountains, they could be no more. However tenuous their well-being, however much they had suffered and would suffer again, they had found a way out of the wilderness.

My grandmother had a reverence for the sun, a holy regard that [9] now is all but gone out of mankind. There was a wariness in her, and an ancient awe. She was a Christian in her later years, but she had come a long way about, and she never forgot her birthright. As a child she had been to the Sun Dances; she had taken part in those annual rites, and by them she had learned the restoration of her people in the presence of Tai-me. She was about seven when the last Kiowa Sun Dance was held in 1887 on the Washita River above Rainy Mountain Creek. The buffalo were gone. In order to consummate the ancient sacrifice—to impale the head of a buffalo bull upon the medicine tree—a delegation of old men journeyed into Texas, there to beg and barter for an animal from the Goodnight herd. She was ten when the Kiowas came together for the last time as a living Sun Dance culture. They could find no buffalo; they had to hang an old hide from the sacred tree. Before the dance could begin, a company of soldiers rode out from Fort Sill under orders to disperse the tribe. Forbidden without cause the essential act of their faith, having seen the wild herds slaughtered and left to rot upon the ground, the Kiowas backed away forever from the medicine tree. That was July 20, 1890, at the great bend of the Washita. My grandmother was there. Without bitterness, and for as long as she lived, she bore a vision of deicide.

Now that I can have her only in memory, I see my grandmother [10] in the several postures that were peculiar to her: standing at the wood stove on a winter morning and turning meat in a great iron skillet; sitting at the south window, bent above her beadwork, and afterwards, when her vision had failed, looking down for a long time into the fold of her hands; going out upon a cane, very slowly as she did when the weight of age came upon her; praying. I remember her most often at prayer. She made long, rambling prayers out of suffering and hope, having seen many things. I was never sure that I had the right to hear, so exclusive were they of all mere custom and company. The last time I saw her she prayed standing by the side of her bed at night, naked to the waist, the light of a kerosene lamp moving upon her dark skin. Her long, black hair, always drawn and braided in the day, lay upon her shoulders and against her breasts like a shawl. I do not speak Kiowa, and I never understood her prayers, but there was something inherently sad in the sound, some merest hesitation upon the syllables of sorrow. She began in a high and descending pitch, exhausting her breath to silence; then again and again—and always the same intensity of effort, of something that is, and is not, like urgency in the human voice. Transported so in the dancing light among the shadows of her room, she seemed beyond the reach of time. But that was illusion; I think I knew then that I should not see her again.

COMPREHENSION

1. Why does Rainy Mountain remind Momaday of his grandmother?

2. What is the significance of the essay's title?

3. What does Momaday mean when he says that his grandmother was born when the Kiowas were living the "last great moment of their history"?

4. How did meeting the Crows change the Kiowas?

5. What effect did the soldiers have on the religion of the Kiowas?

PURPOSE AND AUDIENCE

1. Is Momaday writing simply to express emotions, or does he have other purposes as well? Explain.

2. What assumptions does Momaday make about his audience? What elements of the essay lead you to your conclusion?

3. Why does Momaday include the legend of Devil's Tower in his essay?

STYLE AND STRUCTURE

1. Why does Momaday begin his essay with a description of Rainy Mountain?

2. Find three examples of figurative language in the essay. How do these examples help Momaday convey his point to his readers?

3. In what order does Momaday arrange details in his description of his grandmother?

4. Bracket the narrative passages that Momaday uses in his essay and explain how they help him describe his grandmother.

5. Why does Momaday end his essay with a description of his grandmother praying?

VOCABULARY PROJECTS

1. Define each of the following words as it is used in this selection.

infirm (2)	engender (8)
preeminently (3)	tenuous (8)
nomadic (4)	consummate (9)
luxuriant (7)	impale (9)
billowing (7)	deicide (9)
profusion (7)	inherently (10)

2. Carefully reread paragraph 7. The description in this paragraph contains objective elements, but most of the words convey a subjective impression of the landscape. Study the wording closely and consider alternatives. Then evaluate how well the impression created here suits the rest of Momaday's essay.

3. Why does Momaday use the phrase "seal the soil" in paragraph 7? Would such repetition of initial vowel sounds be appropriate in more objective writing? Why, or why not?

WRITING WORKSHOP

1. Write an essay describing a grandparent or any older person who has had a great influence on you. Make sure that you include background information as well as a physical description.

2. Describe a place that has played an important part in your life. Include a narrative passage that conveys the significance to your readers.

3. Describe a ritual—such as a wedding or a confirmation—that you have witnessed or that you have participated in. Assume that your audience in not familiar with the event you describe.

THEMATIC CONNECTIONS

- "My Mother Never Worked" (p. 64)
- "My Brother and General Crab" (p. 52)

ONCE MORE TO THE LAKE

E. B. White

Elwyn Brooks White was born in 1899 in Mount Vernon, New York. After attending Cornell University, he became a regular contributor to The New Yorker *in 1926. Widely praised for his prose style, White wrote many editorials, features, and essays. In 1957, he moved permanently to his farm in North Brooklin, Maine, where he lived until his death in 1985. He published many books, including the children's story* Charlotte's Web *(1952),* One Man's Meat *(1944), and* The Second Tree from the Corner *(1954). His collected letters were published in 1976 and his* Essays *in 1977. In 1966, he won the presidential Medal of Freedom. "Once More to the Lake" (1941), reprinted from* One Man's Meat, *is a classic essay of personal reminiscence. Using precise detail and vivid language, he masterfully creates the lakeside camp he visited with his son.*

One summer, along about 1904, my father rented a camp on a lake in Maine and took us all there for the month of August. We all got ringworm from some kittens and had to rub Pond's Extract on our arms and legs night and morning, and my father rolled over in a canoe with all his clothes on; but outside of that the vacation was a success and from then on none of us ever thought there was any place in the world like that lake in Maine. We returned summer after summer—always on August 1st for one month. I have since become a salt-water man, but sometimes in summer there are days when the restlessness of the tides and the fearful cold of the sea water and the incessant wind which blows across the afternoon and into the evening make me wish for the placidity of a lake in the woods. A few weeks ago this feeling got so strong I bought myself a couple of bass hooks and a spinner and returned to the lake where we used to go, for a week's fishing and to revisit old haunts. 1

I took along my son, who had never had any fresh water up his nose and who had seen lily pads only from train windows. On the journey over to the lake I began to wonder what it would be like. I wondered how time would have marred this unique, this holy spot—the coves and streams, the hills that the sun set behind, the camps and the paths behind the camps. I was sure that the tarred road 2 would have found it out and I wondered in what other ways it would be desolated. It is strange how much you can remember about places like that once you allow your mind to return into the grooves which lead back. You remember one thing, and that suddenly reminds you of another thing. I guess I remembered clearest of all the early mornings, when the lake was cool and motionless, remembered how the bedroom smelled of the lumber it was made of and of the wet woods whose scent entered through the screen. The partitions in the camp were thin and did not extend clear to the top of the rooms, and as I was always the first up I would dress softly so as not to wake the others, and sneak out into the sweet outdoors and start out in the canoe, keeping close along the shore in the long shadows of the pines. I remembered being very careful never to rub my paddle against the gunwale for fear of disturbing the stillness of the cathedral.

The lake had never been what you would call a wild lake. There were cottages sprinkled around the shores, and it was in farming country although the shores of the lake were quite heavily wooded. Some of the cottages were owned by nearby farmers, and you would live at the shore and eat your meals at the farmhouse. That's what our family did. But although it wasn't wild, it was a fairly large and undisturbed lake and there were places in it which, to a child at least, seemed infinitely remote and primeval. 3

I was right about the tar: it led to within half a mile of the shore. But when I got back there, with my boy, and we settled into a camp near a farmhouse and into the kind of summertime I had known, I could tell that it was going to be pretty much the same as it had been before—I knew it, lying in bed the first morning, smelling the bedroom, and hearing the boy sneak quietly out and go off along the shore in a boat. I began to sustain the illusion that he was I, and therefore, by simple transposition, that I was my father. This sensation persisted, kept cropping up all the time we were there. It was not an entirely new feeling, but in this setting it grew much stronger. I seemed to be living a dual existence. I would be in the middle of some simple act, I would be picking up a bait box or laying down a table fork, or I would be saying something, and suddenly it would be not I but my father who was saying the words or making the gesture. It gave me a creepy sensation. 4

We went fishing the first morning. I felt the same damp moss covering the worms in the bait can, and saw the dragonfly alight on the tip of my rod as it hovered a few inches from the surface of the water. It was the arrival of this fly that convinced me beyond any doubt that everything was as it always had been, that the years 5 were a mirage and there had been no years. The small waves were the same, chucking the rowboat under the chin as we fished at anchor, and the boat was the same boat, the same color green and the ribs broken in the same places, and under the floor-boards the same freshwater leavings and débris—the dead helgramite,* the wisps of moss, the rusty discarded fishhook, the dried blood from yesterday's catch. We stared silently at the tips of our rods, at the dragonflies that came and went. I lowered the tip of mine into the water, tentatively, pensively dislodging the fly, which darted two feet away, poised, darted two feet back, and came to rest again a little farther up the rod. There had been no years between the ducking of this dragonfly and the other one—the one that was part of memory. I looked at the boy, who was silently watching his fly, and it was my hands that held his rod, my eyes watching. I felt dizzy and didn't know which rod I was at the end of.

We caught two bass, hauling them in briskly as though they were   6
mackerel, pulling them over the side of the boat in a businesslike manner without any landing net, and stunning them with a blow on the back of the head. When we got back for a swim before lunch, the lake was exactly where we had left it, the same number of inches from the dock, and there was only the merest suggestion of a breeze. This seemed an utterly enchanted sea, this lake you could leave to its own devices for a few hours and come back to, and find that it had not stirred, this constant and trustworthy body of water. In the shallows, the dark, water-soaked sticks and twigs, smooth and old, were undulating in clusters on the bottom against the clean ribbed sand, and the track of the mussel was plain. A school of minnows swam by, each minnow with its small individual shadow, doubling the attendance, so clear and sharp in the sunlight. Some of the other campers were in swimming, along the shore, one of them with a cake of soap, and the water felt thin and clear and unsubstantial. Over the years there had been this person with the cake of soap, this cultist, and here he was. There had been no years.

Up to the farmhouse to dinner through the teeming, dusty field,   7
the road under our sneakers was only a two-track road. The middle track was missing, the one with the marks of the hooves and the splotches of dried, flaky manure. There had always been three tracks to choose from in choosing which track to walk in; now the choice was narrowed down to two. For a moment I missed terribly the middle alternative. But the way led past the tennis court, and something about the way it lay there in the sun reassured me; the tape

*EDS. NOTE—An insect larva often used as bait.

had loosened along the backline, the alleys were green with plantains and other weeds, and the net (installed in June and removed in September) sagged in the dry noon, and the whole place steamed with midday heat and hunger and emptiness. There was a choice of pie for dessert, and one was blueberry and one was apple, and the waitresses were the same country girls, there having been no passage of time, only the illusion of it as in a dropped curtain—the waitresses were still fifteen; their hair had been washed, that was the only difference—they had been to the movies and seen the pretty girls with the clean hair.

Summertime, oh summertime, pattern of life indelible, the fade-   8
proof lake, the woods unshatterable, the pasture with the sweetfern and the juniper forever and ever, summer without end; this was the background, and the life along the shore was the design, the cottages with their innocent and tranquil design, their tiny docks with the flagpole and the American flag floating against the white clouds in the blue sky, the little paths over the roots of the trees leading from camp to camp and the paths leading back to the outhouses and the can of lime for sprinkling, and at the souvenir counters at the store the miniature birch-bark canoes and the post cards that showed things looking a little better than they looked. This was the American family at play, escaping the city heat, wondering whether the newcomers in the camp at the head of the cove were "common" or "nice," wondering whether it was true that the people who drove up for Sunday dinner at the farmhouse were turned away because there wasn't enough chicken.

It seemed to me, as I kept remembering all this, that those times   9
and those summers had been infinitely precious and worth saving. There had been jollity and peace and goodness. The arriving (at the beginning of August) had been so big a business in itself, at the railway station the farm wagon drawn up, the first smell of the pine-laden air, the first glimpse of the smiling farmer, and the great importance of the trunks and your father's enormous authority in such matters, and the feel of the wagon under you for the long ten-mile haul, and at the top of the last long hill catching the first view of the lake after eleven months of not seeing this cherished body of water. The shouts and cries of the other campers when they saw you, and the trunks to be unpacked, to give up their rich burden. (Arriving was less exciting nowadays, when you sneaked up in your car and parked it under a tree near the camp and took out the bags and in five minutes it was all over, no fuss, no loud wonderful fuss about trunks.)

Peace and goodness and jollity. The only thing that was wrong   10

now, really, was the sound of the place, an unfamiliar nervous sound
of the outboard motors. This was the note that jarred, the one thing
that would sometimes break the illusion and set the years moving.
In those other summertimes all motors were inboard; and when they
were at a little distance, the noise they made was a sedative, an
ingredient of summer sleep. They were one-cylinder and two-cylin-
der engines, and some were make-and-break and some were jump-
spark, but they all made a sleepy sound across the lake. The one-
lungers throbbed and fluttered, and the twin-cylinder ones purred
and purred, and that was a quiet sound too. But now the campers
all had outboards. In the daytime, in the hot mornings, these motors
made a petulant, irritable sound; at night, in the still evening when
the afterglow lit the water, they whined about one's ears like mos-
quitoes. My boy loved our rented outboard, and his great desire was
to achieve singlehanded mastery over it, and authority, and he soon
learned the trick of choking it a little (but not too much), and the
adjustment of the needle valve. Watching him I would remember
the things you could do with the old one-cylinder engine with the
heavy flywheel, how you could have it eating out of your hand if you
got really close to it spiritually. Motor boats in those days didn't
have clutches, and you would make a landing by shutting off the
motor at the proper time and coasting in with a dead rudder. But
there was a way of reversing them, if you learned the trick, by cutting the switch and putting it on again exactly on the final dying
revolution of the flywheel, so that it would kick back against com-
pression and begin reversing. Approaching a dock in a strong following breeze, it was difficult to slow up sufficiently by the ordinary
coasting method, and if a boy felt he had complete mastery over his
motor, he was tempted to keep it running beyond its time and then
reverse it a few feet from the dock. It took a cool nerve, because if
you threw the switch a twentieth of a second too soon you could
catch the flywheel when it still had speed enough to go up past center, and the boat would leap ahead, charging bull-fashion at the
dock.

We had a good week at the camp. The bass were biting well and   11
the sun shone endlessly, day after day. We would be tired at night
and lie down in the accumulated heat of the little bedrooms after the
long hot day and the breeze would stir almost imperceptibly outside
and the smell of the swamp drift in through the rusty screens. Sleep
would come easily and in the morning the red squirrel would be on
the roof, tapping out his gay routine. I kept remembering everything, lying in bed in the mornings—the small steamboat that had

a long rounded stern like the lip of a Ubangi,* and how quietly she ran on the moonlight sails, when the older boys played their mandolins and the girls sang and we ate doughnuts dipped in sugar, and how sweet the music was on the water in the shining night, and what it had felt like to think about girls then. After breakfast we would go up to the store and the things were in the same place—the minnows in a bottle, the plugs and spinners disarranged and pawed over by the youngsters from the boys' camp, the fig newtons and the Beeman's gum. Outside, the road was tarred and cars stood in front of the store. Inside, all was just as it had always been, except there was more Coca-Cola and not so much Moxie and root beer and birch beer and sarsaparilla. We would walk out with a bottle of pop apiece and sometimes the pop would backfire up our noses and hurt. We explored the streams, quietly, where the turtles slid off the sunny logs and dug their way into the soft bottom; and we lay on the town wharf and fed worms to the tame bass. Everywhere we went I had trouble making out which was I, the one walking at my side, the one walking in my pants.

One afternoon while we were there at that lake a thunderstorm came up. It was like the revival of an old melodrama that I had seen long ago with childish awe. The second-act climax of the drama of the electrical disturbance over a lake in America had not changed in any important respect. This was the big scene, still the big scene. The whole thing was so familiar, the first feeling of oppression and heat and a general air around camp of not wanting to go very far away. In midafternoon (it was all the same) a curious darkening of the sky, and a lull in everything that had made life tick; and then the way the boats suddenly swung the other way at their moorings with the coming of a breeze out of the new quarter, and the premonitory rumble. Then the kettle drum, then the snare, then the bass drum and cymbals, then crackling light against the dark, and the gods grinning and licking their chops in the hills. Afterward the calm, the rain steadily rustling in the calm lake, the return of light and hope and spirits, and the campers running out in joy and relief to go swimming in the rain, their bright cries perpetuating the deathless joke about how they were getting simply drenched, and the children screaming with delight at the new sensation of bathing in the rain, and the joke about getting drenched linking the genera-

12

---

*Eds. note—An African tribe whose members wear mouth ornaments that stretch their lips into a saucerlike shape.

tions in a strong indestructible chain. And the comedian who waded in carrying an unbrella.

When the others went swimming my son said he was going in too. 13 He pulled his dripping trunks from the line where they had hung all through the shower, and wrung them out. Languidly, and with no thought of going in, I watched him, his hard little body, skinny and bare, saw him wince slightly as he pulled up around his vitals the small, soggy, icy garment. As he buckled the swollen belt suddenly my groin felt the chill of death.

COMPREHENSION

1. In what ways are the author and his son alike? In what ways are they different?

2. What does White mean when he says, "I seemed to be living a dual existence"?

3. In paragraph 5 White says there seemed to be "no years" between past and present; elsewhere, he senses that things are different. How do you account for these conflicting feelings?

4. Why does White feel disconcerted when he discovers that the road to the farmhouse has two tracks, not three? What do you make of his comment, "now the choice was narrowed down to two"?

5. To what is White referring in the last sentence?

PURPOSE AND AUDIENCE

1. What is the thesis of this essay? Is it stated or implied?

2. Does White expect the ending of his essay to be a surprise to his audience? Explain.

3. To what age group do you think this essay would appeal most? Why?

4. How does White expect his readers to react to his description of the camp?

STYLE AND STRUCTURE

1. Why does White begin his essay with a short narrative about his trip to the lake in 1904? What context does this opening provide for the entire essay?

2. What ideas and images does White repeat throughout his essay? What is the purpose of this repetition?

3. In paragraph 12, White describes a thunderstorm. How does he use language to convey the experience of the storm to his readers?

4. White goes to great lengths to describe how things look, feel, smell, taste, and sound. How does this help him achieve his purpose in this essay?

5. In what way does White's conclusion refer back to the first paragraph of the essay?

VOCABULARY PROJECTS

1. Define each of the following words as it is used in this selection.

placidity (1)	petulant (10)
gunwale (2)	imperceptibly (11)
primeval (3)	melodrama (12)
transposition (4)	premonitory (12)
pensively (5)	perpetuating (12)
jollity (9)	languidly (13)

2. Underline ten words in the essay that refer to one of the five senses. Write a paragraph in which you describe the variety of these words.

3. Make a list of synonyms you could use for these words. How close do you come to capturing White's meaning?

WRITING WORKSHOP

1. Write a description of a scene you remember from your childhood. In your essay discuss how your current view of the scene differs from the view you had when you were a child.

2. Write a description of a person, place, or thing in which you appeal to a reader's five senses.

3. Assume that you are a travel agent. Write a description calculated to bring tourists to the lake. Be specific and stress the benefits that White mentions in his essay.

THEMATIC CONNECTIONS

- "Outsider in a Silent World" (p. 76)
- "The Company Man" (p. 440)

WRITING ASSIGNMENTS FOR DESCRIPTION

1. Choose a character from a work of fiction or film whom you think is truly interesting. Write a descriptive essay in which you demonstrate what makes this character so special.

2. Describe your reaction to a movie, concert, or sports event you have attended. Be certain to include the reactions of the other spectators as well.

3. Locate some photographs of your relatives. Describe three of these pictures, working in narrative details that provide insight into the lives of the people you discuss.

4. Visit a local art museum and select a painting that interests you. Observe it carefully, and write an essay-length description of it. Make certain that you decide on a scheme of organization in advance.

5. Select an object that you are familiar with, and write an objective description of it. Include a diagram if you wish.

6. Assume that you are writing a letter to a pen pal in another country who knows little about life in the United States. Describe to this person something that is typically American—a baseball game, Disneyland, or a drive-in movie, for example.

7. Visit your college library, and write an objective description of the reference section. Be specific, and be sure to select an organizing principle before you begin your essay.

8. Describe your neighborhood to a tourist who knows nothing about it. Include as much specific detail as you can.

9. Describe a color to a blind person. Use imaginative comparisons to communicate your ideas to this individual. ("Green is the color of spring," etc.)

10. Select a magazine picture that indicates a suitable subject for a descriptive essay. Write an essay in which you convey a dominant impression of that subject, and work in narrative details to make the subject come alive to the reader. Include an explicit thesis that communicates the dominant impression.

4

Exemplification

What Is Exemplification?

An *example* is a particular case, a concrete instance that supports a more general assertion or concept. In the following paragraph from *Sexism and Language,* Aileen Pace Nilsen uses a number of well-chosen examples to support her assertion that the armed forces use words that have positive male connotations to encourage recruitment.

> The armed forces, particularly the Marines, use the positive masculine connotation as part of their recruitment psychology. They promote the idea that to join the Marines (or the Army, Navy, or Air Force) guarantees that you will become a man. But this brings up a problem, because much of the work that is necessary to keep a large organization running is what is traditionally thought of as *woman's work.* Now, how can the Marines ask someone who has signed up for a *man-sized job* to do *woman's work?* Since they can't, they euphemize and give the jobs titles that are more prestigious or, at least, don't make people think of females. Waitresses are called *orderlies,* secretaries are called *clerk-typists,* nurses are called *medics,* assistants are called *adjutants,* and cleaning up an area is called *policing the area.* The same kind of word glorification is used in civilian life to bolster a man's ego when he is doing such tasks as cooking and sewing. For example, a *chef* has higher prestige than a *cook* and a *tailor* has higher prestige than a *seamstress.*

You have probably noticed, when watching television talk shows or listening to classroom discussions, that the most interesting and persuasive exchanges take place when those involved illustrate their points with specific examples. It is one thing to say, "The mayor is corrupt and should not be reelected," and another to exemplify his corruption by saying, "The mayor should not be reelected because he has fired two city employees who refused to contribute to his campaign fund, put his family and friends on the city payroll, and used public funds to pay for improvements on his home." The same principle applies to writing, and many of the best essays use examples extensively. Exemplification is used in every kind of writing situation, either as a basic essay pattern or in combination with every other pattern of development, to explain, to add interest, and to persuade.

Examples Explain and Clarify

On a film midterm, you might say, "Even though horror movies seem modern, they really are not." You may think your statement is perfectly clear, but do not be surprised when your examination comes back with a question mark in the margin next to this sentence. After all, your statement goes no further than making a general assertion or claim about horror movies. It is not specific, nor does it anticipate a reader's questions about the ways in which horror movies are not modern. Furthermore, it includes no examples, your best means of ensuring clarity and avoiding ambiguity. To make sure your audience knows exactly what you mean, you should state your point precisely: "Despite the fact that horror movies seem modern, the most memorable ones are adaptations of nineteenth-century Gothic novels."

Then, you could illustrate your point thoroughly by discussing specific films like *Frankenstein*, directed by James Whale, and *Dracula*, directed by Todd Browning, and by linking them with the novels on which they are based. With the benefit of these specific examples, a reader would know that you meant that the literary roots of such movies are in the past, not that their cinematic techniques or production methods are dated. Moreover, a reader would understand which literary sources you meant. With these additions, your point would be clear.

Examples Add Interest

The more relevant detail you provide for your readers, the more interesting and appealing your essay will be. Well-chosen examples provide such detail and add life to relatively bland or straightforward statements. Laurence J. Peter and Raymond Hull skillfully use this technique in their essay "The Peter Principle," which appears later in this chapter. In itself, their assertion that each employee in a system rises to his or her level of incompetence is not particularly engaging. It becomes intriguing, however, when supported by specific examples, such as the cases of the affable foreman who becomes the indecisive supervisor, the exacting mechanic who becomes the disorganized foreman, and the charismatic battlefield general who becomes the impotent and self-destructive field marshal.

When you use exemplification to support your assertions, look for examples that are interesting in themselves. Test the effectiveness of your examples by putting yourself in your readers' place. If you would not find your own essay lively and absorbing, you need to rewrite it with more spirited examples. After all, your goal is to communicate your ideas to your readers, and energetic, imaginative examples can make the difference between an engrossing essay and one that is a chore to read.

Examples Persuade

Although you may use examples simply to help explain an idea or to interest or entertain your readers, examples are also an effective way of convincing others that what you are saying is reasonable and true. A few well-chosen examples can eliminate pages of general, and many times unconvincing, explanations. For instance, a statement on an economics quiz that "rising costs and high unemployment have changed life for many Americans" needs support to be convincing. Noting appropriate examples—that in a typical working-class neighborhood one out of every six primary wage earners is now jobless and that many white-collar workers can no longer afford to go to movies or to eat any beef except hamburger—can persuade a reader that the statement is valid. Similarly, a statement in a biology paper that "despite recent moves to reverse its status, DDT should not be released to commercial users and should continue to be banned" is unconvincing without persuasive examples like these to back it up:

- Although DDT has been banned since December 31, 1972, traces are still being found in the eggs of various fish and water fowl.
- Certain lakes and streams cannot be used for sport and recreation because DDT levels are dangerously high, presumably because of farmland runoff.
- DDT has been found in the milk of a significant number of nursing mothers.

- DDT residues, apparently carried by global air currents, have even been found in meltwater samples from Antarctica.
- Because of its stability as a compound, DDT does not degrade quickly; therefore, existent residues will threaten the environment well into the twenty-first century.

Because examples are often necessary to convince, you should consider both the quality and the quantity of your examples when deciding which ones to include in an essay. Keep in mind that for examples to work, they should be concrete illustrations of your thesis; otherwise, they are beside the point and do not act as support.

Examples Test Your Point

Examples can help you test your ideas as well as the ideas of others. For instance, suppose you plan to write a paper for a composition class about the decline in verbal skills of students nationwide. Your thesis is that writing well is an inborn talent and that teachers can do little to help people write better. But is this really true? Has it been true in your own case? To test your point, you go back over your academic career and brainstorm about the various teachers who tried to help you improve your writing.

As you assemble your list, you remember Mrs. Colson, a teacher you had when you were a junior in high school. She was strict, required lots of writing, and seemed to accept nothing less than perfection. At the time neither you nor your classmates liked her; in fact, her nickname was Warden Colson. But looking back, you recall her private conferences, her organized lessons, and her pointed comments. You also remember her careful review of essay tests and realize that after your year with her, you felt much more comfortable taking such tests. After examining some papers that you saved, you are surprised to see how much your writing actually improved that year. These examples cause you to reevaluate your ideas and revise your thesis. You now think that even though the job is difficult, a good teacher can make a difference in a person's writing.

Using Enough Examples

Brief examples are useful because they allow a writer to pile up evidence quickly and to cover a wide range of possibilities. *Extended examples,* because of their greater detail, can add clarity and interest that brief examples sometimes cannot.

Unfortunately, no general rule exists to tell you whether to use one extended example or many brief examples to support your ideas. Simply stated, the number and type of examples you should use depend on your thesis. If, for instance, your thesis is that an educational institution, like a business, needs careful financial management, a detailed consideration of your own school or university could work well. This one extended example could provide all the detail necessary to make your point. In this case, you would not need to include examples from a number of schools. In fact, too many examples could prove tedious to your readers and undercut your points.

On the other hand, if your thesis were that conflict between sons and fathers is a recurrent theme throughout the works of Franz Kafka, several examples would be necessary. One example would show only that the theme of conflict is present in *one* of Kafka's works. In this case, the more examples you include, the more effectively you prove your point. Of course, for some theses even a great number of examples would not be enough. You would, for instance, have a very difficult time finding enough examples to demonstrate convincingly that children from small families have more successful careers than children from large families. This thesis would require a statistical study to prove its validity.

The most common method of developing an exemplification essay is by combining brief and extended examples. This method takes advantage of the strengths of both types.

Selecting a *sufficient range* of examples is just as important as choosing an appropriate number of examples to support your ideas. If you wanted to convince a reader that Douglas MacArthur was an able general, you would choose examples from more than just the early part of his career. Likewise, if you wanted to argue that outdoor advertising was ruining the scenic view from local highways, you would discuss an area larger than your immediate neighborhood. Your object in each case is to select a cross section of examples appropriate for the boundaries of your topic.

Using Representative Examples

Just as professional pollsters take great pains to ensure that their samples actually do reflect the makeup of the general public, you should make sure that your examples fairly represent the total group you are discussing. If you want to propose a ban on smoking in all public buildings, you should not base your supporting points solely on the benefits of such a ban for restaurants. To be convincing, you would have to widen your scope to include other public places such as government office buildings, hospital lobbies, and movie theaters. For the same reason, one person's experience or one school's problems are not sufficient for a conclusion about many others unless you can establish that the experience or problems are typical.

If you decide that you cannot cite enough representative examples to support your point, reexamine your thesis. Rather than switching to a new topic, you may be able to make your thesis narrower. After all, the only way your paper will be convincing is if your readers believe that your examples and your claim about your topic correspond—that your thesis is supported by your examples and that your examples fairly represent the breadth of your topic.

Of course, your essay will be effective not simply because you use examples effectively but because you keep it focused on your point. Careful use of transitional words and phrases can help you reinforce the connection of examples to thesis ("Another example of successful programs for the homeless. . . . "). A constant danger when using examples is that you may get so involved with one that you wander off into a digression. Disregarding your paper's topic in this way not only could confuse your readers but also could render much of your essay irrelevant. No matter how carefully they are developed, no matter how specific, lively, and appropriate they are, all of your examples must address the main idea of your essay.

STRUCTURING AN EXEMPLIFICATION ESSAY

Essays organized around examples usually begin with an introduction that includes the thesis, which is supported by examples in the body of the essay. Each body paragraph develops a separate example, an aspect of an extended example, or a point illustrated by several brief examples. The conclusion restates the thesis and reinforces the main idea of the essay. At times, variations of this basic pattern are advisable, even necessary. For instance, beginning your paper with a striking example might stimulate your reader's interest and curiosity; ending with one might vividly reinforce your thesis.

Exemplification presents one special organizational problem. In an essay of this type, a large number of examples is not unusual. If these examples are not handled properly, your paper could become a thesis followed by a list or by ten or fifteen very brief, choppy paragraphs. One way to avoid this problem is to select your best examples for full development in separate paragraphs and to discard the others. Another way is to gather related examples together and to group them in paragraphs. Within each paragraph, examples could be arranged in order of increasing importance or persuasiveness, to allow your audience's interest to build. The following informal outline for a paper evaluating the nursing care at a local hospital illustrates one way to arrange examples. Notice how well the author groups his examples under four general categories: *private rooms, semiprivate rooms, emergency wards,* and *outpatient clinics.*

Introduction: Thesis—The quality of nursing care at Albert Einstein Hospital is excellent.
Private rooms
  Example 1:   Responsiveness
  Example 2:   Effective rapport established
  Example 3:   Good bedside care
Semiprivate rooms
  Example 4:   Efficient use of time
  Example 5:   Small ratio of nurses to patients
  Example 6:   Patient-centered care
Emergency wards
  Example 7:   Adequate staffing
  Example 8:   Nurses circulating among patients in the waiting room
  Example 9:   Satisfactory working relationship between doctors and nurses
Outpatient clinics
  Example 10:   Nurses preparing patients
  Example 11:   Nurses assisting during treatment
  Example 12:   Nurses instructing patients after treatment
Conclusion: Restatement of thesis

Exemplification is frequently used in nonacademic writing situations; fiscal reports, memos, progress reports, and proposals can be organized this way. One of the more important uses you may make of the exemplification pattern is in applying for a job. Elizabeth Bensley's letter of application to a prospective employer follows this pattern of development.

295 Main Street
Mount Kisco, NY 10549
October 3, 1988

Mr. Steven Seltzer
The Wall Street Journal
420 Lexington Avenue
New York, NY 10017

Dear Mr. Seltzer:

Opening   Please consider my application for the position of   1
management trainee that you advertised in the October
1, 1988 edition of the Wall Street Journal. My
advisor, Dr. David Sutton, who works as an editorial
consultant to the Journal, has inspired much of my
enthusiasm about my field and about this opportunity
Thesis   to work in your business office. I am confident that
my education and my experience qualify me to fulfill
the responsibilities of this job.

Brief examples   I am presently a senior in the College of Business at   2
Drexel University and will graduate with a degree in
management in June. I have completed courses in
accounting, data processing, economics, management,
and communications. In addition, I have taken a
number of computer courses and have a working
knowledge of systems programming. Throughout my
college career, I have maintained a 3.3 average and
have been secretary of the management society.

Major example   During my latest work-study period, I worked in the   3
business office of the Philadelphia Inquirer. I was
responsible for accounts payable and worked closely
with a number of people in the accounting department.
During my six months in this position, I gained a
working knowledge of the IBM Series Minicomputer,
which recorded charges and payments. Eventually my
supervisor, Ms. Nancy Viamonte, put me in charge of
training and supervising two other work-study
students. While at the Inquirer, I developed a
computer program that verified charges and ensured
the prompt disposition and payment of accounts.

Closing   I believe that my education and my work experience   4
make me a good candidate for your position. I have
enclosed a résumé for your convenience and will be
available for an interview any time after midterms on

```
October 15. I look forward to meeting with you to
discuss my qualifications.

                        Sincerely,

                        Elizabeth Bensley
                        Elizabeth Bensley
```

Points for Special Attention

Organization. Exemplification is ideally suited for letters of application. The only way Elizabeth Bensley can persuasively support her claims about her qualifications for the job is to set forth her experience and knowledge. The body of her letter is divided into two categories: educational record and work-study experience. Each of the body paragraphs has a clear purpose and function. Paragraph 2 contains a series of brief examples all having to do with Elizabeth's educational record. Paragraph 3 contains an extended example that deals with her work-study experience. All of these examples are included to tell the prospective employer what qualifies Elizabeth for the job. In these paragraphs, she uses order of importance to arrange not only her claims but also her examples. Although her academic record is important, in this case it is not as significant to an employer as her experience. Because her practical knowledge directly relates to the position she wants, Elizabeth considers this her strongest point and wisely chooses to present it last.

Elizabeth closes her letter with a request for an interview. In it, she not only asserts her willingness to be interviewed but also gives the date after which she will be available. Because people remember best what they read last, a strong conclusion is as essential here as it is in other writing situations.

Persuasive Examples. To support a thesis convincingly, examples should convey specific information, not just judgments. Saying "I am a good student who works hard at her studies" means very little. It is better to say, as Elizabeth Bensley does, "Throughout my college career, I have maintained a 3.3 average." A letter of application should show a prospective employer how your strengths and background correspond to the employer's needs, and specific examples can help such a reader reach the proper conclusions.

The following essay, by Norman Falzone, illustrates a more traditional use of the example pattern. Written for a psychology class, it answers the question, "Is there too much violence on children's television?"

Violence in the Morning

Introduction   In recent years, television networks have come   1
under increasing attack for the violent programs that
fill their schedules. As we discussed in class,
psychologists and communications experts, such as Dr.
George Gerbner at the University of Pennsylvania, have
formulated scales to measure the death and
destruction that comes into American homes daily.
Sociologists have discussed the possible effects of
this situation on the viewing public. One area that
is currently receiving attention is children's

Thesis   television. As even a brief glance at daily cartoon
shows reveals, children are being exposed to a steady
diet of violence that surpasses that of the prime-
time shows their parents so eagerly watch.

Brief examples   Children's cartoons have traditionally contained   2
(background)   much violence, and this situation is something we
have learned to accept as normal. Consider how much a
part of our landscape the following situations are.
The coyote chases the roadrunner and finds himself
standing in midair over a deep chasm. For a fraction
of a second he looks pathetically at the audience;
then he plunges to the ground. Elmer Fudd puts his
shotgun into a tree where Bugs Bunny is hiding. Bugs
bends the barrel so that, when Elmer pulls the
trigger, the gun discharges into his face. A dog
chases Woody Woodpecker into a sawmill and, unable to
stop, slides into the whirling blade of a circular
saw. As the scene ends, the two halves of the dog
fall to the ground with a clatter.

Extended   Where these so-called traditional cartoons   3
example   depict violence as an isolated occurrence, newer
cartoons portray it as a normal condition of life.
"Transformers" is a good example of this. Every
weekday morning, giant robots capable of changing

shape battle renegade robots that seem intent on
ruling the world. Every day the plot stays the same;
only the particulars of combat change. And every day
the message to young viewers is the same: Only by
violent action can the problems of the world be
solved. For it is only when the Transformers use an
exotic array of destructive weapons to force their
adversaries to retreat that the status quo is
reestablished. Neither the robots nor their human
allies ever attempt to negotiate with the enemy
robots or to find a peaceful solution to their
seemingly endless conflict. Oddly enough no one is
ever killed during all this fighting. Although often
damaged during combat robots are repaired easily, and
human characters seem to avoid serious injury
entirely. It would seem that in an effort to avoid
criticism, the producers of this show have succeeded
in presenting combat as a game in which violence has
no lasting effect on those involved.

Extended
Example   Even more shocking is the violence in "G.I.   4
Joe," a thirty-minute cartoon that is, as its title
suggests, a daily battle between the individuals in a
commando unit (the forces of good) and COBRA (the
forces of evil). In this series violence and evil are
ever present, threatening to overwhelm goodness and
right. Each day COBRA, an organization that appears
to operate freely all over the world, destroys
defense installations, blows up power plants, attacks
cities, or somehow challenges the ingenuity of G.I.
Joe. The two sides have apparently fought to a
stalemate. COBRA's desire to rule the world is at the
heart of the conflict. How COBRA started or how it is
able to operate as freely as it does is never fully
explained. In one episode, COBRA scientists discover
a "computer virus" that can destroy any computer in

which it is placed. COBRA plans to inset this virus into all the police computers in the world to wipe out their records. The G.I. Joe commandos fight a pitched battle on the streets of Las Vegas and eventually find and destroy the virus in the computers of a resort hotel. As is the case with "Transformers," human beings are never killed or seriously injured, but the child viewers of the show must know, even though it is not shown, that many people are killed when lasers explode and buildings fall.

Conclusion (restatement of thesis)

Violence on daily children's television is the rule 5 rather than the exception. Few shows, other than those on cable or public television, attempt to go beyond the simplistic formulas that cartoons follow. As a result, children are being shown that violence is superior to reason and that conflict and threats of violent death are normal conditions for existence. In addition, because human beings never get killed in these cartoons, children are encouraged to see war and fighting as harmless. Perhaps the recently convened government commission to study violence on children's television will help end this situation, but until it does parents will continue to shudder each time their children sit down in front of television for a morning of fun.

Points for Special Attention

Organization.   In his introduction, Norman Falzone establishes the context of his remarks and states his thesis. In the body of his essay, Norman presents the examples that support his thesis. In the second paragraph, he begins with a series of short examples of what he calls traditional children's cartoons, those like "The Roadrunner," "Bugs Bunny," and "Woody Woodpecker," that present isolated violent instances rather than unrelieved violence. He then gives examples of contemporary cartoons. In the third paragraph he uses a major example, "Transformers," to illustrate his assertion that newer cartoons portray violence as a normal condition of life. The fourth paragraph presents another major example, "G.I. Joe," to demonstrate further the extent to which violence pervades children's programs. In his conclusion, Norman sums up his points and ends with an emphatic statement.

Enough Examples. Certainly no single example, no matter how graphic, could adequately support the thesis of this essay. To establish that children's television is violent, Norman must use a number of examples. He therefore presents three brief examples in the second paragraph and an extended example in each of the remaining body paragraphs.

By giving several brief examples and by not dwelling on them, Norman suggests that they represent a still larger group of examples he could have used. By examining two major examples at some length, he also shows that his case is broadly based and that he is not just counting TV programs but analyzing them, too.

Representative Examples. Norman is careful to select examples that illustrate the full range of his subject. He draws from traditional cartoons as well as newer ones, and he presents the plots of these cartoons in enough detail to make them clear to his readers. He also makes sure that his examples are representative, that they are typical of daily cartoons. ("Transformers" and "G.I. Joe" were the two most popular cartoon shows when Norman wrote his essay.)

Effective Examples. All of Norman's examples support his thesis. While developing five examples, he never loses sight of his main idea. Each paragraph in the body of his essay directly addresses one aspect of his thesis. His essay does not wander or get bogged down in needlessly long plot summaries or irrelevant digressions.

The selections that appear in this chapter all depend on exemplification to explain and clarify, to add interest, or to persuade. Some essays use single extended examples; others use series of briefer illustrations.

THE PETER PRINCIPLE

Laurence J. Peter and Raymond Hull

Laurence J. Peter is a professor of education at the University of Southern California, and Raymond Hull (1919-1985) was a writer and dramatist. Together they wrote The Peter Principle, *a 1969 book that so dramatically analyzed American organizations that its title has been absorbed into our language. This selection, the first chapter of* The Peter Principle, *presents the book's thesis along with several supporting examples.*

When I was a boy I was taught that the men upstairs knew what they were doing. I was told, "Peter, the more you know, the further you go." So I stayed in school until I graduated from college and then went forth into the world clutching firmly these ideas and my new teaching certificate. During the first year of teaching I was upset to find that a number of teachers, school principals, supervisors and superintendents appeared to be unaware of their professional responsibilities and incompetent in executing their duties. For example my principal's main concerns were that all window shades be at the same level, that classrooms should be quiet and that no one step on or near the rose beds. The superintendent's main concerns were that no minority group, no matter how fanatical, should ever be offended and that all official forms be submitted on time. The children's education appeared farthest from the administrator's mind. 1

At first I thought this was a special weakness of the school system in which I taught so I applied for certification in another province. I filled out the special forms, enclosed the required documents and complied willingly with all the red tape. Several weeks later, back came my application and all the documents! 2

No, there was nothing wrong with my credentials; the forms were correctly filled out; an official departmental stamp showed that they had been received in good order. But an accompanying letter said, "The new regulations require that such forms cannot be accepted by the Department of Education unless they have been registered at the Post Office to ensure safe delivery. Will you please remail the forms to the Department, making sure to register them this time?" 3

I began to suspect that the local school system did not have a   4
monopoly on incompetence.

As I looked further afield, I saw that every organization contained   5
a number of persons who could not do their jobs.

A UNIVERSAL PHENOMENON

Occupational incompetence is everywhere. Have you noticed it?   6
Probably we all have noticed it.

We see indecisive politicians posing as resolute statesmen and the   7
"authoritative source" who blames his misinformation on "situa-
tional imponderables." Limitless are the public servants who are indolent and insolent; military commanders whose behavioral timidity
belies their dreadnought rhetoric, and governors whose innate ser-
vility prevents their actually governing. In our sophistication, we
virtually shrug aside the immoral cleric, corrupt judge, incoherent
attorney, author who cannot write and English teacher who cannot
spell. At universities we see proclamations authored by administrators whose own office communications are hopelessly muddled, and
droning lectures from inaudible or incomprehensible instructors.

Seeing incompetence at all levels of every hierarchy—political, le-   8
gal, educational and industrial—I hypothesized that the cause was
some inherent feature of the rules governing the placement of employees. Thus began my serious study of the ways in which employees move upward through a hierarchy, and of what happens to them
after promotion.

For my scientific data hundreds of case histories were collected.   9
Here are three typical examples.

Municipal Government File, Case No. 17. J. S. Minion[1] was a   10
maintenance foreman in the public works department of Excelsior
City. He was a favorite of the senior officials at City Hall. They all
praised his unfailing affability.

"I like Minion," said the superintendent of works. "He has good   11
judgment and is always pleasant and agreeable."

This behavior was appropriate for Minion's position: he was not   12
supposed to make policy, so he had no need to disagree with his
superiors.

The superintendent of works retired and Minion succeeded him.   13
Minion continued to agree with everyone. He passed to his foreman

---

[1]Some names have been changed, in order to protect the guilty.

every suggestion that came from above. The resulting conflicts in policy, and the continual changing of plans, soon demoralized the department. Complaints poured in from the Mayor and other officials, from taxpayers and from the maintenance-workers' union.

Minion still says "Yes" to everyone, and carries messages briskly [14] back and forth between his superiors and his subordinates. Nominally a superintendent, he actually does the work of a messenger. The maintenance department regularly exceeds its budget, yet fails to fulfill its program of work. In short, Minion, a competent foreman, became an incompetent superintendent.

Service Industries File, Case No. 3. E. Tinker was exceptionally [15] zealous and intelligent as an apprentice at G. Reece Auto Repair Inc., and soon rose to journeyman mechanic. In this job he showed outstanding ability in diagnosing obscure faults, and endless patience in correcting them. He was promoted to foreman of the repair shop.

But here his love of things mechanical and his perfectionism be- [16] came liabilities. He will undertake any job that he thinks looks interesting, no matter how busy the shop may be. "We'll work it in somehow," he says.

He will not let a job go until he is fully satisfied with it. [17]

He meddles constantly. He is seldom to be found at his desk. He [18] is usually up to his elbows in a dismantled motor and while the man who should be doing the work stands watching, other workmen sit around waiting to be assigned new tasks. As a result the shop is always overcrowded with work, always in a muddle, and delivery times are often missed.

Tinker cannot understand that the average customer cares little [19] about perfection—he wants his car back on time! He cannot understand that most of his men are less interested in motors than in their pay checks. So Tinker cannot get on with his customers or with his subordinates. He was a competent mechanic, but is now an incompetent foreman.

Military File, Case No. 8. Consider the case of the late renowned [20] General A. Goodwin. His hearty, informal manner, his racy style of speech, his scorn for petty regulations and his undoubted personal bravery made him the idol of his men. He led them to many well-deserved victories.

When Goodwin was promoted to field marshal he had to deal, not [21] with ordinary soldiers, but with politicians and allied generalissimos.

He would not conform to the necessary protocol. He could not 22
turn his tongue to the conventional courtesies and flatteries. He
quarreled with all the dignitaries and took to lying for days at a
time, drunk and sulking, in his trailer. The conduct of the war
slipped out of his hands into those of his subordinates. He had been
promoted to a position that he was incompetent to fill.

AN IMPORTANT CLUE!

In time I saw that all such cases had a common feature. The em- 23
ployee had been promoted from a position of competence to a position of incompetence. I saw that, sooner or later, this could happen
to every employee in every hierarchy.

Hypothetical Case File, Case No. 1. Suppose you own a pill-rolling 24
factory, Perfect Pill Incorporated. Your foreman pill roller dies of a
perforated ulcer. You need a replacement. You naturally look among
your rank-and-file pill rollers.

Miss Oval, Mrs. Cylinder, Mr. Ellipse and Mr. Cube all show var- 25
ious degrees of incompetence. They will naturally be ineligible for
promotion. You will choose—other things being equal—your most
competent pill roller, Mr. Sphere, and promote him to foreman.

Now suppose Mr. Sphere proves competent as foreman. Later, 26
when your general foreman, Legree, moves up to Works Manager,
Sphere will be eligible to take his place.

If, on the other hand, Sphere is an incompetent foreman, he will 27
get no more promotion. He has reached what I call his "level of incompetence." He will stay there till the end of his career.

Some employees, like Ellipse and Cube, reach a level of incompe- 28
tence in the lowest grade and are never promoted. Some, like Sphere
(assuming he is not a satisfactory foreman), reach it after one promotion.

E. Tinker, the automobile repair-shop foreman, reached his level of 29
incompetence on the third stage of the hierarchy. General Goodwin
reached his level of incompetence at the very top of the hierarchy.

So my analysis of hundreds of cases of occupational incompetence 30
led me on to formulate *The Peter Principle:*

In a Hierarchy Every Employee Tends
to Rise to His Level of Incompetence

A NEW SCIENCE!

Having formulated the Principle, I discovered that I had inadvert- 31
ently founded a new science, hierarchiology, the study of hierarchies.

The term "hierarchy" was originally used to describe the system 32
of church government by priests graded into ranks. The contemporary meaning includes any organization whose members or employees are arranged in order of rank, grade or class.

Hierarchiology, although a relatively recent discipline, appears to 33
have great applicability to the fields of public and private administration.

THIS MEANS YOU!

My Principle is the key to an understanding of all hierarchal sys- 34
tems, and therefore to an understanding of the whole structure of
civilization. A few eccentrics try to avoid getting involved with hierarchies, but everyone in business, industry, trade-unionism, politics,
government, the armed forces, religion and education is so involved.
All of them are controlled by the Peter Principle.

Many of them, to be sure, may win a promotion or two, moving 35
from one level of competence to a higher level of competence. But
competence in that new position qualifies them for still another promotion. For each individual, for *you*, for *me*, the final promotion is
from a level of competence to a level of incompetence.[1]

So, given enough time—and assuming the existence of enough 36
ranks in the hierarchy—each employee rises to, and remains at, his
level of incompetence. Peter's Corollary states:

In time, every post tends to be occupied by an employee who is incom- 37
petent to carry out its duties.

WHO TURNS THE WHEELS?

You will rarely find, of course, a system in which *every* employee 38
has reached his level of incompetence. In most instances, something
is being done to further the ostensible purposes for which the hierarchy exists.

---

[1]The phenomena of "percussive sublimation" (commonly referred to as "being
kicked upstairs") and of "the lateral arabesque" are not, as the casual observer might
think, exceptions to the Principle. They are only pseudo-promotions. . . .

Work is accomplished by those employees who have not yet reached   39
their level of incompetence.

COMPREHENSION

1. What things disillusioned Laurence Peter during his first year of teaching?

2. What did Peter find out about organizations?

3. What is the Peter Principle? What happens when an employee reaches his "level of incompetence"?

4. What does Peter mean by *hierarchiology?* How did hierarchiology lead him to the Peter Principle?

5. If the Peter Principle operates in hierarchies, who does the work?

PURPOSE AND AUDIENCE

1. Is this essay aimed at a general or a specialized audience? What led you to your conclusion?

2. What is the essay's thesis?

3. The authors place their thesis after the examples. Why do they wait so long to state it?

4. How serious are the authors? What words or phrases indicate whether their purpose is humorous, or serious, or something of both?

STYLE AND STRUCTURE

1. Why do the authors begin the essay with an example? Why do they present a series of brief examples before introducing the "typical case histories"?

2. Why does Peter say he collected hundreds of case histories for data? Why are the three case histories analyzed here typical?

3. Do the authors use brief examples, extended examples, or a combination of both? Why?

4. Does the reliance on hypothetical examples strengthen or weaken the authors' case? Explain.

5. Do the authors use a sufficient range of examples? Explain.

VOCABULARY PROJECTS

1. Define each of the following words as it is used in this selection.

   imponderables (7)   hierarchy (8)
   indolent (7)   minion (10)
   insolent (7)   dismantled (18)
   dreadnought (7)   protocol (22)
   inaudible (7)   subordinates (22)
   incomprehensible (7)   eccentrics (34)
   hypothesized (8)   ostensible (38)

2. Use your college dictionary to find the histories of five of the above words. Write a paragraph summarizing your findings about one word.

3. Do the authors use figurative language in their discussion? Why do they choose to do what they do?

WRITING WORKSHOP

1. Does Laurence Peter overstate his case? Write a letter to him in the form of an exemplification essay pointing out the weaknesses of his position.

2. Study a school, business, or organization with which you are familiar. Write an exemplification essay showing how the Peter Principle applies.

3. Do you know someone who has progressed to the highest level of his or her incompetence? Write an exemplification essay showing how the Peter Principle applies.

THEMATIC CONNECTIONS

- "My Mother Never Worked" (p. 64)
- "The Company Man" (p. 440)

THE PATTERNS OF EATING

PETER FARB AND GEORGE ARMELAGOS

*Peter Farb (1929–1980), naturalist and articulate spokesperson for
conservation, published numerous articles on a variety of aspects
of the sciences and social sciences. He was also the author of* Man's
Rise to Civilization: The Cultural Ascent of the Indians of North
America, Ecology, *and most recently,* Humankind. *George Armelagos is a professor of anthropology at the University of Massachusetts at Amherst. In this essay excerpted from their 1983 book,*
Consuming Passions: The Anthropology of Eating, *they examine
social attitudes as revealed through changes in table manners. To
support their assertions they offer a wide variety of examples from
different historical periods.*

Among the important societal rules that represent one component 1
of cuisine are table manners. As a socially instilled form of conduct,
they reveal the attitudes typical of a society. Changes in table manners through time, as they have been documented for western Europe, likewise reflect fundamental changes in human relationships.
Medieval courtiers saw their table manners as distinguishing them
from crude peasants; but by modern standards, the manners were
not exactly refined. Feudal lords used their unwashed hands to
scoop food from a common bowl and they passed around a single
goblet from which all drank. A finger or two would be extended
while eating, so as to be kept free of grease and thus available for
the next course, or for dipping into spices and condiments—possibly
accounting for today's "polite" custom of extending the finger while
holding a spoon or small fork. Soups and sauces were commonly
drunk by lifting the bowl to the mouth; several diners frequently ate
from the same bread trencher. Even lords and nobles would toss
gnawed bones back into the common dish, wolf down their food, spit
onto the table (preferred conduct called for spitting under it), and
blew their noses into the tablecloth.

By about the beginning of the sixteenth century, table manners 2
began to move in the direction of today's standards. The importance
attached to them is indicated by the phenomenal success of a treatise, *On Civility in Children,* by the philosopher Erasmus, which appeared in 1530; reprinted more than thirty times in the next six

years, it also appeared in numerous translations. Erasmus' idea of good table manners was far from modern, but it did represent an advance. He believed, for example, that an upper class diner was distinguished by putting only three fingers of one hand into the bowl, instead of the entire hand in the manner of the lower class. Wait a few moments after being seated before you dip into it, he advises. Do not poke around in your dish, but take the first piece you touch. Do not put chewed food from the mouth back on your place; instead, throw it under the table or behind your chair.

By the time of Erasmus, the changing table manners reveal a fun-   3
damental shift in society. People no longer ate from the same dish or drank from the same goblet, but were divided from one another by a new wall of constraint. Once the spontaneous, direct, and infor-mal manners of the Middle Ages had been repressed, people began to feel shame. Defecation and urination were now regarded as pri-vate activities; handkerchiefs came into use for blowing the nose; nightclothes were now worn, and bedrooms were set apart as private areas. Before the sixteenth century, even nobles ate in their vast kitchens; only then did a special room designated for eating come into use away from the bloody sides of meat, the animals about to be slaughtered, and the bustling servants. These new inhibitions be-came the essence of "civilized" behavior, distinguishing adults from children, the upper classes from the lower, and Europeans from the "savages" then being discovered around the world. Restraint in eating habits became more marked in the centuries that followed. By about 1800, napkins were in common use, and before long they were placed on the thighs rather than wrapped around the neck; cof-fee and tea were no longer slurped out of the saucer; bread was gen-teelly broken into small pieces with the fingers rather than cut into large chunks with a knife.

Numerous paintings that depict meals—with subjects such as the   4
Last Supper, the wedding at Cana, or Herod's feast—show what din-ing tables looked like before the seventeenth century. Forks were not depicted until about 1600 (when Jacopo Bassano painted one in a Last Supper), and very few spoons were shown. At least one knife is always depicted—an especially large one when it is the only one available for all the guests—but small individual knives were often at each place. Tin disks or oval pieces of wood had already replaced the bread trenchers. This change in eating utensils typified the new table manners in Europe. (In many other parts of the world, no uten-sils at all were used. In the Near East, for example, it was traditional to bring food to the mouth with the fingers of the right hand, the left being unacceptable because it was reserved for wiping the buttocks.) Utensils were employed in part because of a change in the attitude

toward meat. During the Middle Ages, whole sides of meat, or even an entire dead animal, had been brought to the table and then carved in view of the diners. Beginning in the seventeenth century, at first in France but later elsewhere, the practice began to go out of fashion. One reason was that the family was ceasing to be a production unit that did its own slaughtering; as that function was transferred to specialists outside the home, the family became essentially a consumption unit. In addition, the size of the family was decreasing, and consequently whole animals, or even large parts of them, were uneconomical. The cuisines of Europe reflected these social and economic changes. The animal origin of meat dishes was concealed by the arts of preparation. Meat itself became distasteful to look upon, and carving was moved out of sight to the kitchen. Comparable changes had already taken place in Chinese cuisine, with meat being cut up beforehand, unobserved by the diners. England was an exception to the change in Europe, and in its former colonies—the United States, Canada, Australia, and South Africa—the custom has persisted of bringing a joint of meat to the table to be carved.

Once carving was no longer considered a necessary skill among 5 the well-bred, changes inevitably took place in the use of the knife, unquestionably the earliest utensil used for manipulating food. (In fact, the earliest English cookbooks were not so much guides to recipes as guides to carving meat.) The attitude of diners toward the knife, going back to the Middle Ages and the Renaissance, had always been ambivalent. The knife served as a utensil, but it offered a potential threat because it was also a weapon. Thus taboos were increasingly placed upon its use: It was to be held by the point with the blunt handle presented; it was not to be placed anywhere near the face; and most important, the uses to which it was put were sharply restricted. It was not to be used for cutting soft foods such as boiled eggs or fish, or round ones such as potatoes, or to be lifted from the table for courses that did not need it. In short, good table manners in Europe gradually removed the threatening aspect of the knife from social occasions. A similar change had taken place much earlier in China when the warrior was supplanted by the scholar as a cultural model. The knife was banished completely from the table in favor of chopsticks, which is why the Chinese came to regard Europeans as barbarians at their table who "eat with swords."

The fork in particular enabled Europeans to separate themselves 6 from the eating process, even avoiding manual contact with their food. When the fork first appeared in Europe, toward the end of the Middle Ages, it was used solely as an instrument for lifting chunks from the common bowl. Beginning in the sixteenth century, the fork was increasingly used by members of the upper classes—first in Italy, then in France, and finally in Germany and England. By then, social relations in western Europe had so changed that a utensil was needed to spare diners from the "uncivilized" and distasteful necessity of picking up food and putting it into the mouth with the fingers. The addition of the fork to the table was once said to be for reasons of hygiene, but this cannot be true. By the sixteenth century people were no longer eating from a common bowl but from their own plates, and since they also washed their hands before meals, their fingers were now every bit as hygienic as a fork would have been. Nor can the reason for the adoption of the fork be connected with the wish not to soil the long ruff that was worn on the sleeve at the time, since the fork was also adopted in various countries where ruffs were not then in fashion.

Along with the appearance of the fork, all table utensils began to change and proliferate from the sixteenth century onward. Soup was no longer eaten directly from the dish, but each diner used an individual spoon for that purpose. When a diner wanted a second helping from the serving dish, a ladle or a fresh spoon was used. More and more special utensils were developed for each kind of food: soup spoons, oyster forks, salad forks, two-tined fondue forks, blunt butter knives, special utensils for various desserts and kinds of fruit, each one differently shaped, of a different size, with differently numbered prongs and with blunt or serrated edges. The present European pattern eventually emerged, in which each person is provided with a table setting of as many as a dozen utensils at a full-course meal. With that, the separation of the human body from the taking of food became virtually complete. Good table manners dictated that even the cobs of maize were to be held by prongs inserted in each end, and the bones of lamb chops covered by ruffled paper pantalettes. Only under special conditions—as when Western people consciously imitate an earlier stage in culture at a picnic, fish fry, cookout, or campfire—do they still tear food apart with their fingers and their teeth, in a nostalgic reenactment of eating behaviors long vanished. 7

Today's neighborhood barbecue recreates a world of sharing and hospitality that becomes rarer each year. We regard as a curiosity the behavior of hunters in exotic regions. But every year millions of North Americans take to the woods and lakes to kill a wide variety of animals—with a difference, of course: What hunters do for survival we do for sport (and also for proof of masculinity, for male bonding, and for various psychological rewards). Like hunters, too, we stuff ourselves almost whenever food is available. Nibbling on a roasted ear of maize gives us, in addition to nutrients, the satisfac- 8 tion of participating in culturally simpler ways. A festive meal, however, is still thought of in Victorian terms, with the dominant male officiating over the roast, the dominant female apportioning vegetables, the extended family gathered around the table, with everything in its proper place—a revered picture, as indeed it was so painted by Norman Rockwell, yet one that becomes less accurate with each year that passes.

COMPREHENSION

1. According to the authors, what do table manners reveal about a society?

2. At what point in time did table manners move toward today's standards of acceptable behavior? What did this shift indicate about society?

3. In what ways did the table manners of the sixteenth century differ from those of the Middle Ages?

4. How did forks separate Europeans from the eating process?

5. What do the authors feel is the significance of the neighborhood barbecue?

PURPOSE AND AUDIENCE

1. What is the thesis of this selection? Why do the authors state it almost immediately?

2. Is the authors' purpose to instruct, satirize, or entertain? How does their attitude toward modern table manners suggest this purpose?

3. What assumptions do the authors make about their audience's knowledge of the subject? Explain.

STYLE AND STRUCTURE

1. How effective is the introduction to this selection? What strategies do the authors use to arouse reader interest?

2. What major examples do the authors use to support their case?

3. Why do the authors group certain examples together?

4. Do the authors present enough examples to establish their case? Do they offer readers a sufficient range of examples? Are any of the examples irrelevant? Explain.

5. What transitional words and phrases do the authors use to make sure that readers are able to follow the selection's progress from one historical period to the next?

6. What concluding strategy do the authors use in their last paragraph? Why do they mention the conventions of a Victorian meal?

VOCABULARY PROJECTS

1. Define each of the following words as it is used in this selection.

   societal (1)   ruff (6)
   feudal (1)   tine (7)
   condiments (1)   pantalettes (7)
   trencher (1)   apportioning (8)
   treatise (2)

2. In several instances the authors use sarcasm to make a point. Find one example of this technique and discuss how it enables the authors to make their point.

3. Rewrite paragraph 4, substituting your own adjectives for those of the authors to convey your attitude toward sixteenth-century table manners.

WRITING WORKSHOP

1. Write an essay in which you give examples of modern table manners as observed at a typical dinner or a holiday meal with your family.

2. Write an exemplification essay in which you draw from your own experience to support the authors' assertion that table manners reveal the attitudes typical of a society.

3. Write a humorous essay in which you show that your table manners (or those of a friend) are similar to those in practice during the sixteenth century. Be specific, referring to Farb and Armelagos's selection for examples.

THEMATIC CONNECTIONS

- "The Embalming of Mr. Jones" (p. 236)
- "Three Kinds of Discipline" (p. 391)

THE HUMAN COST
OF AN ILLITERATE SOCIETY

Jonathan Kozol

Jonathan Kozol has taught at Yale University and South Boston High School. His books include Death at an Early Age *(1967), which won a National Book Award;* Free Schools *(1972);* The Night Is Dark *(1980); and* On Being a Teacher *(1981). His most recent work is* Rachel and Her Children: Homeless Families in America *(1988). Kozol has been awarded grants from the Guggenheim, Ford, and Rockefeller Foundations. In* Illiterate America *(1985), he discusses the human and financial costs of illiteracy in America, pointing out that more than 35 million people read below the level needed to function in this society and that, in certain cities, almost forty percent of the adult population is functionally illiterate. The following essay is from* Illiterate America *and uses examples to convey to readers what it means to be illiterate in America.*

PRECAUTIONS. READ BEFORE USING.
Poison: Contains sodium hydroxide (caustic soda-lye).
Corrosive: Causes severe eye and skin damage, may cause blindness.
Harmful or fatal if swallowed.
If swallowed, give large quantities of milk or water.
Do not induce vomiting.
Important: Keep water out of can at all times to prevent contents
from violently erupting . . .

—warning on a can of Drano

Questions of literacy, in Socrates' belief, must at length be judged 1
as matters of morality. Socrates could not have had in mind the
moral compromise peculiar to a nation like our own. Some of our
Founding Fathers did, however, have this question in their minds.
One of the wisest of those Founding Fathers (one who may not have
been most compassionate but surely was more prescient than some
of his peers) recognized the special dangers that illiteracy would
pose to basic equity in the political construction that he helped to
shape.

"A people who mean to be their own governors," James Madison 2
wrote, "must arm themselves with the power knowledge gives. A

173

popular government without popular information or the means of acquiring it, is but a prologue to a farce or a tragedy, or perhaps both."

Tragedy looms larger than farce in the United States today. Illiterate citizens seldom vote. Those who do are forced to cast a vote of questionable worth. They cannot make informed decisions based on serious print information. Sometimes they can be alerted to their interests by aggressive voter education. More frequently, they vote for a face, a smile, or a style, not for a mind or character or body of beliefs.   3

The number of illiterate adults exceeds by 16 million the entire vote cast for the winner in the 1980 presidential contest. If even one third of all illiterates could vote, and read enough and do sufficient math to vote in their self-interest, Ronald Reagan would not likely have been chosen president. There is, of course, no way to know for sure. We do know this: Democracy is a mendacious term when used by those who are prepared to countenance the forced exclusion of one third of our electorate. So long as 60 million people are denied significant participation, the government is neither of, nor for, nor by, the people. It is a government, at best, of those two thirds whose wealth, skin color, or parental privilege allows them opportunity to profit from the provocation and instruction of the written word.   4

The undermining of democracy in the United States is one "expense" that sensitive Americans can easily deplore because it represents a contradiction that endangers citizens of all political positions. The human price is not so obvious at first.   5

Since I first immersed myself within this work I have often had the following dream: I find that I am in a railroad station or a large department store within a city that is utterly unknown to me and where I cannot understand the printed words. None of the signs or symbols is familiar. Everything looks strange: like mirror writing of some kind. Gradually I understand that I am in the Soviet Union. All the letters on the walls around me are Cyrillic. I look for my pocket dictionary but I find that it has been mislaid. Where have I left it? Then I recall that I forgot to bring it with me when I packed my bags in Boston. I struggle to remember the name of my hotel. I try to ask somebody for directions. One person stops and looks at me in a peculiar way. I lose the nerve to ask. At last I reach into my wallet for an ID card. The card is missing. Have I lost it? Then I remember that my card was confiscated for some reason, many years before. Around this point, I wake up in a panic.   6

This panic is not so different from the misery that millions of   7 adult illiterates experience each day within the course of their routine existence in the U.S.A.

Illiterates cannot read the menu in a restaurant.   8

They cannot read the cost of items on the menu in the *window* of   9
the restaurant before they enter.

Illiterates cannot read the letters that their children bring home   10
from their teachers. They cannot study school department circulars
that tell them of the courses that their children must be taking if
they hope to pass the SAT exams. They cannot help with homework.
They cannot write a letter to the teacher. They are afraid to visit in
the classroom. They do not want to humiliate their child or themselves.

Illiterates cannot read instructions on a bottle of prescription   11
medicine. They cannot find out when a medicine is past the year of
safe consumption; nor can they read of allergenic risks, warnings to
diabetics, or the potential sedative effect of certain kinds of nonprescription pills. They cannot observe preventive health care admonitions. They cannot read about "the seven warning signs of cancer"
or the indications of blood-sugar fluctuations or the risks of eating
certain foods that aggravate the likelihood of cardiac arrest.

Illiterates live, in more than literal ways, an uninsured existence.   12
They cannot understand the written details on a health insurance
form. They cannot read the waivers that they sign preceding surgical procedures. Several women I have known in Boston have
entered a slum hospital with the intention of obtaining a tubal ligation and have emerged a few days later after having been subjected
to a hysterectomy. Unaware of their rights, incognizant of jargon,
intimidated by the unfamiliar air of fear and atmosphere of ether
that so many of us find oppressive in the confines even of the most
attractive and expensive medical facilities, they have signed their
names to documents they could not read and which nobody, in the
hectic situation that prevails so often in those overcrowded hospitals that serve the urban poor, had even bothered to explain.

Childbirth might seem to be the last inalienable right of any fe-   13
male citizen within a civilized society. Illiterate mothers, as we shall
see, already have been cheated of the power to protect their progeny
against the likelihood of demolition in deficient public schools and,
as a result, against the verbal servitude within which they themselves exist. Surgical denial of the right to bear that child in the first
place represents an ultimate denial, an unspeakable metaphor, a final darkness that denies even the twilight gleamings of our own humanity. What greater violation of our biological, our biblical, our

spiritual humanity could possibly exist than that which takes place nightly, perhaps hourly these days, within such over-burdened and benighted institutions as the Boston City Hospital? Illiteracy has many costs; few are so irreversible as this.

Even the roof above one's head, the gas or other fuel for heating 14 that protects the residents of northern city slums against the threat of illness in the winter months become uncertain guarantees. Illiterates cannot read the lease that they must sign to live in an apartment which, too often, they cannot afford. They cannot manage check accounts and therefore seldom pay for anything by mail. Hours and entire days of difficult travel (and the cost of bus or other public transit) must be added to the real cost of whatever they consume. Loss of interest on the check accounts they do not have, and could not manage if they did, must be regarded as another of the excess costs paid by the citizen who is excluded from the common instruments of commerce in a numerate society.

"I couldn't understand the bills," a woman in Washington, D.C., 15 reports, "and then I couldn't write the checks to pay them. We signed things we didn't know what they were."

Illiterates cannot read the notices that they receive from welfare 16 offices or from the IRS. They must depend on word-of-mouth instruction from the welfare worker—or from other persons whom they have good reason to mistrust. They do not know what rights they have, what deadlines and requirements they face, what options they might choose to exercise. They are half-citizens. Their rights exist in print but not in fact.

Illiterates cannot look up numbers in a telephone directory. Even 17 if they can find the names of friends, few possess the sorting skills to make use of the yellow pages; categories are bewildering and trade names are beyond decoding capabilities for millions of non-readers. Even the emergency numbers listed on the first page of the phone book—"Ambulance," "Police," and "Fire"—are too frequently beyond the recognition of nonreaders.

Many illiterates cannot read the admonition on a pack of ciga- 18 rettes. Neither the Surgeon General's warning nor its reproduction on the package can alert them to the risks. Although most people learn by word of mouth that smoking is related to a number of grave physical disorders, they do not get the chance to read the detailed stories which can document this danger with the vividness that turns concern into determination to resist. They can see the handsome cowboy or the slim Virginia lady lighting up a filter cigarette; they cannot heed the words that tell them that this product is (not "may be") dangerous to their health. Sixty million men and women are condemned to be the unalerted, high-risk candidates for cancer.

Illiterates do not buy "no-name" products in the supermarkets. They must depend on photographs or the familiar logos that are printed on the packages of brand-name groceries. The poorest people, therefore, are denied the benefits of the least costly products.

Illiterates depend almost entirely upon label recognition. Many labels, however, are not easy to distinguish. Dozens of different kinds of Campbell's soup appear identical to the nonreader. The purchaser who cannot read and does not dare to ask for help, out of the fear of being stigmatized (a fear which is unfortunately realistic), frequently comes home with something which she never wanted and her family never tasted.

Illiterates cannot read instructions on a pack of frozen food. Packages sometimes provide an illustration to explain the cooking preparations; but illustrations are of little help to someone who must "boil water, drop the food—*within* its plastic wrapper—in the boiling water, wait for it to simmer, instantly remove."

Even when labels are seemingly clear, they may be easily mistaken. A woman in Detroit brought home a gallon of Crisco for her children's dinner. She thought that she had bought the chicken that was pictured on the label. She had enough Crisco now to last a year—but no more money to go back and buy the food for dinner.

Recipes provided on the packages of certain staples sometimes tempt a semiliterate person to prepare a meal her children have not tasted. The longing to vary the uniform and often starchy content of low-budget meals provided to the family that relies on food stamps commonly leads to ruinous results. Scarce funds have been wasted and the food must be thrown out. The same applies to distribution of food-surplus produce in emergency conditions. Government inducements to poor people to "explore the ways" by which to make a tasty meal from tasteless noodles, surplus cheese, and powdered milk are useless to nonreaders. Intended as benevolent advice, such recommendations mock reality and foster deeper feelings of resentment and of inability to cope. (Those, on the other hand, who cautiously refrain from "innovative" recipes in preparation of their children's meals must suffer the opprobrium of "laziness," "lack of imagination. . . . ")

Illiterates cannot travel freely. When they attempt to do so, they encounter risks that few of us can dream of. They cannot read traffic signs and, while they often learn to recognize and to decipher symbols, they cannot manage street names which they haven't seen before. The same is true for bus and subway stops. While ingenuity can sometimes help a man or woman to discern directions from familiar landmarks, buildings, cemeteries, churches, and the like, most illiterates are virtually immobilized. They seldom wander past the streets and neighborhoods they know. Geographical paralysis becomes a bitter metaphor for their entire existence. They are immobilized in almost every sense we can imagine. They can't move up. They can't move out. They cannot see beyond. Illiterates may take an oral test for drivers' permits in most sections of America. It is a questionable concession. Where will they go? How will they get there? How will they get home? Could it be that some of us might like it better if they stayed where they belong?

Travel is only one of many instances of circumscribed existence.   25
Choice, in almost all its facets, is diminished in the life of an illiterate adult. Even the printed TV schedule, which provides most people with the luxury of preselection, does not belong within the arsenal of options in illiterate existence. One consequence is that the viewer watches only what appears at moments when he happens to have time to turn the switch. Another consequence, a lot more common, is that the TV set remains in operation night and day. Whatever the program offered at the hour when he walks into the room will be the nutriment that he accepts and swallows. Thus, to passivity, is added frequency—indeed, almost uninterrupted continuity. Freedom to select is no more possible here than in the choice of home or surgery or food.

"You don't choose," said one illiterate woman. "You take your   26
wishes from somebody else." Whether in perusal of a menu, selection of highways, purchase of groceries, or determination of affordable enjoyment, illiterate Americans must trust somebody else: a friend, a relative, a stranger on the street, a grocery clerk, a TV copywriter.

"All of our mail we get, it's hard for her to read. Settin' down and   27
writing a letter, she can't do it. Like if we get a bill . . . we take it over to my sister-in-law . . . My sister-in-law reads it."

Billing agencies harass poor people for the payment of the bills   28
for purchases that might have taken place six months before. Utility companies offer an agreement for a staggered payment schedule on a bill past due. "You have to trust them," one man said. Precisely for this reason, you end up by trusting no one and suspecting everyone of possible deceit. A submerged sense of distrust becomes the corollary to a constant need to trust. "They are cheating me . . . I have been tricked . . . I do not know . . . "

Not knowing: This is a familiar theme. Not knowing the right   29
word for the right thing at the right time is one form of subjugation.
Not knowing the world that lies concealed behind those words is a
more terrifying feeling. The longitude and latitude of one's existence
are beyond all easy apprehension. Even the hard, cold stars within
the firmament above one's head begin to mock the possibilities for
self-location. Where am I? Where did I come from? Where will I go?

"I've lost a lot of jobs," one man explains. "Today, even if you're   30
a janitor, there's still reading and writing . . . They leave a note saying, 'Go to room so-and-so . . . ' You can't do it. You can't read it.
You don't know."

"The hardest thing about it is that I've been places where I didn't   31
know where I was. You don't know where you are . . . You're lost."

"Like I said: I have two kids. What do I do if one of my kids starts   32
choking? I go running to the phone . . . I can't look up the hospital
phone number. That's if we're at home. Out on the street, I can't
read the sign. I get to a pay phone. 'Okay, tell us where you are.
We'll send an ambulance.' I look at the street sign. Right there, I
can't tell you what it says. I'd have to spell it out, letter for letter.
By that time, one of my kids would be dead . . . These are the kinds
of fears you go with, every single day . . . "

"Reading directions, I suffer with. I work with chemicals . . .   33
That's scary to begin with . . . "

"You sit down. They throw the menu in front of you. Where do   34
you go from there? Nine times out of ten you say, 'Go ahead. Pick
out something for the both of us.' I've eaten some weird things, let
me tell you!"

Menus. Chemicals. A child choking while his mother searches for   35
a word she does not know to find assistance that will come too late.
Another mother speaks about the inability to help her kids to read:
"I can't read to them. Of course that's leaving them out of something they should have. Oh, it matters. You *believe* it matters! I
ordered all these books. The kids belong to a book club. Donny
wanted me to read a book to him. I told Donny: 'I can't read,' He
said: 'Mommy, you sit down. I'll read it to you.' I tried it one day,
reading from the pictures. Donny looked at me. He said, 'Mommy,
that's not right.' He's only five. He knew I couldn't read . . . "

A landlord tells a woman that her lease allows him to evict her if   36
her baby cries and causes inconvenience to her neighbors. The consequence of challenging his words conveys a danger which appears,
unlikely as it seems, even more alarming than the danger of eviction.
Once she admits that she can't read, in the desire to maneuver for
the time in which to call a friend, she will have defined herself in

terms of an explicit impotence that she cannot endure. Capitulation in this case is preferable to self-humiliation. Resisting the definition of oneself in terms of what one cannot do, what others take for granted, represents a need so great that other imperatives (even one so urgent as the need to keep one's home in winter's cold) evaporate and fall away in face of fear. Even the loss of home and shelter, in this case, is not so terrifying as the loss of self.

"I come out of school. I was sixteen. They had their meetings. The 37 directors meet. They said that I was wasting their school paper. I was wasting pencils . . . "

Another illiterate, looking back, believes she was not worthy of 38 her teacher's time. She believes that it was wrong of her to take up space within her school. She believes that it was right to leave in order that somebody more deserving could receive her place.

Children choke. Their mother chokes another way: on more than 39 chicken bones.

People eat what others order, know what others tell them, struggle 40 not to see themselves as they believe the world perceives them. A man in California speaks about his own loss of identity, of self-location, definition:

"I stood at the bottom of the ramp. My car had broke down on 41 the freeway. There was a phone. I asked for the police. They was nice. They said to tell them where I was. I looked up at the signs. There was one that I had seen before. I read it to them: ONE WAY STREET. They thought it was a joke. I told them I couldn't read. There was other signs above the ramp. They told me to try. I looked around for somebody to help. All the cars was going by real fast. I couldn't make them understand that I was lost. The cop was nice. He told me: 'Try once more.' I did my best. I couldn't read. I only knew the sign above my head. The cop was trying to be nice. He knew that I was trapped. 'I can't send out a car to you if you can't tell me where you are.' I felt afraid. I nearly cried. I'm forty-eight years old. I only said: 'I'm on a one-way street . . . ' "

The legal problems and the courtroom complications that confront 42 illiterate adults have been discussed above. The anguish that may underlie such matters was brought home to me this year while I was working on this book. I have spoken, in the introduction, of a sudden phone call from one of my former students, now in prison for a criminal offense. Stephen is not a boy today. He is twenty-eight years old. He called to ask me to assist him in his trial, which comes up next fall. He will be on trial for murder. He has just knifed and killed a man who first enticed him to his home, then cheated him, and then insulted him—as "an illiterate subhuman."

Stephen now faces twenty years to life. Stephen's mother was illiterate. His grandparents were illiterate as well. What parental curse did not destroy was killed off finally by the schools. Silent violence is repaid with interest. It will cost us $25,000 yearly to maintain this broken soul in prison. But what is the price that has been paid by Stephen's victim? What is the price that will be paid by Stephen?   43

Perhaps we might slow down a moment here and look at the realities described above. This is the nation that we live in. This is a society that most of us did not create but which our President and other leaders have been willing to sustain by virtue of malign neglect. Do we possess the character and courage to address a problem which so many nations, poorer than our own, have found it natural to correct?   44

The answers to these questions represent a reasonable test of our belief in the democracy to which we have been asked in public school to swear allegiance.   45

COMPREHENSION

1. Why is illiteracy a danger to a democratic society?

2. What does Kozol mean when he says that an illiterate person leads a circumscribed existence (paragraph 25)?

3. How does being illiterate limit a person's choices?

4. What are the legal problems and courtroom complications that confront illiterate adults?

5. What does Kozol mean when he says that our reactions to the problem of illiteracy in America test our belief in democracy?

PURPOSE AND AUDIENCE

1. What is Kozol's thesis? Where does he state it?

2. Kozol aims his essay at a general audience. How does he address the needs of this audience? In what ways would his discussion differ if it were intended for an audience of experts?

3. Is Kozol's purpose to inform, persuade, express emotions, or some combination of these three? Does he have additional, more specific purposes as well? Explain.

STYLE AND STRUCTURE

1. Why does Kozol introduce his essay with references to Socrates and James Madison? How does this strategy help him establish his thesis?

2. In paragraph 6 Kozol recounts a dream that he has had. Why does he include this ancedote? How does it help him move from his introduction to the body of his essay?

3. How many examples does Kozol use in his essay? Does he use enough examples to make his case? Explain.

4. How effective is Kozol's use of statistics in this essay? Do the statistics complement or undercut Kozol's illustrations of the personal cost of illiteracy? Explain your answer.

5. Why did Kozol choose to end his essay with the example of Stephen, one of his former students, who is in jail awaiting trial for murder? How does this anecdote help Kozol set up his concluding remarks in paragraphs 44 and 45?

VOCABULARY PROJECTS

1. Define each of the following words as it is used in this selection.

   prescient (1)   incognizant (12)
   farce (2)   jargon (12)
   mendacious (4)   opprobrium (23)
   countenance (4)   concession (24)
   Cyrillic (6)   firmament (29)
   sedative (11)   capitulation (36)
   admonitions (11)

2. Choose any words from the list above that you feel are too difficult for an audience of general readers. In each case, substitute a more accessible word.

3. Look at paragraphs 23 and 24 and determine which words convey Kozol's feelings toward his subject. Rewrite these paragraphs, eliminating as much subjective language as you can. Which version would appeal most to a general audience? To a group of sociologists? To a group of reading teachers?

WRITING WORKSHOP

1. Keep a journal for a day recording the difficulty you would have carrying out your daily routine if you were illiterate.

2. Using your journal entries above, write an essay in which you describe the areas in which you would have difficulty if you could not read. Do not forget to include a thesis and examples to illustrate your points.

3. Using Kozol's essay as source material, write an essay in which your thesis is Madison's statement, "A people who mean to be their own governors must arm themselves with the power knowledge gives." Do not forget to document information that you borrow from Kozol.

THEMATIC CONNECTIONS

- "Outsider in a Silent World" (p. 76)
- "Bilingual Education: The Key to Basic Skills" (p. 490)

PURE AND IMPURE:
THE INTERPLAY OF SCIENCE
AND TECHNOLOGY

Isaac Asimov

Isaac Asimov was born in Russia in 1920 and came to the United States at the age of three with his family. He became a citizen in 1928 and received his Ph.D. in chemistry from Columbia University in 1948. He has written more than three hundred books as well as hundreds of articles. An avid reader of science fiction since boyhood, Asimov achieved recognition with his short story "Nightfall" (1941). He went on to write his best-known works, I Robot (1950), The Foundation Trilogy (1951–53), and The Caves of Steel (1954), which are acknowledged classics of science fiction. In recent years, Asimov has turned his attention to writing books and articles that explain scientific theories to the general public. "Pure and Impure: The Interplay of Science and Technology" questions whether the division between science and technology has any actual basis in reality. To support his thesis he uses several examples that are developed at length throughout the essay.

It is easy to divide a human being into mind and body and to 1 attach far greater importance and reverence to the mind. Similarly, the products of the human mind can be divided into two classes: those that serve to elevate the mind and those that serve to comfort the body. The former are the "liberal arts," the latter, the "mechanical arts."

The liberal arts are those suitable for free men who are in a posi- 2 tion to profit from the labors of others in such a way that they are not compelled to work themselves. The liberal arts deal with "pure knowledge" and are highly thought of, as all things pure must be.

The mechanical arts, which serve agriculture, commerce, and in- 3 dustry, are necessary, too; but as long as slaves, serfs, peasants, and others of low degree know such things, educated gentlemen of leisure can do without them.

Among the liberal arts are some aspects of science. Surely the 4 kinds of studies that have always characterized science—the complex influences that govern the motions of the heavenly bodies, for instance, and that control the properties of mathematical figures and even of the universe itself—are pure enough. As history progressed, though, science developed a low habit of becoming applicable to the work of the world and, as a result, those whose field of mental endeavor lies in the liberal arts (minus science) tend to look down on scientists today as being in altogether too great a danger of dirtying their hands.

Scientists, in response, tend to ape this Greek-inherited snobbishness. They divide science into two parts; one deals only with the difficult, the abstruse, the elegant, the fundamental—in other words, "pure science," a truly liberal art. The other type of science is any branch that goes slumming and becomes associated with such mechanical arts as medicine, agriculture, and industry—clearly a form of impure science. "Impure" is a rather pejorative adjective. It is more common to talk of "basic science" and "applied science." On the other hand, differentiation by adjective alone may not seem enough. The same noun applied to both makes the higher suspect and lends the lower too much credit. There has thus been a tendency to call applied science "technology."

We can therefore speak of "science" and "technology" and we know very well which is the loftier, nobler, more aristocratic, and (in a whisper) the purer of the two. Yet the division is manmade and arbitrary and has no meaning in reality. The advance of knowledge of the physical universe rests on science *and* technology; neither can flourish without the other.

Technology is, indeed, the older of the two. Long before any human being could possibly have become interested in vague speculations about the universe, the hominid precursors of modern human beings were chipping rocks in order to get a sharp edge, and technology was born. Further advances, by hit and miss, trial and error, and even by hard thought, were slow, of course, in the absence of some understanding of basic principles that would guide the technologists in the direction of the possible and inspire them with a grasp of the potential.

Science, as distinct from technology, can be traced back as far as the ancient Greeks who advanced beautiful and intricate speculations. The speculations perhaps tended to become more beautiful, certainly more intricate, but there was no way in which they could have become more in accord with reality. The Greeks, alas, spun their speculations out of deductions based on what they guessed to be principles, and they sharply limited any temptation to indulge in a comparison of their conclusions with the world about them.

It was only when scientists began to observe the real world and to manipulate it that "experimental science" arose. This was in the 16th century, and the most able practitioner was the Italian scientist, Galileo Galilei, who began work toward the end of that century. Thus began the Scientific Revolution. 9

In the 18th century, when enough scientists recognized their responsibility toward the mechanical arts, we had the Industrial Revolution; it reshaped human life. 10

Such is the psychological set of our minds toward a separation of science into pure and impure, basic and applied, useless and useful, intellectual and industrial, that even today it is difficult for people to grasp the frequent and necessary interplay between them. 11

Consider the first great technologist of the modern era, the Scottish engineer, James Watt. Though he did not invent the steam engine, he developed the first one with a condensing chamber and was the first to devise attachments that converted the back-and-forth motion of a piston into the turning of a wheel. He also invented the first automatic feedback devices that controlled the engine's output of steam. In short, beginning in 1769, he developed the first truly practical and versatile mechanism for turning inanimate heat into work and thus started the Industrial Revolution. But was Watt a mere tinkerer? Was he a technologist and nothing more? 12

At the time there lived a Scottish chemist, Joseph Black, who, in his scientific studies of heat in 1764, measured the quantity of heat it takes to boil water. As heat energy pours into water, he found, its temperature goes up rapidly. As water begins to boil, however, vast quantities of heat are absorbed without further rise in temperature. The heat goes entirely into the conversion of liquid to vapor, a phenomenon known as "the latent heat of evaporation." The result is that steam contains far more energy than does hot water at exactly the same temperature. 13

Watt, who knew Black, learned of this latent heat and familiarized himself with the principle involved. That principle guided him in his improvements of the already existing steam engines. Black, in turn, impressed with the exciting application of his discovery, lent Watt a large sum of money to support him in his work. The Industrial Revolution, then, was the product of a fusion of science and technology. 14

Nor is the flow of knowledge entirely in the direction from science toward technology. While many people (even nonscientists) can now recognize that scientific research and discovery, however pure and abstract they may seem, may turn out to have some impure and practical application, few (even among scientists) seem to recognize 15 that, if anything, the flow is stronger in the other direction. Science would stop dead without an input from technology.

In 1581, Galileo, then 17 years old, discovered the principle of the 16 pendulum. In the 1590s, he went on to study the behavior of falling bodies and was greatly hampered by his lack of any device to measure small intervals of time accurately. The first good timepiece was not developed until 1656, when the Dutch scientist, Christiaan Huygens, applied Galileo's principle of the pendulum to construct what we would today call a "grandfather's clock." The principle of the pendulum, by itself, would have done little to advance science. The application of the pendulum principle and the technological development of timepieces made it possible for scientists to make the kind of observations they could never have made before.

In similar fashion, astronomy could not possibly have progressed 17 much past Copernicus without technology. The crucial key to astronomical advance began with spectacle-makers, mere artisans who ground lenses, and with an idle apprentice boy, who, in 1608, played with those lenses—and discovered the principle of the telescope. Galileo built such a telescope and turned it on the heavens. No greater revolution in knowledge has ever occurred in so short a time as the second it took him to turn his telescope on the moon and discover mountains there. In brief, the history of modern science is the history of the development, through technology, of the instruments that are its tools.

Yet tools do not represent the only influence of technology. The 18 products of technology offer a field for renewed speculation. For instance, although Watt had greatly increased the efficiency of the steam engine, it still remained very inefficient. Up to 95 percent of the heat energy of the burning fuel was wasted and was not converted into useful work. A French physicist, Nicolas Carnot, applied himself to this problem. Involving himself with something as technological as the steam engine, he began to consider the flow of heat from a hot body to a cold body and ended up founding the science of thermodynamics (from the Greek for "heat-movement").

Nor is it true that science and technology interacted only in the 19 past. The year 1979 is, by coincidence, a significant year for two great men who seem to typify the very epitome of the purest of science on the one hand and the most practical of technology on the other—Albert Einstein, the greatest scientist since Newton, and Thomas Alva Edison, the greatest inventor since anybody. This year marks the centennial of Einstein's birth. It is also the centennial of Edison's greatest invention, the electric light. How did the work of each man invade the field of the other?

Surely, the theory of relativity, which Einstein originated, is as   20
pure an example of science as one can imagine. The very word "practical" seems a blasphemy when applied to it. Yet the theory of relativity describes the behavior of objects moving at sizable fractions
of the speed of light as nothing else can. Subatomic particles move
at such speeds, and they cannot be studied properly without a consideration of their "relativistic motions." This means that modern
particle accelerators can't exist without taking into account Einstein's theory, and all our present uses of the products of these accelerators would go by the board. We would not have radioisotopes,
for instance, for use in medicine, in industry, in chemical analysis—
and, of course, we would not have them as tools in advancing research into pure science, either.

Out of the theory of relativity, moreover, came deductions that   21
interrelated matter and energy in a definite way (the famous $E = mc^2$). Until Einstein gave us this equation, matter and energy had
been thought to be independent and unconnected entities. Guided
by the theory, we came to see more meaning in energy aspects of
research in subatomic particles, and in the end, the nuclear bomb
was invented and nuclear-power stations were made possible.

Einstein worked outside the field of relativity, too. In 1917, he   22
pointed out that if a molecule is at a high-energy level (a concept
made possible by the purely scientific quantum theory, which had
its origin in 1900) and if it is struck by a photon (a unit of radiation
energy) of just the proper frequency, the molecule drops to lower
energy. It does this because it gives up some of its energy in the
form of a photon of the precise frequency and moving in the precise
direction as the original photon.

Thirty-six years later, in 1953, Charles Hard Townes made use of   23
Einstein's theoretical reasoning to invent the "maser" that could
amplify a short-wave radio ("micro-wave") beam of photons into a
much stronger beam. In 1960, Theodore Harold Maiman extended
the principle to the still shorter-wave photons of visible light and
devised the first "laser." The laser has infinite applications, from
eye surgery to possible use as a war weapon.

And Edison?   24

The net result of his inventions was to spread the use of electricity   25
the world over; to increase greatly the facilities for the generation
and transmission of electricity; to make more important any device
that would make that generation and transmission more efficient
and economical. In short, Edison made the pure-science study of the
flow and behavior of the electric current an important field of study.

Charles Proteus Steinmetz was certainly a technologist. He   26 worked for General Electric and had two hundred patents in his name. Yet he also worked out, in complete mathematical detail, the intricacies of alternating-current circuitry, a towering achievement in pure science. Similar work was done by Oliver Heaviside.

As for Edison himself, his own work on the electric light unwittingly led him in the direction of purity. After he had developed the electric light, he labored for years to improve its efficiency and, in particular, to make the glowing filament last longer before breaking. As was usual for him, he tried everything he could think of. One of his hit-and-miss efforts was to seal a metal wire into the evacuated electric light bulb near, but not touching, the filament. The two were separated by a small gap of vacuum.

Edison then turned on the electric current to see if the presence of the metal wire would somehow preserve the life of the glowing filament. It didn't, and Edison abandoned the approach. However, he noticed that an electric current flowed from the filament to the wire across that vacuum gap. Nothing in Edison's vast practical knowledge of electricity explained this flow of current, but he observed it, wrote it up in his notebooks, and patented it. The phenomenon was called the "Edison effect," and it was Edison's only discovery in pure science—but it arose directly out of his technology.

Did this seemingly casual observation lead to anything? Well, it indicated that an electric current has, associated with it, a flow of matter of a particularly subtle sort—matter that was eventually shown to be electrons, the first subatomic particles to be recognized. Once this was discovered, methods were found to modify and amplify the electron flow in vacuum and, in this way, to control the behavior of an electric current with far greater delicacy than the flipping of switches could. Out of the Edison effect came the huge field of electronics.

There are other examples. A technological search for methods to eliminate static in radiotelephony served as the basis for the development of radio astronomy and the discovery of such phenomena as quasars, pulsars, and the big bang.

The technological development of the transistor brought on an improved way of manipulating and controlling electric currents, and has led to the computerization and automation of society. Computers have become essential tools in both technology and science. A computer was even necessary for the solution of one of the most famous problems in pure mathematics—the four-color problem.

The technological development of a liquid-fuel rocket has led to something as purely astronomical as the mapping, in detail, of Mars and of experiments with its soil.

The fact is that science and technology are one.   33

Just as there is only one species of human being on earth, and all   34
divisions into races, cultures, and nations are but manmade ways
of obscuring that fundamental truth, so there is only one scientific
endeavor on earth—the pursuit of knowledge and understanding—
and all divisions into disciplines and levels of purity are but man-
made ways of obscuring *that* fundamental truth.

COMPREHENSION

1. How does Asimov define the "liberal arts" and the "mechanical
   arts"? According to Asimov, what value does society place on each?

2. Why do scientists divide science into "pure science" and "impure
   science"? Why is science "loftier, nobler, more aristocratic" than
   technology? What is Asimov's opinion of this division?

3. According to Asimov, which is older, science or technology? At what
   point did experimental science arise? How did it set the stage for the
   Industrial Revolution?

4. How do Watt, Galileo, and Carnot demonstrate the interplay of science and technology?

5. What differences does Asimov identify between Edison and
   Einstein? In what way does he say they are alike?

PURPOSE AND AUDIENCE

1. What is Asimov's thesis? At what point does he state it? Why does
   he take so long to get to it?

2. Asimov aims his essay at readers of the *Saturday Review* (educated
   nonscientists). What general information does he expect the audience
   to know about his subject before they begin reading? Explain.

3. Is Asimov writing simply to educate his audience, or does he have a
   persuasive purpose? Explain.

STYLE AND STRUCTURE

1. What is the function of Asimov's introductory paragraphs?

2. Asimov depends primarily on extended examples to support his the-

sis. What are the advantages of this strategy? What would be the effect of using a number of short examples instead of long ones?

3. Does Asimov use enough examples to prove his case? Does he present a wide enough range of examples? Explain.

4. What transitional words and phrases does Asimov use to move his readers from one example to the next?

5. What point does Asimov make in his conclusion? How effective is this conclusion? What other concluding strategy could he have used to end his essay?

VOCABULARY PROJECTS

1. Define each of the following words as it is used in this selection.

abstruse (5)	relativistic (20)
hominid (7)	entities (21)
thermodynamics (18)	filament (27)

2. Throughout his essay, Asimov uses a number of technical terms. Write a paragraph in which you discuss how he helps his audience of nonscientists understand these terms.

3. Asimov uses the passive voice several times in his first six paragraphs (for example, "The products of the human mind can be divided . . . " and "It is more common to talk of 'basic science' and 'applied science' . . . "). What is the effect of this use of the passive voice, and what would be the effect of changing the passive to the active voice (for example, "Philosophers divided the human mind into . . . " and "The Greeks commonly talked of . . . ")?

WRITING WORKSHOP

1. Write an essay in which you defend the study of the liberal arts. Be specific, and use examples from your own experience to support your thesis.

2. Write an exemplification essay in which you either defend or refute the assertion that the liberal arts are highly respected and the mechanical arts are considered "of low degree."

3. Write an essay in which you challenge the stereotypes commonly associated with an arbitrary division similar to the one that Asimov questions (for instance, teachers/students, liberal arts majors/business majors, scholars/athletes, parents/children). Be specific, and use a variety of examples from your experience and from your reading to support your points.

THEMATIC CONNECTIONS

- "A Toast to Progress" (p. 369)
- "Animal Liberation" (p. 501)
- "Animal Rights versus Human Health" (p. 510)

COURTSHIP
THROUGH THE AGES

James Thurber

James Thurber, a popular American humorist, was born in 1894 in Ohio and died in 1961. His first work appeared in 1927 in The New Yorker. *Through the years he has entertained readers with his short stories, sketches, fables, and reminiscences. His works include* Is Sex Necessary? (1929), *written with E. B. White;* My World and Welcome to It *(1942), containing the well-known story "The Secret Life of Walter Mitty";* Thurber Country *(1953); and* The Male Animal *(1940), a comedy written with Elliot Nugent. "Courtship Through the Ages" was published in* The New Yorker *and appeared in* My World and Welcome to It. *In the essay he uses several examples to humorously illustrate the problems experienced by males of all animal species in arousing the interest of females.*

Surely nothing in the astonishing scheme of life can have non-plussed Nature so much as the fact that none of the females of any of the species she created really cared very much for the male, as such. For the past ten million years Nature has been busily inventing ways to make the male attractive to the female, but the whole business of courtship, from the marine annelids up to man, still lumbers heavily along, like a complicated musical comedy. I have been reading the sad and absorbing story in Volume 6 (Cole to Dama) of the *Encyclopaedia Britannica.* In this volume you can learn all about cricket, cotton, costume designing, crocodiles, crown jewels, and Coleridge, but none of these subjects is so interesting as the Courtship of Animals, which recounts the sorrowful lengths to which all males must go to arouse the interest of a lady.

We all know, I think, that Nature gave man whiskers and a mustache with the quaint idea in mind that these would prove attractive to the female. We all know that, far from attracting her, whiskers and mustaches only made her nervous and gloomy, so that man had to go in for somersaults, tilting with lances, and performing feats of parlor magic to win her attention; he also had to bring her candy, flowers, and the furs of animals. It is common knowledge that in

193

spite of all these "love displays" the male is constantly being turned down, insulted, or thrown out of the house. It is rather comforting, then, to discover that the peacock, for all his gorgeous plumage, does not have a particularly easy time in courtship; none of the males in the world do. The first peahen, it turned out, was only faintly stirred by her suitor's beautiful train. She would often go quietly to sleep while he was whisking it around. The *Britannica* tells us that the peacock actually had to learn a certain little trick to wake her up and revive her interest: he had to learn to vibrate his quills so as to make a rustling sound. In ancient times man himself, observing the ways of the peacock, probably tried vibrating his whiskers to make a rustling sound; if so, it didn't get him anywhere. He had to go in for something else; so, among other things, he went in for gifts. It is not unlikely that he got this idea from certain flies and birds who were making no headway at all with rustling sounds.

One of the flies of the family Empidae, who had tried everything, 3 finally hit on something pretty special. He contrived to make a glistening transparent balloon which was even larger than himself. Into this he would put sweetmeats and tidbits and he would carry the whole elaborate envelope through the air to the lady of his choice. This amused her for a time, but she finally got bored with it. She demanded silly little colorful presents, something that you couldn't eat but that would look nice around the house. So the male Empis had to go around gathering flower petals and pieces of bright paper to put into his balloon. On a courtship flight a male Empis cuts quite a figure now, but he can hardly be said to be happy. He never knows how soon the female will demand heavier presents, such as Roman coins and gold collar buttons. It seems probable that one day the courtship of the Empidae will fall down, as man's occasionally does, of its own weight.

The bowerbird is another creature that spends so much time 4 courting the female that he never gets any work done. If all the male bowerbirds became nervous wrecks within the next ten or fifteen years, it would not surprise me. The female bowerbird insists that a playground be built for her with a specially constructed bower at the entrance. This bower is much more elaborate than an ordinary nest and is harder to build; it costs a lot more, too. The female will not come to the playground until the male has filled it up with a great many gifts: silvery leaves, red leaves, rose petals, shells, beads, berries, bones, dice, buttons, cigar bands, Christmas seals, and the Lord knows what else. When the female finally condescends to visit the playground, she is in a coy and silly mood and has to be chased in and out of the bower and up and down the playground before she will quit giggling and stand still long enough even to shake hands. The male bird is, of course, pretty well done in before the chase starts, because he has worn himself out hunting for eyeglass lenses and begonia blossoms. I imagine that many a bowerbird, after chasing a female for two or three hours, says the hell with it and goes home to bed. Next day, of course, he telephones someone else and the same trying ritual is gone through with again. A male bowerbird is as exhausted as a night-club habitué before he is out of his twenties.

The male fiddler crab has a somewhat easier time, but it can 5 hardly be said that he is sitting pretty. He has one enormously large and powerful claw, usually brilliantly colored, and you might suppose that all he had to do was reach out and grab some passing cutie. The very earliest fiddler crabs may have tried this, but, if so, they got slapped for their pains. A female fiddler crab will not tolerate any caveman stuff; she never has and she doesn't intend to start now. To attract a female, a fiddler crab has to stand on tiptoe and brandish his claw in the air. If any female in the neighborhood is interested—and you'd be surprised how many are not—she comes over and engages him in light badinage, for which he is not in the mood. As many as a hundred females may pass the time of day with him and go on about their business. By nightfall of an average courting day, a fiddler crab who has been standing on tiptoe for eight or ten hours waving a heavy claw in the air is in pretty sad shape. As in the case of the males of all species, however, he gets out of bed next morning, dashes some water on his face, and tries again.

The next time you encounter a male web-spinning spider, stop and 6 reflect that he is too busy worrying about his love life to have any desire to bite you. Male web-spinning spiders have a tougher life than any other males in the animal kingdom. This is because the female web-spinning spiders have very poor eyesight. If a male lands on a female's web, she kills him before he has time to lay down his cane and gloves, mistaking him for a fly or a bumblebee who has tumbled into her trap. Before the species figured out what to do about this, millions of males were murdered by ladies they called on. It is the nature of spiders to perform a little dance in front of the female, but before a male spinner could get near enough for the female to see who he was and what he was up to, she would lash out at him with a flat-iron or a pair of garden shears. One night, nobody knows when, a very bright male spinner lay awake worrying about calling on a lady who had been killing suitors right and left. It came to him that this business of dancing as a love display wasn't getting anybody anywhere except the grave. He decided to go in for web-twitching, or strand-vibrating. The next day he tried it on one of the nearsighted girls. Instead of dropping in on her suddenly, he stayed outside the web and began monkeying with one of its strands. He twitched it up and down and in and out with such a lilting rhythm that the female was charmed. The serenade worked beautifully; the female let him live. The *Britannica's* spider-watchers, however, report that this system is not always successful. Once in a while, even now, a female will fire three bullets into a suitor or run him through with a kitchen knife. She keeps threatening him from the moment he strikes the first low notes on the outside strings, but usually by the time he has got up to the high notes played around the center of the web, he is going to town and she spares his life.

Even the butterfly, as handsome a fellow as he is, can't always win a mate merely by fluttering around and showing off. Many butterflies have to have scent scales on their wings. Hepialus carries a powder puff in a perfumed pouch. He throws perfume at the ladies when they pass. The male tree cricket, Oecanthus, goes Hepialus one better by carrying a tiny bottle of wine with him and giving drinks to such doxies as he has designs on. One of the male snails throws darts to entertain the girls. So it goes, through the long list of animals, from the bristle worm and his rudimentary dance steps to man and his gift of diamonds and sapphires. The golden-eye drake raises a jet of water with his feet as he flies over a lake; Hepialus has his powder puff, Oecanthus his wine bottle, man his etchings. It is a bright and melancholy story, the age-old desire of the male for the female, the age-old desire of the female to be amused and entertained. Of all the creatures on earth, the only males who could be figured as putting any irony into their courtship are the grebes and certain other diving birds. Every now and then a courting grebe slips quietly down to the bottom of a lake and then, with a mighty "Whoosh!," pops out suddenly a few feet from his girl friend, splashing water all over her. She seems to be persuaded that this is a purely loving display, but I like to think that the grebe always has a faint hope of drowning her or scaring her to death.

I will close this investigation into the mournful burdens of the male with the *Britannica's* story about a certain Argus pheasant. It appears that the Argus displays himself in front of a female who stands perfectly still without moving a feather. . . . The male Argus the *Britannica* tells about was confined in a cage with a female of another species, a female who kept moving around, emptying ashtrays and fussing with lampshades all the time the male was showing off his talents. Finally, in disgust, he stalked away and began displaying in front of his water trough. He reminds me of a certain male (Homo sapiens) of my acquaintance who one night after dinner asked his wife to put down her detective magazine so that he could read a poem of which he was very fond. She sat quietly enough until he was well into the middle of the thing, intoning with great ardor and intensity. Then suddenly there came a sharp, disconcerting *slap!* It turned out that all during the male's display, the female had been intent on a circling mosquito and had finally trapped it between the palms of her hands. The male in this case did not stalk away and display in front of a water trough; he went over to Tim's and had a flock of drinks and recited the poem to the fellas. I am sure they all told bitter stories of their own about how their displays had been interrupted by females. I am also sure that they all ended up singing "Honey, Honey, Bless Your Heart."

COMPREHENSION

1. What is one of life's more astonishing things according to Thurber?

2. What is a "love display"?

3. Why would Thurber not be surprised if all the male bowerbirds became nervous wrecks?

4. Why do male web-spinning spiders have a more difficult time than other males in the animal kingdom?

5. What is the meaning of Thurber's anecdote about the Argus pheasant (paragraph 8)?

PURPOSE AND AUDIENCE

1. Where does Thurber state his thesis? Why does he place it where he does?

2. In the narrowest sense, Thurber's purpose is to entertain readers by poking fun at the courtship rituals of animals. What other purpose or purposes does he have in mind?

3. Choose several words that convey Thurber's attitude toward his subject. How do these words help him establish his attitude?

STYLE AND STRUCTURE

1. How does Thurber set the stage for the examples he presents? What is his source for the examples in the essay?

2. Is there any logic to the organization of Thurber's examples? Explain your answer.

3. Why does Thurber compare courtship through the ages to a complicated musical comedy?

4. In what way does Thurber relate each new example to the other examples he presents?

5. How does Thurber establish that each of the examples he presents relates to human beings as well as animals?

VOCABULARY PROJECTS

1. Define each of the following words as it is used in this selection.

nonplussed (1)   condescends (4)
annelids (1)   habitué (4)
peahen (2)   rudimentary (7)
sweetmeats (3)   disconcerting (8)

2. What figures of speech does Thurber use in his essay? What function do they serve? (See p. 101, for a review of figures of speech.)

3. Throughout his essay, Thurber uses a mixture of scientific terminology and everyday words. What is the effect of this strategy?

WRITING WORKSHOP

1. Write an essay in which you give examples of ways men try to arouse the interest of women. Or, if you wish, consider how women attempt to interest men.

2. Write an exemplification essay defending or criticizing Thurber's impressions of courtship. How fair or unfair is his portrayal of male-female relationships?

3. Write an exemplification essay in which you describe the most disastrous date you ever had. Use your example to support the thesis that sometimes courting rituals can have unexpected results.

THEMATIC CONNECTIONS

- "I Want a Wife" (p. 435)
- "Euphemism" (p. 454)

WRITING ASSIGNMENTS FOR EXEMPLIFICATION

1. Interview several business people in your community. Explain the Peter Principle to them, and write an essay in which you discuss their feelings about this subject. Take notes as you carry out your interview, and use quotations in your essay.

2. Like Thurber, write a humorous essay about a familiar ritual and the types of people who participate in it.

3. Write an essay in which you establish that you are an optimistic or a pessimistic person. Use two or three extended examples to support your case.

4. If you could change three things at your college or university, what would they be? Use examples from your own experience to support your claims, and be sure to tie the three together with a single thesis.

5. Write an essay about a time in your life when you learned a painful lesson. Use a single extended example to support your thesis.

6. Using your family and friends as examples, write an essay in which you suggest some of the positive and admirable characteristics of Americans.

7. Write an essay in which you give your formula for achieving success in college. You may, if you wish, talk about things like scheduling time, maintaining a high energy level, and learning how to relax. Use examples from your own experience to make your point.

8. Write an exemplification essay in which you discuss how cooperation has helped you achieve some desired goal.

9. Choose an accomplishment that you feel qualifies as one of history's great moments. Write an essay explaining your feelings.

10. Describe two of the most embarrassing incidents you ever experienced. Formulate a thesis that expresses your ideas about these occurrences.

5

Process

WHAT IS PROCESS?

A process essay enumerates the steps in an operation and explains how those steps lead toward its completion. In the following paragraph from "How Dictionaries Are Made," the semanticist S. I. Hayakawa uses process to explain how an editor of a dictionary decides on a word's definition.

> To define a word, then, the dictionary-editor places before him the stack of cards illustrating that word; each of the cards represents an actual use of the word by a writer of some literary or historical importance. He reads the cards carefully, discards some, rereads the rest, and divides up the stack according to what he thinks are the several senses of the word. Finally, he writes his definitions, following the hard-and-fast rule that each definition *must* be based on what the quotations in front of him reveal about the meaning of the word. The editor cannot be influenced by what *he* thinks a given word *ought* to mean. He must work according to the cards or not at all.

Process, like narrative, presents events in chronological order. Unlike a narrative, however, a process essay details a particular series of events that produces the same outcome whenever it is duplicated. Because these events form a sequence that often has a fixed order, clarity is extremely important. Whether your reader is actually to perform the process or simply to understand how it takes place, your paper must make clear the exact order of the individual steps as well as their relationships to one another and to the process as a whole. Therefore, not only must clear, logical transitions exist between the steps in a process, but the steps must be presented in *strict* chronological order—that is, in the order in which they are carried out. Unlike narratives, then, process essays do not use flashbacks or experiment with temporal order.

Instructions and Process Explanations

The two basic kinds of process writing serve different purposes. The purpose of a set of *instructions* is to enable readers to perform the process themselves. Instructions have many practical uses. A recipe, a handout about using your library's card catalog, or an operating manual for your car or your stereo are all written in the form of instructions. So are directions for locating an address or for driving to the beach. Instructions use the present tense and, like commands, the imperative mood: "Disconnect the system, and check the electrical source." Thus instructions speak directly to the readers who are to perform the tasks described.

The purpose of a *process explanation* is not to enable readers to duplicate the process but rather to help them understand the procedure and how it is carried out. Thus, explanation essays can examine anything from how silkworms spin their cocoons to how Michelangelo and Leonardo da Vinci painted their masterpieces on plaster walls and ceilings. A process explanation may employ the first person *(I, we)* or the third *(he, she, it, they)*, the past tense or the present. Because its readers need to understand, not perform, the process, the explanation does not use the second person *(you)* or the imperative mood characteristic of instructions. The style of a process explanation will vary depending on whether a writer is explaining a process that takes place regularly or one that occurred in the past, and on whether the writer or someone else carried out the steps. The chart below suggests some of the options available to writers of process explanations.

	First Person	*Third Person*
Present	"After I pin the pattern to the fabric, I cut it out with a sharp pair of scissors." (habitual process performed by the writer)	"After the photographer places the chemicals in the tray. . . . " (habitual process performed by someone other than the writer)
Past	"After I pinned the pattern to the fabric. . . . " (process performed in the past by the writer)	"When the mixture was cool, he added. . . . " (process performed in the past by someone other than the writer)

Uses of Process Essays

Both instructions and process explanations are used in college writing, and either can serve as the structural pattern for a section of a paper or for an entire piece of writing. For example, in a biology term paper on genetic engineering, you might devote a paragraph to an explanation of the process of amniocentesis; in an editorial on the negative side of fraternity life, you might decide to summarize briefly the process of pledging. On the other hand, an entire paper can be organized around a process pattern. In a literature essay, you might trace the developmental steps through which a fictional character reached new insight; on a finance midterm, you might review the procedure for approving a commercial loan.

Process writing sometimes is used to persuade and at other times is used simply to present information. If its purpose is persuasive, a process paper may take a strong stand like "Applying for public assistance is a needlessly complex process that discourages many potential recipients" or "The process of slaughtering baby seals is inhumane and sadistic." Many process essays, however, aim to communicate nothing more debatable than the idea that learning the procedure for blood typing can introduce students to some basic laboratory techniques. Even in such a case, a process essay should have a clear thesis that gives readers a sense of what the process is and perhaps why it is performed: "Typing your own blood can familiarize you with some fundamental laboratory procedures."

STRUCTURING A PROCESS ESSAY

Like most other essays, a full-length process essay usually consists of three main sections. The introduction names the process and indicates why and under what circumstances it is performed. This section may also include information about materials or preliminary preparations, or it may present an overview of the process, perhaps even listing its major stages. The paper's thesis is also generally stated in the introduction.

To develop the thesis of a short essay, each paragraph in the body of the essay typically treats one major stage of the procedure. Each stage may group several steps, depending on the nature and complexity of the process. These steps are presented in chronological order, interrupted only for essential definitions, explanations, or cautions. Every step must be included and must appear in its proper place. Throughout the body of a process essay, transitional words and phrases ensure that each step, each stage, and each paragraph lead logically to the next. Transitions like *first, second, meanwhile, after this, next, then, when you have finished,* and *finally* establish sequential and chronological relationships that help readers follow the process.

A short process essay may not need a formal conclusion. If an essay does include a conclusion, however, it will, in most cases, reinforce the thesis. The conclusion may also briefly review the procedure's major stages. Such an ending is especially useful if the paper has outlined a very long and complex or particularly technical procedure that may seem complicated to general readers. Finally, the conclusion may summarize the results of the process or explain its significance.

Before you can arrange your ideas into a coherent process essay, you must have a clear understanding of your essay's purpose. As you write, you should keep your readers' needs in mind. When necessary, you should explain the reasons for performing the steps, describe unfamiliar materials or equipment, define uncommon terms, and warn the reader about possible snags during the process. Sometimes you may even need to include illustrations. Besides complete information, your reader needs a clear and consistent discussion without ambiguities or surprises. For this reason, you should avoid unnecessary shifts in tense, person, voice, and mood. You should also include appropriate articles *(a, an,* and *the)* so that your discussion moves smoothly, like an essay, not abruptly, like a cookbook. Careful attention to your essay's consistency as well as to its overall structure will ensure that your readers understand your process explanations and instructions.

Always be careful to depict a process accurately. You should distinguish between what usually or always happens and what occasionally or rarely happens, between necessary steps and incidental ones. You should also mentally test all the steps in sequence to be sure that the process will really work as you explain it. Check carefully for omitted steps or incorrect information. If you are writing from firsthand observation, test your explanation after writing it by observing the process again, if you possibly can. This can help you avoid omissions or mistakes.

Suppose you are taking a midterm examination in a course in childhood and adolescent behavior. One essay question calls for a process explanation: "Trace the stages that children go through in acquiring language." After thinking about the question, you develop the following thesis: "Although individual cases may differ, most children acquire language in a predictable series of stages." You then plan your essay, an extended account of the process by which children learn language, and develop an outline. An informal outline for your essay might look like this:

- Introduction—including thesis and overview of stages
- First stage, two to twelve months: prelinguistic behavior including "babbling" and appropriate responses to nonverbal cues
- Second stage, toward the end of the first year: single words as commands or requests; infant catalogs his or her environment
- Third stage, beginning of second year: expressive jargon, a flow of sounds that imitates adult speech; real words along with jargon
- Fourth and final stage, middle of second year to beginning of third: child begins combining real words into two-word phrases and then longer strings; missing parts of speech appear, and foundations of language are established
- Conclusion and summary

This essay, when completed, will show not only what the stages of the process are but how they relate to one another. It also will develop its thesis that children learn language not at random but through a well-defined process.

The following student essays, Scott Blackman's set of instructions for typing your own blood and Rachel Smith's explanation of how a religious ritual is conducted, illustrate the two types of process essays.

TYPING YOUR OWN BLOOD

Introduction   Typing your own blood is often used as an   1
                introductory laboratory exercise. Even if you do not
Thesis   wish to learn your blood type, the exercise is useful
                because it introduces you to some simple laboratory
                techniques, illustrates the use of basic equipment,
                and prepares you to follow the stages of an orderly
                scientific procedure.

Materials   To type your own blood, you need the following   2
                equipment: alcohol-soaked cotton balls; a sterile
                lancet; a small test tube containing 1 ml. of saline
                solution; anti-A, anti-B, and anti-Rh serums with

individual eye droppers; two microscope slides; a
grease pencil; a Pasteur pipette; three applicator
sticks; and a warm fluorescent light or other low-
heat source.

First stage of process   With the grease pencil, label one slide Rh, and   3
place this slide under the low-heat source. Divide
your cool slide into two equal portions, labeling one
side A and the other B. Apply one drop of anti-A
serum to slide A, one drop of anti-B to slide B, and
one drop of anti-Rh to the warm Rh slide.

Second stage of process   Use an alcohol-soaked cotton ball to swab your   4
middle or ring finger, and allow the excess alcohol
to evaporate. After opening the sterile lancet, prick
the sterile finger once, approximately one-quarter
inch beyond the end of the fingernail. Now, collect
several drops of blood in the test tube containing
the saline solution, and mix the solution. In the
meantime, hold another sterile cotton ball over the
cut to allow the blood to clot.

Third stage of process   Next, using the Pasteur pipette, transfer one   5
drop of the saline solution containing the blood to
each of the anti-A, anti-B, and anti-Rh serums, using
a separate applicator stick to mix each. After two or
three minutes, clumping may have appeared in one or
all of the areas. A-clumping denotes A-type blood,
B-clumping indicates B-type blood, A- and B-clumping
signifies AB blood, and no clumping denotes O blood.
Rh-clumping means that your blood is Rh positive; the
absence of Rh-clumping indicates that you have
Rh-negative blood.

Conclusion   By following the simple steps outlined above,   6
you will learn much that will be of practical value
in your future scientific explorations. As an added
bonus, you will also learn your blood type.

Points for Special Attention

Thesis.   The first paragraph of Scott Blackman's essay includes a thesis that presents the advantages of learning the process of blood typing. By explaining the rationale for the process, the writer makes his purpose clear to his readers.

Structure.   In his paper's introduction, Scott presents reasons the reader might want to carry out the procedure; in his conclusion, he reinforces those reasons. The body of the paper consists of a chronological presentation of a set of steps to be performed, preceded by a precise list of necessary materials. Because his process is such a simple one, Scott did not think he needed to introduce the process with an overview of its steps or to conclude his discussion with a summary.

Purpose and Style.   This set of instructions, written for an introductory course in animal biology, has two specific purposes. It serves as a review exercise for the student author, and it provides other students with all the information they need to duplicate the process. Because it presents instructions rather than an extended explanation of a process, it is written in the second person and in the present tense, with the verbs in the form of commands. These commands, however, are not choppy or abrupt because the essay includes smooth transitions as well as appropriate articles and pronouns.

Detail.   Scott's instructions contain some precise detail: for example, he notes that the cut is to be made "approximately one-quarter inch beyond the end of the fingernail." This detail is based on physiological knowledge about where the cut will produce just enough blood for the test yet do little damage and heal quickly. His advice about using different applicator sticks to avoid inadvertently mixing blood samples shows that he has thought about mistakes his readers might make. Still, he could have supplied even more specific detail. For instance, he could have explained exactly how to prick the finger, how to use a pipette, whether to draw a line with the grease pencil, and so on. Knowing that his readers would have some supervision in their laboratory work, however, Scott decided that the details he included would be sufficient.

In contrast to "Typing Your Own Blood," the next essay is a process explanation.

RIVER BAPTISM

Introduction   What would you think if you were driving in   1
Virginia on a Sunday in August and a group of people
dressed in white robes walked across the road? Your
first reaction might be to assume they were members
of the Ku Klux Klan. You probably would not guess
they were part of a religious ceremony, but in fact
that guess might be the correct one. Once a year in
parts of the South, the citizens celebrate river
baptism. Everyone is welcome to attend, even
sightseers passing through town. A big banner
stretches across the road to announce that this
ceremony is going to take place. To some people the
ceremony might seem outdated, but to those who
participate in it, river baptism is vitally
Thesis   important. This ritual continues to give all involved
a sense of belonging and to remind them of the
strength of their Baptist heritage.

Background   River baptism has its origins in the Biblical   2
story of St. John, who baptized Jesus in the Jordan
River. It is an old tradition of most Southern
Baptists. Decades ago, when tubs and running water
were not available, people who wanted to show their
acceptance of God in their lives would gather by the
river and wash their sins away in the water. When
this act was completed, the reborn Christians would
sing psalms to display their happiness.

Today in my home state of Virginia, this act of   3
baptism is not forgotten, but now, because tubs and
running water are located right in the church, it is
performed only once a year. The first Sunday in
August is the date of the annual river baptism.
Everyone is welcome; in fact, in my hometown not only
residents but also their families are expected to

attend, no matter how far away they have moved. The
process is the same each year.

**First stage in
process:
Preparation**

On the Saturday before the event, the citizens 4
of the town and all family members who are home for
the weekend decorate the street and the waterfront.
They hang the banner from tree to tree and attach
streamers to it. One long, long table is set up. At
this table, decorated like the table of the Last
Supper, the minister and the baptized people will
sit. Houses are also decorated. Everyone in town is
busy trying to get ready for this important day.

**Second stage in
process:
Festivities
begin**

The festivities start at nine on Sunday morning 5
with the choir singing welcoming hymns. The choir
keeps the audience vibrant all day: Baptist choirs
are the most soulful, energetic, and spirited choirs
of all Gospel organizations. From the time the
organist hits the first key until the choir puts down
the tambourines, all the people (especially the
elderly) are out of their chairs.

**Third stage in
process:
Ceremony
begins**

The actual ceremony starts at eleven in the 6
morning. First, the reverend calls everyone to the
throne of worship. He preaches the story of baptism
and why it is important. After the morning sermon,
everyone gets a chance to say a few last words to the
candidates for baptism before the become "new
individuals."

**Fourth stage in
process:
Baptism**

At noon the minister and those who are going to 7
be baptized walk down the hill toward the river. The
minister is dressed in a black robe and the
candidates have on white robes. The family and
friends walk behind them singing the spiritual
"Going up to Yonder," While the audience stops at
the edge of the shore, the minister and the
candidates wade into the river until they are chest

deep in water. Calling them by name, the minister
asks each candidate whether he or she believes in God
and is ready to do God's wishes. If all the questions
are answered correctly, the minister then immerses
the candidate for the so-called sin washing. Then
that Christian comes back on land and rejoices with
his or her family.

Fifth stage in process: Meal

After all the candidates have been baptized, the
big meal is served. This meal consists of fried
chicken, country ham, greens, potato salad, yams,
chitterlings, crabs, corn, pies, cakes, and fruit.
The meal lasts for most of the afternoon--at least two
or three hours--but it is less serious than any other
activity of the day, with people getting to know one
another and visiting with family members. After this
dinner, many people go home to rest for a while.

8

Sixth stage of process: Revival

Five o'clock starts the evening festivities,
which consist of a revival. Here the members and
friends sit in the churchyard and listen to the
minister and choir. The minister preaches about the
meaning of baptism and sin and about how to be a good
Samaritan, and the choir sings until everyone has
nearly fainted from exhaustion and from feeling
spiritually happy and aroused--what we call a case of
the Holy Ghost. At dusk, everyone is issued a candle
that is to be held until the end of the festivities.
After the closing prayer, everyone sings "This
Little Light of Mine," which can be heard throughout
the town. Both participants and observers awaken the
next morning with that song still ringing in their
ears.

9

Conclusion

This ceremony has been repeated each August for
as long as I--and my parents--can remember. It is
always the same, and people in my hometown like this
familiar routine. Rituals like river baptism remind

10

Restatement of thesis	us who we are, and such ceremonies also help to keep our community together and our spiritual heritage alive.

Points for Special Attention

Thesis. Rachel Smith wrote in response to this assignment: "Select a tradition or ritual that has special significance for you, and write an essay in which you not only communicate a sense of what the ritual is like but also explain why it is important." Rachel decided to write about a tradition with which she was very familiar: the ritual of river baptism in her town in Virginia. The wording of the assignment told Rachel that simply describing river baptism would not be enough; the body of her essay could do this, but her thesis would have to make clear why the ritual was so important. To develop her main point—that people's continued loyalty to a routine that has remained essentially unchanged for years has helped to maintain and even to strengthen the Southern Baptist heritage—Rachel logically chose process as her essay's pattern of development.

Structure. Rachel's paper, written for an English composition class, presents an informal overview of the process rather than a complex analysis. She begins with a vivid image of a group of white-robed people and goes on to explain who these people are; she concludes her first paragraph with the thesis her process explanation will support. In the next two paragraphs she presents the background information her audience will need to understand the process. In subsequent paragraphs, beginning with paragraph 4, she presents the various stages in the process of the annual ceremony of river baptism, signaling the start of each new stage with an appropriate topic sentence ("On the Saturday before the event . . . "; "The festivities start . . . "; "The actual ceremony starts . . . "; "At noon . . . "; "After all the candidates have been baptized . . . "; "Five o'clock starts the evening festivities . . . "). Her last paragraph reinforces her thesis.

Purpose and Style. Although Rachel's process essay is clearly based on her own firsthand observations, her purpose is not to share personal experiences but to draw a general conclusion about the importance of the ritual she explains. Therefore, although in her introduction, background, and concluding paragraphs she uses the first person, in the body of her essay she generalizes the process by writing in the third person and by using the present tense, which indicates the process is habitual. When she wishes to place emphasis on the process itself rather than on those involved in it, she uses passive voice ("One long, long table is set up . . . "; " . . . the big meal is served"). Throughout the paper, Rachel's smooth transitions *(first, after, then,* and so on) link sentences and help her readers to follow the process easily.

Detail.   Assuming that her readers, who are not from her predominantly Baptist hometown in Virginia, will not be familiar with the process she describes, Rachel is careful to include detail that will hold her audience's interest and help them to visualize the process. She describes the decorations and the choir, explains the baptism ceremony itself, and names the songs sung and the foods served. Her purpose in providing such detail is not to present a scientifically precise picture but rather to convey a general sense of the events.

The following selections illustrate how varied the purposes of process essays can be. All, however, provide orderly and clear explanations so that readers can follow the process easily.

SLICE OF LIFE

Russell Baker

Russell Baker was born in 1925 in Virginia. After graduating from Johns Hopkins University, he worked as a reporter for the Balti- more Sun *and the* New York Times. *He also contributed to a num- ber of magazines, including* Ladies' Home Journal, McCall's, Sat- urday Evening Post, *and* Sports Illustrated. *He is best known for his syndicated column, "The Observer," where he often treats con- temporary social and political issues in a humorous or satirical manner. He won the Pulitzer Prize in 1979 for distinguished com- mentary. His books include* Poor Russell's Almanac *(1972),* The Up- side Down Man *(1977),* So This Is Depravity *(1980), the autobio- graphical memoir* Growing Up *(1982), and* The Rescue of Miss Yaskell and Other Pipe Dreams *(1983). "Slice of Life," originally a newspaper column, takes a whimsical look at the process of carv- ing a turkey.*

How to carve a turkey: 1

Assemble the following tools—carving knife, stone for sharpening   2
carving knife, hot water, soap, wash cloth, two bath towels, barbells,
meat cleaver. If the house lacks a meat cleaver, an ax may be substi-
tuted. If it is, add bandages, sutures and iodine to above list.

Begin by moving the turkey from roasting pan to a suitable carv-   3
ing area. This is done by inserting the carving knife into the poste-
rior stuffed area of the turkey and the knife-sharpening stone into
the stuffed area under the neck.

Thus skewered, the turkey may be lifted out of the hot grease with   4
relative safety. Should the turkey drop to the floor, however, remove
the knife and stone, roll the turkey gingerly into the two bath towels, wrap them several times around it and lift the encased fowl to
the carving place.

You are now ready to begin carving. Sharpen the knife on the   5
stone and insert it where the thigh joins the torso. If you do this
correctly, which is improbable, the knife will almost immediately encounter a barrier of bone and gristle. This may very well be the joint.
It could, however, be your thumb. If not, execute a vigorous sawing
motion until satisfied that the knife has been defeated. Withdraw
the knife and ask someone nearby, in as testy a manner as possible,

213

why the knives at your house are not kept in better carving condition.

Exercise the biceps and forearms by lifting barbells until they are 6
strong enough for you to tackle the leg joint with bare hands. Wrapping one hand firmly around the thigh, seize the turkey's torso in the other hand and scream. Run cold water over hands to relieve pain of burns.

Now, take a bath towel in each hand and repeat the above maneu- 7
ver. The entire leg should snap away from the chassis with a distinct crack, and the rest of the turkey, obedient to Newton's law about equal and opposite reactions, should roll in the opposite direction, which means that if you are carving at the table the turkey will probably come to rest in someone's lap.

Get the turkey out of the lap with as little fuss as possible, and 8
concentrate on the leg. Use the meat cleaver to sever the sinewy leather which binds the thigh to the drumstick.

If using the alternate, ax method, this operation should be per- 9
formed on a cement walk outside the house in order to preserve the table.

Repeat the above operation on the turkey's uncarved side. You 10
now have two thighs and two drumsticks. Using the wash cloth, soap and hot water, bathe thoroughly and, if possible, go to a movie. Otherwise, look each person in the eye and say, "I don't suppose anyone wants white meat."

If compelled to carve the breast anyhow, sharpen the knife on the 11
stone again with sufficient awkwardness to tip over the gravy bowl on the person who started the stampede for white meat.

While everyone is rushing about to mop the gravy off her slacks, 12
hack at the turkey breast until it starts crumbling off the carcass in ugly chunks.

The alternative method for carving white meat is to visit around 13
the neighborhood until you find someone who has a good carving knife and borrow it, if you find one, which is unlikely.

This method enables you to watch the football game on neighbors' 14
television sets and also creates the possibility that somebody back at your table will grow tired of waiting and do the carving herself.

In this case, upon returning home, cast a pained stare upon the 15
mound of chopped white meat that has been hacked out by the family carving knife and refuse to do any more carving that day. No one who cares about the artistry of carving can be expected to work upon the mutilations of amateurs, and it would be a betrayal of the carver's art to do so.

COMPREHENSION

1. Outline the steps in carving a turkey that Baker presents, and group them into stages.

2. What function is served by the wash cloth? the bath towels? the barbells? the meat cleaver?

3. Like many sets of instructions, this one includes warnings. List some of the disastrous outcomes Baker predicts might occur.

PURPOSE AND AUDIENCE

1. Why does Baker call his essay "Slice of Life"?

2. Does this essay include an explicitly stated thesis? If so, where is it? If not, state the thesis in one sentence.

3. At times, Baker departs from strict chronological order to present an aside. What purpose do these brief digressions serve?

4. Do you think Baker expects his audience to be familiar with the basic process of turkey carving? How can you tell?

5. In general terms, what is this essay's purpose?

STYLE AND STRUCTURE

1. Identify the stylistic clues that distinguish this essay as a set of instructions rather than as a process explanation.

2. What functions do the introductory paragraphs (1 and 2) serve in this essay?

3. Underline the transitional words and phrases that give this essay unity and coherence. Are any other transitions needed? If so, supply them.

4. Baker occasionally lapses into "cookbook style," omitting articles, for instance. Does this use of a particular style weaken or enhance the essay? Explain.

5. Baker frequently employs irony (the use of words to convey the opposite of their literal meaning) and hyperbole (exaggeration for humorous effect). Give two examples of each technique.

6. What is the effect of the essay's conclusion?

VOCABULARY PROJECTS

1. Define each of the following words as it is used in this selection.

   sutures (2)   chassis (7)
   gingerly (4)   sinewy (8)
   execute (5)   compelled (11)
   testy (5)   mutilations (15)

2. At times Baker's vocabulary suggests a surgical procedure. Give examples of words that convey this effect. Why do you think Baker chooses these words?

3. Words may have neutral connotations, or they may be loaded with strong positive or negative associations. To help you understand how a single word's connotation, or suggested meaning, can influence a piece of writing, do the following:

   a. Replace these neutral words with words that have unfavorable connotations.

      moving (3)   maneuver (7)
      lifted (4)   uncarved (10)
      insert (5)

   b. Replace these loaded words with words that have neutral connotations.

      tackle (6)
      stampede (11)
      hack (12)

   How would your substitutions change the essay?

WRITING WORKSHOP

1. Write a set of instructions telling how to perform a physical activity or chore with which you are familiar. In your thesis, try to convince your audience of the benefits the process has for them.

2. Write a straightforward set of instructions explaining how to carve a turkey. Direct your instructions at someone who has never done this before. Use Baker's basic steps, but do not use humor or irony. Pay special attention to the connotations of the words you choose, particularly the descriptive adjectives.

3. Write a humorous set of instructions for one of these processes: how to write a "Dear John" or "Dear Jane" letter; how to bake a cake; how to give a dog a bath.

THEMATIC CONNECTIONS

- "The Patterns of Eating" (p. 167)

MY FIRST CONK

Malcolm X

Malcolm X was born Malcolm Little in Omaha, Nebraska, in 1925, and was assassinated in 1965 by a member of a rival religious group. During his lifetime, Malcolm X was everything from a numbers runner to a Pullman porter to a disciple of Elijah Muhammad, leader of the Black Muslims. The Autobiography of Malcolm X, *from which this excerpt is taken, relates his rise from poverty to national prominence as a lecturer and religious leader. The autobiography is unusual not only in its frankness and vividness, but also in how it was written: It was dictated to Alex Haley, later the author of* Roots. *"My First Conk" explains a ritual procedure that was part of Malcolm X's young manhood and also reflects his adult view of the process. The selection begins as an autobiographical narrative, goes on to explain a process, and ends on a strongly persuasive note.*

Shorty soon decided that my hair was finally long enough to be conked. He had promised to school me in how to beat the barber shops' three- and four-dollar price by making up congolene, and then conking ourselves.

I took the little list of ingredients he had printed out for me, and went to a grocery store, where I got a can of Red Devil lye, two eggs, and two medium-sized white potatoes. Then at a drugstore near the poolroom, I asked for a large jar of vaseline, a large bar of soap, a large-toothed comb and a fine-toothed comb, one of those rubber hoses with a metal spray-head, a rubber apron and a pair of gloves.

"Going to lay on that first conk?" the drugstore man asked me. I proudly told him, grinning, "Right!"

Shorty paid six dollars a week for a room in his cousin's shabby apartment. His cousin wasn't at home. "It's like the pad's mine, he spends so much time with his woman," Shorty said. "Now, you watch me—"

He peeled the potatoes and thin-sliced them into a quart-sized Mason fruit jar, then started stirring them with a wooden spoon as he gradually poured in a little over half the can of lye. "Never use a metal spoon; the lye will turn it black," he told me.

A jelly-like, starchy-looking glop resulted from the lye and po-

217

tatoes, and Shorty broke in the two eggs, stirring real fast—his own conk and dark face bent down close. The congolene turned pale-yellowish. "Feel the jar," Shorty said. I cupped my hand against the outside, and snatched it away. "Damn right, it's hot, that's the lye," he said. "So you know it's going to burn when I comb it in—it burns bad. But the longer you can stand it, the straighter the hair."

He made me sit down, and he tied the string of the new rubber apron tightly around my neck, and combed up my bush of hair. Then, from the big vaseline jar, he took a handful and massaged it hard all through my hair and into the scalp. He also thickly vase-lined my neck, ears and forehead. "When I get to washing out your head, be sure to tell me anywhere you feel any little stinging," Shorty warned me, washing his hands, then pulling on the rubber gloves, and tying on his own rubber apron. "You always got to re-member that any congolene left in burns a sore into your head." 7

The congolene just felt warm when Shorty started combing it in. But then my head caught fire. 8

I gritted my teeth and tried to pull the sides of the kitchen table together. The comb felt as if it was raking my skin off. 9

My eyes watered, my nose was running. I couldn't stand it any longer; I bolted to the washbasin. I was cursing Shorty with every name I could think of when he got the spray going and started soap-lathering my head. 10

He lathered and spray-rinsed, lathered and spray-rinsed, maybe ten or twelve times, each time gradually closing the hot-water fau-cet, until the rinse was cold, and that helped some. 11

"You feel any stinging spots?" 12

"No," I managed to say. My knees were trembling. 13

"Sit back down, then. I think we got it all out okay." 14

The flame came back as Shorty, with a thick towel, started drying my head, rubbing hard. *"Easy, man, easy!"* I kept shouting. 15

"The first time's always worst. You get used to it better before long. You took it real good, homeboy. You got a good conk." 16

When Shorty let me stand up and see in the mirror, my hair hung down in limp, damp strings. My scalp still flamed, but not as badly; I could bear it. He draped the towel around my shoulders, over my rubber apron, and began again vaselining my hair. 17

I could feel him combing, straight back, first the big comb, then the fine-tooth one. 18

Then, he was using a razor, very delicately, on the back of my neck. Then, finally, shaping the sideburns. 19

My first view in the mirror blotted out the hurting. I'd seen some 20 pretty conks, but when it's the first time, on your *own* head, the transformation, after the lifetime of kinks, is staggering.

The mirror reflected Shorty behind me. We both were grinning   21
and sweating. And on top of my head was this thick, smooth sheen of shining red hair—real red—as straight as any white man's.

How ridiculous I was! Stupid enough to stand there simply lost   22
in admiration of my hair now looking "white," reflected in the mirror in Shorty's room. I vowed that I'd never again be without a conk, and I never was for many years.

This was my first really big step toward self-degradation: when I   23
endured all of that pain, literally burning my flesh to have it look like a white man's hair. I had joined that multitude of Negro men and women in America who are brainwashed into believing that the black people are "inferior"—and white people "superior"—that they will even violate and mutilate their God-created bodies to try to look "pretty" by white standards.

Look around today, in every small town and big city, from two-   24
bit catfish and soda-pop joints into the "integrated" lobby of the Waldorf-Astoria, and you'll see conks on black men. And you'll see black women wearing these green and pink and purple and red and platinum-blonde wigs. They're all more ridiculous than a slapstick comedy. It makes you wonder if the Negro has completely lost his sense of identity, lost touch with himself.

You'll see the conk worn by many, many so-called "upper class"   25
Negroes, and, as much as I hate to say it about them, on all too many Negro entertainers. One of the reasons that I've especially admired some of them, like Lionel Hampton and Sidney Poitier, among others, is that they have kept their natural hair and fought to the top. I admire any Negro man who has never had himself conked, or who has had the sense to get rid of it—as I finally did.

I don't know which kind of self-defacing conk is the greater   26
shame—the one you'll see on the heads of the black so-called "middle class" and "upper class," who ought to know better, or the one you'll see on the heads of the poorest, most downtrodden, ignorant black men. I mean the legal-minimum-wage ghetto-dwelling kind of Negro, as I was when I got my first one. It's generally among these poor fools that you'll see a black kerchief over the man's head, like Aunt Jemima; he's trying to make his conk last longer, between trips to the barbershop. Only for special occasions is this kerchief-protected conk exposed—to show off how "sharp" and "hip" its owner is. The ironic thing is that I have never heard any woman, white or black, express any admiration for a conk. Of course, any

white woman with a black man isn't thinking about his hair. But I don't see how on earth a black woman with any race pride could walk down the street with any black man wearing a conk—the emblem of his shame that he is black.

To my own shame, when I say all of this I'm talking first of all 27 about myself—because you can't show me any Negro who ever conked more faithfully than I did. I'm speaking from personal experience when I say of any black man who conks today, or any white-wigged black woman, that if they gave the brains in their heads just half as much attention as they do their hair, they would be a thousand times better off.

COMPREHENSION

1. What exactly is a conk? Why did Malcolm X want to get his hair conked? What did the conk symbolize to him at the time he got it? What did it symbolize at the time he wrote about it?

2. List the materials Shorty asked Malcolm X to buy. Is the purpose of each explained? If so, where?

3. Outline the major stages in the procedure Malcolm X describes. Are they in chronological order? Which, if any of the major stages, are out of place?

PURPOSE AND AUDIENCE

1. Why does Malcolm X write this selection as a process explanation instead of as a set of instructions?

2. This process explanation has an explicit thesis that makes its purpose clear. What is this thesis?

3. *The Autobiography of Malcolm X* was published in 1964, when many blacks got their hair straightened regularly. Is the thesis of the selection still relevant today?

4. Why does Malcolm X include so many references to the pain and discomfort he endured as part of the process?

5. What is the relationship between Malcolm X's personal narrative and the universal statement he makes about conking in this selection?

STYLE AND STRUCTURE

1. Identify some of the transitional words Malcolm X uses to move from step to step.

2. Only about half of this selection is devoted to the process explanation. Where does the process begin? Where does it end?

3. How does the use of dialogue strengthen the process explanation? How does it strengthen Malcolm X's thesis?

4. In paragraphs 22–26, Malcolm X encloses several words in quotation marks, occasionally prefacing them with the phrase *so-called*. What is the effect of these quotation marks?

VOCABULARY PROJECTS

1. Define each of the following words as it is used in this selection.

   vowed (22)   slapstick (24)
   self-degradation (23)   self-defacing (26)
   multitude (23)   downtrodden (26)
   mutilate (23)   emblem (26)

2. Because this is an informal narrative, Malcolm X uses conversational slang terms. Substitute a more formal word for each of the following.

   beat (1)   real (6)
   pad (4)   "sharp" (26)
   glop (6)   "hip" (26)

Evaluate the possible impact of your substitutions. Do they improve the essay or detract from it?

WRITING WORKSHOP

1. Write a process explanation of an unpleasant experience you have often gone through in order to conform to others' standards of physical beauty (for instance, shaving or getting a permanent). Includes a thesis that conveys your disapproval of the process.

2. Rewrite Malcolm X's process explanation as he might have written it when he still thought of conking as a desirable process, worth all the trouble. Include all his steps, but change his thesis and slant your writing to make conking sound painless and worthwhile.

3. Write a set of instructions for a process whose purpose is to transform your appearance—for instance, applying make-up or putting on a tuxedo. Try to inject some humor into your paper.

THEMATIC CONNECTIONS

- "Finishing School" (p. 57)
- "Aria: A Memoir of a Bilingual Childhood" (p. 348)

THE SPIDER AND THE WASP

Alexander Petrunkevitch

*Alexander Petrunkevitch (1875–1964) was a zoologist and a re-
spected authority on spiders. He taught at a number of major universities in the United States and wrote several important scientific books, including* Indes Catalogue of Spiders of North, Central,
and South America *(1911) and* Principles of Classification
*(1952). "The Spider and the Wasp," which presents a vivid descrip-
tion of the process by which a wasp attacks and kills a tarantula,
was first published in 1952 in* Scientific American *and has since
been anthologized many times.*

In the feeding and safeguarding of their progeny insects and spi-   1
ders exhibit some interesting analogies to reasoning and some crass
examples of blind instinct. The case I propose to describe here is
that of the tarantula spiders and their archenemy, the digger wasps
of the genus *Pepsis*. It is a classic example of what looks like intelligence pitted against instinct—a strange situation in which the victim, though fully able to defend itself, submits unwittingly to its
destruction.

Most tarantulas live in the tropics, but several species occur in   2
the temperate zone and a few are common in the southern U.S. Some
varieties are large and have powerful fangs with which they can in-
flict a deep wound. These formidable-looking spiders do not, however, attack man; you can hold one in your hand, if you are gentle,
without being bitten. Their bite is dangerous only to insects and
small mammals such as mice; for man it is no worse than a hornet's
sting.

Tarantulas customarily live in deep cylindrical burrows, from   3
which they emerge at dusk and into which they retire at dawn. Ma-
ture males wander about after dark in search of females and occasionally stray into houses. After mating, the male dies in a few
weeks, but a female lives much longer and can mate several years
in succession. In a Paris museum is a tropical specimen which is said
to have been living in captivity for 25 years.

A fertilized female tarantula lays from 200 to 400 eggs at a time;   4 thus it is possible for a single tarantula to produce several thousand young. She takes no care of them beyond weaving a cocoon of silk to enclose the eggs. After they hatch, the young walk away, find convenient places in which to dig their burrows and spend the rest of their lives in solitude. The eyesight of tarantulas is poor, being limited to a sensing of change in the intensity of light and to the perception of moving objects. They apparently have little or no sense of hearing, for a hungry tarantula will pay no attention to a loudly chirping cricket placed in its cage unless the insect happens to touch one of its legs.

But all spiders, and especially hairy ones, have an extremely deli-   5
cate sense of touch. Laboratory experiments prove that tarantulas can distinguish three types of touch: pressure against the body wall, stroking of the body hair, and riffling of certain very fine hairs on the legs called trichobothria. Pressure against the body, by the finger or the end of a pencil, causes the tarantula to move off slowly for a short distance. The touch excites no defensive response unless the approach is from above where the spider can see the motion, in which case it rises on its hind legs, lifts its front legs, opens its fangs and holds this threatening posture as long as the object continues to move.

The entire body of a tarantula, especially its legs, is thickly   6
clothed with hair. Some of it is short and wooly, some long and stiff. Touching this body hair produces one of two distinct reactions. When the spider is hungry, it responds with an immediate and swift attack. At the touch of a cricket's antennae the tarantula seizes the insect so swiftly that a motion picture taken at the rate of 64 frames per second shows only the result and not the process of capture. But when the spider is not hungry, the stimulation of its hairs merely causes it to shake the touched limb. An insect can walk under its hairy belly unharmed.

The trichobothria, very fine hairs growing from disklike mem-   7
branes on the legs, are sensitive only to air movement. A light breeze makes them vibrate slowly, without disturbing the common hair. When one blows gently on the trichobothria, the tarantula reacts with a quick jerk of its four front legs. If the front and hind legs are stimulated at the same time, the spider makes a sudden jump. This reaction is quite independent of the state of its appetite.

These three tactile responses—to pressure on the body wall, to   8
moving of the common hair, and to flexing of the trichobothria—are so different from one another that there is no possibility of confusing them. They serve the tarantula adequately for most of its needs

and enable it to avoid most annoyances and dangers. But they fail the spider completely when it meets its deadly enemy, the digger wasp *Pepsis*.

These solitary wasps are beautiful and formidable creatures. Most species are either a deep shiny blue all over, or deep blue with rusty wings. The largest have a wing span of about 4 inches. They live on nectar. When excited, they give off a pungent odor—a warning that they are ready to attack. The sting is much worse than that of a bee or common wasp, and the pain and swelling last longer. In the adult stage the wasp lives only a few months. The female produces but a few eggs, one at a time at intervals of two or three days. For each egg the mother must provide one adult tarantula, alive but paralyzed. The mother wasp attaches the egg to the paralyzed spider's abdomen. Upon hatching from the egg, the larva is many hundreds of times smaller than its living but helpless victim. It eats no other food and drinks no water. By the time it has finished its single Gargantuan meal and become ready for wasphood, nothing remains of the tarantula but its indigestible chitinous skeleton. [9]

The mother wasp goes tarantula-hunting when the egg in her ovary is almost ready to be laid. Flying low over the ground late on a sunny afternoon, the wasp looks for its victim or for the mouth of a tarantula burrow, a round hole edged by a bit of silk. The sex of the spider makes no difference, but the mother is highly discriminating as to species. Each species of *Pepsis* requires a certain species of tarantula, and the wasp will not attack the wrong species. In a cage with a tarantula which is not its normal prey, the wasp avoids the spider and is usually killed by it in the night. [10]

Yet when a wasp finds the correct species, it is the other way about. To identify the species the wasp apparently must explore the spider with her antennae. The tarantula shows an amazing tolerance to this exploration. The wasp crawls under it and walks over it without evoking any hostile response. The molestation is so great and so persistent that the tarantula often rises on all eight legs, as if it were on stilts. It may stand this way for several minutes. Meanwhile the wasp, having satisfied itself that the victim is of the right species, moves off a few inches to dig the spider's grave. Working vigorously with legs and jaws, it excavates a hole 8 to 10 inches deep with a diameter slightly larger than the spider's girth. Now and again the wasp pops out of the hole to make sure that the spider is still there. [11]

When the grave is finished, the wasp returns to the tarantula to complete her ghastly enterprise. First she feels it all over once more with her antennae. Then her behavior becomes more aggressive. She [12] bends her abdomen, protruding her sting, and searches for the soft membrane at the point where the spider's legs join its body—the only spot where she can penetrate the horny skeleton. From time to time, as the exasperated spider slowly shifts ground, the wasp turns on her back and slides along with the aid of her wings, trying to get under the tarantula for a shot at the vital spot. During all this maneuvering, which can last for several minutes, the tarantula makes no move to save itself. Finally the wasp corners it against some obstruction and grasps one of its legs in her powerful jaws. Now at last the harassed spider tries a desperate but vain defense. The two contestants roll over and over on the ground. It is a terrifying sight and the outcome is always the same. The wasp finally manages to thrust her sting into the soft spot and holds it there for a few seconds while she pumps in the poison. Almost immediately the tarantula falls paralyzed on its back. Its legs stop twitching; its heart stops beating. Yet it is not dead, as is shown by the fact that if taken from the wasp it can be restored to some sensitivity by being kept in a moist chamber for several months.

After paralyzing the tarantula, the wasp cleans herself by drag- 13
ging her body along the ground and rubbing her feet, sucks a drop of blood oozing from the wound in the spider's abdomen, then grabs a leg of the flabby, helpless animal in her jaws and drags it down to the bottom of the grave. She stays there for many minutes, sometimes for several hours, and what she does all that time in the dark we do not know. Eventually she lays her egg and attaches it to the side of the spider's abdomen with a sticky secretion. Then she emerges, fills the grave with soil carried bit by bit in her jaws, and finally tramples the ground all around to hide any trace of the grave from prowlers. Then she flies away, leaving her descendant safely started in life.

In all this the behavior of the wasp evidently is qualitatively dif- 14
ferent from that of the spider. The wasp acts like an intelligent animal. This is not to say that instinct plays no part or that she reasons as man does. But her actions are to the point; they are not automatic and can be modified to fit the situation. We do not know for certain how she identifies the tarantula—probably it is by some olfactory or chemo-tactile sense—but she does it purposefully and does not blindly tackle a wrong species.

On the other hand, the tarantula's behavior shows only confusion. 15
Evidently the wasp's pawing gives it no pleasure, for it tries to move away. That the wasp is not simulating sexual stimulation is certain because male and female tarantulas react in the same way to its

advances. That the spider is not anesthetized by some odorless secretion is easily shown by blowing slightly at the tarantula and making it jump suddenly. What, then, makes the tarantula behave as
stupidly as it does?

No clear, simple answer is available. Possibly the stimulation by   16
the wasp's antennae is masked by a heavier pressure on the spider's
body, so that it reacts as when prodded by a pencil. But the explanation may be much more complex. Initiative in attack is not in the
nature of tarantulas; most species fight only when cornered so that
escape is impossible. Their inherited patterns of behavior apparently prompt them to avoid problems rather than attack them. For
example, spiders always weave their webs in three dimensions, and
when a spider finds that there is insufficient space to attach certain
threads in the third dimension, it leaves the place and seeks another,
instead of finishing the web in a single plane. This urge to escape
seems to arise under all circumstances, in all phases of life, and to
take the place of reasoning. For a spider to change the pattern of its
web is as impossible as for an inexperienced man to build a bridge
across a chasm obstructing his way.

In a way the instinctive urge to escape is not only easier but often   17
more efficient than reasoning. The tarantula does exactly what is
most efficient in all cases except in an encounter with a ruthless and
determined attacker dependent for the existence of her own species
on killing as many tarantulas as she can lay eggs. Perhaps in this
case the spider follows its usual pattern of trying to escape, instead
of seizing and killing the wasp, because it is not aware of its danger.
In any case, the survival of the tarantula species as a whole is
protected by the fact that the spider is much more fertile than the
wasp.

COMPREHENSION

1. List some of the tarantula's most striking physical features. List
   some of the wasp's most striking physical features.

2. Why *must* the wasp paralyze the tarantula?

3. What does Petrunkevitch see as the single most obvious contrast between the behavior of the wasp and that of the spider?

4. Why, according to Petrunkevitch, does the spider behave with such
   apparent stupidity in its encounter with the wasp?

5. Why is the fact that the tarantula is more fertile than the wasp so
   important?

PURPOSE AND AUDIENCE

1. Does "The Spider and the Wasp" include an explicitly stated thesis? If so, what is it? If not, why not?

2. *Scientific American,* in which "The Spider and the Wasp" first appeared, is a periodical aimed not at scientists but at a well-educated audience with an interest in science. What techniques are used by Petrunkevitch, a zoologist, to arouse and hold the interest of this audience?

3. What do you think is Petrunkevitch's purpose in spending so much more time describing the spider than the wasp? Does he accomplish this end? Explain.

STYLE AND STRUCTURE

1. Where does Petrunkevitch actually begin his discussion of the process by which a wasp kills a tarantula?

2. In the essay's opening paragraphs, Petrunkevitch describes first the spider and then the wasp. How does he indicate his movement from one subject to the other?

3. Why does Petrunkevitch supply detailed descriptions of both the spider and the wasp before he begins to describe the process?

4. In the section of the essay devoted to the process explanation, what transitional words and phrases help readers to follow the steps of the process?

5. What verb tense does Petrunkevitch use in his explanation of the process? Why does he select this tense?

6. In paragraph 11 Petrunkevitch uses an analogy to help readers visualize the tarantula's reaction to the wasp. What is this analogy? Where else does Petrunkevitch use analogies to clarify his explanations?

7. Petrunkevitch makes frequent use of parallelism in his essay. One example of this technique is "They serve the tarantula adequately.... But they fail the spider completely.... " Give some additional examples of parallel constructions. How does parallelism strengthen the essay?

VOCABULARY PROJECTS

1. Define each of the following words as it is used in this selection.
   progeny (1)   crass (1)

unwittingly (1)   chitinous (9)
tactile (8)   olfactory (14)
Gargantuan (9)

2. Although Petrunkevitch knows his audience is not composed of zoologists, his topic requires that he use an occasional technical term. Still, he is careful to accommodate his audience by defining such terms or by placing them in a context that suggests their meaning. Give examples of two or three such technical terms, and explain the concessions Petrunkevitch makes to his audience in each case.

3. At times Petrunkevitch uses distinctly unscientific language—for example, "the wasp pops out of the hole" (11); "her ghastly enterprise" (12). Give other examples of such language, and explain why you think Petrunkevitch uses it.

WRITING WORKSHOP

1. In paragraph 1 Petrunkevitch calls the spider–wasp confrontation "a classic example of what looks like intelligence pitted against instinct—a strange situation in which the victim, though fully able to defend itself, submits unwittingly to its destruction." Write a process essay in which you explain a similar "strange situation" from your own reading or experience—for example, deciding not to respond to a dangerous physical challenge or not to pursue an argument even though you believe you are right.

2. Write a process essay in which you describe an encounter between two people or groups. First describe each in turn, and then give a step-by-step account of their meeting. In your thesis, try to define what the encounter reveals about the two and about their relationship to each other.

3. Describe the process Petrunkevitch outlines from the point of view of either the spider or the wasp. Use first person and present tense.

THEMATIC CONNECTIONS

- "Courtship through the Ages" (p. 193)
- "Murder: Passion and Pathology" (p. 332)

THE MAKER'S EYE: REVISING YOUR OWN MANUSCRIPTS

Donald M. Murray

In this essay, originally published in The Writer, *Donald Murray argues for the importance of the revision process to the writer. Murray, who was born in 1917 and now teaches at the University of New Hampshire, has been a Pulitzer Prize-winning journalist and an editor of* Time *magazine. He has also written various works of fiction, nonfiction, and poetry, as well as the textbooks* A Writer Teaches Writing, Write to Learn, *and* Read to Write. *As he presents the stages in the revision process, Murray illustrates their usefulness to any writer and offers his own views and those of other professional authors.*

When students complete a first draft, they consider the job of writing done—and their teachers too often agree. When professional writers complete a first draft, they usually feel that they are at the start of the writing process. When a draft is completed, the job of writing can begin. 1

That difference in attitude is the difference between amateur and professional, inexperience and experience, journeyman and craftsman. Peter F. Drucker, the prolific business writer, calls his first draft "the zero draft"—after that he can start counting. Most writers share the feeling that the first draft, and all of those which follow, are opportunities to discover what they have to say and how best they can say it. 2

To produce a progression of drafts, each of which says more and says it more clearly, the writer has to develop a special kind of reading skill. In school we are taught to decode what appears on the page as finished writing. Writers, however, face a different category of possibility and responsibility when they read their own drafts. To them the words on the page are never finished. Each can be changed and rearranged, can set off a chain reaction of confusion or clarified meaning. This is a different kind of reading, which is possibly more difficult and certainly more exciting. 3

Writers must learn to be their own best enemy. They must accept the criticism of others and be suspicious of it; they must accept the 4 praise of others and be even more suspicious of it. Writers cannot depend on others. They must detach themselves from their own pages so that they can apply both their caring and their craft to their own work.

Such detachment is not easy. Science fiction writer Ray Bradbury supposedly puts each manuscript away for a year to the day and then rereads it as a stranger. Not many writers have the discipline or the time to do this. We must read when our judgment may be at its worst, when we are close to the euphoric moment of creation. 5

Then the writer, counsels novelist Nancy Hale, "should be critical of everything that seems to him most delightful in his style. He should excise what he most admires, because he wouldn't thus admire it if he weren't . . . in a sense protecting it from criticism." John Ciardi, the poet, adds, "The last act of the writing must be to become one's own reader. It is, I suppose, a schizophrenic process, to begin passionately and to end critically, to begin hot and to end cold; and, more important, to be passion-hot and critic-cold at the same time." 6

Most people think that the principal problem is that writers are too proud of what they have written. Actually, a greater problem for most professional writers is one shared by the majority of students. They are overly critical, think everything is dreadful, tear up page after page, never complete a draft, see the task as hopeless. 7

The writer must learn to read critically but constructively, to cut what is bad, to reveal what is good. Eleanor Estes, the children's book author, explains: "The writer must survey his work critically, coolly, as though he were a stranger to it. He must be willing to prune, expertly and hard-heartedly. At the end of each revision, a manuscript may look . . . worked over, torn apart, pinned together, added to, deleted from, words changed and words changed back. Yet the book must maintain its original freshness and spontaneity." 8

Most readers underestimate the amount of rewriting it usually takes to produce spontaneous reading. This is a great disadvantage to the student writer, who sees only a finished product and never watches the craftsman who takes the necessary step back, studies the work carefully, returns to the task, steps back, returns, steps back, again and again. Anthony Burgess, one of the most prolific writers in the English-speaking world, admits, "I might revise a page twenty times." Roald Dahl, the popular children's writer, states, "By the time I'm nearing the end of a story, the first part will have been reread and altered and corrected at least 150 times. . . . Good writing is essentially rewriting. I am positive of this." 9

Rewriting isn't virtuous. It isn't something that ought to be done.   10
It is simply something that most writers find they have to do to
discover what they have to say and how to say it. It is a condition
of the writer's life.

There are, however, a few writers who do little formal rewriting,   11
primarily because they have the capacity and experience to create
and review a large number of invisible drafts in their minds before
they approach the page. And some writers slowly produce finished
pages, performing all the tasks of revision simultaneously, page by
page, rather than draft by draft. But it is still possible to see the
sequence followed by most writers most of the time in rereading
their own work.

Most writers scan their drafts first, reading as quickly as possible   12
to catch the larger problems of subject and form, then move in closer
and closer as they read and write, reread and rewrite.

The first thing writers look for in their drafts is *information*. They   13
know that a good piece of writing is built from specific, accurate,
and interesting information. The writer must have an abundance of
information from which to construct a readable piece of writing.

Next writers look for *meaning* in the information. The specifics   14
must build a pattern of significance. Each piece of specific information must carry the reader toward meaning.

Writers reading their own drafts are aware of *audience*. They put   15
themselves in the reader's situation and make sure that they deliver
information which a reader wants to know or needs to know in a
manner which is easily digested. Writers try to be sure that they
anticipate and answer the questions a critical reader will ask when
reading the piece of writing.

Writers make sure that the *form* is appropriate to the subject and   16
the audience. Form, or genre, is the vehicle which carries meaning to
the reader, but form cannot be selected until the writer has adequate
information to discover its significance and an audience which needs
or wants that meaning.

Once writers are sure the form is appropriate, they must then look   17
at the *structure,* the order of what they have written. Good writing
is built on a solid framework of logic, argument, narrative, or motivation which runs through the entire piece of writing and holds it
together. This is the time when many writers find it most effective
to outline as a way of visualizing the hidden spine by which the piece
of writing is supported.

The element on which writers may spend a majority of their time   18
is *development.* Each section of a piece of writing must be adequately developed. It must give readers enough information so that

they are satisfied. How much information is enough? That's as diffi- cult as asking how much garlic belongs in a salad. It must be done to taste, but most beginning writers underdevelop, underestimating the reader's hunger for information.

As writers solve development problems, they often have to con- sider questions of *dimension.* There must be a pleasing and effective proportion among all the parts of the piece of writing. There is a continual process of subtracting and adding to keep the piece of writing in balance. 19

Finally, writers have to listen to their own voices. *Voice* is the force which drives a piece of writing forward. It is an expression of the writer's authority and concern. It is what is between the words on the page, what glues the piece of writing together. A good piece of writing is always marked by a consistent, individual voice. 20

As writers read and reread, write and rewrite, they move closer and closer to the page until they are doing line-by-line editing. Writers read their own pages with infinite care. Each sentence, each line, each clause, each phrase, each word, each mark of punctuation, each section of white space between the type has to contribute to the clarification of meaning. 21

Slowly the writer moves from word to word, looking through lan- guage to see the subject. As a word is changed, cut, or added, as a construction is rearranged, all the words used before that moment and all those that follow that moment must be considered and recon- sidered. 22

Writers often read aloud at this stage of the editing process, mut- tering or whispering to themselves, calling on the ear's experience with language. Does this sound right—or that? Writers edit, shift- ing back and forth from eye to page to ear to page. I find I must do this careful editing in short runs, no more than fifteen or twenty minutes at a stretch, or I become too kind with myself. I begin to see what I hope is on the page, not what actually is on the page. 23

This sounds tedious if you haven't done it, but actually it is fun. Making something right is immensely satisfying, for writers begin to learn what they are writing about by writing. Language leads them to meaning, and there is the joy of discovery, of understand- ing, of making meaning clear as the writer employs the technical skills of language. 24

Words have double meanings, even triple and quadruple mean- ings. Each word has its own potential for connotation and denota- tion. And when writers rub one word against the other, they are often rewarded with a sudden insight, an unexpected clarification. 25

The maker's eye moves back and forth from word to phrase to 26 sentence to paragraph to sentence to phrase to word. The maker's eye sees the need for variety and balance, for a firmer structure, for a more appropriate form. It peers into the interior of the paragraph, looking for coherence, unity, and emphasis, which make meaning clear.

I learned something about this process when my first bifocals were prescribed. I had ordered a larger section of the reading portion of the glass because of my work, but even so, I could not contain my eyes within this new limit of vision. And I still find myself taking off my glasses and bending my nose towards the page, for my eyes unconsciously flick back and forth across the page, back to another page, forward to still another, as I try to see each evolving line in relation to every other line.

When does this process end? Most writers agree with the great Russian writer Tolstoy, who said, "I scarcely ever reread my published writings, if by chance I come across a page, it always strikes me: all this must be rewritten; this is how I should have written it."

The maker's eye is never satisfied, for each word has the potential to ignite new meaning. This article has been twice written all the way through the writing process, and it was published four years ago. Now it is to be republished in a book. The editors make a few small suggestions, and then I read it with my maker's eye. Now it has been re-edited, re-revised, re-read, re-re-edited, for each piece of writing to the writer is full of potential and alternatives.

A piece of writing is never finished. It is delivered to a deadline, torn out of the typewriter on demand, sent off with a sense of accomplishment and shame and pride and frustration. If only there were a couple more days, time for just another run at it, perhaps then . . .

COMPREHENSION

1. What difference does Murray identify between how student and professional writers view a first draft? How does he account for this difference? What problem do both share?

2. What special kind of reading skill does Murray say the writer has to develop? Why?

3. How do the professional writers Murray quotes lend support to his thesis?

4. How do professional writers consider audience, form, structure, development, and voice as they revise?

5. Why does the process of revision never actually end?

PURPOSE AND AUDIENCE

1. This essay has an explicitly stated thesis. What is it? Where does it appear?

2. Is Murray's purpose primarily to inform or to persuade? Where does he serve each of these purposes?

3. This essay was written for professional writers, not college students. How does this audience explain the author's decision to write an explanation instead of a set of instructions?

STYLE AND STRUCTURE

1. Murray does not introduce the first step in his process until paragraph 12. Why not?

2. Paragraph 20 begins with the word *finally*, signaling that the last stage in the revision process is being introduced. Where does the discussion of this stage end?

3. Murray occasionally uses analogy to make the writing process concrete and familiar. Identify some of these uses of analogy.

4. Murray occasionally speaks to the reader in the first person. Locate these first-person comments, and explain their effect.

5. Why does Murray end his essay in the middle of a sentence?

VOCABULARY PROJECTS

1. Define each of the following words as it is used in this selection.

   journeyman (2)   schizophrenic (6)
   prolific (2)   connotation (25)
   euphoric (5)   denotation (25)

2. Give three synonyms for each of these words used by Murray in his essay. Be prepared to explain what, if anything, would have been lost if Murray had chosen any of your synonyms instead of his words.

   feeling (2)   prune (8)
   decode (3)   altered (9)
   detach (4)   framework (17)
   dreadful (7)   glues (20)

WRITING WORKSHOP

1. How do you revise your writing? Write an essay in which you explain the steps you take, noting why this process does or does not work for you.

2. Write a set of instructions in which you attempt to convince a younger student of the importance of revision. If you prefer, your essay can focus on the advantages of revising on a computer.

3. Interview a teacher, parent, or older sibling about the way a particular academic subject or skill was taught to them in school. Write an essay explaining the process as you understand it.

THEMATIC CONNECTONS

- "Academic vs. Technical Audiences" (p. 316)

THE EMBALMING
OF MR. JONES

Jessica Mitford

Jessica Mitford was born in England in 1917 and grew up with her four sisters in a protected, wealthy environment. Her sheltered upbringing contrasts sharply with her later involvement in politics and investigative journalism. Her most recent book is Faces of Philip: A Memoir of Philip Toynbee *(1984). Mitford turned her ironic wit on her eccentric family in her autobiographical* Daughters and Rebels *(1960), on left-wing politics in* A Fine Old Conflict *(1977), on the prison system in* Kind and Usual Punishment *(1973), on investigative journalism in* Poison Penmanship *(1979), and on the mortuary business in* The American Way of Death *(1963), from which this excerpt is taken. A scathing criticism of the funeral industry, this book sharpened public scrutiny of the way funerals are handled and also prompted many angry responses from morticians. In "The Embalming of Mr. Jones," Mitford painstakingly and ironically describes the dual process of embalming and restoring a cadaver. Notice as you read how Mitford's meticulous use of detail supports her thesis.*

Embalming is indeed a most extraordinary procedure, and one   1
must wonder at the docility of Americans who each year pay hundreds of millions of dollars for its perpetuation, blissfully ignorant of what it is all about, what is done, how it is done. Not one in ten thousand has any idea of what actually takes place. Books on the subject are extremely hard to come by. They are not to be found in most libraries or bookshops.

In an era when huge television audiences watch surgical opera-   2
tions in the comfort of their living rooms, when, thanks to the animated cartoon, the geography of the digestive system has become familiar territory even to the nursery school set, in a land where the satisfaction of curiosity about almost all matters is a national pastime, the secrecy surrounding embalming can, surely, hardly be attributed to the inherent gruesomeness of the subject. Custom in this regard has within this century suffered a complete reversal. In the early days of American embalming, when it was performed in

the home of the deceased, it was almost mandatory for some relative to stay by the embalmer's side and witness the procedure. Today, family members who might wish to be in attendance would certainly be dissuaded by the funeral director. All others, except apprentices, are excluded by law from the preparation room.

A close look at what does actually take place may explain in large measure the undertaker's intractable reticence concerning a procedure that has become his major *raison d'être*. Is it possible he fears that public information about embalming might lead patrons to wonder if they really want this service? If the funeral men are loath to discuss the subject outside the trade, the reader may, understandably, be equally loath to go on reading at this point. For those who have the stomach for it, let us part the formaldehyde curtain. . . .

The body is first laid out in the undertaker's morgue—or rather, Mr. Jones is reposing in the preparation room—to be readied to bid the world farewell.

The preparation room in any of the better funeral establishments has the tiled and sterile look of a surgery, and indeed the embalmer-restorative artist who does his chores there is beginning to adopt the term "dermasurgeon" (appropriately corrupted by some mortician-writers as "demisurgeon") to describe his calling. His equipment, consisting of scalpels, scissors, augers, forceps, clamps, needles, pumps, tubes, bowls and basins, is crudely imitative of the surgeon's as is his technique, acquired in a nine- or twelve-month post high-school course in an embalming school. He is supplied by an advanced chemical industry with a bewildering array of fluids, sprays, pastes, oils, powders, creams, to fix or soften tissue, shrink or distend it as needed, dry it here, restore the moisture there. There are cosmetics, waxes and paints to fill and cover features, even plaster of Paris to replace entire limbs. There are ingenious aids to prop and stabilize the cadaver: a Vari-Pose Head Rest, the Edwards Arm and Hand Positioner, the Repose Block (to support the shoulders during the embalming), and the Throop Foot Positioner, which resembles an old-fashioned stocks.

Mr. John H. Eckels, president of the Eckels College of Mortuary Science, thus describes the first part of the embalming procedure: "In the hands of a skilled practitioner, this work may be done in a comparatively short time and without mutilating the body other than by slight incision—so slight that it scarcely would cause serious inconvenience if made upon a living person. It is necessary to remove all the blood, and doing this not only helps in the disinfecting, but removes the principal cause of disfigurements due to discoloration."

Another textbook discusses the all-important time element: "The earlier this is done, the better, for every hour that elapses between death and embalming will add to the problems and complications encountered. . . . " Just how soon should one get going on the embalming? The author tells us, "On the basis of such scanty information made available to this profession through its rudimentary and haphazard system of technical research, we must conclude that the best results are to be obtained if the subject is embalmed before life is completely extinct—that is, before cellular death has occurred. In the average case, this would mean within an hour after somatic death." For those who feel that there is something a little rudimentary, not to say haphazard, about this advice, a comforting thought is offered by another writer. Speaking of fears entertained in early days of premature burial, he points out, "One of the effects of embalming by chemical injection, however, has been to dispel fears of live burial." How true; once the blood is removed, chances of live burial are indeed remote. 7

To return to Mr. Jones, the blood is drained out through the veins and replaced by embalming fluid pumped in through the arteries. As noted in *The Principles and Practices of Embalming,* "every operator has a favorite injection and drainage point—a fact which becomes a handicap only if he fails or refuses to forsake his favorites when conditions demand it." Typical favorites are the carotid artery, femoral artery, jugular vein, subclavian vein. There are various choices of embalming fluid. If Flextone is used, it will produce a "mild, flexible rigidity. The skin retains a velvety softness, the tissues are rubbery and pliable. Ideal for women and children." It may be blended with B. and G. Products Company's Lyf-Lyk tint, which is guaranteed to reproduce "nature's own skin texture . . . the velvety appearance of living tissue." Suntone comes in three separate tints: Suntan; Special Cosmetic Tint, a pink shade "especially indicated for young female subjects"; and Regular Cosmetic Tint, moderately pink. 8

About three to six gallons of a dyed and perfumed solution of formaldehyde, glycerin, borax, phenol, alcohol and water is soon circulating through Mr. Jones, whose mouth has been sewn together with a "needle directed upward between the upper lip and gum and brought out through the left nostril," with the corners raised slightly "for a more pleasant expression." If he should be bucktoothed, his teeth are cleaned with Bon Ami and coated with colorless nail polish. His eyes, meanwhile, are closed with flesh-tinted eye caps and eye cement. 9

The next step is to have at Mr. Jones with a thing called a trocar. 10

This is a long, hollow needle attached to a tube. It is jabbed into the abdomen, poked around the entrails and chest cavity, the contents of which are pumped out and replaced with "cavity fluid." This is done, and the hole in the abdomen sewed up, Mr. Jones's face is heavily creamed (to protect the skin from burns which may be caused by leakage of the chemicals), and he is covered with a sheet and left unmolested for a while. But not for long—there is more, much more, in store for him. He has been embalmed, but not yet restored, and the best time to start restorative work is eight to ten hours after embalming, when the tissues have become firm and dry.

The object of all this attention to the corpse, it must be remem- 11
bered, is to make it presentable for viewing in an attitude of healthy repose. "Our customs require the presentation of our dead in the semblance of normality . . . unmarred by the ravages of illness, disease or mutilation," says Mr. J. Sheridan Mayer in his *Restorative Art.* This is rather a large order since few people die in the full bloom of health, unravaged by illness and unmarked by some disfigurement. The funeral industry is equal to the challenge: "In some cases the gruesome appearance of a mutilated or disease-ridden subject may be quite discouraging. The task of restoration may seem impossible and shake the confidence of the embalmer. This is the time for intestinal fortitude and determination. Once the formative work is begun and affected tissues are cleaned or removed, all doubts of success vanish. It is surprising and gratifying to discover the results which may be obtained."

The embalmer, having allowed an appropriate interval to elapse, 12
returns to the attack, but now he brings into play the skill and equipment of sculptor and cosmetician. Is a hand missing? Casting one in plaster of Paris is a simple matter. "For replacement purposes, only a cast of the back of the hand is necessary; this is within the ability of the average operator and is quite adequate." If a lip or two, a nose or an ear should be missing, the embalmer has at hand a variety of restorative waxes with which to model replacements. Pores and skin texture are simulated by stippling with a little brush, and over this cosmetics are laid on. Head off? Decapitation cases are rather routinely handled. Ragged edges are trimmed, and head joined to torso with a series of splints, wires and sutures. It is a good idea to have a little something at the neck—a scarf or high collar—when time for viewing comes. Swollen mouth? Cut out tissue as needed from inside the lips. If too much is removed, the surface contour can easily be restored by padding with cotton. Swollen necks and cheeks are reduced by removing tissue through vertical incisions made down each side of the neck. "When the deceased is

casketed, the pillow will hide the suture incisions . . . as an extra precaution against leakage, the suture may be painted with liquid sealer.''

The opposite condition is more likely to be present itself—that of emaciation. His hypodermnic syringe now loaded with massage cream, the embalmer seeks out and fills the hollowed and sunken areas by injection. In this procedure the backs of the hands and fingers and the under-chin area should not be neglected. 13

Positioning the lips is a problem that recurrently challenges the ingenuity of the embalmer. Closed too tightly, they tend to give a stern, even disapproving expression. Ideally, embalmers feel, the lips should give the impression of being ever so slightly parted, the upper lip protruding slightly for a more youthful appearance. This takes some engineering, however, as the lips tend to drift apart. Lip drift can sometimes be remedied by pushing one or two straight pins through the inner margin of the lower lip and then inserting them between the two front upper teeth. If Mr. Jones happens to have no teeth, the pins can just as easily be anchored in his Armstrong Face Former and Denture Replacer. Another method to maintain lip closure is to dislocate the lower jaw, which is then held in its new position by a wire run through holes which have been drilled through the upper jaws at the midline. As the French are fond of saying, *il faut souffrir pour être belle.** 14

If Mr. Jones has died of jaundice, the embalming fluid will very likely turn him green. Does this deter the embalmer? Not if he has intestinal fortitude. Masking pastes and cosmetics are heavily laid on, burial garments and casket interiors are color-correlated with particular care, and Jones is displayed beneath rose-colored lights. Friends will say, "How *well* he looks." Death by carbon monoxide, on the other hand, can be rather a good thing from the embalmer's viewpoint: "One advantage is the fact that this type of discoloration is an exaggerated form of a natural pink coloration." This is nice because the healthy glow is already present and needs but little attention. 15

The patching and filling completed, Mr. Jones is now shaved, washed and dressed. Cream-based cosmetic, available in pink, flesh, suntan, brunette and blonde, is applied to his hands and face, his hair is shampooed and combed (and, in the case of Mrs. Jones, set), his hands manicured. For the horny-handed son of toil special care must be taken; cream should be applied to remove ingrained grime, 16

---

*EDS. NOTE—It is necessary to suffer in order to be beautiful.

and the nails cleaned. "If he were not in the habit of having them manicured in life, trimming and shaping is advised for better appearance—never questioned by kin."

Jones is now ready for casketing (this is the present participle of the verb "to casket"). In this operation his right shoulder should be depressed slightly "to turn the body a bit to the right and soften the appearance of lying flat on the back." Positioning the hands is a matter of importance, and special rubber positioning blocks may be used. The hands should be cupped slightly for a more lifelike, relaxed appearance. Proper placement of the body requires a delicate sense of balance. It should lie as high as possible in the casket, yet not so high that the lid, when lowered, will hit the nose. On the other hand, we are cautioned, placing the body too low "creates the impression that the body is in a box." 17

Jones is next wheeled into the appointed slumber room where a few last touches may be added—his favorite pipe placed in his hand or, if he was a great reader, a book propped into position. (In the case of little Master Jones a Teddy bear may be clutched.) Here he will hold open house for a few days, visiting hours 10 A.M. to 9 P.M. 18

COMPREHENSION

1. How, according to Mitford, has the public's knowledge of embalming changed? How does she explain this change?

2. To what other professionals does Mitford liken the embalmer? Are these analogies flattering or critical? Explain.

3. What are the major stages of the process of embalming and restoration?

PURPOSE AND AUDIENCE

1. Mitford's purpose in this essay is to convince her audience of something. What is her thesis?

2. Does Mitford expect her audience to agree with her thesis? How can you tell?

3. In one of her books, Mitford refers to herself as a muckraker, one who informs the public of misconduct. Does she achieve this status here? Cite specific examples.

4. Why do you suppose Mitford names the cadaver Mr. Jones?

5. Mitford's tone in this essay is very subjective. What effect does her tone have on you? Does it encourage you to trust her? Should she have presented her facts in a more objective way? Explain.

STYLE AND STRUCTURE

1. Identify the stylistic features that distinguish this process explanation from a set of instructions.

2. In this selection, as in most process essays, a list of necessary materials precedes the procedure. What additional details does Mitford include in her list in paragraph 5? How do these additions affect the reader?

3. Throughout this essay, Mitford uses extensive detail to convey her attitude without directly stating it. Give some examples of this technique.

4. Go through the essay and locate the author's remarks about the language of embalming. How are these comments about euphemisms, newly coined words, and other aspects of the language consistent with Mitford's thesis?

5. Throughout the essay, Mitford quotes a series of experts. How does she use their remarks to support her thesis?

6. What phrases signal Mitford's transitions between stages?

VOCABULARY PROJECTS

1. Define each of the following words as it is used in this selection.

perpetuation (1)	pliable (8)
inherent (2)	repose (11)
mandatory (2)	unravaged (11)
dissuaded (2)	fortitude (11)
intractable (3)	stippling (12)
reticence (3)	emaciation (13)
loath (3)	recurrently (14)
rudimentary (7)	jaundice (15)
haphazard (7)	toil (16)
entertained (7)	

2. Substitute another word for each of the following.

territory (2)	jabbed (10)
gruesomeness (2)	presentable (11)
ingenious (5)	

What effect does each of your changes have on Mitford's meaning?

3. Reread paragraphs 5-9 very carefully. Then, list all the words in this section of the essay that suggest surgical technique and all the words that suggest cosmetic artistry. What do your lists tell you about Mitford's intent in these paragraphs?

WRITING WORKSHOP

1. Rewrite this process explanation as a set of instructions for undertakers, condensing it so that your essay is about five hundred words long. Unlike Mitford, keep your essay objective.

2. In the role of a funeral director, write a letter to Mitford in which you take issue with her essay. Explain the practice of embalming as necessary and practical. Design your process explanation, unlike Mitford's, to defend the practice.

3. Write an explanation of a process which you personally find disgusting—or delightful. Make your attitude clear in your thesis statement and your choice of words.

THEMATIC CONNECTIONS

- "Pure and Impure: The Interplay of Science and Technology" (p. 184)
- "A Toast to Progress" (p 369)

WRITING ASSIGNMENTS FOR PROCESS

1. Write a short explanation of the process you follow when you write an essay. If you compose on a computer, explain the procedure you follow.

2. Write a set of instructions explaining how to get from your home to school (or from any one place to another) on foot or by bicycle or car.

3. Write a consumer-oriented article for your school newspaper in which you explain how to apply for a student loan, a work-study job, a scholarship, or a student internship.

4. List the steps in the process you follow when you study for a major exam. Then, interview a friend about how he or she studies, and take notes about his or her customary procedure. Finally, combine the most helpful strategies into a set of instructions aimed at students entering your school.

5. Write a set of instructions explaining how to use one of these reference works: a thesaurus, the *Readers' Guide to Periodical Literature*, or the *Encyclopaedia Britannica*. If you like, you may substitute another reference work with which you are more familiar.

6. Think of a series of steps in a bureaucratic process, a process you had to go through to accomplish something: registering for classes, registering to vote, getting a driver's license, or applying to college, for instance. Write an essay in which you explain that process.

7. Imagine you have encountered a visitor from another country (or another planet) who is not familiar with a social ritual you take for granted. Try to outline the steps involved in one such ritual—for instance, the Miss America finals; choosing sides for a game; pledging a fraternity or sorority.

8. Write a process essay explaining how you went about putting together a collection, a scrapbook, or an album of some kind. Be sure your essay makes clear why you collected or compiled your materials.

9. Explain how a certain ritual or ceremony is conducted in your religion. Make sure someone of another faith will be able to understand the process.

10. Think of a process you believe should be modified or discontinued. Formulate a persuasive thesis that presents your negative feelings, and then explain the process so that you make your objections to it clear to your readers.

6

Cause and Effect

WHAT IS CAUSE AND EFFECT?

Process describes *how* something happens; cause and effect considers *why* something happens. Cause-and-effect essays examine causes, describe effects, or do both. In the following passage from a newspaper op-ed piece entitled "The Pump on the Well," columnist Tom Wicker considers the effects of a technological advance on a village in India.

> When a solar-powered water pump was provided for a well in India, the village headman took it over and sold the water, until stopped. The new liquid abundance attracted hordes of unwanted nomads. Village boys who had drawn water in buckets had nothing to do, and some became criminals. The gap between rich and poor widened, since the poor had no land to benefit from irrigation. Finally, village women broke the pump, so they could gather again around the well that had been the center of their social lives.
>
> Moral: technological advances have social, cultural and economic consequences, often unanticipated.

Cause and effect, like narration, links situations and events together in time, with causes preceding effects. But causality involves more than sequence: It explains why something happened—or is happening—and it predicts what probably will happen.

Sometimes many different causes can be responsible for one effect. For example, many elements may contribute to an individual's decision to leave his or her native country to live in the United States.

Causes   *Effect*

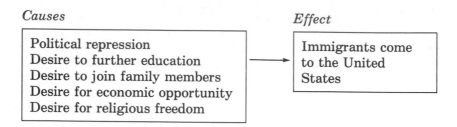

Political repression
Desire to further education
Desire to join family members
Desire for economic opportunity
Desire for religious freedom
→
Immigrants come
to the United
States

Similarly, many different effects can be produced by a single cause. Immigration, for instance, can have both positive and negative effects on a nation.

Cause   *Effects*

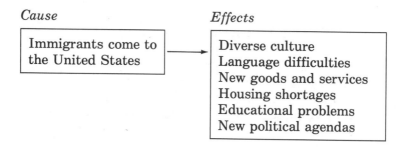

Immigrants come to
the United States
→
Diverse culture
Language difficulties
New goods and services
Housing shortages
Educational problems
New political agendas

Of course, causal relationships are rarely as neat as these boxes suggest. In fact, such relationships are often subtle and complex. As you examine situations that seem suited to cause-and-effect analysis, you will discover that most complex situations involve numerous causes and many different effects. Consider this example.

For nearly twenty years, the college board scores of high school seniors declined steadily. This decline began soon after television became popular, and therefore many people concluded that the two events were connected by cause and effect. The idea is plausible because children did seem to be reading less in order to watch television more and because reading comprehension is one of the chief skills the tests evaluate.

But many other elements might have contributed to the lowering of test scores. During the same period, for example, many schools moved away from required courses and deemphasized traditional subjects and skills, such as reading. Adults were reading less than they used to, and perhaps they were not encouraging their children to read. Furthermore, during the 1960s and 1970s, many colleges changed their policies and admitted students who previously would not have qualified. These new admission standards encouraged students who would have skipped them in earlier years to take the tests. Therefore, the scores may have been lower because they measured the top third of high school seniors rather than the top fifth. In any case, the reason for the lower scores in not clear. Perhaps television was the cause after all, but now—with college board scores rising again while television watching remains constant—nobody knows for sure. In such a case, it is easy—too easy—to claim a cause-and-effect relationship without the evidence to support it.

Just as the lower scores may have had many causes, television watching may have had many effects. For instance, it may have made those same students better observers and listeners, even if they did less well on the standardized written tests. It may have given them a national or even international outlook, instead of a narrow interest in local affairs. In other words, even if watching television may have limited people in some ways, it may have broadened them in others.

To give your readers a complete analysis, you should try to consider all cause and effects, not just the most obvious ones or the first ones you think of. Consider another example. Suppose a professional basketball team, recently stocked with the best players money can buy, has had a miserable season. Because the individual players are talented and because they were successful under other coaches, fans blame the current coach for the team's losing streak and want him fired. But can the coach alone be responsible? Maybe the inability of the players to mesh well as a team is responsible for the losing streak. Perhaps some of the players are suffering from injuries, personal problems, or drug dependency. Or maybe the fans themselves are somehow to blame, for the drop in attendance at games may have affected the team's morale. Clearly, other elements besides the new coach could have caused the losing streak. Indeed, the suspected cause of the team's decline—the coach—may actually have saved the team from total collapse by keeping the players from quarreling with one another. In writing about such a situation, you must carefully identify these complex causes and effects so that your explanation is clear and logical.

Main and Contributory Causes

Even when you have identified several causes of an effect, one is usually more important than the others. That one is the *main cause*, and the others are *contributory causes*. This distinction between the main or most important cause and the contributory or less important cause is vital for planning a cause-and-effect paper. When you can identify the main cause, you can emphasize it in your paper and play down the less important causes. If you properly weigh each factor in your essay, your readers will more easily understand the logic of the relationships you are examining.

How can you tell which is the main, or most important cause? Sometimes the main cause is obvious, but often it is not, as this example shows.

During one recent winter, an abnormally large amount of snow accumulated on the roof of the Civic Center Auditorium in Hartford, Connecticut, and the roof fell in. The newspaper reported that the weight of the snow had caused the collapse, and they were partly right. Other buildings, however, had not been flattened by the snow, so the main cause had to lie elsewhere. Insurance investigators eventually decided that the design of the roof, not the weight of the snow, was the main cause of the disaster.

This diagram outlines the cause-and-effect relationships in the situation summarized above.

Effect	Main Cause	Contributory Cause
Roof collapse	Roof design	Weight of snow

Because often the main cause is not obvious, it is important that you consider the significance of each cause very carefully as you plan your essay—and that you continue to evaluate the relative importance of your main cause and to consider possible alternatives to it as you write and revise.

Immediate and Remote Causes

Another important distinction is the difference between an *immediate* cause and a *remote* cause. An *immediate cause* closely precedes an effect and thus is relatively easy to recognize as a cause. A *remote cause* is less obvious, perhaps because it takes place further in the past or farther away. Building an essay on the assumption that the most obvious cause is the most important can be dangerous as well as shortsighted.

For example, look again at the Hartford roof collapse. Most people agreed that the snow was the immediate, or most obvious, cause of the roof collapse. But further study by insurance investigators considered the remote causes not so readily perceived. The design of the roof was the most important such remote, or less immediately evident, cause of the collapse. In addition, perhaps the materials used in the roof's construction were partly to blame. Maybe maintenance crews had not done their jobs properly, or necessary repairs had not been made. In addition to the snow, any or all of these less apparent but possibly critical elements might have contributed to the disaster. If you were the insurance investigator reporting on the causes of this event, you would want to assess all possible contributing factors rather than just the most obvious. If you did not consider the remote as well as the immediate causes, you would reach an oversimplified and illogical conclusion.

This diagram outlines the cause and-effect relationships in the situation summarized above.

Effect	Immediate Cause	Possible Remote Causes
Roof collapse	Weight of snow	Roof design Roof materials Improper maintenance Repairs not made

In this situation, the remote cause is extremely important; in fact, as we have seen, it is a remote cause—the roof design—that was the main cause of the accident.

The Causal Chain

Sometimes an effect can also be a cause. This is true in a causal chain, where A causes B, B causes C, C causes D, and so on.

A
Cause ⟶ B
        Effect
        (Cause) ⟶ C
                Effect
                (Cause) ⟶ D
                        Effect
                        (Cause) ⟶ E
                                Effect

If your analysis of a situation reveals a causal chain, this discovery can be useful in your writing. The very operation of a causal chain suggests an organizational pattern for a paper, and following the chain automatically keeps you from discussing links out of their logical order. Be careful, however, to keep your emphasis on the causal connections and not to lapse into simple narration.

Here is a simple example of a causal chain: World War II ended in 1945. Beginning in 1946, as thousands of American soldiers returned home, the United States birth rate began a dramatic rise. As the numbers of births increased, the creation of goods and services designed to meet the needs of this growing new population also increased. As advertisers competed to attract this group's attention, the so-called "baby boom generation" became more and more visible. Consequently, it was perceived as more and more powerful—as voters as well as consumers. As a result, this group's emergence has proved to be a major factor in shaping American political, social, cultural, and economic life.

In a causal chain like this one, the result of one action is the cause of another. Leaving out any link in the chain, or putting any link in improper order, destroys the logic and continuity of the chain.

Post Hoc *Reasoning*

When developing a cause-and-effect paper, you must be certain that your conclusions are logical. Simply because event A precedes event B, you must not assume that event A has caused event B. This illogical assumption, called *post hoc* reasoning, equates a chronological sequence with causality. When you fall into this trap, you are really mistaking coincidence for causality—assuming, for instance, that you failed an exam because a black cat crossed your path the day before.

Another situation illustrates *post hoc* reasoning. Until the late nineteenth century, many scientists accepted the notion of spontaneous generation, that is, they believed living things could arise directly from nonliving matter. To support their beliefs, they pointed to specific situations. For example, they observed that maggots, the larvae of the housefly, seemed to arise directly from the decaying bodies of dead animals or from rotting meat.

What these scientists were doing was confusing sequence with causality, assuming that just because the presence of decaying meat preceded the appearance of maggots, the two were connected in a causal relationship. Thus these scientists were guilty of *post hoc* reasoning.

In fact, of course, a logical explanation existed for the appearance of the maggots: Because the dead animals were exposed to the air, flies were free to lay eggs in the animals' bodies. These eggs hatched into maggots. Therefore, the living maggots were not a direct result of the presence of nonliving matter. Although these scientists were applying the best technology and scientific theory of their time, hindsight reveals that their conclusions were not true. In your writing as well as in your observations, it is neither logical nor fair for you to assume that a causal relationship exists in the absence of clear, strong evidence to support the connection.

When you revise a cause-and-effect paper, make sure you have not confused words like *because, therefore*, and *consequently*—words that show a causal relationship—with words like *subsequently, later*, and *afterward*—words that show a chronological relationship. When you use a word like *because*, you are signaling your reader that you are telling *why* something happened; when you use a word like *later* you are only showing what did happen and when.

Being able to perceive and analyze cause-and-effect relationships; to distinguish causes from effects and recognize causal chains; and to sort out immediate from remote, main from contributory, and logical from illogical causes are all skills that will help you write. Understanding the nature of the cause-and-effect relationship will help you to decide when to use this pattern to structure a paper.

STRUCTURING A CAUSE-AND-EFFECT ESSAY

After you have sorted out the cause-and-effect relationships that you will write about, you are ready to plan your paper. You have three basic options: to emphasize causes, to emphasize effects, or to discuss both causes and effects. Often, your assigned topic will suggest which of these options to use. Here are a few likely topics for cause-and-effect treatment:

Emphasis on finding causes	Discuss the causes of the Spanish-American War. (history exam)
	Discuss the factors that have contributed to the declining population of state mental hospitals. (social work paper)

Emphasis on describing or predicting effects	Evaluate the probable effects of moving elementary school children from a highly structured classroom to a relatively open classroom. (education paper) Discuss the impact of World War I on two of Ernest Hemingway's characters. (literature exam)
Discussion of both causes and effects	The 1840s was a volatile decade in Europe. Choose one social, political, or economic event that occurred during those years, analyze its causes, and briefly note how the event influenced later developments in European history. (history exam)

Of course, a cause-and-effect essay should do more than just enumerate causes or effects. For instance, an economics paper treating the major effects of the Vietnam War on the U.S. economy could be a straightforward presentation of factual information—an attempt to inform your readers of the war's economic impact rather than persuade them that these effects justified the war. More likely, however, the paper will indicate the *significance* of the war's effects, not just list them. In fact, cause-and-effect analysis often requires judging and weighing factors, and your assessment of the relative significance of causes or effects may suggest a thesis. Therefore, when you plan your essay, you will want to formulate the thesis statement in light of the relationships among the specific causes or effects you will discuss. This thesis statement should tell your readers three things: the points you will be trying to consider, the positions you will take, and your emphasis on causes, effects, or both. Your thesis may also indicate explicitly or implicitly the cause or effect you consider to be most important and the order in which you will treat your points.

You have several options when it comes to the sequence of causes or effects. One strategy, of course, is chronology—you can present causes or effects in the order in which they occurred. Another option is to introduce the main cause first and then the contributory causes—or to do just the opposite. If you want to stress positive consequences, begin by briefly discussing the negative ones; if you prefer to emphasize negative results, summarize the less important positive effects first. Still another possibility is to begin by disposing of any events and circumstances that were *not* causes and then go on to explain what the real causes were. This method is especially effective if you think your readers are likely to jump to *post hoc* conclusions. Finally, you can begin with the most obvious causes or effects, those most likely to be familiar to your reader, and move on to more subtle factors and then to your analysis and conclusion.

Finding Causes

Suppose you are planning the social work paper mentioned above: "Discuss the causes that have contributed to the declining population of state mental hospitals." Your assignment specifies an effect—the declining population of state mental hospitals—and asks you to discuss possible causes. Some causes might be:

- An increasing acceptance of mental illness in our society
- Prohibitive costs of in-patient care
- Increasing numbers of mental-health professionals, facilitating treatment outside the hospital

Many health professionals, however, believe that the most important cause is the development and use of psychotropic drugs, like chlorpromazine (Thorazine), that have an altering effect on the mind. To emphasize this cause in your paper, you could construct the following thesis statement:

Less important causes | Although society's increasing acceptance of the mentally ill, the high cost of in-patient care, and the rise in the number of health professionals have all been influential in reducing the population of state mental hospitals, the most important cause of this reduction is the development and use of psychotropic drugs.

Effect | Most important cause

This thesis statement fully prepares your readers for your essay. It identifies the causes you will consider, and it also reveals your position—your assessment of the relative significance of these causes. It states the less important causes first and indicates their secondary importance with *although*. In the body of your essay the least important causes would be considered first so that the essay could gradually build up to the most convincing material, the information that is likely to have the greatest impact on the reader. An informal outline for your paper might look like this:

- Introduction—including thesis that identifies the effect and its causes
- First cause: Increased acceptance of the mentally ill
- Second cause: High cost of in-patient care
- Third cause: Rise in the number of health professionals
- Fourth cause: Development and use of psychotropic drugs (the most important cause)
- Conclusion and summary

Describing or Predicting Effects

Suppose you were planning the education paper mentioned earlier: "Evaluate the probable effects of moving elementary school children from a highly structured classroom to a relatively open classroom." You would use a procedure similar to the one above to consider effects rather than find causes. After brainstorming and deciding which specific points to discuss, you might formulate this thesis statement:

> **Cause** Moving children from a highly structured classroom to a relatively open one is desirable because it is likely to encourage more independent play, more flexibility in
> **Effects** forming friendship groups, and ultimately more creativity.

This thesis statement clearly spells out your position by telling the reader the stand you will take and the three main points your essay will consider in support of that stand; the thesis also clearly specifies that these points are effects of the open classroom. After introducing the cause, your essay would treat these three effects in the order in which they are presented in the thesis statement, building up to the most important point. An informal outline of your paper might look like this:

- Introduction—including thesis that identifies the cause and its effects
- First effect: More independent play
- Second effect: More flexible friendship groups
- Third effect: More creativity (the most important effect)
- Conclusion and summary

The following midterm examination, written for a history class, analyzes both causes and effects of the Irish potato famine that occurred during the 1840s. Notice how the writer, Evelyn Pellicane, concentrates on causes but also discusses briefly the effects of this tragedy, just as the exam question directs.

Question: The 1840s was a volatile decade in Europe. Choose one social, political, or economic event that occurred during those years, analyze its causes, and briefly note how the event influenced later developments in European history.

THE IRISH FAMINE, 1845-1849

Thesis   The Irish famine, which brought hardship and   1
tragedy to Ireland during the 1840s, was caused and
prolonged by four basic factors: the failure of the
potato crop, the landlord-tenant system, errors in
government policy, and the long-standing prejudice of
the British toward Ireland.

First cause   The immediate cause of the famine was the   2
failure of the potato crop. In 1845, potato disease
struck the crop, and potatoes rotted in the ground.
The 1846 crop also failed, and before long people
were eating weeds. The 1847 crop was healthy, but
there were not enough potatoes to go around, and in
1848 the blight struck again, leading to more and
more evictions of tenants by landlords.

Second cause   The tenants' position on the land had never been   3
very secure. Most had no leases and could be turned
out by their landlords at any time. If a tenant owed
rent, he was evicted--or, worse, put in prison,
leaving his family to starve. The threat of prison
caused many tenants to leave their land; those who
could leave Ireland did so, sometimes with money
provided by their landlords. Some landlords did try
to take care of their tenants, but most did not. Many
were absentee landlords who spent their rent money
abroad.

Third cause   Government policy errors, while not an immediate   4
cause of the famine, played an important role in
creating an unstable economy and perpetuating
starvation. In 1846, the government decided not to
continue selling corn, as it had during the first
year of the famine, claiming that low-cost purchases
of corn by Ireland had paralyzed British trade by
interfering with free enterprise. Therefore, 1846 saw
a starving population, angry demonstrations, and
panic; even those with money were unable to buy food.
Still the government insisted that, if it sent food
to Ireland, prices would rise in the rest of the
United Kingdom and that this would be unfair to
hardworking English and Scots. As a result, no food
was sent. Throughout the years of the famine, the
British government aggravated an already grave
situation: they did nothing to improve agricultural
operations, to help people adjust to another crop, to
distribute seeds, or to reorder the landlord-tenant
system which made the tenants' position so insecure.

Fourth cause   At the root of this poor government policy was   5
the long-standing British prejudice against the
Irish. Hostility between the two countries went back
some six hundred years, and the British were simply
not about to inconvenience themselves to save the
Irish. When the Irish so desperately needed grain to
replace the damaged potatoes, it was clear that grain
had to be imported from England. This meant, however,
that the Corn Laws, which had been enacted to keep
the price of British corn high by taxing imported
grain, had to be repealed. The British were unwilling
to repeal the Corn Laws. Even when they did supply
corn meal, they made no attempt to explain to the
Irish how to cook this unfamiliar food. Moreover, the

British government was determined to make Ireland pay for its own poor, and so it forced the collection of taxes. Since many landlords just did not have the tax money, they were forced to evict their tenants. The British government's callous and indifferent treatment of the Irish has been called genocide.

Effects   As a result of this devastating famine, the   6
population of Ireland was reduced from about nine million to about six and one-half million. During the famine years, men roamed the streets looking for work, begging when they found none. Epidemics of "famine fever" and dysentery reduced the population drastically. The most important historical result of the famine, however, was the massive emigration to the United States, Canada, and Great Britain of poor, unskilled people who had to struggle to fit into a skilled economy and who brought with them a deep-seated hatred of the British. (This same hatred remained strong in Ireland itself--so strong that at the time of World War II, Ireland, then independent, remained neutral rather than coming to England's aid.) Irish immigrants faced slums, fever epidemics, joblessness, and hostility--even anti-Catholic and anti-Irish riots--in Boston, New York, London, Glasgow, and Quebec. In Ireland itself, poverty and discontent continued, and by 1848 those emigrating from Ireland included a more highly skilled class of farmer, the ones Ireland needed to recover and to survive.

Conclusion   The Irish famine, one of the great tragedies of   7
(includes   the nineteenth century, was a natural disaster
restatement of   compounded by the insensitivity of the British
thesis)   government and the archaic agricultural system of
Ireland. While the deaths that resulted depleted

```
Ireland's resources even more, the men and women who
emigrated to other countries permanently enriched
those nations.
```

Points for Special Attention

Structure.   This is a relatively long essay; if it were not so clearly organized, it would be difficult to follow. Because the essay is to focus primarily on causes, Evelyn first introduces the effect—the famine itself—and then considers its causes. After she has examined the causes, she moves on to the results of the famine, treating the most important result last. In this essay, then, the famine is first treated as an effect and then, toward the end, as a cause. In fact, it is the central link in a causal chain. Evelyn devotes one paragraph to her introduction and one to each cause; she sums up the effects or results in a separate paragraph and devotes the final paragraph to her conclusion. (Depending on a given paper's length and complexity, of course, more—or less—than one paragraph may be devoted to each cause or effect.) An informal outline for her paper might have looked like this:

- Introduction—including thesis
- First cause: Failure of the potato crop
- Second cause: The landlord–tenant system
- Third cause: Errors in government policy
- Fourth cause: British prejudice
- Results of the famine
- Conclusion

Because Evelyn believes that all the causes are very important and that they are interrelated, she does not present them strictly in order of increasing importance. Instead, she begins with the immediate cause of the famine—the failure of the potato crop—and then digs more deeply until she arrives at the most remote cause, British prejudice. The immediate cause is also the main (most important) cause, for the other situations had existed all along.

Transitions.   The cause-and-effect relationships in this essay are both subtle and complex; Evelyn considers a series of interconnected relationships and an intricate causal chain. Throughout the essay, many words suggest cause-and-effect connections: *so, therefore, because, as a result, since, led to, brought about, caused,* and the like. These are the most effective transitions for such an essay.

Answering an Examination Question. Before planning and writing her answer, Evelyn carefully studied the exam question. She noted that it asked for both causes and effects but that its wording directed her to spend more time on causes ("analyze") than on effects ("briefly note"). Consequently, she divides her discussion in accord with these directions and is careful to indicate *explicitly* which are the causes ("government policy . . . played an important role") and which are the results ("The most important historical result . . . ").

Evelyn's purpose is to convey factual information and, in doing so, to demonstrate her understanding of the course material. Her time is limited; rather than waste it choosing a clever opening strategy or making elaborate attempts to engage her audience, Evelyn begins her essay directly (if somewhat abruptly) with a statement of her thesis.

Evelyn has obviously been influenced by outside sources; the ideas in the essay are not completely her own. Because this is an exam, however, and because the instructor is aware that the student based her essay on class notes and assigned readings, she does not have to acknowledge her sources.

All the selections that follow focus on cause-and-effect relationships. Some selections stress causes; others emphasize effects. As those essays illustrate, the cause-and-effect pattern is so versatile that it may be used to examine topics as dissimilar as technology, anthropology, sports, and social change.

WHO KILLED THE BOG MEN
OF DENMARK? AND WHY?

Maurice Shadbolt

Maurice Shadbolt, a native of New Zealand, is a poet, playwright, and novelist. He is the author of Danger Zone *(1975),* Lovelock Version *(1981), and several travel books; he also writes magazine articles such as this one. His most recent book is the historical novel* Season of the Jew *(1987). Mystery stories and archaeological explorations both seek to unearth causes that can explain perplexing situations. This selection combines archaeology and mystery to determine why a group of men died some two thousand years ago. To explain this puzzle, Shadbolt examines the direct and indirect causes of the deaths of the ancient bog men of Denmark.*

Every year in the Danish town of Silkeborg, thousands of visitors 1
file past the face of a murder victim. No one will ever know his name.
It is enough to know that 2000 years ago he was as human as ourselves. That face has moved men and women to poetry, and to tears.

Last summer I journeyed to the lake-girt Danish town and, peer- 2
ing at that face behind glass in a modest museum, I felt awe—for
his every wrinkle and whisker tell a vivid and terrible tale from Denmark's distant past. The rope which choked off the man's breath
is still around his neck. Yet it is a perplexingly peaceful face, inscrutable, one to haunt the imagination.

This strangest of ancient murder mysteries began 27 years ago, 3
on May 8, 1950, when two brothers, Emil and Viggo Højgaard, were
digging peat in Tollund Fen, near Silkeborg. Their spring sowing
finished, the brothers were storing up the umber-brown peat for
their kitchen range, and for warmth in the winter to come. It was a
peaceful task on a sunny morning. Snipe called from the aspens and
firs fringing the dank bowl of the fen, where only heather and coarse
grass grew. Then, at the depth of nine feet, their spades suddenly
struck something.

They were gazing, with fright and fascination, at a face underfoot. 4
The corpse was naked but for a skin cap, resting on its side as if
asleep, arms and legs bent. The face was gentle, with eyes closed and

lips lightly pursed. There was stubble on the chin. The bewildered brothers called the Silkeborg police.

Quick to the scene, the police did not recognize the man as anyone listed missing. Shrewdly guessing the brothers might have blundered into a black hole in Europe's past, the police called in archeologists.

Enter Prof. Peter Glob, a distinguished scholar from nearby Aarhus University, who carefully dislodged a lump of peat from beside the dead man's head. A rope made of two twisted hide thongs encircled his neck. He had been strangled or hanged. But when, and by whom? Glob ordered a box to be built about the corpse and the peat in which it lay, so nothing might be disturbed.

Next day, the box, weighing nearly a ton, was manhandled out of the bog onto a horse drawn cart, on its way for examination at Copenhagen's National Museum. One of Glob's helpers collapsed and died with the hugh effort. It seemed a dark omen, as if some old god were claiming a modern man in place of a man from the past.

Bog bodies were nothing new—since records have been kept, Denmark's bogs have surrendered no fewer than 400—and the preservative qualities of the humic acid in peat have long been known. But not until the 19th century did scientists and historians begin to glimpse the finds and understand that the bodies belonged to remote, murky recesses of European prehistory. None survived long: the corpses were either buried again or crumbled quickly with exposure to light and air.

When peat-digging was revived during and after World War II, bodies were unearthed in abundance—first in 1942 at Store Arden, then in 1946, 1947 and 1948 at Borre Fen. Artifacts found beside them positively identified them as people of Denmark's Early Iron Age, from 400 B.C. to A.D. 400. None, then, was less than 1500 years old, and some were probably much older. The first of the Borre Fen finds—a full-grown male—was to prove especially significant: Borre Fen man, too, had died violently, with a noose about his neck, stron gled or hanged. And his last meal had consisted of grain.

Peter Glob, alongside his artist father (a portraitist and distinguished amateur archeologist), had been digging into Denmark's dim past since he was a mere eight years old. For him, the Tollund man, who had by far the best-preserved head to survive from antiquity, was a supreme challenge. Since 1936, Glob had been living imaginatively with the pagan hunters and farmers of 2000 years ago, fossicking among their corroded artifacts, foraging among the foundations of their simple villages; he knew their habits, the rhythms of their lives. Suddenly, here was a man of that very time. "Majesty and gentleness," he recalls, "seemed to stamp his features as they did when he was alive." What was this enigmatic face trying to tell him?

Glob was intrigued by the fact that so many of the people found   11 in bogs had died violently: strangled or hanged, throats slit, heads battered. Perhaps they had been travelers set upon by brigands, or executed criminals. But there might be a different explanation. These murder victims all belonged to the Danish Iron Age. If they were to be explained away as victims of robber bands, there should be a much greater spread in time—into other ages. Nor would executed criminals all have had so many common traits.

Glob considered the body with care. X rays of Tollund man's ver-   12 tebrae, taken to determine whether he had been strangled or hanged, produced inconclusive results. The condition of the wisdom teeth suggested a man well over 20 years old. An autopsy revealed that the heart, lungs and liver were well preserved; most important, the alimentary canal was undisturbed, containing the dead man's last meal—a 2000 year-old gruel of hand-milled grains and seeds: barley, linseed, flaxseed, knotgrass, among others. Knowledge of prehistoric agriculture made it possible to determine that the man had lived in the first 200 years A.D. The mixture of grains and seeds suggested a meal prepared in winter or early spring.

Since Iron Age men were not vegetarians, why were there no   13 traces of meat? Glob also marveled that the man's hands and feet were soft; he appeared to have done little or no heavy labor in his lifetime. Possibly, then, he was high-ranking in Iron Age society.

Then, on April 26, 1952, peat-digging villagers from Grauballe, 11   14 miles east of Tollund, turned up a second spectacularly well-preserved body, and again Glob was fast to the scene. Unmistakably another murder victim, this discovery was, unlike Tollund man, far from serene. The man's throat had been slashed savagely from ear to ear. His face was twisted with terror, and his lips were parted with a centuries-silenced cry of pain.

Glob swiftly removed the body—still imbedded in a great block   15 of peat—for preservation and study. Carbon-dating of body tissue proved Grauballe man to be about 1650 years old, a contemporary of Constantine the Great. Grauballe man was in extraordinary condition; his fingerprints and footprints came up clearly. Tallish and dark-haired, Grauballe man, like Tollund man, had never done any heavy manual work. He had been slain in his late 30s. Another similarity came to light when Grauballe man's last meal was analyzed: it had been eaten immediately before death and, like Tollund man's, like Borre Fen man's too, it was a gruel of grains and seeds, a meal of winter, or early spring. All three had perished in a similar season.

Who had killed these men of the bogs? Why in winter, or early 16 spring? Why should they—apparently—have led privileged lives? And why the same kind of meals before their sudden ends?

The bodies had told Glob all they could. Now he turned to one of 17 his favorite sources—the Roman historian Tacitus. Nearly 2000 years ago Tacitus recorded the oral traditions of Germanic tribes who inhabited northwest Europe. Tacitus' account of these wild, brave and generous blue-eyed people often shed light into dark corners of Denmark's past. Glob found these lines: "At a time laid down in the distant past, all peoples that are related by blood meet in a sacred wood. Here they celebrate their barbarous rites with a human sacrifice."

Elsewhere, Tacitus wrote: "These people are distinguished by a 18 common worship of Nerthus, or Mother Earth. They believe that she interests herself in human affairs." Tacitus confirmed early spring as a time among the Germanic tribes for offerings and human sacrifice. They were asking the goddess to hasten the coming of spring, and the summer harvest. Men chosen for sacrifice might well have been given a symbolic meal, made up of plant seeds, before being consecrated through death to the goddess—thus explaining the absence of meat. The sacrificial men, with their delicate features, neat hands and feet, might have been persons of high rank chosen by lot for sacrifice, or priests, ritually married to Nerthus.

Tacitus supplied another essential clue: the symbol of Nerthus, he 19 recorded, was a twisted metal "torque," or neck ring, worn by the living to honor the goddess. The leather nooses about the necks of Tollund man and the body from Borre Fen and some earlier bodies were replicas of those neck rings. Glob concluded that it was Nerthus—Mother Earth herself—who had preserved her victims perfectly in her peaty bosom long after those who had fed them into the bogs were dust.

Peter Glob was satisfied. He had found the killer and identified 20 the victims. The centuries-old mystery of Denmark's bog bodies was no more.

COMPREHENSION

1. Identify at least one *result* of each of the following: the Højgaard brothers discover a body; the box containing the body is moved; the humic acid in peat has preservative qualities; peat-digging is revived after World War II.

2. Identify at least one *cause* of each of the following: the man's hands and feet are soft; his last meal was grain; he died a violent death; he has a rope around his neck.

3. From what different sources do the clues about the bog man's murder come?

PURPOSE AND AUDIENCE

1. This essay originally appeared in *The Reader's Digest*, a magazine that prints selections likely to interest a wide general audience. In what ways does this selection qualify?

2. What purpose or purposes might the author have had for writing this essay?

3. What is Shadbolt's thesis?

STYLE AND STRUCTURE

1. In what ways is the structure of this essay similar to that of a modern mystery story? Identify the detective, the clues, and the background research. How is this essay different from a mystery story?

2. Are the style and structure of this essay different from those of a newspaper account? If so, how?

3. The author begins in the first person as if to make himself a part of the story he is relating. Do you think his brief appearance adds to or detracts from the essay's effectiveness? Why?

4. The author begins in the present tense and then uses flashbacks. How would the impact of the essay change if the author had used strict chronological order?

5. Several quotations appear in this essay. Are these direct quotations more convincing than the author's paraphrases would be? Why or why not?

VOCABULARY PROJECTS

1. Define each of the following words as it is used in this selection.

inscrutable (2)	fen (3)
peat (3)	bog (7)
sowing (3)	murky (8)
snipe (3)	artifacts (9)
dank (3)	pagan (10)

fossicking (10)	brigands (11)
foraging (10)	gruel (15)
enigmatic (10)	consecrated (18)

2. The vocabulary of this essay necessarily includes terms used in archaeology and in agriculture. In addition, words and expressions like "murder victim" and "vivid and terrible tale" suggest the language of a murder mystery. List the words and expressions that give the story this atmosphere. Then, try to substitute equivalent expressions that do *not* have this connotation. Do your substitutions deprive the essay of a necessary ingredient, or is the essay essentially unchanged?

WRITING WORKSHOP

1. Write a biographical sketch of the man the Højgaard brothers discovered, establishing the causes of his death.

2. Write an editorial for the Silkeborg daily newspaper in which you discuss the benefits and drawbacks for the town because of the discovery of the bog man.

3. Write an essay unraveling a mystery in your own life; for instance, explain the causes of a friend's strange actions or the reasons your family settled where it did years (or generations) ago.

THEMATIC CONNECTIONS

- "Pure and Impure: The Interplay of Science and Technology" (p. 184)
- "The Embalming of Mr. Jones" (p. 236)
- "Historical Fiction, Fictitious History, and Chesapeake Bay Blue Crabs, or, About Aboutness" (p. 406)

WHO KILLED BENNY PARET?

Norman Cousins

Born in 1912 in New Jersey and educated at Columbia University, Norman Cousins has had a varied career as a journalist and author. He was editor of the Saturday Review *from 1940 to 1978 and has published numerous books, notably the best-selling* Anatomy of an Illness *(1979) about his struggle with a near-fatal condition. Other works include,* Dr. Schweitzer of Lambarene *(1960),* Human Options *(1981),* Healing and Belief *(1982),* The Healing Heart *(1983),* The Words of Albert Schweitzer *(1982), and* Albert Schweitzer's Mission: Healing and Peace *(1985). In the 1962 essay "Who Killed Benny Paret?" Cousins investigates the causes of Paret's death. In answering the question posed by his essay's title, Cousins takes a strong stand against violence in sports.*

Sometime about 1935 or 1936 I had an interview with Mike Jacobs, the prize-fight promoter. I was a fledgling reporter at that time; my beat was education but during the vacation season I found myself on varied assignments, all the way from ship news to sports reporting. In this way I found myself sitting opposite the most powerful figure in the boxing world. 1

There was nothing spectacular in Mr. Jacobs' manner or appearance; but when he spoke about prize fights, he was no longer a bland little man but a colossus who sounded the way Napoleon must have sounded when he reviewed a battle. You knew you were listening to Number One. His saying something made it true. 2

We discussed what to him was the only important element in successful promoting—how to please the crowd. So far as he was concerned, there was no mystery to it. You put killers in the ring and the people filled your arena. You hire boxing artists—men who are adroit at feinting, parrying, weaving, jabbing, and dancing, but who don't pack dynamite in their fists—and you wind up counting your empty seats. So you searched for the killers and sluggers and maulers—fellows who could hit with the force of a baseball bat. 3

I asked Mr. Jacobs if he was speaking literally when he said people came out to see the killer. 4

"They don't come out to see a tea party," he said evenly. "They 5

266

come out to see the knockout. They come out to see a man hurt. If they think anything else, they're kidding themselves."

Recently, a young man by the name of Benny Paret was killed in the ring. The killing was seen by millions; it was on television. In the twelfth round, he was hit hard in the head several times, went down, was counted out, and never came out of the coma. 6

The Paret fight produced a flurry of investigations. Governor Rockefeller was shocked by what happened and appointed a committee to assess the responsibility. The New York State Boxing Commission decided to find out what was wrong. The District Attorney's office expressed its concern. One question that was solemnly studied in all three probes concerned the action of the referee. Did he act in time to stop the fight? Another question had to do with the role of the examining doctors who certified the physical fitness of the fighters before the bout. Still another question involved Mr. Paret's manager; did he rush his boy into the fight without adequate time to recuperate from the previous one? 7

In short, the investigators looked into every possible cause except the real one. Benny Paret was killed because the human fist delivers enough impact, when directed against the head, to produce a massive hemorrhage in the brain. The human brain is the most delicate and complex mechanism in all creation. It has a lacework of millions of highly fragile nerve connections. Nature attempts to protect this exquisitely intricate machinery by encasing it in a hard shell. Fortunately, the shell is thick enough to withstand a great deal of pounding. Nature, however, can protect man against everything except man himself. Not every blow to the head will kill a man—but there is always the risk of concussion and damage to the brain. A prize fighter may be able to survive even repeated brain concussions and go on fighting, but the damage to his brain may be permanent. 8

In any event, it is futile to investigate the referee's role and seek to determine whether he should have intervened to stop the fight earlier. That is not where the primary responsibility lies. The primary responsibility lies with the people who pay to see a man hurt. The referee who stops a fight too soon from the crowd's viewpoint can expect to be booed. The crowd wants the knockout; it wants to see a man stretched out on the canvas. This is the supreme moment in boxing. It is nonsense to talk about prize fighting as a test of boxing skills. No crowd was ever brought to its feet screaming and cheering at the sight of two men beautifully dodging and weaving out of each other's jabs. The time the crowd comes alive is when a man is hit hard over the heart or the head, when his mouthpiece flies 9 out, when the blood squirts out of his nose or eyes, when he wobbles under the attack and his pursuer continues to smash at him with pole-axe impact.

Don't blame it on the referee. Don't even blame it on the fight managers. Put the blame where it belongs—on the prevailing mores that regard prize fighting as a perfectly proper enterprise and vehicle of entertainment. No one doubts that many people enjoy prize fighting and will miss it if it should be thrown out. And that is precisely the point. 10

COMPREHENSION

1. Why, according to Mike Jacobs, do people come to see a prizefight? Does Cousins agree with him?

2. What were the official responses to Paret's death?

3. What was the immediate cause of Paret's death? What remote causes did the investigators consider? What, according to Cousins, is the main cause? (That is, where does the "primary responsibility" lie?)

4. Why does Cousins believe that "it is futile to investigate the referee's role"?

5. Cousins ends his essay with "And that is precisely the point." What is the "point" to which he refers?

PURPOSE AND AUDIENCE

1. This persuasive essay has a strong thesis. What is it?

2. This essay appeared on May 5, 1962, a month after Paret died. What do you suppose its impact was on its audience? Is the impact the same today, or has it changed?

3. Why does Cousins present information about Mike Jacobs in the first two paragraphs?

4. At whom is this essay aimed—boxing enthusiasts, sports writers, or a general audience? What led you to your conclusion?

5. Does Cousins expect his audience to agree with his thesis? How does he try to win their sympathy for his position?

STYLE AND STRUCTURE

1. The essay begins with a brief narrative describing a meeting between Cousins and Mike Jacobs. Where does this narrative introduction end?

2. Once Paret's death is mentioned and the persuasive portion of the essay begins, the introductory narrative never resumes. Why not? Do you think this weakens the essay? Explain.

3. Does Cousins include enough detail to convince readers? Explain. Where, if anywhere, might more detail be helpful?

4. Sort out the complex cause-and-effect relationships discussed in paragraph 9.

5. Look at the last two sentences in paragraph 9. How does the contrast between them advance the essay's thesis?

6. What strategy does Cousins use in his conclusion? Is it effective? Explain.

VOCABULARY PROJECTS

1. Define each of the following words as it is used in this selection.

promoter (1)	maulers (3)
fledgling (1)	lacework (8)
colossus (2)	encasing (8)
feinting (3)	intervened (9)
parrying (3)	

2. The specialized vocabulary of boxing is prominent in this essay, but the facts would apply equally well to any sport in which violence is a potential problem.

   a. Assuming that you are writing a similar essay about football, hockey, rugby, or another sport, substitute appropriate equivalent words for the following:

promoter (1)	killers and sluggers
prize fights (2)	and maulers (3)
in the ring (3)	knockout (5)
boxing artists (3)	referee (7)
feinting, parrying, weaving,	fighters/fight (7)
jabbing, and dancing (3)	

   b. Rewrite this sentence so that it suits the sport you have chosen: "The crowd wants the knockout; it wants to see a man stretched out on the canvas. . . . It is nonsense to talk about prize fighting as a test of boxing skills. No crowd was ever brought to its feet screaming and cheering at the sight of two men beautifully dodging and weaving out of each other's jabs."

WRITING WORKSHOP

1. Write a cause-and-effect essay examining how the demands of the public affect a professional sport. (You might examine violence in

hockey or football, for example, or the ways in which an individual player cultivates an image for the fans.)

2. Write a cause-and-effect essay about a time when you did something you felt was dishonest or unwise in response to peer pressure. Be sure to identify the causes for your actions.

3. Why do you think a young man might turn to a career in boxing? Write a cause-and-effect essay in which you examine his possible motives.

THEMATIC CONNECTIONS

- "38 Who Saw Murder Didn't Call the Police" (p. 70)
- "Shooting an Elephant" (p. 85)
- "The Spider and the Wasp" (p. 222)

TELEVISION:
THE PLUG-IN DRUG

Marie Winn

Born in Czechoslovakia and educated at Radcliffe and Columbia, Marie Winn contributes articles to publications like the New York Times Magazine *and the* Village Voice. *Her books for children include* The Sick Book, The Baby Reader, *and* The Fireside Book of Fun and Game Songs. *In addition to* The Plug-In Drug (1977), *where this selection first appeared, Winn has also authored the adult book* Children Without Childhood. *Her most recent book is* Unplugging the Plug-In Drug (1987). *In "Television: The Plug-In Drug" (originally titled "Family Life"), Winn considers the effects of television on the American family.*

A quarter of a century after the introduction of television into   1
American society, a period that has seen the medium become so deeply ingrained in American life that in at least one state the television set has attained the rank of a legal necessity, safe from repossession in case of debt along with clothes, cooking utensils, and the like, television viewing has become an inevitable and ordinary part of daily life. Only in the early years of television did writers and commentators have sufficient perspective to separate the activity of watching television from the actual content it offers the viewer. In those early days writers frequently discussed the effects of television on family life. However, a curious myopia afflicted those early observers: almost without exception they regarded television as a favorable, beneficial, indeed, wondrous influence upon the family.

"Television is going to be a real asset in every home where there   2
are children," predicts a writer in 1949.

"Television will take over your way of living and change your chil-   3
dren's habits, but this change can be a wonderful improvement," claims another commentator.

"No survey's needed, of course, to establish that television has   4
brought the family together in one room," writes *The New York Times* television critic in 1949.

Each of the early articles about television is invariably accom-   5
panied by a photograph or illustration showing a family cozily sit-

271

ting together before the television set, Sis on Mom's lap, Buddy perched on the arm of Dad's chair, Dad with his arm around Mom's shoulder. Who could have guessed that twenty or so years later Mom would be watching a drama in the kitchen, the kids would be looking at cartoons in their room, while Dad would be taking in the ball game in the living room?

Of course television sets were enormously expensive in those early   6
days. The idea that by 1975 more than 60 percent of American families would own two or more sets was preposterous. The splintering of the multiple-set family was something the early writers could not foresee. Nor did anyone imagine the numbers of hours children would eventually devote to television, the common use of television by parents as a child pacifier, the changes television would effect upon child-rearing methods, the increasing domination of family schedules by children's viewing requirements—in short, the *power* of the new medium to dominate family life.

After the first years, as children's consumption of the new me-   7
dium increased, together with parental concern about the possible effects of so much television viewing, a steady refrain helped to soothe and reassure anxious parents. "Television always enters a pattern of influences that already exist: the home, the peer group, the school, the church and culture generally," write the authors of an early and influential study of television's effects on children. In other words, if the child's home life is all right, parents need not worry about the effects of all that television watching.

But television does not merely influence the child; it deeply influ-   8
ences that "pattern of influences" that is meant to ameliorate its effects. Home and family life has changed in important ways since the advent of television. The peer group has become television-oriented, and much of the time children spend together is occupied by television viewing. Culture generally has been transformed by television. Therefore it is improper to assign to television the subsidiary role its many apologists (too often members of the television industry) insist it plays. Television is not merely one of a number of important influences upon today's child. Through the changes it has made in family life, television emerges as *the* important influence in children's lives today.

Television's contribution to family life has been an equivocal one.   9
For while it has, indeed, kept the members of the family from dispersing, it has not served to bring them *together*. By its domination of the time families spend together, it destroys the special quality that distinguishes one family from another, a quality that depends to a great extent on what a family *does*, what special rituals, games, recurrent jokes, familiar songs, and shared activities it accumulates.

"Like the sorcerer of old," writes Urie Bronfenbrenner, "the televi-   10
sion set casts its magic spell, freezing speech and action, turning
the living into silent statues so long as the enchantment lasts. The
primary danger of the television screen lies not so much in the behavior it produces—although there is danger there—as in the behavior it prevents: the talks, the games, the family festivities and arguments through which much of the child's learning takes place and
through which his character is formed. Turning on the television set
can turn off the process that transforms children into people."

Yet parents have accepted a television-dominated family life so   11
completely that they cannot see how the medium is involved in
whatever problems they might be having. A first-grade teacher reports:

"I have one child in the group who's an only child. I wanted to   12
find out more about her family life because this little girl was quite
isolated from the group, didn't make friends, so I talked to her
mother. Well, they don't have time to do anything in the evening,
the mother said. The parents come home after picking up the child
at the babysitter's. Then the mother fixes dinner while the child
watches TV. Then they have dinner and the child goes to bed. I said
to this mother, 'Well, couldn't she help you fix dinner? That would
be a nice time for the two of you to talk,' and the mother said, 'Oh,
but I'd hate to have her miss "Zoom." It's such a good program!'"

Even when families make efforts to control television, too often   13
its very presence counterbalances the positive features of family life.
A writer and mother of two boys aged 3 and 7 described her family's
television schedule in an article in *The New York Times*:

> We were in the midst of a full-scale War. Every day was a new battle
> and every program was a major skirmish. We agreed it was a bad
> scene all around and were ready to enter diplomatic negotiations. . . .
> In principle we have agreed on 2 1/2 hours of TV a day, "Sesame
> Street," "Electric Company" (with dinner gobbled up in between) and
> two half-hour shows between 7 and 8:30 which enables the grown-ups
> to eat in peace and prevents the two boys from destroying one
> another. Their pre-bedtime choice is dreadful, because, as Josh re-
> cently admitted, "There's nothing much on I really like." So . . . it's
> "What's My Line" or "To Tell the Truth". . . . Clearly there is a need
> for first-rate children's shows at this time. . . .

Consider the "family life" described here: Presumably the father   14
comes home from work during the "Sesame Street"—"Electric
Company" stint. The children are either watching television, gob-
bling their dinner, or both. While the parents eat their dinner in
peaceful privacy, the children watch another hour of television. Then
there is only a half-hour left before bedtime, just enough time for

baths, getting pajamas on, brushing teeth, and so on. The children's evening is regimented with an almost military precision. They watch their favorite programs, and when there is "nothing much on I really like," they watch whatever else is on—because *watching* is the important thing. Their mother does not see anything amiss with watching programs just for the sake of watching; she only wishes there were some first-rate children's shows on at those times.

Without conjuring up memories of the Victorian era with family games and long, leisurely meals, and large families, the question arises: isn't there a better family life available than this dismal, mechanized arrangement of children watching television for however long is allowed them, evening after evening?   15

Of course, families today still do *special* things together at times: go camping in the summer, go to the zoo on a nice Saturday, take various trips and expeditions. But their *ordinary* daily life together is diminished—that sitting around at the dinner table, that spontaneous taking up of an activity, those little games invented by children on the spur of the moment when there is nothing else to do, the scribbling, the chatting, and even the quarreling, all the things that form the fabric of a family, that define a childhood. Instead, the children have their regular schedule of television programs and bedtime, and the parents have their peaceful dinner together.   16

The author of the article in the *Times* notes that "keeping a family sane means mediating between the needs of both children and adults." But surely the needs of adults are being better met than the needs of the children, who are effectively shunted away and rendered untroublesome, while their parents enjoy a life as undemanding as that of any childless couple. In reality, it is those very demands that young children make upon a family that lead to growth, and it is the way parents accede to those demands that builds the relationships upon which the future of the family depends. If the family does not accumulate its backlog of shared experiences, shared *everyday* experiences that occur and recur and change and develop, then it is not likely to survive as anything other than a caretaking institution.   17

FAMILY RITUALS

Ritual is defined by sociologists as "that part of family life that the family likes about itself, is proud of and wants formally to continue." Another text notes that "the development of a ritual by a family is an index of the common interest of its members in the family as a group."   18

What has happened to family rituals, those regular, dependable,   19 recurrent happenings that gave members of a family a feeling of *belonging* to a home rather than living in it merely for the sake of convenience, those experiences that act as the adhesive of family unity far more than any material advantages?

Mealtime rituals, going-to-bed rituals, illness rituals, holiday rit- 20 uals, how many of these have survived the inroads of the television set?

A young woman who grew up near Chicago reminisces about her 21 childhood and gives an idea of the effects of television upon family rituals:

"As a child I had millions of relatives around—my parents both 22 come from relatively large families. My father had nine brothers and sisters. And so every holiday there was this great swoop-down of aunts, uncles, and millions of cousins. I just remember how wonder- ful it used to be. These thousands of cousins would come and every- one would play and ultimately, after dinner, all the women would be in the front of the house, drinking coffee and talking, all the men would be in the back of the house, drinking and smoking, and all the kids would be all over the place, playing hide and seek. Christmas time was particularly nice because everyone always brought all their toys and games. Our house had a couple of rooms with go-through closets, so there was always kids running in a great circle route. I remember it was just wonderful.

"And then all of a sudden one year I remember becoming sud- 23 denly aware of how different everything had become. The kids were no longer playing Monopoly or Clue or the other games we used to play together. It was because we had a television set which had been turned on for a football game. All of that socializing that had gone on previously had ended. Now everyone was sitting in front of the television set, on a holiday, at a family party! I remember being stunned by how awful that was. Somehow the television had become more attractive."

As families have come to spend more and more of their time to- 24 gether engaged in the single activity of television watching, those rituals and pastimes that once gave family life its special quality have become more and more uncommon. Not since prehistoric times when cave families hunted, gathered, ate, and slept, with little time remaining to accumulate a culture of any significance, have families been reduced to such a sameness.

REAL PEOPLE

It is not only the activities that a family might engage in together 25 that are diminished by the powerful presence of television in the home. The relationships of the family members to each other are also affected, in both obvious and subtle ways. The hours that the young child spends in a one-way relationship with television people, an involvement that allows for no communication or interaction, surely affect his relationships with real-life people.

Studies show the importance of eye-to-eye contact, for instance, in real-life relationships, and indicate that the nature of a person's eye-contact patterns, whether he looks another squarely in the eye or looks to the side or shifts his gaze from side to side, may play a significant role in his success or failure in human relationships. But no eye contact is possible in the child-television relationship, although in certain children's programs people purport to speak directly to the child and the camera fosters this illusion by focusing directly upon the person being filmed. (Mr. Rogers is an example, telling the child "I like you, you're special," etc.) How might such a distortion of real-life relationships affect a child's development of trust, of openness, of an ability to relate well to other *real* people? 26

Bruno Bettelheim writes: 27

> Children who have been taught, or conditioned, to listen passively most of the day to the warm verbal communications coming from the TV screen, to the deep emotional appeal of the so-called TV personality, are often unable to respond to real persons because they arouse so much less feeling than the skilled actor. Worse, they lose the ability to learn from reality because life experiences are much more complicated than the ones they see on the screen. . . .

A teacher makes a similar observation about her personal viewing experiences: 28

"I have trouble mobilizing myself and dealing with real people after watching a few hours of television. It's just hard to make that transition from watching television to a real relationship. I suppose it's because there was no effort necessary while I was watching, and dealing with real people always requires a bit of effort. Imagine, then, how much harder it might be to do the same thing for a small child, particularly one who watches a lot of television every day." 29

But more obviously damaging to family relationships is the elimination of opportunities to talk, and perhaps more important, to argue, to air grievances, between parents and children and brothers and sisters. Families frequently use television to avoid confronting their problems, problems that will not go away if they are ignored but will only fester and become less easily resolvable as time goes on. 30

A mother reports: 31

"I find myself, with three children, wanting to turn on the TV set   32
when they're fighting. I really have to struggle not to do it because
I feel that's telling them this is the solution to the quarrel—but it's
so tempting that I often do it."

A family therapist discusses the use of television as an avoidance   33
mechanism:

"In a family I know the father comes home from work and turns   34
on the television set. The children come and watch him and the wife
serves them their meal in front of the set. He then goes and takes a
shower, or works on the car or something. She then goes and has
her own dinner in front of the television set. It's a symptom of a
deeper-rooted problem, sure. But it would help them all to get rid of
the set. It would be far easier to work on what the symptom really
means without the television. The television simply encourages a
double avoidance of each other. They'd find out more quickly what
was going on if they weren't able to hide behind the TV. Things
wouldn't necessarily be better, of course, but they wouldn't be anesthetized."

The decreased opportunities for simple conversation between par-   35
ents and children in the television-centered home may help explain
an observation made by an emergency room nurse at a Boston hospital. She reports that parents just seem to sit there these days
when they come in with a sick or seriously injured child, although
talking to the child would distract and comfort him. "They don't
seem to know *how* to talk to their own children at any length," the
nurse observes. Similarly, a television critic writes in *The New York
Times*: "I had just a day ago taken my son to the emergency ward
of a hospital for stitches above his left eye, and the occasion seemed
no more real to me than Maalot or 54th Street, south-central Los
Angeles. There was distance and numbness and an inability to turn
off the total institution. I didn't behave at all; I just watched. . . . "

A number of research studies substantiate the assumption that   36
television interferes with family activities and the formation of family relationships. One survey shows that 78 percent of the respondents indicated no conversation taking place during viewing except
at specified times such as commercials. The study notes: "The television atmosphere in most households is one of quiet absorption on
the part of family members who are present. The nature of the family social life during a program could be described as 'parallel' rather
than interactive, and the set does seem to dominate family life when
it is on." Thirty-six percent of the respondents in another study indicated that television viewing was the only family activity participated in during the week.

In a summary of research findings on television's effect on family   37
interactions James Gabardino states: "The early findings suggest
that television had a disruptive effect upon interaction and thus presumably human development. . . . It is not unreasonable to ask: 'Is
the fact that the average American family during the 1950s came
to include two parents, two children and a television set somehow
related to the psychosocial characteristics of the young adults of the
1970s?' "

UNDERMINING THE FAMILY

In its effect on family relationships, in its facilitation of parental   38
withdrawal from an active role in the socialization of their children,
and in its replacement of family rituals and special events, television
has played an important role in the disintegration of the American
family. But of course it has not been the only contributing factor,
perhaps not even the most important one. The steadily rising divorce rate, the increase in the number of working mothers, the decline of the extended family, the breakdown of neighborhoods and
communities, the growing isolation of the nuclear family—all have
seriously affected the family.

As Urie Bronfenbrenner suggests, the sources of family break-   39
down do not come from the family itself, but from the circumstances
in which the family finds itself and the way of life imposed upon it
by those circumstances. "When those circumstances and the way of
life they generate undermine relationships of trust and emotional
security between family members, when they make it difficult for
parents to care for, educate and enjoy their children, when there is
no support or recognition from the outside world for one's role as a
parent and when time spent with one's family means frustration of
career, personal fulfillment and peace of mind, then the development
of the child is adversely affected," he writes.

But while the roots of alienation go deep into the fabric of Ameri-   40
can social history, television's presence in the home fertilizes them,
encourages their wild and unchecked growth. Perhaps it is true that
America's commitment to the television experience masks a spiritual vacuum, an empty and barren way of life, a desert of material-
ism. But it is television's dominant role in the family that anesthe-
tizes the family into accepting its unhappy state and prevents it
from struggling to better its condition, to improve its relationships,
and to regain some of the richness it once possessed.

Others have noted the role of mass media in perpetuating an un-   41
satisfactory *status quo*. Leisure-time activity, writes Irving Howe,

"must provide relief from work monotony without making the return to work too unbearable; it must provide amusement without insight and pleasure without disturbance—as distinct from art which gives pleasure through disturbance. Mass culture is thus oriented towards a central aspect of industrial society: the depersonalization of the individual." Similarly, Jacques Ellul rejects the idea that television is a legitimate means of educating the citizen: "Education . . . takes place only incidentally. The clouding of his consciousness is paramount. . . . "

And so the American family muddles on, dimly aware that something is amiss but distracted from an understanding of its plight by an endless stream of television images. As family ties grow weaker and vaguer, as children's lives become more separate from their parents', as parents' educational role in their children's lives is taken over by television and schools, family life becomes increasingly more unsatisfying for both parents and children. All that seems to be left is Love, an abstraction that family members *know* is necessary but find great difficulty giving each other because the traditional opportunities for expressing love within the family have been reduced or destroyed. 42

For contemporary parents, love toward each other has increasingly come to mean successful sexual relations, as witnessed by the proliferation of sex manuals and sex therapists. The opportunities for manifesting other forms of love through mutual support, understanding, nurturing, even, to use an unpopular word, *serving* each other, are less and less available as mothers and fathers seek their independent destinies outside the family. 43

As for love of children, this love is increasingly expressed through supplying material comforts, amusements, and educational opportunities. Parents show their love for their children by sending them to good schools and camps, by providing them with good food and good doctors, by buying them toys, books, games, and a television set of their very own. Parents will even go further and express their love by attending PTA meetings to improve their children's schools, or by joining groups that are acting to improve the quality of their children's television programs. 44

But this is love at a remove, and is rarely understood by children. The more direct forms of parental love require time and patience, steady, dependable, ungrudgingly given time actually spent *with* a child, reading to him, comforting him, playing, joking, and working with him. But even if a parent were eager and willing to demonstrate that sort of direct love to his children today, the opportunities are diminished. What with school and Little League and piano lessons 45 and, of course, the inevitable television programs, a day seems to offer just enough time for a good-night kiss.

COMPREHENSION

1. How did early observers view television? How, in general, does Winn's own view differ from theirs?

2. How has the nature of family television viewing changed since its inception? How does Winn account for this change?

3. How does television keep families apart? In what sense does Winn see television as a threat to the very nature of the family?

4. How does Winn define "family rituals"? How does she believe television has affected these rituals?

5. How, according to Winn, does television affect the relationships of family members to one another?

6. What other factors besides the presence of television does Winn see as having a negative effect on the family?

7. In what sense does television fertilize "the roots of alienation"?

8. Why does Winn believe today's families have such difficulty expressing love?

PURPOSE AND AUDIENCE

1. What purpose might Winn have had in mind when she called the book from which this selection is taken *Unplugging the Plug-In-Drug?*

2. Winn states her thesis in paragraph 8. What is it?

3. In paragraphs 10 and 27, Winn quotes two noted psychologists. What effect does she expect their words to have on her audience?

4. What effect is the young woman's testimony in paragraphs 22–23 calculated to have on Winn's readers?

5. In paragraph 24, Winn makes an analogy between modern families and cave families. What is her purpose in doing this?

STYLE AND STRUCTURE

1. Winn does not state her thesis until paragraph 8. What does she achieve in the paragraphs that precede this?

2. The length of Winn's paragraphs varies considerably. What effect are short paragraphs such as paragraphs 2, 3, 4, and 20 calculated to have?

3. From what different kinds of sources does Winn draw the many quotations she uses in this essay? How does the varied nature of these quotations help support her thesis?

4. This essay includes three headings: "Family Rituals," "Real People," and "Undermining the Family." What functions do these headings serve?

5. In paragraph 38, Winn pauses to summarize the major points she has made so far. Why do you think she does this?

6. Winn's focus in this essay is on the effects of television on the American family. In the last four paragraphs, however, her focus widens, and she touches on television only incidentally. Does this concluding strategy strengthen or weaken her essay? Explain.

VOCABULARY PROJECTS

1. Define each of the following words as it is used in this selection.

myopia (1)	adhesive (19)
ameliorate (8)	fosters (26)
advent (8)	substantiate (36)
subsidiary (8)	facilitation (38)
apologists (8)	perpetuating (41)
equivocal (9)	depersonalization (41)
counterbalances (13)	amiss (42)
regimented (14)	abstraction (42)
mediating (17)	remove (45)

2. One important effect of television has been seen in our vocabulary: television has spawned new words (for example, *sitcom*) and suggested new uses for old words (for instance, *tube*). List as many television-inspired words as you can, and define each.

3. Paragraph 14 presents a somewhat negative picture of family life. Rewrite it, using words with more positive connotations and making other changes as necessary, so that it presents a more appealing view.

WRITING WORKSHOP

1. Write an essay in which you consider the effects (including any possible future effects) of one of these inventions on the American family: the telephone, the personal computer, the microwave oven, the hand-held calculator.

2. Write a cause-and-effect essay in which you discuss the *positive* effects of television on American society.

3. Consider what other causes might have produced some of the same effects Winn identifies, and explore those causes in an essay. For instance, what economic, political, or social events might have contributed to changing the nature of family life? Consider, for example, why the details of family life presented in paragraphs 13–16 and elsewhere do not really characterize many of today's families.

THEMATIC CONNECTIONS

- "Once More to the Lake" (p. 138)
- "Violence in the Morning" (p. 156)
- "The Human Cost of an Illiterate Society" (p. 173)

THE CIVIL RIGHTS MOVEMENT: WHAT GOOD WAS IT?

Alice Walker

Alice Walker was born in Eatonton, Georgia. "The Civil Rights Movement: What Good Was It?" (1966–1967), written when Walker was twenty-three, was later collected in In Search of Our Mothers' Gardens *(1983). In addition to this book, which Walker calls "womanist prose," she has also published two collections of short stories* (In Love and Trouble *and* You Can't Keep a Good Woman Down); *four books of poetry* (Once; Revolutionary Petunias; Goodnight, Willie Lee, I'll See You in the Morning; *and* Horses Make a Landscape Look More Beautiful); *three novels* (The Third Life of Grange Copeland, Meridian, *and* The Color Purple); *and a biography of Langston Hughes.* The Color Purple *won an American Book Award and the Pulitzer Prize for fiction, and it was made into an award-winning film. Walker is also the editor of a collection of readings by Zora Neale Hurston. Pieces reprinted in* In Search of Our Mothers' Gardens *have appeared in publications such as* Ms., *the* New York Times, *the* American Scholar, *and* Mother Jones. "The Civil Rights Movement: What Good Was It?" *Walker's first published essay, won first prize in the* American Scholar *essay contest.*

Someone said recently to an old black lady from Mississippi,   1
whose legs had been badly mangled by local police who arrested her
for "disturbing the peace," that the Civil Rights Movement was
dead, and asked, since it was dead, what she thought about it. The
old lady replied, hobbling out of his presence on her cane, that the
Civil Rights Movement was like herself, "if it's dead, it shore ain't
ready to lay down!"

This old lady is a legendary freedom fighter in her small town in   2
the Delta. She has been severely mistreated for insisting on her
rights as an American citizen. She has been beaten for singing
Movement songs, placed in solitary confinement in prisons for talking about freedom, and placed on bread and water for praying aloud
to God for her jailers' deliverance. For such a woman the Civil
Rights Movement will never be over as long as her skin is black.

It also will never be over for twenty million others with the same "affliction," for whom the Movement can never "lay down," no matter how it is killed by the press and made dead and buried by the white American public. As long as one black American survives, the struggle for equality with other Americans must also survive. This is a debt we owe to those blameless hostages we leave to the future, our children.

Still, white liberals and deserting Civil Rights sponsors are quick   3
to justify their disaffection from the Movement by claiming that it is all over. "And since it is over," they will ask, "would someone kindly tell me what has been gained by it?" They then list statistics supposedly showing how much more advanced segregation is now than ten years ago—in schools, housing, jobs. They point to a gain in conservative politicians during the last few years. They speak of ghetto riots and of the survey that shows that most policemen are admittedly too anti-Negro to do their jobs in ghetto areas fairly and effectively. They speak of every area that has been touched by the Civil Rights Movement as somehow or other going to pieces.

They rarely talk, however, about human attitudes among Negroes   4
that have undergone terrific changes just during the past seven to ten years (not to mention all those years when there was a Movement and only the Negroes knew about it). They seldom speak of changes in personal lives because of the influence of people in the Movement. They see general failure and few, if any, individual gains.

They do not understand what it is that keeps the Movement from   5
"laying down" and Negroes from reverting to their former *silent* second-class status. They have apparently never stopped to wonder why it is always the white man—on his radio and in his newspaper and on his television—who says that the Movement is dead. If a Negro were audacious enough to make such a claim, his fellows might hanker to see him shot. The Movement is dead to the white man because it no longer interests him. And it no longer interests him because he can afford to be uninterested: he does not have to live by it, with it, or for it, as Negroes must. He can take a rest from the news of beatings, killings, and arrests that reach him from North and South—if his skin is white. Negroes cannot now and will never be able to take a rest from the injustices that plague them, for they—not the white man—are the target.

Perhaps it is naive to be thankful that the Movement "saved" a   6
large number of individuals and gave them something to live for, even if it did not provide them with everything they wanted. (Materially, it provided them with precious little that they wanted.) When a movement awakens people to the possibilities of life, it seems un-

fair to frustrate them by then denying what they had thought was offered. But what was offered? What was promised? What was it all about? What good did it do? Would it have been better, as some have suggested, to leave the Negro people as they were, unawakened, unallied with one another, unhopeful about what to expect for their children in some future world?

I do not think so. If knowledge of my condition is all the freedom   7
I get from a "freedom movement," it is better than unawareness, forgottenness, and hopelessness, the existence that is like the existence of a beast. Man only truly lives by knowing; otherwise he simply performs, copying the daily habits of others, but conceiving nothing of his creative possibilities as a man, and accepting someone else's superiority and his own misery.

When we are children, growing up in our parents' care, we await   8
the spark from the outside world. Sometimes our parents provide it—if we are lucky—sometimes it comes from another source far from home. We sit, paralyzed, surrounded by our anxiety and dread, hoping we will not have to grow up into the narrow world and ways we see about us. We are hungry for a life that turns us on; we yearn for a knowledge of living that will save us from our innocuous lives that resemble death. We look for signs in every strange event; we search for heroes in every unknown face.

It was just six years ago that I began to be alive. I had, of course,   9
been living before—for I am now twenty-three—but I did not really know it. And I did not know it because nobody told me that I—a pensive, yearning, typical high-school senior, but Negro—existed in the minds of others as I existed in my own. Until that time my mind was locked apart from the outer contours and complexion of my body as if it and the body were strangers. The mind possessed both thought and spirit—I wanted to be an author or a scientist—which the color of the body denied. I had never seen myself and existed as a statistic exists, or as a phantom. In the white world I walked, less real to them than a shadow; and being young and well hidden among the slums, among people who also did not exist—either in books or in films or in the government of their own lives—I waited to be called to life. And, by a miracle, I was called.

There was a commotion in our house that night in 1960. We had   10
managed to buy our first television set. It was battered and over-priced, but my mother had gotten used to watching the afternoon soap operas at the house where she worked as maid, and nothing could satisfy her on days when she did not work but a continuation of her "stories." So she pinched pennies and bought a set.

I remained listless throughout her "stories," tales of pregnancy,   11 abortion, hypocrisy, infidelity, and alcoholism. All these men and women were white and lived in houses with servants, long staircases that they floated down, patios where liquor was served four times a day to "relax" them. But my mother, with her swollen feet eased out of her shoes, her heavy body relaxed in our only comfortable chair, watched each movement of the smartly coiffed women, heard each word, pounced upon each innuendo and inflection, and for the duration of these "stories" she saw herself as one of them. She placed herself in every scene she saw, with her braided hair turned blond, her two hundred pounds compressed into a sleek size-seven dress, her rough dark skin smooth and *white*. Her husband became "dark and handsome," talented, witty, urbane, charming. And when she turned to look at my father sitting near her in his sweat shirt with his smelly feet raised on the bed to "air," there was always a tragic look of surprise on her face. Then she would sigh and go out to the kitchen looking lost and unsure of herself. My mother, a truly great woman who raised eight children of her own and half a dozen of the neighbors' without a single complaint, was convinced that she did not exist compared to "them." She subordinated her soul to theirs and became a faithful and timid supporter of the "Beautiful White People." Once she asked me, in a moment of vicarious pride and despair, if I didn't think that "they" were "jest naturally smarter, prettier, better." My mother asked this: a woman who never got rid of any of her children, never cheated on my father, was never a hypocrite if she could help it, and never even tasted liquor. She could not even bring herself to blame "them" for making her believe what they wanted her to believe: that if she did not look like them, think like them, be sophisticated and corrupt-for-comfort's-sake like them, she was a nobody. Black was not a color on my mother; it was a shield that made her invisible.

Of course, the people who wrote the soap-opera scripts always 12 made the Negro maids in them steadfast, trusty, and wise in a home-remedial sort of way; but my mother, a maid for nearly forty years, never once identified herself with the scarcely glimpsed black servant's face beneath the ruffled cap. Like everyone else, in her day-dreams at least, she thought she was free.

Six years ago, after half-heartedly watching my mother's soap op- 13 eras and wondering whether there wasn't something more to be asked of life, the Civil Rights Movement came into my life. Like a good omen for the future, the face of Dr. Martin Luther King, Jr., was the first black face I saw on our new television screen. And, as in a fairy tale, my soul was stirred by the meaning for me of his mission—at the time he was being rather ignominiously dumped into a police van for having led a protest march in Alabama—and I fell in love with the sober and determined face of the Movement. The singing of "We Shall Overcome"—that song betrayed by nonbelievers in it—rang for the first time in my ears. The influence that my mother's soap operas might have had on me became impossible. The life of Dr. King, seeming bigger and more miraculous than the man himself, because of all he had done and suffered, offered a pattern of strength and sincerity I felt I could trust. He had suffered much because of his simple belief in nonviolence, love, and brotherhood. Perhaps the majority of men could not be reached through these beliefs, but because Dr. King kept trying to reach them in spite of danger to himself and his family, I saw in him the hero for whom I had waited so long.

What Dr. King promised was not a ranch-style house and an acre 14 of manicured lawn for every black man, but jail and finally freedom. He did not promise two cars for every family, but the courage one day for all families everywhere to walk without shame and unafraid on their own feet. He did not say that one day it will be us chasing prospective buyers out of our prosperous well-kept neighborhoods, or in other ways exhibiting our snobbery and ignorance as all other ethnic groups before us have done; what he said was that we had a right to live anywhere in this country we chose, and a right to a meaningful well-paying job to provide us with the upkeep of our homes. He did not say we had to become carbon copies of the white American middle class; but he did say we had the right to become whatever we wanted to become.

Because of the Movement, because of an awakened faith in the 15 newness and imagination of the human spirit, because of "black and white together"—for the first time in our history in some human relationship on and off TV—because of the beatings, the arrests, the hell of battle during the past years, I have fought harder for my life and for a chance to be myself, to be something more than a shadow or a number, than I had ever done before in my life. Before, there had seemed to be no real reason for struggling beyond the effort for daily bread. Now there was a chance at that other that Jesus meant when He said we could not live by bread alone.

I have fought and kicked and fasted and prayed and cursed and 16 cried myself to the point of existing. It has been like being born again, literally. Just "knowing" has meant everything to me. Knowing has pushed me out into the world, into college, into places, into people.

Part of what existence means to me is knowing the difference be- 17 tween what I am now and what I was then. It is being capable of looking after myself intellectually as well as financially. It is being able to tell when I am being wronged and by whom. It means being awake to protect myself and the ones I love. It means being a part of the world community, and being *alert* to which part it is that I have joined, and knowing how to change to another part if that part does not suit me. To know is to exist: to exist is to be involved, to move about, to see the world with my own eyes. This, at least, the Movement has given me.

The hippies and other nihilists would have me believe that it is all   18 the same whether the people in Mississippi have a movement behind them or not. Once they have their rights, they say, they will run all over themselves trying to be just like everybody else. They will be well fed, complacent about things of the spirit, emotionless, and without the marvelous humanity and "soul" that the Movement has seen them practice time and time again. "What has the Movement done," they ask, "with the few people it has supposedly helped?" "Got them white-collar jobs, moved them into standardized ranch houses in white neighborhoods, given them nondescript gray flannel suits?" "What are these people now?" they ask. And then they answer themselves, "Nothings!"

I would find this reasoning—which I have heard many, many   19 times from hippies and nonhippies alike—amusing if I did not also consider it serious. For I think it is a delusion, a cop-out, an excuse to disassociate themselves from a world in which they feel too little has been changed or gained. The real question, however, it appears to me, is not whether poor people will adopt the middle-class mentality once they are well fed; rather, it is whether they will ever be well fed enough to be able to choose whatever mentality they think will suit them. The lack of a movement did not keep my mother from *wishing* herself bourgeois in her daydreams.

There is widespread starvation in Mississippi. In my own state of   20 Georgia there are more hungry families than Lester Maddox* would like to admit—or even see fed. I went to school with children who ate red dirt. The Movement has prodded and pushed some liberal senators into pressuring the government for food so that the hungry may eat. Food stamps that were two dollars and out of the reach of many families not long ago have been reduced to fifty cents. The price is still out of the reach of some families, and the government, it seems to a lot of people, could spare enough free food to feed its own people. It angers people in the Movement that it does not; they point to the billions in wheat we send free each year to countries

*Eds. Note—Governor of Georgia between 1967 and 1971, Maddox was widely known for his segregationist views.

abroad. Their government's slowness while people are hungry, its unwillingness to believe that there are Americans starving, its stingy cutting of the price of food stamps, make many Civil Rights workers throw up their hands in disgust. But they do not give up. They do not withdraw into the world of psychedelia. They apply what pressure they can to make the government give away food to hungry people. They do not plan so far ahead in their disillusionment with society that they can see these starving families buying identical ranch-style houses and sending their snobbish children to Bryn Mawr and Yale. They take first things first and try to get them fed.

They do not consider it their business, in any case, to say what 21 kind of life the people they help must lead. How one lives is, after all, one of the rights left to the individual—when and if he has opportunity to choose. It is not the prerogative of the middle class to determine what is worthy of aspiration. There is also every possibility that the middle-class people of tomorrow will turn out ever so much better than those of today. I even know some middle-class people of today who are not *all* bad.

I think there are so few Negro hippies because middle-class Ne- 22 groes, although well fed, are not careless. They are required by the treacherous world they live in to be clearly aware of whoever or whatever might be trying to do them in. They are middle class in money and position, but they cannot afford to be middle class in complacency. They distrust the hippie movement because they know that it can do nothing for Negroes as a group but "love" them, which is what all paternalists claim to do. And since the only way Negroes can survive (which they cannot do, unfortunately, on love alone) is with the support of the group, they are wisely wary and stay away.

A white writer tried recently to explain that the reason for the 23 relatively few Negro hippies is that Negroes have built up a "supercool" that cracks under LSD and makes them have a "bad trip." What this writer doesn't guess at is that Negroes are needing drugs less than ever these days for any kind of trip. While the hippies are "tripping," Negroes are going after power, which is so much more important to their survival and their children's survival than LSD and pot.

Everyone would be surprised if the Israelis ignored the Arabs and 24 took up "tripping" and pot smoking. In this country we are the Israelis. Everybody who can do so would like to forget this, of course. But for us to forget it for a minute would be fatal. "We Shall Overcome" is just a song to most Americans, *but we must do it*. Or die.

What good was the Civil Rights Movement? If it had just given 25

290 CAUSE AND EFFECT

this country Dr. King, a leader of conscience, for once in our life-time, it would have been enough. If it had just taken black eyes off white television stories, it would have been enough. If it had fed one starving child, it would have been enough.

If the Civil Rights Movement is "dead," and if it gave us nothing 26 else, it gave us each other forever. It gave some of us bread, some of us shelter, some of us knowledge and pride, all of us comfort. It gave us our children, our husbands, our brothers, our fathers, as men reborn and with a purpose for living. It broke the pattern of black servitude in this country. It shattered the phony "promise" of white soap operas that sucked away so many pitiful lives. It gave us history and men far greater than Presidents. It gave us heroes, selfless men of courage and strength, for our little boys and girls to follow. It gave us hope for tomorrow. It called us to life.

Because we live, it can never die. 27

COMPREHENSION

1. Is this essay's emphasis on finding causes, describing effects, or both?

2. According to Walker, how do white liberals view the civil rights movement?

3. According to Walker, what good *was* the civil rights movement?

4. What was it that called Walker to life at the age of seventeen?

5. With whom did Walker's mother identify as she watched soap operas? Why?

6. Why was Walker so strongly influenced by Dr. King?

7. What, specifically, were the effects of the civil rights movement on Walker herself?

8. What does Walker think the "hippies and other nihilists" would have her believe? What is her reaction to their opinion of the "Movement"?

9. When her essay was written, what did Walker believe still remained to be accomplished?

10. Why does Walker believe there are so few black hippies?

PURPOSE AND AUDIENCE

1. What do you think Walker hoped to accomplish in writing this essay in the late 1960s? Do you think she had different expectations for it when she decided to include it in her 1983 book? Explain.

2. Is Walker writing for an audience that is primarily black, or does she expect to reach a larger interracial audience? How can you tell?

3. What is the essay's thesis?

4. What purpose does Walker's digression about her mother's soap operas serve?

5. What does Walker hope to accomplish with her analogy between blacks and Israelis? Is it as effective an analogy today as it might have been twenty years ago? Explain.

STYLE AND STRUCTURE

1. What advantage does Walker gain by beginning with the anecdote about the elderly woman? What is the connection between this opening and the essay's conclusion?

2. Walker frequently uses *we* in her essay. Whom does she mean by *we*? Why do you think she uses this word?

3. In paragraph 9, Walker announces that she "began to be alive" six years earlier, yet she does not explain this until paragraph 13. What (if anything) does this delay accomplish?

4. Walker frequently uses stylistic techniques that Martin Luther King used—for example, *parallelism* (as in "She has been *beaten* . . . *placed* in solitary confinement . . . and *placed* on bread and water" [paragraph 2]) and *antithesis*, a rhetorical technique in which opposing ideas are expressed within a balanced grammatical structure (for instance, "He did not say we had to become carbon copies of the white American middle class, but he did say we had the right to become whatever we wanted to become" [paragraph 14]). Find another example of each technique. What is the effect?

5. Where in this essay does Walker use narration? Why does she use this technique?

VOCABULARY PROJECTS

1. Define each of the following words as it is used in this selection.

mangled (1)	pensive (9)
deliverance (2)	listless (11)
affliction (2)	hypocrisy (11)
disaffection (3)	coiffed (11)
reverting (5)	innuendo (11)
audacious (5)	urbane (11)
hanker (5)	vicarious (11)
innocuous (8)	ignominiously (13)

292 CAUSE AND EFFECT

nihilists (18)   psychedelia (20)
complacent (18)   prerogative (21)
bourgeois (19)   paternalists (22)

2. What words and expressions used in this essay are not often used today? Are there any expressions you have never heard? How can you explain this?

WRITING WORKSHOP

1. What good, in your opinion, was the civil rights movement? Expanding Walker's focus to include more recent advances—and, if you wish, to include its effects on whites as well as on blacks—write a cause-and-effect essay on this topic.

2. Write a cause-and-effect essay on the topic "The Woman's Movement: What Good Was (or Is) It?" Or, consider the peace movement, the environmental movement, or the nuclear freeze movement. You may focus on positive or negative effects (or both).

3. Write a humorous cause-and-effect essay entitled, "My High School Years: What Good Were They?"

THEMATIC CONNECTIONS

- "An Argument against the Anna Todd Jennings Scholarship" (p. 479)
- "Letter from Birmingham Jail" (p. 516)

THE FATE OF THE EARTH

Jonathan Schell

Born in 1943, Jonathan Schell writes for The New Yorker, *where this essay first appeared. His most recent book is* The Real War: Classic Reporting on the Vietnam War *(1988), a collection of articles that includes his 1967 "The Village of Ben Suc." His other books include* The Abolition *(1984) and* The Fate of the Earth *(1982), a collection of a series of* New Yorker *articles. In the latter book, Schell considers the effects of nuclear holocaust upon the earth's people and institutions, including the possible extinction of mankind. Schell's book, and this excerpt from it, are meant to awaken readers and warn them of the threat that nuclear weapons pose to the world. Through grim, thorough detail and a dispassionate tone, "The Fate of the Earth" describes the effects of a hydrogen bomb dropped on New York City.*

What happened at Hiroshima was less than a millionth part of a 1 holocaust at present levels of world nuclear armament. The more than millionfold difference amounts to more than a difference in magnitude; it is also a difference in kind. The authors of "Hiroshima and Nagasaki"* observe that "an atomic bomb's massive destruction and indiscriminate slaughter involves the sweeping breakdown of all order and existence—in a word, the collapse of society itself," and that therefore "the essence of atomic destruction lies in the totality of its impact on man and society." This is true also of a holocaust, of course, except that the totalities in question are now not single cities but nations, ecosystems, and the earth's ecosphere. Yet with the exception of fallout, which was relatively light at Hiroshima and Nagasaki (because both the bombs were air-burst), the immediate devastation caused by today's bombs would be of a sort similiar to the devastation in those cities. The immediate effects of a twenty-megaton bomb are not different in kind from those of a twelve-and-a-half-kiloton bomb; they are only more extensive. . . . In bursts of both weapons, for instance, there is a radius within which the thermal pulse can ignite newspapers: for the twelve-and-a-half-

*Eds. Note—A comprehensive study, carried out by a group of distinguished Japanese scientists, of the consequences of the bombing of those two cities.

kiloton weapon, it is a little over two miles; for the twenty-megaton weapon, it is twenty-five miles. (Since there is no inherent limit on the size of a nuclear weapon, these figures can be increased indefinitely, subject only to the limitations imposed by the technical capacities of the bomb builder—and of the earth's capacity to absorb the blast. The Soviet Union, which has shown a liking for sheer size in so many of its undertakings, once detonated a sixty-megaton bomb.) Therefore, while the total effect of a holocaust is qualitatively different from the total effect of a single bomb, the experience of individual people in a holocaust would be, in the short term (and again excepting the presence of lethal fallout wherever the bombs were ground-burst), very much like the experience of individual people in Hiroshima. The Hiroshima people's experience, accordingly, is of much more than historical interest. It is a picture of what our whole world is always poised to become—a backdrop of scarcely imaginable horror lying just behind the surface of our normal life, and capable of breaking through into that normal life at any second. Whether we choose to think about it or not, it is an omnipresent, inescapable truth about our lives today that at every single moment each one of us may suddenly become the deranged mother looking for her burned child; the professor with the ball of rice in his hand whose wife has just told him "Run away, dear!" and died in the fires; Mr. Fukai running back into the firestorm; the naked man standing on the blasted plain that was his city, holding his eyeball in his hand; or, more likely, one of millions of corpses. For whatever our "modest hopes" as human beings may be, every one of them can be nullified by a nuclear holocaust.

   One way to begin to grasp the destructive power of present-day nuclear weapons is to describe the consequences of the detonation of a one-megaton bomb, which possesses eighty times the explosive power of the Hiroshima bomb, on a large city, such as New York. Burst some eighty-five hundred feet above the Empire State Building, a one-megaton bomb would gut or flatten almost every building between Battery Park and 125th Street, or within a radius of four and four-tenths miles, or in an area of sixty-one square miles, and would heavily damage buildings between the northern tip of Staten Island and the George Washington Bridge, or within a radius of about eight miles, or in an area of about two hundred square miles. A conventional explosive delivers a swift shock, like a slap, to whatever it hits, but the blast wave of a sizable nuclear weapon endures for several seconds and "can surround and destroy whole buildings" (Glasstone). People, of course, would be picked up and hurled away from the blast along with the rest of the debris. Within the sixty-one square miles, the walls, roofs, and floors of any buildings that had not been flattened would be collapsed, and the people and furniture inside would be swept down onto the street. (Technically, this zone would be hit by various overpressures of at least five pounds per square inch. Overpressure is defined as the pressure in excess of normal atmospheric pressure.) As far away as ten miles from ground zero, pieces of glass and other sharp objects would be hurled about by the blast wave at lethal velocities. In Hiroshima, where buildings were low and, outside the center of the city, were often constructed of light materials, injuries from falling buildings were often minor. But in New York, where the buildings are tall and are constructed of heavy materials, the physical collapse of the city would certainly kill millions of people. The streets of New York are narrow ravines running between the high walls of the city's buildings. In a nuclear attack, the walls would fall and the ravines would fill up. The people in the buildings would fall to the street with the debris of the buildings, and the people in the street would be crushed by this avalanche of people and buildings. At a distance of two miles or so from ground zero, winds would reach four hundred miles an hour, and another two miles away they would reach a hundred and eighty miles an hour. Meanwhile, the fireball would be growing, until it was more than a mile wide, and rocketing upward, to a height of over six miles. For ten seconds, it would broil the city below. Anyone caught in the open within nine miles of ground zero would receive third-degree burns and would probably be killed; closer to the explosion, people would be charred and killed instantly. From Greenwich Village up to Central Park, the heat would be great enough to melt metal and glass. Readily inflammable materials, such as newspapers and dry leaves, would ignite in all five boroughs (though in only a small part of Staten Island) and west to the Passaic River, in New Jersey, within a radius of about nine and a half miles from ground zero, thereby creating an area of more than two hundred and eighty square miles in which mass fires were likely to break out.

   If it were possible (as it would not be) for someone to stand at Fifth Avenue and Seventy-second Street (about two miles from ground zero) without being instantly killed, he would see the following sequence of events. A dazzling white light from the fireball would illumine the scene, continuing for perhaps thirty seconds. Simultaneously, searing heat would ignite everything flammable and start to melt windows, cars, buses, lampposts, and everything else made of metal or glass. People in the street would immediately catch fire, and would shortly be reduced to heavily charred corpses. About five seconds after the light appeared, the blast wave would strike, laden with the debris of a now nonexistent midtown. Some buildings might be crushed, as though a giant fish had squeezed them on all sides, and others might be picked up off their foundations and whirled uptown with the other debris. On the far side of Central Park, the West Side skyline would fall from south to north. The four-hundred-mile-an-hour wind would blow from south to north, die down after a few seconds, and then blow in the reverse direction with diminished intensity. While these things were happening, the fireball would be burning in the sky for the ten seconds of the thermal pulse. Soon huge, thick clouds of dust and smoke would envelop the scene, and as the mushroom cloud rushed overhead (it would have a diameter of about twelve miles) the light from the sun would be blotted out, and day would turn to night. Within minutes, fires, ignited both by the thermal pulse and by broken gas mains, tanks of gas and oil, and the like, would begin to spread in the darkness, and a strong, steady wind would begin to blow in the direction of the blast. As at Hiroshima, a whirlwind might be produced, which would sweep through the ruins, and radioactive rain, generated under the meteorological conditions created by the blast, might fall. Before long, the individual fires would coalesce into a mass fire, which, depending largely on the winds, would become either a conflagration or a firestorm. In a conflagration, prevailing winds spread a wall of fire as far as there is any combustible material to sustain it; in a firestorm, a vertical updraft caused by the fire itself sucks the surrounding air in toward a central point, and the fires therefore converge in a single fire of extreme heat. A mass of either kind renders shelters useless by burning up all the oxygen in the air and creating toxic gases, so that anyone inside the shelters is asphyxiated, and also by heating the ground to such high temperatures that the shelters turn, in effect, into ovens, cremating the people inside them. In Dresden, several days after the firestorm raised there by Allied conventional bombing, the interiors of some bomb shelters were still so hot that when they were opened the inrushing air caused the contents to burst into flame. Only those who had fled their shelters when the bombing started had any chance of surviving. (It is difficult to predict in a particular situation which form the fires will take. In actual experience, Hiroshima suffered a firestorm and Nagasaki suffered a conflagration.)

In this vast theatre of physical effects, all the scenes of agony and death that took place at Hiroshima would again take place, but now involving millions of people rather than hundreds of thousands. Like the people of Hiroshima, the people of New York would be burned, battered, crushed, and irradiated in every conceivable way. The city and its people would be mingled in a smoldering heap. And then, as the fires started, the survivors (most of whom would be on the periphery of the explosion) would be driven to abandon to the flames those family members and other people who were unable to flee, or else to die with them. Before long, while the ruins burned, the processions of injured, mute people would begin their slow progress out of the outskirts of the devastated zone. However, this time a much smaller proportion of the population than at Hiroshima would have a chance of escaping. In general, as the size of the area of devastation increases, the possibilities for escape decrease. When the devastated area is relatively small, as it was at Hiroshima, people who are not incapacitated will have a good chance of escaping to safety before the fires coalesce into a mass fire. But when the devastated area is great, as it would be after the detonation of a megaton bomb, and fires are springing up at a distance of nine and a half miles from ground zero, and when what used to be the streets are piled high with burning rubble, and the day (if the attack occurs in the daytime) has grown impenetrably dark, there is little chance that anyone who is not on the very edge of the devastated area will be able to make his way to safety. In New York, most people would die wherever the blast found them, or not very far from there.

If instead of being burst in the air the bomb were burst on or near the ground in the vicinity of the Empire State Building, the overpressure would be very much greater near the center of the blast area but the range hit by a minimum of five pounds per square inch of overpressure would be less. The range of the thermal pulse would be about the same as that of the air burst. The fireball would be almost two miles across, and would engulf midtown Manhattan from Greenwich Village nearly to Central Park. Very little is known about what would happen to a city that was inside a fireball, but one would expect a good deal of what was there to be first pulverized and then melted or vaporized. Any human beings in the area would be reduced to smoke and ashes; they would simply disappear. A crater roughly three blocks in diameter and two hundred feet deep would open up. In addition, heavy radioactive fallout would be created as dust and debris from the city rose with the mushroom cloud and then fell back to the ground. Fallout would begin to drop almost immediately, contaminating the ground beneath the cloud with levels of radiation many times lethal doses, and quickly killing anyone who might have survived the blast wave and the thermal pulse and might now be attempting an escape; it is difficult to believe that there would be appreciable survival of the people of the city after a megaton ground burst. And for the next twenty-four hours or so more fallout would descend downwind from the blast, in a plume whose directions and length would depend on the speed and the direction of the wind that happened to be blowing at the time of the attack. If the wind was blowing at fifteen miles an hour, fallout of lethal intensity would descend in a plume about a hundred and fifty miles long and as much as fifteen miles wide. Fallout that was sublethal but could still cause serious illness would extend another hundred and fifty miles downwind. Exposure to radioactivity in human beings is measured in units called rems—an acronym for "roentgen equivalent in man." The roentgen is a standard measurement of gamma- and X-ray radiation, and the expression "equivalent in man" indicates that an adjustment has been made to take into account the differences in the degree of biological damage that is caused by radiation of different types. Many of the kinds of harm done to human beings by radiation—for example, the incidence of cancer and of genetic damage—depend on the dose accumulated over many years; but radiation sickness, capable of causing death, results from an "acute" dose, received in a period of anything from a few seconds to several days. Because almost ninety percent of the so-called "infinite-time dose" of radiation from fallout—that is, the dose from a given quantity of fallout that one would receive if one lived for many thousands of years—is emitted in the first week, the one-week accumulated dose is often used as a convenient measure for calculating the immediate harm from fallout. Doses in the thousands of rems, which could be expected throughout the city, would attack the central nervous system and would bring about death within a few hours. Doses of around a thousand rems, which would be delivered some tens of miles downwind from the blast, would kill within two weeks everyone who was exposed to them. Doses of around five hundred rems, which would be delivered as far as a hundred and fifty miles downwind (given a wind speed of fifteen miles per hour), would kill half of all exposed able-bodied young adults. At this level of exposure, radiation sickness proceeds in the three stages observed at Hiroshima. The plume of lethal fallout could descend, depending on the direction of the wind, on other parts of New York State and parts of New Jersey, Pennsylvania, Delaware, Maryland, Connecticut, Massachusetts, Rhode Island, Vermont, and New Hampshire, killing additional millions of people. The circumstances in heavily contaminated areas, in which millions of people were all declining together, over a period of weeks, toward painful deaths, are ones that, like so many of the consequences of nuclear explosions, have been never experienced.

A description of the effects of a one-megaton bomb on New York   6
City gives some notion of the meaning in human terms of a megaton
of nuclear explosive power, but a weapon that is more likely to be
used against New York is the twenty-megaton bomb, which has one
thousand six hundred times the yield of the Hiroshima bomb. The
Soviet Union is estimated to have at least a hundred and thirteen
twenty-megaton bombs in its nuclear arsenal, carried by Bear inter-
continental bombers. In addition, some of the Soviet SS–18 missiles
are capable of carrying bombs of this size, although the actual yields
are not known. Since the explosive power of the twenty-megaton
bombs greatly exceeds the amount necessary to destroy most military targets, it is reasonable to suppose that they are meant for use
against large cities. If a twenty-megaton bomb were air-burst over
the Empire State Building at an altitude of thirty thousand feet, the
zone gutted or flattened by the blast wave would have a radius of
twelve miles and an area of more than four hundred and fifty square
miles, reaching from the middle of Staten Island to the northern
edge of the Bronx, the eastern edge of Queens, and well into New
Jersey, and the zone of heavy damage from the blast wave (the zone
hit by a minimum of two pounds of overpressure per square inch)
would have a radius of twenty-one and a half miles, or an area of
one thousand four hundred and fifty square miles, reaching to the
southernmost tip of Staten Island, north as far as southern Rock-
land County, east into Nassau County, and west to Morris County,
New Jersey. The fireball would be about four and a half miles in
diameter and would radiate the thermal pulse for some twenty seconds. People caught in the open twenty-three miles away from
ground zero, in Long Island, New Jersey, and southern New York
State, would be burned to death. People hundreds of miles away who
looked at the burst would be temporarily blinded and would risk
permanent eye injury. (After the test of a fifteen-megaton bomb on
Bikini Atoll, in the South Pacific, in March of 1954, small animals
were found to have suffered retinal burns at a distance of three hundred and forty-five miles.) The mushroom cloud would be seventy
miles in diameter. New York City and its suburbs would be transformed into a lifeless, flat, scorched desert in a few seconds.

If a twenty-megaton bomb were ground-burst on the Empire   7
State Building, the range of severe blast damage would, as with the
one-megaton ground blast, be reduced, but the fireball, which would
be almost six miles in diameter, would cover Manhattan from Wall
Street to northern Central Park and also parts of New Jersey,
Brooklyn, and Queens, and everyone within it would be instantly

300 CAUSE AND EFFECT

killed, with most of them physically disappearing. Fallout would again be generated, this time covering thousands of square miles with lethal intensities of radiation. A fair portion of New York City and its incinerated population, now radioactive dust, would have risen into the mushroom cloud and would now be descending on the surrounding territory. On one of the few occasions when local fallout was generated by a test explosion in the multi-megaton range, the fifteen-megaton bomb tested on Bikini Atoll, which was exploded seven feet above the surface of a coral reef, "caused substantial contamination over an area of more than seven thousand square miles," according to Glasstone. If, as seems likely, a twenty-megaton bomb ground-burst on New York would produce at least a comparable amount of fallout, and if the wind carried the fallout onto populated areas, then this one bomb would probably doom upward of twenty million people, or almost ten per cent of the population of the United States.

COMPREHENSION

1. What differences does Schell cite between the bombing of Hiroshima and the possible future holocaust he describes? What similarities does he acknowledge?

2. What is the first effect Schell considers? Why does he discuss it first?

3. What effect does Schell focus on in paragraph 3?

4. In paragraph 4, why does Schell maintain that so few people would escape after the blast?

5. What variation on his theme does Schell introduce in paragraph 5? What effects of this new scenario does he consider?

6. What additional possibility is the subject of paragraph 6? Why does Schell feel this possibility is a likely one?

7. According to Schell's essay, what could be the ultimate outcome of a twenty-megaton bomb ground-burst on New York?

PURPOSE AND AUDIENCE

1. Schell's purpose is primarily persuasive, yet he is also presenting factual information. How does the detailed information he presents advance his persuasive purpose?

2. How does Schell ensure that a general audience will be able to understand his points and remain interested in his essay? Consider his use of definition, parenthetical clarification, and analogy.

3. What does Schell hope to accomplish by opening this essay with vivid details from the experience of Hiroshima?

4. What is Schell's thesis? Where is this thesis explicitly stated?

STYLE AND STRUCTURE

1. What tense does Schell use for most of his verbs? Why?

2. This essay has extremely long paragraphs. Why didn't Schell break them up into shorter ones?

3. What is the effect of the parenthetical *as it would not be* at the beginning of paragraph 3?

4. Does Schell's indefinite language, such as *if instead, very little is known*, and *one would expect* in paragraph 5, weaken this argument? Why or why not?

5. How does Schell gradually intensify his argument as he moves from paragraph 5 to paragraph 6 to paragraph 7?

6. How does Schell's style suit his essay? Why does he avoid the sensational style his subject matter might seem to call for?

VOCABULARY PROJECTS

1. Define each of the following words as it is used in this selection.

holocaust (1)	coalesce (3)
ecosystems (1)	conflagration (3)
ecosphere (1)	irradiated (4)
thermal (1)	periphery (4)
inherent (1)	impenetrably (4)
lethal (1)	pulverized (5)
firestorm (1)	vaporized (5)
nullified (1)	acronym (5)
detonation (2)	emitted (5)
velocities (2)	gutted (6)
diminished (3)	

2. Schell's careful choice of words helps him to convey a sense of total devastation. List all the words he uses to convey violence and destructiveness, and then try replacing some of them with words with

neutral connotations. How do your substitutions change the essay's impact?

3. Despite Schell's use of grim detail and strong language throughout the essay, he does achieve the appearance of objectivity and refrains from sensationalism. To see how his essay's impact might have been changed if he had not exercised this restraint, choose one paragraph and substitute more sensational words for Schell's.

WRITING WORKSHOP

1. Consider the impact this essay has had on you or your friends. Write an essay in which you try to predict effects of Schell's work on readers, considering how his ideas might change people's assumptions or plans.

2. Using Schell's information (and being sure to acknowledge it), write a letter to the President of the United States. By outlining the probable effects of the bomb, try to convince the President to support nuclear disarmament. Or, use the same information to convince the President that the U.S. must continue to develop new and stronger atomic weapons to defend itself.

3. Consider the effects on your family or your town of a serious disaster—a fire, a flood, a hurricane or tornado, or a blizzard, for instance. You may discuss events that have actually occurred or speculate about possible effects.

THEMATIC CONNECTIONS

- "Pure and Impure: The Interplay of Science and Technology" (p. 184)
- "The Declaration of Independence" (p. 484)

WRITING ASSIGNMENTS FOR CAUSE AND EFFECT

1. "Who Killed Benny Paret?," "The Fate of the Earth," and "38 Who Saw Murder" all (directly or undirectly) encourage readers to take action rather than remain uninvolved bystanders. Using information gleaned from all three of these essays as examples, write an essay in which you explore the possible consequences of apathy.

2. Both "Letter from Birmingham Jail" and "The Civil Rights Movement: What Good Was It?" consider some of the factors that made the United States ripe for the civil rights movement. Citing these two essays when necessary, write a cause-and-effect essay in which you explore those causes.

3. Various technological and social developments have contributed to the decline of letter writing. One of these is the telephone. Consider some other possible causes and write an essay explaining why letter writing has become less popular. You may also consider the *effects* of this decline.

4. How do you account for the popularity of one of the following phenomena: shopping malls, rock videos, romance novels, fast food, sensationalist tabloids like the *National Enquirer*? Write an essay in which you consider remote as well as immediate causes for the success of the phenomenon you choose.

5. Between 1946 and 1964, the birth rate increased considerably. Some of the effects attributed to this "baby boom" include the 1960s antiwar movement, the increase in the crime rate and the development of feminism. Write an essay in which you explore some possible effects of the baby boom generation's growing older. What trends would you expect to find in the 1990s as the bulk of the baby boomers reach middle age? When they reach retirement?

6. Present a series of events from your life that constitutes a causal chain. Be sure to indicate clearly both the sequence of events and the causal connections among them.

7. In a complete essay, consider the effects, or possible effects, of one of these scientific developments on your life and/or on the lives of your contemporaries: genetic engineering, space exploration, artificial intelligence, in vitro fertilization. Consider negative as well as positive effects.

8. To what do you attribute the rising divorce rate? Be as specific as possible, citing "case studies" of families with which you are familiar.

9. Do some research to determine the causes and/or the effects of one

304 CAUSE AND EFFECT

of these: the Chinese custom of binding women's feet; the practice of patronage of artists by the aristocracy; the building of the Panama Canal; the passage of the Taft-Hartley Act. Write an essay illustrating your findings.

10. Write an essay in which you consider the likely effects of a severe, protracted shortage of one of the following commodities: food, rental housing, medical care, computer hardware, reading matter. You may consider a community-, city-, or statewide shortage or a nation- or worldwide crisis.

7

Comparison
and Contrast

WHAT IS COMPARISON AND CONTRAST?

In a narrow sense, a *comparison* shows how two or more things are similar. A *contrast* shows how they are different. In most writing situations, you will use the two related processes of *comparison and contrast* to consider both similarities and differences. In the following paragraph from *Disturbing the Universe*, Freeman Dyson compares and contrasts two different styles of human endeavor which he calls the "gray" and the "green."

> In everything we undertake, either on earth or in the sky, we have a choice of two styles, which I call the gray and the green. The distinction between the gray and green is not sharp. Only at the extremes of the spectrum can we say without qualification, this is green and that is gray. The difference between green and gray is better explained by examples than by definitions. Factories are gray, gardens are green. Physics is gray, biology is green. Plutonium is gray, horse manure is green. Bureaucracy is gray, pioneer communities are green. Self-reproducing machines are gray, trees and children are green. Human technology is gray, God's technology is green. Clones are gray, clades* are green. Army field manuals are gray, poems are green.

A special form of comparison, called *analogy*, looks for similarities between two essentially *different* things. With analogy you explain one thing by comparing it to a second thing that is more familiar

---

*EDS. NOTE: A group of organisms that evolved from a common ancestor.

than the first. In the following paragraph from *The Shopping Mall High School*, Arthur G. Powell, Eleanor Farrar, and David K. Cohen use analogy to shed light on the nature of American high schools.

> If Americans want to understand their high schools at work, they should imagine them as shopping malls. Secondary education is another consumption experience in an abundant society. Shopping malls attract a broad range of customers with different tastes and purposes. Some shop at Sears, others at Woolworth's or Bloomingdale's. In high schools a broad range of students also shop. They too can select from an astonishing variety of products and services conveniently assembled in one place with ample parking. Furthermore, in malls and schools many different kinds of transactions are possible. Both institutions bring hopeful purveyors and potential purchasers together. The former hope to maximize sales but can take nothing for granted. Shoppers have a wide discretion not only about what to buy but also about whether to buy.

Throughout our lives we are bombarded with countless bits of information from newspapers, television, radio, and personal experience: the police strike in Memphis; city workers walk out in Philadelphia; the Senate debates government spending; the property tax is raised in New Jersey. The list is endless. Yet somehow we must make sense of the jumbled facts and figures that surround us. One way we have of understanding information like this is to put it side by side with other data and then to compare and contrast. Do the police in Memphis have the same complaints as the city workers in Philadelphia? What are the differences between the two situations? Is the national debate on spending analogous to the New Jersey debate on property taxes? How do they differ? We make similar distinctions every day about matters that directly affect us. When we make personal decisions, we consider alternatives, asking ourselves whether one option seems better than another. Should I buy a car with manual or automatic transmission? Should I major in history or business? What job opportunities will each major offer me? Should I register as a Democrat or a Republican, or should I join a smaller political party? What are the positions of each on government spending, welfare, and taxes?

Because this way of thinking is central to our understanding of the world, comparison and contrast is often required in papers and on essay examinations:

Compare and contrast the attitudes toward science and technology expressed in Stanislaw Lem's *Solaris* and Isaac Asimov's *I, Robot*. (science fiction)

What are the similarities and differences between mitosis and meiosis? (biology)

Discuss the relative merits of establishing a partnership and incorporating. (business law)

Discuss the advantages and disadvantages of heterogeneous pupil grouping. (education)

Uses of Comparison and Contrast

You are not likely to sit down and say to yourself, "I think I'll write a comparison-and-contrast essay today. Now what shall I write about?" Instead, you will use comparison and contrast because you have been told to or because you decide it suits your assignment or your purpose. In the examples above, for instance, the instructors have phrased their questions to tell students how to treat the material. When you read the questions, certain key words and phrases—*compare and contrast, similarities and differences, relative merits, advantages and disadvantages*—indicate that you should use a comparison-and-contrast pattern to organize your essay. Sometimes you may not even need such key phrases. Consider the question, "Which of the two Adamses, John or Samuel, had the greatest influence on the timing and course of the American Revolution?" The word *which* is enough to point to a contrast.

Even when you are not given an assignment that is worded to suggest comparison and contrast, your purpose may point to this organization strategy. For instance, when you set out to make an evaluation, you frequently employ comparison and contrast. If you, as a student in hospital management, were asked to evaluate two health delivery systems, you could begin by looking up the standards used by experts in their evaluations. You could then compare each system's performance with those standards, and then contrast the systems with each other, concluding perhaps that both systems met minimum standards but that one was more cost-efficient than the other. Or if you were evaluating this year's new cars for a consumer newsletter, you might establish some criteria—gas economy, handling, comfort, sturdiness, style—and compare and contrast the cars with respect to each criterion. If different cars were best in each category, your readers would have to decide which features mattered most.

Basis of Comparison

Before you can compare or contrast two things, you must determine what elements they have in common. For example, although cats and dogs are very different pets, both can learn from their owners. Cats and dogs may be taught different behaviors in different ways, but these differences can be analyzed because both animals share a common element, that of being trainable. Without a common element, there would be no basis for analysis—that is, no *basis of comparison.*

A comparison should lead you, and thus your reader, beyond the obvious. For instance, at first the idea of a comparison-and-contrast essay based on an analogy between bees and people might seem absurd. After all, these two creatures differ in species, physical structure, and intelligence. Their differences are so obvious that an essay based on them would be pointless. But, with further analysis, you might decide there are quite a few similarities between the two. Both are social animals that live in complex social structures, and both have tasks to perform and roles to fulfill in their societies. Therefore, you would focus your essay on the common elements that seem most provocative—social structures and roles—rather than those elements that lead nowhere—species, physical structure, and intelligence. If you tried to draw an analogy between bees and Volkswagens or humans and golf tees, however, you would run into trouble. Although some points of comparison could be found, they would be trivial. Why bother to point out that both bees and Volkswagens travel great distances or that both people and tees are needed to play golf? Neither statement establishes a significant basis of comparison.

When two subjects are very similar, it is the contrast that is worth writing about. And when two subjects are not very much alike, you should find enlightening similarities.

Selecting Points for Discussion

When you have decided what subjects you will compare and contrast, you brainstorm to find material and then go on to select those points you want to discuss. You do this by determining your emphasis—similarities, differences, or both—and the major emphasis of your paper. If your purpose for comparing two types of house plants is to explain that one is easier to raise than the other, you would contrast points having to do with plant care, not those having to do with plant biology.

When you compare and contrast, make sure that you treat the same, or at least comparable, elements for each subject you discuss. For instance, if you were going to compare and contrast two novels, you might consider the following elements in both works.

Novel A	*Novel B*
Major characters	Major characters
Minor characters	Minor characters
Themes	Themes

A common error that you should avoid is discussing entirely different elements for each subject. Such an approach obscures any basis of comparison that might exist. The two novels, for example, could not be significantly compared or contrasted if you discussed elements such as these:

Novel A	*Novel B*
Major characters	Plot
Minor characters	Author's life
Themes	Symbolism

Thesis Statement

After you decide on the points you want to discuss, you are ready to formulate your thesis statement. This thesis establishes the significance of the comparison or contrast and the relative merits of the items discussed. In a college paper that uses a comparison-and-contrast pattern, a thesis statement almost always strengthens the writing by clarifying its purpose.

As in other essays, your thesis statement should tell your readers what to expect in your essay. It should mention not only the subjects to be compared and contrasted but also the point the comparison is to make. Your thesis should also indicate whether you will concentrate on similarities or differences or whether you will balance the two. In addition, it may list the points of discussion in the order in which they are discussed in the essay. The very structure of your thesis sentence can help to show the focus of your essay. As the following sentences illustrate, a thesis statement can emphasize the central concern of the essay by stating it in the main, rather than the subordinate, clause of the sentence:

> Doctors and nurses perform distinctly different tasks at a hospital; however, their functions overlap when they interact with patients.

> Although Melville's *Moby Dick* and London's *The Sea Wolf* are both about the sea, the major characters, minor characters, and themes of *Moby Dick* establish its greater complexity.

The structure of the first sentence emphasizes similarities, and the structure of the second highlights differences. Moreover, both sentences establish the things to be compared or contrasted as well as the significance or purpose of the juxtaposition.

STRUCTURING A COMPARISON-AND-CONTRAST ESSAY

Like every other type of essay examined in this book, a comparison-and-contrast essay has an introduction, several body paragraphs, and a conclusion. Within the body of your paper, there are two basic comparison-and-contrast patterns you can follow: You can discuss each subject separately, devoting one or more paragraphs to subject A and then the same number to subject B; or you can discuss one common element in each section, making your points about subject A and subject B in turn. As you might expect, both organizational patterns have advantages and disadvantages that you should consider before you use them.

Subject-by-Subject Comparison

When composing a subject-by-subject comparison, you essentially write a separate essay about each subject, but you organize these miniature essays in parallel fashion. In discussing each subject, you use the *same basis of comparison* to guide your selection of supporting points, and you arrange these points in some logical order. Usually you present points in order of increasing significance. The following informal outline illustrates a subject-by-subject comparison:

- Introduction—thesis: Doctors and nurses perform distinctly different tasks at a hospital; however, their functions overlap when they interact with patients.

- Doctor's functions:
    Teaching patients
    Assessing patients
    Dispensing medication
- Nurse's functions:
    Teaching patients
    Assessing patients
    Dispensing medication
- Conclusion

Most often, subject-by-subject comparisons are used for short, uncomplicated papers. In longer papers, where many points are made about each subject, this organizational pattern can put too many demands on your readers, requiring them to keep track of all your points throughout your paper. In addition, because of the size of each section, your paper may sound like two separate essays weakly connected by a transitional phrase. Instead, for longer or more complex papers, it is best to discuss each point of comparison for both subjects together, making your comparisons as you go along.

Point-by-Point Comparison

When you write a point-by-point comparison, your paper is organized differently. Section by section, you first make a point about one subject and then follow it with a comparable point about the other. This alternating pattern continues throughout the body of your essay, until all your comparisons or contrasts have been made. The following informal outline illustrates a point-by-point comparison:

- Introduction—thesis: Melville's *Moby Dick* has more fully developed characters and more complex themes than does London's *The Sea Wolf*.
- Minor characters:
    The Sea Wolf
    Moby Dick
- Major characters:
    The Sea Wolf
    Moby Dick
- Themes:
    The Sea Wolf
    Moby Dick
- Conclusion

Point-by-point comparisons work best for longer, more complicated papers where you discuss exactly the same points in the same order. (If it is not desirable to treat points in the same order for both subjects, then you should consider a subject-by-subject comparison.) In the point-by-point pattern, readers can easily follow comparisons or contrasts and do not have to wait several paragraphs to find out the differences between *Moby Dick* and *The Sea Wolf* or to remember on page six what was said on page three. Nevertheless, it is easy to fall into a monotonous, back-and-forth movement between points when you write a point-by-point comparison. To avoid this, use clear transitions, and vary sentence structure as you move from point to point.

Both of the following essays illustrate comparison and contrast. The first, an examination answer by Jane Czerak, is an example of a subject-by-subject comparison. The second, written by Jeffrey Hasday for his composition class, illustrates a point-by-point comparison.

Question: Choose any two of the novels assigned in the course, and discuss how their views of the future differ. Account if you can for the differences you uncover.

Here is Jane Czerak's answer.

Introduction	When science fiction discusses another world, it 1 is actually discussing our world; and when science fiction discusses the future, it is actually discussing the present. Both Robert Heinlein's Starship Troopers and John Brunner's Stand on Zanzibar are near-future science fiction--supposedly set fifty years from the time they were written.
Thesis (emphasizing differences)	Although these books are alike in some ways, they differ in other ways that reflect the moods of the times in which they were written.
First subject (view of the future)	Starship Troopers takes place in a world that is 2 substantially different from ours. Earth is the center of an empire that encompasses several of the outer planets. Space exploration has led to the colonization of a number of worlds and the inevitable

alien encounter. Consequently, Earth is locked in mortal combat with buglike aliens who are bent on appropriating the living space that people on Earth need to survive. As a result of this struggle, the military has assumed great power. The entire society reflects the values imposed by years of constant warfare. For example, for a person to obtain citizenship, he or she must first serve in the armed forces. Only those who have fought the bugs and survived are granted the right to vote.

First subject (reflection of the past)

In many ways, Starship Troopers reflects the times in which it was written. The 1950s was a decade in which the United States had great faith in military power and in its ability to police the world. Despite the example of Korea, America viewed its atomic arsenal as an umbrella that would protect it from harm. The world of Starship Troopers is one which faces an alien challenge. War is seen as an inevitable result of expansion; only through struggle can human beings establish their right to survive. In this light, the bugs are symbols of all that threatened the United States throughout the 1950s.

3

Second subject (view of the future)

The world of Stand on Zanzibar is very much like ours today. The story takes place in the near future, and the first half of the book is set in New York City. Many of the problems that beset New York today are still present in the future, but they are even more severe. Because of overpopulation, living space is at a premium, and people can afford apartments only by sharing the expense with others. Corporations have assumed great power and virtually run the government. Every facet of life seems to be permeated by television and advertising. People are encouraged to buy as much as they can whenever they can--this in spite of the fact that Earth's resources seem to be

4

declining at an alarming rate. In order to try to
cope with this suicidal way of life, most states have
passed laws strictly limiting the number of children
families can have.

**Second subject
(reflection of
the past)**

Stand on Zanzibar was published in 1968 and very ⁵
accurately expresses the mood of the times. Possibly
because of the joint effects of the war in Vietnam
and the Johnson presidency, Americans were examining
their personal and national goals. The population
explosion, ecology, and corporate power became topics
of great interest. Brunner takes these problems and
speculates about what would happen if Americans
continued their present course of action. The result
is the world of Stand on Zanzibar, where the United
States consumes most of Earth's resources and
continually searches our overextended planet for
more.

Conclusion

Although Starship Troopers and Stand on Zanzibar ⁶
were written only nine years apart, they differ
greatly in their views of the future. Great changes
took place in the United States between 1959 and
1968, and these books reflect the shifts in
priorities and consciousness. Using the near future
as settings for their works, Heinlein and Brunner

**Restatement of
thesis**

create interesting and subtle works which are as
different as the volatile times in which they were
written.

Points for Special Attention

Structure. Jane makes two major points about the two novels
she compares: that they treat the future in different ways and that
this treatment reflects the times in which they were written. Because readers can easily keep these two ideas in mind, a subject-by-
subject discussion was a good strategy for Jane to use. Of course,
she could have chosen a point-by-point discussion and written an

equally convincing paper. Often the choice is a matter of personal preference—a different writer might simply have liked a different strategy better. Because Jane was writing a final examination and time was limited, she chose the strategy that enabled her to organize her essay most quickly and easily.

Transitions. Any comparison-and-contrast essay needs transitions so that its parts are coherent. Without adequate transitions, a point-by-point comparison can produce a series of choppy paragraphs, and a subject-by-subject comparison can read like two separate essays. In addition to connecting the sections of an essay, transitional words and phrases like the following, when used properly, can highlight similarities and differences for your reader:

on the one hand . . . on the other hand . . . even though on the contrary in spite of although despite unlike	Indicate differences
both like likewise similarly	Indicate similarities

Jane could have used these phrases more often than she does, particularly when she shifts from the first subject in her discussion to the second. By adding a transitional phrase, such as *in contrast*, she not only could have emphasized the differences between the two books she is discussing but also could have improved the transition between the two sections of her paper.

Without transition:	The world of *Stand on Zanzibar* is very much like ours today.
With transition:	In contrast to *Starship Troopers*, the world of *Stand on Zanzibar* is very much like ours today.

Topic Sentences. A topic sentence presents the main idea of a paragraph; often it appears as the paragraph's first sentence. Like transitional phrases, topic sentences guide your reader through your paper. When reading a comparison-and-contrast essay, a reader can easily become lost in a jumble of points, especially if the paper is long and complex. Direct, clearly stated topic sentences act as guideposts, alerting your reader to the comparisons and contrasts you are making. Jane's topic sentences are straightforward and reinforce her major points about each book. And, as in any good comparison-and-contrast essay, each of the points discussed in part one of her paper is also discussed in part two. Notice how her topic sentences reinforce this balance:

Starship Troopers takes place in a world that is substantially different from ours.

In many ways, *Starship Troopers* reflects the times in which it was written.

The world of *Stand on Zanzibar* is very much like ours today.

Stand on Zanzibar was published in 1968 and very accurately expresses the mood of the times.

In the following essay, Jeffrey Hasday, who had just finished a work-study period as a technical writer, discusses the differences between writing for academic and technical audiences.

ACADEMIC VS. TECHNICAL AUDIENCES

Introduction

After twelve years of elementary and secondary education and a year of freshman composition, most students have gotten used to writing for an academic audience. They know what this audience expects and what level of information it requires. Admittedly, students are not always correct in their assessments, but even so, they understand the ground rules that govern this writing situation. One thing that I discovered shortly after I began work as a technical writer, however, was that many of the audience assumptions that are true for academic writing are not true for technical or business writing.

Thesis (emphasizing differences)

First point: Academic audience (ability to identify audience)

One of the differences between academic and technical writing is the extent to which writers can identify the audience. An academic audience is easy for students to identify: usually an instructor, and

1

2

in some cases a group of students. The major problem students have is conveying information to this audience in a clear and understandable manner. After being in a class for a number of weeks, though, most students get to know their instructors and their classmates and are able to determine their likes, dislikes, and needs. The audience for a technical report, however, is more difficult to identify. A technical audience usually consists of a supervisor and depending on the importance of the project, any number of other people. When I wrote a technical report, it was not unusual for me to spend a great deal of time just determining who the members of my potential audience would be. Even then, I could not be sure that my report would not circulate beyond the audience that I had identified.

First point: Technical audience

Another difference between academic and technical writing is the extent to which writers can assume an audience's interest in the subject. In academic writing students can usually assume that their audience is interested (or at least will pretend to be interested) in their subject. Whether the instructor's major field of interest is taxation, materials engineering, or Victorian literature, students expect him or her to show interest in upon what they have written. In technical writing, the situation is entirely different. Writers cannot assume that members of their audience have a common set of concerns. A supervisor, for example, might care about the technical side of a problem, while an upper-level manager might be concerned with its business implications. For this reason, one of the most difficult things I had to learn was to address the interests of specific segments of my audience in individual sections of my report.

Second point: Academic audience (audience's interest)

Second point: Technical audience

3

Third point: Academic audience (audience reading)

A final difference between academic and technical writing is the extent to which writers can count on an audience even reading what they have written. In academic writing most students assume that when they hand in a paper, their instructor will read it, comment upon it, grade it, and return it in a reasonable length of time. In fact, students take this condition so much for granted that they have difficulty getting used to its absence in many technical writing situations. Most managers receive a great deal of written material each day, so much that they cannot read it all thoroughly. Consequently, they read only the reports and correspondence that immediately strike them as being important to their jobs. As a result, the first thing that I learned was to place a summary of important information at the beginning of a report so that my audience would see it. I soon discovered that without this summary, a manager would not take the time to read one of my reports.

Third point: Technical audience

Conclusion: Restatement of thesis

The audience that technical writers encounter is more complicated than the audience that most students address in college. Making the transition from academic to technical writing even more difficult for me was the fact that few academic writing situations had prepared me for the kind of writing that I did in my work-study job. An awareness of the differences between the academic and the technical audience, along with a good technical writing course in college, would have made my transition into the world of work a lot easier.

4

5

Points for Special Attention

Structure.   In this point-by-point comparison, Jeffrey is careful to discuss the same points in exactly the same order. By using this strategy, he is able to emphasize the differences between academic and technical writing. With this method of organization he can not only be sure that his readers will follow his comparison, but he can also repeatedly relate each of his three major points to his thesis. Certainly, Jeffrey could have used a subject-by-subject comparison, but then his readers would have had to keep all three points concerning academic writing in mind as they read. This approach would have put too many demands on his readers and thus weakened his essay.

Transitions. Without clear transitions, Jeffrey's readers would have a difficult time determining where a point about academic writing ended and a point about technical writing began. The result would be a jumble of sentences that were not connected to one subject or the other. Jeffrey makes sure that his readers follow his discussion within each of his body paragraphs by connecting the two parts of his comparison with transitional sentences. These sentences make the individual points of contrast clear and thus make the difference between the two kinds of audiences clear.

An academic audience is easy for students to identify: usually an instructor, and in some cases a group of students.
The audience for a technical report, however, is more difficult to identify. In academic writing students can usually assume that their audience is interested (or at least will pretend to be interested) in their subject.
In technical writing, the situation is entirely different.
In academic writing most students assume that when they hand in a paper, their instructor will read it, comment upon it, and return it in a reasonable length of time.
In fact, students take this condition so much for granted that they have difficulty getting used to its absence in many technical writing situations.

Topic Sentences. Jeffrey's topic sentences are clear and straightforward, emphasizing the differences between academic and technical writing. Not only do the topic sentences reinforce the main ideas of each body paragraph, they also remind readers what the main idea of the essay is. Notice that by establishing a parallel structure, the topic sentences form a pattern that helps readers keep track of the thesis as they read.

One of the differences between academic and technical writing is the extent to which writers can identify the audience.

Another difference between academic and technical writing is the extent to which writers can assume an audience's interest in the subject.
A final difference between academic and technical writing is the extent to which writers can count on an audience even reading what they have written.

The selections that follow illustrate both point-by-point and subject-by-subject comparison. Moreover, each uses transitional elements and topic sentences to enhance clarity and to achieve balance between categories. Although the reading selections vary greatly in organization, length, and complexity, each is primarily concerned with the similarities and differences between its subjects.

GRANT AND LEE:
A STUDY IN CONTRASTS

Bruce Catton

*Bruce Catton (1889-1978) was an outstanding authority on the
Civil War. He won both the Pulitzer Prize for history and the National Book Award. Catton edited* American Heritage *and served
as the Director of Information for the United States Department
of Commerce. Among his many books are* Mr. Lincoln's Army
(1951), A Stillness at Appomattox *(1953),* Terrible Swift Sword
(1963), and Gettysburg: The Final Fury *(1974). "Grant and Lee: A
Study in Contrasts," which first appeared in a collection of historical essays entitled* The American Story, *is tightly organized and
has explicit topic sentences and transitions. Further, this essay
identifies not only differences but also important similarities between the two opposing generals.*

When Ulysses S. Grant and Robert E. Lee met in the parlor of a   1
modest house at Appomattox Court House, Virginia, on April 9,
1865, to work out the terms for the surrender of Lee's Army of
Northern Virginia, a great chapter in American life came to a close,
and a great new chapter began.

These men were bringing the Civil War to its virtual finish. To be   2
sure, other armies had yet to surrender, and for a few days the fugitive Confederate government would struggle desperately and
vainly, trying to find some way to go on living now that its chief
support was gone. But in effect it was all over when Grant and Lee
signed the papers. And the little room where they wrote out the
terms was the scene of one of the poignant, dramatic contrasts in
American history.

They were two strong men, these oddly different generals, and   3
they represented the strengths of two conflicting currents that,
through them, had come into final collision.

Back of Robert E. Lee was the notion that the old aristocratic   4
concept might somehow survive and be dominant in American life.

Lee was tidewater Virginia, and in his background were family,   5
culture, and tradition . . . the age of chivalry transplanted to a New
World which was making its own legends and its own myths. He

embodied a way of life that had come down through the age of knighthood and the English country squire. America was a land that was beginning all over again, dedicated to nothing much more complicated than the rather hazy belief that all men had equal rights and should have an equal chance in the world. In such a land Lee stood for the feeling that it was somehow of advantage to human society to have a pronounced inequality in the social structure. There should be a leisure class, backed by ownership of land; in turn, society itself should be keyed to the land as the chief source of wealth and influence. It would bring forth (according to this ideal) a class of men with a strong sense of obligation to the community; men who lived not to gain advantage for themselves, but to meet the solemn obligations which had been laid on them by the very fact that they were privileged. From them the country would get its leadership; to them it could look for the higher values—of thought, of conduct, of personal deportment—to give it strength and virtue.

Lee embodied the noblest elements of this aristocratic ideal.   6
Through him, the landed nobility justified itself. For four years, the Southern states had fought a desperate war to uphold the ideals for which Lee stood. In the end, it almost seemed as if the Confederacy fought for Lee; as if he himself was the Confederacy ... the best thing that the way of life for which the Confederacy stood could ever have to offer. He had passed into legend before Appomattox. Thousands of tired, underfed, poorly clothed Confederate soldiers, long since past the simple enthusiasm of the early days of the struggle, somehow considered Lee the symbol of everything for which they had been willing to die. But they could not quite put this feeling into words. If the Lost Cause, sanctified by so much heroism and so many deaths, had a living justification, its justification was General Lee.

Grant, the son of a tanner on the Western frontier, was everything   7
Lee was not. He had come up the hard way and embodied nothing in particular except the eternal toughness and sinewy fiber of the men who grew up beyond the mountains. He was one of a body of men who owed reverence and obeisance to no one, who were self-reliant to a fault, who cared hardly anything for the past but who had a sharp eye for the future.

These frontier men were the precise opposites of the tidewater   8
aristocrats. Back of them, in the great surge that had taken people over the Alleghenies and into the opening Western country, there was a deep, implicit dissatisfaction with a past that had settled into grooves. They stood for democracy, not from any reasoned conclu-

sion about the proper ordering of human society, but simply because they had grown up in the middle of democracy and knew how it worked. Their society might have privileges, but they would be privileges each man had won for himself. Forms and patterns meant nothing. No man was born to anything, except perhaps to a chance to show how far he could rise. Life was competition.

Yet along with this feeling had come a deep sense of belonging to 9 a national community. The Westerner who developed a farm, opened a shop, or set up in business as a trader, could hope to prosper only as his own community prospered—and his community ran from the Atlantic to the Pacific and from Canada down to Mexico. If the land was settled, with towns and highways and accessible markets, he could better himself. He saw his fate in terms of the nation's own destiny. As its horizons expanded, so did his. He had, in other words, an acute dollars-and-cents stake in the continued growth and development of his country.

And that, perhaps, is where the contrast between Grant and Lee 10 becomes most striking. The Virginia aristocrat, inevitably, saw himself in relation to his own region. He lived in a static society which could endure almost anything except change. Instinctively, his first loyalty would go to the locality in which that society existed. He would fight to the limit of endurance to defend it, because in defending it he was defending everything that gave his own life its deepest meaning.

The Westerner, on the other hand, would fight with an equal te- 11 nacity for the broader concept of society. He fought so because everything he lived by was tied to growth, expansion, and a constantly widening horizon. What he lived by would survive or fall with the nation itself. He could not possibly stand by unmoved in the face of an attempt to destroy the Union. He would combat it with everything he had, because he could only see it as an effort to cut the ground out from under his feet.

So Grant and Lee were in complete contrast, representing two dia- 12 metrically opposed elements in American life. Grant was the modern man emerging; beyond him, ready to come on the stage, was the great age of steel and machinery, of crowded cities and a restless burgeoning vitality. Lee might have ridden down from the old age of chivalry, lance in hand, silken banner fluttering over his head. Each man was the perfect champion of his cause, drawing both his strengths and his weaknesses from the people he led.

Yet it was not all contrast, after all. Different as they were—in 13 background, in personality, in underlying aspiration—these two great soldiers had much in common. Under everything else, they were marvelous fighters. Furthermore, their fighting qualities were really very much alike.

Each man had, to begin with, the great virtue of utter tenacity   14
and fidelity. Grant fought his way down the Mississippi Valley in spite of acute personal discouragement and profound military handicaps. Lee hung on in the trenches at Petersburg after hope itself had died. In each man there was an indomitable quality ... the born fighter's refusal to give up as long as he can still remain on his feet and lift his two fists.

Daring and resourcefulness they had, too; the ability to think   15
faster and move faster than the enemy. These were the qualities which gave Lee the dazzling campaigns of Second Manassas and Chancellorsville and won Vicksburg for Grant.

Lastly, and perhaps greatest of all, there was the ability, at the   16
end, to turn quickly from war to peace once the fighting was over. Out of the way these two men behaved at Appomattox came the possibility of a peace of reconciliation. It was a possibility not wholly realized, in the years to come, but which did, in the end, help the two sections to become one nation again ... after a war whose bitterness might have seemed to make such a reunion wholly impossible. No part of either man's life became him more than the part he played in this brief meeting in the McLean house at Appomattox. Their behavior there put all succeeding generations of Americans in their debt. Two great Americans, Grant and Lee—very different, yet under everything very much alike. Their encounter at Appomattox was one of the great moments of American history.

COMPREHENSION

1. What took place at Appomattox Court House on April 9, 1865? Why did the meeting at Appomattox signal the closing of "a great chapter in American life"?

2. How does Robert E. Lee represent the old aristocracy?

3. How does Ulysses S. Grant represent Lee's opposite?

4. According to Catton, where is it that "the contrast between Grant and Lee becomes most striking"?

5. What similarities does Catton see between the two men?

PURPOSE AND AUDIENCE

1. Catton's purpose in contrasting Grant and Lee is to make a general statement about the differences between two currents in American history. Summarize these differences. Do you think the differences still exist today?

2. Is Catton's purpose in comparing Grant and Lee the same as his purpose in contrasting them? That is, do their similarities also make a statement about America? Explain.

3. State the essay's thesis in your own words.

4. Why do you suppose Catton provides the background for the meeting at Appomattox but presents no information about the dramatic meeting itself?

STYLE AND STRUCTURE

1. Does Catton use subject-by-subject or point-by-point comparison? Why do you think he chose the structure he did?

2. In this essay, topic sentences are extremely important and extremely helpful to the reader. Explain the functions of the following sentences: "Grant . . . was everything Lee was not" (paragraph 7); "So Grant and Lee were in complete contrast . . . " (12); "Yet it was not all contrast, after all" (13); "Lastly, and perhaps greatest of all . . . " (16).

3. Catton carefully uses transitions in his essay. Identify the transitional words or expressions that link each paragraph to the preceding one.

4. Some of Catton's paragraphs (3, 4, 15) are only one or two sentences long. Others (5, 6, 16) are much longer. How can you explain such variation in paragraph length?

5. Most of this essay is devoted to the contrast between Grant and Lee. Where are their similarities mentioned? Why does Catton do this?

VOCABULARY PROJECTS

1. Define each of the following words as it is used in this selection.

   poignant (2)   sanctified (6)
   chivalry (5)   embodied (7)
   deportment (5)   sinewy (7)

obeisance (7)	aspiration (13)
implicit (8)	tenacity (14)
inevitably (10)	fidelity (14)
diametrically (12)	indomitable (14)
burgeoning (12)	reconciliation (16)

2. Look up synonyms for the following words and determine which would and would not have been as good as the original word. Explain your choices.

deportment (5)	diametrically (12)
sanctified (6)	indomitable (14)
obeisance (7)	

3. Locate all the words in the essay that end with the suffix -*ocracy*. Use your college dictionary to determine the meaning of each term and explain how Catton uses these terms in his essay.

WRITING WORKSHOP

1. Write a similar "study in contrasts" about two people you know well—two teachers, your parents, two relatives, two friends—or about two fictional characters with whom you are very familiar. Be sure you include a thesis that draws your essay together.

2. Write a dialogue between two people you know that reveals their contrasting attitudes toward school, work, or any other subject.

3. Compare your attitudes about America with either Grant's or Lee's. Use the method of development that Catton does in his essay.

4. Write an essay about two individuals from periods of American history other than the Civil War to make the same points Catton makes. Do some research if necessary.

THEMATIC CONNECTIONS

- "Historical Fiction, Fictitious History, and Chesapeake Bay Blue Crabs, or, About Aboutness" (p. 406)

FROM SONG TO SOUND:
BING AND ELVIS

Russell Baker

Russell Baker was born in 1925 in Virginia. After graduating from Johns Hopkins University he worked as a reporter for the Baltimore Sun *and the* New York Times. *He has contributed to a number of magazines including* Ladies' Home Journal, McCall's, Saturday Evening Post, *and* Sports Illustrated. *He writes a syndicated column, "The Observer," that often treats contemporary social and political issues in a humorous or satirical manner. He won the Pulitzer Prize in 1979 for distinguished commentary. His books include* Poor Russell's Almanac *(1972),* The Upside Down Man *(1977),* So This is Depravity *(1980), the autobiographical memoir* Growing Up *(1982), and* The Rescue of Miss Yaskell and Other Pipe Dreams *(1983). "From Song to Sound" appeared in "The Observer." In this essay Baker compares two eras as well as the two performers who represented them.*

The grieving for Elvis Presley and the commercial exploitation of   1
his death were still not ended when we heard of Bing Crosby's death
the other day. Here is a generational puzzle. Those of an age to
mourn Elvis must marvel that their elders could really have cared
about Bing, just as the Crosby generation a few weeks ago wondered what all the to-do was about when Elvis died.

Each man was a mass culture hero to his generation, but it tells   2
us something of the difference between generations that each man's
admirers would be hard-pressed to understand why the other could
mean very much to his devotees.

There were similarities that ought to tell us something. Both came   3
from obscurity to national recognition while quite young and became very rich. Both lacked formal music education and went on to
movie careers despite lack of acting skills. Both developed distinctive musical styles which were originally scorned by critics and subsequently studied as pioneer developments in the art of popular
song.

In short, each man's career followed the mythic rags-to-triumph   4
pattern in which adversity is conquered, detractors are given their

comeuppance and estates, fancy cars and world tours become the reward of perseverance. Traditionally this was supposed to be the history of the American business striver, but in our era of committee capitalism it occurs most often in the mass entertainment field, and so we look less and less to the board room for our heroes and more and more to the microphone.

Both Crosby and Presley were creations of the microphone. It 5 made it possible for people with frail voices not only to be heard beyond the third row but also to caress millions. Crosby was among the first to understand that the microphone made it possible to sing to multitudes by singing to a single person in a small room.

Presley cuddled his microphone like a lover. With Crosby the mi- 6 crophone was usually concealed, but Presley brought it out on stage, detached it from its fitting, stroked it, pressed it to his mouth. It was a surrogate for his listener, and he made love to it unashamedly.

The difference between Presley and Crosby, however, reflected 7 generational differences which spoke of changing values in American life. Crosby's music was soothing; Presley's was disturbing. It is too easy to be glib about this, to say that Crosby was singing to, first, Depression America, and, then, to wartime America, and that his audiences had all the disturbance they could handle in their daily lives without buying more at the record shop and movie theater.

Crosby's fans talk about how "relaxed" he was, how "natural," 8 how "casual and easy going." By the time Presley began causing sensations, the entire country had become relaxed, casual and easy going, and its younger people seemed to be tired of it, for Elvis's act was anything but soothing and scarcely what a parent of that placid age would have called "natural" for a young man.

Elvis was unseemly, loud, gaudy, sexual—that gyrating pelvis!— 9 in short, disturbing. He not only disturbed parents who thought music by Crosby was soothing but also reminded their young that they were full of the turmoil of youth and an appetite for excitement. At a time when the country had a population coming of age with no memory of troubled times, Presley spoke to a yearning for disturbance.

It probably helped that Elvis's music made Mom and Dad climb 10 the wall. In any case, people who admired Elvis never talk about how relaxed and easy going he made them feel. They are more likely to tell you he introduced them to something new and exciting.

To explain each man in terms of changes in economic and political 11 life probably oversimplifies the matter. Something in the culture was also changing. Crosby's music, for example, paid great attention to the importance of lyrics. The "message" of the song was as essential to the audience as the tune. The words were usually inane and witless, but Crosby—like Sinatra a little later—made them vital. People remembered them, sang them. Words still had meaning.

Although many of Presley's songs were highly lyrical, in most it wasn't the words that moved audiences; it was the "sound." Rock 'n' roll, of which he was the great popularizer, was a "sound" event. Song stopped being song and turned into "sound," at least until the Beatles came along and solved the problem of making words sing to the new beat. 12

Thus a group like the Rolling Stones, whose lyrics are often elaborate, seems to the Crosby-tuned ear to be shouting only gibberish, a sort of accompanying background noise in a "sound" experience. The Crosby generation has trouble hearing rock because it makes the mistake of trying to understand the words. The Presley generation has trouble with Crosby because it finds the sound unstimulating and cannot be touched by the inanity of the words. The mutual deafness may be a measure of how far we have come from really troubled times and of how deeply we have come to mistrust the value of words. 13

COMPREHENSION

1. List the similarities between Crosby and Presley that Baker discusses.

2. List the differences Baker notes between the two men.

3. How does Baker account for the differences?

4. What, according to Baker's essay, is the difference between *song* and *sound*?

5. What are some nonmusical examples of the "mutual deafness" Baker mentions in his final paragraph?

PURPOSE AND AUDIENCE

1. This column was printed in newspapers all over the country shortly after Bing Crosby died. How does its subject matter make it particularly appropriate for this diverse audience?

2. What is the essay's thesis?

3. At times, Baker seems to be guilty of making unsupported generali-

zations. (For example, he assumes that his readers, like him, have "come to mistrust the value of words.") How do you suppose he expected his audience to react to such assumptions?

STYLE AND STRUCTURE

1. Baker considers both similarities and differences. Why does he deal with similarities first? What sentence signals his move from similarities to differences?

2. Which of the two patterns of organization (subject-by-subject or point-by-point) does Baker use here? Why? Could he have used the other pattern? Why or why not?

3. Paragraphs in this essay are relatively short because their length was determined by narrow newspaper columns. If you were typing this essay on standard paper, would you combine any paragraphs or make any other changes in paragraphing? If so, where?

4. Can you tell by the essay's language whether Baker is a fan of Presley or Crosby or both? If so, how?

5. Baker uses the microphone to illustrate *both* similarities and differences. Could another symbol—the radio or phonograph, for instance—have been used as effectively? Why or why not?

VOCABULARY PROJECTS

1. Define each of the following words as it is used in this selection.

   exploitation (1)   placid (8)
   generational (1)   unseemly (9)
   devotees (2)   gaudy (9)
   mythic (4)   gyrating (9)
   perseverance (4)   gibberish (13)
   surrogate (6)   inanity (13)

2. Make a list of the adjectives that Baker uses to describe both men. What impressions does Baker attempt to convey with these words?

3. Baker encloses certain words and phrases in quotation marks. Locate five examples and explain why Baker does this.

WRITING WORKSHOP

1. Choose any two musicians or groups, and analyze their similarities and differences as performers.

2. Compare and contrast the lyrics of a Bing Crosby song with one sung by Elvis Presley.

3. Write an article for an Elvis Presley fan magazine in which you compare and contrast him with Bing Crosby. Use Baker's facts, but slant them to show Presley in a much more favorable light. If you can, supply additional information to supplement Baker's account.

4. Find newsmagazine accounts of Presley's and Crosby's funerals, and write an essay comparing and contrasting them.

THEMATIC CONNECTIONS

- "Outsider in a Silent World" (p. 76)
- "Television: The Plug-In-Drug" (p. 271)

MURDER: PASSION
AND PATHOLOGY

Ellen Currie

Ellen Currie has written articles for newspapers and magazines and has published a well-received novel, Available Light *(1986). In the following article, which appeared in the* New York Times *in 1986, Currie contrasts Madeleine Smith, who committed a single murder in 1857, with Theodore R. Bundy, who has been linked to the murder of thirty-six women. According to Currie, these crimes as well as the way that people reacted to them reveal us "in a strange and deathly light."*

Henry James,* like many decorous and respectable people, enter- 1
tained a lively interest in murder. He was a fan of the Scottish solicitor William Roughead, who wrote about real-life crime for the first
40 years of this century; James once told Mr. Roughead he was interested in crime because through it "manners and morals become
clearly disclosed." He urged Mr. Roughead to write about "the dear
old human and sociable murders and adulteries and forgeries in
which we are so agreeably at home. And don't tell me, for charity's
sake, that your supply runs short."

Contemporary supplies of murder, adultery and forgery remain 2
abundant. But crime seems to me less sociable these days, if I am
right in taking "sociable" to mean human and comprehensible and
even sympathetic. The crimes get bigger and more horrible, and yet
we are not sufficiently horrified by them; we pay less and less attention to the manners and the morals they disclose.

Look at the difference, for example, between the crimes of Made- 3
leine Smith, who stirred arsenic into her lover's cocoa in 1857, and
the convicted killer Theodore R. Bundy, who has been linked with
the murders of 36 women he didn't even know.

Madeleine Smith, whose case greatly interested Henry James (he 4
called her a "portentous young person"), was the daughter of a Glas-

*Eds note—James, an American writer (1843–1916), was a pioneer of psychologi-
cal realism and master of a rich, complex prose style.

gow architect. In 1855, when she was 19, she crossed paths with a young Frenchman. He was handsome, Mr. Roughead wrote, but "socially impossible." They met in secret and wrote to each other constantly. When they became lovers Miss Smith's letters took on what Mr. Roughead described as "a tropical and abandoned tone." They were indelicate letters, naive and outspoken. Another scholar of crime has pointed out that in a day when sex was supposed to be no more than a woman's bounden duty, Madeleine Smith found it a pagan festival.

Her lover kept her letters, 198 of them. When she accepted an older, richer and more settled suitor, she asked for the letters' return. Wild with jealousy, her lover claimed he would return them only to her father. That prospect drove Miss Smith mad with shame and fear. She bought arsenic. Her lover soon died of arsenic poisoning. She was brought to trial and conducted herself with great dignity. The verdict: not proven.

These people are not admirable, but they are real. Their awful situation is comprehensible; a blown-up, highly colored version of the kind of dilemma ordinary people face. Madeleine Smith's crime was personal. It was a crime of passion.

The case of Ted Bundy is different. To me, it is not "sociable," not comprehensible on any human scale. It is peculiarly impersonal. He didn't even know his victims; they represented an abstraction— women. His are crimes not of passion but pathology. Our reaction to them seems to me to partake of pathology too.

According to the reports I have read, some law enforcement officials say Mr. Bundy may have killed more than 36 young women in sexual crimes across the country. (Like Madeleine Smith, Ted Bundy says he is innocent of any crime.) He has been convicted of battering to death, early on Super Bowl Sunday 1978 in the Chi Omega sorority house at Florida State University, two young women. He hideously beat two more young women in the same house and, blocks away, savaged another young woman. He didn't know any of them. Captured and charged, Mr. Bundy was also indicted in the kidnapping and murder of a 12-year-old girl. He didn't know her, either. He was convicted of all charges. His execution, scheduled for July 3, was indefinitely postponed to give his lawyers time to frame an appeal.

The young women Ted Bundy has been convicted of killing, and is suspected of killing, resemble, an investigator said, "everyone's daughter." Their photographs show the sweet faces of their youth, the long hair of their period. Except for those who loved them, their identities overlap now, and blur. These women are not vivid and defined because they did nothing to bring about their deaths. They were not Ted Bundy's angry and discarded lovers. They did not refuse to return his disastrous, impassioned letters. They didn't know him.

At first all these deaths of pretty young women attracted wide public notice. But once Mr. Bundy was apprehended, the attention was all on his antics and not on the innocent dead. Bundy is a 20th century phenomenon. He is mediagenic. He is handsome, usually described as a former law student and witty, brilliant, charming, polished. Oddly, these latter qualities do not come through in any of the several books about him. Mr. Bundy was once active in Republican politics; there are those who profess to believe that he might ultimately have been elected to high public office had he stayed the course. He has twice made dramatic escapes from custody. He has acted as his own counsel in sensational televised trials. He has been the subject of a television movie. Ted Bundy T-shirts, for, against and smart aleck ("Ted Bundy is a one-night stand"), have enjoyed popularity. So have jingles: "Let's salute the mighty Bundy/Here on Friday, gone on Monday/All his roads lead out of town/It's hard to keep a good man down." Bundy Burgers and a Bundy cocktail had some play in a Colorado Bar. Groupies have gathered at his trials. He gets a lot of mail.

Theodore Bundy is said by psychiatrists to be an antisocial personality, a man without conscience. In a strange, third-person meditation on the killings, Mr. Bundy described the rapes and murders as "inappropriate acting out."

Perhaps Ted Bundy doesn't labor under a conscience. But how about the rest of us? Shouldn't we feel more revulsion, more grief for those young lives? Something vile has happened to our ideas of what is valuable and what is waste. Perhaps we have seen too much evil and on too grand a scale. We are glib and dismissive of the moral issues. We think Mr. Bundy is good for a laugh. We made him a celebrity. (Richard Schickel, in his book "Intimate Strangers," about the nature of celebrity in modern society, contends that multiple murderers have grasped the essentials of the celebrity system better than normal people.)

Crime does disclose on manners and on morals. If people must kill people, I have to put my dollar down on wicked Madeleine Smith. With her sexy letters, poisoned cocoa, caddish lover, she dealt in death. But she is piercingly familiar. Ted Bundy's unspeakable crimes and our cheap reaction to them reveal us to ourselves in a strange and deathly light.

COMPREHENSION

1. What does Currie mean in paragraph 2 when she says that crime seems less sociable these days?

2. What is Currie's opinion of Madeleine Smith's crime?

3. Why is Ted Bundy's crime "not comprehensible on any human scale"?

4. Why does Currie believe Ted Bundy is a twentieth century phenomenon?

5. According to Currie, what does public reaction to Ted Bundy reveal about modern society?

6. What does Currie mean when she says, "I have to put my dollar down on wicked Madeleine Smith" (13)?

PURPOSE AND AUDIENCE

1. At what point does Currie state her thesis? Restate that thesis in your own words.

2. Does Currie expect her audience to agree or disagree with her thesis? How can you tell?

3. Does Currie attempt to establish an identification with her readers or to distance herself from them? Explain.

4. Currie's essay compares two killers in order to serve a specific purpose. What is that purpose?

5. Throughout her essay Currie avoids explicit descriptions of both murderers' crimes. What does she gain or lose by means of this strategy?

STYLE AND STRUCTURE

1. Why does Currie begin her essay with references to Henry James and William Roughead?

2. List the points of comparison that Currie considers. Why does she present those points in the order she does?

3. Does Currie's essay stress the similarities or the differences between the two killers she discusses? Or does she consider the similarities and the differences equally important? Explain.

4. How does Currie signal the shift in her discussion from Madeleine Smith to Ted Bundy?

5. Why does Currie spend more time discussing Ted Bundy than she does discussing Madeleine Smith?

6. How does Currie's conclusion reinforce the essay's purpose?

VOCABULARY PROJECTS

1. Define each of the following words as it is used in this selection.

   decorous (1)   pagan (4)
   solicitor (1)   pathology (7)
   tropical (4)   revulsion (12)
   indelicate (4)   dismissive (12)

2. In paragraph 10 Currie says that Ted Bundy is "mediagenic." Write a paragraph in which you define this coined word and explain how Ted Bundy fits this description.

WRITING WORKSHOP

1. Write an essay in which you compare your thoughts about the health of modern society with those of Ellen Currie. Refer specifically to her thesis and support your views with examples from the media or your own experience as well as with examples from the essay.

2. Compare the contemporary version of a sport such as baseball or boxing with the same sport fifty years ago. Show how changes in the sport disclose changes in the manners and the morals of society. Go to your college library and consult a general reference work or an encyclopedia of sports if you need to gather information.

3. Write a comparison-and-contrast essay in which you illustrate how your ideas about "what is valuable and what is waste" have changed.

THEMATIC CONNECTIONS

- "38 Who Saw Murder Didn't Call the Police" (p. 70)
- 'Who Killed Benny Paret?" (p. 266)

THE ARAB WORLD

Edward T. Hall

Edward T. Hall was born in Webster Groves, Missouri, in 1914. He attended Pomona College, the University of Denver, the University of Arizona, and Columbia University. He has taught anthropology at a number of colleges and universities, most recently at Northwestern University. His articles have appeared in many professional journals, and his published books include Beyond Culture *(1976),* The Hidden Dimension *(1977), and* The Dance of Life: The Other Dimension of Time *(1983). "The Arab World" is excerpted from* The Hidden Dimension *and examines how the Arabs' perceptual world differs from the one occupied by Americans. By studying proxemic patterns—the way people interact closely with one another—Hall reveals the hidden cultural frames that influence perception and that explain the difficulty that Arabs and Americans have understanding one another.*

In spite of over two thousand years of contact, Westerners and 1
Arabs still do not understand each other. Proxemic research reveals
some insights into this difficulty. Americans in the Middle East are
immediately struck by two conflicting sensations. In public they are
compressed and overwhelmed by smells, crowding, and high noise
levels; in Arab homes Americans are apt to rattle around, feeling
exposed and often somewhat inadequate because of too much space!
(The Arab houses and apartments of the middle and upper classes
which Americans stationed abroad commonly occupy are much
larger than the dwellings such Americans usually inhabit.) Both the
high sensory stimulation which is experienced in public places and
the basic insecurity which comes from being in a dwelling that is
too large provide Americans with an introduction to the sensory
world of the Arab.

BEHAVIOR IN PUBLIC

Pushing and shoving in public places is characteristic of Middle 2
Eastern culture. Yet it is not entirely what Americans think it is
(being pushy and rude) but stems from a different set of assumptions concerning not only the relations between people but how one

experiences the body as well. Paradoxically, Arabs consider northern Europeans and Americans pushy, too. This was very puzzling to me when I started investigating these two views. How could Americans who stand aside and avoid touching be considered pushy? I used to ask Arabs to explain this paradox. None of my subjects was able to tell me specifically what particulars of American behavior were responsible, yet they all agreed that the impression was widespread among Arabs. After repeated unsuccessful attempts to gain insight into the cognitive world of the Arab on this particular point, I filed it away as a question that only time would answer. When the answer came, it was because of a seemingly inconsequential annoyance.

While waiting for a friend in a Washington, D.C., hotel lobby and wanting to be both visible and alone, I had seated myself in a solitary chair outside the normal stream of traffic. In such a setting most Americans follow a rule, which is all the more binding because we seldom think about it, that can be stated as follows: as soon as a person stops or is seated in a public place, there balloons around him a small sphere of privacy which is considered inviolate. The size of the sphere varies with the degree of crowding, the age, sex, and the importance of the person, as well as the general surroundings. Anyone who enters this zone and stays there is intruding. In fact, a stranger who intrudes, even for a specific purpose, acknowledges the fact that he has intruded by beginning his request with "Pardon me, but can you tell me . . . ?" 3

To continue, as I waited in the deserted lobby, a stranger walked up to where I was sitting and stood close enough so that not only could I easily touch him but I could even hear him breathing. In addition, the dark mass of his body filled the peripheral field of vision on my left side. If the lobby had been crowded with people, I would have understood his behavior, but in an empty lobby his presence made me exceedingly uncomfortable. Feeling annoyed by this intrusion, I moved my body in such a way as to communicate annoyance. Strangely enough, instead of moving away, my actions seemed only to encourage him, because he moved even closer. In spite of the temptation to escape the annoyance, I put aside thoughts of abandoning my post, thinking, "To hell with it. Why should I move? I was here first and I'm not going to let this fellow drive me out even if he is a boor." Fortunately, a group of people soon arrived whom my tormentor immediately joined. Their mannerisms explained his behavior, for I knew from both speech and gestures that they were Arabs. I had not been able to make this crucial identification by looking at my subject when he was alone because he wasn't talking and he was wearing American clothes. 4

In describing the scene later to an Arab colleague, two contrasting 5
patterns emerged. My concept and my feelings about my own circle
of privacy in a "public" place immediately struck my Arab friend
as strange and puzzling. He said, "After all, it's a public place, isn't
it?" Pursuing this line of inquiry, I found that in Arab thought I
had no rights whatsoever by virtue of occupying a given spot; neither my place nor by body was inviolate! For the Arab, there is no
such thing as an intrusion in public. Public means public. With this
insight, a great range of Arab behavior that had been puzzling, an-
noying, and sometimes even frightening began to make sense. I
learned, for example, that if *A* is standing on a street corner and *B*
wants his spot, B is within his rights if he does what he can to make
A uncomfortable enough to move. In Beirut only the hardy sit in
the last row in a movie theater, because there are usually standees
who want seats and who push and shove and make such a nuisance
that most people give up and leave. Seen in this light, the Arab who
"intruded" on my space in the hotel lobby had apparently selected
if for the very reason I had: it was a good place to watch two doors
and the elevator. My show of annoyance, instead of driving him
away, had only encouraged him. He thought he was about to get me
to move.

Another silent source of friction between Americans and Arabs is 6
in an area that Americans treat very informally—the manners and
rights of the road. In general, in the United States we tend to defer
to the vehicle that is bigger, more powerful, faster, and heavily
laden. While a pedestrian walking along a road may feel annoyed he
will not think it unusual to step aside for a fast-moving automobile.
He knows that because he is moving he does not have the right to
the space around him that he has when he is standing still (as I was
in the hotel lobby). It appears that the reverse is true with the Arabs
who apparently *take on rights to space as they move.* For someone
else to move into a space an Arab is also moving into is a violation
of his rights. It is infuriating to an Arab to have someone else cut
in front of him on the highway. It is the American's cavalier treatment of moving space that makes the Arab call him aggressive and
pushy.

CONCEPTS OF PRIVACY

The experience described above and many others suggested to me 7
that Arabs might actually have a wholly contrasting set of assumptions concerning the body and the rights associated with it. Certainly the Arab tendency to shove and push each other in public and
to feel and pinch women in public conveyances would not be toler-

ated by Westerners. It appeared to me that they must not have any concept of a private zone outside the body. This proved to be precisely the case.

In the Western world, the person is synonymous with an individual inside a skin. And in northern Europe generally, the skin and even the clothes may be inviolate. You need permission to touch either if you are a stranger. This rule applies in some parts of France, where the mere touching of another person during an argument used to be legally defined as assault. For the Arab the location of the person in relation to the body is quite different. The person exists somewhere down inside the body. The ego is not completely hidden, however, because it can be reached very easily with an insult. It is protected from touch but not from words. The dissociation of the body and the ego may explain why the public amputation of a thief's hand is tolerated as standard punishment in Saudi Arabia. It also sheds light on why an Arab employer living in a modern apartment can provide his servant with a room that is a boxlike cubicle approximately 5 by 10 by 4 feet in size that is not only hung from the ceiling to conserve floor space but has an opening so that the servant can be spied on.

As one might suspect, deep orientations toward the self such as the one just described are also reflected in the language. This was brought to my attention one afternoon when an Arab colleague who is the author of an Arab-English dictionary arrived in my office and threw himself into a chair in a state of obvious exhaustion. When I asked him what had been going on, he said: "I have spent the entire afternoon trying to find the Arab equivalent of the English word 'rape'. There is no such word in Arabic. All my sources, both written and spoken, can come up with no more than an approximation, such as 'He took her against her will.' There is nothing in Arabic approaching your meaning as it is expressed in that one word."

Differing concepts of the placement of the ego in relation to the body are not easily grasped. Once an idea like this is accepted, however, it is possible to understand many other facets of Arab life that would otherwise be difficult to explain. One of these is the high population density of Arab cities like Cairo, Beirut, and Damascus. According to the animal studies described in the earlier chapters, the Arabs should be living in a perpetual behavioral sink. While it is probable that Arabs are suffering from population pressures, it is also just as possible that continued pressure from the desert has resulted in a cultural adaptation to high density which takes the form described above. Tucking the ego down inside the body shell not only would permit higher population densities but would explain why it is that Arab communications are stepped up as much as they are when compared to northern European communication patterns. Not only is the sheer noise level much higher, but the piercing look of the eyes, the touch of the hands, and the mutual bathing in the warm moist breath during conversation represent stepped-up sensory inputs to a level which many Europeans find unbearably intense.

The Arab dream is for lots of space in the home, which unfortunately many Arabs cannot afford. Yet when he has space, it is very different from what one finds in most American homes. Arab spaces inside their upper middle-class homes are tremendous by our standards. They avoid partitions because Arabs *do not like to be alone.* The form of the home is such as to hold the family together inside a single protective shell, because Arabs are deeply involved with each other. Their personalities are intermingled and take nourishment from each other like the roots and soil. If one is not with people and actively involved in some way, one is deprived of life. An old Arab saying reflects this value: "Paradise without people should not be entered because it is Hell." Therefore, Arabs in the United States often feel socially and sensorially deprived and long to be back where there is human warmth and contact.

Since there is no physical privacy as we know it in the Arab family, not even a word for privacy, one could expect that the Arabs might use some other means to be alone. Their way to be alone is to stop talking. Like the English, an Arab who shuts himself off in this way is not indicating that anything is wrong or that he is withdrawing, only that he wants to be alone with his own thoughts or does not want to be intruded upon. One subject said that her father would come and go for days at a time without saying a word, and no one in the family thought anything of it. Yet for this very reason, an Arab exchange student visiting a Kansas farm failed to pick up the cue that his American hosts were mad at him when they gave him the "silent treatment." He only discovered something was wrong when they took him to town and tried forcibly to put him on a bus to Washington, D.C., the headquarters of the exchange program responsible for his presence in the U.S.

ARAB PERSONAL DISTANCES

Like everyone else in the world, Arabs are unable to formulate specific rules for their informal behavior patterns. In fact, they often deny that there are any rules, and they are made anxious by suggestions that such is the case. Therefore, in order to determine how the

Arab sets distances, I investigated the use of each sense separately. Gradually, definite and distinctive behavioral patterns began to emerge.

Olfaction occupies a prominent place in the Arab life. Not only is   14
it one of the distance-setting mechanisms, but it is a vital part of a complex system of behavior. Arabs consistently breathe on people when they talk. However, this habit is more than a matter of different manners. To the Arab good smells are pleasing and a way of being involved with each other. To smell one's friend is not only nice but desirable, for to deny him your breath is to act ashamed. Americans, on the other hand, trained as they are not to breathe in people's faces, automatically communicate shame in trying to be polite. Who would expect that when our highest diplomats are putting on their best manners they are also communicating shame? Yet this is what occurs constantly, because diplomacy is not only "eyeball to eyeball" but breath to breath.

By stressing olfaction, Arabs do not try to eliminate all the body's   15
odors, only to enhance them and use them in building human relationships. Nor are they self-conscious about telling others when they don't like the way they smell. A man leaving his house in the morning may be told by his uncle, "Habib, your stomach is sour and your breath doesn't smell too good. Better not talk too close to people today." Smell is even considered in the choice of a mate. When couples are being matched for marriage, the man's go-between will sometimes ask to smell the girl, who may be turned down if she doesn't "smell nice." Arabs recognize that smell and disposition may be linked.

In a word, the olfactory boundary performs two roles in Arab life.   16
It enfolds those who want to relate and separates those who don't. The Arab finds it essential to stay inside the olfactory zone as a means of keeping tab on changes in emotion. What is more, he may feel crowded as soon as he smells something unpleasant. While not much is known about "olfactory crowding," this may prove to be as significant as any other variable in the crowding complex because it is tied directly to the body chemistry and hence to the state of health and emotions. . . . It is not surprising, therefore, that the olfactory boundary constitutes for the Arabs an informal distance-setting mechanism in contrast to the visual mechanisms of the Westerner.

FACING AND NOT FACING

One of my earliest discoveries in the field of intercultural commu-   17
nication was that the position of the bodies of people in conversation

varies with the culture. Even so, it used to puzzle me that a special Arab friend seemed unable to walk and talk at the same time. After years in the United States, he could not bring himself to stroll along, facing forward while talking. Our progress would be arrested while he edged ahead, cutting slightly in front of me and turning sideways so we could see each other. Once in this position, he would stop. His behavior was explained when I learned that for Arabs to view the other person peripherally is regarded as impolite, and to sit or stand back-to-back is considered very rude. You must be involved when interacting with Arabs who are friends.

One mistaken American notion is that Arabs conduct all conver- 18 sations at close distances. This is not the case at all. On social occasions, they may sit on opposite sides of the room and talk across the room to each other. They are, however, apt to take offense when Americans use what are to them ambiguous distances, such as the four- to seven-foot social-consultative distance. They frequently complain that Americans are cold or aloof or "don't care." This was what an elderly Arab diplomat in an American hospital thought when the American nurses used "professional" distance. He had the feeling that he was being ignored, that they might not take good care of him. Another Arab subject remarked, referring to American behavior, "What's the matter? Do I smell bad? Or are they afraid of me?"

Arabs who interact with Americans report experiencing a certain 19 flatness traceable in part to a very different use of the eyes in private and in public as well as between friends and strangers. Even though it is rude for a guest to walk around the Arab home eying things, Arabs look at each other in ways which seem hostile or challenging to the American. One Arab informant said that he was in constant hot water with Americans because of the way he looked at them without the slightest intention of offending. In fact, he had on several occasions barely avoided fights with American men who apparently thought their masculinity was being challenged because of the way he was looking at them. As noted earlier, Arabs look each other in the eye when talking with an intensity that makes most Americans highly uncomfortable.

INVOLVEMENT

As the reader must gather by now, Arabs are involved with each 20 other on many different levels simultaneously. Privacy in a public place is foreign to them. Business transactions in the bazaar, for example, are not just between buyer and seller, but are participated in by everyone. Anyone who is standing around may join in. If a grownup sees a boy breaking a window, he must stop him even if he doesn't know him. Involvement and participation are expressed in other ways as well. If two men are fighting, the crowd must intervene. On the political level, *to fail to intervene* when trouble is brewing is to take sides, which is what our State Department always seems to be doing. Given the fact that few people in the world today are even remotely aware of the cultural mold that forms their thoughts, it is normal for Arabs to view *our* behavior as though it stemmed from *their* own hidden set of assumptions.

FEELINGS ABOUT ENCLOSED SPACES

In the course of my interviews with Arabs the term "tomb" kept cropping up in conjunction with enclosed space. In a word, Arabs don't mind being crowded by people but hate to be hemmed in by walls. They show a much greater overt sensitivity to architectural crowding than we do. Enclosed space must meet at least three requirements that I know of if it is to satisfy the Arabs: there must be plenty of unobstructed space in which to move around (possibly as much as a thousand square feet); very high ceilings—so high in fact that they do not normally impinge on the visual field; and, in addition, there must be an unobstructed view. It was spaces such as these in which the Americans referred to earlier felt so uncomfortable. One sees the Arab's need for a view expressed in many ways, even negatively, for to cut off a neighbor's view is one of the most effective ways of spiting him. In Beirut one can see what is known locally as the "spite house." It is nothing more than a thick, four-story wall, built at the end of a long fight between neighbors, on a narrow strip of land for the express purpose of denying a view of the Mediterranean to any house built on the land behind. According to one of my informants, there is also a house on a small plot of land between Beirut and Damascus which is completely surrounded by a neighbor's wall built high enough to cut off the view from all windows. 21

BOUNDARIES

Proxemic patterns tell us other things about Arab culture. For example, the whole concept of the boundary as an abstraction is almost impossible to pin down. In one sense, there are no boundaries. "Edges" of town, yes, but permanent boundaries out in the country (hidden lines), no. In the course of my work with Arab subjects I had a difficult time translating our concept of a boundary 22 into terms which could be equated with theirs. In order to clarify the distinctions between the two very different definitions, I thought it might be helpful to pinpoint acts which constituted trespass. To date, I have been unable to discover anything even remotely resembling our own legal concept of trespass.

Arab behavior in regard to their own real estate is apparently an   23
extension of, and therefore consistent with, their approach to the body. My subjects simply failed to respond whenever trespass was mentioned. They didn't seem to understand what I meant by this term. This may be explained by the fact that they organize relationships with each other according to closed systems rather than spatially. For thousands of years Moslems, Marinites, Druses, and Jews have lived in their own villages, each with strong kin affiliations. Their hierarchy of loyalties is: first to one's self, then to kinsman, townsman, or tribesman, co-religionist and/or countryman. Anyone not in these categories is a stranger. Strangers and enemies are very closely linked, if not synonymous, in Arab thought. Trespass in this context is a matter of who you are, rather than a piece of land or a space with a boundary that can be denied to anyone and everyone, friend and foe alike.

In summary, proxemic patterns differ. By examining them it is   24
possible to reveal cultural frames that determine the structure of a given people's perceptual world. Perceiving the world differently leads to differential definitions of what constitutes crowded living, different interpersonal relations, and a different approach to both local and international politics. . . .

COMPREHENSION

1. By what two conflicting sensations in the Middle East is an American immediately struck?

2. How does Hall explain the pushing and shoving in public that he says is characteristic of Middle Eastern culture? In what way does the Arab sense of "public" extend to the rights of the road? How can the American's sense of "moving space" cause friction?

3. How does the Arab sense of privacy differ from the Western sense of privacy?

4. According to Hall, what part does olfaction play in Arab life? What effect do American concepts of personal distance have on Arabs?

5. What do patterns of proximity reveal about the Arab's perceptual world?

PURPOSE AND AUDIENCE

1. What is Hall's purpose in describing the ways that Arabs interact when they are close to one another?

2. What is the thesis of this essay? At what point does Hall state it? Why does he state it where he does?

3. What assumptions does Hall make about his audience's knowledge of Arab culture? How does Hall characterize his readers? Explain.

4. What is Hall's attitude toward Arabs? Does he treat his subject with dignity? Does he seem to condescend? Give examples from the essay to support your assertions.

STYLE AND STRUCTURE

1. How does the introduction of this essay prepare readers for the discussion to follow?

2. Does Hall use a subject-by-subject or a point-by-point method of comparison, or a combination of both? What is the advantage of the strategy that he uses?

3. How does Hall use headings to emphasize the ideas that he discusses? How do these headings help readers keep track of the comparison?

4. In paragraph 3 Hall introduces an example that he develops for several paragraphs. What point does this example illustrate, and how effective is this strategy?

5. Does Hall discuss too many points? Should he have just concentrated on the points that he could develop in depth? Do the short discussions at the end of the essay add to the readers' understanding?

6. Is Hall guilty of overgeneralizing? Are sentences like the following fair and accurate: "Olfaction occupies a prominent place in the Arab life"?

VOCABULARY PROJECTS

1. Define each of the following words as it is used in this selection.

proxemic (1)   peripherally (17)
paradoxically (2)   bazaar (20)
inviolate (3)   Marinites (23)
olfaction (14)   Druses (23)

2. For what English words does Hall say that the Arabs have no equivalents? Write a paragraph in which you discuss the significance of this fact.

3. Throughout this essay Hall includes small bits of dialogue. What is the function of this dialogue, and how does it help Hall achieve his purpose?

WRITING WORKSHOP

1. Write an essay in which you compare the value that you place on privacy to the value that Hall says Arabs place on privacy.

2. Write an essay in which you compare your "hierarchy of loyalities" to the one that Hall presents in paragraph 23.

3. Compare the hidden cultural frames that exist for your peer group, family, or ethnic group to the ones that Hall identifies for Arabs.

THEMATIC CONNECTIONS

- "The Patterns of Eating" (p. 167)
- "American Regional Costume" (p. 384)

ARIA: A MEMOIR
OF A BILINGUAL CHILDHOOD

Richard Rodriguez

*Born in San Francisco in 1944 to Mexican-American parents, Rich-
ard Rodriguez learned to speak English when he was in elementary
school. He graduated from Stanford University and went on to do
graduate work in English Renaissance literature and to teach at
the University of California at Berkeley, often feeling he was an
outsider. He is now a writer and journalist living in Mexico City.
Rodriguez has written articles for many magazines and journals
including* Harper's, *the* New York Times, Saturday Review, *and*
American Scholar. *In a series of autobiographical essays revised
and collected in the book* The Hunger of Memory *(1982), Rodriguez
explores his ambivalent feelings about what he gained—and lost—
by leaving his immigrant culture and entering American society.
In this excerpt from the book, an essay that was originally
published in* American Scholar, *Rodriguez compares the conflicting pulls of home and school, family and outsiders, Spanish and
English.*

I remember to start with that day in Sacramento—a California 1
now nearly thirty years past—when I first entered a classroom, able
to understand some fifty stray English words.

The third of four children, I had been preceded to a neighborhood 2
Roman Catholic school by an older brother and sister. But neither
of them had revealed very much about their classroom experiences.
Each afternoon they returned, as they left in the morning, always
together, speaking in Spanish as they climbed the five steps of the
porch. And their mysterious books, wrapped in shopping-bag paper,
remained on the table next to the door, closed firmly behind them.

An accident of geography sent me to a school where all my class- 3
mates were white, many the children of doctors and lawyers and
business executives. All my classmates certainly must have been
uneasy on that first day of school—as most children are uneasy—to
find themselves apart from their families in the first institution of
their lives. But I was astonished.

The nun said, in a friendly but oddly impersonal voice, "Boys and 4 girls, this is Richard Rodriguez." (I heard her sound out: *Richard Road-ree-guess*.) It was the first time I had heard anyone name me in English. "Richard," the nun repeated more slowly, writing my name down in her black leather book. Quickly I turned to see my mother's face dissolve in a watery blur behind the pebbled glass door.

Many years later there is something called bilingual education— a scheme proposed in the late 1960s by Hispanic-American social activists, later endorsed by a congressional vote. It is a program that seeks to permit non-English-speaking children, many from lower-class homes, to use their family language as the language of school. (Such is the goal its supporters announce.) I hear them and am forced to say no: It is not possible for a child—any child—ever to use his family's language in school. Not to understand this is to misunderstand the public uses of schooling and to trivialize the nature of intimate life—a family's "language."

Memory teaches me what I know of these matters; the boy reminds the adult. I was a bilingual child, a certain kind—socially disadvantaged—the son of working-class parents, both Mexican immigrants.

In the early years of my boyhood, my parents coped very well in America. My father had steady work. My mother managed at home. They were nobody's victims. Optimism and ambition led them to a house (our home) many blocks from the Mexican south side of town. We lived among *gringos* and only a block from the biggest, whitest houses. It never occurred to my parents that they couldn't live wherever they chose. Nor was the Sacramento of the fifties bent on teaching them a contrary lesson. My mother and father were more annoyed than intimidated by those two or three neighbors who tried initially to make us unwelcome. ("Keep your brats away from my sidewalk!") But despite all they achieved, perhaps because they had so much to achieve, any deep feeling of ease, the confidence of "belonging" in public was withheld from them both. They regarded the people at work, the faces in crowds, as very distant from us. They were the others, *los gringos*. That term was interchangeable in their speech with another, even more telling, *los americanos*.

I grew up in a house where the only regular guests were my relations. For one day, enormous families of relatives would visit and there would be so many people that the noise and the bodies would spill out to the backyard and front porch. Then, for weeks, no one came by. (It was usually a salesman who rang the doorbell.) Our house stood apart. A gaudy yellow in a row of white bungalows. We were the people with the noisy dog. The people who raised pigeons and chickens. We were the foreigners on the block. A few neighbors smiled and waved. We waved back. But no one in the family knew the names of the old couple who lived next door; until I was seven years old, I did not know the names of the kids who lived across the street.

In public, my father and mother spoke a hesitant, accented, not always grammatical English. And they would have to strain—their bodies tense—to catch the sense of what was rapidly said by *los gringos*. At home they spoke Spanish. The language of their Mexican past sounded in counterpoint to the English of public society. The words would come quickly, with ease. Conveyed through those sounds was the pleasing, soothing, consoling reminder of being at home.

During those years when I was first conscious of hearing, my mother and father addressed me only in Spanish; in Spanish I learned to reply. By contrast, English (*inglés*), rarely heard in the house, was the language I came to associate with *gringos*. I learned my first words of English overhearing my parents speak to strangers. At five years of age, I knew just enough English for my mother to trust me on errands to stores one block away. No more.

I was a listening child, careful to hear the very different sounds of Spanish and English. Wide-eyed with hearing, I'd listen to sounds more than words. First, there were English (*gringo*) sounds. So many words were still unknown that when the butcher or the lady at the drugstore said something to me, exotic polysyllabic sounds would bloom in the midst of their sentences. Often the speech of people in public seemed to me very loud, booming with confidence. The man behind the counter would literally ask, "What can I do for you?" But by being so firm and so clear, the sound of his voice said that he was a *gringo*; he belonged in public society.

I would also hear then the high nasal notes of middle-class American speech. The air stirred with sound. Sometimes, even now, when I have been traveling abroad for several weeks, I will hear what I heard as a boy. In hotel lobbies or airports, in Turkey or Brazil, some Americans will pass, and suddenly I will hear it again—the high sound of American voices. For a few seconds I will hear it with pleasure, for it is now the sound of *my* society—a reminder of home. But inevitably—already on the flight headed for home—the sound fades with repetition. I will be unable to hear it anymore.

When I was a boy, things were different. The accent of *los gringos* was never pleasing nor was it hard to hear. Crowds at Safeway or at bus stops would be noisy with sound. And I would be forced to edge away from the chirping chatter above me.

I was unable to hear my own sounds, but I knew very well that I 14 spoke English poorly. My words could not stretch far enough to form complete thoughts. And the words I did speak I didn't know well enough to make into distinct sounds. (Listeners would usually lower their heads, better to hear what I was trying to say.) But it was one thing for *me* to speak English with difficulty. It was more troubling for me to hear my parents speak in public: their high-whining vowels and guttural consonants; their sentences that got stuck with "eh" and "ah" sounds; the confused syntax; the hesitant rhythm of sounds so different from the way *gringos* spoke. I'd notice, moreover, that my parents' voices were softer than those of *gringos* we'd meet.

I am tempted now to say that none of this mattered. In adulthood 15 I am embarrassed by childhood fears. And, in a way, it didn't matter very much that my parents could not speak English with ease. Their linguistic difficulties had no serious consequences. My mother and father made themselves understood at the county hospital clinic and at government offices. And yet, in another way, it mattered very much—it was unsettling to hear my parents struggle with English. Hearing them, I'd grow nervous, my clutching trust in their protection and power weakened.

There were many times like the night at a brightly lit gasoline 16 station (a blaring white memory) when I stood uneasily, hearing my father. He was talking to a teenaged attendant. I do not recall what they were saying, but I cannot forget the sounds my father made as he spoke. At one point his words slid together to form one word—sounds as confused as the threads of blue and green oil in the puddle next to my shoes. His voice rushed through what he had left to say. And, toward the end, reached falsetto notes, appealing to his listener's understanding. I looked away to the lights of passing automobiles. I tried not to hear anymore. But I heard only too well the calm, easy tones in the attendant's reply. Shortly afterward, walking toward home with my father, I shivered when he put his hand on my shoulder. The very first chance that I got, I evaded his grasp and ran on ahead into the dark, skipping with feigned boyish exuberance.

But then there was Spanish. *Español*: my family's language. *Es-* 17 *pañol*: the language that seemed to me a private language. I'd hear strangers on the radio and in the Mexican Catholic church across town speaking in Spanish, but I couldn't really believe that Spanish was a public language, like English. Spanish speakers, rather, seemed related to me, for I sensed that we shared—through our language—the experience of feeling apart from *los gringos*. It was thus a ghetto Spanish that I heard and I spoke. Like those whose lives are bound by a barrio, I was reminded by Spanish of my separateness from *los otros, los gringos* in power. But more intensely than for most barrio children—because I did not live in a barrio—Spanish seemed to me the language of home. (Most days it was only at home that I'd hear it.) It became the language of joyful return.

A family member would say something to me and I would feel myself specially recognized. My parents would say something to me and I would feel embraced by the sounds of their words. Those sound said: *I am speaking with ease in Spanish. I am addressing you in words I never use with* los gringos. *I recognize you as someone special, close, like no one outside. You belong with us. In the family.* 18

(Ricardo.) 19

At the age of five, six, well past the time when most other children no longer easily notice the difference between sounds uttered at home and words spoken in public, I had a different experience. I lived in a world magically compounded of sounds. I remained a child longer than most; I lingered too long, poised at the edge of language—often frightened by the sounds of *los gringos*, delighted by the sounds of Spanish at home. I shared with my family a language that was startlingly different from that used in the great city around us. 20

For me there were none of the gradations between public and private society so normal to a maturing child. Outside the house was public society; inside the house was private. Just opening or closing the screen door behind me was an important experience. I'd rarely leave home all alone or without reluctance. Walking down the sidewalk, under the canopy of tall trees, I'd warily notice the—suddenly—silent neighborhood kids who stood warily watching me. Nervously, I'd arrive at the grocery store to hear there the sounds of the *gringo*—foreign to me—reminding me that in this world so big, I was a foreigner. But then I'd return. Walking back toward our house, climbing the steps from the sidewalk, when the front door was open in summer, I'd hear voices beyond the screen door talking in Spanish. For a second or two, I'd stay, linger there, listening. Smiling, I'd hear my mother call out, saying in Spanish (words): "Is that you, Richard?" All the while her sounds would assure me: *You are home now; come closer; inside. With us.* 21

"Si," I'd reply. 22

Once more inside the house I would resume (assume) my place in the family. The sounds would dim, grow harder to hear. Once more at home, I would grow less aware of that fact. It required, however, 23 no more than the blurt of the doorbell to alert me to listen to sounds all over again. The house would turn instantly still while my mother went to the door. I'd hear her hard English sounds. I'd wait to hear her voice return to soft-sounding Spanish, which assured me, as surely as did the clicking tongue of the lock on the door, that the stranger was gone.

Plainly, it is not healthy to hear such sounds so often. It is not healthy to distinguish public words from private sounds so easily. I remained cloistered by sounds, timid and shy in public, too dependent on voices at home. And yet it needs to be emphasized: I was an extremely happy child at home. I remember many nights when my father would come back from work, and I'd hear him call out to my mother in Spanish, sounding relieved. In Spanish, he'd sound light and free notes he never could manage in English. Some nights I'd jump up just at hearing his voice. With *mis hermanos* I would come running into the room where he was with my mother. Our laughing (so deep was the pleasure!) became screaming. Like others who know the pain of public alienation, we transformed the knowledge of our public separateness and made it consoling—the reminder of intimacy. Excited, we joined our voices in a celebration of sounds. *We are speaking now the way we never speak out in public. We are alone—together,* voices sounded, surrounded to tell me. Some nights, no one seemed willing to loosen the hold sounds had on us. At dinner, we invented new words. (Ours sounded Spanish, but made sense only to us.) We pieced together new words by taking, say, an English verb and giving it Spanish endings. My mother's instructions at bedtime would be lacquered with mock-urgent tones. Or a word like *si* would become, in several notes, able to convey added measures of feeling. Tongues explored the edges of words, especially the fat vowels. And we happily sounded that military drum roll, the twirling roar of the Spanish *r*. Family language: my family's sounds. The voices of my parents and sisters and brother. Their voices insisting: *You belong here. We are family members. Related. Special to one another. Listen!* Voices singing and sighing, rising, straining, then surging, teeming with pleasure that burst syllables into fragments of laughter. At times it seemed there was steady quiet only when, from another room, the rustling whispers of my parents faded and I moved closer to sleep.

COMPREHENSION

1. What things made Rodriguez ill at ease on his first day of school? In what ways was he different from the other children?

2. What does Rodriguez mean when he says that his parents were "no-body's victims"?

3. To the young Rodriguez, how did the sounds of English differ from the sounds of Spanish? Why did Spanish seem to be a private language?

4. What does Rodriguez mean in paragraph 24 when he says, "It is not healthy to distinguish public words from private sounds so easily"?

5. In addition to the differences between public and private language, what other oppositions does Rodriguez encounter?

6. Does Rodriguez consider his experiences to be similar to or different from those faced by other Mexican–American children? What statements in the essay lead you to your conclusion?

PURPOSE AND AUDIENCE

1. What is Rodriguez's thesis? Where does he state it?

2. Is Rodriguez writing this essay to enlighten, persuade, debunk, educate, or entertain? Explain.

3. This essay is addressed to a well-educated audience largely made up of *los gringos*. What concessions does Rodriguez make to this audience?

4. Does Rodriguez consider his audience to be hostile or friendly? well informed or misinformed? Explain your answer.

STYLE AND STRUCTURE

1. What is the function of the occasional words of Spanish Rodriguez uses?

2. Why are some passages italicized?

3. Rodriguez's essay does not move in a straight line from one time period or episode to the next; different periods blend together. How is this indefinite sense of time consistent with the aims of the essay? What would this essay have gained or lost if Rodriguez had presented events in chronological order?

4. What transitional words and phrases does Rodriguez use to indicate comparisons?

5. How does the use of dialogue strengthen Rodriguez's essay?

6. In the first four paragraphs, Rodriguez uses a flashback to highlight an episode that occurred when he was a child. How does this technique set the stage for the thesis?

7. Does Rodriguez present his ideas objectively or subjectively? Could he be accused of sentimentalizing the nature of family life and its reliance on a "private language"? Explain.

8. Find two examples of Rodriguez's use of figurative language in this essay. How do the figures of speech add to the impact of the essay?

9. What ideas does Rodriguez choose to emphasize in his conclusion? Why does he choose these?

VOCABULARY PROJECTS

1. Define each of the following words as it is used in this selection.
   bilingual (5)   guttural (14)
   polysyllabic (11)   barrio (17)

2. What Spanish words does Rodriguez use in this essay? Does he make sure that his English-speaking readers understand their meaning? What effect does he achieve by including them? Write a paragraph in which you explain your reaction to their use.

WRITING WORKSHOP

1. Think of a time when you felt like an outsider from a group. Write an essay in which you compare your ideas with those held by the members of the group.

2. Has anyone you know come from a family whose private language, unique culture, or special customs set them apart from you and your family? Write an essay in which you compare your family and the person that you know and explain how these differences manifested themselves.

3. Write an essay in which you respond to Rodriguez's thesis that it is not possible for a child to use his or her private language in school. Compare your ideas about the public uses of language with the ideas that Rodriguez expresses in paragraph 5.

THEMATIC CONNECTIONS

- "Bilingual Education: The Key to Basic Skills" (p. 490)
- "Bilingual Education: Outdated and Unrealistic" (p. 495)

WRITING ASSIGNMENTS FOR COMPARISON AND CONTRAST

1. Find a description of the same event in two different magazines or newspapers. Write a comparison-and-contrast essay in which you discuss the similarities and differences of these two stories.

2. Go to the library and locate two children's books, one written in the 1950s and one written today. Write an essay discussing which elements are the same and which are different. Include a thesis that makes a point about the relative merits of the two books.

3. Write a comparison-and-contrast essay in which you show how your increased knowledge of an academic subject has either increased or decreased your enthusiasm for it.

4. Think of a relative or friend you knew when you were a child. Consider how your opinion of this person has changed and how it has remained the same. Write an essay in which you demonstrate this opinion.

5. Compare your ethnic group with another ethnic group. In an essay discuss how your customs are similar and how they are different.

6. Choose two different sports, and write an essay in which you discuss how the players are similar and how they are different.

7. Watch a local television news show and then a national news broadcast. Write an essay in which you compare the two television shows, paying particular attention to the news content and to the broadcasting styles of the journalists.

8. Write an essay in which you compare your own early memories of school with those of Richard Rodriguez.

9. Interview your grandmother or mother and write an essay comparing the role of women today with their role in the past.

10. Write an essay in which you compare any two groups that have divergent values: parents vs. children, readers vs. nonreaders, vegetarians vs. meat-eaters, drinkers vs. nondrinkers, singles vs. marrieds, and so on.

11. Prepare a thorough outline comparing and contrasting two-year colleges and four-year colleges. The outline may follow either the point-by-point or subject-by-subject format. Then, using your outline as a guide, write an essay on this topic.

8

Classification and Division

WHAT IS CLASSIFICATION AND DIVISION?

Division is the process of breaking a whole into parts; classification is the act of sorting individual items into categories. In the following paragraph from "Fans," Paul Gallico divides sports fans into categories based on what sport they watch.

The fight crowd is a beast that lurks in the darkness behind the fringe of white light shed over the first six rows by the incandescents atop the ring, and is not to be trusted with pop bottles or other hardware. The tennis crowd is the pansy of all the great sports mobs and is always preening and shushing itself. The golf crowd is the most unwieldy and most sympathetic, and is the only horde given to mass production of that absurd noise written generally as "tsk tsk tsk tsk," and made between tongue and teeth with head-waggings to denote extreme commiseration. The baseball crowd is the most hysterical, the football crowd the best-natured and the polo crowd the most aristocratic. Racing crowds are the most restless, wrestling crowds the most tolerant, and soccer crowds the most easily incitable to riot and disorder. Every sports crowd takes on the characteristics of the individuals who compose it. Each has its particular note of hysteria, its own little cruelties, mannerisms, and bad mannerisms, its own code of sportsmanship and its own method of expressing its emotions.

Through classification and division, we can arrange seemingly random ideas by putting scattered bits of information into useful, coherent order. By breaking a large group into smaller categories and bringing separate items together into particular categories we are able to identify relationships between the whole and its parts and to recognize similarities and differences among the parts themselves. (Remember, though, that simply enumerating representative examples does not constitute classification; when you classify, you always sort individual examples into categories according to some grouping principle.)

Because it is so fundamental, classification and division has many applications. In countless practical situations it brings order to chaos. Items in a Sunday newspaper are *classified* in clearly defined sections—international news, sports, travel, entertainment, comics, and so on—so that hockey scores, for example, are not mixed up with real estate listings. Similarly, department stores are *divided* into different departments so that managers can assign merchandise to particular areas and shoppers can know where to look for a particular item. Without such organization, merchandise might be anywhere in a store. Thus order is brought to newspapers and department stores—like supermarkets, biological hierarchies, and libraries—when a whole is divided into categories or sections and individual items are assigned to one or another of these subgroups.

When you classify, you usually divide as well; division and classification almost always go hand in hand. But dividing and classifying are not exactly the same. When you classify, you begin with individual items and sort them into categories. Most things have several different attributes, and so they can be classified in any of several different ways. Take as an example the students who attend your school. The most obvious way to classify these individuals might be according to their year in college—freshman, sophomore, junior, or senior. But you could also classify students according to their major, racial or ethnic background, home state, grade point average, political affiliation, or any number of other principles. The principle you choose would depend on how you wished to think about the members of this large and diverse group.

Division is essentially the opposite of classification. You start with a whole (an entire class) that you divide into its individual parts—smaller, more specific classes, called subclasses. For example, you might start with the large, general class *television shows* and divide it into smaller subclasses: *comedy, drama, action/adventure*, and so forth. You could divide each of these subclasses still further—*action/adventure*, for example, might include *westerns, police shows*, and so on—and each of these subclasses could be further divided as well. Eventually you would need to determine a particular principle to help you classify specific works: *genre, target audience*, or *setting*, for instance. The principle you use depends on your purpose.

Three guidelines can help ensure proper division and classification:

1. All the categories should result from the same principle; otherwise your categories will overlap and confuse you when you try to classify particular items. If you are dividing *television shows* into *westerns, police shows,* and the like, it is not logical to include the subclass *children's programs,* for this subclass results from one principle—target audience—while the others result from another principle, genre. Similarly, if you are classifying undergraduates at your school according to their year, you cannot include the subclass *scholarship students.*
2. All of the subclasses should be on the same level. In the series *comedy, drama, action/adventure,* and *westerns,* the last of these items, *westerns,* does not belong because it is on a lower level—that is, it is a subclass of *action/adventure.* Likewise, *sophomores* (a subclass of *undergraduates*) does not belong in the series *undergraduates, graduate students, extension students.*
3. You should treat all subclasses that are significant and relevant to your discussion and include enough subclasses to make your point, with no important omissions and no repetitions. In a review of the fall television lineup, the series *sitcoms, soap operas, police shows,* and *detective shows* is incomplete because it omits important subclasses like *sports, news, game shows, talk shows,* and *documentaries;* moreover, it is repetitive because *detective shows* may include some *police shows.* In the same way, the series *freshmen, sophomores, juniors,* and *transfers* is also illogical: The important group *seniors* has been omitted, while *transfers* is repetitive because it may include *freshmen, sophomores,* and *juniors.*

Using Classification and Division

Classification and division can bring order to the writing process. When you brainstorm, as Chapter 1 explains, you first consider your larger topic, listing all the related points you can think of. Next, you *divide* your topic into logical categories and *classify* the items on your brainstorming list into one category or another, perhaps narrowing, expanding, or eliminating some categories—or some points—as you go along. This picking and choosing, sorting and grouping, reduces your material until it is manageable and eventually suggests your thesis and the main points of your essay.

Because of the way they are worded, certain topics and questions require you to use classification, division, or both as the pattern for developing an essay. Suppose you are asked, "What kinds of policies can be used to direct and control the national economy?" Here the word *kinds* suggests classification and division. Other words, such as *types, varieties,* and *categories* can also serve as clues.

Structuring a Classification-and-Division Essay

Once you decide to use classification and division as your pattern of development, you need to plan your essay. If your topic consists of many individual items that you want to group into well-established categories, your main task will be to classify. If your topic consists of a large class that you want to partition, your main task will be to divide. In general, however, you will use both processes to be certain that your analysis is complete. And regardless of your initial vantage point, the result will be the same—a system that categorizes the members of a group.

When you classify and divide information, you must decide what principle you are going to use—what quality you regard your items as having in common. Your system must be logical and consistent. Just as a clear basis of comparison determines the points in a comparison-and-contrast essay, so a clear principle of classification and division determines the system you use to categorize items. Every group of people, things, or ideas can be categorized in many ways; your purpose in classifying and dividing determines which principle you use. When you are in line at the bookstore with only twenty dollars, the cost of different books may be your only principle of selection. As you carry your books across campus, however, weight may matter more. Finally, as you study and read, the quality of your books should be paramount. Similarly, when you organize an essay, your principle of classification and division is determined by your writing situation—your assignment, your purpose, your audience, and your special knowledge and interests.

Once you define your principle and apply it to your topic, you must select your categories by dividing a whole class into parts and grouping a number of different items together within each part. Next, you should decide how you will treat the categories in your essay. Just as a comparison-and-contrast essay makes comparable points about its subjects, so your classification-and-division essay should treat all categories similarly. When you discuss comparable points for each, you ensure that your reader sees your distinctions among categories and understands your definition of each category.

Finally, arrange your categories in some logical order, preferably so that one leads to the next and the least important yields to the most important. Such an order ensures that your reader sees how the categories relate and how significant each is. Whatever this order, it should be consistent with your purpose and support your thesis.

Like other essays, the classification-and-division essay must have a thesis. This thesis should identify your subject, enumerate the categories you will discuss, and perhaps show readers the relationships of your categories to one another and to the subject as a whole. But in most academic writing, your essay's goal is to communicate more than such simple information. For this reason, your thesis may also do more—for example, it may convince your readers why your categories are significant or establish the relative value of your categories. Listing different kinds of investments would be pointless if you did not evaluate the strengths and weaknesses of each and then make recommendations based on your assessment. Similarly, a term paper about a writer's major works would accomplish little if it merely categorized his or her writings. Instead, your arrangement should communicate your view of these works to your reader, perhaps demonstrating that some deserve higher public regard than others.

Once you have formulated your essay's main idea and established your subclasses, you should plan your classification-and-division papers around the same three major sections that other essays have: introduction, body, and conclusion. Your introduction should orient your readers by mentioning your topic, the principle by which your material is divided and classified, and the individual subclasses you plan to discuss. Your paper's thesis should also usually be stated in the introduction. Once your readers have this information, they can easily follow your paper as it develops. In the subsequent body paragraphs, you should treat the categories one by one in the order in which your introduction presents them. Finally, your conclusion should restate your thesis, summing up the points you have made, and then perhaps move on to consider their implications.

Classification

Suppose that you are preparing a term paper for an American literature course on Mark Twain's nonfiction works. You have read *Roughing It, Life on the Mississippi,* and *The Innocents Abroad.* Besides these books derived from his experiences, you have read Twain's autobiography. This work, in turn, led you to some of his correspondence and essays. When you realize that the works you have studied can easily be classified as four different types of Twain's nonfiction—travel books, essays, letters, and autobiography—you decide to use classification and division to structure your essay. Therefore, you first divide the large class, *Twain's nonfiction prose*, into major subclasses—his travel books, essays, autobiography, and letters. Then you go on to classify the individual works—that is, to assign the works you plan to discuss to these subclasses, which you could then discuss one at a time. Your categories make sense to you as a way to organize your paper, but you know that you also need a strong thesis statement so that your paper does more than just list his nonfiction works. You decide that you want to persuade readers to reconsider the reputations of some of these works, and you formulate your thesis accordingly. You might then prepare a formal outline like this one for the body of your paper:

    I. Travel books
      A. *Roughing It*
      B. *The Innocents Abroad*
      C. *Life on the Mississippi*
    II. Essays
      A. "Fenimore Cooper's Literary Offenses"
      B. "How To Tell A Story"
      C. "The Awful German Language"
    III. Letters
      A. To W. D. Howells
      B. To his family
    IV. Autobiography

Because this will be a long term paper, each of the outline's divisions will have several subdivisions, and each subdivision might require several paragraphs.

Once your term paper is finished, you are confident that it will be clear and persuasive despite its length because you have carefully considered each of the characteristics of an effective classification. Because you were careful to apply only *one* principle of classification when you grouped Twain's nonfiction works according to literary genre, your categories do not overlap. You selected this principle rather than another—for example, theme, subject matter, stage in his career, or contemporary critical reception—because it suited your purpose. If you had written your term paper for a political science course, you might have decided to examine Twain as a social critic by classifying his works according to the amount or kind of political commentary in each. Literary genre, however, was an appropriate principle of classification for the writing situation at hand. If you had divided Twain's works into novels, essays, short stories, letters, and political works, for instance, you would have mixed two principles of classification—genre and content. As a result, a highly political novel like *The Gilded Age* would have fit more than one category. You also made certain that all your subclasses were on the same level (you could not, for example, treat Twain's essays, letters, autobiography, and *Roughing It* as your four major divisions). And, you included all relevant subclasses. Had you left out the subclass *essays,* for example, you would have been unable to classify several significant works of nonfiction.

In addition, you arranged your subclasses so they would support your thesis. Because you challenged the dominance of Twain's travel books, you discussed them briefly early in your paper. Similarly, the autobiography made your best case for the merit of the other nonfiction works and thus was most effective placed last. Of course, you could have arranged your categories in several other orders, such as shorter to longer works or least to most popular, depending on the details of your argument.

Finally, you are certain that you have treated your categories comparably. In fact, you verified this by identifying each main point in your rough draft and cross-checking the order of points from category to category. You knew your case would be weakened if you inadvertently skipped style in your discussion of Twain's letters after you had included it for every other category. This omission might lead your readers to suspect either that you could not discuss this point because you had not done enough research on the letters or that you had ignored the point because the style of his letters did not measure up somehow. Your careful organization, however, prevented such questions by your readers.

Division

When you plan a paper such as the essay on Mark Twain's works, your main task is classification. When you do not plan to devote much attention to individual items in each category, however, your main task is division. Suppose you are planning a paper for your finance course on managing a model portfolio. You want to discuss general kinds of investments rather than specific investment opportunities, so you mainly rely on division—the process of breaking a whole into parts—to analyze your topic. Based on your preliminary research, you decide to concentrate on the categories of investments usually considered by a new investor with a moderate income, namely stocks, bonds, real estate, and mutual funds. Based on this division, you formulate your thesis: "Carefully selected stocks, bonds, and real estate are all sound investments, but the beginner would be best advised to invest in mutual funds."

You realize that the body of your essay should devote a paragraph or two to each category in turn, explaining the same aspects of each kind of investment so that their relative merits are clear. If in your discussion of stocks you consider stability, ease of liquidation, and potential for long-term growth, you know you should consider the same points—and no others—for bonds, real estate, and mutual funds. If you consider different points, your treatment will be unbalanced, and your readers will be confused.

If you were assigned a long paper, you might want to treat each type of investment in further detail by dividing it into smaller subclasses. In this way, you could distinguish between common and preferred stocks, municipal and corporate bonds, commercial and residential real estate, and stock and money-market mutual funds. For a short paper, however, such subdivisions would not be practical. You would have only enough space to concentrate on more general distinctions between broader categories or to limit your topic to one subdivision. You might prepare the following informal outline for a short paper on a model investment portfolio:

Introduction:	Thesis—Carefully selected stocks, bonds, and real estate are all sound investments, but the beginner would be best advised to invest in mutual funds.
First category:	Advantages and disadvantages of stocks
Second category:	Advantages and disadvantages of bonds
Third category:	Advantages and disadvantages of real estate
Fourth category:	Advantages and disadvantages of mutual funds, emphasizing advantages
Conclusion:	Including restatement of thesis

The following essay was written by Roger Bauer for a course in American literature. The essay divides a whole entity—fiction of the American West—into four parts, or elements, using a principle of division common in literary analysis.

THE WESTERN: MORE THAN JUST "POPULAR" LITERATURE

Introduction   A work of popular fiction—a detective story, a   1

gothic novel, or a Western, for example—is usually

not regarded very highly by literary critics. This
evaluation is justified in most cases. All too often
in popular fiction characters are familiar
stereotypes, plot devices are predictable (and
sometimes improbable), settings are overly familiar
or only vaguely described, and themes are simplistic
or undeveloped. To some extent, these characteristics
apply to fiction of the American West--not only to
contemporary Westerns, but also to those novels and
stories that have achieved status as classics. Still,

Thesis (identifies four elements to be discussed) although clichéd characters and trite plots dominate
even classic Westerns, a strong sense of place and
timeless themes give the Western the power to
transcend the "popular fiction" category.

First element: Characters Readers encounter familiar characters in novels   2
and short stories with Western settings. The cast of
characters is likely to include at least a few of the
following: the cowboy, the dance hall girl, the
sheriff, the deputy, the madam, the miner, the
schoolmarm, the Easterner, the gambler, the rancher,
the hired hand, the store owner, the preacher, the
traveling salesman, and assorted cavalry soldiers,
cattle rustlers, Indians, and Mexicans. These people
are seldom fully developed; rather, they are stock
characters who play exactly the roles readers expect
them to play. Some classic stories, such as "The
Outcasts of Poker Flat" and "Stage to Lordsburg"
gather an assortment of these characters together in
an isolated setting, playing them off against one
another in a way that emphasizes their function as
types rather than individuals. The plot elements are

Second element: Plot just as predictable. Sometimes a gang will terrorize
innocent settlers or ranchers or townspeople, as in
Shane; sometimes a desperado will be on the loose, as
in "The Bride Comes to Yellow Sky." There may be a

showdown on a dusty street, as in "The Tin Star,"
or an ambush, as in "Stage to Lordsburg." Scenes of
chase and capture are staples from James Fenimore
Cooper to Louis L'Amour, and standard boy-meets-girl
plots can be traced from The Virginian to current
popular novels.

Third element: Setting

But the Western has the potential to transcend   3
the limits of these familiar materials. A particular
strength is its geographical setting, which provides
it with an unusually varied landscape and some
magnificent scenery. The setting in Western fiction
is special for a variety of reasons. First, the West
is beautiful and exotic. Second, the West is huge:
Towns are widely separated, and characters travel
great distances. As a result, a sense of loneliness
and isolation pervades the Western. Third, the West
is frightening and unpredictable, characterized by
untamed landscapes, wild animals, and terrifying
extremes of weather. The harshness and
unpredictability of the climate are especially
frightening to newcomers to the West (and to
readers). Still, the very extreme conditions
(tornadoes, blizzards, desert sun) and unfamiliar
topography (mesas, plains, canyons) that are so
disturbing are also fascinating. Ultimately, the
setting can be friend or enemy: Zane Grey's Riders of
the Purple Sage ends with its lovers isolated in a
canyon by a rock slide; in Max Brand's "Wine on the
Desert," a man dies of thirst in the hostile sun. In
these and other Western stories, the setting is a
powerful presence that is always strongly felt.

Fourth element: Theme

Perhaps even more powerful than the setting are   4
the themes of the Western--themes found in all great
literature. Each of these themes adds interest to the
Western, giving it substance and stature. One such

theme is the classic conflict between East and West, civilization and the wilderness, illustrated in novels as diverse as Cooper's The Prairie and Wister's The Virginian. (In The Virginian, as in Crane's "The Bride Comes to Yellow Sky," it is the woman who is the symbol of civilization.) Typically, the East is portrayed as rigid, sterile, and limiting, while the West is natural and spontaneous, untamed and beautiful. Another classic theme frequently seen in Western literature is the initiation theme. Here a young man or a boy (or, occasionally, a girl) is initiated into the mysteries of adulthood through participation in a physical test of his courage--for example, a fist fight, a gun battle, or a feat of strength. This theme is developed in "The Tin Star" as well as in High Noon, the film based on this story. A third theme frequently explored in Western fiction is the journey or search. The vast spaces and dangerous climate and topography of the West make it an ideal setting for this theme. In works as diverse as Charles Portis's novel True Grit, Louis L'Amour's Down the Long Hills, and the classic John Ford film The Searchers, the journey figures prominently. Whether the quest is for a long lost relative, for land or gold or silver, or for knowledge or experience, the search theme dominates many works of Western literature, particularly longer works.

Conclusion (restates thesis) Balancing the familiar plot elements and stereotypical characters of Western fiction are two other elements, setting and theme, that set it apart from other kinds of popular fiction. In addition to its vivid settings and universal themes, the Western also boasts a strong sense of history and an identity as a uniquely American genre. These two qualities

```
should give it a lasting importance consistent with
its continuing popularity.
```

Points for Special Attention

Thesis.   Roger Bauer's purpose in writing this essay was not just to describe the fiction of the American West but also to evaluate it. Consequently, his thesis presents his assessment of the genre's literary value, and his body paragraphs support his position with analysis and examples.

Organization.   Roger planned his essay carefully, and his organization scheme keeps the four elements he discusses distinct; in addition, both the space he allots to each element and the order in which he presents them conveys his emphasis to his readers. Thus paragraph 2 combines a discussion of the two elements Roger does not consider to be particularly noteworthy; in paragraphs 3 and 4 he goes on to give fuller treatment to the two elements of major importance to his thesis, setting and theme. Because he considers some elements to be more important than others, his treatment of the four categories is necessarily unequal. Still, Roger is careful to provide specific examples from various works of Western literature in all four cases.

Transition between Categories.   Roger uses clear transitional sentences to introduce each individual element of literature he discusses: "Readers encounter familiar characters in novels and short stories with Western settings"; "The plot elements are just as predictable"; "A particular strength is its geographical setting, which provides it with an unusually varied landscape and some magnificent scenery"; and "Perhaps even more powerful than the setting are the themes of the Western—themes found in all great literature." To indicate his shift from what he considers less important elements to more significant ones, Roger uses another strong transition: "But the Western has the potential to transcend the limits of these familiar materials." Each of these transitional sentences not only distinguishes the four elements from one another but also conveys Roger's direction and emphasis to his readers.

Writing about Literature.   Because he is writing for a course in American literature, Roger pays special attention to certain conventions that apply to writing about literature. He uses present tense when referring to literary works, and he places titles of short stories within quotation marks and underlines titles of novels and films. Also, he presents his interpretations and evaluations straightforwardly, without using unnecessary phrases like *In my opinion* and *I think.*

In the following paper, written for a freshman composition class, Andrew Striker classifies different kinds of technological advances to make a point about the society that produced them.

A TOAST TO PROGRESS

Introduction   Perhaps the most notable feature of our   1
civilization is our desire to change or improve
nature. Throughout the twentieth century,
particularly in recent years, the United States has
made many technological advances in an effort to
improve the lives of its citizens. When considered
together, three kinds of technological advances in
particular reveal the true nature of the United

Thesis States in the eighties: It is a nation of great
promise, but one that is limited by its own
imperfections and frivolity.

First category   The first kind of technological advance, the   2
kind that demonstrates the enormous advances in
medical technology that are taking place in our
society, is typified by the artificial heart.
Presently, artificial hearts are most effective as
temporary hearts for people awaiting transplants. In
a matter of years, however, artificial hearts may
function as well as healthy organic ones. The many
other lifesaving developments like the artificial
heart--CAT scans, fetal surgery, organ transplants,
synthetic hormones, and the like--are only part of
this category of advances. Life-improving advances--
electronic wheelchairs, skin grafts, laser surgery,
in vitro fertilization, and all kinds of computer
technology--also reveal the promise of our century's
technology.

Second category   The second type of technological advance, the [3] kind that reveals our society's imperfection, is represented by artificial sweetener. This category includes technological developments that seem to offer promise but which in fact have a negative side. Artificial sweeteners, for example, play a part in helping Americans to avoid consuming unhealthful sugars, but studies have suggested that they may be carcinogenic. Other developments too seemed at first to offer solutions for some of society's problems but have turned out to have a dark side. These include aerosol sprays, which have been found to threaten our atmosphere's ozone layer, and various "miracle" drugs that have been found to cause health problems and fetal deformities. Far less serious, but still disturbing, is a seemingly beneficial invention like the microwave oven. This appliance does make it possible for us to cook food more quickly, but it is rapidly creating a generation of families eating hurried, separate, silent meals. In addition, we have the digital watches--designed to be precise, these could conceivably produce a generation of children who do not understand the meaning of the word "counterclockwise"--and the walkman, designed to cut down on noise and improve sound but in fact a major contributor to the impersonal, antisocial nature of life in the eighties. Such "advances" demonstrate our society's technological imperfections.

Third category   It is the third type of advance, however, that [4] reveals the most about the United States in the twentieth century. In this category fall technological inventions that cater to fashion but do not save, or even significantly improve, any lives. Passive exercise machines and fat-suctioning surgery lead the list. Other inventions of dubious value include tanning salons and water beds. As relatively useless as they may be, advances of this type may demand as much time and energy from scientists, and as much money for research and development, as lifesaving or life-improving inventions. This final category of advance is perhaps best typified not by the artificial heart, not by artificial sweetener-- but by artificial turf.

Conclusion   Technology touches every part of our lives. At   5 its best, it can change--or save--our lives. At its worst, it can threaten or even destroy us. The three categories of technological advances typified by the artificial turf--and our reactions to them--all reveal something about the spirit and the character of our nation. We may insist that our goal is progress, but we are often willing to settle for less.

Points for Special Attention

Thesis and Support.   Andrew's assignment was to write an essay on the topic "What do some of the recent technological advances made in the United States reveal about the society that has created and used them?" The essay was to have an explicit thesis. Andrew's thesis, clearly stated in the last sentence of his first paragraph, is supported by a series of examples grouped into three categories. His essay shows how useful classification can be in organizing a variety of diverse examples.

Parallel Treatment of Categories.   Each of Andrew's three categories is clearly identified and distinguished from the others, and each is given similar treatment. For instance, each category is illustrated with examples calculated both to show the range of advances and to characterize them, and each category is memorably identified by one key development: artificial heart, artificial sweetener, artificial turf.

Transitions.   The topic sentences of Andrew's body paragraphs serve as transitions that help move his readers from one group of technological advances to another. In these sentences repetition and parallelism ("The first kind of advance . . . "; "The second type of technological advance . . . "; "It is the third type of advance, however, . . . ") link the paragraphs to one another as well as to the essay's thesis. Within each paragraph, words and phrases like *however, also, other developments,* and *such advances* connect ideas between sentences, thus contributing to the essay's coherence and unity.

Each of the following essays uses classification and division as its pattern of development. In some cases, the pattern is used to explain ideas; in others, it is used to persuade the reader.

COLLEGE PRESSURES

William Zinsser

Born in 1922 and educated at Princeton, William Zinsser has been a writer and editor as well as a teacher of writing. He was a feature and editorial writer for the New York Herald Tribune, *where he also served as drama editor, and he taught English at Yale from 1970 to 1979. His books include* On Writing Well: An Informal Guide to Writing Nonfiction *(1976) and* Writing with a Word Processor *(1983) as well as several works on American culture. He now serves as executive editor of the Book-of-the-Month Club. In "College Pressures," written for* Country Journal *magazine in 1979, Zinsser analyzes the different forces contributing to the anxiety of college students at Yale.*

Dear Carlos: I desperately need a dean's excuse for my chem midterm which will begin in about 1 hour. All I can say is that I totally blew it this week. I've fallen incredibly, inconceivably behind.   1

Carlos: Help! I'm anxious to hear from you. I'll be in my room and won't leave it until I hear from you. Tomorrow is the last day for. . . .   2

Carlos: I left town because I started bugging out again. I stayed up all night to finish a take home make-up exam & am typing it to hand in on the 10th. It was due on the 5th. P.S. I'm going to the dentist. Pain is pretty bad.   3

Carlos: Probably by Friday I'll be able to get back to my studies. Right now I'm going to take a long walk. This whole thing has taken a lot out of me.   4

Carlos: I'm really up the proverbial creek. The problem is I really *bombed* the history final. Since I need that course for my major. . . .   5

Carlos: Here follows a tale of woe. I went home this weekend, had to help my Mom, & caught a fever so didn't have much time to study. My professor.   6

Carlos: Aargh! Nothing original but everything's piling up at once. To be brief, my job interview.   7

Hey Carlos, good news! I've got mononucleosis.   8

Who are these wretched supplicants, scribbling notes so laden   9
with anxiety, seeking such miracles of postponement and balm?
They are men and women who belong to Bradford College, one of
the twelve residential colleges at Yale University, and the messages
are just a few of the hundreds that they left for their dean, Carlos
Hortas—often slipped under his door at 4 A.M.—last year.

But students like the ones who wrote those notes can also be   10
found on campuses from coast to coast—especially in New England
and at many other private colleges across the country that have
high academic standards and highly motivated students. Nobody
could doubt that the notes are real. In their urgency and their gal-
lows humor they are authentic voices of a generation that is panicky
to succeed.

My own connection with the message writers is that I am master   11
of Branford College. I live in its Gothic quadrangle and know the
students well. (We have 485 of them.) I am privy to their hopes and
fears—and also to their stereo music and their piercing cries in the
dead of night ("Does anybody *ca-a-are?*). If they went to Carlos to
ask how to get through tomorrow, they come to me to ask how to
get through the rest of their lives.

Mainly I try to remind them that the road ahead is a long one and   12
that it will have more unexpected turns than they think. There will
be plenty of time to change jobs, change careers, change whole attitudes and approaches. They don't want to hear such liberating
news. They want a map—right now—that they can follow unswerv-
ingly to career security, financial security, Social Security and, presumably, a prepaid grave.

What I wish for all students is some release from the clammy grip   13
of the future. I wish them a chance to savor each segment of their
education as an experience in itself and not as a grim preparation
for the next step. I wish them the right to experiment, to trip and
fall, to learn that defeat is as instructive as victory and is not the
end of the world.

My wish, of course, is naive. One of the few rights that America   14
does not proclaim is the right to fail. Achievement is the national
god, venerated in our media—the million-dollar athlete, the wealthy
executive—and glorified in our praise of possessions. In the presence
of such a potent state religion, the young are growing up old.

I see four kinds of pressure working on college students today;   15
economic pressure, parental pressure, peer pressure, and self-
induced pressure. It is easy to look around for villains—to blame the
colleges for charging too much money, the professors for assigning
too much work, the parents for pushing their children too far, the

students for driving themselves too hard. But there are no villains, only victims.

"In the late 1960s," one dean told me, "the typical question that 16 I got from students was 'Why is there so much suffering in the world?' or 'How can I make a contribution?' Today it's 'Do you think it would look better for getting into law school if I did a double major in history and political science, or just majored in one of them?'" Many other deans confirmed this pattern. One said: "They're trying to find an edge—the intangible something that will look better on paper if two students are about equal."

Note the emphasis on looking better. The transcript has become 17 a sacred document, the passport to security. How one appears on paper is more important than how one appears in person. *A* is for Admirable and *B* is for Borderline, even though, in Yale's official system of grading, *A* means "excellent" and *B* means "very good." Today, looking very good is no longer good enough, especially for students who hope to go on to law school or medical school. They know that entrance into the better schools will be an entrance into the better law firms and better medical practices where they will make a lot of money. They also know that the odds are harsh. Yale Law School, for instance, matriculates 170 students from an applicant pool of 3,700; Harvard enrolls 550 from a pool of 7,000.

It's all very well for those of us who write letters of recommenda- 18 tion for our students to stress the qualities of humanity that will make them good lawyers or doctors. And it's nice to think that admission officers are really reading our letters and looking for the extra dimension of commitment or concern. Still, it would be hard for a student not to visualize these officers shuffling so many transcripts studded with *A*s that they regard a *B* as positively shameful.

The pressure is almost as heavy on students who just want to 19 graduate and get a job. Long gone are the days of the "gentleman's C," when students journeyed through college with a certain relaxation, sampling a wide variety of courses—music, art, philosophy, classics, anthropology, poetry, religion—that would send them out as liberally educated men and women. If I were an employer I would rather employ graduates who have this range and curiosity than those who narrowly pursued safe subjects and high grades. I know countless students whose inquiring minds exhilarate me. I like to hear the play of their ideas. I don't know if they are getting *A*s or *C*s, and I don't care. I also like them as people. The country needs them, and they will find satisfying jobs. I tell them to relax. They can't.

Nor can I blame them. They live in a brutal economy. Tuition, 20 room, and board at most private colleges now comes to at least $7,000, not counting books and fees. This might seem to suggest that the colleges are getting rich. But they are equally battered by inflation. Tuition covers only 60 percent of what it costs to educate a student, and ordinarily the remainder comes from what colleges receive in endowments, grants, and gifts. Now the remainder keeps being swallowed by the cruel costs—higher every year—of just opening the doors. Heating oil is up. Insurance is up. Postage is up. Health-premium costs are up. Everything is up. Deficits are up. We are witnessing in America the creation of a brotherhood of paupers—colleges, parents, and students, joined by the common bond of debt.

21   Today it is not unusual for a student, even if he works part time at college and full time during the summer, to accrue $5,000 in loans after four years—loans that he must start to repay within one year after graduation. Exhorted at commencement to go forth into the world, he is already behind as he goes forth. How could he not feel under pressure throughout college to prepare for this day of reckoning? I have used "he," incidentally, only for brevity. Women at Yale are under no less pressure to justify their expensive education to themselves, their parents, and society. In fact, they are probably under more pressure. For although they leave college superbly equipped to bring fresh leadership to traditionally male jobs, society hasn't yet caught up with this fact.

22   Along with economic pressure goes parental pressure. Inevitably, the two are deeply intertwined.

23   I see many students taking pre-medical courses with joyless tenacity. They go off to their labs as if they were going to the dentist. It saddens me because I know them in other corners of their life as cheerful people.

24   "Do you want to go to medical school?" I ask them.

25   "I guess so," they say, without conviction, or "Not really."

26   "Then why are you going?"

27   "Well, my parents want me to be a doctor. They're paying all this money and . . . "

28   Poor students, poor parents. They are caught in one of the oldest webs of love and duty and guilt. The parents mean well; they are trying to steer their sons and daughters toward a secure future. But the sons and daughters want to major in history or classics or philosophy—subjects with no "practical" value. Where's the payoff on the humanities? It's not easy to persuade such loving parents that the humanities do indeed pay off. The intellectual faculties developed by studying subjects like history and classics—an ability to synthe-

size and relate, to weigh cause and effect, to see events in perspective—are just the faculties that make creative leaders in business or almost any general field. Still, many fathers would rather put their money on courses that point toward a specific profession—courses that are pre-law, pre-medical, pre-business, or, as I sometimes heard it put, "pre-rich."

But the pressure on students is severe. They are truly torn. One 29 part of them feels obligated to fulfill their parents' expectations, after all, their parents are older and presumably wiser. Another part tells them that the expectations that are right for their parents are not right for them.

I know a student who wants to be an artist. She is very obviously 30 an artist and will be a good one—she has already had several modest exhibits. Meanwhile she is growing as a well-rounded person and taking humanistic subjects that will enrich the inner resources out of which her art will grow. But her father is strongly opposed. He thinks that an artist is a "dumb" thing to be. The student vacillates and tries to please everybody. She keeps up with her art somewhat furtively and takes some of the "dumb" courses her father wants her to take—at least they are dumb courses for her. She is a free spirit on a campus of tense students—no small achievement in itself—and she deserves to follow her muse.

Peer pressure and self-induced pressure are also intertwined, and 31 they begin almost at the beginning of freshman year.

"I had a freshman student I'll call Linda," one dean told me, "who 32 came in and said she was under terrible pressure because her roommate, Barbara, was much brighter and studied all the time. I couldn't tell her that Barbara had come in two hours earlier to say the same thing about Linda."

The story is almost funny—except that it's not. It's symptomatic 33 of all the pressures put together. When every student thinks every other student is working harder and doing better, the only solution is to study harder still. I see students going off to the library every night after dinner and coming back when it closes at midnight. I wish they could sometimes forget about their peers and go to a movie. I hear the clacking of typewriters in the hours before dawn. I see the tension in their eyes when exams are approaching and papers are due: *"Will I get everything done?"*

Probably they won't. They will get sick. They will get "blocked." 34 They will sleep. They will oversleep. They will bug out. *Hey Carlos, help!*

Part of the problem is that they do more than they are expected 35 to do. A professor will assign five-page papers. Several students will start writing ten-page papers to impress him. Then more students will write ten-page papers, and a few will raise the ante to fifteen. Pity the poor student who is still just doing the assignment.

"Once you have twenty or thirty percent of the student population deliberately overexerting," one dean points out, "it's bad for everybody. When a teacher gets more and more effort from his class, the student who is doing normal work can be perceived as not doing well. The tactic works, psychologically." 36

Why can't the professor just cut back and not accept longer papers? He can, and he probably will. But by then the term will be half over and the damage done. Grade fever is highly contagious and not easily reversed. Besides, the professor's main concern is with his course. He knows his students only in relation to the course and doesn't know that they are also overexerting in their other courses. Nor is it really his business. He didn't sign up for dealing with the student as a whole person and with all the emotional baggage the student brought along from home. That's what deans, masters, chaplains, and psychiatrists are for. 37

To some extent this is nothing new: a certain number of professors have always been self-contained islands of scholarship and shyness, more comfortable with books than with people. But the new pauperism has widened the gap still further, for professors who actually like to spend time with students don't have as much time to spend. They also are overexerting. If they are young, they are busy trying to publish in order not to perish, hanging by their finger nails onto a shrinking profession. If they are old and tenured, they are buried under the duties of administering departments—as departmental chairmen or members of committees—that have been thinned out by the budgetary axe. 38

Ultimately it will be the students' own business to break the circles in which they are trapped. They are too young to be prisoners of their parents' dreams and their classmates' fears. They must be jolted into believing in themselves as unique men and women who have the power to shape their own future. 39

"Violence is being done to the undergraduate experience," says Carlos Hortas. "College should be open-ended: at the end it should open many, many roads. Instead, students are choosing their goal in advance, and their choices narrow at they go along. It's almost as if they think that the country has been codified in the type of jobs that exist—that they've got to fit into certain slots. Therefore, fit into the best-paying slot. 40

"They ought to take chances. Not taking changes will lead to a 41 life of colorless mediocrity. They'll be comfortable. But something in the spirit will be missing."

I have painted too drab a portrait of today's students, making 42 them seem a solemn lot. That is only half of their story; if they were were so dreary I wouldn't so thoroughly enjoy their company. The other half is that they are easy to like. They are quick to laugh and to offer friendship. They are not introverts. They are usually kind and are more considerate of one another than any student generation I have known.

Nor are they so obsessed with their studies that they avoid sports 43 and extracurricular activities. On the contrary, they juggle their crowded hours to play on a variety of teams, perform with musical and dramatic groups, and write for campus publications. But this in turn is one more cause of anxiety. They are too many choices. Academically, they have 1,300 courses to select from; outside class they have to decide how much spare time they can spare and how to spend it.

This means that they engage in fewer extracurricular pursuits 44 than their predecessors did. If they want to row on the crew and play in the symphony they will eliminate one; in the '60s they would have done both. They also tend to choose activities that are self-limiting. Drama, for instance, is flourishing in all twelve of Yale's residential colleges as it never has before. Students hurl themselves into these productions—as actors, directors, carpenters, and technicians with a dedication to create the best possible play, knowing that the day will come when the run will end and they can get back to their studies.

They also can't afford to be the willing slave of organizations like 45 the *Yale Daily News*. Last spring at the one-hundredth anniversary banquet of that paper—whose past chairmen include such once and future kings as Potter Stewart, Kingman Brewster, and William F. Buckley, Jr.*—much was made of the fact that the editorial staff used to be small and totally committed and that "newsies" routinely worked fifty hours a week. In effect they belonged to a club; Newsies is how they defined themselves at Yale. Today's student will write one or two articles a week, when he can, and he defines himself as a student. I've never heard the word Newsie except at the banquet.

If I have described the modern undergraduate primarily as a 46

---

*EDS. NOTE—Stewart is a former U.S. Supreme Court Justice; Brewster is a former president of Yale; and Buckley is a conservative editor and columnist.

driven creature who is largely ignoring the blithe spirit inside who keeps trying to come out and play, it's because that's where the crunch is, not only at Yale but throughout American education. It's why I think we should all be worried about the values that are nurturing a generation so fearful of risk and so goal-obsessed at such an early age.

I tell students that there is no one "right" way to get ahead—that 47 each of them is a different person, starting from a different point and bound for a different destination. I tell them that change is a tonic and that all the slots are not codified nor the frontiers closed. One of my ways of telling them is to invite men and women who have achieved success outside the academic world to come and talk informally with my students during the year. They are heads of companies or ad agencies, editors of magazines, politicians, public officials, television magnates, labor leaders, business executives, Broadway producers, artists, writers, economists, photographers, scientists, historians—a mixed bag of achievers.

I ask them to say a few words about how they got started. The 48 students assume that they started in their present profession and knew all along that it was what they wanted to do. Luckily for me, most of them got into their field by a circuitous route, to their surprise, after many detours. The students are startled. They can hardly conceive of a career that was not pre-planned. They can hardly imagine allowing the hand of God or chance to nudge them down some unforeseen trail.

COMPREHENSION

1. What advice does Zinsser give to students when they bring their problems to him?

2. What does Zinsser wish for his students? Why does he believe his wish is naive?

3. What are the four kinds of pressures Zinsser identifies?

4. Whom does Zinsser blame for the existence of the pressures? Explain.

5. How, according to Zinsser, is his evaluation of students different from their own and from their potential employers' assessments?

6. Why does Zinsser believe that women are probably under even more pressure than men?

7. Why does Zinsser believe that the dean's story about Linda and Barbara is "symptomatic of all the pressures put together"?

8. How does what Zinsser calls the "new pauperism" affect professors?

9. Who, according to Zinsser, is ultimately responsible for eliminating college pressures? Explain.

10. In what sense are sports and extracurricular activities another source of anxiety for students? How do students adapt to this pressure?

11. Why are students surprised at what the "achievers" Zinsser brings in to speak to them have to say?

PURPOSE AND AUDIENCE

1. In your own words, state Zinsser's thesis.

2. On what kind of audience do you think this essay would have the most significant impact: students, teachers, parents, potential employers, graduate school admissions committees, or college administrators? Explain.

3. Is Zinsser's intent in this essay simply to expose a difficult situation or to effect change? Explain

4. What does Zinsser hope to accomplish in paragraphs 42–46? How might the essay be different without this section?

5. What assumptions does Zinsser make about his audience? Are they valid? Explain.

STYLE AND STRUCTURE

1. Evaluate the essay's introductory strategy. What impact does Zinsser hope the notes to Carlos will have on his readers? Do they have the desired impact? Explain.

2. Identify the boundaries of the actual classification. How does Zinsser introduce the first category? How does he indicate that his treatment of the final category is complete?

3. What function do paragraphs 22 and 31 serve in the essay?

4. Zinsser is careful to explain that when he refers to students as *he*, he includes female students as well. However, he also refers to professors as *he* (for example, in paragraphs 35–37). Assuming that not

all professors at Yale are male, what other stylistic options does Zinsser have in this situation?

5. At various points in this essay Zinsser quotes deans and students at Yale. What is the effect of these quotations?

6. Zinsser notes that his categories are "intertwined." In what ways do the categories overlap? Does this overlap weaken the essay? Explain.

7. What, if anything, seems to determine the order in which Zinsser introduces his categories? Is this order effective?

VOCABULARY PROJECTS

1. Define each of the following words as it is used in this selection.

proverbial (5)	exhorted (21)
supplicants (9)	tenacity (23)
balm (9)	faculties (28)
privy (11)	blithe (46)
venerated (14)	tonic (47)
intangible (16)	codified (47)
accrue (21)	

2. At times Zinsser uses religious language—*national god, sacred document*—to describe the students' quest for success. Identify other examples of such language, and explain why it is used.

WRITING WORKSHOP

1. Zinsser believes Yale students' drive for success is typical of that faced by students at other colleges. Do you agree, or are the pressures you experience as a college student different from the ones Zinsser describes? Classify your own college pressures, and write an essay with a thesis that takes a strong stand against the forces responsible for the pressures.

2. Zinsser sees today's college students as part of "a generation that is panicky to succeed." Do you agree? Write a classification essay in which you support a thesis about college students' drive for success by categorizing students you know on the basis of either the degree of their need to succeed or the different ways in which they wish to succeed.

3. Zinsser takes a negative view of the college pressures he identifies. Using his four categories, write an essay that argues that, in the long run, these pressures are not only necessary but valuable.

THEMATIC CONNECTIONS

- "My First Conk" (p. 217)
- "The Company Man" (p. 440)

AMERICAN REGIONAL COSTUME

Alison Lurie

Born in 1926, Alison Lurie graduated from Radcliffe College. She is currently a Professor of English at Cornell University. Recipient of several prestigious fellowships, foundation grants, and other awards, Lurie is the author of seven novels, including The War Between the Tates *(1974) and* Only Children *(1979), which present satirical portraits of the upper middle class. She has also written fiction for children. Her latest novel is* The Truth about Lorin Jones *(1988).* The Language of Clothes *(1981), from which "American Regional Costume" is excerpted, considers in detail what our clothes tell us about ourselves and about others.*

Even today, when the American landscape is becoming more and more homogeneous, there is really no such thing as an all-American style of dress. A shopping center in Maine may superficially resemble one in Georgia or California, but the shoppers in it will look different, because the diverse histories of these states have left their mark on costume.

Regional dress in the United States, as in Britain, can best be observed at large national meetings where factors such as occupation and income are held relatively constant. At these meetings regional differences stand out clearly, and can be checked by looking at the name tags Americans conventionally wear to conventions. Five distinct styles can be distinguished: (1) Old New England, (2) Deep South, (3) Middle American, (4) Wild West and (5) Far West or Californian. In border areas, outfits usually combine regional styles.

Americans who do not travel much within their own country often misinterpret the styles of other regions. Natives to the Eastern states, for instance, may misread Far Western clothing as indicating greater casualness—or greater sexual availability—than is actually present. The laid-back-looking Los Angeles executive in his open-chested sports shirt and sandals may have his eye on the main chance to an extent that will shock his Eastern colleague. The reverse error can also occur: a Southern Californian may discover with surprise that the sober-hued, buttoned-up New Englander he or she has just met is bored with business and longing to get drunk or hop into bed.

NORTHEAST AND SOUTHEAST: PURITANS AND PLANTERS

The drab, severe costumes of the Puritan settlers of New England,   4
and their suspicion of color and ornament as snares of the devil, have left their mark on the present-day clothes of New Englanders. At any large meeting people from this part of the country will be dressed in darker hues—notably black, gray and navy—often with touches of white that recall the starched collars and cuffs of Puritan costume. Fabrics will be plainer (though heavier and sometimes more expensive) and styles simpler, with less waste of material: skirts and lapels and trimmings will be narrower. More of the men will also wear suits and shoes made in England (or designed to look as if they had been made in England). The law of camouflage also operates in New England, where gray skies and dark rectangular urban landscapes are not unknown.

The distinctive dress of the Deep South is based on a climate that   5
did not demand heavy clothing and an economy that for many years exempted middle- and upper-class whites from all manual labor and made washing and ironing cheap. Today the planter's white suits and fondness for fine linen and wife's and daughters' elaborate and fragile gowns survive in modern form. At our imaginary national meeting the male Southerners will wear lighter-colored suits—pale grays and beiges—and a certain dandyism will be apparent, expressing itself in French cuffs, more expensive ties, silkier materials and wider pin stripes. The women's clothes will be more flowery, with a tendency toward bows, ruffles, lace and embroidery. If they are white, they will probably be as white as possible; a pale complexion is still the sign of a Southern lady, and female sun tans are unfashionable except on tourists.

MIDWEST AND WILD WEST: PIONEERS AND COWBOYS

The American Midwest and Great Plains states were settled by   6
men and women who had to do their own work and prided themselves on it. They chose sturdy, practical clothes that did not show the dirt, washed and wore well and needed little ironing, made of gingham and linsey-woolsey and canvas. From these clothes descends the contemporary costume of Middle Americans. This style is visible to everyone on national television, where it is worn by most

news announcers, politicians, talk-show hosts and actors in commercials for kitchen products. A slightly dowdier version appears in the Sears and Montgomery Ward catalogues. But even when expensive, Middle American fashion is apt to lag behind fashion as it is currently understood back East; it is also usually more sporty and casual. The pioneer regard for physical activity and exercise is still strong in this part of the country, and as a result the Midwesterners at our convention will look healthier and more athletic—and also somewhat beefier—than their colleagues from the cold, damp Northeast and the hot humid South. Their suits will tend toward the tans and browns of plowed cornfields rather than the grays of Eastern skies. More of them will wear white or white-on-white shirts, and their striped or foulard ties will be brighter and patterned on a larger scale than those purchased in sober New York and Boston.

The traditional Western costume, of course, was that of the cowboy on the range. Perhaps because of the isolation of those wide open spaces, this is the style which has been least influenced by those of other regions. At any national convention the Wild Westerners will be the easiest to identify. For one thing, they are apt to be taller—either genetically or with the help of boots. Some may appear in full Western costume, that sartorial equivalent of a "he-went-thataway" drawl; but even the more conservative will betray, or rather proclaim, their regional loyalty through their dress, just as in conversation they will from time to time use a ranching metaphor, or call you "pal" or "pardner." A man in otherwise conventional business uniform will wear what looks like cowboy boots, or a hat with an enlarged brim and crown. Women, too, are apt to wear boots, and their jackets and skirts may have a Western cut, especially when viewed from the rear. Some may wear red or navy-blue bandanna-print shirts or dresses, or an actual cotton-print bandanna knotted around their necks.

THE FAR WEST: ADVENTURERS AND BEACH BOYS

The men and women who settled the Far West were a mixed and rather raffish lot. Restlessness, the wish for excitement, the hope of a fortune in gold and sometimes a need to escape the law led them to undertake the long and dangerous journey over mountains and deserts, or by sea round Cape Horn. In more than one sense they were adventurers, and often desperadoes—desperate people. California was a territory where no one would ask about your past, where unconventionality of character and behavior was easily accepted. Even today when, as the country song puts it, "all the gold in California is in a bank in the middle of Beverly Hills in somebody else's name," the place has the reputation of an El Dorado. Men and women willing to risk everything on long odds in the hope of a big hit, or eager to put legal, financial and personal foul-ups behind them, often go west.

Present day California styles are still in many ways those of adventurers and eccentrics. Whatever the current fashion, the California version will be more extreme, more various and—possibly because of the influence of the large Spanish-American population—much more colorful. Clothes tend to fit more tightly than is considered proper elsewhere, and to expose more flesh: an inability to button the shirt above the diaphragm is common in both sexes. Virtuous working-class housewives may wear outfits that in any other part of the country would identify them as medium-priced whores; reputable business and professional men may dress in a manner which would lose them most of their clients back east and attract the attention of the Bureau of Internal Revenue if not of the police.

Southern Californians, and many other natives of what is now called the Sun Belt (an imaginary strip of land stretching across the bottom of the United States from Florida to Santa Barbara, but excluding most of the Old South), can also be identified by their year-round sun tans, which by middle age have often given the skin the look of old, if expensive and well-oiled, leather. The men may also wear the getup known as Sun Belt Cool: a pale beige suit, open-collared shirt (often in a darker shade than the suit), cream-colored loafers and aviator sunglasses. The female version of the look is similar, except that the shoes will be high-heeled sandals.

REGIONAL DISGUISE: SUNBELT PURITANS AND URBAN COWBOYS

Some long-time inhabitants of California and the other sartorially distinct regions of the United States refuse to wear the styles characteristic of that area. In this case the message is clear: they are unhappy in that locale and/or do not want anyone to attribute to them the traits associated with it. Such persons, if depressed, may adopt a vague and anonymous mode of dress; if in good spirits they may wear the costume of some other region in order to proclaim their sympathy with it. In terms of speech, what we have then is not a regional accent, but the conscious adoption of a dialect by a outsider.

In the urban centers of the West and Far West bankers and financial experts of both sexes sometimes adopt an Eastern manner of

388 CLASSIFICATION AND DIVISION

speech and a Wall Street appearance in order to suggest reliability and tradition. And today in Southern California there are professors who speak with Bostonian accents, spend their days in the library stacks, avoid the beach and dress in clothes that would occasion no comment in Harvard Yard. New arrivals to the area sometimes take these men and women for visiting Eastern lecturers, and are surprised to learn that they have lived in Southern California for thirty or forty years, or have even been born there.

The popularity of the various regional styles of American costume, like that of the various national styles, is also related to economic and political factors. Some years ago modes often originated in the Far West and the word "California" on a garment was thought to be an allurement. Today, with power and population growth shifting to the Southwestern oil-producing states, Wild West styles—particularly those of Texas—are in vogue. This fashion, of course, is not new. For many years men who have never been nearer to a cow than the local steakhouse have worn Western costume to signify that they are independent, tough and reliable. In a story by Flannery O'Connor, for instance, the sinister traveling salesman is described as wearing "a broad-brimmed stiff gray hat of the kind used by businessmen who would like to look like cowboys"—but, it is implied, seldom succeed in doing so. 13

The current popularity of Western costume has been increased by the turn away from foreign modes that has accompanied the recent right-wing shift in the United States politics. In all countries periods of isolationism and a belligerently ostrichlike stance toward the rest of the world have usually been reflected in a rejection of international modes in favor of national styles, often those of the past. Today in America the cowboy look is high fashion, and even in New York City the streets are full of a variety of Wild West types. Some are dressed in old-fashioned, well-worn Western gear; others in the newer, brighter and sleeker outfits of modern ranchers; while a few wear spangled, neon-hued Electric Cowboy and Cowgirl costumes of the type most often seen on Texas country-rock musicians. 14

COMPREHENSION

1. In general, how does Lurie account for the differences in dress that occur from region to region?

2. What scenario does Lurie establish to highlight the differences among regions? Why does she feel this is an appropriate setting?

3. How many categories of American regional dress does Lurie identify? What are they?

4. Why, according to Lurie, do residents of New England tend to wear dark clothing? Why do residents of the Deep South favor light-colored, elaborate styles? How does Lurie account for the contemporary dress of Midwest and Great Plains Americans?

5. Which group does Lurie believe is the easiest to identify? Why does she think this group's dress is the most distinctive?

6. How does Lurie characterize the settlers of the Far West? How have the traits she identifies influenced their dress?

7. Why, according to Lurie, do certain people refuse to wear the styles of clothing that characterize their region?

8. To what does Lurie attribute the recent popularity of Western dress?

PURPOSE AND AUDIENCE

1. Does this essay have an explicitly stated thesis? If so, where does it appear?

2. Is Lurie's intent in this essay to proclaim the superiority of one region's dress over another's, or does she have another motive? How can you tell?

3. In theory at least, every American reader of Lurie's essay will fit into one of her categories. How do you think readers will react to Lurie's descriptions? Does she take their possible reactions into account? Explain.

STYLE AND STRUCTURE

1. In addition to classification and division, Lurie's essay also uses cause and effect, description, and comparison and contrast. Give examples of her use of each strategy.

2. In paragraph 11, Lurie makes a comparison between dress and speech. In what respects are regional dress and regional speech comparable? How are they different? What is the point of her comparison?

3. What principle of classification and division is used in this essay?

4. What scheme does Lurie follow in arranging her categories?

5. Does Lurie include the same kind of information in each section of her essay? Explain.

6. Lurie quotes Flannery O'Connor in paragraph 13 and a country song in paragraph 8. What does each quotation add to the essay?

VOCABULARY PROJECTS

1. Define each of the following words as it is used in this selection.

   homogeneous (1)   foulard (6)
   superficially (1)   sartorial (7)
   Puritan (4)   raffish (8)
   dandyism (5)   allurement (13)
   gingham (6)   isolationism (14)
   linsey-woolsey (6)   belligerently (14)

2. List the adjectives Lurie uses to sketch the principal characteristics of each category of American regional dress. Suggest two or three additional adjectives to describe each region's dress.

3. In this essay Lurie juxtaposes the vocabulary of casual conversation (such as slang terms) with words that suggest a sociological or anthropological perspective. Give several examples of each kind of term. What is the effect of this juxtaposition?

WRITING WORKSHOP

1. What styles of dress are dominant on your college's campus? Establish four or five categories, and write an essay in which you classify students on the basis of dress.

2. Choose a style of dress popularized by a well-known sports or entertainment figure. Analyze the components of this personality's typical costume and write a classification-and-division essay in which you describe each of its aspects in turn.

3. Consider the ways in which films, television shows, musicians, and recreational pursuits affect the styles in which people dress. Then, write a classification-and-division essay on fashion fads.

THEMATIC CONNECTIONS

- "The Patterns of Eating" (p. 167)
- "My First Conk" (p. 217)

THREE KINDS OF DISCIPLINE

John Holt

John Holt was born in 1923 and educated at Yale. He taught elementary school and high school and lectured extensively on educational issues; in addition, he served as a visiting lecturer at Harvard and at the University of California at Berkeley. He founded Growing Without Schooling *magazine in 1977. In addition to numerous magazine articles on education, Holt is the author of* How Children Fail *(1964),* How Children Learn *(1967),* The Underachieving School *(1969),* Freedom and Beyond *(1972),* Escape from Childhood *(1974),* Instead of Education *(1976),* Never Too Late *(1978), and* Teach Your Own *(1981). He died in 1985. In "Three Kinds of Discipline," excerpted from* Freedom and Beyond, *Holt distinguishes among three uses of the word* discipline *by defining each use.*

A child, in growing up, may meet and learn from three different 1 kinds of disciplines. The first and most important is what we might call the Discipline of Nature or of Reality. When he is trying to do something real, if he does the wrong thing or doesn't do the right one, he doesn't get the result he wants. If he doesn't pile one block right on top of another, or tries to build on a slanting surface, his tower falls down. If he hits the wrong key, he hears the wrong note. If he doesn't hit the nail squarely on the head, it bends, and he has to pull it out and start with another. If he doesn't measure properly what he is trying to build, it won't open, close, fit, stand up, fly, float, whistle, or do whatever he wants it to do. If he closes his eyes when he swings, he doesn't hit the ball. A child meets this kind of discipline every time he tries to *do* something, which is why it is so important in school to give children more chances to do things, instead of just reading or listening to someone talk (or pretending to). This discipline is a good teacher. The learner never has to wait long for his answer, it usually comes quickly, often instantly. Also it is clear, and very often points toward the needed correction; from what happened he can not only see that what he did was wrong, but also why, and what he needs to do instead. Finally, and most important, the giver of the answer, call it Nature, is impersonal, impartial, and indifferent. She does not give opinions, or make judgments: she cannot be wheedled, bullied, or fooled; she does not get angry or disappointed; she does not praise or blame; she does not remember past failures or hold grudges; with her one always gets a fresh start, this time is the one that counts.

The next discipline we might call the Discipline of Culture, of 2 Society, of What People Really Do. Man is a social, a cultural animal. Children sense around them this culture, this network of agreements, customs, habits, and rules binding the adults together. They want to understand it and be a part of it. They watch very carefully what people around them are doing and want to do the same. They want to do right, unless they become convinced they can't do right. Thus children rarely misbehave seriously in church, but sit as quietly as they can. The example of all those grownups is contagious. Some mysterious ritual is going on, and children, who like rituals, want to be part of it. In the same way, the little children that I see at concerts or operas, though they may fidget a little, or perhaps take a nap now and then, rarely make any disturbance. With all those grownups sitting there, neither moving nor talking, it is the most natural thing in the world to imitate them. Children who live among adults who are habitually courteous to each other, and to them, will soon learn to be courteous. Children who live surrounded by people who speak a certain way will speak that way, however much we may try to tell them that speaking that way is bad or wrong.

The third discipline is the one most people mean when they speak 3 of discipline—the Discipline of Superior Force, of sergeant to private, of "you do what I tell you or I'll make you wish you had." There is bound to be some of this in a child's life. Living as we do surrounded by things that can hurt children, or that children can hurt, we cannot avoid it. We can't afford to let a small child find out from experience the danger of playing in a busy street, or of fooling with the pots on the top of a stove, or of eating up the pills in the medicine cabinet. So, along with other precautions, we say to him, "Don't play in the street, or touch things on the stove, or go into the medicine cabinet, or I'll punish you." Between him and the danger too great for him to imagine we put a lesser danger, but one he can imagine and maybe therefore wants to avoid. He can have no idea of what it would be like to be hit by a car, but he can imagine being shouted at, or spanked, or sent to his room. He avoids these substitutes for the greater danger until he can understand it and avoid it for its own sake. But we ought to use this discipline only when it is necessary to protect the life, health, safety, or well-being of people or other living creatures, or to prevent destruction of things that people care about. We ought not to assume too long, as we usually do, that a child cannot understand the real nature of the danger from which we want to protect him. The sooner he avoids the danger, not to escape our punishment, but as a matter of good sense, the better. He can learn that faster than we think. In Mexico, for example, where people drive their cars with a good deal of spirit, I saw many children no older than five or four walking unattended on the streets. They understood about cars, they knew what to do. A child whose life is full of the threat and fear of punishment is locked into babyhood. There is no way for him to grow up, to learn to take responsibility for his life and acts. Most important of all, we should not assume that having to yield to the threat of our superior force is good for the child's character. It is never good for *anyone's* character. To bow to superior force makes us feel impotent and cowardly for not having had the strength or courage to resist. Worse, it makes us resentful and vengeful. We can hardly wait to make someone pay for our humiliation, yield to us as we were once made to yield. No, if we cannot always avoid using the Discipline of Superior Force, we should at least use it as seldom as we can.

There are places where all three disciplines overlap. Any very demanding human activity combines in it the disciplines of Superior Force, of Culture, and of Nature. The novice will be told, "Do it this way, never mind asking why, just do it that way, that is the way we always do it." But it probably *is* just the way they always do it, and usually for the very good reason that it is a way that has been found to work. Think, for example, of ballet training. The student in a class is told to do this exercise, or that; to stand so; to do this or that with his head, arms, shoulders, abdomen, hips, legs, feet. He is constantly corrected. There is no argument. But behind these seemingly autocratic demands by the teacher lie many decades of custom and tradition, and behind that, the necessities of dancing itself. You cannot make the moves of classical ballet unless over many years you have acquired, and renewed every day, the needed strength and suppleness in scores of muscles and joints. Nor can you do the difficult motions, making them look easy, unless you have learned hundreds of easier ones first. Dance teachers may not always agree on all the details of teaching these strengths and skills. But no novice could learn them all by himself. You could not go for a night or two to watch the ballet and then, without any other knowledge at all, teach yourself how to do it. In the same way, you would be unlikely to learn any complicated and difficult human activity without drawing heavily on the experience of those who know it better. But the point is that the authority of these experts or teachers stems from, grows out of their greater competence and experience, the fact that what they do *works,* not the fact that they happen to be the teacher and as such have the power to kick a student out of the class. And the further point is that children are always and everywhere attracted to that competence, and ready and eager to submit themselves to a discipline that grows out of it. We hear constantly that children will never do anything unless compelled to by bribes or threats. But in their private lives, or in extracurricular activities in school, in sports, music, drama, art, running a newspaper, and so on, they often submit themselves willingly and wholeheartedly to very intense disciplines, simply because they want to learn to do a given thing well. Our Little-Napoleon football coaches, of whom we have too many and hear far too much, blind us to the fact that millions of children work hard every year getting better at sports and games without coaches barking and yelling at them.

COMPREHENSION

1. Name the three kinds of discipline Holt identifies in his essay, and briefly define each.

2. Why does Holt believe it is so important for a child to have the opportunity to "do things," rather than just to read and listen?

3. Why does Holt consider the first kind of discipline to be "a great teacher"?

4. Why do children tend to imitate the behavior of adults?

5. What, according to Holt, do most people mean by "discipline"? What role does Holt believe this kind of discipline should play in a child's life?

6. Holt acknowledges that the three kinds of discipline overlap. What extended example does he use to illustrate this?

7. What does Holt consider to be the best motivation for discipline in children?

PURPOSE AND AUDIENCE

1. What does Holt hope to accomplish by distinguishing among the three kinds of discipline? How do you know?

2. Holt expects his essay to be read by parents and educators—readers who have a built-in interest in his topic. Find examples of how Holt's

knowledge of this audience's needs and expectations has influenced his presentation.

3. What do you think Holt expects the example about the Mexican children to contribute to his essay? Explain.

STYLE AND STRUCTURE

1. Why do you think Holt chose not to begin his essay by listing the three kinds of discipline?

2. How does the use of repetition and parallelism in paragraph 1 ("If he hits," "If he doesn't hit," "If he doesn't measure," etc., and "She does not," "she cannot," etc.) enhance the points Holt is making there?

3. What determines the paragraph divisions of the first three paragraphs?

4. How do the topic sentences of this essay help to link the paragraphs into a coherent whole?

5. Ideally, a classification-and-division essay will have categories that are mutually exclusive. Does Holt's admission in paragraph 4 that all three of his disciplines overlap weaken his essay? What justification can you offer for this overlap?

VOCABULARY PROJECTS

1. Define each of the following words as it is used in this selection.
   wheedled (1)   autocratic (4)
   impotent (3)   suppleness (4)
   novice (4)

2. The word *discipline,* which is central to this essay, has a number of different meanings. Consulting a good desk dictionary, summarize in one paragraph all the meanings the word may have when it is used as a noun. You will need to expand the dictionary entry with examples to write an effective paragraph.

WRITING WORKSHOP

1. Write a classification-and-division essay in which you distinguish among kinds of rewards or kinds of punishments that a parent or teacher can use when disciplining children. Direct your essay to an audience of teachers or parents of young children. Your thesis state-

ment should indicate the relative merits of the different rewards or punishments you examine.

2. Classify parents—your own and those of your friends—on the basis of what kind of discipline they practice (how strict or lenient they are, how consistent they are, or how creative their practices are, for example). Take a stand in favor of one kind of discipline.

3. Write an essay in which you classify children according to their behavior in school, sports, or social situations. You may create categories like "the model child," "the leader," "the extrovert," and "the bully" to help you organize your discussion. Be sure to describe typical members of each category fully, and include examples where necessary.

THEMATIC CONNECTIONS

- "Shooting an Elephant" (p. 85)
- "Aria: A Memoir of a Bilingual Childhood" (p. 348)

RULE OF LAW

Joseph Lelyveld

Born in 1937, Joseph Lelyveld graduated from Harvard Univer-
sity. Currently the Foreign Editor for the New York Times, *Lely-*
veld has also reported for the Times *in India, Hong Kong, and the*
United States. In addition, he has served twice as the Times *corre-*
spondent in South Africa. In 1984 he received a Guggenheim Fel-
lowship, and he has twice been the recipient of the George Polk
Memorial Award, once for his reports on South Africa. In his 1985
book Move Your Shadow, *Lelyveld is sharply critical of South Af-*
rica's system of apartheid. "Rule of Law," excerpted from Move
Your Shadow, *explains how the apartheid system mandates the*
irrational and arbitrary classification of blacks into various
groups. In this sense apartheid is "the ultimate divide-and-rule
strategy."

It's time to talk law. Where other regimes have no difficulty tyran- 1
nizing their citizens under the cloak of constitutions guaranteeing
universal human rights, South Africa's white rulers have been unusually conscientious about securing statutory authority for their
abuses. When a right, even a birthright, such as citizenship, is to be
annulled, it is always done with a law. Most whites are uncompre-
hending of the argument that law is brought into disrepute when
it is used to destroy habeas corpus, the presumption of innocence,
equality before the law, and various other basic freedoms. Law is
law. It's the principle of order and therefore of civilization, the antithesis advanced by the white man to what he knows as a matter
of tribal lore, his own, to be Africa's fundamental thesis: anarchy.
Excessive liberty, in his view, is what threatens civilization; law is
what preserves it. The opposing view that law might preserve liberty is thus held to be a contradiction; in Africa, a promise of surrender. On this basis, it has been possible to build apartheid not simply
as the sum of various kinds of segregation, or the disenfranchise-
ment of the majority, but as a comprehensive system of racial dominance. A decade after the South African authorities announced
their intention to move away from "hurtful and unnecessary discrimination," I thought I would get the feel of the basic statutes by
holding them in my hands as you might if you were apprizing an

eggplant or a melon. Some laws, especially those reserving the best industrial jobs for whites, had been repealed. Others, such as the Prohibition of Mixed Marriages Act, seemed destined for repeal as part of a calculated effort to lower the level of ignominy attaching to the system. I wanted to feel, literally to weigh, what remained.

What remained weighed slightly more than ten pounds when I   2 stepped on a scale with an up-to-date volume of all the laws in South Africa that relate specifically to blacks—laws, that is, that can normally be broken only by blacks (or by persons of other racial groups only when they interfere with the state's master plan for blacks). The figure of ten pounds had to be halved immediately because the volume of 4,500 pages contained both the Afrikaans and English version of sixty-four basic statutes that regulate the lives of blacks. These then amounted to about 2,250 closely printed pages, weighing about five pounds. But the small print that followed the statutes indicated that they had given rise to some 2,000 regulations, adding two or three pounds at least. These, in turn, would have given rise to hundreds or maybe thousands of official circulars that were not in the public domain but were treated as law by the officials who regulate blacks. And that was only the racial law for blacks. There were also laws, regulations, and circulars for coloreds and Indians, running to hundreds of additional pages and another couple of pounds. And there were laws, regulations, and circulars relating to the administration of the Group Areas Act, the basic statute guaranteeing absolute resident segregation. Gathering all the materials for a precise weighing was more than I could manage; but the basic corpus of South African racial law still ran to more than 3,000 pages, and when all the regulations and circulars were added in, its dead weight was bound to be well over ten pounds. Apartheid was not wasting away. For argument's sake, there was enough of it left to give someone a concussion. And this still did not include the mass of draconian security laws and the other legislation restricting political association and expression, which are certainly oppressive but not as distinctively South African.

Of course, the impact of apartheid cannot be measured in pounds.   3 A South African Gogol may contrive a way someday to measure it in "dead souls." But I could measure it only by trying to witness the system in operation, at the points where it impinges on individual lives, especially in the mazelike structure of courts and official bureaus it has established to channel black laborers in and out of areas of economic opportunity while minimizing their chances of establishing permanent residence with their families. If this structure were suddenly dismantled, if whites stopped regulating black lives, there would still be migrant workers by the hundreds of thousands in South Africa and millions of impoverished blacks. There would still be wealthy suburbs, hugh ranches, black townships, and squalid rural areas. But it would then be possible to think of the society as a whole and talk rationally about its needs. Apartheid ensures that the language for such a discussion hardly exists. It does so for its own cunning reasons. Once you think of the society as a whole, it is impossible not to think of the distribution of land—50,000 white farmers have twelve times as much land for cultivation and grazing as 14 million rural blacks—or of the need to relieve the pressure in those portions of the countryside that have been systematically turned into catchment areas for surplus black population.

If South Africa were viewed as one country, it might be possible 4 to recognize a glaring fact about its social geography: the existence of an almost continuous scimitar-shaped belt of black rural poverty, stretching for more than 1,000 miles from the northeastern Transvaal through the Swazi and Zulu tribal areas and down into the two "homelands" for Xhosa-speaking blacks in the eastern Cape, a belt that is inhabited by about 7 million people, amounting to nearly 30 percent of the black population. Instead, in the layered, compartmentalized consciousness that apartheid insidiously shapes, these blacks are dispersed in Venda, Gazankulu, Lebowa, KwaZulu, Transkei, and Ciskei: foreign places, hard to find on maps, another galaxy.

In apartheid's terms, it is revolutionary or at least eccentric to 5 think of this band of poverty as South Africa's problem. Apartheid thus raises the stakes, deliberately compounding mass rural poverty in order to preserve white privilege and power. It is the ultimate divide-and-rule strategy, dividing the land into racially designated areas and bogus homelands and the population into distinct racial castes and subcastes of which I can count at least eight: the whites, who are free to do anything except move into an area designated as nonwhite; the coloreds and Indians, who can move freely in the country but are barred from owning land in more than 95 percent of it; and the blacks, who are subdivided by law into six distinct impermeable or semipermeable categories.

The broad distinction between urban and rural blacks is only the 6 beginning of this process of alienation. The urban blacks come in two subcastes: the "insiders," as they are now sometimes called, and the "commuters." The insiders are conceded to have a certain immunity to arbitrary expulsion, amounting to a right of permanent residence in what is acknowledged to be South Africa. The circumstances of the urban commuters appear to be exactly the same, except that the townships in which they reside are not deemed, as a result of gerrymandering, to fall within the boundaries of some homeland. Although they may be only a short bus ride from a South African city such as Pretoria, Durban, or East London, no farther than the blacks of Soweto are from Johannesburg, they are regarded by South African law as foreign or on their way to becoming foreign. But such commuters can still get "special" licenses of limited duration making them "authorized work seekers" in an urban area.

This means they are still far better off than a second group of commuters who must be regarded as a separate subcaste because they commute to the industrial centers from homeland areas that remain essentially rural. These rural commuters are on a distinctly lower level of the hierarchy, but it can be argued that they are the most privileged or, rather, least abused of the four distinguishable subcastes of rural blacks. The rural commuters generally travel much longer distances to work than the urban commuters, live in officially designated "closer settlements" without such amenities as running water or electricity, rather than organized townships, and get their jobs through the state's network of labor bureaus. They generally work on annual contracts like migrant laborers, but at least they come home to their families at night and on weekends.   7

The migrants, the next subcaste, live in urban townships or on the mines and sugar plantations in barrackslike single-sex hostels, usually for eleven months of every year; it is theoretically possible for some of them to acquire a right of urban residence after ten or fifteen years but practically impossible for them to acquire a house in which to exercise it.   8

Blacks who live in the white rural areas as farm laborers make up the next subcaste; by tradition they receive more of their compensation in kind—sacks of mealie (corn) meal usually—than in cash, but wages are gradually coming into vogue. And finally, there are the homeland blacks, who live their whole lives in the black rural areas. Of these, a tiny elite is employed by the homeland governments as officials, teachers, or police; others are employed as menials. But overall the former tribal reserves provide gainful employment for fewer that 20 percent of the young blacks reared within their borders, only 12 percent, according to a statistic let slip by a white Cabinet minister who was trying to counter extremist arguments during a political campaign that too much was done for blacks. The rest of the homeland blacks—those who cannot become migrants themselves—are mainly dependent on the wages of migrants, or scratch out a meager existence as subsistence cultivators on exhausted soil, or are unemployed and wholly destitute. The life-   9

threatening protein deficiency known as kwashiorkor and the starvation condition known as marasmus are endemic among children
in this group. Reliable statistics are spotty, but in some black rural
areas in a country that has been aptly described as the Saudi Arabia
of minerals, it appears that scarcely 50 percent of the children who
are alive at birth survive past the age of five.

A lopsided social structure is not peculiar to South Africa. What   10
is peculiar is the fact that it is legally mandated and rigorously imposed on the basis of race. It is impossible to change caste without
an official appeals board ruling that you are a different color from
what you were originally certified to be. These miraculous transformations are tabulated and announced on an annual basis. In my
first year back in South Africa, 558 coloreds became whites, 15
whites became coloreds, 8 Chinese became whites, 7 whites became
Chinese, 40 Indians became coloreds, 20 coloreds became Indians,
79 Africans became coloreds, and 8 coloreds became Africans. The
spirit of this grotesque self-parody, which results from the delibera-
tions of an official body known as the Race Classification Board, is
obviously closer to Grand Guignol than the Nuremberg Laws; in
other words, it's sadistic farce. "Look, man, it's all a game, it's all
a big joke," I was assured once by a Cape Town colored who had
managed to get himself reclassified as a white, a transformation
sometimes described in Afrikaans by the term *verblankingsproses*
("whitening process").

"When you're in Rome," the man said, "what are you? A bloody   11
German? Hell, no, you're a Roman! Self-preservation is the only
rule."

The legal definitions that attach to the various categories of racial   12
caste are vague, overlapping, and sometimes contradictory. A
white, by one of the definitions, is "any person who in appearance
obviously is or who is generally accepted as a white person, other
than a person who, although in appearance obviously a white person, is generally accepted as a colored person." In other words, a
rose is a rose is maybe not a rose. "A colored person," this same
statute holds, is "any person who is not a member of the white
group or of the black group."* But a colored can also be any woman
"to whichever race, class or tribe she may belong" who marries a
colored man, or a white man who marries a colored woman. Mixed
marriages may have been illegal throughout the apartheid era—as
they were, lest we forget, in a majority of American states within

---

*Unless, of course, he is an Indian, who may be the same color but is legally set
apart on the basis of ethnicity, most of the time, anyhow.

living memory—but even when the South African law prohibiting them is finally repealed, there will still be this other racial statute to bar mixed couples from living in white areas.

Apartheid never concerned itself with mixed marriages between browns and blacks. They remained legal. It was only the white race that had to be preserved. Carel Boshoff, a theology professor at Pretoria University and son-in-law of Hendrik Verwoerd, informed me as if it were a matter of incontrovertible facts that a group could be diluted by 6 or 7 percent and still maintain its "identity." In fact, Afrikaner researchers in this esoteric field have concluded that 6.9 percent is the probable proportion of "colored blood" in their veins. Racism, it then may be deduced, is no more that 93.1 percent in their doctrine. Nevertheless, classification remains the essence of the system. No one—least of all a black—has the right to classify himself as simply a South African. Thus the single most important determinant of status and rights in South Africa remains the accident of birth. Most white South Africans would dispute this assertion, but then most white South Africans have insulated themselves from any knowledge of how the system works. 13

COMPREHENSION

1. How, according to Lelyveld, does the view of the South African white rulers toward the concept of law differ from the view held by other regimes?

2. What does Lelyveld's physically weighing the documents pertaining to South African racial law demonstrate to him?

3. What does Lelyveld believe would remain the same if the apartheid system were dismantled? What does he think would change?

4. What "glaring fact" does Lelyveld believe would be apparent if South Africa were to be viewed as one country?

5. What does Lelyveld classify in "Rule of Law"? List the categories he identifies.

6. What is the relationship between Lelyveld's classification and the points he makes about South African law?

7. What, according to Lelyveld, is particularly unusual about South Africa's "lopsided social structure"?

8. In paragraph 13 Lelyveld observes that "classification remains the essence of the system." Explain.

9. In paragraph 3 Lelyveld says that he was able to measure the impact of the apartheid system "only by trying to witness the system in operation"; in paragraph 13 he asserts that "most white South Africans have insulated themselves from any knowledge of how the system works." What point do these two statements, taken together, make about the apartheid system?

10. What does Lelyveld mean when he says that "the single most important determinant of status and rights in South Africa remains the accident of birth" (13)?

PURPOSE AND AUDIENCE

1. Identify the selection's thesis. Then, restate that thesis in a single sentence that explains the significance of the classification Lelyveld presents.

2. *Move Your Shadow,* the book from which "Rule of Law" is excerpted, was published in the United States. What assumptions does Lelyveld make about the reaction of his American audience to his subject? How can you tell?

3. In paragraph 12 Lelyveld notes that until quite recently marriages between blacks and whites were illegal in the United States. What is his purpose in including this information?

4. Lelyveld uses the first person (*I*) in his discussion. What effect does he expect this voice to have on his audience?

5. Throughout "Rule of Law" Lelyveld quotes and paraphrases government officials and refers to specific government statutes. What motives does he have for doing so?

6. What does Lelyveld hope to accomplish in paragraph 10 by enumerating the "miraculous transformations"?

STYLE AND STRUCTURE

1. Where does Lelyveld actually begin his classification? How does he introduce it? Where does the classification end?

2. What transitions does Lelyveld use to indicate movement from one category of his classification to the next?

3. From what principle of classification does Lelyveld derive his categories?

4. What determines the order in which Lelyveld introduces his categories? Is this the most effective order? Explain.

5. Lelyveld's attitude toward apartheid is clearly highly critical. How does his language reveal his negative attitude? Give specific examples.

6. Do any of Lelyveld's categories overlap? Explain.

VOCABULARY PROJECTS

1. Define each of the following words as it is used in this selection.

disrepute (1)	castes (5)
antithesis (1)	impermeable (5)
anarchy (1)	gerrymandering (6)
disenfranchisement (1)	hostels (8)
apprizing (1)	kind (9)
ignominy (1)	menials (9)
corpus (2)	destitute (9)
draconian (2)	endemic (9)
cunning (3)	incontrovertible (13)
catchment (3)	esoteric (13)
scimitar (4)	deduced (13)
insidiously (4)	

2. Some terms that Lelyveld uses are indigenous to South Africa (*apartheid*) and others have a special meaning there (*colored*). Identify as many such terms as you can, and define each.

3. Use a dictionary to help you to determine the origin of each of these words: *corpus, draconian, gerrymander, theology, apartheid.*

WRITING WORKSHOP

1. Classify the people in your neighborhood or city, or the students at your school, according to the degree of privilege each group enjoys. To help you keep your groups from overlapping, give each group a name that distinguishes it from the others.

2. Devise a classification system for a group of novels, films, or television shows, classifying the individual items on the basis of their portrayal of a particular minority group.

3. Imagine a society of the future, either an ideal one or a nightmare world. Classify its citizens in a way that will support your thesis about the desirability of such a society.

THEMATIC CONNECTIONS

- "Shooting an Elephant" (p. 85)
- "The Untouchable" (p. 430)

HISTORICAL FICTION, FICTITIOUS HISTORY, AND CHESAPEAKE BAY BLUE CRABS, OR, ABOUT ABOUTNESS

John Barth

John Barth, award-winning novelist and writer of numerous short stories and essays, was born in 1930 in Cambridge, Maryland, and was educated at Johns Hopkins University. He has taught at Pennsylvania State University, the State University of New York at Buffalo, and Johns Hopkins. Barth's published works include The Floating Opera, The End of the Road, The Sot-Weed Factor, Giles Goat Boy, Lost in the Funhouse, Letters, Chimera *(winner of the 1973 National Book Award for fiction), and* Sabbatical *(1982). The essay that follows began as a 1979 talk delivered to a dinner meeting of the Dorchester County Historical Society in Cambridge, Maryland; it also appeared in* The Friday Book, *a 1984 collection of Barth's essays and lectures. A slightly amended version of the talk, reproduced here, was published in the July 15, 1979,* Washington Post Sunday Magazine. *In his remarks, Barth classifies Chesapeake Bay blue crabs into five categories to make a point about the written representation of historical events.*

This article will not quite be about what its title says it's about: historical fiction and fictitious history. 1

The fact is, I recently finished writing a novel called *Letters* that happens to involve the Chesapeake Bay area and to some extent its history, particularly the late 1960s and the period of the 1812 War; 20 years ago I published another, *The Sot-Weed Factor*, set in colonial Maryland. Both are more or less "historical" fiction, and for both I did a respectable amount of homework on the periods involved. But it was a novelist's homework, not a historian's, and novelists are the opposite of icebergs: 90 percent of what I once knew about this region's history, and have since forgotten, is in plain view on the surface of those two novels, where it serves its fictive purposes without making the author any sort of authority. Since *The Sot-Weed Factor* isn't finally "about" colonial Maryland at all, any 2

406

more than *Letters* is really "about" the burning of Washington in
1814 or the burning of Cambridge, [Maryland] in 1967, I'm already
uncertain which of their historical details are real and which I
dreamed up.

For example, I recall a fine anecdote about the first murder ever
committed by white folks in colonial Maryland. It happened not
long after the original settlers disembarked from the *Ark* and the
Dove in 1632: fellow killed his wife, or vice-versa. No problem appre-
hending the murderer, who obligingly confessed at once. The trouble
was, there were no courts to try him in, no statutes to try him under,
and no jails to sentence him to. So the Governor's Council, by a rap
of the gavel, turned itself into a board of inquest, took depositions,
and found a true bill; turned itself into a court, heard the case, and
found the defendant guilty of murder, turned itself into a legislative
body and ruled that murder is against the law; turned itself back
into a court and sentenced the guilty party to hang; then commuted
the sentence lest there be, in all this improvising, a miscarriage of
justice. That solved *their* problem; *my* problem, an occupational haz-
ard of storytellers, is that I can't remember how much of this story
is history and how much is fiction.

Fictitious history is something that my *Letters* novel *is* more or
less about: false documents, falsified documents, forged and doctored letters and the like, in the history of History. But I'd rather
you read the novel when Putnam's brings it out in the fall.

The next thing that these remarks will emphatically not be about
is Mr. James A. Michener's recent best-selling novel *about* the Chesapeake Bay/Choptank River area, my native turf. Mr. Michener and
I are respectful acquaintances, but I can't comment about his novel
about the Chesapeake for the excellent reason that I haven't read
it; and I haven't read it, as I've explained to the author, because
I've been too busy for the past seven years writing my own.

But my books, as aforedeclared, are *not* finally about tidewater
Maryland and its history. There are obvious differences in the way
history and fiction are about what they're about; there are differences just as important, but maybe less obvious, in the way different kinds of fiction are about what they're about. These different
kinds of "aboutness" are my topic here: I want to speak about
aboutness.

Now, storytellers and Chesapeake Bay blue crabs have something
in common: they usually approach what they're after sideways. I
shall say what I have to say about aboutness by way of five different Chesapeake Bay blue crabs—rather, five pictures or other representations of crabs. Never mind that you can't see them all; I'll de-

scribe them to our purpose. Anyhow, the first of the five crab representations I don't have before me, and the fifth doesn't exist. We shall use our imaginations, as both fictionists and historians do, in their different ways.

The first rendition of a blue crab that I want you to imagine is   8 one of those large preserved ones mounted on a wall plaque on the wall of some local seafood restaurant. Doesn't matter which restaurant, or which crab. Let's notice certain things about it.

First and obviously, it isn't "fiction": it's made from mortal re-   9 mains of an actual, "historical" animal, preserved by a taxidermist. The degree of realism in the representation is therefore considerable, though it's relative and so to speak "historical": we have the skeleton only; the living, breathing breast is gone, and with it the feel, taste, smell, etc. of the real thing. Its sensory aspects have been reduced to just one, really: the visual aspect. It looks a lot like a crab, even though the colors are a sort of mortician's approximation of life; there can be no question about its general external accuracy. If we consider what the purposes of such a representation are— which is another way of asking what this crab is "about"—I think we'll agree that it has at least five: 1) to help decorate the restaurant; 2) in doing so, to evoke the tidewater atmosphere by means of a bit of natural-historical realism and thereby 3) to whet our appetites for what we've come there for; in other words, and on the bottom line, 4) to sell seafood dinners at a profit to the owners of the crab and of the restaurant, while incidentally 5) standing as a historical record of an actual crab caught somewhere in the surrounding waters. We'll return to these purposes presently.

Our second and third blue crabs were both rendered by staff art-   10 ists of the National Geographic Magazine as illustrations for accompanying text. Number two is color foldout entitled "Marsh Fauna": it has a lot of other things in it besides the blue crab; he or she is tucked down in the lower right-hand corner, about to grab an anchovy lunch. Number three is a pen-and-ink drawing entitled "Blue crab: main cog in an 'immense protein factory.'" In both of these representations, as in the first one, there's considerable realism in the way of anatomical or biological accuracy. The colors aren't quite right, of course, even in the foldout, and the drawing is in black and white, as no actual blue crab ever was. Both of them translate the three dimensions of historical blue crabs into two dimensions. And both, unlike the first one, represent no individual, "historical" crab, but rather a generalized, typical, "fictitious" crab. The foldout painting adds an improbable amount of other simultaneous ecological action—all sorts of Marsh Fauna engaged in eating one another up; more such action than anybody ever saw at once, even in Indian times—and it presumes further to show us what's going on under the water and inside the mudflats. But we don't object to this exaggeration of the "historical" facts, because we understand the instructional-scientific purpose of the foldout: namely, to illustrate the actual ecology of a Chesapeake marsh by distorting the time-frame, by cutting away certain factual barriers to normal human vision, and by moving the whole scene from the inconvenient reality of three physical dimensions (plus scale, motion, smell, feel, taste, and sound) to the convenience of two visual dimensions, scaled down, frozen in action, and approximated in color. We don't mistake it for reality, though it's inspired by reality. We don't mistake it for science, though it grows out of science. We don't mistake it for fine art, either, though the artist is properly called a staff artist and is good at his/her trade. We would not likely frame and hang the original on our walls as art, much less expect to see it in the National Gallery or the Louvre or the Metropolitan—though I confess that my particular copy has been carried around with me for some seven years, from Buffalo to Boston to Baltimore, to remind me of all the life and death that goes on constantly in the place I was writing about.

The pen drawing, crab number three—"Blue crab: main cog" [11] etc.—is even more striking, and our reaction to it more interesting to think about. It's a meticulously realistic drawing; we're likely to admire it even more than the color foldout, not only because the detail is finer, but because, paradoxically, it is at the same time more realistic and farther removed from reality than those other crab images. Not only are feel, taste, sound, smell, scale, depth, motion, and environment removed (not to mention literal life), but also any attempt to approximate the actual color of the subject. The very black-and-whiteness of the drawing, and the absence of any background, make us sharply aware that this is an ink-drawing, not the real thing; and that awareness enhances rather than diminishes our pleasure in it. In fact, this drawing might be said to be not only "about" the Chesapeake Bay blue crab, but about pen and ink as well, and shading and foreshortening and such—in other words, it's partly about the art of drawing—and we admire it, if we do, precisely because the artist is able to evoke the reality of blue crabs with material so far removed from that reality as a pen and black ink and white paper. Number three here we might actually hang with pleasure on the wall of our office, or our kitchen, if we had the original well matted and framed, even though its bottom-line purpose, like that of the mounted crab earlier, is to sell us something: in this case, not restaurant meals for profit, but subscriptions to the organ of a non-profit scientific and educational society. And even though we realize, consciously or intuitively, that number three is "about" line and shape and shading as well as "about" the blue crab and, by extension, about the life and culture of the Chesapeake Bay estuarine system, we don't expect to see this drawing in a museum of fine art, for the simple but important reason that it's more about the crab than about the medium of drawing, and while it's professionally admirable draftsmanship, something tells us that there's a difference between competent, accurate draftsmanship and fine art.

Our fourth crab image is crawling up my necktie as I write: a gold-plated tie-tac in the semblance of a crab, purchased as a gift and worn as a souvenir. It is not *Callinectes sapidus*, the Chesapeake blue crab. Its carapace more resembles something in the Dungeness or purple marsh crab family—but it isn't purple, and there's no detail to speak of beyond the correct number and location of the legs. It's a stylized version of a crab, designed for inexpensive manufacture and retail sale at a high profit margin to people like myself who may like to be reminded, when they put their neckties on, or remind others whom they then see, that the world contains objects somewhat like this called *crabs,* fun to catch and good to eat, and maybe, by extension, that the world contains the Chesapeake Bay and Eastern Shore thereof: interesting and even beautiful places to work and play and live in, with more or less interesting cultural, political, and geological history; and, by further extension yet, that the wearer of the tie-tac, while he knows the difference not only between it and a real crab but also between it and a realistic representation of a crab, nevertheless enjoys being reminded, even crudely, of the real thing and its associations, and reminding others likewise. He might even be reminding you that he's *part* of the real thing, or once was, or wishes he were: a member of the tidewater culture, or a familiar of it.

In this case, the purpose of the designer (we don't even use the term *staff artist*) is to make some money by trading inexpensively (to him- or herself) on these innocent wishes and pleasures of ours. My tie-tac is not *about* crabs in any remarkable, thoughtful, interesting, or even careful way. Nor is it *about* the art of costume jewelry in any remarkable, thoughtful, interesting, or careful way—as a gold brooch by Benvenuto Cellini cast by the lost-wax method from an actual fly or beetle might be, for example. What it's about, from the designer's point of view, is low-budget commercialized nostalgia; from the wearer's point of view, it's about the gratification or advertisement of that nostalgia. The wearer's motives, we might notice in passing, are relatively innocent; the manufacturer's are relatively mercenary. I shall return to this point

There is a curious phenomenon involved here that can make an   14
artist tear his hair, though it's perfectly understandable and, up to a point, forgivable. Anyone who happens to have traveled through the Netherlands will have found that Dutch gift shops are as full of toy wooden shoes and cheap china windmills as tidewater Maryland gift shops are of junk-art mallard duck prints and fake goose decoys and so much stuff with cattails and skipjacks and tongboats on it, often so clumsily or cheaply rendered, that one feels like setting out at once for Honolulu or Montreal or even Ohio, where they've scarcely heard of such things; or else for the Dorchester County marshes, where there's nothing between oneself and the real McCoy. But the curious thing is that the main purchasers of this sentimental-picturesque junk, after the tourists, are the natives. The Dutch happen to love very much their dikes and canals and windmills and wooden shoes and tulips; so much so that even when the outside of a Dutch farmhouse is surrounded by the genuine article, the inside is likely to be decorated with plastic tulips stuck in simulated *Klompen* made out of imitation Delftware imported from Hong Kong. The same goes for Eastern Shore folk, I've noticed, and I daresay it goes for any other people who happen to love their culture and/or its history.

What's likely to drive an artist bananas is certainly not this inno-   15
cent enjoyment of their culture by its natives, even when that culture is trivialized, vulgarized, and commercially exploited by outsiders or by insiders (often the worst offenders). When the artist tears his/her hair, or at least rolls his/her eyes, is when people mistake the junk for quality stuff: when they lose sight of the difference between a true and honest backfin crabcake, for example, and some third-rate restaurant's version of the same thing, whether that restaurant is a fast-food joint or a pretentious, high-overhead rip-off. Third rate is third rate, no matter how impressive the packaging and promotion. I don't suppose that any native Chesapeaker would be taken in by a third-rate crabcake masquerading as gourmet food—and gourmet food is what a *first*-rate crabcake is. I wish I could be as confident of native judgment in the other matter, to which we now return.

The fifth and last rendition of a blue crab in this series, like the   16
first, I don't have before me, but for a different reason: I don't believe it exists yet. It's the one which, if it did exist, might very well hang in the Louvre, or the National Gallery, or the Amsterdam Rijks museum, even though the people who came to see it might

never have seen a blue crab, live or steamed, or know where Maryland is, unless they looked it up or came around the world to visit because they loved the drawing so. I wish there were a Rembrandt drawing of a crab, blue or otherwise, to illustrate my point; but they don't have *Callinectes sapidus* in the North Sea, and Rembrandt didn't go in much for still lifes anyhow, though he *was* very big on windmills and canal boats. The best I could find in my library is a reproduction of a Rembrandt pen-and-wash drawing of a different animal: two birds of paradise, done in whites and grey-yellows about 1637, five years after Lord Baltimore's first colonists stepped ashore in Maryland and committed the first recorded murder in the Old Line State. The original does in fact hang in the Louvre. I invite you to notice two things about it.

First, there's much less *information* about birds of paradise in 17 Rembrandt's drawing than there is about the Common Egret or the Long-Billed Marsh Wren in the "Marsh Fauna" foldout. The Rembrandt would not be much use to a birdwatcher for field identification, whereas the foldout even shows us what the birds eat and where they find it. The second thing to notice is the caption commentary by the critic who put my library-volume together, a professor of fine arts at Harvard's Fogg Museum: "The way these exotic birds fill the page," Professor Slive remarks, "is as admirable as Rembrandt's depiction of the different weights and textures of the feathers on their heads, necks, bodies, and great tails."

This is an extension of what we noted about the blue-crab drawing 18 in pen and ink: a lot of the reality of birds of paradise is in Rembrandt's drawing, no doubt; maybe even more than of crab-reality in the National Geographic staff artist's. But it isn't there by meticulous copying of detail (not to mention color, size, depth, feel, sound, smell, motion, and lice under the wings). The Rembrandt is certainly "about" birds of paradise, but as Professor Slive's commentary makes clear, it's at least as much *about* the composition of forms on the page, the arrangements of darks and lights, the suggestion of weights and textures by quick and masterful strokes of the pen and the brush: in other words, it's about as much about the art of drawing as it is about what it's a drawing *of,* and since it's about both of these things in a masterful way, it hangs in the Louvre instead of in a Route 50 emporium for the Ocean City trade.

We could go further and imagine a version by some 20th-century 19 Rembrandt in which that former kind of "aboutness," the bird of paradise itself, might fly the coop altogether. If the second kind of aboutness were still powerful and fine enough, the work mightn't be in the Louvre, but it might well be in the Museum of Modern Art or the National Gallery's new East Wing, with the other abstractionists: painting that is entirely, or almost entirely, about itself and its materials; in which the "subject," if any, is just a point of departure, like the melody-line among good jazz musicians.

The aim of my remarks is plain: the analogy between these several 20 categories of crab-art and some different ways in which a piece of writing can be "about" a place, such as the lower Eastern Shore of Maryland, and/or about a historical moment, such as the guerilla warfare of Joseph Whaland's Loyalist Picaroons in the Dorchester marshes during the Revolutionary War, or the Cambridge race riots of the 1960s.

The mounted prize crabs on the restaurant wall, let's say, are like 21 the documents of history: those early-19th-century wills in the Dorchester County Courthouse, for example, where black human beings and bedroom furniture are given away in the same sentence. From such documentary shucks and sheds, the historiographer tries to infer what happened in a human place and time: he reconstructs the political, social-economic, and cultural past; how things hung together and were done, their causes and effects. If he's knowledgeable and scrupulous, he keeps speculation and conscious bias to a minimum and tries to beware the unconscious biases and cultural assumptions that he can doubtless never entirely avoid. The result will be the verbal equivalent of that National Geographic foldout: a good deal of information efficiently, attractively, and authoritatively presented, which we might even read for pleasure as well as for reference. It isn't literature, in the capital-L sense of the term (unless the author happens to be a Herodotus or a Carlyle), but it's honest and useful work, usually low-paying and done mainly for the love of knowledge, like pure science.

The historical novelist, too, might make use of those documentary 22 crabshells and dramatize not only what happened, but what it might have felt like to be a live human being experiencing that history in that place.

There's a much greater likelihood here that the author will project 23 his/her contemporary sensibility back onto our ancestors—one large reason why most historical fiction is a pretty fishy rendition of a crab—but we're talking about *fiction* now, and since our bottom line in reading fiction is to illuminate our own experience of life, a case can be made for that kind of distortion. Anyhow, if the novelist happens to be a fine literary artist like Charles Dickens (I'm thinking now of his novel "about" the French Revolution), what he turns out won't be a proper historical novel at all, but a work of literature. *A Tale of Two Cities* is obviously not about the French Revolution in the way that Carlyle's *History of the French Revolution* is, not to mention the actual documents of the Reign of Terror: it's about love, loyalty, and self-sacrifice among human beings pungently rendered, not among puppets sent down from Central Casting. The same goes for Tolstoy's *War and Peace* or Stendhal's *Charterhouse of Parma:* they're about the Napoleonic wars, for sure—but so is Puccini's opera *Tosca*—and that fact is the least interesting thing about those works of art, even though their authors happen to have done their homework.

But now I'm ahead of my hardcrabs. It should be added, before we leave the crabshells and the foldouts, that the forged and doctored and suppressed documents of history—from the 9th-century *Donation of Constantine* which "justified" the Holy Roman Empire, to the 20th-century falsified reports that led to the Tonkin Gulf Resolution—share the same bottom line with faked restaurant atmosphere: to sell us a bill of goods. Even the honest historian, to be sure, wants to sell us his point of view, though not particularly for gain, and not by distorting the evidence systematically to fit a thesis. And good historical novelists such as Robert Graves or Mary Renault are like good restaurateurs: they're not in business for their health, but they apparently enjoy what they're doing and do it well, at a small or large profit, and they don't stuff their crab imperial full of breadcrumbs and cheap mayonnaise, or sell claw meat at backfin prices. [24]

Their books might be compared to that pen-and-ink drawing in the National Geographic advertisement. So might that lovely nonfiction work of William Warner's, *Beautiful Swimmers:* full of honest information about *Callinectes sapidus* and its environment, skillfully presented, rich in detail, ably written, and attractively illustrated. Great literature it may not be, in the Louvre/National Gallery sense, but it surely ranks with the best writing *about* the Chesapeake area. [25]

Now: about the literary equivalent of my tie-tac, the less said the better: its perpetrators are over-publicized already. These are your flat-out, big-time, big-money book-of-the-monthers, the James Rouses of literature, who move in on a culture or a subject and "work it up" like a real-estate developer with high-rise megabucks under a low profile. It's tempting to say "under a low-*brow* profile," but your tie-tac writers are often smart cookies indeed, even civilized and likeable, though the size of their egos is breathtaking. Their belief that what they manufacture is Literature is as remarkable as if James Rouse were to mistake Columbia, Maryland, for Athens, Greece; rather, it *would* be remarkable, if not that so many [26] innocent readers (but almost no critics or other writers) make the same mistake. I daresay Mr. Rouse doesn't confuse himself with Pericles of Athens; but to hear Mr. Leon Uris talk about his novel *Exodus*, for example, is to wonder whether he's not confusing his version with Moses'. It ought to be astonishing that the same people who can't be fooled when it comes to overcooked rockfish or over-ripe cantaloupes, and who stopped Rouse & Co. from "developing" Wye Island—that these same sturdy and expert native citizens can read a trite commercial novel and believe that they've taken in a genuine work of art about their place and its history, even about themselves, when in fact they've *been* taken in by a superficial— though not necessarily cynical—piece of Route 50 merchandise.

I say it *ought* to be astonishing. Of course it isn't, for the innocent reason I mentioned before. If we love our territory, we're apt to en- 27 joy being reminded of it. We ought to be indignant at a stock rendi-tion of it into novels or films or TV mini-series—but alas, most of us know more about our local seafood, and about whatever our regu-lar daily business is, than we do about the human heart, the human spirit, the human passions of our fellow women and men, and the human language that such things can be expressed in. So instead of making something honest out of a tie-tac novel—like a doorstop— we're apt to think, "Now by golly he's got that part right: your skip-jack has one mast and your bugeye has two," and feel sort of proud to see it said in best-selling print, God forgive and assist us.

I mentioned the human passions and human language: we have 28 now arrived at the Louvre and those Rembrandt birds. But instead of describing the literary equivalent of our imaginary Rembrandt blue crab, I'll close with what seems to me to be three reasonable rules of thumb for culling beautiful literary swimmers from the other kind. I hope three rules of thumb won't make us all thumbs; the culling is important to our literary ecology.

Rule No. 1: Fiction about history almost never becomes part of the 29 *history of fiction.* Or, to put it another way: novels that are directly and mainly *about* a particular culture and its heritage seldom be-come part of that culture's cultural heritage. There may be excep-tions—we think of Faulkner's fiction about the American South, or Isaac Bashevis Singer's fiction about Polish-Jewish life before the Holocaust—but I believe that such apparent exceptions prove the rule: namely, that the more a novel's *main* interest is in the time and place it's "about," the less likely it is to be a significant work of literature in its own right, though it might certainly be good light entertainment of the costume-drama sort. Aristotle, the first writer in history to describe the difference between historians and poets, says in the *Poetics* that the historian tells us how things were, while the poet tells us how they might have been, or ought ideally to have been. The trouble with much official history, by this famous and useful distinction, is that it's poetry: it tells us how its sponsor wishes things had been. "History is the propaganda of the winners." And the trouble with most historical fiction is that it's so concerned with getting the "facts" straight—as given in the documents of history—that the artistic truth gets lost. The data might be correct, but the hearts and minds and souls of the characters come from Hollywood, not from human history. On the other hand, high-school students reading Shakespeare's *Julius Caesar* like to point out the anachronism of the clock's striking in Act II: there were no clocks in Caesar's Rome. But of course Shakespeare's play isn't about Caesar's Rome: it's about Caesar and Brutus, and the poet has them right. Even if he didn't, historically, it wouldn't matter, since the *real* subjects are pride and conflicting loyalties, not Caesar and Brutus; and the play is one of the treasures of English literature, not of Roman history. Like *Romeo and Juliet,* it is so English to the bone that it can pretend to be about Italy and never mention England at all.

Rule No. 2 is Rule No. 1 turned inside out: *The literature that finally matters in any culture is almost never principally* about *that culture.* The 18th-century historian Edward Gibbon remarks that in the Koran, the bible of Islam, there is no mention of camels. The contemporary Argentine writer Jorge Luis Borges quoted this remark of Gibbon's when he himself was being criticized for not being Argentinian enough, because he never wrote about tangos and gauchos riding over the pampas. Borges went on to say that if the Koran had been written by Arab nationalists, there would no doubt be caravans of camels on every page; but the actual authors of the Koran were so unselfconsciously Arabian that they took camels for granted, and didn't feel pressed to turn the holy book of Islam into a regional zoo. The same might go for blue crabs and Canada geese in the Great Eastern Shore Novel, if one ever gets written, and the reason for this Aristotle also tells us plainly: that the true subject of literature is not the events of history or the features of a particular place, but "the experience of human life, its happiness and its misery." That's what Faulkner's and Singer's stories are truly about: not Southern life or Jewish life, but human life, which they get at by making use of their intimate knowledge of Southerners and of Jews, respectively, and then by writing fiction that rises above its Southernness or its Jewishness.

This is what another Nobel Prize-winner, Thomas Mann, meant 31
when he wrote in 1903: "What an artist talks *about* is never the
main point; it is the raw material, in and for itself indifferent, out of
which, with bland and serene mastery, he creates his work of art."
The French writer Alain Robbe-Grillet goes even further. " . . . the
genuine writer," he declares, "has nothing to say. . . . He has only a
way of speaking." And Homer, the daddy of us all, is equally radical
on the subject of poetry and history: he makes the famous remark
in the *Odyssey* that "wars are fought so that poets will have something to sing about"—with the clear implication that the songs are
finally more important than the wars which are their ostensible subject. Most fiction *about* a place and time never rises above that place
and time. When a real artist such as Faulkner or Singer or Mark
Twain or Nathaniel Hawthorne or Homer happens to find inspira
tion in a particular region or period, it's likely to be because he finds
in that region or period a symbol of his real concerns, which will
be the passions of the human breast and the possibilities of human
language.

That fetches us to *Rule No. 3*, illustrated both by Crab No. 3 (that 32
National Geographic graphic) and by the Rembrandt drawing:
Whatever else it is about, great literature is almost always also
about itself. On rare occasions it may even be *mainly* about itself;
though it's almost never *exclusively* about itself, even when it seems
to be. And the same may go for such remarks as these, even when
they claim to be about "aboutness."

COMPREHENSION

1. In what sense is the first crab Barth describes "historical" rather
   than "fictional"? What purposes does this crab serve?

2. What attributes do the second and third blue crabs have in common? How do they differ from each other? How do they differ from
   the first crab?

3. What purposes do the second and third crabs serve?

4. In what sense is crab number three "partly about the art of drawing"? Why, however, is it "more about the crab"?

5. Is the fourth crab "historical" or "fictional"? Explain. What purpose is it intended to serve? What is it "about"?

6. In what important respect is the fifth blue crab different from all
   the others? Is it "historical" or "fictional"?

7. Does Barth introduce his categories in random order, or is there some logic to their order? Explain.

8. What categories of historical writing does Barth identify in paragraphs 21–26? According to Barth, what purpose does each kind of writing serve?

9. Why, according to Barth, do so many readers mistake a work of "trite commercial" historical fiction for "a genuine work of art about their place and its history"?

10. Paraphrase Barth's three rules for distinguishing "beautiful literary swimmers from the other kind."

11. Is Barth's essay "about" crabs, history, or literature? Or, is it about art? Explain.

PURPOSE AND AUDIENCE

1. What assumptions might Barth have been able to make about the original audience for this essay—members of a historical society—that he could not make about the audience who read the essay in the *Washington Post Sunday Magazine?*

2. Barth made very few changes in the talk when he revised it for his magazine article. Should he have made more changes? For instance, should he have added or deleted any information? Explain.

3. What is Barth's intent in beginning his essay with a five-paragraph introduction telling what it will *not* be about? How successful is this strategy?

4. In paragraph 20 Barth explains his essay's aim. Paraphrase his explanation. Is his general purpose to persuade his readers or to inform them?

5. What thesis does Barth's classification support?

STYLE AND STRUCTURE

1. Identify the five categories into which Barth classifies Chesapeake Bay blue crabs. What organizing principle(s) govern his classification?

2. Where in his essay does Barth shift his focus from crabs to history? How does he indicate this shift to his audience?

3. Throughout his essay, Barth mentions writers of popular historical fiction, "good historical novelists," "fine literary artists," and other

writers and historians. How do his discussions of these writers strengthen his essay?

4. Although Barth has edited his talk, many of the original conversational elements remain. Identify some of these expressions. Should the talk have been edited further to delete such elements? Explain.

5. Although Barth's subject is serious, even scholarly, his essay frequently includes contractions and informal expressions like *drive an artist bananas* and *smart cookies.* Do such expressions lessen the impact or the credibility of the essay? Explain.

6. At various points in his essay (for example, paragraphs 9 and 29–32) Barth includes numbered lists; he also distinguishes the five kinds of crabs by numbering them. What does such numbering achieve? Does it have a negative as well as a positive effect? Explain.

7. In paragraphs 10 and 15 Barth uses *his/her* to refer to the singluar antecedent *artist;* in paragraph 21, however, he refers to the antecedent *historiographer* as *he,* and in paragraph 24 he uses *his* to refer to *historian.* Why do you think he makes this distinction? What other stylistic options are available to him?

8. At several places in his essay Barth notes that he is not finished with a particular point, and that he plans to discuss it further. Identify these comments. Do they add to the essay's coherence, or are they a distraction? Explain.

9. In paragraphs 14 and 15 Barth wanders from his discussion of crabs. Do these paragraphs constitute an unwarranted digression, or do they contribute something to the essay? Explain.

10. What do Barth's references to historical events—for instance, in paragraphs 3 and 16—contribute to his essay?

11. In paragraph 20 Barth begins to develop an analogy between his five "categories of crab-art" and something else. What is the other element to which the categories of crabs are analogous?

12. In general, does Barth approach his categories with objectivity, or does he reveal any biases for or against certain categories? How can you tell?

VOCABULARY PROJECTS

1. Define each of the following words as it is used in this selection.

   fictionists (7)   taxidermist (9)
   rendition (8)   meticulously (11)

paradoxically (11)	sensibility (23)
semblance (12)	pungently (23)
carapace (12)	perpetrators (26)
stylized (12)	stock (27)
tidewater (12)	culling (28)
historiographer (21)	anachronism (29)
infer (21)	

2. Barth coins a word—*aboutness*—that is central to his discussion. Write a two- or three-sentence definition of *aboutness*.

3. Coin words to name each of the five categories of crabs Barth identifies.

WRITING WORKSHOP

1. Choose three pictures that offer different artistic representations of the same subject. Write an essay in which you identify and name the three categories of pictures and discuss the purposes of each. If you can, give several examples of additional pictures that would fall into each of the three groups. In your thesis, draw a conclusion about the relative merits of the three types of representations.

2. Consider the kinds of books you read. Devise several distinct categories and write an essay in which you assess the value of each kind of book. You may classify the books according to subject matter, degree of difficulty, format, purpose, or any other principle you choose.

THEMATIC CONNECTIONS

- "The Spider and the Wasp" (p. 222)
- The Declaration of Independence (p. 484)
- "A Modest Proposal" (p. 544)

WRITING ASSIGNMENTS FOR CLASSIFICATION AND DIVISION

1. Choose a film you have seen recently and make a chart of all the different elements that you consider significant—plot, direction, acting, special effects, and so on. Then fill in your chart, further subdividing each category (for instance, listing each of the special effects). Using this chart as an organizational guide, evaluate the film.

2. Write an essay in which you classify the teachers you have had into several distinct categories. Be sure to give each category a name, and make certain your essay has a thesis that makes a judgment about the relative effectiveness of the teachers in each group.

3. Choose the same topic treated by one of the essays in this chapter—kinds of discipline, ways of reading, and so on—and devise your own categories. Write an essay based on your system of classification and division.

4. Do some research to help you identify the subclasses of a large class of animals or plants. Write an essay in which you enumerate and describe the subclasses in each class for an audience of elementary school students.

5. Consider the large class *sports*. Working as quickly as possible, list all the different sports you can think of. Then devise a system of classification that includes all the sports you have identified, and write an essay that demonstrates the superiority of one class of sports over the others.

6. Classify television shows according to type (action, drama, etc.), audience (preschoolers, school-age children, adults, etc.), or any other logical principle. Write an essay based on your system of classification, making sure to include a thesis. For instance, you might assert that the relative popularity of one kind of program over the other reveals something about television watchers, or that one kind of program shows signs of becoming obsolete.

7. Write a lighthearted essay discussing kinds of snack foods, toys, shoppers, parties, vacations, weight-loss diets, hair styles, or drivers.

8. Write an essay in which you assess the relative merits of one of the following: politicians, news broadcasts, or microcomputers.

9. What kinds of survival skills does a student need to get through college successfully? Write a classification-and-division essay in which you identify and discuss several kinds of skills, indicating why each category is important.

10. Classify the characters of a favorite author. Include a thesis that makes a point about the writer's work.

9

Definition

WHAT IS DEFINITION?

A definition tells what a term means and how it is different from other terms in its class. In the following paragraph from *The Medical Detectives,* Berton Roueché defines *hysteria.*

The word "hysteria" derives from the Greek *hystera,* meaning "uterus." This curious name reflects Hippocrates' notion of the point of origin of the disturbance. "For hysterical maidens," he wrote, "I prescribe marriage, for they are cured by pregnancy." His view prevailed in medicine until well into the nineteenth century, and is perhaps still prevalent in the lingering lay association of women and hysteria. The term "mass hysteria" is also a lay survival. The phenomenon is now preferably known to science as "collective obsessional behavior." Collective obsessions occur throughout the animal world (the cattle stampede, the flocking of starlings on the courthouse roof), and the human animal, despite—or maybe because of—its more finely tuned mentality, seems exquisitely susceptible to them. Manifestations among the human race take many forms. These range in social seriousness from the transient tyranny of the fad (skate-boards, Farrah Fawcett-Majors, jogging, Perrier with a twist) and the eager lockstep of fashion (blue jeans, hoopskirts, stomping boots, white kid gloves, the beard, the wig) to the delirium of the My Lai massacre and the frenzy of the race riot and the witch hunt. Epidemic obsessional behavior differs from its companion compulsions in one prominent respect. It is not, as Alan C. Kerckhoff and Kurt W. Back, both of Duke University, have noted in "The June Bug: A Study of Hysterical Contagion" (1968), "an active response to some element in the situation; it is a passive experience. The actors do not *do* something so much as something happens to them."

Any time you take an examination, you are likely to encounter questions that require definitions. You might be asked to define *be-*

423

haviorism, tell what a *cell* is, explain the meaning of the literary term *naturalism,* include a clear, comprehensive definition of *mitosis* in your answer, or define *authority.* Such exam questions cannot always be answered in one or two sentences. They call for definitions that often require several paragraphs.

Most people think of definition in terms of dictionaries, which give brief, succinct explanations of what words mean. But *definition* has much wider application. It also includes explaining what something, or even someone, *is*—that is, its essential nature. Sometimes a definition can be given in a sentence. At other times it requires a paragraph, an essay, or even a whole book. These longer, more complex definitions are called *extended definitions.*

Extended definitions are useful for many academic assignments besides exams. A thoughtful definition can clarify precise terms as well as more general concepts central to any academic discipline. Definitions can explain abstractions like *freedom* or controversial terms like *right to life* or slang terms whose meanings may vary from locale to locale or change as time passes. In various situations, a definition can be essential because a term has more than one meaning, because you are using it in an uncommon way, or because you suspect the term is unfamiliar to your readers.

Many extended-definition essays contain shorter definitions like those in the dictionary. Moreover, essays with other dominant patterns of development often incorporate brief definitions of terms to clarify points or establish basic information that equips the reader to follow the rest of the discussion. Whether it appears in another kind of essay or acts as a center for an extended definition, the brief dictionary or formal definition establishes the essential meaning of a term.

Formal or Dictionary Definitions

Thumb through any dictionary, and you will see pages of words followed by definitions. These definitions all follow a standard three-part structure: first they present the *term* to be defined, then the general *class* it is a part of, and finally the *qualities that differentiate* it from the other terms in the same class.

Term	Class	Differentiation
Behaviorism	is a theory	that regards the objective facts of a subject's actions as the only valid basis for psychological study.

Term	Class	Differentiation
A cell	is a unit of protoplasm	with a nucleus, cytoplasm, and an enclosing membrane.
Naturalism	is a literary movement	whose original adherents believed that writers should treat life with scientific objectivity.
Mitosis	is the process	of nuclear division of cells, consisting of prophase, metaphase, anaphase, and telophase.
Authority	is the power	to command and require obedience.

Supplying a dictionary definition of each term you use is seldom necessary or desirable. Readers generally will either know what a word means or be able to look it up easily. Sometimes, however, defining your terms is essential—for example, when a word has several meanings, each of which might fit your context, or when you want to use a word in a special way. Occasionally a brief formal definition may be part of a longer definition essay; there it can introduce the extended definition or even help to establish the essay's thesis. Remember, all such definitions include the term, its class, and its distinguishing qualities—the three components that pinpoint what something is and what it is not.

Extended or Essay-Length Definitions

An extended definition includes the three basic parts of a formal definition—the term, its class, and its distinguishing characteristics. Beyond these essentials, an extended definition does not follow a set pattern. Instead, it adapts whatever techniques best suit the term being defined and the writing situation. In fact, any of the essay patterns explored in this book can be used to structure a definition essay. As you plan your essay, jotting down your ideas about the term or subject, a pattern consistent with your essay's purpose may emerge. Working out the term's formal definition may also suggest distinctions or illustrations around which a pattern can grow. The formal definitions of the five terms discussed earlier might be extended using five different patterns of development.

Exemplification. To explain what *behaviorism* is, you could give examples. Carefully chosen cases exemplifying behaviorist assumptions and methods could show how this theory of psychology applies in different situations. Through these examples your reader could see exactly how behaviorism works and what it can and cannot account for. Often, giving examples can be the clearest way to explain something unusual, especially when it is unfamiliar to your readers. If you were defining dreams as "the symbolic representation of mental states," those words might convey little to readers who did not know much about psychology. But a few examples could help you make your point. Many students have dreams about taking exams—perhaps dreaming that they are late for the test, that they remember nothing about the course, or that they are writing their answers with disappearing ink. You might explain the nature of dreams by interpreting these particular dreams, which may symbolize anxiety about a particular course or about school in general.

Description.   You can explain the nature of something by describing it. For example, the concept of a *cell* would be difficult to grasp from the formal definition alone, but your readers would understand the cell more clearly if you were to explain what it looks like, possibly with the aid of a diagram or two. Concentrating on the cell membrane, cytoplasm, and nucleus, you could detail each structure's appearance and function. With these clear descriptions, your reader would be aided in visualizing the whole cell and understanding its workings. Of course, there is more to description than the visual. You could define Italian cooking by describing the taste and smell, as well as the appearance, of veal parmigiana, and you could define a disease partly by describing how its symptoms feel to a patient.

Comparison and Contrast.   An extended definition of *naturalism* could employ a comparison-and-contrast structure. Naturalism is one of several major movements in American literature, and its literary aims could be contrasted with those of other literary movements like romanticism or realism. Or you could compare and contrast the plots and characters of several naturalistic works with those of romantic or realistic works. When defining something unfamiliar, you can compare it to something similar but more familiar to your readers. For example, your readers may never have heard of the Chinese dish called sweet and sour cabbage, but you can help them understand it by saying that it tastes like cole slaw. You may also define a thing by contrasting it with something very much unlike it, especially if the two have some qualities in common. One way to explain the British sport of rugby is by contrasting it with American football, which is more violent.

Process. An extended definition of *mitosis* should be organized as a process analysis because mitosis is a process. You could explain the stages of mitosis, making sure that you point out the transition from one phase to another. By tracing the process from stage to stage for the reader, you could be certain that this type of cell division is clearly defined. Similarly, some objects must be defined in terms of what they do. A computer is a machine that *does* what other computers do, not something that *looks* like other computers, and so an extended definition of a computer would probably include a process analysis.

Classification. Finally, you could define *authority* using classification and division. Based on Max Weber's model, you could divide the class *authority* into subclasses such as traditional authority, charismatic authority, and legal-bureaucratic authority. Then, through parallel discussions explaining how each type of authority is legitimized, you could clarify this very broad term for your reader. In both extended and formal definitions, classification can be very useful. By saying what class an object belong to, you are explaining what kind of thing it is. For instance, monetarism is an economic theory; *The Adventures of Huckleberry Finn* is a novel; emphysema is a disease. And by dividing that class into subclasses, you can be more specific. Emphysema is not merely a disease, it is a disease of the lungs, which classifies it with tuberculosis but not with appendicitis.

Each of these patterns of development helps define by emphasizing a central, essential characteristic of the subject. Naturally, other options are also available. Cause and effect or narration can be used to structure definition papers, as can any combination of patterns. Additionally, a few techniques are unique to definition:

- You can define a term by using *synonyms* (using words with similar meanings)
- You can define a term by using *negation* (telling what it is *not*)
- You can define a term by using *enumeration* (listing its characteristics)
- You can define a term by discussing its *origin* (examining the word's derivation, original meaning, or usages)

Although your definitions and definition essays may take many forms, you should be certain that they are clear and that they actually define. You should be sure you provide a true definition, not just a descriptive statement such as "Happiness is a pizza and a six-pack." Likewise, repetition is not definition, so do not include the term you are defining in your definition. For instance, explaining that "abstract art is a school of artists whose works are abstract" clarifies nothing for your reader. Finally, define as precisely as possible. Name the class of the term you are defining—state, for example, "mitosis is *a process in which* a cell divides" rather than "mitosis is *when* a cell divides." In addition, define this class as narrowly and as accurately as possible. Be specific when you differentiate your term from other members of its narrowed class. Only careful attention to the language and structure of your definition can ensure that your meaning will be clear to your reader.

STRUCTURING A DEFINITION ESSAY

Like any other paper, a definition essay should have an introduction, a body, and a conclusion. Although the wording of a dictionary definition is objective, an extended definition may not be. It may show the term being defined in a special light determined by your attitude toward the subject, by your purpose in defining the term, and by your audience. Therefore, your extended-definition paper about literary naturalism could argue that the significance of this movement's major works has been underestimated by literary scholars. Or, you could define *authority* in order to criticize its abuses. In such cases the thesis provides a center for a definition essay and makes it more than just a catalog of facts.

Suppose that you are assigned a short paper in your introductory psychology course. You decide to examine *behaviorism.* First, you have to recognize that your topic entails a definition. If the topic can be summed up in a form such as "The true nature of A is B" or "A means B," then it is a definition. Of course, you can define *behaviorism* as a *word* in a sentence, or possibly two. But to explain the meaning of the *concept* of behaviorism and its position in the history and current knowledge of psychology, you must go beyond the dictionary into the world.

Second, you have to decide what kinds of explanation are most suitable for your topic and for your intended audience. If you are trying to define *behaviorism* for readers who know very little about psychology, you might use comparisons that relate behaviorism to your readers' experiences, such as how they were brought up by their parents or how they trained their pets. You might use examples, but the examples would relate not to psychological experiments or clinical treatment but to experiences in everyday life. If, on the other hand, you direct your paper to your psychology instructor, who obviously already knows what behaviorism is, your purpose is to show that you know too. One way to show that you understand a theory is to compare it with other theories that claim to explain human behavior. Another is to give examples of how it works in practice. You might also choose to give some of the background and history of the theory. (In a term paper you might even include all of these strategies.) After considering your paper's scope and audience, you might decide that because behaviorism is still somewhat controversial, your best strategy is to supplement a formal definition with examples showing how behaviorist assumptions and methods are applied in specific situations, drawing on your class notes and your textbook. These examples will support your thesis that behaviorism is a valid approach for treating certain psychological dysfunctions. In combination, your examples will define *behaviorism* as it is understood today.

An informal outline for your essay might look like this:

Introduction:	Thesis—Contrary to its critics' assertions, behaviorism is a valid approach for treating a wide variety of psychological dysfunctions.
Background:	An introductory definition of behaviorism, including its origins and evolution
First example:	The use of behaviorism to help psychotics function in an institutional setting
Second example:	The use of behaviorism to treat neurotic behavior, such as chronic anxiety, a phobia, or a pattern of destructive acts
Third example:	The use of behaviorism to treat normal but antisocial or undesirable behavior, such as heavy smoking or overeating
Conclusion:	Restatement of thesis

Notice how the three examples in this paper define behaviorism with the complexity, detail, and breadth that a formal definition could not duplicate. It is more like a textbook explanation—and, in fact, textbook explanations are often written as extended definitions.

The following student essay, written by Ajoy Mahtab for a composition course, defines the untouchables, a caste whose members are shunned in India. In his essay, Ajoy, who grew up in Calcutta, presents a thesis that is sharply critical of the practice of ostracizing untouchables.

THE UNTOUCHABLE

**Introduction:
Background**

A word that is extremely common in India yet uncommon to the point of incomprehension in the West is the word <u>untouchable</u>. It is a word that has had extremely sinister connotations throughout India's history. A rigorously worked out caste system existed in Indian society. At the top of the social ladder sat the Brahmins, the clan of the priesthood. These people had renounced a material world for a spiritual one. Below them came the Kshatriyas, or the warrior caste. This caste included the kings and all their nobles along with their armies. Third on the social ladder were the Vaishyas, who were the merchants of the land. Trade was their only form of livelihood. Last came the Shudras--the menials. Shudras were employed by the prosperous as sweepers and laborers. Originally a person's caste was determined only by his profession. Thus if the son of a merchant joined the army, he automatically converted from a Vaishya to a Kshatriya. However, the system soon became hereditary and rigid. Whatever one's occupation, one's caste was determined from birth according to the caste of one's father.

1

Outside of this structure were a group of people, human beings treated worse than dogs and shunned far more than lepers, people who were not considered even human, people who defiled with their very touch. These were the Achhoots: The untouchables.

2

**Formal
definition**

The word <u>untouchable</u> is commonly defined as "that which cannot or should not be touched." In India, however, it was taken to a far greater extreme. The

History

untouchables of a village lived in a separate community downwind of the borders of the village. They had a separate water supply, for they would make

the village water impure if they were to drink of it.
When they walked they were made to bang two sticks
together continuously so that passersby could avoid
the untouchable's shadow. Tied to their waists,
trailing behind them, was a broom that would clean
the ground they had walked on. The list goes on. The
penalty for not following any of these rules was
death for the untouchable and, in many instances, for
the entire untouchable community.

**Present
situation**

One of the pioneers of the fight against
untouchability was Mahatma Gandhi. Thanks to his
efforts and those of many others, untouchability no
longer presents anything like the horrific picture
painted above. In India today, recognition of
untouchability is punishable by law. Theoretically
there is no such thing as untouchability anymore. But
old traditions linger on, and such a deep-rooted fear
passed down from generation to generation is not
going to disappear overnight. Even today, caste is an
important factor in most marriages. Most Indian
surnames reveal a person's caste immediately, and so
it is a difficult thing to hide. The shunning of the
untouchable is more prevalent in South India, where
the general public is much more devout, than in the
North. Some people would rather starve than share
food and water with an untouchable. This concept is a
little difficult to accept in the West, but it is a
true one all the same.

3

Example

I remember an incident from my childhood. I
could not have been more than eight or nine at the
time. I was on a holiday staying at my family's house
on the river Ganges. There was a festival going on
and, as is customary, we were giving the servants
small presents. I was handing them out when an old

4

lady, bent with age, slowly hobbled into the room. She stood in the far corner of the room all alone, and no one so much as looked at her. When the entire line ended, she stepped hesitantly forward and stood in front of me, looking down at the ground. She then held a cloth stretched out in front of her. I was a little confused about how I was supposed to hand her her present since both her hands were occupied holding the cloth. Then, with the help of prompting from someone behind me, I found out that I was supposed to drop the gift into the cloth without touching the cloth itself. It was only later that I found out that she was an untouchable. This was the first time I had actually come face to face with prejudice, and it felt like a slap in the face. That incident was burned into my memory, and I do not think I will ever forget it.

Conclusion begins

The word <u>untouchable</u> is not often used in the West, and when it is, it is generally used as a complimentary term. For example, an avid fan might say of an athelete, "He was absolutely untouchable. Nobody could even begin to compare with him." It seems rather ironic that in one culture a word should be so favorable and in another so derogatory. Why does a word that gives happiness in one part of the world cause pain in another? Why does the same word have different meanings to different people around the globe? Why do certain words cause rifts and others forge bonds? I do not think anyone can tell me the answer. 5

Conclusion continues

No actual parallel can be found in the world today that can compare to the horrors of untouchability. For an untouchable, life itself was a crime. The day was spent just trying to stay alive. 6

Thesis   From the misery of the untouchables, the world should
learn a lesson: Isolating and punishing any group of
people is dehumanizing and immoral.

Points for Special Attention

Thesis. Ajoy Mahtab's assignment was to write an extended definition of a term he expected would be unfamiliar to his audience. Because he had strong feelings about the unjust treatment of the untouchables, Ajoy wanted his essay to have a strong thesis that communicated his disapproval. Still, because he knew his American classmates would need a good deal of background information before they would be willing to accept such a thesis, he decided not to present it in his introduction but rather to lead up to it gradually and state it at the end of his essay.

Structure. Ajoy's introduction establishes the direction of his essay by introducing the word he will define; he then places this word in context by explaining India's rigid caste system. In paragraph 2 he presents the formal definition of the word *untouchable* and goes on to sketch the term's historical framework. Paragraph 3 explains the status of the untouchables in present-day India, and paragraph 4 gives a vivid example of Ajoy's first encounter with an untouchable. As he begins his conclusion in paragraph 5, Ajoy brings his readers back to the word his essay defines. Here he uses two strategies to add interest: He contrasts one contemporary American usage of *untouchable* with its derogatory meaning in India, and he asks a series of rhetorical questions. In paragraph 6 Ajoy uses a summary of his position to lead in to his thesis.

Patterns of Development. This essay uses a number of the strategies commonly encountered in extended definitions: It includes a formal definition, it explains the term's origin, and it enumerates some of the term's characteristics. In addition, the essay uses several familiar patterns of development to develop an extended definition of the word *untouchable*. For instance, paragraph 1 uses *classification and division* to explain India's caste system; paragraphs 2 and 3 use *brief examples* to illustrate the plight of the untouchable; and paragraph 4 presents a *narrative*. Each of these patterns enriches the definition.

No one pattern is more appropriate than another for a definition paper. In fact, combining several patterns may most effectively define the significant aspects of your term. Your choice of pattern or patterns should evolve naturally from your knowledge of your material, your purpose, and the needs of your audience. The essays that follow employ exemplification, comparison and contrast, narration, and other methods of developing extended definitions.

I WANT A WIFE

Judy Syfers

Judy Syfers was born in San Francisco in 1937 and graduated from the University of Iowa. Now divorced, she has been a housewife, worked as a secretary, written articles on social issues, edited a newsletter, and been involved in the feminist movement. "I Want a Wife" appeared in the first issue of Ms. magazine in December 1971, and it has been reprinted widely in a variety of publications. In an ironic tone, Syfers presents her definition of what society considers the ideal wife.

I belong to that classification of people known as wives. I am A 1
Wife. And, not altogether incidentally, I am a mother.

Not too long ago a male friend of mine appeared on the scene fresh 2
from a recent divorce. He had one child, who is, of course, with his
ex-wife. He is looking for another wife. As I thought about him while
I was ironing one evening, it suddenly occurred to me that I, too,
would like to have a wife. Why do I want a wife?

I would like to go back to school so that I can become economi- 3
cally independent, support myself, and if need be, support those dependent upon me. I want a wife who will work and send me to school.
And while I am going to school I want a wife to take care of my
children. I want a wife to keep track of the children's doctor and
dentist appointments. And to keep track of mine, too. I want a wife
to make sure my children eat properly and are kept clean. I want a
wife who will wash the children's clothes and keep them mended. I
want a wife who is a good nurturant attendant to my children, who
arranges for their schooling, makes sure that they have an adequate
social life with their peers, takes them to the park, the zoo, etc. I
want a wife who takes care of the children when they are sick, a
wife who arranges to be around when the children need special care,
because, of course, I cannot miss classes at school. My wife must
arrange to lose time at work and not lose the job. It may mean a
small cut in my wife's income from time to time, but I guess I can
tolerate that. Needless to say, my wife will arrange and pay for the
care of the children while my wife is working.

I want a wife who will take care of *my* physical needs. I want a 4

435

wife who will keep my house clean. A wife who will pick up after my children, a wife who will pick up after me. I want a wife who will keep my clothes clean, ironed, mended, replaced when need be, and who will see to it that my personal things are kept in their proper place so that I can find what I need the minute I need it. I want a wife who cooks the meals, a wife who is a *good* cook. I want a wife who will plan the menus, do the necessary grocery shopping, prepare the meals, serve then pleasantly, and then do the cleaning up while I do my studying. I want a wife who will care for me when I am sick and sympathize with my pain and loss of time from school. I want a wife to go along when our family takes a vacation so that someone can continue to care for me and my children when I need a rest and change of scene.

I want a wife who will not bother me with rambling complaints   5
about a wife's duties. But I want a wife who will listen to me when I feel the need to explain a rather difficult point I have come across in my course of studies. And I want a wife who will type my papers for me when I have written them.

I want a wife who will take care of the details of my social life.   6
When my wife and I are invited out by my friends, I want a wife who will take care of the babysitting arrangements. When I meet people at school that I like and want to entertain, I want a wife who will have the house clean, will prepare a special meal, serve it to me and my friends, and not interrupt when I talk about things that interest me and my friends. I want a wife who will have arranged that the children are fed and ready for bed before my guests arrive so that the children do not bother us. I want a wife who takes care of the needs of my guests so that they feel comfortable, who makes sure that they have an ashtray, that they are passed the hors d'oeu-vres, that they are offered a second helping of the food, that their wine glasses are replenished when necessary, that their coffee is served to them as they like it. And I want a wife who knows that sometimes I need a night out by myself.

I want a wife who is sensitive to my sexual needs, a wife who   7
makes love passionately and eagerly when I feel like it, a wife who makes sure that I am satisfied. And, of course, I want a wife who will not demand sexual attention when I am not in the mood for it. I want a wife who assumes the complete responsibility for birth control, because I do not want more children. I want a wife who will remain sexually faithful to me so that I do not have to clutter up my intellectual life with jealousies. And I want a wife who understands that *my* sexual needs may entail more than strict

adherence to monogamy. I must, after all, be able to relate to people as fully as possible.

If, by chance, I find another person more suitable as a wife than the wife I already have, I want the liberty to replace my present wife with another one. Naturally, I will expect a fresh, new life; my wife will take the children and be solely responsible for them so that I am left free. 8

When I am through with school and have a job, I want my wife to quit working and remain at home so that my wife can more fully and completely take care of a wife's duties. 9

My God, who *wouldn't* want a wife? 10

COMPREHENSION

1. In one sentence, define what Syfers means by *wife*. Does this ideal wife actually exist? Explain.

2. List some of the specific duties of the wife Syfers describes.

3. Into what five general categories does Syfers arrange these duties?

4. What complaints does Syfers apparently have about the life she actually leads? To what does she seem to attribute her problems?

5. Under what circumstances does Syfers say she would consider leaving her wife? What would happen to the children if she left?

PURPOSE AND AUDIENCE

1. What does Syfers hope to accomplish in this essay?

2. This essay was first published in *Ms.* magazine. In what sense is it appropriate for the audience of this feminist publication?

3. Does this essay have an explicitly stated thesis? If so, where is it? If the thesis is implied, paraphrase it.

4. Do you think Syfers *really* wants the kind of wife she describes? Explain.

STYLE AND STRUCTURE

1. Which rhetorical strategies does Syfers use in developing her definition? Where does she use each pattern?

2. Throughout the essay, Syfers repeats the words "I want a wife." What is the effect of this repetition?

3. What does Syfers mean when she says in paragraph 1, "I am A Wife. And, not altogether incidentally, I am a mother."? Why does she capitalize "A Wife"?

4. What is the effect of Syfers's use of the expression *of course* in paragraph 2 ("He had one child, who is, of course, with his ex-wife."); paragraph 4 (" . . . a wife who arranges to be around when the children need special care, because, of course, I cannot miss classes at school"); and paragraph 7 ("And, of course, I want a wife who will not demand sexual attention when I am not in the mood for it.")?

5. The first and last paragraphs of this essay are quite brief. Does this weaken the essay? Explain.

6. In enumerating the wife's duties, Syfers frequently uses the verb *arrange*. What other verbs does she use repeatedly? How do these verbs help her make her point?

7. Syfers never uses the personal pronouns *he* or *she* to refer to the wife. Why not?

VOCABULARY PROJECTS

1. Define each of the following words as it is used in this selection.

nurturant (3)	adherence (7)
replenished (6)	monogamy (7)

2. Going beyond the dictionary definitions, decide what Syfers means to suggest by the following words. Is she using any of those words sarcastically? Explain.

proper (4)	demand (7)
pleasantly (4)	clutter up (7)
bother (6)	suitable (8)
necessary (6)	free (8)

3. Comment on Syfers's use of phrases like *needless to say* (paragraph 3), *after all* (paragraph 7), *by chance* (paragraph 8), and *naturally* (paragraph 8). What do these expressions contribute to the sentences in which they appear?

WRITING WORKSHOP

1. Write an essay in which you define your ideal spouse.

2. Write an essay entitled, "I Want a Husband." Taking an ironic

stance, use society's notions of the ideal husband to help you shape your definition.

3. Read "The Company Man" (p. 440). Using ideas gleaned from that essay and "I Want a Wife," as well as your own ideas, write a definition essay called "The Ideal Couple." Your essay can be serious or humorous. Support your definition with examples.

THEMATIC CONNECTIONS

- "My Mother Never Worked" (p. 64)
- "If Shakespeare Had Had a Sister" (p. 564)

THE COMPANY MAN

Ellen Goodman

Ellen Goodman was born in 1941 in Newton, Massachusetts. After graduating from Radcliffe College in 1963, she worked as a researcher for Newsweek *and as a feature writer for the* Detroit Free Press. *She began working at the* Boston Globe *in 1967, and today she writes a regular column, "At Large," which has been syndicated since 1976. In 1975 she published* Close to Home, *a collection of her columns, and, in 1979,* Turning Points, *an examination of changes in men's and women's lives as a result of the feminist movement. In 1980 she was awarded the Pulitzer Prize for commentary. Other collections of her columns are* At Large *(1981) and* Keeping in Touch *(1985). "The Company Man" from* Close to Home, *defines what clinicians call a* workaholic. *Goodman develops her definition with an extended example of a man who literally worked himself to death.*

He worked himself to death, finally and precisely, at 3:00 A.M Sunday morning. 1

The obituary didn't say that, of course. It said that he died of a 2 coronary thrombosis—I think that was it—but everyone among his friends and acquaintances knew it instantly. He was a perfect Type A, a workaholic, a classic, they said to each other and shook their heads—and thought for five or ten minutes about the way they lived.

This man who worked himself to death finally and precisely at 3 3:00 A.M. Sunday morning—on his day off—was fifty-one years old and a vice-president. He was, however, one of six vice-presidents, and one of three who might conceivably—if the president died or retired soon enough—have moved to the top spot. Phil knew that.

He worked six days a week, five of them until eight or nine at 4 night, during a time when his own company had begun the four-day week for everyone but the executives. He worked like the Important People. He had no outside "extracurricular interests," unless, of course, you think about a monthly golf game that way. To Phil, it was work. He always ate egg salad sandwiches at his desk. He was, of course, overweight, by 20 or 25 pounds. He thought it was okay, though, because he didn't smoke.

On Saturdays, Phil wore a sports jacket to the office instead of a 5
suit, because it was the weekend.

He had a lot of people working for him, maybe sixty, and most of 6
them liked him most of the time. Three of them will be seriously
considered for his job. The obituary didn't mention that.

But it did list his "survivors" quite accurately. He is survived by 7
his wife, Helen, forty-eight years old, a good woman of no particular
marketable skills, who worked in an office before marrying and
mothering. She had, according to her daughter, given up trying to
compete with his work years ago, when the children were small. A
company friend said, "I know how much you will miss him." And
she answered, "I already have."

"Missing him all these years," she must have given up part of 8
herself which had cared too much for the man. She would be "well ,
taken care of."

His "dearly beloved" eldest of the "dearly beloved" children is a 9
hard-working executive in a manufacturing firm down South. In the
day and a half before the funeral, he went around the neighborhood
researching his father, asking the neighbors what he was like. They
were embarrassed.

His second child is a girl, who is twenty-four and newly married. 10
She lives near her mother and they are close, but whenever she was
alone with her father, in a car driving somewhere, they had nothing
to say to each other.

The youngest is twenty, a boy, a high-school graduate who has 11
spent the last couple of years, like a lot of his friends, doing enough
odd jobs to stay in grass and food. He was the one who tried to grab
at his father, and tried to mean enough to him to keep the man at
home. He was his father's favorite. Over the last two years, Phil
stayed up nights worrying about the boy.

The boy once said, "My father and I only board here." 12

At the funeral, the sixty-year-old company president told the 13
forty-eight-year-old widow that the fifty-one-year-old deceased had
meant much to the company and would be missed and would be hard
to replace. The widow didn't look him in the eye. She was afraid
he would read her bitterness and, after all, she would need him to
straighten out the finances—the stock options and all that.

Phil was overweight and nervous and worked too hard. If he 14
wasn't at the office, he was worried about it. Phil was a Type A, a
heart-attack natural. You could have picked him out in a minute
from a lineup.

So when he finally worked himself to death, at precisely 3:00 A.M. 15
Sunday morning, no one was really surprised.

By 5:00 P.M. the afternoon of the funeral, the company president   16
had begun, discreetly of course, with care and taste, to make inquiries about his replacement. One of three men. He asked around:
"Who's been working the hardest?"

COMPREHENSION

1. In one sentence, define *the company man.* What does the extended
   example add to the meaning that this one-sentence definition lacks?

2. When Phil's widow is told by a friend, "I know how much you will
   miss him," she answers, "I already have." What does she mean?

3. Why does Phil's oldest son go around the neighhood researching his
   father?

4. Why doesn't Phil's widow look the company president in the eye?

5. What does Goodman tell us about Phil's job—what he actually did
   at the office? Why?

6. What kind of man will the company president seek for Phil's replacement?

PURPOSE AND AUDIENCE

1. What point is Goodman trying to make in this essay?

2. What assumptions does Goodman make about her readers? Considering who she expects to read her essay, what effect does she hope it to
   have?

3. Why does Goodman imply her thesis and not state it?

STYLE AND STRUCTURE

1. Why does Goodman state the time of Phil's death both at the beginning and at the end of her essay?

2. Is there a reason why Goodman waits until the end of paragraph 3
   before she uses "the company man's" name?

3. How does Goodman support her assertions about Phil?

4. What is the effect of the dialogue that Goodman presents?

5. Goodman tells Phil's story in a flat, impersonal way. How does this
   tone help her achieve her purpose?

6. Why does Goodman put quotation marks around the phrases *extra-curricular interests, survivors, missing him all these years, well taken care of,* and *dearly beloved*?

7. What rhetorical patterns does Goodman use to define her subject?

VOCABULARLY PROJECTS

1. Define each of the following words as it is used in this selection.
   coronary thrombosis (2)   conceivably (3)
   workaholic (2)   stock options (13)
   classic (2)

2. This essay's style and vocabulary are quite informal. Substitute a more formal word or expression for each of the following:
   top spot (3)   grab at (11)
   okay (4)   all that (13)
   odd jobs (11)   a heart-attack natural (14)

Make sure each of your choices sounds natural in the context of its sentence. How do your substitutions change the sentences in which they appear?

WRITING WORKSHOP

1. Write an essay defining the workaholic student (or the procrastinating student), using an extended example. As Goodman does, use a series of details and dialogue to support your thesis.

2. Write a definition essay in which you define the company man, but use comparison and contrast or process to organize your definition.

3. Write a brief obituary for Phil, one that might appear in his company's trade magazine. Using the title "A Valued Employee," develop the obituary as a definition essay. Your aim is to show readers what traits such an employee must have.

THEMATIC CONNECTIONS

- "Three Kinds of Discipline" (p. 391)
- "I Want a Wife" (p. 435)

TO NOBLE COMPANIONS

Gail Godwin

Gail Godwin was born in 1937 and received a B.A. degree from the University of North Carolina and M.A. and Ph.D. degrees from the University of Iowa. Godwin has worked as a reporter for the Miami Herald *and taught literature at the University of Iowa. She is best known as a novelist, author of* The Perfectionists, Glass People, The Odd Woman, Violet Clay, A Mother and Two Daughters, *and* The Finishing School, *but she is also a writer of short stories and essays. Her most recently published novel is* A Southern Family *(1987). In "To Noble Companions," first published in the August 1973 issue of* Harper's Magazine, *Godwin presents her definition of a friend.*

The dutiful first answer seems programmed into us by our meager expectations: "A friend is one who will be there in times of trouble." But I believe this is a skin-deep answer to describe skin-deep friends. There is something irresistible about misfortune to human nature, and standbys for setbacks and sicknesses (as long as they are not too lengthy, or contagious) can usually be found. They can be *hired*. What I value is not the "friend" who, looming sympathetically above me when I have been dashed to the ground, appears gigantically generous in the hour of my reversal; more and more I desire friends who will endure my ecstasies with me, who possess wings of their own and who will fly with me. I don't mean this as arrogance (I am too superstitious to indulge long in that trait), and I don't fly all that often. What I mean is that I seek (and occasionally find) friends with whom it is possible to drag out all those beautiful, old, outrageously *aspiring* costumes and rehearse together for the Great Roles; persons whose qualities groom me and train me up for love. It is for these people that I reserve the glowing hours, too good not to share. It is the existence of these people that reminds me that the words "friend" and "free" grew out of each other. (OE *freo*, not in bondage, noble, glad; OE *freon*, to love; OE *freond*, friend.)

When I was in the eighth grade, I had a friend. We were shy and "too serious" about our studies when it was becoming fashionable with our classmates to acquire the social graces. We said little at school, but she would come to my house and we would sit down with pencils and paper, and one of us would say: "Let's start with a train whistle today." We would sit quietly together and write separate poems or stories that grew out of a train whistle. Then we would read them aloud. At the end of that school year, we, too, were transformed into social creatures and the stories and poems stopped.

When I lived for a time in London, I had a friend. He was in despair and I was in despair, but our friendship was based on the small flicker of foresight in each of us that told us we would be sorry later if we did not explore this great city because we had felt bad at the time. We met every Sunday for five weeks and found many marvelous things. We walked until our despairs resolved themselves and then we parted. We gave London to each other.   3

For almost four years I have had a remarkable friend whose imagination illumines mine. We write long letters in which we often discover our strangest selves. Each of us appears, sometimes prophetically, sometimes comically, in the other's dreams. She and I agree that, at certain times, we seem to be parts of the same mind. In my most sacred and interesting moments, I often think: "Yes, I must tell _____." We have never met.   4

It is such exceptional (in a sense divine) companions I wish to salute. I have seen the glories of the world reflected briefly through our encounters. One bright hour with their kind is worth more to me than a lifetime guarantee of the services of a Job's comforter whose "helpful" lamentations will only clutter the healing silence necessary to those darkest moments in which I would rather be my own best friend.   5

COMPREHENSION

1. What possible definitions of *friend* does Godwin reject as she moves toward the definition she considers most accurate?

2. What does Godwin mean in paragraph 1 when she says, "I desire friends who . . . possess wings of their own and who will fly with me"?

3. What qualities do the three friends Godwin describes in paragraphs 2–4 share? How are they different from one another?

4. In what sense does Godwin see the kind of friends she salutes in this essay as "divine"?

5. What does Godwin mean in paragraph 6 when she says that there are times at which she would rather be her own best friend?

6. Enumerate some of the qualities Godwin hopes to find in a friend.

7. What, according to Godwin, is a friend? Use the opinions supplied in the essay to help you formulate a one-sentence definition.

PURPOSE AND AUDIENCE

1. In paragraph 1 Godwin supplies a bit of etymology, touching on the origin of the word *friend* and its association with the word *free*. What is her motive for doing so?

2. Beyond offering a definition of *friend*, what is Godwin's purpose in writing this essay?

3. What is Godwin's thesis?

STYLE AND STRUCTURE

1. What patterns of development does Godwin use to work through her definition?

2. Where in her definition does Godwin use negation?

3. In paragraphs 2–4 Godwin discusses three different friends she has had. How do their stories help to support her definition?

4. What stylistic device does Godwin use to link paragraphs 2, 3, and 4?

5. Godwin's essay is very brief, and she presents only the sketchiest portraits of individual friends she has had. Would more concrete, more fully developed characterizations have strengthened her essay? Explain.

6. The language in this essay tends to convey extremes of emotion—either very positive or very negative. For example, Godwin uses positive phrases like *gigantically generous* and *glowing hours* and negative expressions like *dashed to the ground* and *in despair*. Identify as many examples of such language as you can. What does the contrast between these two sets of terms contribute to Godwin's essay?

7. The last sentence of Godwin's essay is quite long. How could it be divided into shorter sentences? Would such revision strengthen or weaken the essay's conclusion?

VOCABULARY PROJECTS

1. Define each of the following words as it is used in this selection.
   dutiful (1)   meager (1)

looming (1)   illumines (4)
aspiring (1)   lamentations (5)

2. Some of the adjectives in the last two paragraphs of this brief essay convey the idea of light; some words convey religious allusions. List all the words that suggest either religion or light, and explain why Godwin chooses to cluster such words together in her concluding paragraphs.

WRITING WORKSHOP

1. Write an essay in which you define what you consider to be the *worst* kind of friend. Be sure to explain in your thesis why the "friend" you describe is different from a true friend.

2. Write a definition essay in which you define a more conventional kind of friend than Godwin's ideal. Use as your thesis Godwin's "dutiful first answer": "A friend is someone who will be there in times of trouble." Develop your definition with several extended examples or with a narrative.

THEMATIC CONNECTIONS

- "My Brother and General Crab" (p. 52)
- "Finishing School" (p. 57)

DYSLEXIA

Eileen Simpson

This selection, an excerpt from Reversals: A Personal Account of Victory over Dyslexia, *defines a developmental disorder that afflicts some twenty-three million Americans—and has afflicted noted figures like Hans Christian Andersen, W. B. Yeats, Thomas Edison, and Woodrow Wilson. Eileen Simpson, a psychotherapist and the author of short stories, a novel, and the recently published* Orphans: Real and Imaginary *(1987), struggled all her life with her handicap and was able to overcome it by gaining an understanding of what dyslexia is. Here she presents a working definition for her readers, comparing the examples she selects with her own experience as a child.*

Dyslexia (from the Greek, *dys*, faulty, + *lexis*, speech, cognate 1
with the Latin *legere*, to read), developmental or specific dyslexia as
it's technically called, the disorder I suffered from, is the inability
of otherwise normal children to read. Children whose intelligence is
below average, whose vision or hearing is defective, who have not
had proper schooling, or who are too emotionally disturbed or brain-
damaged to profit from it belong in other diagnostic categories.
They, too, may be unable to learn to read, but they cannot properly
be called dyslexics.

For more than seventy years the essential nature of the affliction 2
has been hotly disputed by psychologists, neurologists, and educators. It is generally agreed, however, that it is the result of a neuro-
physiological flaw in the brain's ability to process language. It is
probably inherited, although some experts are reluctant to say this
because they fear people will equate "inherited" with "untreatable."
Treatable it certainly is: not a disease to be cured, but a malfunction
that requires retraining.

Reading is the most complex skill a child entering school is asked 3
to develop. What makes it complex, in part, is that letters are less
constant than objects. A car seen from a distance, close to, from
above, or below, or in a mirror still looks like a car even though the
optical image changes. The letters of the alphabet are more whimsi-

cal. Take the letter *b*. Turned upside down it becomes a *p*. Looked at in a mirror, it becomes a *d*. Capitalized, it becomes something quite different, a *B*. The *M* upside down is a *W*. The *E* flipped over becomes Ǝ. This reversed *E* is familiar to mothers of normal children who have just begun to go to school. The earliest examples of art work they bring home often have I LOVƎ YOU written on them.

Dyslexics differ from other children in that they read, spell, and   4
write letters upside down and turned around far more frequently and for a much longer time. In what seems like a capricious manner, they also add letters, syllables, and words, or, just as capriciously, delete them. With palindromic words (was–saw, on–no), it is the order of the letters rather than the orientation they change. The new word makes sense, but not the sense intended. Then there are other words where the changed order—"sorty" for story—does not make sense at all.

The inability to recognize that g, *g*, and G are the same letter, the   5
inability to maintain the orientation of the letters, to retain the order in which they appear, and to follow a line of text without jumping above or below it—all the results of the flaw—can make of an orderly page of words a dish of alphabet soup.

Also essential for reading is the ability to store words in memory   6
and to retrieve them. This very particular kind of memory dyslexics lack. So, too, do they lack the ability to hear what the eye sees, and to see what they hear. If the eyes sees "off," the ear must hear "off" and not "of," or "for." If the ear hears "saw," the eye must see that it looks like "saw" on the page and not "was." Lacking these skills, a sentence or paragraph becomes a coded message to which the dyslexic can't find the key.

It is only a slight exaggeration to say that those who learned to   7
read without difficulty can best understand the labor reading is for a dyslexic by turning a page of text upside down and trying to decipher it.

While the literature is replete with illustrations of the way these   8
children write and spell, there are surprisingly few examples of how they read. One, used for propaganda purposes to alert the public to the vulnerability of dyslexics in a literate society, is a sign warning that behind it are guard dogs trained to kill. The dyslexic reads:

Wurring
Guard God
Patoly

for

Warning
Guard Dog
Patrol

and, of course, remains ignorant of the danger.

   Looking for a more commonplace example, and hoping to recap- 9
ture the way I must have read in fourth grade, I recently observed
dyslexic children at the Educational Therapy Clinic in Princeton,
through the courtesy of Elizabeth Travers, the director. The first
child I saw, eight-year-old Anna (whose red hair and brown eyes reminded me of myself at that age), had just come to the Clinic and
was learning the alphabet. Given the story of "Little Red Riding
Hood," which is at the second grade level, she began confidently
enough, repeating the title from memory, then came to a dead stop.
With much coaxing throughout, she read as follows:

> Grandma you a top. Grandma [looks over at picture of Red Riding
> Hood]. Red Riding Hood [long pause, presses index finger into the
> paper. Looks at me for help. I urge: Go ahead] the a [puts head close
> to the page, nose almost touching] on Grandma

for

> Once upon a time there was a little girl who had a red coat with a red
> hood. Etc.

   "Grandma" was obviously a memory from having heard the 10
story read aloud. Had I needed a reminder of how maddening my
silences must have been to Miss Henderson, and how much patience
is required to teach these children, Anna, who took almost ten minutes to read these few lines, furnished it. The main difference between Anna and me at that age is that Anna clearly felt no need to
invent. She was perplexed, but not anxious, and seemed to have infinite tolerance for her long silences.

   Toby, a nine-year old boy with superior intelligence, had a year 11
of tutoring behind him and could have managed "Little Red Riding
Hood" with ease. His text was taken from the *Reader's Digest's
Reading Skill Builder,* Grade IV. He read:

> A kangaroo likes as if he had but truck together warm. His saw neck
> and head do not . . . [Here Toby sighed with fatigue] seem to feel
> happy back. They and tried and so every a tiger Moses and shoots
> from lonesome day and shouts and long shore animals. And each farm
> play with five friends . . .

He broke off with the complaint, "This is too hard, Do I have to   12
read any more?"

His text was: 13

> A kangaroo looks as if he had been put together wrong. His small
> neck and head do not seem to fit with his heavy back legs and thick
> tail. Soft eyes, a twinkly little nose and short front legs seem strange
> on such a large strong animal. And each front paw has five fingers,
> like a man's hand.

An English expert gives the following bizarre example of an   14
adult dyslexic's performance:

> An the bee-what in the tel mother of the biothodoodoo to the majoram
> or that emldrate enl enl Krastrel, mestrlet to Ketra lotombreldl to ra
> from treido as that.

His text, taken from a college catalogue the examiner happened   15
to have close at hand, was:

> It shall be in the power of the college to examine or not every licenti-
> ate, previous to his admission to the fellowship, as they shall think
> fit.

That evening when I read aloud to Auntie for the first time, I   16
probably began as Toby did, my memory of the classroom lesson
keeping me close to the text. When memory ran out, and Auntie did
not correct my errors, I began to invent. When she still didn't stop
me, I may well have begun to improvise in the manner of this patient—anything to keep going and keep up the myth that I was reading—until Auntie brought the "gibberish" to a halt.

COMPREHENSION

1. In one sentence, define *dyslexia.*

2. How are dyslexics different from normal children who are just learning to read and write?

3. What essential skills for reading do dyslexics lack?

4. Why did Simpson visit the Educational Therapy Clinic?

5. How is Anna's behavior different from the behavior of Simpson as a
   child? How can you account for this difference?

6. Why did Simpson, like other dyslexics, resort to "improvising" when she read aloud?

PURPOSE AND AUDIENCE

1. In paragraph 2, Simpson suggests her purpose in defining *dyslexia*. What is this purpose?

2. Does this essay include an explicitly stated thesis? If so, what is it? If not, state the thesis in one sentence.

3. Does Simpson expect her audience to be familiar with dyslexia? How can you tell?

STYLE AND STRUCTURE

1. In paragraph 1, Simpson uses formal definition and negation. Locate an example of each technique.

2. In the body of her essay, Simpson develops her definition with examples, description, and comparison and contrast. Find examples of each technique.

3. In presenting examples of the reading performances of dyslexics, Simpson begins with an eight-year-old child, moves to a nine-year-old child with superior intelligence, and concludes with an adult. Why does she organize her examples in this manner?

4. Simpson concludes her essay with a personal note. Is this an effective conclusion? Why, or why not?

VOCABULARY PROJECTS

1. Define each of the following words as it is used in this selection.

cognate (1)	palindromic (4)
developmental (1)	orientation (5)
neurologists (2)	replete (8)
neuro-physiological (2)	vulnerability (8)
whimsical (3)	literate (8)
capricious (4)	commonplace (9)

2. Simpson uses a variety of terms to characterize dyslexia as a treatable condition, not a hopeless disease—for instance, *disorder* (paragraph 1), *affliction, flaw,* and *malfunction* (paragraph 2). Look up each of these four words in a good desk dictionary and make sure you understand how they differ. Then, compile a list of near synonyms for

each. Are there any contexts in the essay in which you believe one of these synonyms would be more appropriate than the word Simpson uses? Explain.

3. In paragraph 1, Simpson explains the derivation of the word *dyslexia*. List all the other words you can think of that are formed from the Greek *dys* (faulty) or *lexis* (speech) or the Latin *legere* (to read). Check a dictionary to make sure your choices are correct.

WRITING WORKSHOP

1. Write an essay in which you define a handicap you have or a handicap you are familiar with through the experiences of a friend or family member. Use examples and any other appropriate techniques to develop your definition.

2. Use what you now know about dyslexia to write an essay in which you define a similar handicap by comparing and contrasting it with dyslexia.

3. Even without a handicap, you have probably found some task or skill very difficult to master, though others found it easy. Name and define the "condition" that hindered your learning, using whatever techniques are appropriate for your definition.

THEMATIC CONNECTIONS

- "The Human Cost of an Illiterate Society" (p. 173)
- "Bilingual Education: The Key to Basic Skills" (p. 490)

EUPHEMISM

Neil Postman

Born in 1931 and currently Professor of Media Ecology at New York University, Neil Postman is widely known for his essays and books advocating radical education reform. In addition to contributing to periodicals like the Atlantic *and* The Nation, *Postman is the author of* Teaching as a Conserving Activity *(1980),* The Disappearance of Childhood *(1982), and most recently* Amusing Ourselves to Death: Public Discourse in the Age of Show Business *(1985); coauthor of* Linguistics: A Revolution in Teaching *(1966) and* Teaching as a Subversive Activity *(1969); and author of* Crazy Talk, Stupid Talk: How We Defeat Ourselves by the Way We Talk and What to Do About It *(1976), in which "Euphemism" appeared. Here he discusses the value of using euphemisms in speaking and writing, considering the political as well as the linguistic implications.*

A euphemism is commonly defined as an auspicious or exalted term (like "sanitation engineer") that is used in place of a more down-to-earth term (like "garbage man"). People who are partial to euphemisms stand accused of being "phony" or of trying to hide what it is they are really talking about. And there is no doubt that in some situations the accusation is entirely proper. For example, one of the more detestable euphemisms I have come across in recent years in the term "Operation Sunshine," which is the name the U.S. Government gave to some experiments it conducted with the hydrogen bomb in the South Pacific. It is obvious that the government, in choosing this name, was trying to expunge the hideous imagery that the bomb evokes and in so doing committed, as I see it, an immoral act. This sort of process—giving pretty names to essentially ugly realities—is what has given euphemizing such a bad name. And people like George Orwell have done valuable work for all of us in calling attention to how the process works. But there is another side to euphemizing that is worth mentioning, and a few words here in its defense will not be amiss.

To begin with, we must keep in mind that things do not have "real" names, although many people believe that they do. A garbage man is not "really" a "garbage man," any more than he is really a "sanitation engineer." And a pig is not called a "pig" because it is so dirty, nor a shrimp a "shrimp" because it is so small. There are things, and then there are the names of things, and it is considered a fundamental error in all branches of semantics to assume that a name and a thing are one and the same. It is true, of course, that a name is usually so firmly associated with the thing it denotes that it is extremely difficult to separate one from the other. That is why, for example, advertising is so effective. Perfumes are not given names like "Bronx Odor," and an automobile will never be called "The Lumbering Elephant." Shakespeare was only half right in saying that a rose by any other name would smell as sweet. What we call things affects how we will perceive them. It is not only harder to sell someone a "horse mackerel" sandwich than a "tuna fish" sandwich, but even though they are the "same" thing, we are likely to enjoy the taste of tuna more than that of the horse mackerel. It would appear that human beings almost naturally come to *identify* names with things, which is one of our more fascinating illusions. But there is some substance to this illusion. For if you change the names of things, you change how people will regard them, and that is as good as changing the nature of the thing itself.

Now, all sorts of scoundrels know this perfectly well and can make us love almost anything by getting us to transfer the charm of a name to whatever worthless thing they are promoting. But at the same time and in the same vein, euphemizing is a perfectly intelligent method of generating new and useful ways of perceiving things. The man who wants us to call him a "sanitation engineer" instead of a "garbage man" is hoping we will treat him with more respect than we presently do. He wants us to see that he is of some importance to our society. His euphemism is laughable only if we think that he is not deserving of such notice or respect. The teacher who prefers us to use the term "culturally different children" instead of "slum children" is euphemizing, all right, but is doing it to encourage us to see aspects of a situation that might otherwise not be attended to.

The point I am making is that there is nothing in the process of euphemizing itself that is contemptible. Euphemizing is contemptible when a name makes us see something that is not true or diverts our attention from something that is. The hydrogen bomb kills. There is nothing else that it does. And when you experiment with it, you are trying to find out how widely and well it kills. Therefore, to call such an experiment "Operation Sunshine" is to suggest a purpose for the bomb that simply does not exist. But to call "slum children" "culturally different" is something else. It calls attention, for example, to legitimate reasons why such children might feel alienated from what goes on in school.

I grant that sometimes such euphemizing does not have the intended effect. It is possible for a teacher to use the term "culturally different" but still be controlled by the term "slum children" (which the teacher may believe is their "real" name). "Old people" may be called "senior citizens," and nothing might change. And "lunatic asylums" may still be filthy, primitive prisons though they are called "mental institutions." Nonetheless, euphemizing may be regarded as one of our more important intellectual resources for creating new perspectives on a subject. The *attempt* to rename "old people" "senior citizens" was obviously motivated by a desire to give them a political identity, which they not only warrant but which may yet have important consequences. In fact, the fate of euphemisms is very hard to predict. A new and seemingly silly name may replace an old one (let us say, "chairperson" for "chairman") and for years no one will think or act any differently because of it. And then, gradually, as people begin to assume that "chairperson" is the "real" and proper name (or "senior citizen" or "tuna fish" or "sanitation engineer"), their attitudes begin to shift, and they will approach things in a slightly different frame of mind. There is a danger, of course, in supposing that a new name can change attitudes quickly or always. There must be some authentic tendency or drift in the culture to lend support to the change, or the name will remain incongruous and may even appear ridiculous. To call a teacher a "facilitator" would be such an example. To eliminate the distinction between "boys" and "girls" by calling them "childpersons" would be another.

But to suppose that such changes never "amount to anything" is to underestimate the power of names. I have been astounded not only by how rapidly the name "blacks" has replaced "Negroes" (a kind of euphemizing in reverse) but also by how significantly perceptions and attitudes have shifted as an accompaniment to the change.

The key idea here is that euphemisms are a means through which a culture may alter its imagery and by so doing subtly change its style, its priorities, and its values. I reject categorically the idea that people who use "earthy" language are speaking more directly or with more authenticity than people who employ euphemisms. Saying that someone is "dead" is not to speak more plainly or honestly than saying he has "passed away." It is, rather, to suggest a different conception of what the event means. To ask where the "shithouse" is, is no more to the point than to ask where the "restroom" is. But in the difference between the two words, there is expressed a vast difference in one's attitude toward privacy and propriety. What I am saying is that the process of euphemizing has no moral content. The moral dimensions are supplied by what the words in question express, what they want us to value and to see. A nation that calls experiments with bombs "Operation Sunshine" is very frightening. On the other hand, a people who call "garbage men" "sanitation engineers" can't be all bad.

COMPREHENSION

1. What is a euphemism? Give examples.

2. What, according to Postman, "has given euphemizing such a bad name"?

3. In paragraph 2, what misconception does Postman set out to correct? Why?

4. What does Postman see as the value of euphemizing? What are its potential dangers?

5. What does Postman mean in paragraph 6 when he refers to the shift from *Negroes* to *blacks* as "a kind of euphemizing in reverse"?

PURPOSE AND AUDIENCE

1. What is Postman's purpose in writing this essay, besides just defining *euphemism*? What is his thesis?

2. What attitude does Postman assume his audience already has about euphemizing? How do you know this?

3. In paragraph 1, Postman introduces the "detestable" euphemism *Operation Sunshine*; he brings it up again in paragraphs 4 and 7. What effect does the repetition of this term have on the reader? Does this effect in any way counter the essay's purpose? Why, or why not?

STYLE AND STRUCTURE

1. On what technique does Postman rely most heavily in developing his definition?

2. Where does Postman define *euphemism* through its effects?

3. Most of Postman's paragraphs are of similar length; paragraph 6, however, is much shorter. What might account for this?

4. What information in the conclusion echoes the essay's introduction? Is this repetition an effective closing technique? Explain.

VOCABULARY PROJECTS

1. Define each of the following words as it is used in this selection.

   auspicious (1)   denotes (2)
   exalted (1)   incongruous (5)
   expunge (1)   facilitator (5)
   semantics (2)   categorically (7)

2. List as many euphemisms for professions (for instance, *sanitation engineer* for *garbage collector*) as you can. How do each of these euphemisms change your conception of the occupation? What other categories of words are frequently euphemized? How do you account for this tendency?

WRITING WORKSHOP

1. Write an essay in which you define *euphemism* by presenting examples. Begin by listing all the euphemisms you can; then, classify them into related groups. In your thesis, make a point about the kinds of words people euphemize.

2. Write a definition essay whose purpose is to convince your readers of the potential dangers of euphemizing. Use examples to support your thesis.

THEMATIC CONNECTIONS

- "The Embalming of Mr. Jones" (p. 236)
- "Politics and the English Language" (p. 572)

WRITING ASSIGNMENTS FOR DEFINITION

1. Choose a document or ritual that plays a significant part in your religious or cultural heritage. Define it, using any pattern or combination of patterns you choose but making sure to include a formal definition somewhere in your essay. Assume your readers are not familiar with the term you are defining.

2. Using a series of examples drawn from personal experience to support your thesis, define *superstition, courage,* or *eccentricity.*

3. The professional essays in this chapter define family and occupational roles, a handicap, and a term associated with language. Write an essay in which you too define one of these topics—for instance, a stepmother (family role), the modern baseball player (occupational role), agoraphobia (handicap), or hyperbole (term associated with language).

4. Do some research to learn the meaning of one of these medical terms: angina, migraine, Hodgkin's disease, Down's Syndrome, tubal ligation, osteoporosis, poliomyelitis, Alzheimer's disease. Then, write a definition essay explaining the term to an audience of college students with no background in medicine.

5. Use an extended example to support a thesis in an essay that defines racism, sexism, or another type of bigoted behavior.

6. Choose a term that is central to one of your courses—for instance, *naturalism, behaviorism,* or *authority*—and write an essay in which you define the term. Your audience is made up of students who have not yet taken the course. You may begin with an overview of the term's origin if you believe this is appropriate; then, develop your essay with examples, comparisons, and the like that will facilitate your audience's understanding of the term.

7. Assuming your audience is a group from a culture not familiar with modern pastimes, write a definition essay in which you describe the form and function of a Frisbee, a Barbie doll, a G.I. Joe action figure, a jump rope, a boomerang, or baseball cards.

8. Review any one of the following narrative essays from chapter 2, and use it to help you develop an extended definition of one of the following terms:
   "Finishing School"—prejudice
   "My Mother Never Worked"—work
   "38 Who Saw Murder Didn't Call the Police"—apathy
   "Outsider in a Silent World"—responsibility
   "Shooting an Elephant"—role expectation

10

Argumentation

WHAT IS ARGUMENTATION?

Argumentation is a reasoned, logical way of convincing an audience of the soundness of a position, belief, or conclusion. Argumentation takes a stand—supported by evidence—and urges people to share the writer's perspective and insights. In the following paragraph from "Test-Tube Babies: Solution or Problem?" Ruth Hubbard argues that before we endorse further development of the technology that allows for the creation of test-tube babies, we must carefully consider the consequences.

> In vitro fertilization of human eggs and the implantation of early embryos into women's wombs are new biotechnologies that may enable some women to bear children who have hitherto been unable to do so. In that sense, it may solve their particular infertility problems. On the other hand, this technology poses unpredictable hazards since it intervenes in the process of fertilization, in the first cell divisions of the fertilized egg, and in the implantation of the embryo into the uterus. At present we have no way to assess in what ways and to what extent these interventions may affect the women or the babies they acquire by this procedure. Since the use of the technology is only the beginning, the financial and technical investments it represents are still modest. It is therefore important that we, as a society, seriously consider the wisdom of implementing and developing it further.

Unlike an informal exchange of opinion, formal arguments follow rules designed to ensure that ideas are presented fairly and logically. The first rules governing argument were formulated thousands of years ago by the ancient Greeks. They designed their rules to apply to public speaking, but as you will see in this chapter, the techniques of argument apply to writing as well.

One purpose of argument is to convince reasonable people to accept your position. Another is simply to defend your position, to establish its validity even if other people cannot be convinced to agree. A third purpose of argumentation is to question or refute some position you believe to be misguided, untrue, or evil, without necessarily offering an alternative of your own. (You could, for example, question a political party's platform without presenting one of your own.)

Argumentation and Persuasion

Although *persuasion* and *argument* are terms frequently used interchangeably in everyday speech, they are quite different. *Persuasion* is a general term used to describe a technique a writer uses to move an audience to adopt a belief or follow a course of action. To persuade an audience a writer relies on various appeals—to the *emotions,* to *reason,* or to *ethics.*

Argument is the appeal to reason. In an argument a writer connects a series of statements in an orderly way so that they lead to a conclusion. Argument is different from persuasion in that it does not try to move an audience to action; its primary purpose is to demonstrate to an audience that certain ideas are valid and that others are not. Unlike persuasion, argumentation has a formal structure: To support a conclusion, an argument makes points, supplies evidence, establishes a logical chain of reasoning, refutes opposing arguments, and accommodates the views of an audience.

As the readings in this section demonstrate, most effective argumentation essays appeal to the emotions as well as to reason. For example, you could use a combination of logical and emotional appeals to argue against lowering the drinking age in your state from twenty-one to eighteen years of age. You could appeal to *reason* by constructing an argument that leads to the conclusion that the state should not condone policies that have a high probability of injuring or killing citizens. You could support your conclusion by presenting statistics that show that alcohol-related traffic accidents kill more teenagers than disease does. You could also discuss a study that shows that states with a lower drinking age have more fatal traffic accidents than states with a higher drinking age. In addition, you could appeal to the *emotions* by telling a particularly sad story about an eighteen-year-old alcoholic or by pointing out how an increased number of accidents involving drunk drivers would cost taxpayers more money and could even cost some their lives. These appeals to your audience's emotions could strengthen your argument and widen its appeal.

What appeals you choose and how you balance them depend in part on your purpose and your sense of your audience. But ethical questions are also involved. Some extremely effective means of persuasion are quite simply unfair. Although most people would agree that lies, threats, and appeals to greed and prejudice are unacceptable ways of motivating an audience to action, such appeals are commonly used in political campaigns, international diplomacy, and daily conversation. Still, in your college writing you should use only those appeals to emotion that most people would perceive as being fair. In addition, because so much of the persuasive writing that you do in college requires you to adhere to the rules of argument, your primary means of convincing an audience should be the appeal to reason.

Choosing a Topic

In an argumentative essay, as in all writing, choosing the right topic is important. It should be one in which you have an intellectual or emotional interest. Nevertheless, you should be openminded and willing to consider all sides of a question. If the evidence goes against your position, you should be able to change your thesis or even the subject. And you should be able, in advance, to consider your topic from other people's viewpoints so that you understand what they believe and can build a logical case. If you cannot, then you should abandon your topic and pick another one that you can deal with more objectively.

Other factors should also influence your selection of a topic. You should be well informed about your topic. In addition, you should select a limited issue, narrow enough to be treated effectively in the space available to you, or confine your discussion to a particular aspect of a broad issue. You should also consider your purpose— what you expect your argument to accomplish and how you wish your audience to respond. If your topic is so far-reaching that you cannot identify what you want to convince a reader to think, or so idealistic that your expectations are impossible or unreasonable, your essay will not be effective.

Taking a Stand

After you have chosen your topic, you are ready to take your stand—to state the position you will argue in the form of a thesis. Consider the following thesis statement:

Solar power is the best available solution to the impending energy crisis.

This thesis says that you believe there will be an energy crisis in the future, that there is more than one possible solution to the crisis, and that solar energy is a better solution than any other. In your argument you will have to support each of these three assertions logically and persuasively. Here is an opposing thesis on the same topic:

Solar power is not a good solution to the energy crisis.

This thesis states that solar power could not solve such a crisis, at least not by itself. This is a simpler position to argue, with only one assertion that requires support. That is not to say, of course, that it is more valid.

Before going any further, you should examine your thesis to make sure that it is *debatable*. There is no point in arguing a statement of fact or a point that people accept as self-evident. For example, most people would agree with the following assertion: "Immigrants have contributed much to the development of the United States." A good argumentative thesis, however, would contain a proposition that has at least two sides and could function as the basis of an argument: "Because immigrants have contributed much to the development of the United States, immigration quotas should be eliminated." A good way to test the suitability of your thesis for an argumentation essay is to formulate an *antithesis*, a statement that asserts the opposite position. If you can, you can be certain that your thesis is indeed debatable: "Even though immigrants have contributed much to the United States, immigration quotas should *not* be eliminated."

It is also wise to test your own attitude toward your thesis. If you are so convinced you are right that you cannot understand or respect opposing views and the people who hold them, you do not have the objectivity you need to develop a sound and persuasive argument. Argument is demanding, and it requires clear thought and a reasonably cool head. Of course you should care about your subject and believe your position is right, but the strength of your conviction alone will not guarantee a strong argument.

Analyzing Your Audience

Before writing any essay, you should analyze the characteristics, values, and interests of your audience. Once you know who your audience will be, you need to assess what beliefs or opinions they are likely to hold and whether they are friendly, neutral, or hostile to your thesis. It is probably best to assume that some, if not most, of your readers are at least skeptically neutral and possibly hostile. That assumption will keep you from making claims you cannot support. If your position is controversial, you should assume an informed and determined opposition is looking for holes in your argument.

Often you begin with a purpose in mind but must decide on an audience. If you want to make something happen, who has the power to do it? Whom do you have to persuade, and how would those readers respond to your efforts? Sometimes you will need to appeal to several different audiences, tailoring your persuasive method and approach to each.

Each of these considerations influences your approach to your subject. For example, it would be relatively easy to convince college students that tuition should be lowered or instructors that salaries should be raised. You could be reasonably sure, in advance, that each group would be friendly and would agree with your position. But argument requires more than telling people what they already believe. It would be much harder to convince college students that tuition should be raised to pay for an increase in instructors' salaries or to persuade instructors to forgo raises so that tuition can remain the same. Yet these are the kinds of challenges that arguments must routinely meet. Whether your readers are mildly sympathetic, neutral, or even hostile to your position, your purpose is to change their views to match your own more closely. Remember, your audience will not just take your word for things. You must provide evidence that will support your thesis and reasoning that will lead to your conclusion.

Gathering Evidence

All the points that you make in your paper must be supported. If they are not, your audience will dismiss them as irrelevant or unclear. Sometimes you can support a statement with appeals to emotion, but most of the time you support the points of your argument by appealing to reason—by providing *evidence*, material presented in support of your claim.

As you gather evidence and assess its effectiveness, keep in mind that evidence in an argumentative essay never proves anything conclusively. If it did there would be no debate and hence no point in arguing. The best that evidence can do is convince your audience that an assertion is reasonable and worth believing. Choose your evidence with this goal in mind.

Evidence can consist of fact or opinion. *Facts* are statements that most people agree are true and that can be verified independently. Examples are the most common type of factual evidence, but statistics—evidence expressed as numbers—are also factual. It is a *fact*, for example, that since 1945 more than 45,000 people a year have been killed in automobile accidents on the nation's highways. Facts may be drawn from your own experience as well as from reading and observation. It may be a fact that you yourself have had a serious automobile accident. Quite often, facts alone are not enough to support an assertion. In such cases, you need *opinions,* interpretations of facts. To connect your facts about automobile accidents to the assertion that installation of automatic airbags on all cars could dramatically reduce deaths, you could cite the opinions of experts—consumer advocate Ralph Nader, for example. His statements, along with the facts you have assembled and your own interpretations of those facts, could convince readers that your solution to the problem of highway deaths is promising.

Keep in mind that not all opinions are equal. You may form opinions based on personal experience and observation and use such opinions to support an argument. Still, the opinions of experts are more convincing than are those of individuals who have less experience with or knowledge of an issue. Your personal opinions can be excellent evidence provided you are knowledgeable about your subject, but they seldom constitute enough evidence to support a major assertion of your argument. In the final analysis, what is important is not just the quality of the evidence, but also the credibility of the person offering the evidence.

As soon as you decide on a topic, you should begin to gather as much evidence as you can. Brainstorm to think of experiences and observations that would support your claims. If your topic is technical or demands support beyond your own knowledge of the subject, go to the library and search the card catalog, periodical indexes, and reference books to locate the information that you need.

When selecting and reviewing material, remember three things about your evidence:

1. *Your evidence should be relevant.* Your evidence should support your thesis and should contribute to the argument that you are making. As you present evidence, you may concentrate so much on a specific example that you lose sight of the point you are supporting. As a result, you digress from your point,

and your readers become confused. In arguing against mandatory AIDS testing for all government workers, one student
made the point that AIDS was not yet of epidemic proportions.
To illustrate this point he offered a discussion of the bubonic
plague in fourteenth-century Europe. Although interesting,
this example was not relevant because the writer did not link
his discussion to his assertions about AIDS. To show its rele-
vance he could, for instance, have compared estimates of the
number of people who died of the bubonic plague during a single year with the number who have died of AIDS during a single year.

2. *Your evidence should be representative.* Your evidence should
represent the *full* range of opinions about your subject, not just
one side or the other. Examples and expert opinions should be
typical, not aberrant. Suppose you were writing an argumentation essay in which you supported the building of a trash-to-
steam plant in your city. To support your thesis you present
the example of Baltimore, which has a successful trash-to-
steam program. As you consider your evidence, you should ask
yourself if Baltimore's experience with trash-to-steam is typical. Did other cities in different regions of the country have
less success? Look especially hard at opinions that disagree
with the position you plan to take. They will help you understand your opposition and enable you to refute it effectively
when you write your paper.

3. *Your evidence should be sufficient.* Your evidence should be
sufficient to support your claims. The amount of evidence that
you need depends on your audience and your thesis. It stands
to reason that you would use fewer examples in a two-page paper than in a ten-page research assignment. Similarly, an audience that is favorably disposed to your thesis might need only
one or two examples to be convinced, while a skeptical audience would need many more. As you develop your thesis, consider the level of support that you will need as you write your
paper. You may decide that a narrower, more limited thesis
might be easier to support than one that is more expansive.

What kind of evidence might change a reader's mind? That depends on the readers, on the issue, and on the facts at hand. You need
to put yourself in the place of your readers and ask what would make
them agree with your thesis. Why should a student agree to pay
higher tuition? You might concede that tuition is high but point out
that it has not been raised for three years, while the college's costs

have kept going up. Heating and maintaining the buildings cost more and professors' salaries have failed to keep pace with the cost of living, with the result that several excellent teachers have recently left the college for higher-paying jobs. Furthermore, cuts in government funding have already caused a reduction in the number of courses offered. How could you convince a professor to agree to accept no raise at all, especially in light of the fact that faculty salaries have not kept up with inflation? You could say that because government cuts in funding have already reduced course offerings and because the government has also reduced funds for loans for the many students from families whose incomes average $20,000 or less, any further rise in tuition to pay faculty salaries might cause many students to drop out—and that in turn would cost some instructors their jobs. As you can see, the evidence and reasoning you use in an argument depend to a great extent on whom you want to persuade and what you know about them.

Dealing with the Opposition

When gathering evidence, you should keep in mind that you must deal effectively with arguments against your position. You should address the most obvious—and sometimes the not-so-obvious—objections to your case. Try to anticipate the objections that a reasonable person would have to your thesis. By directly addressing these objections in your essay, you go a long way toward convincing readers that your arguments are sound. In classical rhetoric, this part of an argument is called *refutation* and is considered essential to making the strongest case possible on behalf of your thesis.

You can refute opposing arguments by showing that they are unsound, unfair, or weak. Frequently, you present contrasting evidence to show the weakness of your opponent's case. Careful definition and exacting cause-and-effect analysis may also prove effective. In the following passage from the essay "Politics and the English Language," (p. 572) George Orwell refutes an opponent's argument:

> I said earlier that the decadence of our language is probably curable. Those who deny this would argue, if they produced an argument at all, that language merely reflects existing social conditions, and that we cannot influence its development by any direct tinkering with words and constructions. So far as the general tone or spirit of a language goes, this may be true, but it is not true in detail. Silly words and expressions have often disappeared, though not through any evolutionary process but owing to the conscious actions of a minority.

Orwell begins by stating the point he wants to make. He goes on to define the argument against his position, and then he defines its weakness. Later in the paragraph Orwell bolsters his argument by presenting two examples that support his point. When refuting an argument, you should not distort an opponent's argument or make it seem weaker than it actually is. This technique, called *creating a straw man*, can backfire and actually turn fair-minded readers against you.

When an opponent's argument is so compelling that it cannot be easily dismissed, you should acknowledge its strength. By conceding that the point is well taken, you reenforce the impression that you are a fair-minded person. If possible, point out the limitations of the opposing position and then move your argument to more solid ground. Many times a strong point represents only *one* element in a multifaceted problem. For this reason your ability to use process and classification and division will be important in establishing the strengths of your argument.

When planning your argumentative essay, you should write down all the objections to your thesis that you can identify. As you marshal your evidence, you can then decide which points you will refute. Remember, though, that careful readers will expect you to refute intelligently the most compelling of your opponent's arguments.

Deductive and Inductive Argument

In argument, you may move from evidence to conclusion in two basic ways. One is called *deductive reasoning*. It proceeds from a general premise or assumption to a specific conclusion, and it is what most people mean when they speak of logic. Using strict logical form, deduction holds that if all the statements in the argument are true, the conclusion must also be true. The other is *inductive reasoning*. It proceeds from individual observations to a more general conclusion and uses no strict form. It requires only that all the relevant evidence be stated and that the conclusion fit the evidence better than any other conclusion would. Most written arguments use a combination of deductive and inductive reasoning, but here it is simpler to discuss them separately.

Deductive Arguments.   The basic form of a deductive argument is a *syllogism*. A syllogism consists of a major premise, which is a general statement; a minor premise, which is a related but more specific statement; and a conclusion, which has to be drawn from those premises. For example:

Major premise: All Olympic runners are fast.
Minor premise: John is an Olympic runner.
  Conclusion: Therefore, John is fast.

As you can see, if you grant each of the premises, then you must also grant the conclusion—and it is the only conclusion that you can properly draw. You cannot say that John is slow, because that contradicts the premises, nor can you say that John is tall, because that goes beyond the premises.

Of course this argument seems obvious, and it is much simpler than an argumentative essay would be. But a deductive argument can be powerful, and its premises can be fairly elaborate. The Declaration of Independence has at its core a deductive argument that might be summarized in this way:

Major premise: Tyrannical rulers deserve no loyalty.
Minor premise: King George III is a tyrannical ruler.
  Conclusion: Therefore, King George III deserves no loyalty.

The major premise is one of those truths that the Declaration claims is self-evident. Much of the Declaration consists of evidence to support the minor premise that King George is a tyrannical ruler. And the conclusion, because it is drawn from those premises, has the force of irrefutable logic: The king deserves no loyalty from his American subjects, who are therefore entitled to revolt against him.

When a conclusion follows logically from the major and minor premises, then the argument is said to be *valid*. But if the syllogism is not logical, the argument is not valid and the conclusion is not sound. For example:

Major premise: All dogs are animals.
Minor premise: All cats are animals.
  Conclusion: Therefore, all dogs are cats.

Of course the conclusion is absurd. But how did we wind up with such a ridiculous conclusion when both premises are obviously true? The answer is that although both cats and dogs are animals, cats are not included in the major premise of the syllogism. Thus the form of the syllogism is defective, and the argument is invalid. Here is another example of an invalid argument:

Major premise: All dogs are animals.
Minor premise: Ralph is an animal.
  Conclusion: Therefore, Ralph is a dog.

Even without using formal logic, most of us can tell that there is a problem with this conclusion. This error in logic occurs when the minor premise refers to a term in the major premise *(animals)* that is *undistributed*—that is, it covers only items in the class denoted *(dogs)*. In the major premise, *dogs* is the distributed term; it designates *all dogs.* The minor premise, however, refers not to *dogs* but to *animals,* and *animals* is undistributed because it refers only to animals that are dogs. Just because, as the minor premise establishes, Ralph is an animal, it does not follow that he is also a dog. He could be a cat, a horse, or even a human being.

But even if a syllogism is valid—that is, correct in its form—its conclusion will not necessarily be *true.* For example:

Major premise: All dogs are brown.
Minor premise: My poodle Toby is a dog.
Conclusion: Therefore, Toby is brown.

As it happens, Toby is black. The conclusion is false because the major premise is false: Many dogs are not brown. If Toby had actually been brown, the conclusion would have been correct, but only by chance, not by logic. To be *sound,* the syllogism must be both logical and true.

The advantage of a deductive argument is that if you convince your audience to accept your major and minor premises, they should also accept your conclusion. The problem is to establish your basic assumptions. You try to select premises that you know your audience accepts or that are self-evident—that is, premises that most people would believe to be true. Do not think, however, that "most people" is made up only of your friends and acquaintances. Think, too, of those who may hold different views. If you think that your premises are too controversial or difficult to establish firmly, you should use inductive reasoning.

Inductive Arguments. Inductive arguments move from specific examples or facts to a general conclusion. Unlike deduction, induction has no distinctive form, and its conclusions are less definitive than those of syllogisms whose forms are valid and whose premises are clearly true. Still, there is a sequence of events that is common to much inductive thinking and to some writing based on that thinking. First, usually, you decide on a question to be answered—or, especially in scientific work, a tentative answer to such a question, called a *hypothesis.* Then you gather all the evidence you can find that is relevant to the question and that may be important to finding the answer. Finally you draw a conclusion, often called an *inference,* that answers the question and takes the evidence into account. Here is a very simple example:

Question: How did that living-room window get broken?
Evidence: There is a baseball on the living-room floor.
           The baseball was not there this morning.
           Some children were playing baseball this afternoon.
           They were playing in the vacant lot across from the window.
           They stopped playing a little while ago.
           They aren't in the vacant lot now.
Conclusion: One of the children hit or threw the ball through the window.
           Then they all ran away.

The conclusion seems obvious. That is because it takes all of the evidence into account. But if it turned out that the children had been playing softball, not baseball, that one additional piece of evidence would make the conclusion very doubtful—and the true answer would be much harder to infer. And just because the conclusion is believable you cannot necessarily assume it is true. Even if the children had been playing baseball, the window could have been broken in some other way. Perhaps a bird flew against it, and perhaps the baseball in the living room had been there unnoticed all day, so that the second piece of "evidence" is not true.

Because inductive arguments tend to be more complicated than this example, how can you move from the evidence you have collected to a sound conclusion? That crucial step can be a big one, and indeed it is sometimes called an *inductive leap.* With induction, conclusions are never certain, only highly probable. Although the form of induction does not point to any particular type of conclusion the way deduction does, making sure that your evidence is relevant, representative, and sufficient (see pp. 466–67) can increase the probability of your conclusion's being sound. In addition, the more information you gather, the better your chances of establishing the connection between your evidence and your conclusion.

Considering alternate conclusions is a good way to avoid reaching an unjustified or false conclusion. In the example above, a hypothesis something like this might follow the question:

Hypothesis: Those children playing baseball broke the living-room window.

Many people stop reasoning at this point, without considering the evidence. When the gap between your evidence and your conclusion is too great, you can be accused of reaching a hasty conclusion or one that is not borne out by the facts. This well-named error is called *jumping to a conclusion* because it amounts to a premature inductive leap. In induction, the hypothesis is merely the starting point. The rest of the inductive process continues as if the question were still to be answered—as in fact it is until all the evidence has been taken into account.

Fallacies of Argument

Fallacies are statements that may look like arguments but are not logically defensible and may actually be deceptive. When detected they can backfire and turn even a sympathetic audience against your position. Here are some of the more common fallacies that you should try to avoid.

Begging the Question.   Begging the question is a logical fallacy that assumes in the premise what the arguer is trying to prove in the conclusion. This tactic asks us to agree that certain points are self-evident when they are not.

> The unfair and shortsighted legislation that limits free trade is clearly a threat to the American economy.

Restrictions against free trade may or may not be unfair and shortsighted, but emotionally loaded language does not constitute proof. The statement begs the question because it assumes what it should be proving—that restrictive legislation is dangerous.

Argument from Analogy.   An analogy is a comparison of two unlike things. Although analogies can explain an abstract or unclear idea and can be quite convincing, they never prove anything. When you base an argument on an analogy and ignore important dissimilarities between the two things being compared, you create a fallacy.

> The overcrowded conditions in some parts of our city have forced people together like rats in a cage. Like rats, they will eventually turn on one another, fighting and killing until a balance is restored. It is therefore necessary that we vote to appropriate funds to build low-cost housing.

No evidence is offered that people behave like rats under these or any conditions. Simply because two things have some characteristics in common, the conclusion does not necessarily follow that they are alike in other respects.

Personal Attack (Argument *Ad Hominem*). This fallacy tries to turn attention away from the facts of an issue by attacking the motives or character of one's opponents.

> The public should not take seriously Dr. Mason's plan for upgrading county health services. He is a former alcoholic whose second wife recently divorced him.

This attack on Dr. Mason's character says nothing about the quality of his plan. Sometimes there is a connection between a person's private and public lives—for example, a case of conflict of interest. But no evidence of such a connection is given here.

Hasty or Sweeping Generalization. This fallacy occurs when a general principle is applied mistakenly to a special case.

> Because preschool programs help children form social relationships, Amy and Fred Winkler should send their son Marc to nursery school.

Perhaps Marc would benefit from nursery school, perhaps not. Like many other children he may be shy, or frail in health, or otherwise not ready for the experience. General rules nearly always have exceptions, and the case in point may be one of those exceptions.

False Dilemma (Either/Or Fallacy). This kind of argument assumes that there are only two alternatives when more exist.

> We must choose between life and death, between total disarmament and nuclear war. There can be no neutrality on this issue.

An argument like this misrepresents issues and forces people to choose between extremes instead of exploring more moderate possibilities.

Equivocation. This fallacy occurs when you change the meaning of a key term at some point in your argument. Equivocation makes it seem as if your conclusion follows from your premises when it actually does not.

As a human endeavor computers are a praiseworthy and even remarkable accomplishment. But how human can we hope to be if we rely on computers to make our decisions?

The use of *human* in the first sentence refers to the entire human race. In the second sentence human means "merciful" or civilized. By subtly shifting this term to refer to qualities characteristic of people as opposed to machines, the writer makes his argument seem more sound than it is.

Red Herring. This fallacy occurs when you change the focus of an argument to divert your audience from the actual issue. Very often this is done to move an argument from a weak position to a stronger one

So far Mr. Bradley, our state representative, has spent months debating the proposed tax bill. The governor has said that he needs the revenue that this bill offers, but Mr. Bradley refuses to support him. One can only wonder if Mr. Bradley has nothing better to do in his own district than to spend so much time opposing the governor.

The focus of this argument should be the merits of the tax bill. Instead, the writer shifts to the irrelevant issue of Mr. Bradley's spending too much time opposing the governor.

You Also (*Tu Quoque*.) This fallacy occurs when you assert that an opponent's argument has no value because the opponent does not follow his or her own advice. In other words, you accuse an opponent of acting in a way that is not in line with his or her stated position ("you do it too").

How can that judge favor mandatory drug testing? During his confirmation hearings, he admitted having smoked marijuana.

Appeal to Doubtful Authority. Often people will attempt to bolster an argument with references to experts or famous people. These appeals are valid when the person you are quoting or referring to is an expert in the area you are discussing. You commit a fallacy, however, when you cite individuals who have no expertise concerning the issue with which you are concerned.

According to Ted Koppel, interest rates will decline during the next fiscal year.

Although Ted Koppel is a competent television interviewer, he has no background in business or finance. In the final analysis, his pronouncements about interest rates are no more than an opinion, or, at best, an educated guess.

Misleading Statistics.   This fallacy occurs when the person arguing misrepresents statistical evidence in an attempt to influence an audience.

> Women will never be competent electricians; 50 percent of the women in the electrical technology section failed the exam.

Here the writer has neglected to mention that there were only two women in the course. Because this statistic is not based on a big enough sample, it cannot be used as evidence to support the argument.

***Post Hoc, Ergo Propter Hoc* (After This, Therefore Because of This).**   This fallacy, known as *post hoc* reasoning, assumes that because two events occur close together in time, the first must cause the second.

> Every time a Republican is elected president a recession follows. If we want to avoid another recession, we should elect a Democrat.

This statement makes a mistaken connection between Republican presidents and recessions. Even if we were to grant the truth of the assertion that recessions always occur during the tenure of Republican presidents, no causal connection has been established. (See pp. 250–51)

***Non Sequitur* (It Does Not Follow).**   This fallacy occurs when irrelevant evidence is used to support an assertion.

> Disarmament weakened America after World War I. Disarmament also weakened America after the Vietnam War. Considering this evidence, we should not continue to negotiate with the Soviet Union.

The effects of disarmament in the past have nothing to do with current negotiations with the Soviet Union. For this reason they are irrelevant to the soundness of any current treaty.

STRUCTURING AN ARGUMENTATIVE ESSAY

An argumentative essay, like other kinds of essays, has an introduction stating a thesis and a conclusion. But the body of an argumentative essay has its own special structure, originating with the ancient Greeks and used, with variations, ever since. The Declaration of Independence generally follows the classical design: introduction, thesis statement, outline of the argument, proof of the thesis, refutation of opposing arguments, and conclusion.

Jefferson begins the Declaration of Independence by presenting the issue that the document addresses: the obligation of the people of the American colonies to tell the world why they must separate from Great Britain. Next Jefferson states his thesis that because of the tyranny of the British king, the colonies must replace his rule with another form of government. In the body of the Declaration of Independence, he offers as evidence twenty-eight examples of injustice endured by the American colonies. Following the evidence, Jefferson anticipates possible counterarguments and rebuts them by explaining how time and time again the colonists have appealed to the British for redress, but without result. In his concluding paragraph, Jefferson restates the thesis and reinforces it one final time. He ends with a flourish: He speaks for the representatives of the states, explicitly dissolving all connections between England and America.

Not all arguments, however, follow this pattern. Your material, your thesis, your purpose, your audience, the type of argument you are writing, and the limitations of your assignment ultimately determine the strategies you use. Nevertheless, the typical argumentative essay may include presentation of evidence; connecting the evidence with the thesis by induction, deduction, or a combination of the two; and refuting opposing evidence and arguments.

Introduction: Introduce the issue.
State the thesis.
Body: Induction—offer evidence to support the thesis.
Deduction—use syllogisms to support the thesis.
State the arguments against the thesis and refute them.
Conclusion: Sum up the argument if it is long and complex.
Restate the thesis.
Make a forceful closing statement.

If your thesis is especially novel or controversial, the refutation of opposing arguments may come first. Peter Singer uses this technique in his essay "Animal Liberation." For the same reason, opposing positions may even be mentioned in the introduction—provided they are discussed later in the argument.

Suppose your journalism instructor has given you the following assignment: "Select a controversial topic that interests you, and write a brief editorial. Direct your editorial to readers who do not share your views, and try to convince them that your position is reasonable. Be sure to acknowledge the view your audience holds and to refute any criticisms of your argument that you can anticipate." You are especially well informed about one local issue because you have just read a series of articles on it. A citizens group has formed to lobby for a local ordinance that would authorize spending tax dollars for parochial schools in your community. Because you have also recently studied the constitutional doctrine of separation of church and state in your American history class, you know you could argue fairly and strongly against the position taken by this group.

An informal outline of your essay might look like this:

Introduce the issue:	Should public tax revenues be spent on aid to parochial schools?
Thesis:	Despite the pleas of citizen groups like Parochial School Parents United, using tax dollars to support church-affiliated schools directly violates the United States Constitution.
Evidence (deduction):	Explain general principle of separation of church and state in the Constitution.
Evidence (induction):	Present recent examples of court cases interpreting and applying this principle.
Evidence (deduction):	Interpret how the Constitution and the court cases apply to your community's situation.
Anticipate and refute opposition:	Specify and answer arguments used by Parochial School Parents United. Concede the point that many families can no longer afford the cost of a parochial school education.
Conclusion:	Sum up the argument, restate the thesis, and end with a strong closing statement.

The following editorial, written by Matt Daniels for his college newspaper, illustrates a number of the techniques discussed above.

An Argument against the Anna Todd Jennings Scholarship^x

Introduction   Recently, a dispute has arisen over the   1
"Caucasian-restricted" Anna Todd Jennings
scholarship. Anna Jennings died in 1955 and
Summary of   established a trust that granted a scholarship of up
controversy
to $15,000 for a deserving student. Unfortunately,
Anna Jennings, who had certain racist views, limited
her scholarship to "Caucasian students." After much
debate with family and friends, I, a white, well-
qualified, and definitely deserving student, have
decided not to apply. It is my view that despite
Thesis   arguments to the contrary, applying for the Anna Todd
Jennings scholarship furthers the racist ideas that
were held by its founder.

Argument   Most people would agree that racism in any form   2
(deductive) is an evil that should be opposed. The Anna Todd
Premises lead
to conclusion Jennings scholarship is a subtle but nonetheless
dangerous expression of racism. It explicitly
discriminates against blacks, Asians, Hispanics,
Native Americans, and others. By providing a
scholarship for whites only, Anna Jennings frustrates
the aspirations of groups who until recently had been
virtually shut out of the educational mainstream. On
this basis alone, students should refuse to apply and
should actively work to encourage the school to
challenge the racist provisions of Anna Todd
Jennings's will. Such challenges have been upheld by
the courts: The striking down of a similar clause in
the will of the eighteenth-century financier Stephen
Girard is one recent example.

Argument   The school itself must share some blame in this   3
(inductive) case. Students who applied for the Anna Todd Jennings

---

*Eds Note—This essay discusses a true situation; however, we have changed the
name of the scholarship.

Evidence

scholarship were unaware of its restrictions. The director of the financial aid office has admitted that he knew about the racial restrictions of the scholarship but thought that students should have the right to apply anyway. In addition, the materials distributed by the financial aid office gave no indication that the award was limited to Caucasians. Students were required to fill out forms, submit financial statements, and forward transcripts. In addition to this material, all students were told to attach a recent photograph to their application. Little did the applicants realize that the sole purpose of this innocuous little picture was to separate whites from nonwhites. The school has been in collusion with the administrators of the Anna Todd

Conclusion (based on evidence)

Jennings trust. By keeping secret the restrictions of the scholarship, the school has put students, most of whom are not racists and who support the goals of affirmative action, in the position of unwittingly endorsing Anna Jennings's racism.

Refutation of opposing argument

The problem that faces students is how best to   4
deal with the benefaction of a racist. A recent edition of the school paper contained several letters saying that students should accept Anna Jennings's scholarship money. One student said, "If we do not take that money and use our education to topple the barriers of prejudice, we are giving the money to those who will use the money in an opposite fashion." This argument, although seemingly attractive, is flawed. If an individual accepts a scholarship with racial restrictions, then he or she would seem to endorse the principles behind it. If you do not want to appear to endorse racism, then you should reject the scholarship, even if this action

causes you hardship or gives your adversary a
momentary advantage. To do otherwise is to further
the cause of the individual who set up the
scholarship. The best way to register a protest is to
work to change the requirement for the scholarship
and to encourage others not to apply as long as the
racial restrictions exist.

Refutation of opposing argument

Another student made the point that a number of   5
other restricted scholarships are available at the
school but no one seems to question them. For
example, one is for the children of veterans, another
is for women, and yet another is earmarked for
blacks. Certainly all these scholarships do have
restrictions, but to say that all restrictions are
the same is to make a hasty generalization. Women,
blacks, and the children of veterans are groups whose
special treatment is justified. Both women and blacks
have been discriminated against for years, and many
educational opportunities have been denied them.
Earmarking scholarships for them is simply a means of
restoring some measure of equality. The children of
veterans have been singled out because their parents
have rendered extraordinary service to their county.
Whites, however, do not fall into either of these
categories. Special treatment for them is based
solely on race and has nothing to do with any
objective standard of need or merit.

Restatement of thesis

Conclusion

I hope that by refusing to apply for the Anna   6
Todd Jennings scholarship, I have encouraged other
students to think about the issues involved in their
own decisions. All of us have a responsibility to
ourselves and to society. If we truly believe that
racism in all its forms is evil, then we have to make
a choice between student loans and hypocrisy. Faced

with these options, our decision should be clear.

Concluding statement

Accept the loss of funds as an opportunity to explore your values and to fight for principles in which you believe; if you do, this opportunity is worth far more than any scholarship.

Points for Special Attention

Gathering Evidence. Because of his involvement with his subject, Matt Daniels was able to provide examples from his own experience to make his point and did not have to do library research. This does not mean, however, that Matt did not spend a lot of time thinking about ideas and selecting evidence. He had to review the requirements for the scholarship and decide on the arguments that he would make. In addition, he reviewed an article that appeared in the school newspaper and the letters that students wrote in response to the article. He then chose facts that would help sustain interest and add authority to his points.

Certainly statistics, studies, and expert testimony, if they exist, would strengthen Matt's argument. But even without such evidence, an argument such as this one, based on strong logic and personal experience, can be quite compelling.

Refuting Opposing Arguments. Matt devotes two paragraphs to presenting and refuting arguments made by students who believed they should apply for the scholarship despite its racial restrictions. He begins this section by asking a rhetorical question—a question asked not for information but to further the argument. He goes on to present what he considers to be the two strongest arguments against his thesis—that students should take the money and work to fight racism and that other scholarships at the school have restrictions. Matt counters these arguments by identifying a flaw in the logic of the first argument and by pointing to a fallacy, a hasty generalization, in the second.

Audience. Because his essay was an editorial for his college newspaper, Matt assumed an audience of general readers who were familiar with the issue he was discussing. Letters to the editor of the paper convinced him that his position was unusual, and he concluded that his readers, mostly students and instructors, would have to be persuaded that his points were valid. For this reason he is careful to present himself as a reasonable person, to explain issues that he believes are central to his case, and to avoid *ad hominem* attacks. In addition, he avoids sweeping generalizations and name-calling and goes into great detail to support his assertions and to convince his readers that his points are worth considering.

Organization.   Matt uses several strategies discussed earlier in the chapter. He begins his essay by introducing the issue he is going to discuss and then states his thesis: Applying for the Anna Todd Jennings scholarship furthers the racist ideas that were held by its founder.

Because Matt had given a good deal of thought to his subject, he was able to construct two fairly strong arguments to support his position. His first argument is deductive. He begins by stating a premise that he believes is self evident. Most people agree that racism should be opposed. The rest of his argument follows a straightforward deductive pattern:

Major premise: Racism is an evil that should be opposed.
Minor premise: The Anna Todd Jennings scholarship is racist.
   Conclusion: Therefore, the Anna Todd Jennings scholarship should be opposed.

Matt ends his argument with a piece of factual evidence—the relatively recent successful challenge to Stephen Girard's will   that reenforces his conclusion.

Matt's second argument is inductive, asserting that the school has put students in the position of unknowingly supporting racism. The argument begins with Matt's hypothesis and presents the fact that the school actually knew about the racism restrictions of the scholarship and that they did nothing to make students aware of them. According to Matt, the school's knowledge and tacit approval of the situation lead to the conclusion that the school is in collusion with the administrators who manage the scholarship.

In his fourth and fifth paragraphs, Matt anticipates and refutes two criticisms of his argument. Although his conclusion is rather brief, it does effectively reinforce and support his main idea. Matt ends his essay by recommending a course of action to his fellow stu dents.

The essays that follow represent a wide variety of historical and topical perspectives. Each, however, presents an argument to support a controversial thesis. As you read each essay, try to identify the strategies that each author uses to convince readers.

THE DECLARATION OF INDEPENDENCE

Thomas Jefferson

Thomas Jefferson was born in what is now Albemarle County, Virginia, in 1743. He attended The College of William and Mary and in 1767 became a lawyer. He served in the Virginia House of Burgesses and became known as a leading patriot. As a result, he was named a delegate to the Continental Congress and was chosen to draft the Declaration of Independence, which was then amended by the Congress. After the Revolution, he was governor of Virginia, then a member of the Continental Congress, minister to France, Secretary of State in Washington's first cabinet, Vice President to John Adams, and President from 1801 to 1809. During his retirement Jefferson designed and founded the University of Virginia. He died on July 4, 1826. The Declaration of Independence challenges a basic assumption of the age in which it was written—the divine right of kings. To accomplish his ends, Jefferson followed many of the principles of argumentative writing. Unlike many modern revolutionary manifestos, the Declaration of Independence is a model of clarity and precision that attempts to establish and support its thesis by means of irrefutable logic and reason.

When in the course of human events, it becomes necessary for one 1 people to dissolve the political bands which have connected them with another, and to assume among the powers of the earth, the separate and equal station to which the Laws of Nature and of Nature's God entitle them, a decent respect to the opinions of mankind requires that they should declare the causes which impel them to the separation.

We hold these truths to be self-evident, that all men are created 2 equal, that they are endowed by their Creator with certain unalienable rights, that among these are life, liberty and the pursuit of happiness. That to secure these rights, governments are instituted among men, deriving their just powers from the consent of the governed. That whenever any form of government becomes destructive of these ends, it is the right of the people to alter or to abolish it, and to institute new government, laying its foundation on such principles and organizing its powers in such form, as to them shall seem most likely to effect their safety and happiness. Prudence, indeed, will dictate that governments long established should not be changed for light and transient causes; and accordingly all experience hath shown, that mankind are more disposed to suffer, while evils are sufferable, than to right themselves by abolishing the forms to which they are accustomed. But when a long train of abuses and usurpations, pursuing invariably the same object, evinces a design to reduce them under absolute despotism, it is their right, it is their duty, to throw off such government, and to provide new guards for their future security. Such has been the patient sufferance of these Colonies; and such is now the necessity which constrains them to alter their former systems of government. This history of the present King of Great Britain is a history of repeated injuries and usurpations, all having in direct object the establishment of an absolute tyranny over these States. To prove this, let facts be submitted to a candid world.

He has refused his assent to laws, the most wholesome and necessary for the public good. 3

He has forbidden his Governors to pass laws of immediate and pressing importance, unless suspended in their operation till his assent should be obtained; and when so suspended, he has utterly neglected to attend to them. 4

He has refused to pass other laws for the accommodation of large districts of people, unless those people would relinquish the right of representation in the legislature, a right inestimable to them and formidable to tyrants only. 5

He has called together legislative bodies at places unusual, uncomfortable, and distant from the depository of their public records, for the sole purpose of fatiguing them into compliance with his measures. 6

He has dissolved representative houses repeatedly, for opposing with manly firmness his invasions on the rights of the people. 7

He has refused for a long time, after such dissolutions, to cause others to be elected; whereby the legislative powers, incapable of annihilation, have returned to the people at large for their exercise; the State remaining in the meantime exposed to all the dangers of invasion from without and convulsions within. 8

He has endeavoured to prevent the population of these states; for that purpose obstructing the laws for naturalization of foreigners; refusing to pass others to encourage their migration hither, and raising the conditions of new appropriations of lands. 9

He has obstructed the administration of justice, by refusing his 10
assent to laws for establishing judiciary powers.

He has made judges dependent on his will alone, for the tenure of 11
their offices, and the amount and payment of their salaries.

He has erected a multitude of new offices, and sent hither swarms 12
of officers to harass our people, and eat out their substance.

He has kept among us, in times of peace, standing armies without 13
the consent of our legislatures.

He has affected to render the military independent of and superior 14
to the civil power.

He has combined with others to subject us to a jurisdiction for- 15
eign to our constitution, and unacknowledged by our laws; giving
his assent to their acts of pretended legislation:

For quartering large bodies of armed troops among us: 16

For protecting them, by a mock trial, from punishment for any 17
murders which they should commit on the inhabitants of these
States:

For cutting off our trade with all parts of the world: 18

For imposing taxes on us without our consent: 19

For depriving us in many cases of the benefits of trial by jury: 20

For transporting us beyond seas to be tried for pretended offences: 21

For abolishing the free system of English laws in a neighbouring 22
Province, establishing therein an arbitrary government, and enlarg-
ing its boundaries so as to render it at once an example and fit instrument for introducing the same absolute rule into these Colonies:

For taking away our Charters, abolishing our most valuable laws, 23
and altering fundamentally the forms of our governments:

For suspending our own legislatures, and declaring themselves in- 24
vested with power to legislate for us in all cases whatsoever.

He has abdicated government here, by declaring us out of his pro- 25
tection and waging war against us.

He has plundered our seas, ravaged our coasts, burnt our towns, 26
and destroyed the lives of our people.

He is at this time transporting large armies of foreign mercenaries 27
to complete the works of death, desolation and tyranny, already begun with circumstances of cruelty and perfidy scarcely paralleled in
the most barbarous ages, and totally unworthy the head of a civilized nation.

He has constrained our fellow citizens taken captive on the high 28
seas to bear arms against their country, to become the executioners
of their friends and brethren, or to fall themselves by their hands.

He has excited domestic insurrections amongst us, and has en- 29
deavoured to bring on the inhabitants of our frontiers, the merciless

Indian savages, whose known rule of warfare, is an undistinguished destruction of all ages, sexes, and conditions.

In every stage of these oppressions we have petitioned for redress in the most humble terms: our repeated petitions have been answered only by repeated injury. A prince whose character is thus marked by every act which may define a tyrant is unfit to be the ruler of a free people.   30

Nor have we been wanting in attention to our British brethren. We have warned them from time to time of attempts by their legislature to extend an unwarrantable jurisdiction over us. We have reminded them of the circumstances of our emigration and settlement here. We have appealed to their native justice and magnanimity, and we have conjured them by the ties of our common kindred to disavow those usurpations, which would inevitably interrupt our connections and correspondence. They too have been deaf to the voice of justice and of consanguinity. We must, therefore, acquiesce in the necessity, which denounces our separation, and hold them, as we hold the rest of mankind, enemies in war, in peace friends.   31

We, therefore, the Representatives of the United States of America, in General Congress assembled, appealing to the Supreme Judge of the world for the rectitude of our intentions, do, in the name, and by authority of the good people of these Colonies, solemnly publish and declare, That these United Colonies are, and of right ought to be, Free and Independent States; that they are absolved from all allegiance to the British Crown, and that all political connection between them and the state of Great Britain, is and ought to be totally dissolved; and that as Free and Independent States, they have full power to levy war, conclude peace, contract alliances, establish commerce, and to do all other acts and things which Independent States may of right do. And for the support of this declaration, with a firm reliance on the protection of Divine Providence, we mutually pledge to each other our lives, our fortunes, and our sacred honor.   32

COMPREHENSION

1. What "truths" does Jefferson assert are "self-evident"?

2. What does Jefferson say is the source from which governments derive their powers?

3. What reasons does Jefferson give to support his premise that the United States should break away from Great Britain?

4. What conclusions about the British crown does Jefferson draw from the facts he presents?

PURPOSE AND AUDIENCE

1. What is the major premise of Jefferson's argument? Should Jefferson have done more to establish the truth of his premise?

2. The Declaration of Independence was written during a period now referred to as the Age of Reason. In what ways has Jefferson tried to make his document reasonable?

3. For what audience is the document intended? Would all people have been likely to accept it?

4. How does Jefferson attempt to convince his audience that he is reasonable? Does Jefferson anticipate and refute the opposition?

5. In paragraph 31, following the list of grievances, why does Jefferson address his "British brethren"?

STYLE AND STRUCTURE

1. Construct an outline of the Declaration of Independence.

2. Is the Declaration of Independence an example of inductive or deductive reasoning?

3. How does Jefferson create smooth and logical transitions from one paragraph to another?

4. Why does Jefferson list all of his twenty-eight grievances?

5. Jefferson begins the last paragraph of the Declaration of Independence with "We, therefore. . . . " What clues about the intent of the document do these words give?

6. What particular words does Jefferson use that are rare today?

VOCABULARY PROJECTS

1. Define each of the following words as it is used in this selection.

station (1)	transient (2)
impel (1)	usurpations (2)
self-evident (2)	evinces (2)
endowed (2)	despotism (2)
deriving (2)	sufferance (2)
prudence (2)	candid (2)

depository (6)	arbitrary (22)
dissolutions (8)	insurrections (29)
annihilation (8)	disavow (31)
appropriations (9)	consanguinity (31)
tenure (11)	rectitude (32)
jurisdiction (15)	levy (32)

2. Underline ten words that have negative connotations. Discuss how Jefferson uses these words to help him make his point and how words with more neutral connotations would affect his case.

WRITING WORKSHOP

1. Write an argumentative essay from the point of view of King George III, and try to convince the colonists that they should not break away from Great Britain. If you can, refute several of the points Jefferson lists in the Declaration.

2. Following Jefferson's example, write a declaration of independence from your school, job, family, or any other institution with which you are connected.

3. Write an essay in which you state a grievance that you share with other members of some group, and then argue for the best way to eliminate it.

THEMATIC CONNECTIONS

- "Grant and Lee: A Study in Contrasts" (p. 321)
- "Rule of Law" (p. 397)
- "Civil Disobedience" (p. 552)

BILINGUAL EDUCATION:
THE KEY TO BASIC SKILLS

Angelo Gonzalez

Angelo Gonzalez is the educational director of ASPIRA of New York, a Hispanic advocacy and civic organization. His essay and the next, by Richard Rodriguez, originally appeared as companion pieces in an educational supplement to the New York Times. *In his essay, Gonzalez argues forcefully for the continuation of full funding for bilingual education programs in the United States. Using evidence from various sources, he relies primarily on an appeal to reason.*

If we accept that a child cannot learn unless taught through the language he speaks and understands; that a child who does not speak or understand English must fall behind when English is the dominant medium of instruction; that one needs to learn English so as to be able to participate in an English-speaking society; that self-esteem and motivation are necessary for effective learning; that rejection of a child's native language and culture is detrimental to the learning process: then any necessary effective educational program for limited or no English-speaking ability must incorporate the following: 1

- Language arts and comprehensive reading programs taught in the child's native language. 2
- Curriculum content areas taught in the native language to further comprehension and academic achievement. 3
- Intensive instruction in English. 4
- Use of materials sensitive to and reflecting the culture of children within the program. 5

MOST IMPORTANT GOAL

The mastery of basic reading skills is the most important goal in primary education since reading is the basis for much of all subsequent learning. Ordinarily, these skills are learned at home. But 6 where beginning reading is taught in English, only the English-speaking child profits from these early acquired skills that are prerequisites to successful reading development. Reading programs taught in English to children with Spanish as a first language wastes their acquired linguistic attributes and also impedes learning by forcing them to absorb skills of reading simultaneously with a new language.

Both local and national research data provide ample evidence for   7
the efficacy of well-implemented programs. The New York City Board of Education Report on Bilingual Pupil Services for 1982–83 indicated that in all areas of the curriculum—English, Spanish and mathematics—and at all grade levels, students demonstrated statistically significant gains in tests of reading in English and Spanish and in math. In all but two of the programs reviewed, the attendance rates of students in the program, ranging from 86 to 94 percent, were higher than those of the general school population. Similar higher attendance rates were found among students in high school bilingual programs.

At Yale University, Kenji Hakuta, a linguist, reported recently   8
on a study of working-class Hispanic students in the New Haven bilingual program. He found that children who were the most bilingual, that is, who developed English without the loss of Spanish, were brighter in both verbal and nonverbal tests. Over time, there was an increasing correlation between English and Spanish—a finding that clearly contradicts the charge that teaching in the home language is detrimental to English. Rather the two languages are interdependent within the bilingual child, reinforcing each other.

ESSENTIAL CONTRIBUTION

As Jim Cummins of the Ontario Institute for Studies in Educa-   9
tion has argued, the use and development of the native language makes an essential contribution to the development of minority children's subject-matter knowledge and academic learning potential. In fact, at least three national data bases—the National Assessment of Educational Progress, National Center for Educational Statistics-High School and Beyond Studies, and the Survey of Income and Education—suggest that there are long-term positive effects among high school students who have participated in bilingual-education programs. These students are achieving higher scores on tests of verbal and mathematics skills.

These and similar findings buttress the argument stated persua-   10
sively in the recent joint recommendation of the Academy for Edu-

cational Development and the Hazen Foundation, namely, that America needs to become a more multilingual nation and children who speak a non-English language are a national resource to be nurtured in school.

Unfortunately, the present Administration's educational policies would seem to be leading us in the opposite direction. Under the guise of protecting the common language of public life in the United States, William J. Bennett, the Secretary of Education, unleashed a frontal attack on bilingual education. In a major policy address, he engaged in rhetorical distortions about the nature and effectiveness of bilingual programs, pointing only to unnamed negative research findings to justify the Administration's retrenchment efforts. 11

Arguing for the need to give local school districts greater flexibility in determining appropriate methodologies in serving limited-English-proficient students, Mr. Bennett fails to realize that, in fact, districts serving large numbers of language-minority students, as is the case in New York City, do have that flexibility. Left to their own devices in implementing legal mandates, many school districts have performed poorly at providing services to all entitled language-minority students. 12

A HARSH REALITY

The harsh reality in New York City for language-minority students was documented comprehensively last month by the Educational Priorities Panel. The panel's findings revealed that of the 113,831 students identified as being limited in English proficiency, as many as 44,000 entitled students are not receiving any bilingual services. The issue at hand is, therefore, not one of choice but rather violation of the rights of almost 40 percent of language-minority children to equal educational opportunity. In light of these findings the Reagan Administration's recent statements only serve to exacerbate existing inequities in the American educational system for linguistic-minority children. Rather than adding fuel to a misguided debate, the Administration would serve these children best by insuring the full funding of the 1984 Bilingual Education Reauthorization Act as passed by the Congress. 13

COMPREHENSION

1. What three elements does Gonzalez believe are necessary for any effective educational program for students of limited or no English-speaking ability?

2. According to Gonzalez, what is the most important goal in primary education?

3. What is the effect of teaching beginning reading in English to children whose first language is Spanish?

4. How does local and national research support Gonzalez's claims?

5. According to Gonzalez, how are the rights of 40 percent of language-minority students being violated? What does he think the government should do to correct this situation?

PURPOSE AND AUDIENCE

1. Does Gonzalez address his readers as if they are familiar or unfamiliar with the problem he is discussing? Explain.

2. At what point does Gonzalez state his thesis? What are the advantages or disadvantages of this placement?

3. Does Gonzalez ever attempt to appeal to his readers' emotions? Explain.

STYLE AND STRUCTURE

1. Does Gonzalez use inductive or deductive reasoning to reach the conclusion he states at the end of paragraph 1? How sound is his reasoning?

2. Does Gonzalez use statistics, personal experience, or the opinions of experts to support his assertions? Given his credentials, why does he not rely more on his own testimony?

3. At what point in the essay does Gonzalez use inductive reasoning?

4. Gonzalez does not refute any of the major arguments against his position. Would doing so have strengthened his essay?

5. In what way do headings emphasize major points in the essay?

6. How effective is Gonzalez's conclusion? What points does he choose to emphasize? Would another type of conclusion have been better? Explain.

VOCABULARY PROJECTS

1. Define each of the following words as it is used in this selection.

medium (1)   linguistic (6)
detrimental (1)   attributes (6)

impede (6)   rhetorical (11)
efficacy (7)   exacerbate (13)
buttress (10)

2. In the last paragraph of his essay, Gonzalez refers to children who do not speak or understand English as *language-minority children.* How does he expect this phrase to affect his readers?

3. Throughout his essay Gonzalez refers to *bilingual educational programs.* Write a paragraph in which you define as best you can what Gonzalez means by this term.

WRITING WORKSHOP

1. Write an essay in which you argue for or against Gonzalez's assertion that not teaching in a non-English-speaking child's native language is a violation of his or her rights.

2. Do you agree or disagree with the joint recommendations of the Academy for Educational Development and the Hazen Foundation that America needs to become a more multilingual nation? Write an essay in which you argue for your position.

3. Critics of bilingual education have said that programs that put emphasis on a native language other than English delay children's ability to learn English. They believe that non-English-speaking children would be better served by programs that educated them in English and that offered them tutoring and counseling. Write an essay in which you argue for or against this suggestion.

THEMATIC CONNECTIONS

- "Aria: A Memoir of a Bilingual Childhood" (p. 348)
- "Bilingual Education: Outdated and Unrealistic" (p. 495)

BILINGUAL EDUCATION: OUTDATED AND UNREALISTIC

Richard Rodriguez

Born in 1944 in San Francisco to Mexican-American parents, Richard Rodriguez learned to speak English when he was in elementary school. He graduated from Stanford University and went on to do graduate work in Renaissance literature and to teach at the University of California at Berkeley. He is now a writer and journalist living in Mexico City. Rodriguez, who has published essays in many magazines and journals, caused considerable controversy with his autobiography The Hunger of Memory *(1982), in which he argues against bilingual education programs and affirmative action. The following essay is a response to "Bilingual Education: The Key to Basic Skills" by Angelo Gonzalez and, like it, addresses the question of whether bilingual education programs should be continued in the public schools.*

How shall we teach the dark-eyed child *ingles?* The debate continues much as it did two decades ago. 1

Bilingual education belongs to the 1960's, the years of the black civil rights movement. Bilingual education became the official Hispanic demand; as a symbol, the English-only classroom was intended to be analogous to the segregated lunch counter; the locked school door. Bilingual education was endorsed by judges and, of course, by politicians well before anyone knew the answer to the question: Does bilingual education work? 2

Who knows? *Quien sabe?* 3

The official drone over bilingual education is conducted by educationalists with numbers and charts. Because bilingual education was never simply a matter of pedagogy, it is too much to expect educators to resolve the matter. Proclamations concerning bilingual education are weighted at bottom with Hispanic political grievances and, too, with middle-class romanticism. 4

No one will say it in public; in private, Hispanics argue with me about bilingual education and every time it comes down to memory. Everyone remembers going to that grammar school where students were slapped for speaking Spanish. Childhood memory is offered as 5

495

parable; the memory is meant to compress the gringo's long history of offenses against Spanish, Hispanic culture, Hispanics.

It is no coincidence that, although all of America's ethnic groups   6
are implicated in the policy of bilingual education, Hispanics, particularly Mexican-Americans, have been its chief advocates. The English words used by Hispanics in support of bilingual education are words such as "dignity," "heritage," "culture." Bilingualism becomes a way of exacting from gringos a grudging admission of contrition—for the 19th-century theft of the Southwest, the relegation of Spanish to a foreign tongue, the injustice of history. At the extreme, Hispanic bilingual enthusiasts demand that public schools "maintain" a student's sense of separateness.

Hispanics may be among the last groups of Americans who still   7
believe in the 1960's. Bilingual-education proposals still serve the romance of that decade, especially of the late 60's, when the heroic black civil rights movement grew paradoxically wedded to its opposite—the ethnic revival movement. Integration and separatism merged into twin, possible goals.

With integration, the black movement inspired middle-class   8
Americans to imitations—the Hispanic movement; the Gray Panthers; feminism; gay rights. Then there was withdrawal, with black glamour leading a romantic retreat from the anonymous crowd.

Americans came to want it both ways. They wanted in and they   9
wanted out. Hispanics took to celebrating their diversity, joined other Americans in dancing rings around the melting pot.

MYTHIC METAPHORS

More intently than most, Hispanics wanted the romance of their   10
dual cultural allegiance backed up by law. Bilingualism became proof that one could have it both ways, could be a full member of public America and yet also separate, privately Hispanic. "Spanish" and "English" became mythic metaphors, like country and city, describing separate islands of private and public life.

Ballots, billboards, and, of course, classrooms in Spanish. For   11
nearly two decades now, middle-class Hispanics have had it their way. They have foisted a neat ideological scheme on working-class children. What they want to believe about themselves, they wait for the child to prove that it is possible to be two, that one can assume the public language (the public life) of America, even while remaining what one was, existentially separate.

Adulthood is not so neatly balanced. The tension between public   12
and private life is intrinsic to adulthood—certainly middle-class

adulthood. Usually the city wins because the city pays. We are mass people for more of the day than we are with our intimates. No Congressional mandate or Supreme Court decision can diminish the loss.

I was talking the other day to a carpenter from Riga, in the Soviet 13 Republic of Latvia. He has been here six years. He told me of his having to force himself to relinquish the "luxury" of reading books in Russian or Latvian so he could begin to read books in English. And the books he was able to read in English were not of a complexity to satisfy him. But he was not going back to Riga.

Beyond any question of pedagogy there is the simple fact that a 14 language gets learned as it gets used, fills one's mouth, one's mind, with the new names for things.

The civil rights movement of the 1960's taught Americans to deal 15 with forms of discrimination other than economic—racial, sexual. We forget class. We talk about bilingual education as an ethnic issue; we forget to notice that the program mainly touches the lives of working-class immigrant children. Foreign-language acquisition is one thing for the upper-class child in a convent school learning to curtsy. Language acquisition can only seem a loss for the ghetto child, for the new language is psychologically awesome, being, as it is, the language of the bus driver and Papa's employer. The child's difficulty will turn out to be psychological more than linguistic because what he gives up are symbols of home.

PAIN AND GUILT

I was that child! I faced the stranger's English with pain and guilt 16 and fear. Baptized to English in school, at first I felt myself drowning—the ugly sounds forced down my throat—until slowly, slowly (held in the tender grip of my teachers), suddenly the conviction took; English was my language to use.

What I yearn for is some candor from those who speak about bilin- 17 gual education. Which of its supporters dares speak of the price a child pays—the price of adulthood—to make the journey from a working-class home into a middle-class schoolroom? The real story, the silent story of the immigrant child's journey is one of embarrassments in public; betrayal of all that is private; silence at home; and at school the hand tentatively raised.

Bilingual enthusiasts bespeak an easier world. They seek a lin- 18 guistic solution to a social dilemma. They seem to want to believe that there is an easy way for the child to balance private and public, in order to believe that there is some easy way for themselves.

Ten years ago, I started writing about the ideological implications   19
of bilingual education. Ten years from now some newspaper may
well invite me to contribute another Sunday supplement essay on
the subject. The debate is going to continue. The bilingual establishment is now inside the door. Jobs are at stake. Politicians can only
count heads; growing numbers of Hispanics will insure the compliance of politicians.

Publicly, we will continue the fiction. We will solemnly address   20
this issue as an educational question, a matter of pedagogy. But
privately, Hispanics will still seek from bilingual education as admission from the gringo that Spanish has value and presence. Hispanics
of middle class will continue to seek the romantic assurance of separateness. Experts will argue. Dark-eyed children will sit in the classroom. Mute.

COMPREHENSION

1. How long has the debate over bilingual education continued?

2. What does Rodriguez mean when he says that bilingual education
   belongs to the 1960s?

3. According to Rodriguez, what are the implications of bilingualism
   having become the official Hispanic demand? How does this public
   stand differ from what Hispanics say in private?

4. Explain what Rodriguez means in paragraph 9 when he says that
   Hispanics, like other Americans, wanted it both ways.

5. In what way have middle-class Hispanics "foisted a neat ideological
   scheme on working-class children"?

6. According to Rodriguez, what is the real story of the journey from a
   working-class Hispanic home into a middle-class classroom?

PURPOSE AND AUDIENCE

1. At what point does Rodriguez state his thesis? Why does he choose
   this strategy?

2. Rodriguez realizes that his *New York Times* audience is largely non-
   Hispanic. What concessions does he make to this audience? What
   changes would he make if he were addressing Hispanic readers?

3. Does Rodriguez see his audience as hostile, friendly, or neutral? Explain.

STYLE AND STRUCTURE

1. Unlike Gonzalez, Rodriguez uses personal observations as support for his argument. What is the effect of this evidence? Would he have done better using the numbers and charts of "educationists"?

2. Does Rodriguez appeal to reason, to emotion, or to both? Explain the advantages and disadvantages of his strategy.

3. Explain the use that Rodriguez makes of rhetorical questions.

4. What point does Rodriguez make in paragraph 13 by introducing the example of the carpenter from Riga?

5. Why in paragraph 16 does Rodriguez abruptly shift into the first person? What does he hope to gain with this strategy?

6. How optimistic or pessimistic is Rodriguez in his conclusion? Why does he choose to end his essay on this note?

VOCABULARY PROJECTS

1. Define each of the following words as it is used in this selection.

analogous (2)	mythic (10)
drone (4)	metaphor (10)
gringo (5)	pedagogy (14)
contrition (6)	ideological (19)
relegation (6)	mute (20)
paradoxically (7)	

2. In the first part of his essay, Rodriguez uses Spanish words and phrases. Write a paragraph in which you discuss his reasons for doing so.

3. Rodriguez draws a distinction between public and private languages. Write a paragraph or two in which you define these terms.

WRITING WORKSHOP

1. Write an essay in which you argue for or against Rodriguez's statement that it is not possible to assume the public language of America while remaining essentially separate. Use examples from your own experience to support your points.

2. In a recent article, Sally Peterson, an elementary school teacher and the president of the Learning English Advocates Drive, said, "Bilingual education is a successful financial institution, and like a sacred cow in California; to oppose it you immediately become a racist." Us-

ing this quotation as one piece of evidence, write an essay in which you agree or disagree with Rodriguez's assertion that proclamations about bilingual education were never a matter of pedagogy.

3. In 1986 California passed a law declaring English the state's official language. Some advocates of English said that the law was necessary to ensure that Spanish did not supplant English in the state. Opponents of the law said that there was no danger of this situation occurring and that those who supported the law were trying to suppress Hispanic culture. At present, twelve other states have statutes making English their official language. Write an essay in which you argue for or against such a statute in your state. If your instructor gives you permission, go to the library and find some articles that discuss this issue.

THEMATIC CONNECTIONS

- "Aria: A Memoir of a Bilingual Childhood" (p. 348)
- "Bilingual Education: The Key to Basic Skills" (p. 490)

ANIMAL LIBERATION

Peter Singer

Peter Singer was born in 1946 in Melbourne, Australia. He attended the University of Melbourne and Oxford, where he was a Radcliffe lecturer in philosophy. He has written Democracy and Disobedience *and published articles in both professional journals and magazines, including the* New York Times Magazine *and the* New York Review of Books. *While at Oxford, Singer became interested in the treatment of animals. After meeting others who shared his involvement, he became a vegetarian and began thinking seriously about the ethics of using animals for food or experimentation. The research he did culminated in* Animal Liberation *(1975), a book that is credited with supplying the philosophical underpinnings of the animal rights movement. The following essay, excerpted from this book, focuses on the problem of animal experimentation. Using a series of analogies, Singer refutes some of the criticism that has been leveled against those who, like himself, oppose using animals for scientific experimentation.*

When are experiments on animals justifiable? Upon learning of the nature of many contemporary experiments, many people react by saying that all experiments on animals should be prohibited immediately. But if we make our demands as absolute as this, the experimenters have a ready reply: Would we be prepared to let thousands of humans die if they could be saved by a single experiment on a single animal?

This question is, of course, purely hypothetical. There never has been and there never could be a single experiment that saves thousands of lives. The way to reply to this hypothetical question is to pose another: Would the experimenter be prepared to carry out his experiment on a human orphan under six months old if that were the only way to save thousands of lives?

If the experimenter would not be prepared to use a human infant then his readiness to use nonhuman animals reveals an unjustifiable form of discrimination on the basis of species, since adult apes, monkeys, dogs, cats, rats, and other mammals are more aware of what is happening to them, more self-directing, and, so far as we can tell, at least as sensitive to pain as a human infant. (I specified that the human infant be an orphan to avoid the complications of the feelings of parents, although in so doing I am being overfair to the experimenter, since the nonhuman animals used in experiments are not orphans and in many species the separation of mother and young clearly causes distress for both.)

There is no characteristic that human infants possess to a higher degree than adult nonhuman animals, unless we are to count the infant's potential as a characteristic that makes it wrong to experiment on him. Whether this characteristic should count is controversial—if we count it, we shall have to condemn abortion along with experiments on infants, since the potential of the infant and the fetus is the same. To avoid the complexities of this issue, however, we can alter our original question a little and assume that the infant is one with severe and irreversible brain damage that makes it impossible for him ever to develop beyond the level of a six-month-old infant. There are, unfortunately, many such human beings, locked away in special wards throughout the country, many of them long since abandoned by their parents. Despite their mental deficiencies, their anatomy and physiology is in nearly all respects identical with that of normal humans. If, therefore, we were to force-feed them with large quantities of floor polish, or drip concentrated solutions of cosmetics into their eyes, we would have a much more reliable indication of the safety of these products for other humans than we now get by attempting to extrapolate the results of tests on a variety of other species. The radiation experiments, the heatstroke experiments, and many other experiments described earlier in this chapter could also have told us more about human reactions to the experimental situation if they had been carried out on retarded humans instead of dogs and rabbits.

So whenever an experimenter claims that his experiment is important enough to justify the use of an animal, we should ask him whether he would be prepared to use a retarded human at a similar mental level to the animal he is planning to use. If his reply is negative, we can assume that he is willing to use a nonhuman animal only because he gives less consideration to the interests of members of other species than he gives to members of his own—and this bias is no more defensible than racism or any other form of arbitrary discrimination.

Of course, no one would seriously propose carrying out the experiments described in this chapter on retarded humans. Occasionally it has become known that some medical experiments have been performed on humans without their consent, and sometimes on retarded humans; but the consequences of these experiments for the human subjects are almost always trivial by comparison with what is standard practice for nonhuman animals. Still, these experiments on humans usually lead to an outcry against the experimenters, and rightly so. They are, very often, a further example of the arrogance of the research worker who justifies everything on the grounds of increasing knowledge. If experimenting on retarded, orphaned humans would be wrong, why isn't experimenting on nonhuman animals wrong? What difference is there between the two, except for the mere fact that, biologically, one is a member of our species and the other is not? But *that*, surely, is not a morally relevant difference, any more than the fact that a being is not a member of our race is a morally relevant difference.

Actually the analogy between speciesism and racism applies in   7 practice as well as in theory in the area of experimentation. Blatant speciesism leads to painful experiments on other species, defended on the grounds of its contribution to knowledge and possible usefulness for our species. Blatant racism has led to painful experiments on other races, defended on the grounds of its contribution to knowledge and possible usefulness for the experimenting race. Under the Nazi regime in Germany, nearly 200 doctors, some of them eminent in the world of medicine, took part in experiments on Jews and Russian and Polish prisoners. Thousands of other physicians knew of these experiments, some of which were the subject of lectures at medical academies. Yet the records show that the doctors sat through medical reports of the infliction of horrible injuries on these "lesser races" and then proceeded to discuss the medical lessons to be learned from them without anyone making even a mild protest about the nature of the experiments. The parallels between this attitude and that of experimenters today toward animals are striking. Then, as now, the subjects were frozen, heated, and put in decompression chambers. Then, as now, these events were written up in a dispassionate scientific jargon. The following paragraph is taken from a report by a Nazi scientist of an experiment on a human being, placed in a decompression chamber; it could equally have been taken from accounts of recent experiments in this country on animals:

> After five minutes spasms appeared; between the sixth and tenth minute respiration increased in frequency, the TP [test person] losing consciousness. From the eleventh to the thirtieth minute respiration slowed down to three inhalations per minute, only to cease entirely at the end of that period ... about half an hour after breathing had ceased, an autopsy was begun.

Then, as now, the ethic of pursuing knowledge was considered sufficient justification for inflicting agony on those who are placed beyond the limits of genuine moral concern. Our sphere of moral concern is far wider than that of the Nazis; but so long as there are sentient beings outside it, it is not wide enough.

To return to the question of when an experiment might be justifiable. It will not do to say: "Never!" In extreme circumstances, absolutist answers always break down. Torturing a human being is almost always wrong, but it is not absolutely wrong. If torture were the only way in which we could discover the location of a nuclear time bomb hidden in a New York City basement, then torture would be justifiable. Similarly, if a single experiment could cure a major disease, that experiment would be justifiable. But in actual life the benefits are always much, much more remote, and more often than not they are nonexistent. So how do we decide when an experiment is justifiable? 8

We have seen that the experimenter reveals a bias in favor of his own species whenever he carries out an experiment on a nonhuman for a purpose that he would not think justified him in using a human being, even a retarded human being. This principle gives us a guide toward an answer to our question. Since a speciesist bias, like a racist bias, is unjustifiable, an experiment cannot be justifiable unless the experiment is so important that the use of a retarded human being would also be justifiable. 9

This is not an absolutist principle. I do not believe that it could *never* be justifiable to experiment on a retarded human. If it really were possible to save many lives by an experiment that would take just one life, and there were *no other way* those lives could be saved, it might be right to do the experiment. But this would be an extremely rare case. Not one tenth of one percent of the experiments now being performed on animals would fall into this category. Certainly none of the experiments described in this chapter could pass this test. 10

It should not be thought that medical research would grind to a halt if the test I have proposed were applied, or that a flood of untested products would come onto the market. So far as new products are concerned it is true that, as I have already said, we would have to make do with fewer of them, using ingredients already known to be safe. That does not seem to be any great loss. But for testing really essential products, as well as for other areas of research, alternative methods not requiring animals can be and would be found. Some alternatives exist already and others would develop more rap- 11 idly if the energy and resources now applied to experimenting on animals were redirected into the search for alternatives.

At present scientists do not look for alternatives *simply because*   12
they do not care enough about the animals they are using. I make this assertion on the best possible authority, since it has been more or less admitted by Britain's Research Defense Society, a group which exists to defend researchers from criticism by animal welfare organizations. A recent article in the *Bulletin* of the National Society for Medical Research (the American equivalent of the Research Defence Society) described how the British group successfully fought off a proposed amendment to the British law regulating experiments that would have prohibited any experiment using live animals if the purpose of that experiment could be achieved by alternative means not involving animals. The main objections lodged by the Research Defense Society to this very mild attempt at reform were, first, that in some cases it may be cheaper to use animals than other methods, and secondly, that:

> in some cases alternatives may exist but they may be unknown to an investigator. With the vast amount of scientific literature coming out of even a very narrow field of study it is possible that an investigator may not know all that is now known about techniques or results in a particular area. . . .

(This ignorance would make the experimenter liable to prosecution under the proposed amendment.)

What do these objections amount to? The first can mean only one   13
thing: that economic considerations are more important than the suffering of animals; as for the second, it is a strong argument for a total moratorium on animal experiments until every experimenter has had time to read up on the existing reports of alternatives available in his field and results already obtained. Is it not shocking that experimenters may be inflicting agony on animals only because they have not kept up with the literature in their field literature that may contain reports of methods of achieving the same results without using animals? Or even reports of similar experiments that have been done already and are being endlessly repeated?

The objections of the Research Defence Society to the British   14
amendment can be summed up in one sentence: the prevention of animal suffering is not worth the expenditure of extra money or of the time the experimenter would need to read the literature in his

field. And of this "defense," incidentally, the National Society for Medical Research has said:

> The Research Defence Society of Great Britain deserves the plaudits of the world's scientific community for the manner in which it expressed its opposition to this sticky measure.

It would not be appropriate here to go into the alternatives to animal experiments that are already available. The subject is a highly technical one, more suited for researchers than for the general reader. But we already have the means to reduce greatly the number of animals experimented upon, in techniques like tissue culture (the culture of cells or groups of cells in an artificial environment); mathematical or computer models of biological systems; gas chromatography and mass spectrometry; and the use of films and models in educational instruction. Considering how little effort has been put into this field, the early results promise much greater progress if the effort is stepped up.

In some important areas improvements can easily be made without using animals. Although thousands of animals have been forced to inhale tobacco smoke for months and even years, the proof of the connection between tobacco usage and lung cancer was based on data from clinical observations of humans.

The US government is pouring billions of dollars into research on cancer. Much of it goes toward animal experiments, many of them only remotely connected with fighting cancer—experimenters have been known to relabel their work "cancer research" when they found they could get more money for it that way than under some other label. Of all cancers, lung cancer is the biggest killer. We know that smoking causes 80–85 percent of all lung cancer—in fact this is a "conservative" estimate, according to the director of the National Cancer Institute. In a case like this we must ask ourselves: can we justify inflicting lung cancer on thousands of animals when we know that we could virtually wipe out the disease by eliminating the use of tobacco? And if people are not prepared to give up tobacco, can it be right to make animals suffer the cost of their decision to continue smoking?

Of course, it must be admitted that there are some fields of scientific research that will be hampered by any genuine consideration of the interests of animals used in experimentation. No doubt there have been genuine advances in knowledge which would not have been attained as easily or as rapidly without the infliction of pain on animals. The ethical principle of equal consideration of interests does rule out some means of obtaining knowledge, and other means may be slower or more expensive. But we already accept such restrictions on scientific enterprise. We do not believe that our scientists have a general right to perform painful or lethal experiments on human beings without their consent, although there are cases in which such experiments would advance knowledge far more rapidly than any alternative method. My proposal does no more than broaden the scope of this existing restriction on scientific research.

Finally, it is important to realize that the major health problems   19
of the world largely continue to exist, not because we do not know how to prevent disease and keep people healthy, but because no one is putting the manpower and money into doing what we already know how to do. The diseases that ravage Asia, Africa, Latin America, and the pockets of poverty in the industrialized West, are diseases that, by and large, we know how to cure. They have been eliminated in communities which have adequate nutrition, sanitation, and health care. Those who are genuinely concerned about improving health and have medical qualifications would probably make a more effective contribution to human health if they left the laboratories and saw to it that our existing stock of medical knowledge reaches those who need it most.

COMPREHENSION

1. How does Singer answer the charge that if animal experimentation were stopped, thousands of people who could be saved by a single experiment would die?

2. What arguments does Singer present to support his point that if experimenters would not carry out an experiment on a human orphan under six months old, then they should not carry out the same experiment on an animal?

3. According to Singer, how are racism and speciesism similar?

4. How effective is Singer's analogy between racism and speciesism? Does Singer ignore important differences between racism and speciesism when he makes his analogy? Explain.

5. Under what circumstances does Singer consider experimentation on animals justifiable?

6. At present why do scientists fail to look for alternatives to animal experimentation? What alternatives does Singer suggest? What are scientists' objections to these alternatives?

7. Why, according to Singer, do the major health problems of the world continue to exist? What action does he suggest to scientists who are genuinely concerned with saving human lives?

PURPOSE AND AUDIENCE

1. Does Singer assume that his readers support or oppose his position? Explain.

2. How does Singer attempt to convince his readers that he is not an extremist?

3. What is the thesis of this essay? Is it stated or implied? Explain.

STYLE AND STRUCTURE

1. Why does Singer begin his essay with a question? At what point does he answer the question?

2. In paragraph 4 Singer draws an analogy between retarded human infants and animals. Why does he use this tactic? Can Singer be accused of oversimplifying his case?

3. Why does Singer include a quotation in paragraph 7? How effective is this strategy? Could this tactic have an effect other than the one Singer intended?

4. What points does Singer concede to his opposition? What major arguments against his position does Singer refute? How effective is his refutation?

5. Why in paragraph 12 does Singer spend so much time discussing what he admits is a "very mild attempt at reform"?

6. In his conclusion Singer tells those who want to improve human health to leave the laboratories and deliver health care to those who need it most. Is Singer setting up a red herring? Explain.

VOCABULARY PROJECTS

1. Define each of the following words as it is used in this selection.

hypothetical (2)	absolutist (10)
anatomy (4)	moratorium (13)
physiology (4)	chromatography (15)
eminent (7)	spectrometry (15)
decompression (7)	

2. In his essay, Singer refers to animals as *nonhuman animals*. What idea does he hope to convey with this usage?

3. Throughout the body of his essay, Singer draws a parallel between racism and speciesism. Write a paragraph in which you define and then contrast the two terms.

WRITING WORKSHOP

1. Write an argumentative essay in which you answer Singer's question, "If experimenting on retarded, orphaned humans would be wrong, why isn't experimenting on nonhuman animals wrong?" Refer to specific points in Singer's essay and tell why you agree or disagree with them.

2. Write an essay in which you respond to Singer's charge of speciesism. Do you agree that human beings are indeed guilty of speciesism, or do you, like Albert Rosenfeld (p. 510), believe that no advance in medicine would be made without experiments on animals?

3. Write an essay in which you address the question of whether scientists should be allowed to experiment on prisoners, on the terminally ill, or on the elderly.

THEMATIC CONNECTIONS

- "Shooting an Elephant" (p. 85)
- "Pure and Impure: The Interplay of Science and Technology" (p. 184)
- "Animal Rights versus Human Health" (p. 510)

ANIMAL RIGHTS
VERSUS HUMAN HEALTH

Albert Rosenfeld

Albert Rosenfeld is a professor of biology at the University of Texas, Galveston. He also is a journalist and has written a number of books and articles on medical and scientific topics. The following article appeared in Science '81 *and addresses the arguments made by Peter Singer (see p. 501) and others who say that animal experimentation should be strictly limited or, in many cases, eliminated entirely. In his essay, Rosenfeld makes the case that despite its drawbacks, animal experimentation is a necessary means of gaining scientific information.*

Stray dogs and cats by the hundreds of thousands roam the streets of our cities. Usually they wind up in animal shelters, where hard-pressed staffs must find ways to dispose of them. One legitimate disposal route has been the research laboratory. But in southern California—with its impressive collection of research centers—antivivisectionists and animal rights groups recently have been leaning hard on animal shelters, effectively cutting off much of the supply.

About 30 years ago Los Angeles voters soundly defeated a proposal to prohibit the release of animals for laboratory use. But today, with new proposals being submitted to city councils and county boards, the results could well be different. And the new proposals are much more sweeping. They would, for instance, create review boards for all animal experimentation, requiring researchers to justify in advance any experiment they were planning and to submit a detailed research protocol before even applying for a grant. Alarmed, a group of southern California investigators have organized a committee for animal research in medicine.

"Most scientists don't realize the danger," says Caltech neurobiologist John M. Allman, who uses monkeys to study the organization of the brain. "Such movements in the past—in this country, at least—have largely been the efforts of small, fragmented, and relatively ineffective groups. But this new movement is carefully orchestrated, well organized, and well financed. Moreover, this is not just a local issue. It is going on intensively at the national and even at the international level. We'd be foolish to underestimate these people. They have clout. And if they attain their goals, it will effectively kill a lot of important research."

To doubly ensure the protection of human experimental subjects, a number of restrictions and regulations that admittedly are burdensome have been adopted over recent years. They take a great deal of time and energy. They generate a considerable amount of extra paper work. They often slow research (indeed, make some projects impossible) and render it much more difficult and costly at a time when budgets are shrinking and inflation is making further inroads. While these procedures are accepted as the price of seeing that human subjects volunteer freely and with fully informed consent, are we willing to pay a similar price on behalf of animal subjects who can in no way either give or withhold consent?

It is easy to look at the history of animal experimentation and compile a catalog of horrors. Or, for that matter, to look around today and find research projects that might be hard to justify. But the day is long past when a researcher can take any animal and do anything he pleases to it with a total disregard for its welfare and comfort. "People don't realize," says Allman, "that we are already extensively reviewed. In my work I must follow the ethical codes laid down by the National Institutes of Health and the American Physiological Society, among others. And we might have a surprise visit at any time from the U.S. Department of Agriculture's inspectors. It's the USDA field veterinarians who do the enforcing. Believe me, these inspections are anything but routine, and these fellows have a great deal of power. Because their reports can adversely affect federal funding, their recommendations are, in reality, orders.

"More than that, we are all required to keep detailed reports on all our animal experiments. And if pain or surgery is involved, we must tell them what anesthetics we used and in what dosages, what postoperative pain relievers and care were given, and so on. These reports are filed annually with the USDA, and they keep tabs on what goes on all over the country."

For all these precautions, however, it is fair to say that millions of animals—probably more rats and mice than any other species—are subjected to experiments that cause them pain, discomfort, and distress, sometimes lots of it over long periods of time. If you want to study the course of a disease with a view to figuring out its causes and possible therapies, there is no way that the animal to whom you give the disease is going to be happy about it. All new forms of

medication or surgery are tried out on animals first. Every new substance that is released into the environment, or put on the market,
is tested on animals.

In fact, some of the tests most objected to by animal advocates   8
are those required by the government. For instances, there is a figure called the LD-50 (short for "lethal dose for 50 percent") that
manufacturers are required to determine for any new substance. In
each such case, a great many animals are given a lot of the stuff to
find out how much it takes to kill half of them—and the survivors
aren't exactly in the pink.

The animal rights advocates, except for the more extreme and un-   9
compromising types, are not kooks or crackpots. They tend to be
intelligent, compassionate individuals raising valid ethical questions, and they probably serve well as consciousness raisers. It is
certainly their prerogative—or anyone's—to ask of a specific project: Is this research really necessary? (What's "really necessary" is
of course not always obvious.)

But it's important that they not impose their solutions on society.   10
It would be tragic indeed—when medical science is on the verge of
learning so much more that is essential to our health and welfare—if
already regulation-burdened and budget-crunched researchers were
further hampered.

In 1975, Australian philosopher Peter Singer wrote his influential   11
book called *Animal Liberation,* in which he accuses us all of
"speciesism"—as reprehensible, to him, as racism or sexism. He
freely describes the "pain and suffering" inflicted in the "tyranny of
human over nonhuman animals" and sharply challenges our biblical
license to exercise "dominion over the fish of the sea, and over the
fowl of the air, and over every living thing that moveth upon the
Earth."

Well, certainly we are guilty of speciesism. We do act as if we   12
had dominion over other living creatures. But domination also entails
some custodial responsibility. And the questions continue to be
raised: Do we have the right to abuse animals? To eat them? To
hunt them for sport? To keep them imprisoned in zoos—or, for that
matter, in our households? Especially to do experiments on these
creatures who can't fight back? To send them into orbit, spin them
on centrifuges, run them through mazes, give them cancer, perform
experimental surgery?

Hardly any advance in either human or veterinary medicine—   13
cure, vaccine, operation, drug, therapy—has come about without experiments on animals. And it may be impossible to get the data we
need to determine the hazards of, say, radiation exposure or environ-

mental pollutants without animal testing. I certainly sympathize with the demand that we look for ways to get the information we want without using animals. Most investigators are delighted when they can get their data by means of tissue cultures or computer simulations. But as we look for alternative ways to get information, do we meanwhile just do without?

I wonder about those purists who seek to halt all animal experimentation on moral grounds: Do they also refuse, for themselves and others, to accept any remedy—or information—that was gained through animal experimentation? And do they ask themselves if they have the right to make such moral decisions on behalf of all the patients in cancer wards and intensive care units and on behalf of all the victims of the maladies that afflict our species? And what of the future generations that will be so afflicted but who might not have been—had the animal rightists not intervened? 14

COMPREHENSION

1. How are current proposals to prohibit the release of animals for laboratory use different from ones of thirty years ago?

2. According to John M. Allman, why do most scientists fail to realize the danger of the movement to prohibit the use of animals for research in medicine?

3. What steps do scientists take to protect human experimental subjects? What are the arguments against following the same procedures with animal subjects?

4. According to Rosenfeld, can pain, discomfort, and distress ever be eliminated from animal experimentation? Explain.

5. What is Rosenfeld's response to Peter Singer's charge of "speciesism"? What does Rosenfeld say to those "purists" who would like to halt all animal experimentation on moral grounds?

PURPOSE AND AUDIENCE

1. What arguments against his thesis does Rosenfeld anticipate?

2. Where does Rosenfeld state his thesis? Why does he place it where he does?

3. What does Rosenfeld hope to achieve by citing Peter Singer?

STYLE AND STRUCTURE

1. Why does Rosenfeld begin his essay with a discussion of stray dogs and cats? Does this focus on stray animals misrepresent the issue?

2. Identify each quotation that Rosenfeld uses in his essay and explain its function. What other kinds of evidence does he use to support his points? Does he use enough evidence? Explain.

3. What points does Rosenfeld concede to his opposition? What is the effect of these concessions on readers?

4. Is Rosenfeld's argument primarily inductive or deductive? Explain.

5. Does Rosenfeld include any elements of persuasion in his essay? Explain.

6. Is Rosenfeld's summary of Peter Singer's argument accurate and fair? How effectively does he refute Singer's point?

7. In his conclusion, Rosenfeld accuses the animal rights people of hypocrisy. Is this tactic fair? Or is Rosenfeld trying to turn attention away from the issue by making an *ad hominem* attack? Explain.

VOCABULARY PROJECTS

1. Define each of the following words as it is used in this selection.
   antivivisectionists (1)
   anesthetics (6)
   prerogative (9)
   reprehensible (11)

2. What terms does Rosenfeld use that indicate that his essay is aimed at an audience of nonscientists? What changes in his vocabulary would he have to make if he were writing to a group of biologists?

3. Throughout his essay Rosenfeld avoids detailed descriptions of animal experimentation. Find a point in the essay where Rosenfeld mentions a specific experiment. Rewrite the experiment adding descriptive adverbs and adjectives. Would including your description in the essay support or undercut Rosenfeld's argument?

WRITING WORKSHOP

1. Write an essay in which you discuss society's right to sacrifice the rights of the individual for the greater good. Should society have the right, for example, to forbid smokers from smoking? to make drivers wear seat belts? to force people to take drug tests?

2. Write a short argument in which you explain the restrictions that you believe are necessary to safeguard the rights of animals. You may use statements from either Rosenfeld's or Singer's essay to support your points. Do not forget to document all information from your sources.

3. Write an argument based on the following thesis statement: "People who want to stop animal experimentation have no right to make decisions that could affect the lives of thousands of people."

THEMATIC CONNECTIONS

- "The Embalming of Mr. Jones" (p. 236)
- "Animal Liberation" (p. 501)

LETTER
FROM BIRMINGHAM JAIL

Martin Luther King, Jr.

Martin Luther King, Jr., was born in 1929 in Atlanta, Georgia, and assassinated in 1968 in Memphis, Tennessee. He graduated from Morehouse College in 1948 and received his B.D. from the Crozer Theological Seminary in Chester, Pennsylvania, in 1951. After receiving his Ph.D. from Boston University in 1954, he became pastor of the Dexler Avenue Baptist Church in Montgomery, Alabama. With his involvement in the Montgomery bus boycott (1955–1956) King's prominence increased swiftly. In 1957 he was elected head of the Southern Christian Leadership Conference. During this time he developed a philosophy of nonviolent direct protest that would characterize his actions throughout the rest of his career. In 1963, King launched a campaign against segregation in Birmingham, Alabama, but he met fierce opposition from police as well as white moderates who saw him as dangerous. Arrested and jailed for eight days, King wrote his "Letter from Birmingham Jail" to white clergymen to explain his actions and to answer those who urged him to call off the demonstrations. Having much in common with the Declaration of Independence, the "Letter from Birmingham Jail" is a well-reasoned defense of demonstrations and civil disobedience.

April 16, 1963

My Dear Fellow Clergymen:

While confined here in the Birmingham city jail, I came across your recent statement calling my present activities "unwise and untimely." Seldom do I pause to answer criticism of my work and ideas. If I sought to answer all the criticisms that cross my desk, my secretaries would have little time for anything other than such correspondence in the course of the day, and I would have no time for constructive work. But since I feel that you are men of genuine good will and that your criticisms are sincerely set forth, I want to try to answer your statement in what I hope will be patient and reasonable terms.

I think I should indicate why I am here in Birmingham, since you 2
have been influenced by the view which argues against "outsiders
coming in." I have the honor of serving as president of the Southern
Christian Leadership Conference, an organization operating in every
southern state, with headquarters in Atlanta, Georgia. We have
some eighty-five affiliated organizations across the South, and one
of them is the Alabama Christian Movement for Human Rights.
Frequently we share staff, educational, and financial resources with
our affiliates. Several months ago the affiliate here in Birmingham
asked us to be on call to engage in a nonviolent direct-action program if such were deemed necessary. We readily consented, and
when the hour came we lived up to our promise. So I, along with
several members of my staff, am here because I was invited here. I
am here because I have organizational ties here.

But more basically, I am in Birmingham because injustice is here. 3
Just as the prophets of the eighth century B.C. left their villages and
carried their "thus saith the Lord" far beyond the boundaries of
their home towns, and just as the Apostle Paul left his village of
Tarsus and carried the gospel of Jesus Christ to the far corners
of the Greco-Roman world, so am I compelled to carry the gospel of
freedom beyond my own home town. Like Paul, I must constantly
respond to the Macedonian call for aid.

Moreover, I am cognizant of the interrelatedness of all communi- 4
ties and states. I cannot sit idly by in Atlanta and not be concerned
about what happens in Birmingham. Injustice anywhere is a threat
to justice everywhere. We are caught in an inescapable network of
mutuality, tied in a single garment of destiny. Whatever affects one
directly, affects all indirectly. Never again can we afford to live with
the narrow, provincial, "outside agitator" idea. Anyone who lives
inside the United States can never be considered an outsider anywhere within its bounds.

You deplore the demonstrations taking place in Birmingham. But 5
your statement, I am sorry to say, fails to express a similar concern
for the conditions that brought about the demonstrations. I am sure
that none of you would want to rest content with the superficial
kind of social analysis that deals merely with effects and does not
grapple with underlying causes. It is unfortunate that demonstrations are taking place in Birmingham, but it is even more unfortunate that the city's white power structure left the Negro community
with no alternative.

In any nonviolent campaign there are four basic steps: collection 6
of the facts to determine whether injustices exist; negotiation; self-
purification; and direct action. We have gone through all these steps

in Birmingham. There can be no gainsaying the fact that racial injustice engulfs this community. Birmingham is probably the most thoroughly segregated city in the United States. Its ugly record of brutality is widely known. Negroes have experienced grossly unjust treatment in courts. There have been more unsolved bombings of Negro homes and churches in Birmingham than in any other city in the nation. These are the hard, brutal facts of the case. On the basis of these conditions, Negro leaders sought to negotiate with the city fathers. But the latter consistently refused to engage in good-faith negotiation.

Then, last September, came the opportunity to talk with leaders of Birmingham's economic community. In the course of the negotiations, certain promises were made by the merchants—for example, to remove the stores' humiliating racial signs. On the basis of these promises, the Reverend Fred Shuttlesworth and the leaders of the Alabama Christian Movement for Human Rights agreed to a moratorium on all demonstrations. As the weeks and months went by, we realized that we were the victims of a broken promise. A few signs, briefly removed, returned; the others remained. 7

As in so many past experiences, our hopes had been blasted, and the shadow of deep disappointment settled upon us. We had no alternative except to prepare for direct action, whereby we would present our very bodies as means of laying our case before the conscience of the local and the national community. Mindful of the difficulties involved, we decided to undertake a process of self-purification. We began a series of workshops on nonviolence, and we repeatedly asked ourselves: "Are you able to accept blows without retaliating?" "Are you able to endure the ordeal of jail?" We decided to schedule our direct-action program for the Easter season, realizing that except for Christmas, this is the main shopping period of the year. Knowing that a strong economic-withdrawal program would be the by-product of direct action, we felt that this would be the best time to bring pressure to bear on the merchants for the needed change. 8

Then it occurred to us that Birmingham's mayoral election was coming up in March, and we speedily decided to postpone action until after election day. When we discovered that the Commissioner of Public Safety, Eugene "Bull" Connor, had piled up enough votes to be in the run-off, we decided again to postpone action until the day after the run-off so that the demonstrations could not be used to cloud the issues. Like many others, we waited to see Mr. Connor defeated, and to this end we endured postponement after postpone- 9 ment. Having aided in this community need, we felt that our direct-action program could be delayed no longer.

You may well ask, "Why direct action? Why sit-ins, marches, and 10
so forth? Isn't negotiation a better path?" You are quite right in calling for negotiation. Indeed, this is the very purpose of direct action. Nonviolent direct action seeks to create such a crisis and foster such a tension that a community which has constantly refused to negotiate is forced to confront the issue. It seeks so to dramatize the issue that it can no longer be ignored. My citing the creation of tension as part of the work of the nonviolent-resistor may sound rather shocking. But I must confess that I am not afraid of the word "tension." I have earnestly opposed violent tension, but there is a type of constructive, nonviolent tension which is necessary for growth. Just as Socrates felt that it was necessary to create a tension in the mind so that individuals could rise from the bondage of myths and half-truths to the unfettered realm of creative analysis and objective appraisal, so must we see the need for nonviolent gad-flies to create the kind of tension in society that will help men rise from the dark depths of prejudice and racism to the majestic heights of understanding and brotherhood.

The purpose of our direct-action program is to create a situation 11
so crisis-packed that it will inevitably open the door to negotiation. I therefore concur with you in your call for negotiation. Too long has our beloved Southland been bogged down in a tragic effort to live in monologue rather than dialogue.

One of the basic points in your statement is that the action that 12
I and my associates have taken in Birmingham is untimely. Some have asked: "Why didn't you give the new city administration time to act?" The only answer that I can give to this query is that the new Birmingham administration must be prodded about as much as the outgoing one, before it will act. We are sadly mistaken if we feel that the election of Albert Boutwell as mayor will bring the millennium to Birmingham. While Mr. Boutwell is a much more gentle person than Mr. Connor, they are both segregationists, dedicated to maintenance of the status quo. I have hoped that Mr. Boutwell will be reasonable enough to see the futility of massive resistance to desegregation. But he will not see this without pressure from devotees of civil rights. My friends, I must say to you that we have not made a single gain in civil rights without determined legal and nonviolent pressure. Lamentably, it is an historical fact that privileged groups seldom give up their privileges voluntarily. Individuals may see the moral light and voluntarily give up their unjust posture; but, as

Reinhold Niebuhr* has reminded us, groups tend to be more immoral than individuals.

We know through painful experience that freedom is never voluntarily given by the oppressor; it must be demanded by the oppressed. Frankly, I have yet to engage in a direct-action campaign that was "well timed" in the view of those who have not suffered unduly from the disease of segregation. For years now I have heard the word "Wait!" It rings in the ear of every Negro with piercing familiarity. This "Wait" has almost always meant "Never." We must come to see, with one of our distinguished jurists, that "justice too long delayed is justice denied." 13

We have waited for more than 340 years for our constitutional and God-given rights. The nations of Asia and Africa are moving with jetlike speed toward gaining political independence, but we still creep at horse-and-buggy pace toward gaining a cup of coffee at a lunch counter. Perhaps it is easy for those who have never felt the stinging darts of segregation to say, "Wait." But when you have seen vicious mobs lynch your mothers and fathers at will and drown your sisters and brothers at whim; when you have seen hate-filled policemen curse, kick, and even kill your black brothers and sisters; when you see the vast majority of your twenty million Negro brothers smothering in an airtight cage of poverty in the midst of an affluent society; when you suddenly find your tongue twisted and your speech stammering as you seek to explain to your six-year-old daughter why she can't go to the public amusement park that has just been advertised on television, and see tears welling up in her eyes when she is told that Funtown is closed to colored children, and see ominous clouds of inferiority beginning to form in her little mental sky, and see her beginning to distort her personality by developing an unconscious bitterness toward white people; when you have to concoct an answer for a five-year-old son who is asking, "Daddy, why do white people treat colored people so mean?"; when you take a cross-country drive and find it necessary to sleep night after night in the uncomfortable corners of your automobile because no motel will accept you; when you are humiliated day in and day out by nagging signs reading "white" and "colored"; when your first name becomes "nigger," your middle name becomes "boy" (however old you are) and your last name becomes "John," and your wife and mother are never given the respected title "Mrs."; when you are harried by day and haunted by night by the fact that you are a Negro, living constantly at tiptoe stance, never quite knowing what to expect 14

*EDS. NOTE—American religious and social thinker (1892–1971).

next, and are plagued with inner fears and outer resentments; when you are forever fighting a degenerating sense of "nobodiness"—then you will understand why we find it difficult to wait. There comes a time when the cup of endurance runs over, and men are no longer willing to be plunged into the abyss of despair. I hope, sirs, you can understand our legitimate and unavoidable impatience.

You express a great deal of anxiety over our willingness to break laws. This is certainly a legitimate concern. Since we so diligently urge people to obey the Supreme Court's decision of 1954 outlawing segregation in the public schools, at first glance it may seem rather paradoxical for us consciously to break laws. One may well ask: "How can you advocate breaking some laws and obeying others?" The answer lies in the fact that there are two types of laws: just and unjust. I would be the first to advocate obeying just laws. One has not only a legal but a moral responsibility to obey just laws. Conversely, one has a moral responsibility to disobey unjust laws. I would agree with St. Augustine that "an unjust law is no law at all."   15

Now, what is the difference between the two? How does one determine whether a law is just or unjust? A just law is a man-made code that squares with the moral law or the law of God. An unjust law is a code that is out of harmony with the moral law. To put it in the terms of St. Thomas Aquinas*: An unjust law is a human law that is not rooted in eternal law and natural law. Any law that uplifts human personality is just. Any law that degrades human personality is unjust. All segregation statutes are unjust because segregation distorts the soul and damages the personality. It gives the segregator a false sense of superiority and the segregated a false sense of inferiority. Segregation, to use the terminology of the Jewish philosopher Martin Buber, substitutes an "I-it" relationship for an "I-thou" relationship and ends up relegating persons to the status of things. Hence segregation is not only politically, economically, and sociologically unsound, it is morally wrong and sinful. Paul Tillich** has said that sin is separation. Is not segregation an existential expression of man's tragic separation, his awful estrangement, his terrible sinfulness? Thus it is that I can urge men to obey the 1954 decision of the Supreme Court, for it is morally right; and I can urge them to disobey segregation ordinances, for they are morally wrong.   16

Let us consider a more concrete example of just and unjust laws.   17

*EDS. NOTE—Italian philosopher and theologian (1225–1274)
**EDS. NOTE—American philosopher and theologian (1886–1965)

An unjust law is a code that a numerical or power majority group compels a minority group to obey but does not make binding on itself. This is *difference* made legal. By the same token, a just law is a code that a majority compels a minority to follow and that it is willing to follow itself. This is *sameness* made legal.

Let me give another explanation. A law is unjust if it is inflicted on a minority that, as a result of being denied the right to vote, had no part in enacting or devising the law. Who can say that the legislature of Alabama which set up that state's segregation laws was democratically elected? Throughout Alabama all sorts of devious methods are used to prevent Negroes from becoming registered voters, and there are some counties in which, even though Negroes constitute a majority of the population, not a single Negro is registered. Can any law enacted under such circumstances be considered democratically structured? 18

Sometimes a law is just on its face and unjust in its application. For instance, I have been arrested on a charge of parading without a permit. Now, there is nothing wrong in having an ordinance which requires a permit for a parade. But such an ordinance becomes unjust when it is used to maintain segregation and to deny citizens the First-Amendment privilege of peaceful assembly and protest. 19

I hope you are able to see the distinction I am trying to point out. In no sense do I advocate evading or defying the law, as would the rabid segregationist. That would lead to anarchy. One who breaks an unust law must do so openly, lovingly, and with a willingness to accept the penalty. I submit that an individual who breaks a law that conscience tells him is unjust, and who willingly accepts the penalty of imprisonment in order to arouse the conscience of the community over its injustice, is in reality expressing the highest respect for law. 20

Of course, there is nothing new about this kind of civil disobedience. It was evidenced sublimely in the refusal of Shadrach, Meshach, and Abednego to obey the laws of Nebuchadnezzar, on the ground that a higher moral law was at stake. It was practiced superbly by the early Christians, who were willing to face hungry lions and the excruciating pain of chopping blocks rather than submit to certain unjust laws of the Roman Empire. To a degree, academic freedom is a reality today because Socrates practiced civil disobedience. In our own nation, the Boston Tea Party represented a massive act of civil disobedience. 21

We should never forget that everything Adolf Hitler did in Germany was "legal" and everything the Hungarian freedom fighters did in Hungary was "illegal." It was "illegal" to aid and comfort a 22

Jew in Hitler's Germany. Even so, I am sure that, had I lived in Germany at the time, I would have aided and comforted my Jewish brothers. If today I lived in a Communist country where certain principles dear to the Christian faith are suppressed, I would openly advocate disobeying that country's anti-religious laws.

I must make two honest confessions to you, my Christian and Jewish brothers. First, I must confess that over the past few years I have been gravely disappointed with the white moderate. I have almost reached the regrettable conclusion that the Negro's great stumbling block in his stride toward freedom is not the White Citizen's Counciler or the Ku Klux Klanner, but the white moderate, who is more devoted to "order" than to justice; who prefers a negative peace which is the absence of tension to a positive peace which is the presence of justice; who constantly says, "I agree with you in the goal you seek, but I cannot agree with your methods of direct action"; who paternalistically believes he can set the timetable for another man's freedom; who lives by a mythical concept of time and who constantly advises the Negro to wait for a "more convenient season." Shallow understanding from people of good will is more frustrating than absolute misunderstanding from people of ill will. Lukewarm acceptance is much more bewildering than outright rejection.

I had hoped that the white moderate would understand that law and order exist for the purpose of establishing justice and that when they fail in this purpose they become the dangerously structured dams that block the flow of social progress. I had hoped that the white moderate would understand that the present tension in the South is a necessary phase of the transition from an obnoxious negative peace, in which the Negro passively accepted his unjust plight, to a substantive and positive peace, in which all men will respect the dignity and worth of human personality. Actually, we who engage in nonviolent direct action are not the creators of tension. We merely bring to the surface the hidden tension that is already alive. We bring it out in the open, where it can be seen and dealt with. Like a boil that can never be cured so long as it is covered up but must be opened with all its ugliness to the natural medicines of air and light, injustice must be exposed, with all the tension its exposure creates, to the light of human conscience and the air of national opinion, before it can be cured.

In your statement you assert that our actions, even though peaceful, must be condemned because they precipitate violence. But is this a logical assertion? Isn't this like condemning a robbed man because his possession of money precipitated the evil act of robbery?

Isn't this like condemning Socrates because his unswerving commitment to truth and his philosophical inquiries precipitated the act by the misguided populace in which they made him drink hemlock? Isn't this like condemning Jesus because his unique God-consciousness and never-ceasing devotion to God's will precipitated the evil act of crucifixion? We must come to see that, as the federal courts have consistently affirmed, it is wrong to urge an individual to cease his efforts to gain his basic constitutional rights because the quest may precipitate violence. Society must protect the robbed and punish the robber.

I had also hoped that the white moderate would reject the myth concerning time in relation to the struggle for freedom. I have just received a letter from a white brother in Texas. He writes: "All Christians know that the colored people will receive equal rights eventually, but it is possible that you are in too great a religious hurry. It has taken Christianity almost two thousand years to accomplish what it has. The teachings of Christ take time to come to earth." Such an attitude stems from a tragic misconception of time, from the strangely irrational notion that there is something in the very flow of time that will inevitably cure all ills. Actually, time itself is neutral; it can be used either destructively or constructively. More and more I feel that the people of ill will have used time much more effectively than have the people of good will. We will have to repent in this generation not merely for the hateful words and actions of the bad people, but for the appalling silence of the good people. Human progress never rolls in on wheels of inevitability; it comes through the tireless efforts of men willing to be co-workers with God, and without his hard work, time itself becomes an ally of the forces of social stagnation. We must use time creatively, in the knowledge that the time is always ripe to do right. Now is the time to make real the promise of democracy and transform our pending national elegy into a creative psalm of brotherhood. Now is the time to lift our national policy from the quicksand of racial injustice to the solid rock of human dignity.

You speak of our activity in Birmingham as extreme. At first I was rather disappointed that fellow clergymen would see my nonviolent efforts as those of an extremist. I began thinking about the fact that I stand in the middle of two opposing forces in the Negro community. One is a force of complacency, made up in part of Negroes who, as a result of long years of oppression, are so drained of self-respect and a sense of "somebodiness" that they have adjusted to segregation; and in part of a few middle-class Negroes who, because of a degree of academic and economic security and because in some ways they profit by segregation, have become insensitive to the problems of the masses. The other force is one of bitterness and hatred, and it comes perilously close to advocating violence. It is expressed in the various black nationalist groups that are springing up across the nation, the largest and best-known being Elijah Muhammad's Muslim movement. Nourished by the Negro's frustration over the continued existence of racial discrimination, this movement is made up of people who have lost faith in America, who have absolutely repudiated Christianity, and who have concluded that the white man is an incorrigible "devil."

I have tried to stand between these two forces, saying that we need emulate neither the "do-nothingism" of the complacent nor the hatred and despair of the black nationalist. For there is the more excellent way of love and nonviolent protest. I am grateful to God that, through the influence of the Negro church, the way of nonviolence became an integral part of our struggle.   28

If this philosophy had not emerged, by now many streets of the South would, I am convinced, be flowing with blood. And I am further convinced that if our white brothers dismiss as "rabble-rousers" and "outside agitators" those of us who employ nonviolent direct action, and if they refuse to support our nonviolent efforts, millions of Negroes will, out of frustration and despair, seek solace and security in black-nationalist ideologies—a development that would inevitably lead to a frightening racial nightmare.   29

Oppressed people cannot remain oppressed forever. The yearning for freedom eventually manifests itself, and that is what has happened to the American Negro. Something within has reminded him of his birthright of freedom, and something without has reminded him that it can be gained. Consciously or unconsciously, he has been caught up by the *Zeitgeist*, and with his black brothers of Africa and his brown and yellow brothers of Asia, South America, and the Caribbean, the United States Negro is moving with a sense of great urgency toward the promised land of racial justice. If one recognizes this vital urge that has engulfed the Negro community, one should readily understand why public demonstrations are taking place. The Negro has many pent-up resentments and latent frustrations, and he must release them. So let him march; let him make prayer pilgrimages to the city hall; let him go on freedom rides—and try to understand why he must do so. If his repressed emotions are not released in nonviolent ways, they will seek expression through violence; this is not a threat but a fact of history. So I have not said to my people, "Get rid of your discontent." Rather, I have tried to say that this normal and healthy discontent can be channeled into the   30 creative outlet of nonviolent direct action. And now this approach is being termed extremist.

But though I was initially disappointed at being categorized as an extremist, as I continued to think about the matter I gradually gained a measure of satisfaction from the label. Was not Jesus an extremist for love: "Love your enemies, bless them that curse you, do good to them that hate you, and pray for them which despitefully use you, and persecute you." Was not Amos an extremist for justice: "Let justice roll down like waters and righteousness like an ever-flowing stream." Was not Paul an extremist for the Christian gospel: "I bear in my body the marks of the Lord Jesus." Was not Martin Luther an extremist: "Here I stand; I cannot do otherwise, so help me God." And John Bunyan: "I will stay in jail to the end of my days before I make a butchery of my conscience." And Abraham Lincoln: "This nation cannot survive half slave and half free." And Thomas Jefferson: "We hold these truths to be self-evident, that all men are created equal. . . . " So the question is not whether we will be extremists, but what kind of extremists we will be. Will we be extremists for hate or for love? Will we be extremists for the preservation of injustice or for the extension of justice? In that dramatic scene on Calvary's hill three men were crucified. We must never forget that all three were crucified for the same crime—the crime of extremism. Two were extremists for immorality, and thus fell below their environment. The other, Jesus Christ, was an extremist for love, truth, and goodness, and thereby rose above his environment. Perhaps the South, the nation, and the world are in dire need of creative extremists. 31

I had hoped that the white moderate would see this need. Perhaps I was too optimistic; perhaps I expected too much. I suppose I should have realized that few members of the oppressor race can understand the deep groans and passionate yearnings of the oppressed race, and still fewer have the vision to see that injustice must be rooted out by strong, persistent, and determined action. I am thankful, however, that some of our white brothers in the South have grasped the meaning of this social revolution and committed themselves to it. They are still all too few in quantity, but they are big in quality. Some—such as Ralph McGill, Lillian Smith, Harry Golden, James McBride Dabbs, Ann Braden, and Sarah Patton Boyle—have written about our struggle in eloquent and prophetic terms. Others have marched with us down nameless streets of the South. They have languished in filthy, roach-infested jails, suffering the abuse and brutality of policemen who view them as "dirty nigger-lovers." Unlike so many of their moderate brothers and sisters, 32 they have recognized the urgency of the moment and sensed the need for powerful "action" antidotes to combat the disease of segregation.

Let me take note of my other major disappointment. I have been so greatly disappointed with the white church and its leadership. Of course, there are some notable exceptions. I am not unmindful of the fact that each of you has taken some significant stands on this issue. I commend you, Reverend Stallings, for your Christian stand on this past Sunday, in welcoming Negroes to your worship service on a nonsegregated basis. I commend the Catholic leaders of this state for integrating Spring Hill College several years ago.   33

But despite these notable exceptions, I must honestly reiterate that I have been disappointed with the church. I do not say this as one of those negative critics who can always find something wrong with the church. I say this as a minister of the gospel, who loves the church; who was nurtured in its bosom; who has been sustained by its spiritual blessings and who will remain true to it as long as the cord of life shall lengthen.   34

When I was suddenly catapulted into the leadership of the bus protest in Montgomery, Alabama, a few years ago, I felt we would be supported by the white church. I felt that the white ministers, priests, and rabbis of the South would be among our strongest allies. Instead, some have been outright opponents, refusing to understand the freedom movement and misrepresenting its leaders; all too many others have been more cautious than courageous and have remained silent behind the anesthetizing security of stained-glass windows.   35

In spite of my shattered dreams, I came to Birmingham with the hope that the white religious leadership of this community would see the justice of our cause and, with deep moral concern, would serve as the channel through which our just grievances could reach the power structure. I had hoped that each of you would understand. But again I have been disappointed.   36

There was a time when the church was very powerful—in the time when the early Christians rejoiced at being deemed worthy to suffer for what they believed. In those days the church was not merely a thermometer that recorded the ideas and principles of popular opinion; it was a thermostat that transformed the mores of society. Whenever the early Christians entered a town, the people in power became disturbed and immediately sought to convict the Christians for being "disturbers of the peace" and "outside agitators." But the Christians pressed on, in the conviction that they were "a colony of heaven," called to obey God rather than man. Small in number, they   37 were big in commitment. They were too God-intoxicated to be "astronomically intimidated." By their effort and example they brought an end to such ancient evils as infanticide and gladiatorial contests.

Things are different now. So often the contemporary church is a weak, ineffectual voice with an uncertain sound. So often it is an archdefender of the status quo. Far from being disturbed by the presence of the church, the power structure of the average community is consoled by the church's silent—and often even vocal—sanction of things as they are. 38

But the judgment of God is upon the church as never before. If today's church does not recapture the sacrificial spirit of the early church, it will lose its authenticity, forfeit the loyalty of millions, and be dismissed as an irrelevant social club with no meaning for the twentieth century. Every day I meet young people whose disappointment with the church has turned into outright disgust. 39

Perhaps I have once again been too optimistic. Is organized religion too inextricably bound to the status quo to save our nation and the world? Perhaps I must turn my faith to the inner spiritual church, the church within the church, as the true *ekklesia** and the hope of the world. But again I am thankful to God that some noble souls from the ranks of organized religion have broken loose from the paralyzing chains of conformity and joined us as active partners in the struggle for freedom. They have left their secure congregations and walked the streets of Albany, Georgia, with us. They have gone down the highways of the South on torturous rides for freedom. Yes, they have gone to jail with us. Some have been dismissed from their churches, have lost the support of their bishops and fellow ministers. But they have acted in the faith that right defeated is stronger than evil triumphant. Their witness has been the spiritual salt that has preserved the true meaning of the gospel in these troubled times. They have carved a tunnel of hope through the dark mountain of disappointment. 40

I hope the church as a whole will meet the challenge of this decisive hour. But even if the church does not come to the aid of justice, I have no despair about the future. I have no fear about the outcome of our struggle in Birmingham, even if our motives are at present misunderstood. We will reach the goal of freedom in Birmingham and all over the nation, because the goal of America is freedom. Abused and scorned though we may be, our destiny is tied up with 41

*EDS. NOTE—Greek word for the early Christian church.

America's destiny. Before the pilgrims landed at Plymouth, we were here. Before the pen of Jefferson etched the majestic words of the Declaration of Independence across the pages of history, we were here. For more than two centuries our forebears labored in this country without wages; they made cotton king; they built the homes of their masters while suffering gross injustice and shameful humiliation—and yet out of a bottomless vitality they continued to thrive and develop. If the inexpressible cruelties of slavery could not stop us, the opposition we now face will surely fail. We will win our freedom because the sacred heritage of our nation and the eternal will of God are embodied in our echoing demands.

Before closing I feel impelled to mention one other point in your statement that has troubled me profoundly. You warmly commended the Birmingham police force for keeping "order" and "preventing violence." I doubt that you would have so warmly commended the police force if you had seen its dogs sinking their teeth into unarmed, nonviolent Negroes. I doubt that you would so quickly commend the policemen if you were to observe their ugly and inhumane treatment of Negroes here in the city jail; if you were to watch them push and curse old Negro women and young Negro girls; if you were to see them slap and kick old Negro men and young boys; if you were to observe them, as they did on two occasions, refuse to give us food because we wanted to sing our grace together. I cannot join you in your praise of the Birmingham police department.   42

It is true that the police have exercised a degree of discipline in handling the demonstrators. In this sense they have conducted themselves rather "nonviolently" in public. But for what purpose? To preserve the evil system of segregation. Over the past few years I have consistently preached that nonviolence demands that the means we use must be as pure as the ends we seek. I have tried to make clear that it is wrong to use immoral means to attain moral ends. But now I must affirm that it is just as wrong, or perhaps even more so, to use moral means to preserve immoral ends. Perhaps Mr. Connor and his policemen have been rather nonviolent in public, as was Chief Pritchett in Albany, Georgia, but they have used the moral means of nonviolence to maintain the immoral end of racial injustice. As T. S. Eliot has said, "The last temptation is the greatest treason: To do the right deed for the wrong reason."   43

I wish you had commended the Negro sit-inners and demonstrators of Birmingham for their sublime courage, their willingness to suffer, and their amazing discipline in the midst of great provoca-   44 tion. One day the South will recognize its real heroes. They will be the James Merediths,* with the noble sense of purpose that enables them to face jeering and hostile mobs, and with the agonizing loneliness that characterizes the life of the pioneer. They will be old, oppressed, battered Negro women, symbolized in a seventy-two-year-old woman in Montgomery, Alabama, who rose up with a sense of dignity and with her people decided not to ride segregated buses, and who responded with ungrammatical profundity to one who inquired about her weariness: "My feets is tired, but my soul is at rest." They will be the young high school and college students, the young ministers of the gospel and a host of their elders, courageously and nonviolently sitting in at lunch counters and willingly going to jail for conscience' sake. One day the South will know that when these disinherited children of God sat down at lunch counters, they were in reality standing up for what is best in the American dream and for the most sacred values in our Judaeo-Christian heritage, thereby bringing our nation back to those great wells of democracy which were dug deep by the founding fathers in their formulation of the Constitution and the Declaration of Independence.

Never before have I written so long a letter. I'm afraid it is much   45
too long to take your precious time. I can assure you that it would have been much shorter if I had been writing from a comfortable desk, but what else can one do when he is alone in a narrow jail cell, other than write long letters, think long thoughts, and pray long prayers?

If I have said anything in this letter that overstates the truth and   46
indicates an unreasonable impatience, I beg you to forgive me. If I have said anything that understates the truth and indicates my having a patience that allows me to settle for anything less than brotherhood, I beg God to forgive me.

I hope this letter finds you strong in the faith. I also hope that   47
circumstances will soon make it possible for me to meet each of you, not as an integrationist or a civil-rights leader but as a fellow clergyman and a Christian brother. Let us all hope that the dark clouds of racial prejudice will soon pass away and the deep fog of misunderstanding will be lifted from our fear-drenched communities, and in some not too distant tomorrow the radiant stars of love and brotherhood will shine over our great nation with all their scintillating beauty.

Yours for the cause of Peace and Brotherhood,
Martin Luther King, Jr.

*EDS. NOTE—First black to enroll at the University of Mississippi.

COMPREHENSION

1. Martin Luther King, Jr., says that he seldom answers criticism. Why does he decide to do so in this instance?

2. Why do the other clergymen consider King's activities to be "unwise and untimely"?

3. What reasons does King give for the demonstrations? Why does he think it is too late for negotiations?

4. What does King say *wait* means to blacks?

5. What are the two types of laws King defines? What is the difference between the two?

6. Why is King disappointed in the white moderates?

7. What does King find illogical about the claim that the actions of his followers precipitate violence?

8. What two forces does King say he stands between?

9. Why is King disappointed in the white church?

PURPOSE AND AUDIENCE

1. Why, in the first paragraph, does King establish his setting (the Birmingham city jail) and define his intended audience?

2. Why does King begin his letter with a reference to his audience as "men of genuine good will"? Is this phrase ironic in light of his later criticism of them?

3. What indication is there that King is writing his letter to an audience other than his fellow clergymen?

4. What is the thesis of this letter? Is it stated or implied?

5. Why does King so carefully outline for his audience the reasons why he is in Birmingham?

STYLE AND STRUCTURE

1. Where does King seek to establish that he is a reasonable person? Why does he open with "My Dear Fellow Clergymen"?

2. Where does King address the objections of his audience?

3. At what point does King introduce the problem that is the subject of his letter?

4. What facts or examples does King use to support his thesis?

5. As in the Declaration of Independence, transitions are important in King's letter. Identify the transitional words and phrases that connect the different parts of his argument.

6. Why does King cite Jewish, Catholic, and Protestant philosophers to support his position?

7. King relies heavily on an appeal to authority (Augustine, Aquinas, Buber, Tillich, etc.). Why does he use this technique?

8. King uses both induction and deduction in his letter. Find an example of each, and explain how they function in the argument.

9. Throughout the body of his letter, King criticizes his audience of white moderates. In his conclusion, he seeks to reeestablish a harmonious relationship with them. How does he do this?

VOCABULARY PROJECTS

1. Define each of the following words as it is used in this selection.

affiliates (2)	anarchy (20)
cognizant (4)	elegy (26)
mutuality (4)	incorrigible (27)
provincial (4)	emulate (28)
gainsay (6)	reiterate (34)
unfettered (10)	intimidate (37)
millennium (12)	infanticide (37)
devotee (12)	inextricably (40)
estrangement (16)	scintillating (47)
ordinances (16)	

2. Locate five allusions to the Bible in this essay. How do these allusions help King make his point?

3. In paragraph 14 King refers to his "cup of endurance." To what is this a reference? How is the original phrase worded?

WRITING WORKSHOP

1. Write an argumentative essay in which you support a deeply held belief of your own. Assume that your audience, like King's, is not openly hostile to your position.

2. Assume that you are a black militant writing a letter to Martin Luther King, Jr. Argue that King's methods do not go far enough. Be sure to address potential objections to your position. You might want

to go to the library and read some newspapers and magazines from the 1960s to help you prepare your argument.

3. Read the newspaper for several days, and collect articles about a controversial subject in which you are interested. Using the information from the articles, take a position on the issue, and write an essay supporting it.

THEMATIC CONNECTIONS

- "Rule of Law" (p. 397)
- "Civil Disobedience" (p. 552)

WRITING ASSIGNMENTS FOR ARGUMENTATION

1. Write an essay in which you discuss a teacher's right to strike. Address the major arguments against your position and maintain an objective stance.

2. Assume that a library in your town has decided that certain books are objectionable and has removed them from the shelves. Write a letter to the local paper in which you argue for or against the library's actions. Make a list of the major arguments that you could refute and address some of them in your essay. Remember to respect the rights of your audience and to address them in a respectful manner.

3. Write an essay in which you argue for or against the right of a woman to keep her baby after she has agreed to be a surrogate mother.

4. Write an essay in which you discuss how far down the evolutionary ladder an animal must be before it is suitable for experimentation. Is, for example, a frog more suitable than a dog? a monkey more suitable than a human being?

5. Assume that you are a person who remained loyal to King George III during the American Revolution. Write a letter to Thomas Jefferson presenting the reasons for your stance.

6. Go to the library and read the accounts of some criminal cases that resulted in the death penalty. Write an essay in which you present your arguments either in favor of or against the death penalty. Do not forget to give credit to your sources.

7. Write an argumentative essay in which you discuss whether there are any situations in which a person has an obligation to go or not to go to war.

8. Write an essay in which you discuss whether the racial situation in America has gotten better, gotten worse, or remained the same since Martin Luther King, Jr., wrote "Letter from Birmingham Jail."

9. In the Declaration of Independence, Jefferson says that all individuals are entitled to "life, liberty, and the pursuit of happiness." Write an essay in which you argue that these rights are not absolute.

10. Write an argumentative essay on one of these topics: Should high school students be required to take sex education courses? Should fraternities/sororities be abolished? Should teachers be required to pass periodic competency tests? Should the legal drinking age be raised (or lowered)? Should any workers be required to submit to random drug testing?

ESSAYS FOR FURTHER READING

THE MYTH OF THE CAVE

Plato

The Greek philosopher Plato (427?–347 B.C.) was a pupil and friend of Socrates. Plato founded a school in Athens called the Academy where, until his death, he instructed students in philosophy and mathematics. Plato's most famous works are in the form of dialogues, thirty of which involve Socrates as the central speaker. Socrates was convinced that it was his duty to guide his fellow Athenians to intellectual and moral improvement. In his role as social critic, Socrates made many enemies, and in 399 B.C., he was accused of corrupting the youth of Athens, brought to trial, and executed. Like Socrates, Plato believed that true knowledge rests in an individual's awareness of the Good. Plato, however, took Socrates's ideas further and tried to construct a harmonious philosophical system. To illustrate his ideas about the Good, Plato introduces the myth of the cave in Book VII of his utopian work, the Republic. Here Socrates tells Glaucon how men are chained facing the wall of a cave, mistaking the shadows they see for reality. According to Plato, people can be brought to apprehend their shadow state and can move out of the cave toward enlightenment.

And now, I said, let me show in a figure how far our nature is 1
enlightened or unenlightened:—Behold! human beings living in an underground den, which has a mouth open toward the light and reaching all along the den; here they have been from their childhood, and have their legs and necks chained so that they cannot move, and can only see before them, being prevented by the chains from turning round their heads. Above and behind them a fire is blazing at a distance, and between the fire and the prisoners there is a raised way; and you will see, if you look, a low wall built along the way, like the screen which marionette players have in front of them, over which they show the puppets.

I see. 2

And do you see, I said, men passing along the wall carrying all 3
sorts of vessels, and statues and figures of animals made of wood and stone and various materials, which appear over the wall? Some of them are talking, others silent.

You have shown me a strange image, and they are strange pris-   4
oners.

Like ourselves, I replied; and they see only their own shadows, or   5
the shadows of one another, which the fire throws on the opposite
wall of the cave?

True, he said; how could they see anything but the shadows if they   6
were never allowed to move their heads?

And of the objects which are being carried in like manner they   7
would only see the shadows?

Yes, he said.   8

And if they were able to converse with one another, would they   9
not suppose that they were naming what was actually before them?

Very true.   10

And suppose further that the prison had an echo which came from   11
the other side, would they not be sure to fancy when one of the
passers-by spoke that the voice which they heard came from the
passing shadow?

No question, he replied.   12

To them, I said, the truth would be literally nothing but the   13
shadows of the images.

That is certain.   14

And now look again, and see what will naturally follow if the pris-   15
oners are released and disabused of their error. At first, when any
of them is liberated and compelled suddenly to stand up and turn
his neck round and walk and look toward the light, he will suffer
sharp pains; the glare will distress him, and he will be unable to see
the realities of which in his former state he had seen the shadows;
and then conceive some one saying to him, that what he saw before
was an illusion, but that now, when he is approaching nearer to being and his eye is turned toward more real existence, he has a clearer
vision—what will be his reply? And you may further imagine that
his instructor is pointing to the objects as they pass and requiring
him to name them—will he not be perplexed? Will he not fancy that
the shadows which he formerly saw are truer than the objects which
are now shown to him?

Far truer.   16

And if he is compelled to look straight at the light, will he not   17
have a pain in his eyes which will make him turn away to take refuge
in the objects of vision which he can see, and which he will conceive
to be in reality clearer than the things which are now being shown
to him?

True, he said.   18

And suppose once more, that he is reluctantly dragged up a steep   19
and rugged ascent, and held fast until he is forced into the presence
of the sun himself, is he not likely to be pained and irritated? When
he approaches the light his eyes will be dazzled, and he will not be
able to see anything at all of what are now called realities.

Not all in a moment, he said.   20

He will require to grow accustomed to the sight of the upper   21
world. And first he will see the shadows best, next the reflections of
men and other objects in the water, and then the objects themselves;
then he will gaze upon the light of the moon and the stars and the
spangled heaven; and he will see the sky and the stars by night better than the sun or the light of the sun by day.

Certainly.   22

Last of all he will be able to see the sun, and not mere reflections   23
of him in the water, but he will see him in his own proper place, and
not in another; and he will contemplate him as he is.

Certainly.   24

He will then proceed to argue that this is he who gives the season   25
and the years, and is the guardian of all that is in the visible world,
and in a certain way the cause of all things which he and his fellows
have been accustomed to behold?

Clearly, he said, he would first see the sun and then reason about   26
him.

And when he remembered his old habitation, and the wisdom of   27
the den and his fellow-prisoners, do you not suppose that he would
felicitate himself on the change, and pity them?

Certainly, he would.   28

And if they were in the habit of conferring honors among them-   29
selves on those who were quickest to observe the passing shadows
and to remark which of them went before, and which followed after,
and which were together; and who were therefore best able to draw
conclusions as to the future, do you think that he would care for
such honors and glories, or envy the possessors of them? Would he
not say with Homer,

> Better to be the poor servant of a poor master,

and to endure anything, rather than think as they do and live after
their manner?

Yes, he said, I think that he would rather suffer anything than   30
entertain these false notions and live in this miserable manner.

Imagine once more, I said, such one coming suddenly out of the   31 sun to be replaced in his old situation; would he not be certain to have his eyes full of darkness?

To be sure, he said.   32

And if there were a contest, and he had to compete in measuring   33
the shadows with the prisoners who had never moved out of the den, while his sight was still weak, and before his eyes had become steady (and the time which would be needed to acquire this new habit of sight might be very considerable), would he not be ridiculous? Men would say of him that up he went and down he came without his eyes; and that it was better not even to think of ascending; and if any one tried to loose another and lead him up to the light, let them only catch the offender, and they would put him to death.

No question, he said.   34

This entire allegory, I said, you may now append, dear Glaucon,   35
to the previous argument; the prison-house is the world of sight, the light of the fire is the sun, and you will not misapprehend me if you interpret the journey upwards to be the ascent of the soul into the intellectual world according to my poor belief, which, at your desire, I have expressed—whether rightly or wrongly God knows. But, whether true or false, my opinion is that in the world of knowledge the idea of good appears last of all, and is seen only with an effort; and, when seen, is also inferred to be the universal author of all things beautiful and right, parent of light and of the lord of light in this visible world, and the immediate source of reason and truth in the intellectual; and that this is the power upon which he who would act rationally either in public or private life must have his eye fixed.

I agree, he said, as far as I am able to understand you.   36

Moreover, I said, you must not wonder that those who attain to   37
this beatific vision are unwilling to descend to human affairs; for their souls are ever hastening into the upper world where they desire to dwell; which desire of theirs is very natural, if our allegory may be trusted.

Yes, very natural.   38

And is there anything surprising in one who passes from divine   39
contemplations to the evil state of man, misbehaving himself in a ridiculous manner; if, while his eyes are blinking and before he has become accustomed to the surrounding darkness, he is compelled to fight in courts of law, or in other places, about the images or the shadows of images of justice, and is endeavoring to meet the conceptions of those who have never yet seen absolute justice?

Anything but surprising, he replied.   40

Any one who has common sense will remember that the bewilder-   41 ments of the eyes are of two kinds, and arise from two causes, either from coming out of the light or from going into the light, which is true of the mind's eye, quite as much as of the bodily eye; and he who remembers this when he sees any one whose vision is perplexed and weak, will not be too ready to laugh; he will first ask whether that soul of man has come out of the brighter life, and is unable to see because unaccustomed to the dark, or having turned from darkness to the day is dazzled by excess of light. And he will count the one happy in his condition and state of being, and he will pity the other; or, if he have a mind to laugh at the soul which comes from below into the light, there will be more reason in this than in the laugh which greets him who returns from above out of the light into the den.

That, he said, is a very just distinction.   42

But then, if I am right, certain professors of education must be   43
wrong when they say that they can put a knowledge into the soul which was not there before, like sight into blind eyes.

They undoubtedly say this, he replied.   44

Whereas, our argument shows that the power and capacity of   45
learning exists in the soul already; and that just as the eye was unable to turn from darkness to light without the whole body, so too the instrument of knowledge can only by the movement of the whole soul be turned from the world of becoming into that of being, and learn by degrees to endure the sight of being, and of the brightest and best of being, or in other words, of the good.

Very true.   46

And must there not be some art which will effect conversion in   47
the easiest and quickest manner; not implanting the faculty of sight, for that exists already, but has been turned in the wrong direction, and is looking away from the truth?

Yes, he said, such an art may be presumed.   48

And whereas the other so-called virtues of the soul seem to be akin   49
to bodily qualities, for even when they are not originally innate they can be implanted later by habit and exercise, the virtue of wisdom more than anything else contains a divine element which always remains, and by this conversion is rendered useful and profitable; or, on the other hand, hurtful and useless. Did you never observe the narrow intelligent flashing from the keen eye of a clever rogue—how eager he is, how clearly his paltry soul sees the way to his end; he is the reverse of blind, but his keen eyesight is forced into the service of evil, and he is mischievous in proportion to his cleverness?

Very true, he said.   50

But what if there had been a circumcision of such natures in the   51 days of their youth; and they had been severed from those sensual pleasures, such as eating and drinking, which, like leaden weights, were attached to them at their birth, and which drag them down and turn the vision of their souls upon the things that are below—if, I say, they had been released from these impediments and turned in the opposite direction, the very same faculty in them would have seen the truth as keenly as they see what their eyes are turned to now.

Very likely.   52

Yes I said; and there is another thing which is likely, or rather a   53
necessary inference from what has preceded, that neither the uneducated and uninformed of the truth, nor yet those who never make an end of their education, will be able ministers of State; not the former, because they have no single aim of duty which is the rule of all their actions, private as well as public; nor the latter, because they will not act at all except upon compulsion, fancying that they are already dwelling apart in the islands of the blest.

Very true, he replied.   54

Then, I said, the business of us who are the founders of the State   55
will be to compel the best minds to attain that knowledge which we have already shown to be the greatest of all—they must continue to ascend until they arrive at the good; but when they have ascended and seen enough we must not allow them to do as they do now.

What do you mean?   56

I mean that they remain in the upper world: but this must not be   57
allowed. They must be made to descend again among the prisoners in the den, and partake of their labors and honors, whether they are worth having or not.

But is not this unjust? he said; ought we to give them a worse life,   58
when they might have a better?

You have again forgotten, my friend, I said, the intention of the   59
legislator, who did not aim at making any one class in the State happy above the rest: the happiness was to be in the whole State, and he held the citizens together by persuasion and necessity, making them benefactors of the State, and therefore benefactors of one another; to this end he created them, not to please themselves, but to be his instruments in binding up the State.

True, he said, I had forgotten.   60

Observe, Glaucon, that there will be no injustice in compelling our   61
philosophers to have a care and providence of others; we shall explain to them that in other States, men of their class are not obliged to share in the toils of politics: and this is reasonable, for they grow up at their own sweet will, and the government would rather not

have them. Being self-taught, they cannot be expected to show any gratitude for a culture which they have never received. But we have brought you into the world to be rulers of the hive, kings of your-selves and of the other citizens, and have educated you far better and more perfectly than they have been educated, and you are better able to share in the double duty. Wherefore each of you, when his turn comes, must go down to the general underground abode, and get the habit of seeing in the dark. When you have acquired the habit, you will see ten thousand times better than the inhabitants of the den, and you will know what the several images are, and what they represent, because you have seen the beautiful and just and good in their truth. And thus our State which is also yours will be a reality, and not a dream only, and will be administered in a spirit unlike that of other States, in which men fight with one another about shadows only and are distracted in the struggle for power, which in their eyes is a great good. Whereas the truth is that the State in which the rulers are most reluctant to govern is always the best and most quietly governed, and the State in which they are most eager, the worst.

Quite true, he replied.   62

And will our pupils, when they hear this, refuse to take their turn   63
at the toils of State, when they are allowed to spend the greater part
of their time with one another in the heavenly light?

Impossible, he answered; for they are just men, and the com-   64
mands which we impose upon them are just; there can be no doubt
that every one of them will take office as a stern necessity, and not
after the fashion of our present rulers of State.

Yes, my friend, I said; and there lies the point. You must contrive   65
for your future rulers another and better life than that of a ruler,
and then you may have a well-ordered State; for only in the State
which offers this, will they rule who are truly rich, not in silver and
gold, but in virtue and wisdom, which are the true blessings of life.
Whereas if they go to the administration of public affairs, poor and
hungering after their own private advantage, thinking that hence
they are to snatch the chief good, order there can never be; for they
will be fighting about office, and the civil and domestic broils which
thus arise will be the ruin of the rulers themselves and of the whole
State.

Most true, he replied.   66

And the only life which looks down upon the life of political ambi-   67
tion is that of true philosophy. Do you know of any other?

Indeed, I do not, he said.   68

And those who govern ought not to be lovers of the task? For, if   69
they are, there will be rival lovers, and they will fight.

No question.   70

Who then are those whom we shall compel to be guardians? Surely   71
they will be the men who are wisest about affairs of State, and by
whom the State is best administered, and who at the same time have
other honors and another and a better life than that of politics?

They are the men, and I will choose them, he replied.   72

And now shall we consider in what way such guardians will be   73
produced, and how they are to be brought from darkness to light—
as some are said to have ascended from the world below to the gods?

By all means, he replied.   74

The process, I said, is not the turning over of an oyster-shell, but   75
the turning round of a soul passing from a day which is little better
than night to the true day of being, that is, the ascent from below
which we affirm to be true philosophy?

Quite so.   76

A MODEST PROPOSAL

For Preventing the Children of Poor People in Ireland from Being a Burden to Their Parents or Country, and for Making Them Beneficial to the Public

Jonathan Swift

Jonathan Swift (1667–1745) was born in Dublin. His father, who was English, died before Swift was born, and his mother deserted him. His uncle took charge of his education, and in 1694 Swift was ordained an Anglican priest. During the next twenty years, Swift was repeatedly frustrated in his attempts to gain advancement in England. Finally, in 1714, he accepted a minor appointment as Dean of St. Patrick's Cathedral, Dublin. During this time Swift wrote on many political and religious topics. Swift's satire reached its climax in his masterpiece Gulliver's Travels *(1726). In 1729 Swift achieved national prominence in Ireland with the publication of his satirical pamphlet "A Modest Proposal." In it, he offers the suggestion that the children of the poor could be sold to the rich as food. And this way, says Swift, the parents of the children could improve their financial condition as well as alleviate the famine that was ravaging Ireland.*

1   It is a melancholy object to those who walk through this great town or travel in the country, when they see the streets, the roads, and cabin doors, crowded with beggars of the female sex, followed by three, four, or six children, all in rags and importuning every passenger for an alms. These mothers, instead of being able to work for their honest livelihood, are forced to employ all their time in strolling to beg sustenance for their helpless infants: who as they grow up either turn thieves for want of work, or leave their dear native country to fight for the pretender in Spain, or sell themselves to the Barbadoes.

2   I think it is agreed by all parties that this prodigious number of children in the arms, or on the backs, or at the heels of their mothers, and frequently of their fathers, is in the present deplorable state of

the kingdom a very great additional grievance; and, therefore, whoever could find out a fair, cheap, and easy method of making these
children sound, useful members of the commonwealth, would deserve so well of the public as to have his statue set up for a preserver
of the nation.

But my intention is very far from being confined to provide only 3
for the children of professed beggars; it is of a much greater extent,
and shall take in the whole number of infants at a certain age who
are born of parents in effect as little able to support them as those
who demand our charity in the streets.

As to my own part, having turned my thoughts for many years 4
upon this important subject, and maturely weighed the several
schemes of our projectors, I have always found them grossly mistaken in their computation. It is true, a child just dropped from its
dam may be supported by her milk for a solar year, with little other
nourishment; at most not above the value of 2s.,* which the mother
may certainly get, or the value in scraps, by her lawful occupation
of begging; and it is exactly at one year old that I propose to provide
for them in such a manner as instead of being a charge upon their
parents or the parish, or wanting food and raiment for the rest of
their lives, they shall on the contrary contribute to the feeding, and
partly to the clothing, of many thousands.

There is likewise another great advantage in my scheme, that it 5
will prevent those voluntary abortions, and that horrid practice of
women murdering their bastard children, alas! too frequent among
us! sacrificing the poor innocent babes I doubt more to avoid the
expense than the shame, which would move tears and pity in the
most savage and inhuman breast.

The number of souls in this kingdom being usually reckoned one 6
million and a half, of these I calculate there may be about 200,000
couple whose wives are breeders; from which number I subtract
30,000 couple who are able to maintain their own children (although
I apprehend there cannot be so many, under the present distress
of the kingdom); but this being granted, there will remain 170,000
breeders. I again subtract 50,000 for those women who miscarry, or
whose children die by accident or disease within the year. There only
remain 120,000 children of poor parents annually born. The question
therefore is, how this number shall be reared and provided for?
which, as I have already said, under the present situation of affairs,

*EDS. NOTE—2s. = two shillings. Later in the essay, Swift speaks of "*l*" and
"*d*," that is, of pounds and pence.

is utterly impossible by all the methods hitherto proposed. For we can neither employ them in handicraft or agriculture; we neither build houses (I mean in the country) nor cultivate land; they can very seldom pick up a livelihood by stealing, till they arrive at six years old, except where they are of towardly parts; although I confess they learn the rudiments much earlier; during which time they can, however, be properly looked upon only as probationers; as I have been informed by a principal gentleman in the county of Cavan, who protested to me that he never knew above one or two instances under the age of six, even in a part of the kingdom so renowned for the quickest proficiency in that art.

I am assured by our merchants, that a boy or a girl before twelve   7
years old is no saleable commodity; and even when they come to this age they will not yield above 3*l*. or 3*l*. 2*s*. 6*d*. at most on the exchange; which cannot turn to account either to the parents or kingdom, the charge of nutriment and rags having been at least four times that value.

I shall now therefore humbly propose my own thoughts, which I   8
hope will not be liable to the least objection.

I have been assured by a very knowing American of my acquaint-   9
ance in London, that a young healthy child well nursed is at a year old a most delicious, nourishing, and wholesome food, whether stewed, roasted, baked, or broiled; and I make no doubt that it will equally serve in a fricassee or a ragout.

I do therefore humbly offer it to public consideration that of the   10
120,000 children already computed, 20,000 may be reserved for breed, whereof only one-fourth part to be males; which is more than we allow to sheep, black cattle, or swine; and my reason is, that these children are seldom the fruits of marriage, a circumstance not much regarded by our savages; therefore one male will be sufficient to serve four females. That the remaining 100,000 may, at a year old, be offered in sale to the persons of quality and fortune through the kingdom; always advising the mother to let them suck plentifully in the last month, so as to render them plump and fat for a good table. A child will make two dishes at an entertainment for friends; and when the family dines alone, the fore or hind quarter will make a reasonable dish, and seasoned with a little pepper or salt will be very good boiled on the fourth day, especially in winter.

I have reckoned upon a medium that a child just born will weigh   11
12 pounds, and in a solar year, if tolerably nursed, will increase to 28 pounds.

I grant this food will be somewhat dear, and therefore very proper   12 for landlords, who, as they have already devoured most of the parents, seem to have the best title to the children.

Infant's flesh will be in season throughout the year, but more plentiful in March, and a little before and after: for we are told by a grave author, an eminent French physician, that fish being a prolific diet, there are more children born in Roman Catholic countries about nine months after Lent than at any other season; therefore, reckoning a year after Lent, the markets will be more glutted than usual, because the number of popish infants is at least three to one in this kingdom: and therefore it will have one other collateral advantage, by lessening the number of papists among us.

I have already computed the charge of nursing a beggar's child (in which list I reckon all cottagers, laborers, and four-fifths of the farmers) to be about *2s.* per annum, rags included; and I believe no gentleman would repine to give *10s.* for the carcass of a good fat child, which, as I have said, will make four dishes of excellent nutritive meat, when he has only some particular friend or his own family to dine with him. Thus the squire will learn to be a good landlord, and grow popular among the tenants; the mother will have *8s.* net profit, and be fit for work till she produces another child.

Those who are more thrifty (as I must confess the times require) may flay the carcass; the skin of which artificially dressed will make admirable gloves for ladies, and summer boots for fine gentlemen.

As to our city of Dublin, shambles may be appointed for this purpose in the most convenient parts of it, and butchers we may be assured will not be wanting: although I rather recommend buying the children alive, and dressing them hot from the knife as we do roasting pigs.

A very worthy person, a true lover of his country, and whose virtues I highly esteem, was lately pleased in discoursing on this matter to offer a refinement upon my scheme. He said that many gentlemen of this kingdom, having of late destroyed their deer, he conceived that the want of venison might be well supplied by the bodies of young lads and maidens, not exceeding fourteen years of age nor under twelve; so great a number of both sexes in every country being not ready to starve for want of work and service; and these to be disposed of by their parents, if alive, or otherwise by their nearest relations. But with due deference to so excellent a friend and so deserving a patriot, I cannot be altogether in his sentiments; for as to the males, my American acquaintance assured me from frequent experience that their flesh was generally tough and lean, like that of our schoolboys by continual exercise, and their taste disagreeable; and to fatten them would not answer the charge. Then as to the females, it would, I think, with humble submission be a loss to the public, because they soon would become breeders themselves: and besides, it is not improbable that some scrupulous people might be apt to censure such a practice (although indeed very unjustly), as a little bordering upon cruelty; which, I confess, has always been with me the strongest objection against any project, how well soever intended.

But in order to justify my friend, he confessed that this expedient 18 was put into his head by the famous Psalmanazar, a native of the island Formosa, who came from thence to London about twenty years ago: and in conversation told my friend, that in his country when any young person happened to be put to death, the executioner sold the carcass to persons of quality as a prime dainty; and that in his time the body of a plump girl of fifteen, who was crucified for an attempt to poison the emperor, was sold to his imperial majesty's prime minister of state, and other great mandarins of the court, in joints from the gibbet, at 400 crowns. Neither indeed can I deny, that if the same use were made of several plump girls in this town, who without one single groat to their fortunes cannot stir abroad without a chair, and appear at the playhouse and assemblies in foreign fineries which they never will pay for, the kingdom would not be the worse.

Some persons of a desponding spirit are in great concern about 19 that vast number of poor people, who are aged, diseased, or maimed, and I have been desired to employ my thoughts what course may be taken to ease the nation of so grievous an encumbrance. But I am not in the least pain upon that matter, because it is very well known that they are every day dying and rotting by cold and famine, and filth and vermin, as fast as can be reasonably expected. And as to the young laborers, they are now in as hopeful a condition: they cannot get work, and consequently pine away for want of nourishment, to a degree that if at any time they are accidentally hired to common labor, they have not strength to perform it; and thus the country and themselves are happily delivered from the evils to come.

I have too long digressed, and therefore shall return to my sub- 20 ject. I think the advantages by the proposal which I have made are obvious and many, as well as the highest importance.

For first, as I have already observed, it would greatly lessen the 21 number of papists, with whom we are yearly overrun, being the principal breeders of the nation as well as our most dangerous enemies; and who stay at home on purpose to deliver the kingdom to the Pretender, hoping to take their advantage by the absence of so many good Protestants, who have chosen rather to leave their country than stay at home and pay tithes against their conscience to an Episcopal curate.

Secondly, the poor tenants will have something valuable of their own, which by law may be made liable to distress and help to pay their landlord's rent, their corn and cattle being already seized, and money a thing unknown. 22

Thirdly, whereas the maintenance of 100,000 children from two years old and upward, cannot be computed at less that *10s.* a-piece per annum, the nation's stock will be thereby increased £50,000 per annum, beside the profit of a new dish introduced to the tables of all gentlemen of fortune in the kingdom who have any refinement in taste. And the money will circulate among ourselves, the goods being entirely of our own growth and manufacture. 23

Fourthly, the constant breeders, beside the gain of *8s.* sterling per annum by the sale of their children, will be rid of the charge of maintaining them after the first year. 24

Fifthly, this food would likewise bring great custom to taverns, where the vintners will certainly be so prudent as to procure the best receipts for dressing it to perfection, and consequently have their houses frequented by all the fine gentlemen, who justly value themselves upon their knowledge in good eating; and a skillful cook, who understands how to oblige his guests, will contrive to make it as expensive as they please. 25

Sixthly, this would be a great inducement to marriage, which all wise nations have either encouraged by rewards or enforced by laws and penalties. It would increase the care and tenderness of mothers toward their children, when they were sure of a settlement for life to the poor babes, provided in some sort by the public, to their annual profit instead of expense. We should see an honest emulation among the married women, which of them would bring the fattest child to the market. Men would become as fond of their wives during the time of their pregnancy as they are now of their mares in foal, their cows in calf, their sows when they are ready to farrow; nor offer to beat or kick them (as is too frequent a practice) for fear of a miscarriage. 26

Many other advantages might be enumerated. For instance, the addition of some thousand carcasses in our exportation of barreled beef, the propagation of swine's flesh, and improvement in the art of making good bacon, so much wanted among us by the great destruction of pigs, too frequent at our table; which are no way comparable in taste or magnificence to a well-grown, fat, yearling child, which roasted whole will make a considerable figure at a lord 27 mayor's feast or any other public entertainment. But this and many others I omit, being studious of brevity.

Supposing that 1,000 families in this city would be constant cus- 28
tomers for infants' flesh, besides others who might have it at merry-meetings, particularly at weddings and christenings, I compute that Dublin would take off annually about 20,000 carcasses; and the rest of the kingdom (where probably they will be sold somewhat cheaper) the remaining 80,000.

I can think of no one objection that will possibly be raised against 29
this proposal, unless it should be urged that the number of people will be thereby much lessened in the kingdom. This I freely own, and it was indeed one principal design in offering it to the world. I desire the reader will observe, that I calculate my remedy for this one individual kingdom of Ireland and for no other that ever was, is, or I think ever can be upon earth. Therefore let no man talk to me of other expedients: of taxing our absentees at 5s. a pound: of using neither clothes nor household furniture except what is of our own growth and manufacture: of utterly rejecting the materials and instruments that promote foreign luxury: of curing the expensive-ness of pride, vanity, idleness, and gaming in our women: of intro-ducing a vein of parsimony, prudence, and temperance: of learning to love our country, in the want of which we differ even from Laplanders and the inhabitants of Topinamboo: of quitting our ani-mosities and factions, not acting any longer like the Jews, who were murdering one another at the very moment their city was taken: of being a little cautious not to sell our country and conscience for nothing: of teaching landlords to have at least one degree of mercy toward their tenants: lastly, of putting a spirit of honesty, industry, and skill into our shopkeepers; who, if a resolution could now be taken to buy only our native goods, would immediately unite to cheat and exact upon us in the price, the measure, and the goodness, nor could ever yet be brought to make one fair proposal of just deal-ing, though often and earnestly invited to it.

Therefore I repeat, let no man talk to me of these and the like 30
expedients, till he has at least some glimpse of hope that there will be ever some hearty and sincere attempt to put them in practice.

But as to myself, having been wearied out for many years with 31
offering vain, idle, visionary thoughts, and at length utterly despair-ing of success, I fortunately fell upon this proposal; which, as it is wholly new, so it has something solid and real, of no expense and little trouble, full in our own power, and whereby we can incure no danger of disobliging England. For this kind of commodity will not bear exportation, the flesh being of too tender a consistence to admit

a long continuance in salt, although perhaps I could name a country which would be glad to eat up our whole nation without it.

After all, I am not so violently bent upon my own opinion as to   32 reject any offer proposed by wise men, which shall be found equally innocent, cheap, easy, and effectual. But before something of that kind shall be advanced in contradiction to my scheme, and offering a better, I desire the author or authors will be pleased maturely to consider two points. First, as things now stand, how they will be able to find food and raiment for 100,000 useless mouths and backs. And secondly, there being a round million of creatures in human figure throughout this kingdom, whose subsistence put into a common stock would leave them in debt 2,000,000l. sterling, adding those who are beggars by profession to the bulk of farmers, cottagers, and laborers, with the wives and children who are beggars in effect; I desire those politicians who dislike my overture, and may perhaps be so bold as to attempt an answer, that they will first ask the parents of these mortals, whether they would not at this day think it a great happiness to have been sold for food at a year old in the manner I prescribe, and thereby have avoided such a perpetual scene of misfortunes as they have since gone through by the oppression of landlords, the impossibility of paying rent without money or trade, the want of common sustenance, with neither house nor clothes to cover them from the inclemencies of the weather, and the most inevitable prospect of entailing the like or greater miseries upon their breed for ever.

I profess, in the sincerity of my heart, that I have not the least   33 personal interest in endeavoring to promote this necessary work, having no other motive than the public good of my country, by advancing our trade, providing for infants, relieving the poor, and giving some pleasure to the rich. I have no children by which I can propose to get a single penny; the youngest being nine years old, and my wife past child-bearing.

CIVIL DISOBEDIENCE

Henry David Thoreau

Henry David Thoreau (1817–1862) was born in Concord, Massachusetts, and graduated from Harvard in 1837. After teaching school in Concord, he lived for two years with Ralph Waldo Emerson, noted American essayist, poet, and philosopher, who had a strong influence on Thoreau's thinking. Thoreau contributed to The Dial *and other periodicals, and, after an 1839 trip with his brother, wrote* A Week on the Concord and Merrimack Rivers. *From July 4, 1845, until September 6, 1847, Thoreau lived alone in a hut he built at Walden Pond, Massachusetts, where he wrote his best-known book,* Walden *(1854). Here, he felt, he was able not only to appreciate the wonders of nature but also to embrace simplicity and individualism. During this period he spent a night in jail for refusing, in protest against the United States Government's involvement in the Mexican War, to pay a poll tax. To explain this act of principle, Thoreau wrote* Civil Disobedience *(1849) after he was released. In this essay he outlines his philosophy of passive resistance, which holds that acts of individual conscience are more important than the law.*

I heartily accept the motto, "that government is best which governs least;" and I should like to see it acted up to more rapidly and systematically. Carried out, it finally amounts to this, which also I believe—"That government is best which governs not at all;" and when men are prepared for it, that will be the kind of government which they will have. Government is at best but an expedient; but most governments are usually, and all governments are sometimes, inexpedient. The objections which have been brought against a standing army, and they are many and weighty, and deserve to prevail, may also at last be brought against a standing government. The standing army is only an arm of the standing government. The government itself, which is only the mode which the people have chosen to execute their will, is equally liable to be abused and perverted before the people can act through it. Witness the present Mexican war, the work of comparatively a few individuals using the standing government as their tool; for, in the outset, the people would not have consented to this measure.

This American government—what is it but a tradition, though a   2
recent one, endeavoring to transmit itself unimpaired to posterity,
but each instant losing some of its integrity? It has not the vitality
and force of a single living man; for a single man can bend it to his
will. It is a sort of wooden gun to the people themselves. But it is
not the less necessary for this; for the people must have some complicated machinery or other, and hear its din, to satisfy that idea of
government which they have. Governments show thus how successfully men can be imposed on, even impose on themselves, for their
own advantage. It is excellent, we must all allow. Yet this government never of itself furthered any enterprise, but by the alacrity
with which it got out of its way. *It* does not keep the country free.
It does not settle the West. *It* does not educate. The character inherent in the American people has done all that has been accomplished;
and it would have done somewhat more, if the government had not
sometimes got in its way. For government is an expedient by which
men would fain succeed in letting one another alone; and, as has
been said, when it is most expedient, the governed are most let alone
by it. Trade and commerce, if they were not made of india-rubber,
would never manage to bounce over the obstacles which legislators
are continually putting in their way; and if one were to judge these
men wholly by the effects of their actions and not partly by their
intentions, they would deserve to be classed and punished with
those mischievous persons who put obstructions on the railroads.

But, to speak practically and as a citizen, unlike those who call   3
themselves no-government men, I ask for, not at once no government, but *at once* a better government. Let every man make known
what kind of government would command his respect, and that will
be one step toward obtaining it.

After all, the practical reason why, when the power is once in the   4
hands of the people, a majority are permitted, and for a long period
continue, to rule is not because they are most likely to be in the
right, nor because this seems fairest to the minority, but because
they are physically the strongest. But a government in which the
majority rule in all cases cannot be based on justice, even as far as
men understand it. Can there not be a government in which majorities do not virtually decide right and wrong, but conscience? in
which majorities decide only those questions to which the rule of
expediency is applicable? Must the citizen ever for a moment, or in
the least degree, resign his conscience to the legislator? Why has
every man a conscience, then? I think that we should be men first,
and subjects afterwards. It is not desirable to cultivate a respect for
the law, so much as for the right. The only obligation which I have

a right to assume is to do at any time what I think right. It is truly enough said that a corporation has no conscience; but a corporation of conscientious men is a corporation *with* a conscience. Law never made men a whit more just; and, by means of their respect for it, even the well-disposed are daily made the agents of injustice. A common and natural result of an undue respect for law is, that you may see a file of soldiers, colonel, captain, corporal, privates, powder-monkeys, and all, marching in admirable order over hill and dale to the wars, against their wills, ay, against their common sense and consciences, which makes it very steep marching indeed, and produces a palpitation of the heart. They have no doubt that it is a damnable business in which they are concerned; they are all peaceably inclined. Now, what are they? Men at all? or small movable forts and magazines, at the service of some unscrupulous man in power? Visit the Navy-Yard, and behold a marine, such a man as an American government can make, or such as it can make a man with its black arts—a mere shadow and reminiscence of humanity, a man laid out alive and standing, and already, as one may say, buried under arms with funeral accompaniments, though it may be,—

> "Not a drum was heard, not a funeral note,
> As his corse to the rampart we hurried;
> Not a soldier discharged his farewell shot
> O'er the grave where our hero was buried."

The mass of men serve the state thus, not as men mainly, but as machines, with their bodies. They are the standing army, and the militia, jailers, constables, *posse comitatus,** etc. In most cases there is no free exercise whatever of the judgment or of the moral sense; but they put themselves on a level with wood and earth and stones; and wooden men can perhaps be manufactured that will serve the purpose as well. Such command no more respect than men of straw or a lump of dirt. They have the same sort of worth only as horses and dogs. Yet such as these even are commonly esteemed good citizens. Others—as most legislators, politicians, lawyers, ministers, and office-holders—serve the state chiefly with their heads; and, as they rarely make any moral distinctions, they are as likely to serve the devil, without *intending* it, as God. A very few—as heroes, patriots, martyrs, reformers in the great sense, and *men*—serve the state with their consciences also, and so necessarily resist it for the most part; and they are commonly treated as enemies by it. A wise

*EDS. NOTE—(Latin.) A group of people assembled to aid in law enforcement.

man will only be useful as a man, and will not submit to be "clay," and "stop a hole to keep the wind away," but leave that office to his dust at least:—

> "I am too high-born to be propertied,
> To be a secondary at control,
> Or useful serving-man and instrument
> To any sovereign state throughout the world."

He who gives himself entirely to his fellow-men appears to them useless and selfish; but he who gives himself partially to them is pronounced a benefactor and philanthropist.   6

How does it become a man to behave toward this American government today? I answer, that he cannot without disgrace be associated with it. I cannot for an instant recognize that political organization as *my* government which is the *slave's* government also.   7

All men recognize the right of revolution; that is, the right to refuse allegiance to, and to resist, the government, when its tyranny or its inefficiency are great and unendurable. But almost all say that such is not the case now. But such was the case, they think, in the Revolution of '75. If one were to tell me that this was a bad government because it taxed certain foreign commodities brought to its ports, it is most probable that I should not make an ado about it, for I can do without them. All machines have their friction; and possibly this does enough good to counter-balance the evil. At any rate, it is a great evil to make a stir about it. But when the friction comes to have its machine, and oppression and robbery are organized, I say, let us not have such a machine any longer. In other words, when a sixth of the population of a nation which has undertaken to be the refuge of liberty are slaves, and a whole country is unjustly overrun and conquered by a foreign army, and subjected to military law, I think that it is not too soon for honest men to rebel and revolutionize. What makes this duty the more urgent is the fact that the country so overrun is not our own, but ours is the invading army.   8

*   *   *

Practically speaking, the opponents to a reform in Massachusetts are not a hundred thousand politicians at the South, but a hundred thousand merchants and farmers here, who are more interested in commerce and agriculture than they are in humanity, and are not prepared to do justice to the slave and to Mexico, *cost what it may.* I quarrel not with far-off foes, but with those who, near at home,   9 coöperate with, and do the bidding of, those far away, and without whom the latter would be harmless. We are accustomed to say, that the mass of men are unprepared; but improvement is slow, because the few are not materially wiser or better than the many. It is not so important that many should be as good as you, as that there be some absolute goodness somewhere; for that will leaven the whole lump. There are thousands who are *in opinion* opposed to slavery and the war, who yet in effect do nothing to put an end to them; who, esteeming themselves children of Washington and Franklin, sit down with their hands in their pockets, and say that they know not what to do, and do nothing; who even postpone the question of freedom to the question of free trade, and quietly read the prices-current along with the latest advices from Mexico, after dinner, and, it may be, fall asleep over them both. What is the price-current of an honest man and patriot today? They hesitate, and they regret, and sometimes they petition; but they do nothing in earnest and with effect. They will wait, well disposed, for others to remedy the evil, that they may no longer have it to regret. At most, they give only a cheap vote, and a feeble countenance and God-speed, to the right, as it goes by them. There are nine hundred and ninety-nine patrons of virtue to one virtuous man. But it is easier to deal with the real possessor of a thing than with the temporary guardian of it.

All voting is a sort of gaming, like checkers or backgammon, with   10
a slight moral tinge to it, a playing with right and wrong, with moral questions; and betting naturally accompanies it. The character of the voters is not staked. I cast my vote, perchance, as I think right; but I am not vitally concerned that that right should prevail. I am willing to leave it to the majority. Its obligation, therefore, never exceeds that of expediency. Even voting *for the right* is *doing* nothing for it. It is only expressing to men feebly your desire that it should prevail. A wise man will not leave the right to the mercy of chance, nor wish it to prevail through the power of the majority. There is but little virtue in the action of masses of men. When the majority shall at length vote for the abolition of slavery, it will be because they are indifferent to slavery, or because there is but little slavery left to be abolished by their vote. *They* will then be the only slaves. Only *his* vote can hasten the abolition of slavery who asserts his own freedom by his vote.

I hear of a convention to be held at Baltimore, or elsewhere, for   11
the selection of a candidate for the Presidency, made up chiefly of editors, and men who are politicians by profession; but I think, what is it to any independent, intelligent, and respectable man what deci-

sion they may come to? Shall we not have the advantage of his wisdom and honesty, nevertheless? Can we not count upon some independent votes? Are there not many individuals in the country who do not attend conventions? But no: I find that the respectable man, so called, has immediately drifted from his position, and despairs of his country, when his country has more reason to despair of him. He forthwith adopts one of the candidates thus selected as the only *available* one, thus proving that he is himself *available* for any purposes of the demagogue. His vote is of no more worth than that of any unprincipled foreigner or hireling native, who may have been bought. O for a man who is a *man*, and, as my neighbor says, has a bone in his back which you cannot pass your hand through! Our statistics are at fault: the population has been returned too large. How many *men* are there to a square thousand miles in this country? Hardly one. Does not America offer any inducement for men to settle here? The American has dwindled into an Odd Fellow—one who may be known by the development of his organ of gregariousness, and a manifest lack of intellect and cheerful self-reliance; whose first and chief concern, on coming into the world, is to see that the almshouses are in good repair; and, before yet he has lawfully donned the virile garb, to collect a fund for the support of the widows and orphans that may be; who, in short, ventures to live only by the aid of the Mutual Insurance company, which has promised to bury him decently.

It is not a man's duty, as a matter of course, to devote himself to [12] the eradication of any, even the most enormous, wrong; he may still properly have other concerns to engage him; but it is his duty, at least, to wash his hands of it, and, if he gives it no thought longer, not to give it practically his support. If I devote myself to other pursuits and contemplations, I must first see, at least, that I do not pursue them sitting upon another man's shoulders. I must get off him first, that he may pursue his contemplations too. See what gross inconsistency is tolerated. I have heard some of my townsmen say, "I should like to have them order me out to help put down an insurrection of the slaves, or to march to Mexico—see if I would go"; and yet these very men have each, directly by their allegiance, and so indirectly, at least, by their money, furnished a substitute. The soldier is applauded who refuses to serve in an unjust war by those who do not refuse to sustain the unjust government which makes the war; is applauded by those whose own act and authority he disregards and sets at naught; as if the state were penitent to that degree that it hired one to scourge it while it sinned, but not to that degree that it left off sinning for a moment. Thus, under the name

of Order and Civil Government, we are all made at last to pay hom-
age to and support our own meanness. After the first blush of sin
comes its indifference; and from immoral it becomes, as it were, *un-
moral*, and not quite unnecessary to that life which we have made.

The broadest and most prevalent error requires the most disinter- 13
ested virtue to sustain it. The slight reproach to which the virtue of
patriotism is commonly liable, the noble are most likely to incur.
Those who, while they disapprove of the character and measures of
a government, yield to it their allegiance and support are undoubtedly its most conscientious supporters, and so frequently the most
serious obstacles to reform. Some are petitioning the State to dissolve the Union, to disregard the requisitions of the President. Why
do they not dissolve it themselves—the union between themselves
and the State—and refuse to pay their quota into its treasury? Do
not they stand in the same relation to the State that the State does
to the Union? And have not the same reasons prevented the State
from resisting the Union which have prevented them from resisting
the State?

How can a man be satisfied to entertain an opinion merely, and 14
enjoy *it?* Is there any enjoyment in it, if his opinion is that he is
aggrieved? If you are cheated out of a single dollar by your neighbor,
you do not rest satisfied with knowing that you are cheated, or with
saying that you are cheated, or even with petitioning him to pay
you your due; but you take effectual steps at once to obtain the
full amount, and see that you are never cheated again. Action from
principle, the perception and the performance of right, changes
things and relations; it is essentially revolutionary, and does not
consist wholly with anything which was. It not only divides States
and churches, it divides families; ay, it divides the *individual,* sepa-
rating the diabolical in him from the divine.

Unjust laws exist: shall we be content to obey them, or shall we 15
endeavor to amend them, and obey them until we have succeeded,
or shall we transgress them at once? Men generally, under such a
government as this, think that they ought to wait until they have
persuaded the majority to alter them. They think that, if they
should resist, the remedy would be worse than the evil. But it is the
fault of the government itself that the remedy *is* worse than the evil.
It makes it worse. Why is it not more apt to anticipate and provide
for reform? Why does it not cherish its wise minority? Why does it
cry and resist before it is hurt? Why does it not encourage its citizens to be on the alert to point out its faults, and *do* better than it
would have them? Why does it always crucify Christ, and excommu-

nicate Copernicus and Luther, and pronounce Washington and Franklin rebels?

* * *

I do not hesitate to say, that those who call themselves Abolitionists should at once effectually withdraw their support, both in person and property, from the government of Massachusetts, and not wait till they constitute a majority of one, before they suffer the right to prevail through them. I think that it is enough if they have God on their side, without waiting for that other one. Moreover, any man more right than his neighbors constitutes a majority of one already.   16

I meet this American government, or its representative, the State government, directly, and face to face, once a year—no more—in the person of its tax-gatherer; this is the only mode in which a man situated as I am necessarily meets it; and it then says distinctly, Recognize me; and the simplest, the most effectual, and, in the present posture of affairs, the indispensablest mode of treating with it on this head, of expressing your little satisfaction with and love for it, is to deny it then. My civil neighbor, the tax-gatherer, is the very man I have to deal with—for it is, after all, with men and not with parchment that I quarrel—and he has voluntarily chosen to be an agent of the government. How shall he ever know well what he is and does as an officer of the government, or as a man, until he is obliged to consider whether he shall treat me, his neighbor, for whom he has respect, as a neighbor and well-disposed man, or as a maniac and disturber of the peace, and see if he can get over this obstruction to his neighborliness without a ruder and more impetuous thought or speech corresponding with his action. I know this well, that if one thousand, if one hundred, if ten men whom I could name—if ten *honest* men only—ay, if *one* HONEST man, in this State of Massachusetts, *ceasing to hold slaves*, were actually to withdraw from this copartnership, and be locked up in the county jail therefor, it would be the abolition of slavery in America. For it matters not how small the beginning may seem to be: what is once well done is done forever. But we love better to talk about it: that we say is our mission. Reform keeps many scores of newspapers in its service, but not one man. If my esteemed neighbor, the State's ambassador, who will devote his days to the settlement of the question of human rights in the Council Chamber, instead of being threatened with the prisons of Carolina, were to sit down the prisoner of Massachusetts, that State which is so anxious to foist the sin of slavery upon her   17

560 ESSAYS FOR FURTHER READING

sister—though at present she can discover only an act of inhospitality to be the ground of a quarrel with her—the Legislature would not wholly waive the subject the following winter.

Under a government which imprisons any unjustly, the true place 18 for a just man is also a prison. The proper place to-day, the only place which Massachusetts has provided for her freer and less desponding spirits, is in her prisons, to be put out and locked out of the State by her own act, as they have already put themselves out by their principles. It is there that the fugitive slave, and the Mexican prisoner on parole, and the Indian come to plead the wrongs of his race should find them; on that separate, but more free and honorable, ground, where the State places those who are not *with* her, but *against* her—the only house in a slave State in which a free man can abide with honor. If any think that their influence would be lost there, and their voices no longer afflict the ear of the State, that they would not be as an enemy within its walls, they do not know by how much truth is stronger than error, nor how much more eloquently and effectively he can combat injustice who has experienced a little in his own person. Cast your whole vote, not a strip of paper merely, but your whole influence. A minority is powerless while it conforms to the majority; it is not even a minority then; but it is irresistible when it clogs by its whole weight. If the alternative is to keep all just men in prison, or give up war and slavery, the State will not hesitate which to choose. If a thousand men were not to pay their tax-bills this year, that would not be a violent and bloody measure, as it would be to pay them, and enable the State to commit violence and shed innocent blood. This is, in fact, the definition of a peaceable revolution, if any such is possible. If the tax-gatherer, or any other public officer, asks me, as one has done, "But what shall I do?" my answer is, "If you really wish to do anything, resign your office." When the subject has refused allegiance, and the officer has resigned his office, then the revolution is accomplished. But even suppose blood should flow. Is there not a sort of blood shed when the conscience is wounded? Through this wound a man's real manhood and immortality flow out, and he bleeds to an everlasting death. I see this blood flowing now.

I have contemplated the imprisonment of the offender, rather than 19 the seizure of his goods—though both will serve the same purpose—because they who assert the purest right, and consequently are most dangerous to a corrupt State, commonly have not spent much time in accumulating property. To such the State renders comparatively small service, and a slight tax is wont to appear exorbitant, particularly if they are obliged to earn it by special labor with their hands.

If there were one who lived wholly without the use of money, the State itself would hesitate to demand it of him. But the rich man—not to make any invidious comparison—is always sold to the institution which makes him rich. Absolutely speaking, the more money, the less virtue; for money comes between a man and his objects, and obtains them for him; and it was certainly no great virtue to obtain it. It puts to rest many questions which he would otherwise be taxed to answer; while the only new question which it puts is the hard but superfluous one, how to spend it. Thus his moral ground is taken from under his feet. The opportunities of living are diminished in proportion as what are called the "means" are increased. The best thing a man can do for his culture when he is rich is to endeavor to carry out those schemes which he entertained when he was poor. Christ answered the Herodians according to their condition. "Show me the tribute-money," said he;—and one took a penny out of his pocket;—if you use money which has the image of Caesar on it, and which he has made current and valuable, that is, *if you are men of the State*, and gladly enjoy the advantages of Caesar's government, then pay him back some of his own when he demands it. "Render therefore to Caesar that which is Caesar's, and to God those things which are God's"—leaving them no wiser than before as to which was which; for they did not wish to know.

When I converse with the freest of my neighbors, I perceive that, whatever they may say about the magnitude and seriousness of the question, and their regard for the public tranquillity, the long and the short of the matter is, that they cannot spare the protection of the existing government, and they dread the consequences of their property and families of disobedience to it. For my own part, I should not like to think that I ever rely on the protection of the State. But, if I deny the authority of the State when it presents its tax-bill, it will soon take and waste all my property, and so harass me and my children without end. This is hard. This makes it impossible for a man to live honestly, and at the same time comfortably, in outward respects. It will not be worth the while to accumulate property; that would be sure to go again. You must hire or squat somewhere, and raise but a small crop, and eat that soon. You must live within yourself, and depend upon yourself always tucked up and ready for a start, and not have many affairs. A man may grow rich in Turkey even, if he will be in all respects a good subject of the Turkish government. Confucius said: "If a state is governed by the principles of reason, poverty and misery are subjects of shame; if a state is not governed by the principles of reason, riches and honors are the subjects of shame." No: until I want the protection of Massachusetts to be extended to me in some distant Southern port, where my liberty is endangered, or until I am bent solely on building up an estate at home by peaceful enterprise, I can afford to refuse allegiance to Massachusetts, and her right to my property and life. It costs me less in every sense to incur the penalty of disobedience to the State than it would to obey. I should feel as if I were worth less in that case.

Some years ago, the State met me in behalf of the Church, and 21 commanded me to pay a certain sum toward the support of a clergyman whose preaching my father attended, but never I myself. "Pay," it said, "or be locked up in the jail." I declined to pay. But, unfortunately, another man saw fit to pay it. I did not see why the schoolmaster should be taxed to support the priest, and not the priest the schoolmaster; for I was not the State's schoolmaster, but I supported myself by voluntary subscription. I did not see why the lyceum should not present its tax-bill, and have the State to back its demand, as well as the Church. However, at the request of the selectmen, I condescended to make some such statement as this in writing:—"Know all men by these presents, that I, Henry Thoreau, do not wish to be regarded as a member of any incorporated society which I have not joined." This I gave to the town clerk; and he has it. The State, having thus learned that I did not wish to be regarded as a member of that church, has never made a like demand on me since; though it said that it must adhere to its original presumption that time. If I had known how to name them, I should then have signed off in detail from all the societies which I never signed on to; but I did not know where to find a complete list.

I have paid no poll-tax for six years. I was put into a jail once on 22 this account, for one night; and, as I stood considering the walls of solid stone, two or three feet thick, the door of wood and iron, a foot thick, and the iron grating which strained the light, I could not help being struck with the foolishness of that institution which treated me as if I were mere flesh and blood and bones to be locked up. I wondered that it should have concluded at length that this was the best use it could put me to, and had never thought to avail itself of my services in some way. I saw that, if there was a wall of stone between me and my townsmen, there was a still more difficult one to climb or break through before they could get to be as free as I was. I did not for a moment feel confined, and the walls seemed a great waste of stone and mortar. I felt as if I alone of all my townsmen had paid my tax. They plainly did not know how to treat me, but behaved like persons who are underbred. In every threat and in every compliment there was a blunder; for they thought that my chief desire was to stand the other side of that stone wall. I could not but smile to see how industriously they locked the door on my meditations, which followed them out again without let or hindrance, and *they* were really all that was dangerous. As they could not reach me, they had resolved to punish my body; just as boys, if they cannot come at some person against whom they have a spite, will abuse his dog. I saw that the State was half-witted, that it was timid as a lone woman with her silver spoons, and that it did not know its friends from its foes, and I lost all my remaining respect for it, and pitied it.

Thus the State never intentionally confronts a man's sense, intellectual or moral, but only his body, his senses. It is not armed with superior wit or honesty, but with superior physical strength. I was not born to be forced. I will breathe after my own fashion. Let us see who is the strongest. What force has a multitude? They only can force me who obey a higher law than I. They force me to become like themselves. I do not hear of *men* being *forced* to live this way or that by masses of men. What sort of life were that to live? When I meet a government which says to me, "Your money or your life," why should I be in haste to give it my money? It may be in a great strait, and not know what to do: I cannot help that. It must help itself; do as I do. It is not worth the while to snivel about it. I am not responsible for the successful working of the machinery of society. I am not the son of the engineer. I perceive that, when an acorn and a chestnut fall side by side, the one does not remain inert to make way for the other, but both obey their own laws, and spring and grow and flourish as best they can, till one, perchance, overshadows and destroys the other. If a plant cannot live according to its nature, it dies; and so a man. 23

IF SHAKESPEARE
HAD HAD A SISTER

Virginia Woolf

Author of essays, reviews, and novels, Virginia Woolf was born in 1882 into a prominent, well-educated London family. With her husband, Leonard Woolf, she founded the Hogarth Press, which published works by many well-known writers—including those who came to be known as the Bloomsbury group after the area of London in which Woolf lived. Woolf's own published books include the novels Mrs. Dalloway *(1922),* To the Lighthouse *(1927), and* Orlando *(1928) and the essay collections* The Common Reader *(1925) and* A Room of One's Own *(1929). Woolf committed suicide in 1941. "If Shakespeare Had Had a Sister," the selection that follows, is excerpted from* A Room of One's Own, *a book based on lectures Woolf delivered at Cambridge University. The book's premise is that women, historically denied both financial support and uninterrupted time ("a room of one's own") in which to write, have naturally been unable to produce as much written work as their male counterparts. "If Shakespeare Had Had a Sister" considers the many obstacles facing an Elizabethan woman who might wish to become an independent, well-educated professional. The selection's concluding paragraph is the last paragraph of* A Room of One's Own.*

Perhaps now it would be better to give up seeking for the truth, and receiving on one's head an avalanche of opinion hot as lava, discoloured as dish-water. It would be better to draw the curtains; to shut out distractions; to light the lamp; to narrow the enquiry and to ask the historian, who records not opinions but facts, to describe under what conditions women lived, not throughout the ages, but in England, say in the time of Elizabeth.

For it is a perennial puzzle why no woman wrote a word of that extraordinary literature when every other man, it seemed, was capable of song or sonnet. What were the conditions in which women lived, I asked myself; for fiction, imaginative work that is, is not dropped like a pebble upon the ground, as science may be; fiction is like a spider's web, attached ever so lightly perhaps, but still attached to life at all four corners. Often the attachment is scarcely perceptible; Shakespeare's plays, for instance, seem to hang there complete by themselves. But when the web is pulled askew, hooked up at the edge, torn in the middle, one remembers that these webs are not spun in midair by incorporeal creatures, but are the work of suffering human beings, and are attached to grossly material things, like health and money and the houses we live in.

I went, therefore, to the shelf where the histories stand and took down one of the latest, Professor Trevelyan's *History of England.* Once more I looked up Women, found "position of," and turned to the pages indicated. "Wife-beating," I read, "was a recognised right of man, and was practised without shame by high as well as low. . . . Similarly," the historian goes on, "the daughter who refused to marry the gentleman of her parent's choice was liable to be locked up, beaten and flung about the room, without any shock being inflicted on public opinion. Marriage was not an affair of personal affection, but of family avarice, particularly in the 'chivalrous' upper classes. . . . Betrothal often took place while one or both of the parties was in the cradle, and marriage when they were scarcely out of the nurses' charge." That was about 1470, soon after Chaucer's time. The next reference to the position of women is some two hundred years later, in the time of the Stuarts. "It was still the exception for women of the upper and middle class to choose their own husbands, and when the husband had been assigned, he was lord and master, so far at least as law and custom could make him. Yet even so," Professor Trevelyan concludes, "neither Shakespeare's women nor those of authentic seventeenth-century memoirs, like the Verneys and the Hutchinsons, seem wanting in personality and character." Certainly, if we consider it, Cleopatra must have had a way with her; Lady Macbeth, one would suppose, had a will of her own; Rosalind, one might conclude, was an attractive girl. Professor Trevelyan is speaking no more than the truth when he remarks that Shakespeare's women do not seem wanting in personality and character. Not being a historian, one might go even further and say that women have burnt like beacons in all the works of all the poets from the beginning of time—Clytemnestra, Antigone, Cleopatra, Lady Macbeth, Phèdre, Cressida, Rosalind, Desdemona, the Duchess of Malfi, among the dramatists; then among the prose writers: Millamant, Clarissa, Becky Sharp, Anna Karenine, Emma Bovary, Madame de Guermantes—the names flock to mind, nor do they recall women "lacking in personality and character." Indeed, if women had no existence save in the fiction written by men, one would imagine her a person of the utmost importance; very various; heroic and mean; splendid and sordid; infinitely beautiful and hideous in the extreme; as great as a man, some think even greater. But this is woman in fiction. In fact, as Professor Trevelyan points out, she was locked up, beaten and flung about the room.

A very queer, composite being thus emerges. Imaginatively she is of the highest importance; practically she is completely insignificant. She pervades poetry from cover to cover; she is all but absent from history. She dominates the lives of kings and conquerors in fiction; in fact she was the slave of any boy whose parents forced a ring upon her finger. Some of the most inspired words, some of the most profound thoughts in literature fall from her lips; in real life she could hardly read, could scarcely spell, and was the property of her husband.

It was certainly an odd monster that one made up by reading the historians first and the poets afterwards—a worm winged like an eagle; the spirit of life and beauty in a kitchen chopping up suet. But these monsters, however amusing to the imagination, have no existence in fact. What one must do to bring her to life was to think poetically and prosaically at one and the same moment, thus keeping in touch with fact—that she is Mrs. Martin, aged thirty-six, dressed in blue, wearing a black hat and brown shoes; but not losing sight of fiction either—that she is a vessel in which all sorts of spirits and forces are coursing and flashing perpetually. The moment, however, that one tries this method with the Elizabethan woman, one branch of illumination fails; one is held up by the scarcity of facts. One knows nothing detailed, nothing perfectly true and substantial about her. History scarcely mentions her.

* * *

Here am I asking why women did not write poetry in the Elizabethan age, and I am not sure how they were educated; whether they were taught to write; whether they had sitting-rooms to themselves; how many women had children before they were twenty-one; what, in short, they did from eight in the morning till eight at night. They had no money evidently; according to Professor Trevelyan they were married whether they liked it or not before they were out of the nursery, at fifteen or sixteen very likely. It would have been extremely odd, even upon this showing, had one of them suddenly written the plays of Shakespeare, I concluded, and I thought of that old gentleman, who is dead now, but was a bishop, I think, who declared that it was impossible for any woman, past, present, or to come, to have the genius of Shakespeare. He wrote to the papers about it. He also told a lady who applied to him for information that cats do not as a matter of fact go to heaven, though they have, he added, souls of a sort. How much thinking those old gentlemen used to save one! How the borders of ignorance shrank back at their approach! Cats do not go to heaven. Women cannot write the plays of Shakespeare.

Be that as it may, I could not help thinking, as I looked at the words of Shakespeare on the shelf, that the bishop was right at least in this; it would have been impossible, completely and entirely, for any woman to have written the plays of Shakespeare in the age of Shakespeare. Let me imagine, since facts are so hard to come by, what would have happened had Shakespeare had a wonderfully gifted sister, called Judith, let us say. Shakespeare himself went, very probably—his mother was an heiress—to the grammar school, where he may have learnt Latin—Ovid, Virgil and Horace—and the elements of grammar and logic. He was, it is well known, a wild boy who poached rabbits, perhaps shot a deer, and had, rather sooner than he should have done, to marry a woman in the neighbourhood, who bore him a child rather quicker than was right. That escapade sent him to seek his fortune in London. He had, it seemed, a taste for the theatre; he began by holding horses at the stage door. Very soon he got work in the theatre, became a successful actor, and lived at the hub of the universe, meeting everybody, knowing everybody, practising his art on the boards, exercising his wits in the streets, and even getting access to the palace of the queen. Meanwhile his extraordinarily gifted sister, let us suppose, remained at home. She was as adventurous, as imaginative, as agog to see the world as he was. But she was not sent to school. She had no chance of learning grammar and logic, let alone of reading Horace and Virgil. She picked up a book now and then, one of her brother's perhaps, and read a few pages. But then her parents came in and told her to mend the stockings or mind the stew and not moon about with books and papers. They would have spoken sharply but kindly, for they were substantial people who knew the conditions of life for a woman and loved their daughter—indeed, more likely than not she was the apple of her father's eye. Perhaps she scribbled some pages up in an apple loft on the sly, but was careful to hide them or set fire to them. Soon, however, before she was out of her teens, she was to be betrothed to the son of a neighbouring wool-stapler. She cried out that marriage was hateful to her, and for that she was severely beaten by her father. Then he ceased to scold her. He begged her instead not to hurt him, not to shame him in this matter of her marriage. He would give her a chain of beads or a fine petticoat, he said; and there were tears in his eyes. How could she disobey him? How could she break his heart? The force of her own gift alone drove her to it. She made a small parcel of her belongings, let herself down by a rope one summer's night and took the road to London. She was not seventeen.

The birds that sang in the hedge were not more musical than she was. She had the quickest fancy, a gift like her brother's, for the tune of words. Like him, she had a taste for the theatre. She stood at the stage door; she wanted to act, she said. Men laughed in her face. The manager—a fat, loose-lipped man—guffawed. He bellowed something about poodles dancing and women acting—no woman, he said, could possibly be an actress. He hinted—you can imagine what. She could get no training in her craft. Could she even seek her dinner in a tavern or roam the streets at midnight? Yet her genius was for fiction and lusted to feed abundantly upon the lives of men and women and the study of their ways. At last—for she was very young, oddly like Shakespeare the poet in her face, with the same grey eyes and rounded brows—at last Nick Greene the actor-manager took pity on her; she found herself with child by that gentleman and so—who shall measure the heat and violence of the poet's heart when caught and tangled in a woman's body?—killed herself one winter's night and lies buried at some cross-roads where the omnibuses now stop outside the Elephant and Castle.*

That, more or less, is how the story would run, I think, if a woman in Shakespeare's day had had Shakespeare's genius. But for my part, I agree with the deceased bishop, if such he was—it is unthinkable that any woman in Shakespeare's day should have had Shakespeare's genius. For genius like Shakespeare's is not born among labouring, uneducated, servile people. It was not born in England among the Saxons and the Britons. It is not born today among the working classes. How, then, could it have been born among women whose work began, according to Professor Trevelyan, almost before they were out of the nursery, who were forced to it by their parents and held to it by all the power of law and custom? Yet genius of a sort must have existed among women as it must have existed among the working classes. Now and again an Emily Brontë or a Robert Burns blazes out and proves its presence. But certainly it never got itself on to paper. When, however, one reads of a witch being ducked, of a woman possessed by devils, of a wise woman selling herbs, or even of a very remarkable man who had a mother, then I think we are on the track of a lost novelist, a suppressed poet, of some mute and inglorious Jane Austen, some Emily Brontë who dashed her brains out on the moor or mopped and mowed about the highways crazed with the torture that her gift had put her to. Indeed, I would venture to guess that Anon, who wrote so many poems without signing them, was often a woman. It was a woman Edward Fitzgerald, I think, suggested who made the ballads and the folk-songs, crooning

8

*EDS. NOTE—An old, established English pub, the Elephant and Castle is a well-known landmark from which a South East London neighborhood takes its name.

them to her children, beguiling her spinning with them, or the length
of the winter's night.

This may be true or it may be false—who can say?—but what is   9
true in it, so it seemed to me, reviewing the story of Shakespeare's
sister as I had made it, is that any woman born with a great gift in
the sixteenth century would certainly have gone crazed, shot herself, or ended her days in some lonely cottage outside the village,
half witch, half wizard, feared and mocked at. For it needs little skill
in psychology to be sure that a highly gifted girl who had tried to
use her gift for poetry would have been so thwarted and hindered
by other people, so tortured and pulled asunder by her own contrary
instincts, that she must have lost her health and sanity to a certainty. No girl could have walked to London and stood at a stage
door and forced her way into the presence of actor-managers without
doing herself a violence and suffering an anguish which may have
been irrational—for chastity may be a fetish invented by certain societies for unknown reasons—but were none the less inevitable.
Chastity had then, it has even now, a religious importance in a woman's life, and has so wrapped itself round with nerves and instincts
that to cut it free and bring it to the light of day demands courage
of the rarest. To have lived a free life in London in the sixteenth
century would have meant for a woman who was poet and playwright a nervous stress and dilemma which might well have killed
her. Had she survived, whatever she had written would have been
twisted and deformed, issuing from a strained and morbid imagination. And undoubtedly, I thought, looking at the shelf where there
are no plays by women, her work would have gone unsigned. That
refuge she would have sought certainly. It was the relic of the sense
of chastity that dictated anonymity to women even so late as the
nineteenth century. Currer Bell, George Eliot, George Sand, all the
victims of inner strife as their writings prove, sought ineffectively
to veil themselves by using the name of a man. Thus they did hom-
age to the convention, which if not implanted by the other sex was
liberally encouraged by them (the chief glory of a woman is not to
be talked of, said Pericles, himself a much-talked-of man), that pub-
licity in women is detestable.

*   *   *

That woman, then, who was born with a gift of poetry in the six-   10
teenth century, was an unhappy woman, a woman at strife against
herself. All the conditions of her life, all her own instincts, were hostile
to the state of mind which is needed to set free whatever is in the brain.
But what is the state of mind that is most propitious to the act of creation, I asked? Can one come by any notion of the state that furthers

and makes possible that strange activity? Here I opened the volume containing the Tragedies of Shakespeare. What was Shakespeare's state of mind, for instance, when he wrote *Lear* and *Antony and Cleopatra?* It was certainly the state of mind most favourable to poetry that has ever existed. But Shakespeare himself said nothing about it. We only know casually and by chance that he "never blotted a line." Nothing indeed was ever said by the artist himself about his state of mind until the eighteenth century perhaps. Rousseau perhaps began it. At any rate, by the nineteenth century self-consciousness had developed so far that it was the habit for men of letters to describe their minds in confessions and autobiographies. Their lives also were written, and their letters were printed after their deaths. Thus, though we do not know what Shakespeare went through when he wrote *Lear,* we do know what Carlyle went through when he wrote the *French Revolution;* what Flaubert went through when he wrote *Madame Bovary;* what Keats was going through when he tried to write poetry against the coming of death and the indifference of the world.

And one gathers from this enormous modern literature of confession and self-analysis that to write a work of genius is almost always a feat of prodigious difficulty. Everything is against the likelihood that it will come from the writer's mind whole and entire. Generally material circumstances are against it. Dogs will bark; people will interrupt; money must be made; health will break down. Further, accentuating all these difficulties and making them harder to bear is the world's notorious indifference. It does not ask people to write poems and novels and histories; it does not need them. It does not care whether Flaubert finds the right word or whether Carlyle scrupulously verifies this or that fact. Naturally, it will not pay for what it does not want. And so the writer, Keats, Flaubert, Carlyle, suffers, especially in the creative years of youth, every form of distraction and discouragement. A curse, a cry of agony, rises from those books of analysis and confession. "Mighty poets in their misery dead"— that is the burden of their song. If anything comes through in spite of all this, it is a miracle, and probably no book is born entire and uncrippled as it was conceived. 11

But for women, I thought, looking at the empty shelves, these difficulties were infinitely more formidable. In the first place, to have a room of her own, let alone a quiet room or a sound-proof room, was out of the question, unless her parents were exceptionally rich or very noble, even up to the beginning of the nineteenth century. Since her pin money, which depended on the good will of her father, was only enough to keep her clothed, she was debarred from such alleviations as came even to Keats or Tennyson or Carlyle, all poor men, from a walking tour, a little journey to France, from the 12 separate lodging which, even if it were miserable enough, sheltered them from the claims and tyrannies of their families. Such material difficulties were formidable; but much worse were the immaterial. The indifference of the world which Keats and Flaubert and other men of genius have found so hard to bear was in her case not indifference but hostility. The world did not say to her as it said to them, Write if you choose; it makes no difference to me. The world said with a guffaw, Write? What's the good of your writing?

* * *

I told you in the course of this chapter that Shakespeare had a sister; but do not look for her in Sir Sidney Lee's life of the poet. She died young—alas, she never wrote a word. She lies buried under where the omnibuses now stop, opposite the Elephant and Castle. Now my belief is that this poet who never wrote a word and was buried at the cross-roads still lives. She lives in you and in me, and in many other women who are not here tonight, for they are washing up the dishes and putting the children to bed. But she lives; for great poets do not die; they are continuing presences; they need only the opportunity to walk among us in the flesh. This opportunity, as I think, it is now coming within your power to give her. For my belief is that if we live another century or so—I am talking of the common life which is the real life and not of the little separate lives which we live as individuals—and have five hundred a year each of us and rooms of our own; if we have the habit of freedom and the courage to write exactly what we think; if we escape a little from the common sitting-room and see human beings not always in their relation to each other but in relation to reality; and the sky, too, and the trees or whatever it may be in themselves; if we look past Milton's bogey; for no human being should shut out the view; if we face the fact, for it is a fact, that there is no arm to cling to, but that we go alone and that our relation is to the world of reality and not only to the world of men and women, then the opportunity will come and the dead poet who was Shakespeare's sister will put on the body which she has so often laid down. Drawing her life from the lives of the unknown who were her forerunners, as her brother did before her, she will be born. As for her coming without that preparation, without that effort on our part, without that determination that when she is born again she shall find it possible to live and write her poetry, that we cannot expect, for that would be impossible. But I maintain that she would come if we worked for her, and that so to work, even in poverty and obscurity, is worth while.

POLITICS AND THE
ENGLISH LANGUAGE

George Orwell

"Politics and the English Language" was first published in 1946 in the London monthly Horizon. *It was reprinted in 1950 in* Shooting an Elephant and Other Essays. *In this essay, Orwell focuses on what he sees as the "decadence of our language." He argues for the upgrading of English and the elimination of the well-worn words and phrases that enable some in our society to defend the indefensible. (For biographical information on George Orwell, see page 85.)*

Most people who bother with the matter at all would admit that the English language is in a bad way, but it is generally assumed that we cannot by conscious action do anything about it. Our civilization is decadent and our language—so the argument runs—must inevitably share in the general collapse. It follows that any struggle against the abuse of language is a sentimental archaism, like preferring candles to electric light or hansom cabs to aeroplanes. Underneath this lies the half-conscious belief that language is a natural growth and not an instrument which we shape for our own purpose.

Now, it is clear that the decline of a language must ultimately have political and economic causes: it is not due simply to the bad influence of this or that individual writer. But an effect can become a cause, reinforcing the original cause and producing the same effect in an intensified form, and so on indefinitely. A man may take to drink because he feels himself to be a failure, and then fail all the more completely because he drinks. It is rather the same thing that is happening to the English language. It becomes ugly and inaccurate because our thoughts are foolish, but the slovenliness of our language makes it easier for us to have foolish thoughts. The point is that the process is reversible. Modern English, especially written English, is full of bad habits which spread by imitation and which can be avoided if one is willing to take the necessary trouble. If one gets rid of these habits one can think more clearly, and to think clearly is a necessary first step towards political regeneration: so that the fight against bad English is not frivolous and is not the exclusive concern of professional writers. I will come back to this presently, and I hope that by that time the meaning of what I have said here will have become clearer. Meanwhile, here are five specimens of the English language as it is now habitually written.

These five passages have not been picked out because they are especially bad—I could have quoted far worse if I had chosen—but because they illustrate various of the mental vices from which we now suffer. They are a little below the average, but are fairly representative samples. I number them so that I can refer back to them when necessary:

"(1) I am not, indeed, sure whether it is not true to say that the Milton who once seemed not unlike a seventeenth-century Shelley had not become, out of an experience ever more bitter in each year, more alien [sic] to the founder of that Jesuit sect which nothing could induce him to tolerate."
        Professor Harold Laski (Essay in *Freedom of Expression*).

"(2) Above all, we cannot play ducks and drakes with a native battery of idioms which prescribes such egregious collocations of vocables as the Basic *put up with* for *tolerate* or *put at a loss* for *bewilder.*"
        Professor Lancelot Hogben *(Interglossa).*

"(3) On the one side we have the free personality: by definition it is not neurotic, for it has neither conflict nor dream. Its desires, such as they are, are transparent, for they are just what institutional approval keeps in the forefront of consciousness; another institutional pattern would alter their number and intensity; there is little in them that is natural, irreducible, or culturally dangerous. But *on the other side,* the social bond itself is nothing but the mutual reflection of these self-secure integrities. Recall the definition of love. Is not this the very picture of a small academic? Where is there a place in this hall of mirrors for either personality or fraternity?
        Essay on psychology in *Politics* (New York)

"(4) All the 'best people' from the gentlemen's clubs, and all the frantic fascist captains, united in common hatred of Socialism and bestial horror of the rising tide of the mass revolutionary movement, have turned to acts of provocation, to foul incendiarism, to medieval legends of poisoned wells, to legalize their own destruction of proletarian organizations, and rouse the agitated petty-bourgeoisie to chauvinistic fervour on behalf of the fight against the revolutionary way out of the crisis."
        Communist pamphlet.

"(5) If a new spirit *is* to be infused into this old country, there is one thorny and contentious reform which must be tackled, and that is the humanization and galvanization of the B.B.C. Timidity here will bespeak cancer and atrophy of the soul. The heart of Britain may be sound and of strong beat, for instance, but the British lion's roar at present is like that of Bottom in Shakespeare's *Midsummer Night's Dream*—as gentle as any sucking dove. A virile new Britain cannot continue indefinitely to be traduced in the eyes or rather ears, of the world by effete languors of Langham Place, brazenly masquerading as 'standard English.' When the Voice of Britain is heard at nine o'clock, better far and infinitely less ludicrous to hear aitches honestly dropped than the present priggish, inflated, inhibited, school-ma'amish arch braying of blameless bashful mewing maidens!"

Letter in *Tribune*

Each of these passages has faults of its own, but, quite apart from   4
avoidable ugliness, two qualities are common to all of them. The first is staleness of imagery: the other is lack of precision. The writer either has a meaning and cannot express it, or he inadvertently says something else, or he is almost indifferent as to whether his words mean anything or not. This mixture of vagueness and sheer incompetence is the most marked characteristic of modern English prose, and especially of any kind of political writing. As soon as certain topics are raised, the concrete melts into the abstract and no one seems to think of turns of speech that are not hackneyed: prose consists less and less of *words* chosen for the sake of their meaning, and more and more of *phrases* tacked together like the sections of a prefabricated hen-house. I list below, with notes and examples, various of the tricks by means of which the work of prose-construction is habitually dodged:

DYING METAPHORS

A newly invented metaphor assists thought by evoking a visual   5
image, while on the other hand a metaphor which is technically "dead" (e.g., *iron resolution*) has in effect reverted to being an ordinary word and can generally be used without loss of vividness. But in between these two classes there is a huge dump of worn-out metaphors which have lost all evocative power and are merely used because they save people the trouble of inventing phrases for themselves. Examples are: *Ring the changes on, take up the cudgels for, toe the line, ride roughshod over, stand shoulder to shoulder with, play into the hands of, no axe to grind, grist to the mill, fishing in troubled waters, on the order of the day, Achilles' heel, swan song,*

hotbed. Many of these are used without knowledge of their meaning (what is a "rift," for instance?), and incompatible metaphors are frequently mixed, a sure sign that the writer is not interested in what he is saying. Some metaphors now current have been twisted out of their original meaning without those who use them even being aware of the fact. For example, *toe the line* is sometimes written *tow the line.* Another example is *the hammer and the anvil,* now always used with the implication that the anvil gets the worst of it. In real life it is always the anvil that breaks the hammer, never the other way about: a writer who stopped to think what he was saying would be aware of this, and would avoid perverting the original phrase.

OPERATORS OR VERBAL FALSE LIMBS

These save the trouble of picking out appropriate verbs and nouns, and at the same time pad each sentence with extra syllables which give it an appearance of symmetry. Characteristic phrases are: *render inoperative, militate against, make contact with, be subjected to, give rise to, give grounds for, have the effect of, play a leading part (role) in, make itself felt, take effect, exhibit a tendency to, serve the purpose of,* etc., etc. The keynote is the elimination of simple verbs. Instead of being a single word, such as *break, stop, spoil, mend, kill,* a verb becomes a *phrase,* made up of a noun or adjective tacked on to some general-purpose verb such as *prove, serve, form, play, render.* In addition, the passive voice is wherever possible used in preference to the active, and noun constructions are used instead of gerunds (*by examination of* instead of *by examining*). The range of verbs is further cut down by means of the *-ize* and *de-* formation, and the banal statements are given an appearance of profundity by means of the *not un-* formation. Simple conjunctions and prepositions are replaced by such phrases as *with respect to, having regard to, the fact that, by dint of, in view of, in the interests of, on the hypothesis that;* and the ends of sentences are saved from anticlimax by such resounding commonplaces as *greatly to be desired, cannot be left out of account, a development to be expected in the near future, deserving of serious consideration, brought to a satisfactory conclusion,* and so on and so forth.

PRETENTIOUS DICTION

Words like *phenomenon, element, individual* (as noun)*, objective, categorical, effective, virtual, basic, primary, promote, constitute, exhibit, exploit, utilize, eliminate, liquidate,* are used to dress up simple statements and give an air of scientific impartiality to biased judgments. Adjectives like *epoch-making, epic, historic, unforgettable, triumphant, age-old, inevitable, inexorable, veritable,* are used to dignify the sordid processes of international politics, while writing that aims at glorifying war usually takes on an archaic colour, its characteristic words being: *realm, throne, chariot, mailed fist, trident, sword, shield, buckler, banner, jackboot, clarion.* Foreign words and expressions such as *cul de sac, ancien régime, deus ex machina, mutatis mutandis, status quo, gleichschaltung, weltanschauung,* are used to give an air of culture and elegance. Except for the useful abbreviations *i.e., e.g.,* and *etc.,* there is no real need for any of the hundreds of foreign phrases now current in English. Bad writers, and especially scientific, political and sociological writers, are nearly always haunted by the notion that Latin or Greek words are grander than Saxon ones, and unnecessary words like *expedite, ameliorate, predict, extraneous, deracinated, clandestine, subaqueous* and hundreds of others constantly gain ground from their Anglo-Saxon opposite numbers.[1] The jargon peculiar to Marxist writing (*hyena, hangman, cannibal, petty bourgeois, these gentry, lacquey, flunkey, mad dog, White Guard,* etc.) consists largely of words and phrases translated from Russian, German or French; but the normal way of coining a new word is to use a Latin or Greek root with the appropriate affix and, where necessary, the *-ize* formation. It is often easier to make up words of this kind (*deregionalize, impermissible, extramarital, nonfragmentatory* and so forth) than to think up the English words that will cover one's meaning. The result, in general, is an increase in slovenliness and vagueness.

MEANINGLESS WORDS

In certain kinds of writing, particularly in art criticism and literary criticism, it is normal to come across long passages which are almost completely lacking in meaning.[2] Words like *romantic, plastic,* 8

---

[1] An interesting illustration of this is the way in which the English flower names which were in use till very recently as being ousted by Greek ones, *snapdragon* becoming *antirrhinum, forget-me-not* becoming *myosotis,* etc. It is hard to see any practical reason for this change of fashion: it is probably due to an instinctive turning-away from the more homely word and a vague feeling that the Greek word is scientific.

[2] Example: "Comfort's catholicity of perception and image, strangely Whitmanesque in range, almost the exact opposite of aesthetic compulsion, continues to evoke that trembling atmospheric accumulative hinting at a cruel, and inexorably serene timelessness. . . . Wrey Gardiner scores by aiming at simple bull's-eyes with precision. Only they are not so simple, and through this contented sadness runs more than the surface bitter-sweet of resignation." *(Poetry Quarterly.)*

values, human, dead, sentimental, natural, vitality, as used in art criticism, are strictly meaningless in the sense that they not only do not point to any discoverable object, but are hardly ever expected to do so by the reader. When one critic writes, "The outstanding feature of Mr. X's work is its living quality," while another writes, "The immediately striking thing about Mr. X's work is its peculiar deadness," the reader accepts this as a simple difference of opinion. If words like *black* and *white* were involved, instead of the jargon words *dead* and *living,* he would see at once that language was being used in an improper way. Many political words are similarly abused. The word *Fascism* has now no meaning except in so far as it signifies "something not desirable." The words *democracy, socialism, freedom, patriotic, realistic, justice,* have each of them several different meanings which cannot be reconciled with one another. In the case of a word like *democracy,* not only is there no agreed definition, but the attempt to make one is resisted from all sides. It is almost universally felt that when we call a country democratic we are praising it: consequently the defenders of every kind of régime claim that it is a democracy, and fear that they might have to stop using the word if it were tied down to any one meaning. Words of this kind are often used in a consciously dishonest way. That is, the person who uses them has his own private definition, but allows his hearer to think he means something quite different. Statements like *Marshall Pétain* was a true patriot, The Soviet Press is the freest in the world, The Catholic Church is opposed to persecution,* are almost always made with intent to deceive. Other words used in variable meanings, in most cases more or less dishonestly, are: *class, totalitarian, science, progressive, reactionary, bourgeois, equality.*

Now that I have made this catalogue of swindles and perversions, 9 let me give another example of the kind of writing that they lead to. This time it must of its nature be an imaginary one. I am going to translate a passage of good English into modern English of the worst sort. Here is a well-known verse from *Ecclesiastes:*

"I returned and saw under the sun, that the race is not to the swift, nor the battle to the strong, neither yet bread to the wise, nor yet riches to men of understanding, nor yet favour to men of skill; but time and chance happeneth to them all."

Here it is in modern English:

*Eds. Note—World War I French military hero who became chief of state of the Vichy government in unoccupied France during World War II. After the war he was tried and found guilty of collaboration and treason.

"Objective consideration of contemporary phenomena compels the conclusion that success or failure in competitive activities exhibits no tendency to be commensurate with innate capacity, but that a considerable element of the unpredictable must invariably be taken into account."

This is a parody, but not a very gross one. Exhibit (3), above, for instance, contains several patches of the same kind of English. It will be seen that I have not made a full translation. The beginning and ending of the sentence follow the original meaning fairly closely, but in the middle the concrete illustrations—race, battle, bread— dissolve into the vague phrase "success or failure in competitive activities." This had to be so, because no modern writer of the kind I am discussing—no one capable of using phrases like "objective consideration of contemporary phenomena"—would ever tabulate his thoughts in that precise and detailed way. The whole tendency of modern prose is away from concreteness. Now analyse these two sentences a little more closely. The first contains forty-nine words but only sixty syllables, and all its words are those of everyday life. The second contains thirty-eight words of ninety syllables: eighteen of its words or from Latin roots, and one from Greek. The first sentence contains six vivid images, and only one phrase ("time and chance") that could be called vague. The second contains not a single fresh, arresting phrase, and in spite of its ninety syllables it gives only a shortened version of the meaning contained in the first. Yet without a doubt it is the second kind of sentence that is gaining ground in modern English. I do not want to exaggerate. This kind of writing is not yet universal, and outcrops of simplicity will occur here and there in the worst-written page. Still, if you or I were told to write a few lines on the uncertainty of human fortunes, we should probably come much nearer to my imaginary sentence than to the one from *Ecclesiastes*. 10

As I have tried to show, modern writing at its worst does not consist in picking out words for the sake of their meaning and inventing images in order to make the meaning clearer. It consists in gumming together long strips of words which have already been set in order by someone else, and making the results presentable by sheer humbug. The attraction of this way of writing is that it is easy. It is easier—even quicker, once you have the habit—to say *In my opinion it is a not unjustifiable assumption that* than to say *I think*. If you use ready-made phrases, you not only don't have to hunt about for words; you also don't have to bother with the rhythms of your sentences, since these phrases are generally so arranged as to be more or less euphonious. When you are composing in a hurry—when you 11 are dictating to a stenographer, for instance, or making a public speech—it is natural to fall into a pretentious, Latinized style. Tags like *a consideration which we should do well to bear in mind* or *a conclusion to which all of us would readily assent* will save many a sentence from coming down with a bump. By using stale metaphors, similes and idioms, you save much mental effort, at the cost of leaving your meaning vague, not only for your reader but for yourself. This is the significance of mixed metaphors. The sole aim of a metaphor is to call up a visual image. When these images clash—as in *The Fascist octopus has sung its swan song, the jackboot is thrown into the melting pot*—it can be taken as certain that the writer is not seeing a mental image of the objects he is naming; in other words he is not really thinking. Look again at the examples I gave at the beginning of this essay. Professor Laski (1) uses five negatives in fifty-three words. One of these is superfluous, making nonsense of the whole passage, and in addition there is the slip *alien* for akin, making further nonsense, and several avoidable pieces of clumsiness which increase the general vagueness. Professor Hogben (2) plays ducks and drakes with a battery which is able to write prescriptions, and, while disapproving of the everyday phrase *put up with,* is unwilling to look *egregious* up in the dictionary and see what it means. (3), if one takes an uncharitable attitude towards it, is simply meaningless: probably one could work out its intended meaning by reading the whole of the article in which it occurs. In (4), the writer knows more or less what he wants to say, but an accumulation of stale phrases chokes him like tea leaves blocking the sink. In (5), words and meaning have almost parted company. People who write in this manner usually have a general emotional meaning—they dislike one thing and want to express solidarity with another—but they are not interested in the detail of what they are saying. A scrupulous writer, in every sentence that he writes, will ask himself at least four questions, thus: What am I trying to say? What words will express it? What image or idiom will make it clearer? Is this image fresh enough to have an effect? And he will probably ask himself two more: Could I put it more shortly? Have I said anything that is avoidably ugly? But you are not obliged to go to all this trouble. You can shirk it by simply throwing your mind open and letting the ready-made phrases come crowding in. They will construct your sentences for you—even think your thoughts for you, to a certain extent—and at need they will perform the important service of partially concealing your meaning even from yourself. It is at this point that the special connection between politics and the debasement of language becomes clear.

In our time it is broadly true that political writing is bad writing. 12

Where it is not true, it will generally be found that the writer is some kind of rebel, expressing his private opinions and not a "party line." Orthodoxy, or whatever colour, seems to demand a lifeless, imitative style. The political dialects to be found in pamphlets, leading articles, manifestos. White Papers and the speeches of undersecretaries do, of course, vary from party to party, but they are all alike in that one almost never finds in them a fresh, vivid, homemade turn of speech. When one watches some tired hack on the platform mechanically repeating the familiar phrases—*bestial atrocities, iron heel, bloodstained tyranny, free peoples of the world, stand shoulder to shoulder*—one often has a curious feeling that one is not watching a live human being but some kind of dummy: a feeling which suddenly becomes stronger at moments when the light catches the speaker's spectacles and turns them into blank discs which seem to have no eyes behind them. And this is not altogether fanciful. A speaker who uses that kind of phraseology has gone some distance towards turning himself into a machine. The appropriate noises are coming out of his larynx, but his brain is not involved as it would be if he were choosing his words for himself. If the speech he is making is one that he is accustomed to make over and over again, he may be almost unconscious of what he is saying, as one is when one utters the responses in church. And this reduced state of consciousness, if not indispensable, is at any rate favourable to political conformity.

In our time, political speech and writing are largely the defence of the indefensible. Things like the continuance of British rule in India, the Russian purges and deportations, the dropping of the atom bombs on Japan, can indeed be defended, but only by arguments which are too brutal for most people to face, and which do not square with the professed aims of political parties. Thus political language has to consist largely of euphemism, question-begging and sheer cloudy vagueness. Defenseless villages are bombarded from the air, the inhabitants driven out into the countryside, the cattle machine-gunned, the huts set on fire with incendiary bullets: this is called *pacification*. Millions of peasants are robbed of their farms and sent trudging along the roads with no more than they can carry: this is called *transfer of population* or *rectification of frontiers*. People are imprisoned for years without trial, or shot in the back of the neck or sent to die of scurvy in Artic lumber camps: this is called *elimination of unreliable elements*. Such phraseology is needed if one wants to name things without calling up mental pictures of them. Consider for instance some comfortable English professor defending Russian totalitarianism. He cannot say outright, "I believe in killing off your opponents when you can get good results by doing so." Probably, therefore, he will say something like this:

"While freely conceding that the Soviet régime exhibits certain   14
features which the humanitarian may be inclined to deplore, we
must, I think, agree that a certain curtailment of the right to political opposition is an unavoidable concomitant of transitional periods, and that the rigours which the Russian people have been
called upon to undergo have been amply justified in the sphere of
concrete achievement."

The inflated style is itself a kind of euphemism. A mass of Latin   15
words falls upon the facts like soft snow, blurring the outlines and
covering up all the details.The great enemy of clear language is in-
sincerity. When there is a gap between one's real and one's declared
aims, one turns as it were instinctively to long words and exhausted
idioms, like a cuttlefish squirting out ink. In our age there is no such
thing as "keeping out of politics." All issues are political issues, and
politics itself is a mass of lies, evasions, folly, hatred and schizo-
phrenia. When the general atmosphere is bad, language must suffer.
I should expect to find—this is a guess which I have not sufficient
knowledge to verify—that the German, Russian and Italian languages have all deteriorated in the last ten or fifteen years, as a
result of dictatorship.

But if thought corrupts language, language can also corrupt   16
thought. A bad usage can spread by tradition and imitation, even
among people who should and do know better. The debased language that I have been discussing is in some ways very convenient.
Phrases like *a not unjustifiable assumption, leaves much to be desired, would serve no good purpose, a consideration which we should
do well to bear in mind,* are a continuous temptation, a packet of
aspirins always at one's elbow. Look back through this essay, and
for certain you will find that I have again and again committed the
very faults I am protesting against. By this morning's post I have
received a pamphlet dealing with conditions in Germany. The author tells me that he "felt impelled" to write it. I open it at random,
and here is almost the first sentence that I see: "(The Allies) have
an opportunity not only of achieving a radical transformation of
Germany's social and political structure in such a way as to avoid
a nationalistic reaction in Germany itself, but at the same time of
laying the foundations of a co-operative and unified Europe." You
see, he "feels impelled" to write—feels, presumably, that he has
something new to say—and yet his words, like cavalry horses answering the bugle, group themselves automatically into the familiar
dreary pattern. This invasion of one's mind by ready-made phrases
(lay the foundations, achieve a radical transformation) can only be
prevented if one is constantly on guard against them, and every
such phrase anaesthetizes a portion of one's brain.

I said earlier that the decadence of our language is probably cura-   17
ble. Those who deny this would argue, if they produced an argument
at all, that language merely reflects existing social conditions, and
that we cannot influence its development by any direct tinkering
with words and constructions. So far as the general tone or spirit of
a language goes, this may be true, but it is not true in detail. Silly
words and expressions have often disappeared, not through any evolutionary process but owing to the conscious action of a minority.
Two recent examples were *explore every avenue* and *leave no stone
unturned,* which were killed by the jeers of a few journalists. There
is a long list of flyblown metaphors which could similarly be got rid
of if enough people would interest themselves in the job; and it
should also be possible to laugh the *not un-* formation out of existence,[3] to reduce the amount of Latin and Greek in the average sentence, to drive out foreign phrases and strayed scientific words, and,
in general, to make pretentiousness unfashionable. But all these are
minor points. The defence of the English language implies more
than this, and perhaps it is best to start by saying what it does *not*
imply.

To begin with it has nothing to do with archaism, with the salvag-   18
ing of obsolete words and turns of speech, or with the setting up of
a "standard English" which must never be departed from. On the
contrary, it is especially concerned with the scrapping of every word
or idiom which has outworn its usefulness. It has nothing to do with
correct grammar and syntax, which are of no importance so long as
one makes one's meaning clear, or with the avoidance of American-
isms, or with having what is called a "good prose style." On the
other hand it is not concerned with fake simplicity and the attempt
to make written English colloquial. Nor does it even imply in every
case preferring the Saxon word to the Latin one, though it does imply using the fewest and shortest words that will cover one's meaning. What is above all needed is to let the meaning choose the word,
and not the other way about. In prose, the worst thing one can do
with words is to surrender to them. When you think of a concrete
object, you think wordlessly, and then, if you want to describe the
thing you have been visualizing you probably hunt about till you
find the exact words that seem to fit. When you think of something
abstract you are more inclined to use words from the start, and unless you make a conscious effort to prevent it, the existing dialect

---

[3]One can cure oneself of the *not un-* formation by memorizing this sentence: *A not
unblack dog was chasing a not unsmall rabbit across a not ungreen field.*

will come rushing in and do the job for you, at the expense of blurring or even changing your meaning. Probably it is better to put off using words as long as possible and get one's meaning as clear as one can through pictures or sensations. Afterwards one can choose—not simply *accept*—the phrases that will best cover the meaning, and then switch round and decide what impression one's words are likely to make on another person. This last effort of the mind cuts out all stale or mixed images, all prefabricated phrases, needless repetitions, and humbug and vagueness generally. But one can often be in doubt about the effect of a word or a phrase, and one needs rules that one can rely on when instinct fails. I think the following rules will cover most cases:

(i)   Never use a metaphor, simile or other figure of speech which you are used to seeing in print.
(ii) Never use a long word where a short one will do.
(iii) If it is possible to cut a word out, always cut it out.
(iv) Never use the passive where you can use the active.
(v)   Never use a foreign phrase, a scientific word or a jargon word if you can think of an everyday English equivalent.
(vi) Break any of these rules sooner than say anything outright barbarous.

These rules sound elementary, and so they are, but they demand a deep change of attitude in anyone who has grown used to writing in the style now fashionable. One could keep all of them and still write bad English, but one could not write the kind of stuff that I quoted in those five specimens at the beginning of this article.

I have not here been considering the literary use of language, but merely language as an instrument for expressing and not for concealing or preventing thought. Stuart Chase and others have come near to claiming that all abstract words are meaningless, and have used this as a pretext for advocating a kind of political quietism. Since you don't know what Fascism is, how can you struggle against Fascism? One need not swallow such absurdities as this, but one ought to recognize that the present political chaos is connected with the decay of language, and that one can probably bring about some improvement by starting at the verbal end. If you simplify your English, you are freed from the worst follies of orthodoxy. You cannot speak any of the necessary dialects, and when you make a stupid remark its stupidity will be obvious, even to yourself. Political language—and with variations this is true of all political parties, from Conservatives to Anarchists—is designed to make lies sound truthful and murder respectable, and to give an appearance of solidity to

19

pure wind. One cannot change this all in a moment, but one can at least change one's own habits, and from time to time one can even, if one jeers loudly enough, send some worn-out and useless phrase—some *jackboot, Achilles' heel, hotbed, melting pot, acid test, veritable inferno* or other lump of verbal refuse—in the dustbin where it belongs.

Glossary

Abstract/Concrete two kinds of language. Abstract words are names for concepts or qualities that cannot be directly seen or touched: *love, justice, emotion, concern, evil, anguish.* Concrete words vividly refer to objects or qualities that *can* be perceived by the senses: *green, fountain pen, ink-blot, leaky, overflowing, stain.* Concrete phrases that give the reader a complete and vivid visual picture are **images.** (See also **Images.**)

Abstract words are necessary at times to express ideas, but when used without concrete supporting detail they are very vague. The abstract phrase "The speaker was overcome with emotion" could mean almost anything, but the addition of concrete language clarifies the meaning: "He clenched his fist and shook it at the crowd" (anger); "He began to teeter and grabbed hold of the edge of the podium; at the same time his mouth went dry and no sound came out" (fear); "He wiped tears from his eyes with a blue cloth, shook his head, and stepped away from the microphone" (sadness).

Allusions brief references to people, objects, events, statements, or situations that readers are expected to recognize. Making an allusion is a way of evoking a vivid impression in very few words. "The gardener opened the gate and suddenly we found ourselves in Eden" suggests in one word (Eden) the stunning beauty of the garden that the writer visited. Allusions typically refer to literature ("The mayor is a Scrooge who will not even listen to our suggestions for a municipal sculpture garden.") or to historical or biblical figures or events.

Analogy a form of comparison that considers similarities between two essentially different items. By making an analogy, writers are able to explain one element by comparing it to another that is more familiar ("Money is like muck, not good unless it be spread."). Analogies can clarify abstract or technical information

585

by presenting it to the reader in simpler, more concrete terms. *Analogous* means "very similar, parallel": "The effect of pollution on the environment is analogous to that of cancer on the body."

Antithesis   the name for a debatable viewpoint opposite from the one that is expressed in a **thesis**. The thesis of an argumentative essay must be debatable—that is, it should have one or more antitheses. One way a writer can test the strength of the thesis is to try to formulate an antithesis. If no antithesis exists, the writer's thesis is not debatable.

Antonym   a word opposite in meaning to another word. *Beautiful* is the antonym of *ugly*. A word may have several antonyms; other antonyms for *ugly* might be *pretty, handsome,* or *attractive*. **Synonym** is the antonym of *antonym*.

Argumentation   the form of writing that takes a stand on an issue and attempts to convince readers to agree by presenting a logical sequence of points supported by ample evidence. Argumentation may be reinforced by appeals to the readers' emotions. See Chapter 10.

Audience   the people "listening" to a writer's words. Each piece of writing has not only something to say but someone to say it to. Writers who are sensitive to their audience will carefully choose a tone, examples, and allusions that their readers will understand and react to. Displaying such sensitivity is like making eye contact in a conversation; it engages the reader.

Even if a writer's thoughts are articulate and strong, they may seem weak if the writer has not written with the particular audience in mind. A work of writing for children would need to use relatively brief sentences and accessible language. A good article attempting to persuade high school teenagers not to use drugs would use examples and allusions pertinent to a teenager's life. Different examples would need to be chosen if the writer were addressing middle-aged members of Alcoholics Anonymous.

Basis of Comparison   the term for the fundamental similarity between two or more things that allows a writer to compare them. In a comparison of how two different towns react to foreign immigrants, the basis of comparison might be that both towns have a rapidly expanding immigrant population. (If one of the towns did not have any immigrants, a comparison between the two dealing with immigrants would be impossible.) A basis for comparison may be thought of as justification: Could you defend the comparison in your paper if someone challenged the point of it? If so, you have a strong basis of comparison.

The lack of an obvious basis of comparison should not rule out creative comparisons, however. You may see a strong connection between two situations that have not previously been discussed together. Comparing two objects that appear vastly different can sometimes lead to an interesting and unique paper, as long as the two items have essential similarities. For example, you could compare a building with a tree because they share the same essential architectural pattern, or compare quantum mechanics with Buddhist philosophy because of the similar intuitive thought patterns they both require for understanding, as Fritjof Capra has done in *The Tao of Physics*. A paper's very lack of an obvious basis of comparison can provoke the reader's curiosity and disbelief at the outset, allowing the writer to present a strong defense in the pages that follow. Such an unexpected comparison is particularly effective for papers discussing abstract philosophical ideas or ideas that must be intuitively understood. The more diverse the elements of the comparison, however, the stronger the basis of comparison must be.

Brainstorming   See **Invention**

Causal Chain   the term for a sequence of events that are linked through a domino effect—one event causes another event that causes another event. Describing a causal chain can provide an essay with a simple, logical, and dynamic structure.

Cause and Effect   the pattern of development that discusses either the reasons for an occurrence or the observed or predicted consequences. Often both causes and effects are presented in the same essay. See Chapter 6.

Causes   the reasons for an event, situation, or phenomenon. An *immediate cause* is an obvious one; a *remote cause* is a more obscure, less easily perceived one. The *main cause* is the one that is the most important cause, whether immediate or remote. Other, less important causes that nevertheless encourage the effect in some way (for instance, by speeding it up or providing favorable circumstances for it) are called *contributory causes.*

Chronological Order   the sequence in which events occur. Chronological order is a simple and common way to organize a narrative; it is also the structure that process essays follow.

Classification and Division   related methods of organizing information. *Classification* involves searching for common characteristics among scattered items and grouping them accordingly, thereby giving order to previously random information. In contrast, *division* breaks up an entity into smaller groups or elements, providing for a more detailed and managable discussion. Classification generalizes; division specifies. See Chapter 8.

Cliché See **Diction**

Coherence the tight relationship between all the parts of a good piece of writing. Such a relationship ensures that the writing will make clear sense to readers. For a piece of writing to be coherent, it must be logical and orderly, with effective **transitions** making the movement between sentences and paragraphs clear.

Colloquialisms expressions that are generally appropriate for conversation and informal writing but not for formal writing in college, business, or professional settings. Words often have two types of meaning, a dictionary meaning (which is considered appropriate for formal writing in the way that a tuxedo would be appropriate for a diplomatic banquet) and a different, informal meaning that is used colloquially. For example, the formal definition of the word *aggravate* is "to make worse" ("Continual medical expenses aggravated their efforts to save money."). Colloquially, however, *aggravate* means "to irritate" (this usage should be avoided in formal writing).

Some colloquial expressions are acceptable in conversation but not in writing. For instance, you should write *center on*, not *center around; enthusiastic about,* not *enthused about;* and *very sorry,* not *good and sorry.* Writers are also speakers, and so they must be careful not to be too casual in their writing. (See also **Diction.**)

Comparison and Contrast two patterns of development, often found together. In a general sense, *comparison* shows how two or more things are alike; *contrast* shows how they are different. In a *subject-by-subject comparison,* the comparison is organized by subject rather than by points. Although the subjects are compared in the thesis, they are discussed separately in similarly structured sections in the body of the essay. This kind of pattern works best for short, simple comparisons or for papers concerned with only a few points of comparison, where the reader can easily perceive the similarities between subjects. A *point-by-point comparison* is a comparison organized by points discussed rather than by subject. Typically, each paragraph in the essay raises a new issue and compares each subject in relation to the issue. This kind of pattern works well with complex, detailed comparisons. See Chapter 7.

Conclusion the group of sentences or, in the case of a long paper, paragraphs that brings an essay to a close. To *conclude* means not only "to end" but also "to resolve." Although the purpose of the conclusion is not to resolve all the issues and questions raised in the essay, the conclusion is the place to show that they *have* been resolved, that all the points made have been supported by adequate evidence, and that the thesis of the paper is indeed reasonable. Conclusions should show that the writer is not just glad to be finished writing but also committed to what has been expressed. The conclusion is the writer's last chance to leave an impression with the readers, and the impression it leaves should be one of confidence.

Two commonly used weak endings should be avoided: 1) introducing new points or afterthoughts, suggesting that the writer has forgotten to discuss something in the body of the paper and is not ready to end the essay; and 2) apologizing or qualifying the thesis, leaving the impression that the essay is in charge of the writer rather than that the writer is in charge of the essay. Conclusions should give the whole essay a sense of completeness and unity.

Several possible ways of concluding an essay include the following:

1. Restating the thesis and/or giving a summary of the points made in the essay, perhaps also suggesting the implications or significance of the topic
2. Recommending a course of action or a solution to a problem that has been discussed in the essay
3. Making a prediction
4. Ending with an embellishment, such as a quotation, an anecdote, or a question, that indirectly supports and strengthens the thesis (and does not back away from it).

Several of these methods resemble methods that can be used in introducing essays. Sometimes during the **writing process** an original ending will be relocated to the beginning or a beginning will become an end. Although **introductions** and conclusions often convey similar information, an introduction generally focuses more on provoking the reader's interest and a conclusion on leaving the reader convinced that the thesis has been supported.

Concrete   See **Abstract/Concrete**

Connotation/Denotation   two terms that refer to the meanings of words. A word's denotation is its dictionary definition. Connotations are the word's associations, the meanings or feelings that are suggested beyond the word's literal meaning. The word *home* denotes one's place of residence, but it also connotes warmth and a sense of belonging.

Connotations are important in subjective writing; writers who are aware of connotations can carefully choose words that evoke the precise mood they want to convey. Connotations reveal a writer's attitude toward something and indicate how an audience should respond—if they should pity, sympathize with, or fear a person, for example.

English is such a rich language that many words have similar denotations; however, all words have at least slightly different connotations. The adjectives *thoughtful*, *reflective*, and *pensive* all denote the quality of thinking a lot, but they differ in degree and in association. *Thoughtful* implies "considerate, caring towards other people" as well as "full of thought." *Reflective* connotes "self-conscious" and sometimes "reminiscent." *Pensive* suggests deeper and more sober thought; it often suggests "withdrawn" and "melancholy."

Connotations may reveal or even conceal societal attitudes. Not being aware of connotations can sometimes be damaging. By using words with sexist or racist connotations, for example, a writer may unintentionally insult readers.

Contributory Cause   See **Causes**

Deduction   the method of reasoning that presents a general premise and shows how it leads to a specific conclusion. (See also **Syllogism**.) The opposite of deduction is **induction**, which begins with specific evidence and moves to a general conclusion. Deduction and induction may be effectively used together. See Chapter 10.

Definition   an explanation of a word's meaning. It may be a brief *formal definition* (as it appears in a dictionary) or a longer *extended definition* that elaborates on the formal definition through **exemplification, narration, classification,** or other rhetorical strategies, or that argues in favor of a particular meaning. An extended definition can be an effective pattern of development for an essay. See Chapter 9.

Denotation   See **Connotation/Denotation**

Description   a pattern of development that presents a word picture of a thing, a person, a situation, or a series of events through sensory details. See Chapter 3.

Diction   the specific words and kinds of words that a writer chooses. The kind of diction a writer uses depends on the purpose of a piece of writing and on its audience. For instance, expressive writing might use poetic language while business writing would avoid it in favor of the most direct words possible. A newsletter for computer engineers might use specialized technical words that would need defining in a textbook chapter for students learning computer engineering.

Many kinds of diction should be avoided in college writing as well as in business and professional writing. These include:

- *Contractions* (write *will not* instead of *won't* and *they are* instead of *they're*)
- *Slang* (write *car*, not *wheels*; avoid words like *lousy, awesome, cool*)
- *Conversational fillers* (*I mean, you know*)
- *Unnecessary words and redundant phrases* (write *consensus*, not *consensus of opinion*, and *unique*, not *very unique*)
- *Bland words* (whenever possible, replace *good, nice, very, fine* with stronger, more specific and colorful words)
- *Colloquial uses of words* (write *enthusiastic*, not *enthused*, and *center on*, not *center around*)—See **Colloquialisms**
- *Pretentious words or jargon* (such as *disinformation* for *falsehood* or *lie*; *prioritize options* for *set priorities*)
- *Euphemisms* (write *died* rather than *passed on*)
- *Sexist language* (write *the writer ... he or she* or *the writers ... they*, not *the writer ... he*; write *police officer* and *firefighter*, not *policeman* and *fireman*.)
- *Clichés* (overused expressions such as *hustle and bustle; Beauty is in the eye of the beholder; A picture is worth a thousand words; To make a long story short....*"

In writing the first draft of an essay, try to use precise and colorful language. Then review word choices and eliminate or strengthen any weak phrases that you discover.

Digression a remark or series of remarks that wanders from the main point of a discussion. In the case of a personal narrative, a digression could prove entertaining because of its very irrelevance but in other kinds of writing it interrupts and confuses the development of the essay. Writers should be especially careful when giving examples not to get so involved with developing the example that they fail to connect it to the idea they are illustrating.

Division See **Classification and Division**

Dominant Impression the mood or quality that is emphasized in a piece of writing.

Enumeration a list of a series of items. The introduction of a **classification-and-division** essay may enumerate the categories to be discussed, and the introduction of a **process** essay may enumerate the steps in the process.

Essay a short work of nonfiction writing on a single topic that usually expresses the author's impressions or opinions. The word *es-*

say also means "an attempt." In this sense, an essay as a work of writing is never the last word on a subject but only the best attempt that can be made. An essay may be organized around one or several of the patterns of development presented in this book. A *formal essay* generally has a serious purpose and tone, formal diction (as opposed to colloquial language), and a tight structure based on a logical progression of ideas. An *informal essay* tends to offer a more entertaining viewpoint and therefore may employ colloquial expressions and a looser structure.

Evidence   statements composed of facts and opinions. *Facts*, in the form of examples or statistics, may be drawn from research or personal experience, and *opinions* may represent the conclusions of experts or your own ideas. Evidence for an analytical literature paper might include lines and passages from the work being discussed or quotations from literary critics; a historical research paper would probably draw on historical accounts, statistics, and the findings of scholars.

Example   a concrete, specific illustration used to support general points being made. An example may, among other things, be a brief historical account, a personal anecdote, or a summary of a passage from a work of literature.

Exemplification   the pattern of development that uses a single extended **example** or a series of examples to support a thesis. See Chapter 4.

Fallacies   statements that resemble plausible arguments but are not. They are often persuasive, but they unfairly manipulate readers to win agreement. Fallacies include begging the question; argument for analogy; personal attack (*ad hominem*); hasty or sweeping generalizations; false dilemma (the either/or fallacy); equivocation; red herring; you also (*tu quoque*); appeal to doubtful authority; and misleading statistics. See Chapter 10.

Figures of Speech (also **Figurative Language**)   imaginative comparisons that indirectly suggest to readers another meaning beyond their literal one. Three of the most common figures of speech are *similes, metaphors,* and *personifications.*

A simile makes a comparison using *like* or *as* ("Hills Like White Elephants"—Ernest Hemingway). A metaphor compares two things without using *like* or *as* ("Not yet would they veer southward to the caldron of the land that lay below"—N. Scott Momaday). Personification describes animals or objects as if they were human ("the chair slouched"; "bees grumbled over the rose bush"; "the wind sighed outside the window").

Other figures of speech include *hyperbole* and *understatement.*

Freewriting See **Invention**

Hyperbole is a deliberate exaggeration for emphasis or humorous effect: "I froze to death out in the storm"; "She has hundreds of boyfriends"; "Clothes these days seem to cost a million dollars"; "Last year passed by in a second." The opposite of hyperbole is understatement, which has similar intended effects: "The people who live near the power plant are not exactly looking forward to another Chernobyl in their backyards."

Imagery a set of verbal pictures of sensory experiences. These pictures, conveyed through concrete details, make a description vivid and immediate to the reader. Some images are literal ("The cows were so white they almost glowed in the dark.") while some are more figurative ("The black and white cows looked like maps, with the continents in black and the seas in white."). A pattern of imagery (repeated images of, for example, shadows, forests, fire) in a work of writing may build up its own set of associations and become a **symbol** with a special meaning.

Immediate Cause See **Causes**

Induction the method of reasoning that first presents specific evidence and then draws a general conclusion based on this evidence. Induction is the opposite of **deduction**, which moves from a general premise to a specific conclusion. The two forms of logic may be used together effectively in an essay. See Chapter 10.

Introduction an essay's opening. Depending on the scope of the essay, it may be one paragraph or several paragraphs long—or even a few pages long in a lengthy research paper. In an introduction a writer wants to encourage the audience to read the essay that follows. This prompting involves carefully choosing a tone and diction that invites the readers and does not alienate them, as well as indicating either explicitly or implicitly what the paper is about and in what direction it will go. If an introduction is not interesting and lively, it may discourage readers.

Several possible ways of introducing an essay include the following:

1. Directly stating the thesis
2. Defining a relevant term or concept
3. Telling an anecdote or story that pertains to the thesis
4. Asking a provoking question
5. Beginning with a quotation

Invention (also Prewriting) the initial preparatory stage of writing in which a writer explores the writing assignment, focuses ideas, and ultimately decides on a thesis for an essay. A writer might begin by thinking through the requirements of the assignment—the purpose, the length of the essay, and the audience. Several of the following specific invention techniques can then help the writer to proceed.

Freewriting is an indirect method that allows the writer to back off from the subject and thus move beyond writer's block. Freewriting involves writing quickly, without stopping, for a fixed period of time on any subject. The goal of this strategy is to free-associate to discover ideas to write about.

Looping involves isolating one idea from a piece of freewriting and using this idea as a focus for a new piece of freewriting. Looping may be repeated if it is effective in generating new ideas.

Another invention technique uses *questions for probing* to explore a subject. These questions encourage a dialogue in the writer's mind; they allow the writer to delve deeper and deeper into the subject and also to think about which questions can most productively be explored in an essay.

Brainstorming is an invention technique that involves listing everything that comes to mind about the writing topic. It is a chance to be creative and to be drawn in new, even surprising directions.

Using one or more of these methods, writers should be able to come up with a tentative thesis and then begin work on the essay itself. See Chapter 1.

Irony   language that points to a discrepancy between two different levels of meaning. *Verbal irony* is characterized by a gap between what is actually stated and what is really meant, which is often the opposite in meaning—for instance, "such a heavenly aroma" (referring to the smell from dirty socks); "his humble abode" (referring to a millionaire's estate), or "Let's go boating" (referring to a trickle of water that is supposed to be a river). Deliberately insincere and biting irony is called *sarcasm*—for example, "That's okay, I love it when you drop dishes on the floor and break them."

Another kind of irony is *thematic* rather than verbal. It points to a twist of fate, a discrepancy between what was intended and what actually happened. This kind of irony is present when a character, trying to scare away a rival, ends up being scared away himself.

A more sophisticated, kind of irony occurs when the reader understands more about what is happening in a story than the rather naïve character who is telling the story does. For example, the narrator might tell an anecdote very simply and honestly and explain at the end how puzzled he was by other people's reactions, while it is obvious to the reader from the story's events that the narrator has made a fool of himself because of his gullibility.

Looping See **Invention**

Main Cause See **Causes**

Narration the pattern of development that tells a story. See Chapter 2.

Objective/Subjective terms that refer to the degree to which an author's personal point of view is present in the writing. An *objective description* is a distanced, factual picture presented in as plain and direct a manner as possible. Objective description tries to avoid opinions and interpretations. Pure objectivity is difficult to achieve, however, because people's perceptions are often colored by their past experiences and their personal values and biases. Still, certain forms of writing—science papers, technical reports, and news articles, for example—strive for *objective language* that is plain, direct, and free of value judgments.

   Descriptions that do contain value judgments (*a saintly woman, a stud*) are subjective. Although objective language is distanced from an event or object, *subjective language* is involved. A subjective description focuses on the author's relationship to the event rather than on the event itself, conveying not just a factual record of details but also their significance. Subjective language, the language generally used in personal narratives and editorials, may include poetic words and impressionistic descriptions. It purposely avoids colorless, utilitarian language in favor of words that impart a judgment or emotional response to a description (*stride, limp, meander, pace, hobble, stroll, plod, glide,* or *shuffle* instead of *walk; snicker, snort, chuckle, titter, giggle,* or *guffaw* instead of *laugh*). Subjective language also includes **figures of speech.** See Chapter 3.

Objective Description, Objective Language See **Objective/Subjective**

Paragraph the basic unit of an essay. A paragraph is composed of related sentences that together express one of the ideas in the essay. The **unifying idea** of a paragraph is often stated in a single **topic sentence.** Paragraphs are also graphic symbols on the page, mapping the progress of the ideas in the essay and also providing visual relief to the reader.

Parallelism the use of similar grammatical elements within or between sentences. For a sentence to exhibit parallelism, any elements of equal importance—for example, paired elements or elements in a series—must be presented in the same form. "I like hiking, skiing, and to cook" is not parallel because *hiking* and *skiing* share the gerund form (*-ing*) of the verbs while *to cook* is the infinitive form. Revised for parallelism, the sentence could read either "I like hiking, skiing, and cooking" or "I like to hike, to ski, and to cook."

As a stylistic technique, parallelism can provide emphasis and cohesion, effectively linking elements in a sentence or a series of sentences through repetition of a grammatical form or a particular phrase—for example, "Walk groundly, talk profoundly, drink roundly, sleep soundly" (William Hazlitt). Parallelism is a powerful oratorical technique often employed by politicians and evangelists: "Until justice is blind to color, until education is unaware of race, until opportunity is unconcerned with the color of men's skins, emancipation will be a proclamation but not a fact" (Lyndon B. Johnson).

Paraphrase   the restatement of another person's words in your own words. It is particularly necessary in a source-based paper where the purpose is to direct information gathered during research into pointed statements that support the ideas in the paper. Only information that is uniquely worded (for instance, Marie Winn's labeling television a "plug-in-drug") or extremely difficult to paraphrase should be quoted directly. For example, Jonathan Kozol's "Illiterates cannot travel freely. When they attempt to do so, they encounter risks that few of us can dream of" (p. 177) might be paraphrased like this: "According to Jonathan Kozol, people who cannot read find travel extremely risky."

Persuasion   a method of convincing an audience that relies on various appeals to win support of an opinion or to move readers to action. See "Argument and Persuasion," Chapter 10.

Plagiarism   presenting the words or ideas of someone else as if they were your own. It should always be avoided.

***Post Hoc* Reasoning**   the fallacy of looking back at two events that have occurred in chronological sequence and wrongly assuming that the first event caused the second.

Prewriting   See Invention

Process (also **Process Explanation**)   the pattern of development that presents a series of steps in a procedure, such as a laboratory experiment, in chronological order. See Chapter 5.

Prose   speech or writing as opposed to poetic verse.

Purpose   the reason for writing. Purpose is the end a writer wants to achieve. A writer's purpose may, for example, be to entertain readers with an amusing story, inform them about dangerous disease, move them to action by enraging them with an example of injustice, or change their perspective in some way by revealing a hidden dimension of a person or situation. To give an essay **coherence** and power, a writer should always keep its purpose or purposes in mind. One good way for a reader to become more deeply involved with a work of writing is to ask, "Why did this writer write this?" See Chapter 1

Refutation the attempt to counter an opposing argument by revealing its weaknesses. Three of the most common weaknesses are logical flaws in the argument, inadequate evidence, and irrelevance. Refutation greatly strengthens an argument by showing that the writer is aware of the complexity of the issue and has considered opposing viewpoints.

Remote Cause See **Causes**

Rhetoric the study and art of effective communication through prose.

Rhetorical question a question asked for effect and not meant to be answered.

Sarcasm See **Irony**

Satire writing that uses wit, irony, and ridicule to attack foolishness. Satire has a different purpose from comedy, which usually intends simply to entertain. For an example of ironic satire, see Jonathan Swift's "A Modest Proposal," page 544.

Subjective See **Objective/Subjective**

Summary See **Conclusions**

Syllogism a basic form of deductive reasoning. Every syllogism includes three parts, 1) a major premise that makes a general statement ("confinement is physically and psychologically damaging"); 2) a minor premise that makes a related but more specific statement ("zoos confine animals"); and 3) a conclusion drawn from these two premises ("therefore, zoos are physically and psychologically damaging to animals"). See Chapter 10.

Symbol an occurrence, being, or thing that represents something more than its literal meaning.

Synonym a word with the same denotative meaning as another word. A synonym for *loud* is *noisy*. Most words in the English language have several or many synonyms; however, each synonym has a unique nuance or connotation. (See also **Connotation /Denotation**.)

Topic Sentence a sentence stating the main idea of a paragraph. Often, but not always, the topic sentence opens the paragraph.

Thesis the name for an essay's main idea, an idea that all the points made in the paragraphs of the essay support. In addition to conveying the essay's main idea, the thesis should indicate the writer's approach to the subject and express the writer's purpose (the reason for writing). It may also indicate the pattern of development that will structure the essay. A thesis may be stated explicitly or implied. Depending on the writer's purpose, a thesis may be *expressive, informative,* or *persuasive.*

The thesis a writer develops in the early stages of the essay is usually a *tentative* or *working thesis,* one that serves as a guide while the writer thinks through the essay. Ultimately, however, the thesis should define a point of view that can be fully discussed in the body of the essay. A good thesis is much more than a statement of fact; it allows room for development. See Chapter 1. (See also **Antithesis.**)

Transitions   links between ideas in a work of writing. They may be words, sentences, or sometimes even paragraphs. The ideas themselves should be organized in a way that makes sense logically and sequentially, with each new sentence and paragraph building on the last. However, shifts in emphasis or subject matter can be unsettling to readers unless pivotal phrases and sentences guide them, reminding them where they have been and showing them the direction in which they are now moving.

Transitions between paragraphs bridge a larger gap than transitions between sentences; the last sentence of a paragraph might hint at what the next paragraph will discuss, and the first sentence of a new paragraph may echo a fragment of the preceding paragraph and indicate how that idea relates to a new idea. Transitional sentences often aid coherence by clarifying the relationship between thesis and support.

Within and between paragraphs, transition may be enhanced by the repetition of an essay's key words or concepts, by the use of pronouns to refer to nouns in previous sentences, and by the use of transitional expressions. Some of the more useful transitional expressions are listed below.

- To show chronological sequence: *simultaneously, meanwhile, afterward, then, subsequently, soon, at the same time, since, first (second, third ...)*
- To indicate spatial relationships: *nearby, beside, facing, adjacent to, in front of, behind*
- To indicate results: *consequently, therefore, as a result, because*
- To indicate contrast: *in contrast, conversely, but, however, yet, on the other hand, still, nevertheless*
- To indicate similarity: *similarly, likewise, in the same way*

- To indicate addition: *first, second, third, also, in addition, furthermore, finally*
- To indicate movement from general to specific: *in fact, for example, for instance*

Unifying Idea the central point or concept expressed in a paragraph. This idea is often expressed in a topic sentence.

Unity the desirable attribute of a paragraph in which every sentence relates directly to the paragraph's main idea.

Writing Process the name given to the sequence of tasks a writer undertakes when writing an essay. During **invention,** or **prewriting,** the writer gathers information and ideas and focuses them into a workable topic. During the *arrangement* stage, the writer organizes these ideas into a logical sequence.

During *drafting and revision,* the essay is actually written and then reworked. These stages occur in no fixed order; many effective writers move back and forth among them. This process reveals that writing is not simply a way of expressing ideas that are clear in the writer's mind; it is actually a way of thinking and learning that can help writers to discover new ideas and new connections among ideas.

Richard Rodriguez, "Aria: A Memoir of a Bilingual Childhood." From *Hunger of Memory* by Richard Rodriguez. Copyright © 1982 by Richard Rodriguez. Reprinted by permission of David R. Godine, Publishers.

CLASSIFICATION AND DIVISION

William K. Zinsser, "College Pressures." From *Blair & Ketchum's Country Journal*. Copyright © 1979 by William K. Zinsser. Reprinted by permission of the author.

Alison Lurie, "American Regional Costumes." From *The Language of Cloths* by Alison Lurie. Copyright © 1981 by Alison Lurie. Reprinted by permission of Random House, Inc.

John Holt, "Three Kinds of Discipline." From *Freedom and Beyond* by John Holt. Copyright © 1972 by The Estate of John C. Holt. Reprinted by permission of The Estate of John C. Holt.

John Barth, "Historical Fiction, Fictitious History, and Chesapeake Bay Blue Crabs, or About Aboutness." Reprinted by permission of International Creative Management, Inc. [First published in The Washington Post Sunday Magazine.] Copyright © by John Barth.

Joseph Lelyveld, "Rule of Law." From *Move Your Shadow: South Africa Black and White* by Joseph Lelyveld. Copyright © 1985 by Joseph Lelyveld. Reprinted by permission of Times Books, a division of Random House, Inc.

DEFINITION

Judy Syfers, "Why I Want a Wife." Copyright © 1970 by Judy Syfers. Reprinted by permission of the author.

Ellen Goodman, "The Company Man." Copyright © 1981 by The Washington Post Company. Reprinted by permission of Summit Books, a division of Simon & Schuster, Inc.

Gail Godwin, "To Noble Companions." Copyright © 1973 by Harper's Magazine. All rights reserved. Reprinted from the August issue by special permission.

Eileen Simpson, "Dyslexia." From *Reversals* by Eileen Simpson. Copyright © 1979 by Eileen Simpson. Reprinted by permission of Houghton Mifflin Company.

Neil Postman, "Euphemism." From *Crazy Talk, Stupid Talk* by Neil Postman. Copyright © 1976 by Neil Postman. Reprinted by arrangement of Delacorte Press. All rights reserved.

ARGUMENTATION

Angelo Gonzalez, "Bilingual Education: The Key to Basic Skills." Copyright © 1985 by The New York Times Company. Reprinted by permission.

Richard Rodriguez, "Bilingual Education: Outdated and Unrealistic." Copyright © 1985 by The New York Times Company. Reprinted by permission.

Peter Singer, "Animal Liberation." Reprinted by permission of the author from *Animal Liberation: A New Ethnic for the Treatment of Animals*, New York Review/Random House 1975, Avon Discuss 1977. Copyright © 1975 by Peter Singer.

Albert Rosenfeld, "Animal Rights versus Human Health." Reprinted by permission from the June issue of Science '81. Copyright © 1981 by the American Association for the Advancement of Science.

Martin Luther King, Jr., "Letter from Birmingham Jail." From *Why We Can't Wait* by Martin Luther King, Jr. Copyright © 1963 by Martin Luther King, Jr. Reprinted by permission of Harper & Row, Publishers, Inc.

ESSAYS FOR FURTHER READING

Virginia Woolf, "If Shakespeare Had Had a Sister." From *A Room of One's Own* by Virginia Woolf. Copyright © 1929 by Harcourt Brace Jovanovich, Inc.; renewed 1957 by Leonard Woolf. Reprinted by permission by Harcourt Brace Jovanovich, Inc.

George Orwell, "Politics and the English Language." Copyright © 1946 by Sonia Brownell Orwell and renewed 1974 by Sonia Orwell. From *Shooting an Elephant and Other Essays* by George Orwell. Reprinted by permission of Harcourt Brace Jovanovich, Inc., The Estate of the late Sonia Brownell Orwell, and Martin Secker & Warburg Ltd.

Index of
Terms, Authors,
and Titles